The International Law
of Human Rights

THE INTERNATIONAL
LAW OF
HUMAN RIGHTS

PAUL SIEGHART

CLARENDON PRESS · OXFORD
1983

Oxford University Press, Walton Street, Oxford OX2 6DP

London Glasgow New York Toronto
Delhi Bombay Calcutta Madras Karachi
Kuala Lumpur Singapore Hong Kong Tokyo
Nairobi Dar es Salaam Cape Town
Melbourne Auckland
and associates in
Beirut Berlin Ibadan Mexico City Nicosia

Published in the United States by
Oxford University Press, New York

OXFORD is a trade mark of Oxford University Press

British Library Cataloguing in Publication Data

The International law of human rights.
  1. Civil rights (International law)
  I. Sieghart, Paul
  341.4'81   K3240
  ISBN 0-19-876096-5

Library of Congress Cataloging in Publication Data

Sieghart, Paul.
  The international law of human rights.

  Bibliography: p.
  Includes index.
  1. Civil rights (International law)   I. title.
  K3240.4.S49 1982   341.4'81   82-14248
  ISBN 0-19-876096-5

Typeset by Joshua Associates, Oxford
Printed in Great Britain
at Hazell, Watson & Viney
Aylesbury, Bucks

This book is humbly dedicated to the millions of individuals who have needlessly suffered and perished, over many centuries and in many cultures, through the denial of their human rights and fundamental freedoms; and to the countless more who will be unjustly deprived, oppressed, and persecuted before the rule of the international law of human rights can become fully established.

GENERAL ARRANGEMENT

This book is divided into four Parts. Part I describes the framework. The authentic English texts of the substantive Articles in the eight major international human rights instruments are then set out, ordered according to their subject-matter, in Parts II and III. These texts are in each case followed by cross-references, some textual comment, a brief history (where relevant) of the right concerned, a digest of jurisprudence — that is, interpretation and application by competent independent institutions[1] — and a summary of the contents of any relevant subsidiary instruments. Part IV reproduces the procedural Articles, with a minimum of necessary comment. At the end of the book, two Tables give respectively the status of the relevant instruments on 1 January 1982, and references to all the jurisprudence cited, with explanations of the abbreviations used for these.

In order to save much space, the international instruments and institutions are generally referred to in abbreviated form, in italic capitals for instruments (e.g. *ICES* for the International Covenant on Economic, Social and Cultural Rights), and in roman capitals for institutions (e.g. UNESCO for the United Nations Educational, Scientific and Cultural Organisation). The abbreviations used are explained in the Lists of Instruments and Institutions which follow the Table of Contents. Articles and paragraphs of the instruments are also given in abbreviated form: thus, sub-paragraph (*e*) of paragraph 3 of Article 6 of the Council of Europe Convention for the Protection of Human Rights and Fundamental Freedoms is referred to as *EHR* 6(3)(*e*). Two instruments have not yet entered into force, and the institution that one of them envisages has not yet been established; these are throughout referred to in square brackets: [*AFR*], [AFCM], and [*CT*]; so are a few other drafts which have not yet been adopted.

Again, to save space, the Preambles to the instruments are not reproduced, nor are marginal notes or headings, or the transitional provisions relating to signature, ratification, entry into force, amendment, etc.

[1] Throughout the book, the word 'jurisprudence' is used in this sense only; not in the sense of 'philosophy of law', in which it is still sometimes used by teachers of law in English-speaking countries.

vii

For ease of reference and cross-reference, all the material is organized into sections and sub-sections (always, and exclusively, described by the symbol '§'); so that, for example, §14.3 forms the third sub-section of §14, and §14.3.4 forms the fourth sub-division of §14.3. These numbers are repeated in the top outside corner of each page, and exclusively used for cross-references. Running page numbers are given at the bottom of each page, but have no other function.

The individual Articles considered here are not reproduced in the order in which they appear in the instruments to which they belong, but in the order of the different sections and sub-sections of the book to which they relate (and therefore, on a few occasions, more than once). At the end of the volume, there is an Index showing where they are to be found in it. For the texts of the major instruments (other than [*AFR*][2]) in their original order, the reader is referred to I. Brownlie (ed.), *Basic Documents on Human Rights* (2nd ed. 1981). That work also contains the texts of some of the subsidiary instruments; many of these are also reprinted in the UN publication *Human Rights: a Compilation of International Instruments*.

No material is included unless it has become available before 1 January 1982.

---

[2] The full text of [*AFR*] is reprinted in *The Review* of the International Commission of Jurists, No. 27, December 1981.

TABLE OF CONTENTS

Table of Contents

Table of Contents

Table of Contents

Table of Contents

LIST OF INSTRUMENTS

| | Year of | | |
	Adoption	Entry into force	Abbreviation
Global			
United Nations Charter	1945	1945	*UNCH*
Universal Declaration of Human Rights	1948		*UDHR*
American Declaration of the Rights and Duties of Man	1948		*ADRD*
International Covenant on Economic, Social and Cultural Rights	1966	1976	*ICES*
International Covenant on Civil and Political Rights	1966	1976	*ICPR*
Optional Protocol thereto	1966	1976	*ICPR OP*
Regional			
Council of Europe Convention for the Protection of Human Rights and Fundamental Freedoms	1950	1953	*EHR*
First Protocol thereto	1952	1954	*EHR P1*
Second Protocol thereto	1963	1970	*EHR P2*
Third Protocol thereto	1963	1970	*EHR P3*
Fourth Protocol thereto	1963	1968	*EHR P4*
Fifth Protocol thereto	1966	1971	*EHR P5*
European Social Charter	1961	1965	*ESC*
American Convention on Human Rights	1969	1978	*AMR*
[African Charter on Human and Peoples' Rights]	1981		*[AFR]*
Subsidiary			
Convention on the Prevention and Punishment of the Crime of Genocide	1948	1951	*CG*
International Convention on the Suppression and Punishment of the Crime of *Apartheid*	1973	1976	*CA*

xv

List of Instruments

	Year of Adoption	Year of Entry into force	Abbreviation
Convention on the Elimination of all Forms of Racial Discrimination	1965	1969	*CD*
[Convention on the Elimination of Torture]			*[CT]*
Convention Relating to the Status of Refugees	1951	1954	*CR*
Convention Relating to the Status of Stateless Persons	1954	1960	CS_1
Convention on the Reduction of Statelessness	1961	1975	CS_2
Convention on the Elimination of all Forms of Discrimination against Women	1979	1981	CW_1
Convention on the Political Rights of Women	1952	1954	CW_2
Convention on the Nationality of Married Women	1957	1958	CW_3
Convention on Consent to Marriage, Minimum Age for Marriage and Registration of Marriages	1962	1964	*CM*
Convention against Discrimination in Education	1960	1962	*CE*
Protocol thereto	1962	1968	
Slavery Convention (as amended by 1953 Protocol)	1926	1927	SC_1
Supplementary Convention on the Abolition of Slavery, the Slave Trade, and Institutions and Practices similar to Slavery	1956	1957	SC_2
Convention for the Suppression of the Traffic in Persons and of the Exploitation of the Prostitution of Others	1949	1951	*CP*
Convention on the International Right of Correction	1952	1962	*CC*

ILO

	Year of Adoption	Year of Entry into force	Abbreviation
Convention concerning Forced Labour	1930	1932	*ILO 29*

List of Instruments

	Year of		
		Entry into	
	Adoption	force	Abbreviation
Convention concerning Freedom of Association and Protection of the Right to Organise	1948	1950	*ILO 87*
Convention concerning the Application of the Principles of the Right to Organise and to Bargain Collectively	1949	1951	*ILO 98*
Convention concerning Equal Remuneration for Men and Women Workers for Work of Equal Value	1951	1953	*ILO 100*
Convention concerning the Abolition of Forced Labour	1957	1959	*ILO 105*
Convention concerning Discrimination in Respect of Employment and Occupation	1958	1960	*ILO 111*
Convention concerning Employment Policy	1964	1966	*ILO 122*
Convention concerning Protection and Facilities to be Afforded to Workers' Representatives in the Undertaking	1971	1973	*ILO 135*

Notes

1. The abbreviations for international *instruments* (as opposed to institutions) are printed throughout in *italics*.
2. Global instruments have four letters, regional ones three, and subsidiary ones two (with a numbered suffix where more than one instrument is *in pari materia*).
3. Instruments not yet in force on 1 January 1982 are shown in square brackets.
4. Apart from the Preambles, marginal notes, and headings, and certain transitional provisions, the texts of the global and regional instruments are reprinted in the present work. Those of most of the subsidiary instruments and ILO Conventions may be found in the UN publication *Human Rights: a Compilation of International Instruments*.
5. Subsidiary instruments which only apply regionally are not considered in the present work.

LIST OF INSTITUTIONS

Note
As [AFR] has not yet entered into force, [AFCM] has not yet been established.

PREFACE

It is a matter of common observation in all human societies that people may treat each other 'well' or 'badly', depending on whether they are motivated by love, generosity, gratitude, co-operation, and creativity; or by hatred, greed, envy, competitiveness, and destructiveness. Deeply buried somewhere in that observation are the origins of what are today called 'human rights', and the legal rules associated with them.

All human beings display certain needs which must be satisfied if they are even to survive, let alone to grow, develop their potential, and contribute to the development of the potentials of others. Those needs are often painfully frustrated by unavoidable causes such as disease, or other natural calamities. It is the paramount objective of human rights law — both national and international — to seek to protect individuals from man-made, and so avoidable, suffering inflicted on them through deprivation, exploitation, oppression, persecution, and other forms of maltreatment by organized and powerful groups of other human beings. In order to approach that objective, human rights law uses the classical transformations of political philosophers and lawyers: from needs to moral claims, and from those claims to 'rights', founded first on morality, and ultimately on positive and enforceable law.

The word 'revolution' is much abused, especially in human affairs. Strictly, it should only be used where there has been a real discontinuity in a process: a 'quantum jump' profoundly distinguishing what comes after from what went before. Without that, changes are evolutionary rather than revolutionary, however much the pace of change may itself accelerate. What has prompted the preparation and publication of this book is an event which, even by that restrictive definition, can properly be described as a recent revolution in human affairs comparable with those of 1789, 1848, and 1917, namely the birth of *international* human rights law after the Second World War — itself a cluster of events constituting, by the scale and extent of the avoidable suffering which it and its immediate antecedents imposed upon humanity, a major discontinuity in the recorded history of human affairs.

Until then, how a sovereign State treated its own citizens was, in the consistent tradition of international law, a matter exclusively for its own sovereign determination, and beyond the scope of legitimate criticism by others. Today — for the first time in the history of mankind — that is no longer the case: such matters are now the subject of the *legitimate* concern of all mankind, and capable of objective assessment and judgment by reference to common standards of internationally agreed, and legally binding, rules — collectively known as 'international human rights law', and in effect for many of the world's nations, at all events in the form of treaty law, only since 1976.

Design

The purpose of this book is to set out the substantive content of this new corpus of law in a form designed for easy reference. But something must first be said about that design.

Preface

Once needs have been transformed successively into claims and rights, there is a temptation to try to classify them, and the ingenuity of the human intellect has devised many forms of classification. Claims and rights — whether moral or legal — may be arbitrarily divided into those that are positive or negative, personal or social, individual or collective, cheap or expensive to satisfy, bourgeois or socialist, primary or derivative, sequential or parallel; and there are many other such antinomies. None of them is adopted in this book. Here, only one distinction is used: where international law as it is now in force formally declares, guarantees, and attempts to protect a particular human right, the formulation by which it does that is set out and considered. Where it does not — or not yet — that 'right' is mentioned, if at all, only parenthetically. There is an extensive literature about *lex ferenda* in the field of human rights, but this book deliberately confines itself[1] to the *lex lata*.

Its underlying premise is that a distinction can and should be made between what various commentators believe human rights ought to be, and what international law now says they are. The former is fit subject-matter for moral philosophers, social and political scientists, and others, using the methods of academic study and disputation. The latter is more suitable for lawyers, using their particular skills in the interpretation of legal texts and the application of the results to particular cases. The book therefore restricts itself to the international instruments now in force which declare the law of human rights, and avoids questioning whether those instruments are good, bad, or indifferent; whether they are exhaustive or incomplete; whether they reflect right values or wrong ones; and whether they are based on principle or expediency — or, if both, whether they strike a desirable balance between the two. It is intended as a book of law, not of morality, philosophy, or politics.

For that reason, it seeks to avoid all reference to the 'implementation' of human rights — that is, to the manifold and important efforts made by many agencies to ensure that such rights are in fact better observed and protected,[2] and the various factual techniques for monitoring whether they are — let alone references to the actual observance of human rights, or lack of it, in different countries in the world today. For that reason also, it has nothing to say about the present politics, or the future development, of international human rights law. As the youngest of all existing legal systems, the rate at which it is changing is still high, and so is the potential for its development. But the purpose of this work is simply to describe its content as it now stands, rather than to speculate on what it may hereafter become.

Disclaimers

The literature on human rights is immense; by comparison, the existing literature on human rights *law* still seems small. Even less yet exists about *international* human rights law, in force in Europe since 1953, and in the form of global treaties only since 1976. What there is, though generally of high quality, tends to be confined to commentaries either on a particular text (such as the European Convention on Human Rights and Fundamental Freedoms), or on a particular

---

[1] Except that it includes consideration of two human rights treaties which have not yet formally entered into force, but are expected to do so within the useful lifetime of the work.

[2] For instance, the 1980 edition of *United Nations Action in the Field of Human Rights* alone runs to 380 double-column pages.

human right or group of rights, or on procedure. It is also invariably academic in the best sense of being scholarly, thorough, and above all discursive.

What is instead attempted here is a plain handbook for practitioners and students of what international human rights law now consists of; what it says and (where this raises doubts) what that means; and how it works — as well as an elementary (and at this stage necessarily incomplete) apparatus of reference for further research. Practising lawyers above all need annotated codes of the law they have to apply. The primary purpose of a book such as this one is that a Ruritanian lawyer, faced with a point of human rights law to which he does not know the answer, and endowed with no more than a working knowledge of the English language, should be able to use it to find the human right concerned, see whether any of the instruments of international human rights law recognizes and protects it, to what extent and subject to what restrictions, check whether Ruritania is a party to that instrument and whether it has made any relevant reservations or derogations — or, if it is not a party, whether it can be said to be bound by any relevant customary international law — and so conclude whether he can take the point either in his own courts or before one of the new international institutions. With any luck, he may also find some help on how to frame and argue the point, perhaps from other cases which have already been decided somewhere.

In order to fulfil that function, the entire work is necessarily assertive rather than discursive, and practical rather than academic. Its primary data are the texts themselves (*le droit écrit*) and, where their meaning is not sufficiently clear, any guidance which can be obtained from past interpretations and applications by competent independent institutions[3] (*la jurisprudence*[4]). Its function is not to argue for or against the rightness or desirability of those data, but merely to assemble them in a form convenient for those who need to know what the law *is*, either for their studies or for the benefit of their clients. I have therefore refrained from expressing any views of my own, and resisted many temptations to discuss, rather than describe, the subject-matter. Even in the sub-sections headed 'Comment', I have attempted no more than some simple analysis and comparison of the language of the texts under consideration there.

Because the whole subject is so new, there has been very little time for the competent international institutions to refine the texts of the instruments by authoritative interpretation: even the European Court of Human Rights, established since 1958, had by 1 January 1982 delivered judgments interpreting the Convention over which it has jurisdiction in only thirty-six cases. But many of the rights and freedoms now enumerated in international human rights law have been protected for rather longer by the constitutions and national laws of individual nations — sometimes, as in the case of the United Kingdom, France, and the United States of America, for two centuries or even more. During that time, the superior courts of those countries have had many opportunities to interpret and apply the provisions by which those rights and freedoms were nationally protected. Such interpretations will generally be treated as having

---

[3] No account is taken here of interpretations provided by political organs, such as Committees of Ministers, Parliamentary Assemblies, or entities composed of governmental representatives.

[4] Some teachers of law in English-speaking countries still use the word 'jurisprudence' in the sense of 'philosophy of law'. But it is used here only in its other sense, now universal in the rest of the world, of the formal interpretation and application of laws by courts, tribunals, and other independent institutions competent to pronounce on them.

authority within the country concerned; where those courts apply a rule of *stare decisis*, their authority can even be binding. However, in international human rights law interpretations adopted by national courts can at best only be persuasive authority. Besides, the new international canon does not always use precisely the same forms of words as those to be found in national constitutions or legislation, and any national jurisprudence may therefore not always be readily transferable to the international forum. Nonetheless, in appropriate places, I have made at least a start on including material from some superior national courts about national provisions which seem to be *in pari materia*.

In order to cater for the majority of practitioners and students who know their national legal systems but probably know rather less about international law (which is a fairly recondite speciality), there are also some introductory chapters designed to provide a framework for what follows. These are even more lacking in academic depth than those which follow: their sole purpose is to furnish the necessary minimum of a frame of reference for any reader who does not have it already.

What has been said so far requires no particular apology: the obvious shortcomings are an unavoidable consequence of the design. But there are others for which I cannot plead that excuse.

As a practitioner rather than a professional researcher, my resources for assembling the material collected here have necessarily been limited, both in time and in access to the relevant sources. It is that, and not the subject-matter itself, which accounts for many defects of which I am only too conscious. Any Eurocentricity, for example, is due far more to that factor than to the historical accident that the main unfolding of coherent theories of human rights took place in cultures of European origin in the eighteenth and nineteenth centuries of the Christian era, that the lawyers who first devised the means of transmuting those theories into legal provisions — first nationally, and now internationally — were almost without exception trained in the two main European legal traditions, and that the most extensive international jurisprudence so far is that of the Council of Europe institutions located in Strasbourg, France.

Living in England, with neither the time nor the funds for study visits abroad, I have had to confine myself to the material available here. That has necessarily meant that I have not been able to consult a great deal even of what I know exists, and could have been most valuable — as, for example, the *travaux préparatoires* of the international treaties, or the 'country reports' rendered under several of their supervision procedures, let alone the law reports of many nations whose supreme or constitutional courts may have had to pass on texts similar, or even identical, to those considered here. Nor have I had the time to give enough attention to a third, and in practice very important, source of law, especially in the international field, namely *la doctrine*: the considered writings published by learned teachers of the law.

It may be that future editions will be able to repair at least some of these omissions, especially if readers of this one will be kind enough to point them out to me.

Acknowledgements

Most books of these dimensions are nowadays written with the support of an academic institution, a charitable foundation, or more often both. This one has enjoyed no such bounty — except to the extent that the valuable research contributed to it by Nihal Jayawickrama, a former Permanent Secretary of the

Preface

Ministry of Justice of Sri Lanka, was carried out as part of a study for a Ph.D., supported by a generous grant from the Leverhulme Trust Fund, at the School of Oriental and African Studies in London, and he was able to consult the material available there and at the Institute of Advanced Legal Studies, as well as the growing and important reference centre at the British Institute of Human Rights, also made possible only through the generosity of the Leverhulme Trust Fund. I am most grateful to him for the great deal of work which he has done, principally on the jurisprudence of Strasbourg and of national courts, and to all those institutions for giving him their support.

As nothing quite like this has been written before, I have thought it right to submit the typescript for scrutiny, at various stages of its progress, to some of the distinguished men who have themselves played major roles in creating its subject-matter: Professor John Humphrey, now at the University of Western Ontario, the first Director of the UN Division of Human Rights and the author of the first draft of the Universal Declaration of·Human Rights; James Fawcett, the longest-serving President of the European Commission of Human Rights; Professor Torkel Opsahl of the University of Oslo, a member both of that Commission and of the UN Human Rights Committee; and Sir Ian Sinclair and David Edwards of the Foreign and Commonwealth Office in London. I am greatly indebted to them all for the unstinting generosity with which they have given of their time and expertise, and the many valuable suggestions they have made. Without their help, there would be far more defects in this book than there still are. It of course goes without saying that the sole responsibility for those that remain is mine.

Here I must also acknowledge my profound debt to the late Sir John Foster, Queen's Counsel and Fellow of All Souls College, Oxford. He was the first to stimulate, and over many years of friendship consistently supported, my interest in a subject to whose development he had himself contributed so much — as an English Member of Parliament, at the Council of Europe, in the International Commission of Jurists and its British section *Justice*, and elsewhere. This book may serve as a personal memorial to him: his death just three days after the final typescript was delivered to the publisher was a sad and irreplaceable loss.

My devoted thanks are due to many others for their contributions: Leah Levin of the UK United Nations Association, who never failed to trace and find even the most recondite material; Laurie Wiseberg of Human Rights Internet, who was able to collect voluminous publications in Washington, DC which were nowhere to be found in the UK; Klaus Sampson of the ILO, and Frits Hondius, Costas Indianos and Franco Millich of the Council of Europe, who supplied much valuable material about the work of their respective institutions; Kéba Mbaye, then First President of the Supreme Court of Senegal and now a Judge of the International Court of Justice, who kept me up to date with progress on the new African Charter; Alex Milne of Gray's Inn, who kindly volunteered his help with some research; and Paul Hofseth of Oslo, who supplied some interesting information about Old Norse law.

My deepest debt of all is due to the two people who have carried the greatest share of the burden of preparation. Kim Chisholm has cheerfully typed, copied, and collated successive drafts, and endless additions and corrections, of the entire manuscript, and has prepared the Index of Articles. And my wife has not only been generously tolerant of an obsession that has occupied most of my spare time over the last three years; in addition, she volunteered to take on the

Preface

unrewarding task of extracting and collating all the innumerable references from the footnotes, and preparing the bulk of Table B.

But perhaps the final acknowledgement should go to the many members of my profession who have in fact written most of this book — the draftsmen and interpreters of the texts here considered. The modern public tends to treat lawyers collectively with a degree of suspicion. Yet, at every stage of the development of both national and international human rights law, those who drafted, negotiated, advocated, and ultimately agreed the texts which govern it today were all lawyers; and so were — and are — the judges of the national and international tribunals who have interpreted and applied them. Few outside their own profession now remember who they all were. Their monuments are not found in statues erected in public places, legends of lives taken and wounds inflicted in wars or battles, businesses founded, or buildings constructed or paid for. They stand instead in the texts and judgments they have written, and in the far-reaching effects these have had, and will continue to have, on the lives of countless people who have never even heard of them.

Gray's Inn,   PAUL SIEGHART
London, England
February 1982

Part I

The Framework

§1. HISTORICAL AND JURIDICAL BACKGROUND

This section attempts to describe, in outline, the processes by which both national and international human rights law have come into being, as well as the relationship of this law with other branches of national and international law.

§1.1 The development of laws

Any group in which human beings associate together for any length of time requires some mechanism to ensure its collective stability. Among other things, that mechanism must assure a predictable degree of conformity by the members of the group to some coherent *rules of conduct*. Such rules are normative or prescriptive: they call on the members of the group to do some things, and to refrain from doing others, in given circumstances. Their mere existence will not of course guarantee that the actual conduct of the members of the group will always conform with them. But in order to maximize such conformity, the rules will generally also prescribe incentives towards that end, in the form either of rewards for conformity, or of punishments or other sanctions for infringement. All this is the case as much for families, clubs, companies, co-operatives, political parties, and trade unions as it is for more heterogeneous communities such as villages, towns, provinces, and nations.

Before any such set of rules can be categorized as a set of *laws*, it must satisfy certain conditions. There is a wide range of opinion among jurists as to what those conditions are, and some will therefore use the concept of 'law' in a much wider, or a much narrower, sense than others (see §1.6).

Like many other things devised by man, laws are subject to a process of development — continuous and evolutionary most of the time, and only on rare occasions discontinuous and revolutionary. Such processes tend to follow certain consistent sequences, and to exhibit some typical phases. It is therefore difficult to make much sense of any set of laws at any given time, let alone to understand them fully, without some knowledge of the processes by which they have developed.[1] Probably more than for any other discipline, history is an essential component of the study of law. In order to make sense of modern national and international human rights law, it is therefore desirable to have at least some understanding of the processes by which laws develop.[2]

---

[1] For example, it is difficult to understand the modern legal systems of many Continental European countries without some knowledge of the laws of the Roman Empire and the Napoleonic codification; or that of the modern USA without some grounding in the law of England, at least up to the eighteenth century. Again, the secular laws of modern Muslim countries make little sense without some understanding of the history of Islam.

[2] The processes described in this sub-section are general rather than particular, and outline a sequence of phases which has in fact been followed during the development of a number of known legal systems, without however describing the particular history of any one of them. No specific legal system has followed that sequence precisely, and there are a few that have followed markedly different ones. There have also been great variations in the

3

Laws generally have their beginnings in small permanent groups such as tribes and village communities, where they are founded essentially on the consensus of the members of the group. So, for example, a simple agricultural settlement might have a law prescribing that, if A kills B, B's relatives are bound — or at least entitled (in the sense that they will not be exposed to any sanctions, or even disapproval, from the rest of the group) — to kill A by way of reprisal; but such a law might also provide that this obligation or entitlement will cease if A, usually with prescribed formalities, tenders compensation for the loss of B's life in the form of 'blood money'.[3] Many laws rely at this stage for their enforcement, in some such way as this, on self-help — which may take the form of reprisal by (or on behalf of) a person injured through their breach, with the active or tacit consent of the rest of the community which treats the law-breaker as an 'outlaw' no longer entitled to their protection, and so allows 'private' sanctions to be imposed on him.

But reprisals, and especially revenge, have practical as well as theoretical demerits. In particular, they tend to destabilize the group and so fail to serve the principal end of laws. If revenge is legitimate, there will be little to restrain A's relatives from killing those among B's relatives who have taken part in the counter-killing of A. Thereupon, the B family may feel impelled to take yet more lives; other families may align themselves with one faction or the other, and eventually the entire community may find itself engaged in a divisive and destructive vendetta, to its collective detriment.[4]

For that reason, the progressive reduction of the entitlement to reprisal — and indeed to self-help in general — is a consistent feature of legal development. But in order to achieve this, an alternative sanction for breach of the law must be made available, not less efficacious and reliable than the remedy of self-help in the hands of the person injured by the breach. And whoever wishes to impose such an alternative sanction, to the exclusion of the one it replaces, must have an effective monopoly of force within the community, which he is willing (and ultimately bound) to make generally available both to enforce the new 'public' sanction, and to restrain recourse to the use of private self-help.

As contact, trade, and interdependence between small communities increase, tendencies develop towards the harmonization and universalization of their local laws. A common phenomenon is the emergence at some stage of a strong military or religious leader, concerned to weld together a number of smaller communities into a greater whole, and to that end seeking to impose upon them, by force or persuasion, a single set of laws. Those laws then serve not only to regulate conduct within the larger community, but also to define it and encourage its cohesion. At that stage, the maintenance and enforcement of the common set of laws generally become the task, and the monopoly, of one or more specialized groups within the larger community, to the exclusion of the different local groups which had before maintained their own different laws for themselves; and the replacement of diverse local sets of laws by a single one for the larger community tends to progress in the measure in which the specialized group responsible for

times taken over successive phases. What is sketched here should therefore not be taken as in any sense prescriptive, and even insofar as it appears to be descriptive it describes only an idealized and typical sequence, rather than a specific and historically verifiable one.

[3] For a detailed description of how such a customary legal system operated in early Norse communities, probably before around 900 AD, see the *Gulatingslovi*, translated from the old Norwegian by Knut Robberstad (3rd ed., Oslo, 1969), 205–15.
[4] As in the case of the Guelphs and the Ghibellines in pre-Renaissance Italy.

the maintenance of the common set of laws is able to exercise an effective monopoly of force. That monopoly, even today, constitutes the first claim, and in a very real sense the primary definitive characteristic, of a State.

In an extreme form, a single monopoly of force may extend so far that it covers communities and peoples whose laws and customs were originally quite different from the laws and customs of those who came to govern them. That is one aspect of the phenomenon of 'imperialism', exemplified by numerous periods during which the representatives of a single (and often quite small) people have succeeded in establishing an effective monopoly of force over many other peoples, often in distant colonies. Such imperial peoples have included Egyptians, Persians, Macedonians, Romans, Arabs, Normans, Chinese, Moguls, Turks, Spaniards, Portuguese, English, Russians, Austrians, French, Germans and several others. In each case, they tried (and often at least partially succeeded) to impose their own laws permanently upon their subject peoples. But in each case also, they learned lessons from the pre-existing laws of those peoples. The leading example is what the Romans called the *ius gentium*, the common features they identified among the laws of their subject tribes. That concept came to serve as a source, first for the laws of the Roman Empire itself, and later both for a theory of 'natural law' (see §1.3) and for the 'general principles of law recognized by civilized nations' which formed one of the sources of the Law of Nations (see §1.4).

§1.2 Hierarchies of laws

In the course of such a development, it may take a substantial time before the necessary monopoly of force can be established. During that period, local and central laws may co-exist, though they generally regulate different matters. Thus, there may be a stage where there is a single law, centrally enforced, about the taking of human life, and different laws, locally enforced, about such things as land tenure and inheritance. But even after the communities constituting a State have become fully welded together, the State may not need, or wish, to acquire exclusive responsibility for all the laws in all its regions, or in all the fields of conduct of its citizens. Within the limits set by the central authorities, different communities may be left free to make and enforce their own rules.

In such cases, it is convenient to think of the different sets of laws concerned as being ranked in a hierarchical order, in which one set is considered 'superior' to another if (but only if) it is able to prescribe limits for the other's contents. In a developed legal system, hierarchies of that kind will often contain several ranks. One especially important rank is that which regulates the nature and functions of the groups within the State who exercise the task of making and maintaining its laws, and with it the State's monopoly of force. Many different configurations of such groups are possible in theory; at different times and in different places a fair number have been tried in practice; and they all present various advantages and disadvantages. The total task can be conveniently divided into three separate functions, now commonly performed in many States by three different institutions:

(1) *legislatures* responsible for making new laws, and for changing or repealing old ones;

(2) *judicatures* responsible for interpreting and applying existing laws;
(3) *executives* responsible (among other things) for the exercise of the State's monopoly of force.

The nature, form, and powers of these institutions, and the relationships between them, are today commonly regulated by a separate set of rules or laws, called the State's 'constitution'. With three exceptions,[5] the constitutions of all modern States are embodied in a single written instrument. Within such a State, constitutional law prescribes the limits of the content of all other laws, and so ranks highest in the hierarchy of laws: so, for example, the legislature can only make laws which the constitution allows it to make, and cannot itself change the constitution; in their turns, the judiciary can only apply, and the executive only enforce, the constitutionally valid laws which the legislature has made. And the constitution can only be changed by some procedure (such as, for example, a plebiscite or referendum) which is laid down in the constitution itself, and which is different from — and usually slower and more complicated than — the procedure for changing 'ordinary' laws.

However, the allocation of these three functions to separate institutions is a comparatively late development; for long periods in the history of many States, more than one of these functions (and often all of them) were vested in the same institution, frequently a hereditary ruler. While he seldom exercised all of them in every detail, the constitutional theory was that the power to exercise them was his, and that if others in fact exercised them they could do so only by delegation from him, and in his name. The famous dictum of the French King Louis XIV, *'l'état, c'est moi,'* quite correctly represented the political theory and reality of that stage of French constitutional development.

§1.3 Emergence of domestic human rights law

In periods of absolute rule, constitutional changes are apt to be no more than changes in the person or family of the ruler, either by succession on death (sometimes disputed and resolved by civil war), or by foreign conquest. However, though in theory an absolute ruler may proclaim whatever laws he pleases, in practice he is constrained by what his subjects can be forced, cajoled, or persuaded to accept. The more powerful of those subjects may therefore be able to procure the ruler to proclaim laws which are in their interests rather than his, as for example in the case of the English Magna Carta Libertatum in the thirteenth century.

In practice, any ruler can only maintain himself in power with the active support of a sufficient number of other power-holders within his society, and the passive acquiescence — however reluctant — of most of the rest of his subjects. Such support will diminish if his conduct, and the laws he proclaims, are perceived to be bad — either in the sense of being morally wrong, or in the sense of being contrary to the general interest, or to a particular and powerful interest. In the case of laws, a special concept — that of *justice* — is apt to be used for assessing whether they are good or bad. This concept, like that of law itself, has no universally accepted definition. It has meant different things to different people, in different societies at different times, and it still does today.[6]

---

[5] Israel, New Zealand, and the United Kingdom.
[6] Compare, for example, C. K. Allen, *Aspects of Justice* (Stevens, 1958); H. Kelsen,

Tenable judgements on the quality of a set of national laws can therefore only be made by reference to the perception of justice in the particular society at the particular time. So, for example, the Christian canon lawyers in western Europe from at least the twelfth century onwards applied the test of conformity of a secular ruler's law with their understanding of divine law, condemning it, if it failed to conform, with the maxim *lex iniusta non est lex*. The test of conformity with God-given laws is to be found also in many other religious cultures, of which the Jews, the ancient Greeks,[7] and Islam are the best-documented examples.

The practical importance of all this lies in the concept of *legitimacy*. In the measure that a particular ruler's laws are shown to be unjust, the legitimacy of his rule is put into question; in the same measure, legitimacy is acquired by those who refuse to obey such laws, and who may be driven first to resist the ruler, and in extreme cases even to rebel against him in order to overthrow him. Without a claim to legitimacy, they would have no tenable case for undertaking the necessary disobedience, subversion, or violence. It therefore becomes especially important, at all stages in the development of legal systems, to devise consistent theories of the legitimacy of laws. Any such theory requires a standard of values — and especially of justice — against which existing laws can be measured. Such a standard must necessarily be superior to the laws themselves, and will therefore constitute the highest rank in the legal hierarchy. The major difficulty is to find a plausible source for that standard.

Claims have been put forward for several such sources. Religious institutions derive their ultimate standards from 'divine law', as revealed by God to man in some Holy Scripture. In western Europe during the Middle Ages, that standard was widely applied, and served to confer legitimacy upon many secular rulers, as well as upon the opponents of some others. But a single uncritical Christian faith began to be questioned by the Renaissance in the fifteenth century, became fragmented by the Reformation in the sixteenth and seventeenth, and was openly challenged by the Enlightenment in the eighteenth and the rapid advances of natural science in the nineteenth. As a result, other grounds had to be found to support standards against which to judge a ruler's laws.

The search for such grounds coincided with, and formed much of the content of, the development of political philosophy during that period. Among the outstanding contributors to this field were the Britons Hobbes, Burke, Locke, Hume, Bentham, and Mill; the Frenchmen Montaigne, Rousseau, Voltaire, Montesquieu, de Tocqueville, and Proud'hon; the Germans Marx and Nietzsche; and the Russian Lenin. Their work both reflects, and contributed to, the development of the theory of the legitimacy of State power. But that work had its effect on real politics as well as on political theory. Quite apart from the economic interests involved, and the tensions of religious sectarianism, the challenge to the legitimacy of the Stuart monarchs in Great Britain — the last in that

What is Justice? (Berkeley, 1960); R. B. Brandt (ed.); *Social Justice* (Prentice-Hall, 1962); J. Rawls, *A Theory of Justice* (OUP, 1972); B. Barry, *The Liberal Theory of Justice* (OUP, 1973); R. Nozik, *Anarchy, State and Utopia* (Blackwell, 1974); D. Miller, *Social Justice* (OUP, 1976); R. Dworkin, *Taking Rights Seriously* (Duckworth, 1978); and J. R. Lucas, *On Justice* (Clarendon, 1980).

[7] See, for example, H. Lauterpacht, *International Law and Human Rights*, 80–3; M. Cranston, *What are Human Rights?*, 9–10.

country to claim the 'divine right of Kings'[8] — was one of the major causes of both the Civil War of 1642-51, and of the 'bloodless revolution' in 1688.

In the year of that revolution, the British Parliament enacted a 'Bill of Rights'. That statute, like Magna Carta, is widely regarded as an early human rights instrument, though its text in fact more closely resembles a settlement reached between different interest groups after a period of instability. However, it was on any view an instrument of constitutional law, adumbrating a new period in which historical discontinuities such as civil wars, revolutions, or foreign conquests were more apt to result in discontinuous constitutional change. That process reached its climax at the end of the next century, with the almost simultaneous rebellion of Britain's American colonies and the French Revolution. In each case, the successful rebels saw merit in enshrining in one or more great texts — the Declaration of Independence and the Bill of Rights in America, and the *déclaration des droits de l'homme et du citoyen* in France — values which had inspired them in the struggle against their respective *anciens régimes*.

It is striking how profoundly those documents differ from the British Bill of Rights of only a century earlier. The difference constitutes a permanent monument to the work of the philosophers who had had so profound an influence on the development of political theory during that century. For the great American and French texts of 1776, 1789, and 1791 for the first time set forth principles which are instantly recognizable as propositions of modern human rights law, properly so called. Those principles may be summarized as follows:

∽ (1) The *principle of universal inherence*: every human being has certain rights, capable of being enumerated and defined, which are not conferred on him by any ruler, nor earned or acquired by purchase, but which inhere in him by virtue of his humanity alone.

∽ (2) The *principle of inalienability*: no human being can be deprived of any of those rights, by the act of any ruler or even by his own act.[9]

∽ (3) The *Rule of Law*: where rights conflict with each other, the conflicts must be resolved by the consistent, independent and impartial application of just laws in accordance with just procedures.

But the ground of those principles was less than clear: in part, the Creator was still being invoked; some were asserted as 'self-evident' truths. A theory of 'natural' law, founded in part on Stoic philosophy and the Roman concept of *ius gentium*, was also being revived and developed.[10] So was the theory of the 'social contract', according to which rulers derive their authority only from some notional agreement under which their peoples have delegated to

---

[8] Though that right had already come under challenge in the previous century in the Netherlands, whose States-General declared, in their Act of Abjuration from Philip II of Spain of 26 July 1581, 'that God did not create the subjects for the benefit of the Prince, to do his bidding in all things whether godly or ungodly, right or wrong, and to serve him as slaves, but the Prince for the benefit of the subjects, without which he is no Prince.'

[9] Or, in a democracy, even by the will of the majority of the sovereign people.

[10] This brief sentence does scant justice to the complexity and sophistication of theories of natural law, and to the pervasive influence they have had on legal and political theory and practice for more than two millenia, and down to the present day. See, on this subject, the section on 'The Law of Nature and the Rights of Man' in Lauterpacht, *op. cit.* 73 ff.; F. Castberg, *Natural Law and Human Rights: An idea-historical survey*.

them the power of government during those peoples' pleasure, and subject to implied but ascertainable conditions.

Closely associated with these propositions were others bearing on the theoretical basis and practical form of the institutions of the State, mainly directed to the replacement of the single institution of monarchy by those of a democratic republic.

The rights listed in the respective catalogues at that time all took the form of 'freedoms' — that is, they defined areas of conduct which were stated to be beyond the scope of regulation or interference by the State, whether through the enactment of laws or otherwise.

To put these principles into effect, the new United States of America and the new French Republic used the method of a written constitution, which served both to create and to define the functions of the institutions of the new State, and to declare and entrench (in the USA by the set of constitutional amendments known as the Bill of Rights) the catalogue of fundamental rights. Since then, that method has been adopted by virtually every other nation in the world,[11] usually in the wake of some major discontinuity in its history. In all those nations today, therefore, the constitution occupies the highest rank in the hierarchy of laws, and any catalogue of fundamental rights or freedoms there set out constrains the field within which their legislatures, executives and judiciaries have legitimate power to function.

However, since the end of the eighteenth century, these catalogues have been much expanded. They are now no longer confined to 'freedoms' from State intervention, but include many rights that can only be realized through positive action by the State. This expansion owes much to the development, in the early nineteenth century, of the new political theory of socialism. In accordance with that theory, it is not enough for the State to abstain from intervention in some of its citizens' areas of conduct: the State should intervene actively in the redress of injustice and inequality, especially of a social or economic kind. Indeed, the citizens have a right to require the State to intervene in such fields. Today, such 'programme' rights are included in the catalogue of fundamental rights of many countries, regardless of whether or not they formally describe themselves as 'socialist'.[12]

§1.4 The Law of Nations

From earliest times, different communities have entered into relationships with each other — whether friendly, as in the case of trade; or hostile, as in the case of war. For such relationships too, as for those between individuals within a group, rules of conduct have evolved, and have passed through a process of development similar in some (but not all) respects to those of 'domestic' or 'national' legal systems. Those rules also have varied from place to place, and from time to time. However, over the centuries certain consistent traditions developed in the ways in which relationships between rulers, representing their

---

[11] The first to follow the French and US examples were the Netherlands (1798), Sweden (1809), Spain (1812), Norway (1814), Belgium (1831), Liberia (1847), Sardinia (1848), Denmark (1849), and Prussia (1850).

[12] The way for this was led by the Papal encyclical *Rerum Novarum* in 1891, and the first nations to incorporate such rights in their constitutions were Mexico (1917), Russia (1918), and Germany (1919). On the categorization of the different human rights and freedoms, see generally §13.

nations or States, were conducted. In due course, those traditions came to be collectively described as a set of laws — the Law of Nations or, in more modern usage, international law.[13]

Today, international law is concerned with an enormous range of subject matters, from maritime trade to the allocation of radio frequencies. But there is still one important difference between the system of international law and domestic legal systems: in the community composed of the nation states, there is no single legislature, nor is there a single institution with a monopoly of force. Accordingly, international law can only be created by the consent of the States who are its subjects, and can only be enforced by individual and collective sanctions imposed by those subjects themselves, rather than by some superior institution. If a private individual fails to perform a legally binding contract he has made with another, that other can obtain an order against him from a national court for the payment of compensation, and that order can be made effective through the forcible seizure of the defendant's assets by some court official exercising his State's monopoly of force. But if a State defaults on a contract it has made with another State, there is no directly comparable enforcement procedure: failing the voluntary payment of compensation, the other State can only resort to self-help or reprisal — perhaps by itself seizing assets of the defaulting State located within its own territory, restricting or terminating trade or diplomatic relations, or, as the ultimate reprisal, going to war. It may also seek to enlist the support of other members of the community of nations in imposing collective sanctions on its adversary, but whether it succeeds will depend at least as much on those other States' own political interests as on any rules of international law.

Accordingly, international law even today rests essentially on consent, and can be enforced only by self-help, and individual or collective sanctions imposed on 'outlaws'. To that extent, despite the complexity and sophistication of the matters which it now regulates, and the means by which it regulates them, it can still be (and often is) described as 'primitive' in form, comparable in this respect with the laws of a simple agricultural settlement rather than with the legal system of a modern nation state.

The consent from which the rules of international law are derived may be signified in different ways. The most obvious is an express contract or treaty, imposing obligations by which all the State Parties to it agree to be bound. Such 'treaty law' constitutes a large part of modern international law. Consent may however also be inferred from the established and consistent practice of States in conducting their relationships with each other: the equivalent of the Roman *ius gentium*, and of 'customary' law in other domestic legal systems, especially those based on uncodified traditions such as the Anglo-Saxon ones. So, for example, codes of conduct or multilateral declarations of common policy which are not themselves treaties may, over time, provide enough evidence of consistent practice to become rules of international law. And, once those rules are so firmly established as to form part of the international *ius*

---

[13] One of the necessary premises for such a set of laws is the existence of a set of discrete entities to which they can apply: in this case, sovereign States. This could be said to be no more than a convenient fiction, since it cloaks the fact that no such entities exist in reality: nations and states are in fact no more than the aggregates of the individuals who compose them, and the territory and material objects over which they have physical control. It could therefore be argued that international law is in reality no more than a convenient and elegant construct, whose practical importance lies only in the effect that it can have on the minds and consciences of individuals, and through those on their conduct.

cogens, they bind even States that have never evinced any express consent to be bound by them — as, for example, newly independent States joining the international community for the first time.

In short, unlike modern national legal systems, international law is initially created by obligations voluntarily *assumed* by its subjects; only when that process is far advanced can it be said that the law *imposes* obligations on those subjects. However, though there is no single supranational institution that can exercise a monopoly of force to ensure conformity with the rules of international law, this does not mean that they can be ignored with impunity. As in simple agricultural settlements, the member states of the modern international community depend heavily on each others' goodwill, and it would be contrary to the interests of any of them to outlaw themselves entirely from it. Here again, the concept of legitimacy is crucial: any government that so conducts itself as to put its own legitimacy into serious question in the international community risks not only legitimate sanctions and even reprisals from the other members of that community, but legitimate resistance and perhaps even rebellion within its own territory. There are in fact today very strong pressures on most nation states to comply with their obligations under international law.

§1.5 The doctrine of national sovereignty

Since the beginnings of the Law of Nations, one of its fundamental principles was that of national sovereignty, which reserves to each sovereign State the exclusive right to take any action it thinks fit, provided only that the action does not interfere with the rights of other States, and is not prohibited by international law on that or any other ground.

According to that principle, a sovereign State has complete freedom of action, in international law, to deal with its own nationals ('personal sovereignty') and with its own territory ('territorial sovereignty'), to make use of the public domain (the high seas, the atmosphere, and outer space), to enter into legal relationships with other sovereign States, to become a member of international organizations of 'universal vocation' — and, originally, to make war, though the scope of that sovereign freedom has now been reduced to the use of force in self-defence, and the right to remain neutral when others are at war.

It follows from this principle that, in all matters falling within the 'domestic jurisdiction' of any State, international law does not permit any interference, let alone any intervention, by any other State. Such matters do not fall within the concern of international law. Accordingly, so long as 'personal' sovereignty continued to be regarded as falling exclusively within the domestic jurisdiction of sovereign States, 'what a government did to its own citizens was its own affair and beyond the reach of international law or legal intervention by other States'.[14]

However, matters stood differently in the case of aliens. As part of its national sovereignty, a State was always entitled to demand respect for its own nationals abroad, for any maltreatment of them could constitute a violation of the 'personal' sovereignty of the State to which they belonged. Accordingly, international law from early times imposed (and still imposes) an obligation on States to make their territories safe for the nationals of other States, even

---

[14] J. P. Humphrey, 'The International Law of Human Rights', in *The Present State of International Law and other Essays* (1973).

while there was no such obligation for their own nationals. In time an international minimum standard for such safety was developed, requiring the protection of the lives, liberty, and property of all aliens, both in every State's domestic law and in fact. Moreover, the standard was an objective one, and could often require better protection than the domestic law in fact provided, either for aliens or for citizens. The standard included the administration of justice, so that a 'manifest' denial of justice, for instance through denial of a fair hearing, fell short of it.[15]

In the result, international law for a long time demanded substantial protection for the aliens within a State, while demanding none for the State's own citizens. But even that demand flowed only from the doctrine of national sovereignty itself — so that, if a State fell short of the requirement to protect another State's nationals, for example by expropriating their property, the compensation was due to the other State whose 'personal' sovereignty had been violated, not to the individual whose property had been taken. Whether that State chose to pass the compensation on to the injured individual was, in international law, entirely its own affair.

And, for centuries, one proposition remained without challenge: by reason of the doctrine of national sovereignty, the Law of Nations could not recognize *any* rights vested in *any* individual against *any* sovereign State — his own or another.

§1.6 Legal positivism

As has already been mentioned in §1.3, legal and political theorists have encountered substantial difficulties in devising tenable grounds for assessing the legitimacy, or the justice, of laws. Both 'divine' law and 'natural' law have been prayed in aid for that purpose, but each of these depends for its conviction on belief either in a divinity or in a moral dimension that permeates the natural world. Neither of these beliefs is objectively verifiable, and so neither divine nor natural law carries much conviction for unbelievers. In the late nineteenth and early twentieth centuries, therefore, there grew up a marked reaction against such attempts at systematic legal theology, in parallel with a similar reaction against the then current pursuit of systematic metaphysics in philosophy. In both cases, the reaction took the form of 'positivism', a school of thought distinguished by its refusal to treat as meaningful any proposition whose truth could not be objectively demonstrated in the material world. To the positivist, such propositions are not so much false, as simply devoid of meaning or substance.

In particular, for the strict legal positivist the only laws which may properly be called by that name are those which can demonstrably be enforced: if a rule of conduct cannot be enforced, it is (to him) meaningless to describe it as a law. Nor are there true hierarchies of laws: all laws are of equal status, and valid only to the extent to which they can be enforced. From which it necessarily follows that no meaningful distinction can be drawn between good and bad

---

[15] 'To undertake to examine the justice of a definitive sentence is an attack on the jurisdiction of him who has passed it. The prince, therefore, ought not to interfere in the causes of his subjects in foreign countries, and grant them his protection, excepting in cases where justice is refused, or palpable and evident injustice done, or rules and forms openly violated, or, finally, an odious distinction made, to the prejudice of his subjects, or of foreigners in general', *Law of Nations* (Chitty's ed. 1869), 165.

laws, or just and unjust ones. And, consistently with that position, some strict legal positivists denied the very existence of international law as such, on the ground that there were no means by which the rules comprised in that alleged canon could be consistently enforced.

§1.7 Emergence of international human rights law

By the nineteenth century, international law was developing a doctrine of the legitimacy of 'humanitarian intervention' in cases where a State committed atrocities against its own subjects which 'shocked the conscience of mankind'. This provided a limited exception to the doctrine of national sovereignty. It was invoked largely against the Ottoman Empire: in 1827 on behalf of the Greek people, by France in Syria in 1860-1, and again in 1876 when around 12,000 Christians were massacred by irregular Ottoman troops in what is today Bulgaria. On a strict view of the doctrine of national sovereignty, that was the exclusive concern of the sovereign Ottoman State, and not the business of anyone else. Nonetheless, by invoking the doctrine of humanitarian intervention in public and Parliamentary speeches, the British Liberal politician Gladstone succeeded in promoting a foreign policy designed to support the freedom of the people of Bulgaria.

This process continued, albeit slowly. Following the First World War, Minority Treaties were concluded — with the new League of Nations as a guarantor — which sought to protect the rights of linguistic and ethnic minorities within the new State territories created by the Treaties of Versailles and St Germain, and these may be seen as precursors of modern international human rights instruments.[16]

The same period saw the beginning of international collaboration in a number of specific 'humanitarian' fields. The abolition of national slavery and the international slave trade began to be pursued from the early part of the nineteenth century, and by 1885 the General Act of the Berlin Conference on Central Africa was able to affirm that 'trading in slaves is forbidden in conformity with the principles of international law'. Later, through the influence of the Red Cross movement, international treaties (the 'Hague Conventions' and ultimately the 'Geneva Conventions') were adopted in order to limit the suffering caused by wars, and to regulate the treatment of prisoners of war. The International Labour Organisation was established in 1919, and soon began to promote a succession of international conventions designed to protect industrial workers from gross exploitation, and to improve their working conditions.[17] The League of Nations took a continuing interest in humanitarian matters and in at least some aspects of human rights. And the first true international human rights treaty — the Slavery Convention — was adopted in 1926 and entered into force in the following year.

[16] Especially Article 4 of the German-Polish Convention on Upper Silesia of 1922, which broke new ground in guaranteeing rights of individuals — including the rights to life, liberty, and the free exercise of religion, and equal treatment before the law — even against States whose own nationals they were. A Pole and a Czech were the first private individuals in the history of international law to establish personal rights against a State as a result of this treaty: *Steiner and Gross* v. *The Polish State*, Upper Silesian Arbitral Tribunal, Cases Nos. 188 and 287, *Annual Digest* 1927-8.

[17] Even before the formal establishment of the ILO, two multilateral labour conventions were concluded in Berne, Switzerland, in 1906: one against night work by women, and the other against the use of white phosphorus in the manufacture of matches.

Nonetheless, during the first part of the twentieth century the theory of legal positivism remained in the ascendant. Combined with a strict application of the doctrine of national sovereignty, it effectively excluded the possibility of judging, and therefore criticizing, the treatment of any people by its own government. The apotheosis — and the consequent downfall — of that position came in National Socialist Germany in the late 1930s and early 1940s, where historically unprecedented atrocities were perpetrated by the régime there and then lawfully in power upon some millions of its own citizens. Many of those atrocities were carried out with complete legality under National Socialist legislation: the domestic laws authorized, and paralleled, the pernicious injustice of the acts. Moreover, those laws had been enacted by a legislature lawfully installed under the constitution of a sovereign State. According to the strict doctrine of national sovereignty, any foreign criticism of those laws was therefore formally illegitimate; according to the strict positivist position, it was also meaningless.

And precisely the same position could be, and was, taken in relation to the atrocities perpetrated at much the same time upon some millions of its citizens by the régime then legitimately in power in the USSR.

§1.8 International human rights law since 1945

While those events spelt unprecedented tragedy for huge numbers of people, they also spelt the *reductio ad absurdum* of strict legal positivism, and of a strict application of the doctrine of national sovereignty. When the Second World War which they had unleashed ended, the victorious nations determined to introduce into international law new concepts designed to outlaw such events for the future, in order to make their recurrence at least less probable.[18] The means adopted were the establishment of new intergovernmental organizations such as the United Nations, the Council of Europe and the Organisation of American States, and the development within those fora of a new branch of international law, specifically concerned with the relations between governments and their own subjects. Many systems of domestic human rights law lay ready to hand, and catalogues of human rights and fundamental freedoms had already long since been incorporated in the national constitutions of many States. What was now required was to formulate an up-to-date catalogue, and to incorporate this into binding international law — first in the form of a Universal Declaration (in fact adopted in 1948), and thereafter through multilateral treaties, under which sovereign States would consent to be bound by the obligation to respect and secure the human rights there specified within their own territories, for all individuals (including their own citizens) over whom they had jurisdiction.

Since then, several such treaties have entered into force, which are considered

---

[18] The landmarks in this movement were the Atlantic Charter of 14 August 1941, with its call for 'freedom from fear and want'; the Declaration of 1 January 1942 by the 26 'United Nations' then fighting the Axis powers, to the effect 'that complete victory over their enemies is essential to defend life, liberty, independence and religious freedom, and to preserve human rights and justice in their own lands as well as in other lands'; and the Dumbarton Oaks Proposals in 1944 for the establishment of the UN which would, among other things, 'promote respect for human rights and fundamental freedoms' — the phrase to which the San Francisco conference of the following year added the words '. . . for all, without distinction as to race, sex, language or religion.'

in detail in later Parts of this book. These now impose obligations on many governments as to what they may or may not do to individuals over whom they are able to exercise State power. To the extent of those obligations, the strict doctrine of national sovereignty has been cut down in two crucial respects. First, how a State treats its own subjects is now the legitimate concern of international law. Secondly, there is now a superior international standard, established by common consent, which may be used for judging the domestic laws and the actual conduct of sovereign States within their own territories and in the exercise of their internal jurisdictions, and may therefore be regarded as ranking in the hierarchy of laws even above national constitutions.

Accordingly, the need for standards founded on systems of divine or natural law has disappeared, and with it the need for the legal positivist to object to them. To judge whether a national law is good or bad, just or unjust, recourse is no longer necessary to the Creator or to Nature, or to belief in either of them.[19] Instead, one may refer to the rules of international human rights law, as defined in the relevant instruments which have been brought into existence since 1945.[20] If the strict legal positivist still wishes to object, he can point out that these rules are not yet enforceable, even against governments that have assented to them, by any formal procedure that can compel compliance in all circumstances. Technically, that remains true so long as there is no supranational institution having a monopoly of force. Yet, under the pressures of the international community, many nations have already modified their laws and practices in order to conform more closely with these international obligations, especially in the case of the regional human rights conventions (see, for example, §§2.5 and 2.6).

However, it undoubtedly remains the case that too many other nations have not yet accepted, or do not yet conform, or conform only inadequately, with the new obligations under international human rights law. But it seems at least doubtful whether that fact can support a fundamental objection to the meaning or validity of this entire area of law, any more than the continued prevalence of crime in many places can be used to support an argument that all criminal law is fundamentally meaningless and invalid.

Another objection which is sometimes heard is that 'human rights' are an exclusively Western concept, whose 'imposition' on the rest of the world constitutes a form of intellectual, political, or legal neo-colonialism or neo-imperialism. But that is in fact quite fallacious. Concepts of legitimacy, the justice of laws, the integrity and dignity of the individual, safeguards against arbitrary rule, freedom from oppression and persecution, individual participation in collective endeavours (including the government of the community), and the like are to be found in very similar form in every civilization throughout the world, and throughout history, whose aspirations have ever been recorded. Besides, the international instruments in which these concepts are now formulated have been freely negotiated, adopted, and ratified by many nations in all parts of the world, covering the entire spectrum of existing cultural, religious and political orientations.

---

[19] References to both of them were deleted from the draft of *UDHR* shortly before its adoption: see J. P. Humphrey, 'The Universal Declaration of Human Rights: its history, impact and juridical character' in B. G. Ramcharan (ed.), *Human Rights: 30 Years After the Universal Declaration*, 27.
[20] 'They transfer the inalienable and natural rights of the individual from the venerable but controversial orbit of the law of nature to the province of positive law': Lauterpacht, *op cit.*, 159.

§1.9 The structure of modern international human rights law

The instruments concerned fall into several categories. They are reviewed in §2, and the texts of the eight that have the widest scope are set out, with appropriate supporting material, in Parts II, III, and IV of this book. But it may be helpful to give here a brief sketch of the general structure of the new system.

The modern international law-making process almost invariably begins with the adoption of a Declaration or Resolution by a major organ of an intergovernmental organization, such as the General Assembly of the United Nations. Such an instrument does not by itself create new international law, though over time it may come to be cited as evidence of the consistent practice of States, and so of the consent necessary for the development of a new rule of international law. Following such a declaration or resolution, attempts may be made to convert its principles into the form of a detailed and binding treaty, negotiated in the same (though sometimes in a different) inter-governmental forum. When such a treaty enters into force, it will immediately create specific obligations in international law for those States which become parties to it. Major treaties of wide general import are then often followed by more specific ones, dealing with narrower topics in greater detail. In the field of international human rights law, many such resolutions and declarations have been adopted, and a number of such treaties is now in force. They fall into three broad categories: global, regional, and subsidiary.

The global and regional human rights treaties (which are the main subject-matter of the present work) have much in common, and are distinguished mainly by the forum in which they have been adopted, and therefore the States which are, or can become, parties to them. Their common features are these:

(1) They specify the particular obligations of all their State Parties in respect of certain 'human rights and fundamental freedoms' of all the persons within their territories and subject to their jurisdictions (see §6).
(2) They contain general provisions applying to the protection or realization of all those rights (see §§7–12).
(3) They define and circumscribe the rights and freedoms concerned (see Part III).
(4) They establish institutions and procedures for the international supervision, interpretation, and application of their substantive provisions (see Part IV).

The subsidiary treaties (which are often referred to, but not reprinted, in the present work) are distinguished from the global and regional ones principally by the fact that each of them deals only with one human right, or a small number of related rights; at the same time, the obligations which they impose on their State Parties are usually much more specific and detailed, being designed to provide concrete means for the protection or realization of the right or rights with which they deal.

What all these treaties have in common, and what makes the legal code which they collectively constitute unprecedented in international law, is that — by agreement between the State Parties among themselves — they define and create specific rights for the individuals over whom those States are able to exercise power, but who are not themselves parties to the instruments. In effect, they create *iura quaesita tertio* for hundreds of millions of the world's human population[21] (see also §1.12).

---

[21] 'The individual has acquired a status and a stature which have transformed him from

The concept of a 'right' is of course familiar to all lawyers, as is the general principle that for every right there must be a correlative duty, imposed on someone other than the holder of the right. So, for example, the owner of a house has the right to occupy it and to exclude others from its occupation; those others have a correlative duty not to trespass on his property. Again, the driver of a motor vehicle on a highway has a duty not to endanger others; if he damages someone else through a breach of that duty, the victim will acquire a right to compensation. All rights and duties of that kind are acquired and created by some act or event, such as purchase, inheritance, the making of a contract, or the happening of a traffic accident; those rights may likewise be transferred, disposed of or extinguished by other acts or events. But 'human' rights are distinguished from other rights by two principal features. First, they are not acquired, nor can they be transferred, disposed of or extinguished, by any act or event: according to the classical theory, now reflected in the international standards, they 'inhere' universally in all human beings, throughout their lives, in virtue of their humanity alone, and they are 'inalienable'.[22] Secondly, their primary correlative duties fall on States and their public authorities, not on other individuals. Three important consequences flow from those distinctions.

§1.10 Non-discrimination

The first is that, in respect of 'ordinary' rights, it is often perfectly legitimate to differentiate between different individuals in different circumstances, and for different reasons. The law may, for example, impose more stringent obligations on those who practise medicine than on those who practise landscape gardening. In computing the compensation for loss of earnings payable to the victim of a traffic accident, it may award a larger sum to a banker than to a bus-driver. It may give an insurer the right to avoid a contract for the mere non-disclosure of a material fact, and yet decline to give any such right to a trader in commodities.

But because of the reflection in the modern international canon of the twin principles of 'universal inherence' and 'inalienability', no such differentiation is today permissible in the case of 'human' rights. In respect of these, the law must treat all members of the protected class with complete equality, regardless of their particular circumstances, features or characteristics. Indeed, the concept of 'non-discrimination' is so central to international human rights law that all but one of the major instruments prescribe it in an Article of general application, expressed to extend to all the specific rights which they declare (see §7).

That policy is soundly based on experience. The pretext for many of the worst violations of human rights which have been perpetrated in the world's history has been discrimination, directed at different times and places against

an object of international compassion into a subject of international right.' Lauterpacht, *op. cit.*, 4. In fact, that principle was first applied by the High Court of Danzig in the *Zappot Street Crossing Case*, Annual Digest 1933–4, No. 104, following the Advisory Opinion of the Permanent Court of International Justice on *The Jurisdiction of the Courts of Danzig*, Annual Digest 1927–8, No. 187.

[22] That, at least, is the general principle. But, as so often in the field of law, it is subject to exceptions. If, for example, capital punishment for murder is regarded as compatible with a 'human' right to life, it can only be on the basis that, by choosing to commit murder, the murderer 'alienates' that right for himself.

groups as disparate as slaves, serfs, women, or races differing in skin colour from a dominant group; religious, ethnic, or linguistic minorities such as Christians, Jews, Armenians, Muslims, and Hindus; or the members of hereditary castes or social classes — not to mention those holding unorthodox political or other opinions. All such grounds of discrimination are therefore now expressly forbidden in the major instruments, and many of the subsidiary instruments are devoted to particular aspects of them.

It does not of course follow that modern international human rights law adopts a simplistic philosophy of egalitarianism. On the contrary, it is the recognition that all human beings differ from each other, and that each individual is unique, which underlies the concept of the integrity and dignity of the individual person which human rights law is primarily concerned to protect. This does not require that all persons must be treated alike in all circumstances; what it requires is that, regardless of their many differences, they are entitled to protection from those man-made and avoidable impositions of oppressive power which would restrict the development of their individual potentials. Thus, regardless of their personal characteristics, they must not be tortured, or enslaved, or arbitrarily killed, or imprisoned without a fair trial if they are accused of a crime, nor must they be deprived of the opportunity of gaining their living by work of their choice, or of fair access to food, clothing, housing, education, and health services. Equality of treatment is required only in respect of the rights and freedoms — often called 'fundamental' — which are inherent in their individual humanity, and which are necessary to enable their personal diversity to develop and manifest itself.[23]

§ 1.11 The Rule of Law

Secondly, national systems may differ widely in the 'ordinary' rights they protect, and the means by which they protect them. One system may treat trespass on land as a crime, another as a civil wrong, and yet another may not impose any sanctions for it at all. Some rights may be justiciable in the courts; for others, the competence may lie with an administrative agency. The circumstances in which a right can be established and enjoyed may be laid down in a set of binding rules, or be a matter for the exercise of someone's unfettered discretion.

By contrast, the 'Rule of Law' is a fundamental principle of human rights law.[24] Within a State, rights must themselves be protected by law; and any disputes about them must not be resolved by the exercise of some arbitrary discretion, but must be consistently capable of being submitted for adjudication to a competent, impartial, and independent tribunal, applying procedures which will ensure full equality and fairness to all the parties, and determining the question in accordance with clear, specific, and pre-existing laws, known and openly proclaimed (see § 22).

The application of the Rule of Law is of particular importance for establishing the boundaries of the different human rights. It is a commonplace of both

[23] See, on this subject, the judgments of the International Court of Justice in the *South-West Africa Cases (Second Phase)*, ICJ Reports 1966, and especially the (dissenting) opinion of Judge Tanaka at 284–316.

[24] For a useful collection of texts relating to the Rule of Law, see *The Rule of Law and Human Rights: Principles and Definitions*, International Commission of Jurists (Geneva, 1966).

law and experience that the claims of different individuals constantly conflict with each other: indeed, a 'legal right' can usefully be defined as that part of a person's claim in some field which the law invests with sufficient legitimacy to allow and enable it to prevail over the conflicting claims of others. In common with all other specifications of legal rights, therefore, human rights law provides boundaries for the rights which it enumerates. With very few exceptions such as the freedoms from torture and slavery, each human right is made subject to restrictions and limitations in order to accommodate the rights of others. To take just one example, the right to freedom of expression is not drawn so widely as to entitle everyone, with impunity, to defame their neighbours, put life and limb at risk by falsely shouting 'Fire!' in a crowded assembly, or imperil the fairness of a criminal trial by conducting a public press campaign against the accused.

At the same time, such restrictions and limitations must be used only to establish the proper boundaries of the protected right, and not as a pretext for eroding the core of the right itself, let alone for destroying it altogether. It is therefore crucially important that, whenever any conflict of this kind arises, it should be decided by a tribunal which is independent of all the parties concerned, not subject to any external pressures, competent to establish all the relevant facts with complete impartiality, and able to apply known and established legal rules consistently to the resolution of the conflict. Those are the fundamental requirements of the Rule of Law.

Two common fallacies should perhaps be mentioned here. First, laymen who have not themselves examined the texts of the instruments are apt to dismiss the entire concept of 'human rights' as a piece of unrealistic idealism (or, in the words of Bentham's famous stricture upon natural law, 'nonsense upon stilts'), on the ground that all such rights are far too wide and vague ever to be realized in practice. Only a detailed study of the treaty texts themselves will show that they have in fact been drafted with all the legal precision necessary to apply them to real situations, and that their restriction and limitation clauses outline clear and sufficient boundaries for all those rights and freedoms for which that is necessary in order to ensure the orderly conduct of a human society.

But a superficial glance at those clauses of restriction and limitation often evokes another fallacy, namely that they are so wide as to take away, for all practical purposes, the rights which they qualify. In coming to that conclusion, the layman is necessarily unaware of a fundamental rule of construction of any legal text, enshrined for centuries in the maxim *verba chartarum semper interpretantur contra proferentem* and reflected also in the basic principle of international law that treaty obligations must be performed 'in good faith'.[25] This rule requires that, where a text confers a legal right, anyone who wishes to take advantage of some other provision of that text to restrict or limit the right conferred has the burden of establishing that his case falls clearly and unambiguously within the terms of that other provision, interpreted objectively and as narrowly as its exact words will allow. In short, the primary right must always prevail unless the precise exception or limitation is clearly and affirmatively shown to apply in the particular case (see §8).

One must always remember that the texts of the instruments are *legal* texts, designed to be interpreted and applied according to established legal rules. Here too, therefore, the Rule of Law provides essential support for the maintenance of the rights and freedoms enumerated in those texts.

[25] See now the Vienna Convention of the Law of Treaties, Art. 31(1).

19

§1.12 Remedies for violation

Lastly, the function of a national government in relation to 'human' rights is different from its function in relation to 'ordinary' rights. For the latter, the government's only concerns are to provide an adequate framework of domestic laws to define who has what rights, against whom, and in what circumstances; to provide tribunals to apply and interpret those laws in cases of dispute; and to put its monopoly of force at the disposal of those tribunals in order to enforce their decisions, and so provide effective remedies for infringements of the rights concerned. And since clear laws, ready access to tribunals, and effective remedies for the infringement of rights all tend to encourage stability and orderliness within a society, it is in the obvious interests of national governments to provide all these.

By contrast, 'human' rights are primarily claims against the public authorities of the State itself — either to remain free from interference by them, or to require them to act in some specific fashion. For any human right, the correlative duty falls in the first instance on the authorities of the State itself, not on other members of the community.[26] But apart from altruism, idealism, or long-term enlightened self-interest, power-holders may not always perceive any obvious advantage for themselves in accepting restrictions on their own power over others. The case, after all, is not one for mobilizing the State's monopoly of force against those who break its laws, but rather for constraining that monopoly by 'superior' rules, and sometimes even for calling for its exercise against its own possessors.

Many States of course already have domestic laws — and especially constitutions — which restrict and regulate the use of the State's monopoly of force, and independent tribunals in which the State itself can be called to account, and which can enforce their decisions against it. In such States, human rights are to that extent already protected by *national* human rights law. But only governments can make that protection effective, and the obligation to ensure that they do can in its turn be most effectively imposed on them through the operation of *international* law.

In the traditional view,[27] the *subjects* of international law — that is, those having rights and being bound by obligations under it — are sovereign States, in practice represented by their governments. The *objects* of international human rights law — that is, the beneficiaries of the rights protected or guaranteed — are individuals, in their turn the 'subjects' of those States, their governments and their laws.[28] That necessarily creates an asymmetry: those whose rights are

---

[26] But the duty may extend to the enactment of domestic laws to protect the human rights of individuals within the State's jurisdiction from *all* violations, and the provision of effective remedies if they are violated by private interests as well as by the State itself: see §§ 4.4 and 6.6. Some national constitutions — notably those of socialist States — also impose general duties and responsibilities on individuals. But the international human rights treaties tend to prefer the method of limiting some of the rights they define by reference to the rights of others, rather than by imposing duties owed to abstract entities.

[27] For an extended critique of this view, see the section 'The subjects of the Law of Nations' in Lauterpacht, *op cit.*, 3 ff. And when the government of Uruguay put forward precisely this contention to HRC, the Committee dismissed it as 'devoid of legal foundation' in cases where the State concerned had recognized the Committee's competence to receive and consider individual communications under *ICPR OP* (see § 27.3): *Antonaccio v. Uruguay* (R. 14/63) published 14 December 1981.

[28] But those 'objects' have in fact always been subjects of international law in at least one respect, namely in the area of 'international crime' (see § 5.3).

being protected are not themselves parties to the treaties, while those whom the treaties oblige to protect these rights do not obtain an obvious correlative benefit from the assumption of that obligation.[29] In the more common symmetrical (technically, synallagmatic) contract, each party receives benefits in return for the obligations which it assumes, and therefore retains a strong negotiating position throughout the period, after its conclusion, when the obligations under the contract fall to be performed; if one party fails to perform its part of the bargain, the other becomes entitled to do likewise, so that there is a powerful incentive on all parties to perform, rather than be deprived of the benefits flowing to them from the contract. But where the contract is made among debtors for the benefit of a class of unidentified creditors who are not themselves parties to it, and are not therefore bound to give anything in return, those creditors do not retain any negotiating power after the contract has been concluded.

For that reason, there needs to be some procedure under which individuals have an effective remedy if their human rights are violated by a State which, under international law, has become bound to respect those rights. All the major treaties therefore impose upon their State Parties an express obligation to provide such a remedy in their internal fora. But that is not by itself enough, for a State which deliberately fails to perform the obligation to respect a human right may, with equal deliberation, fail to perform the obligation to provide a domestic remedy for the resulting violation.

Accordingly, the major treaties also establish *international* institutions designed to provide at least some recourse if any State Party fails to provide adequate domestic remedies. The forms both of the institutions and of the recourse vary widely, ranging from no more than a Committee entitled to consider and comment on reports prepared by the State Parties themselves, to international Courts having full jurisdiction to determine complaints of violations by individuals, and to render judgements binding upon the States concerned. Quite apart from their practical effects, the mere existence and jurisdiction of these institutions has now finally established the principle that the individual person is more than an 'object' of international law: like the States (which in reality are themselves no more than collections of individuals), he is a *subject* of international law, entitled under it to claim legal rights, and to have recourse at the international level for violations of those rights if he cannot obtain redress from the national institutions of the State that has violated them.

[29] As the International Court of Justice put it, in its Advisory Opinion on *Reservations to the Genocide Convention* (ICJ Reports 1951, 15 at 23): 'In such a convention the Contracting States do not have any interests of their own; they merely have, one and all, a common interest, namely, the accomplishment of those high purposes which are the *raison d'être* of the convention. Consequently, in a convention of this type one cannot speak of individual advantages or disadvantages to States or of the maintenance of a perfect contractual balance between rights and duties.'

EUCM has made the same point in *Austria v. Italy* (788/60) YB 4, 138: 'The purpose of the High Contracting Parties in concluding the Convention was not to concede to each other reciprocal rights and obligations in pursuance of their individual national interests but to realise the aims and ideals of the Council of Europe, as expressed in its Statute, and to establish a common public order of the free democracies of Europe with the object of safeguarding their common heritage of political traditions, ideals, freedom and the rule of law; . . . The obligations undertaken by the High Contracting Parties in the Convention are essentially of an objective character, being designed rather to protect the fundamental rights of individual human beings from infringements by any of the High Contracting Parties than to create subjective and reciprocal rights for the High Contracting Parties themselves.'

In this context, the independence and impartiality of the relevant tribunal is of course crucial. It is enshrined in the venerable maxim *nemo iudex in causa sua*, and the central importance of that precept has been consistently demonstrated in international human rights law. Where that law assigns a supervisory function to an institution composed of governmental representatives, the results have so far ranged from the negligible, through the anodyne, to the blatantly political. That is hardly surprising: it may often not suit a government to criticise another State with which it is concerned to maintain friendly relations for strategic or economic reasons, nor are most governments anxious to invite counter-criticism of their own records in the field of human rights. In matters of foreign policy, self-interest and expediency are apt to outweigh high principle. That may be perfectly defensible if the objective is the preservation or advancement of national interests, but it is bound to restrict — if it does not totally paralyse — the pursuit of the objective of supporting and enforcing the rights of individuals against governments.

By contrast, the institutions whose members serve 'in a personal capacity' are not handicapped by such conflicts of interest. They have therefore been able to develop, through many decided cases, a substantial body of jurisprudence of high quality in the international law of human rights, which is considered in Parts II and III of the present work. Though it is self-evident that human rights have their political as well as their legal aspects, these institutions have consistently sought to separate the two from each other. For that reason, since the present work is intended as a book of law and not of politics, it confines its consideration of jurisprudence only to that of the *independent* institutions.

For lawyers, the principle utility of that jurisprudence lies in the clarification which it furnishes for the *boundaries* of human rights: the central areas are usually clear enough. A finding of fact by an international tribunal that an applicant has been subjected to extreme physical brutality by a State's security forces in order to induce him to divulge the names of clandestine trade union organisers, and that this amounted to a violation of his right not to be tortured, may be of the first importance for him, and expose the State concerned to international condemnation as a lawbreaker. But it adds nothing to the clarification of the law — unlike, say, a finding that some less brutal conduct constituted 'degrading treatment', but did not amount to 'torture'. Again, it is obvious that to shut down a newspaper which has criticized the government, sequestrate its property, confiscate its records, and imprison its editor, all violate the right to freedom of expression. But for lawyers it is more important to know whether a less flagrant restriction on that right — say the enforcement of an absolute duty of professional secrecy on members of the medical profession — may be justified on the ground that it protects the rights of others. For that reason, the importance of the jurisprudence increases as it approaches the margins of the field, and it is therefore on those cases that the present work places its emphasis — rather than on the many others which can do no more than give a melancholy description of the massive violations of central human rights which still take place in far too many parts of the world.

International human rights law is very young, and therefore still displays a certain frailty. It is an observable fact that the governments of a number of States, even though now formally bound by it, have so far been less than diligent in performing their obligations. The task of assuring its growth and vigour therefore now rests very largely on the international institutions called upon to supervise the performance of those State obligations, and to pronounce upon complaints of violation.

Over a quarter of a century, the independent European institutions at Strasbourg have deservedly established a high reputation in this field for their integrity, expertise, fairness, and realism, and their decisions have already led to many important changes in the laws and administrative practices of Member States of the Council of Europe. As the increasing number of other independent international institutions get into their stride, establish and develop procedures and precedents, and earn public respect for their determinations, their voices will come to be more widely heard and what they have to say will add its weight to the mounting pressures on those members of the international community whose performance still lags behind their promise. And — perhaps politically most important of all — those determinations will supply the essential legitimacy for any sanctions which other members of that community may be minded to impose upon the laggards, and for the resistance of their internal opponents.

It would of course be naïve to expect that international human rights law will miraculously abolish the oppression and exploitation of man by his fellows. But by making at least some of these visibly illegitimate, it can help to diminish their intensity and their extent, and so justify a position of guarded optimisim about its prospective utility.

§2. REVIEW OF THE INTERNATIONAL INSTRUMENTS

This section provides a brief summary of the genesis and contents of the existing international human rights instruments. For the eight principal ones, the Articles of general application are set out in full and considered in Part II of the present work, and the Articles defining the rights and freedoms guaranteed in Part III. Those two Parts also contain digests of the relevant jurisprudence — that is, the formal interpretations and applications of the Articles concerned by the competent independent international institutions established by the treaties to supervise their provisions (see below), and also by some superior national courts. The Articles which provide for international supervision, interpretation and application, and sometimes also enforcement, are finally set out in Part IV.

§2.1 The United Nations Charter (*UNCH*)

The United Nations are an inter-governmental organization, whose constituent instrument is its Charter (*UNCH*), signed at San Fransisco, USA, on 26 June 1945. Article 1 includes, among its purposes,

'(3) to achieve international co-operation . . . in promoting and encouraging respect for human rights and for fundamental freedoms for all . . .'

Articles 55 and 56 (see §6.1) record the 'pledge' of the UN Member States to take joint and separate action to achieve

'(c) universal respect for, and observance of, human rights and fundamental freedoms for all . . .'

For the juridical effect of these provisions in international law, see §6.1.

§2.2 The Universal Declaration of Human Rights (*UDHR*)

The first catalogue of human rights and fundamental freedoms enumerated by the UN was *UDHR*, a declaration of the UN General Assembly (UNGA) adopted in Paris, France, on 10 December 1948. At that time, the UN had 56 members: 48 voted in favour, none against, and 8 (Byelorussia, Czechoslovakia, Poland, Saudi Arabia, South Africa, Ukraine, the USSR, and Yugoslavia) abstained.

The catalogue of human rights and fundamental freedoms set out in *UDHR* contains 28 Articles, followed by a further Article on duties and limitations, and another on abuse. For a brief discussion of the juridical status of this instrument in international law today, see §6.2.

24

§2.3 The International Covenant on Civil and Political Rights (*ICPR*)

At the same time, and on the assumption that *UDHR* would not impose sufficiently binding obligations, the UN Commission on Human Rights (CHR) proceeded with the drafting of Covenants on human rights designed to become legally binding on the UN's Member States. That work began in 1947, and was not completed until 1954, when two Covenants were presented to the UNGA: *ICPR* and *ICES*. It took a further twelve years before the UNGA adopted these in 1966.

The division into two of the single *UDHR* catalogue reflected certain ideological and political differences between two major groups of negotiating States: unlike all the other major instruments, for example, neither of the Covenants mentions any right to property. The division has also been supported by the argument that the grant or concession of most of the rights defined in *ICPR* lies in the simple power of national governments, which are able if they wish to protect or guarantee them by legislation or administrative action, whereas most of the rights described in *ICES* are said to depend for their realization on the progressive economic development of a country, which may take many years and does not lie exclusively within the power of its government[1] (but see §13).

ICPR contains 27 Articles defining and circumscribing, in much greater detail than *UDHR*, a variety of rights and freedoms, and imposing (in Article 2) an absolute and immediate obligation on each of the State Parties to 'respect and ensure' these rights 'to all individuals within its territories and subject to its jurisdiction'. The instrument also establishes a Human Rights Committee (HRC) having competence in three matters:

(1) to comment on reports to be submitted by the State Parties on the measures they have adopted to comply with their obligations under the Covenant;
(2) to investigate complaints by State Parties of failures by other State Parties to fulfil their obligations under the Covenant;
(3) under an Optional Protocol (*ICPR OP*), to investigate complaints from victims of such failures.

Although *ICPR* was adopted by the UNGA in 1966, it did not come into force (by deposit of the thirty-fifth instrument of ratification) until 23 March 1976. Since then, the accession of other countries both to the Covenant and to its Optional Protocol has proceeded apace, and Table A lists the States which were bound by these treaties on 1 January 1982. HRC has entered on its task, adopted Rules of Procedure, and carried out a substantial volume of work, including the thorough examination of many State reports, and the consideration of a number of complaints under the Optional Protocol (see §27). The jurisprudence to which these have given rise is noted in the appropriate sections in Parts II and III below.

---

[1] See, for example, Cranston, *What are Human Rights?*, 66–7.

§2.4 The International Covenant on Economic Social and Cultural Rights (*ICES*)

This instrument, drafted in parallel with *ICPR*, has followed the same history. Presented to the UNGA in 1954 and adopted in 1966, it did not enter into force until 3 January 1976, and has been ratified or acceded to by many more States since then. Those bound by it on 1 January 1982 are again listed in Table A.

This Covenant contains 15 Articles defining, in detail, a set of rights largely derived from *UDHR*. But in this instance the obligation assumed by the State Parties (in Article 2) is qualified and progressive: unlike *ICPR*, each of them only 'undertakes to take steps . . . to the maximum of its available resources . . . with a view to achieving progressively the full realisation of the rights recognised . . . by all appropriate means.'

ICES contains no provisions for interpretation and application. Instead, it provides a reporting procedure, through the UN Secretary-General, to the UN Economic and Social Council (ECOSOC), which may transmit the State reports to CHR, may obtain reports from the UN specialised agencies, and has power to report to the General Assembly with 'recommendations of a general nature'. In fact ECOSOC has not so far referred these reports to CHR, but has set up a sessional working group of its own to examine them (see §31). It has not yet made any recommendations about them. However, some jurisprudence which has emanated from a competent independent ILO Committee under this procedure is noted in the appropriate sections in Part III below.

§2.5 The European Convention on Human Rights and Fundamental Freedoms (*EHR*)

The history of the UN Covenants exemplifies the difficulties of negotiating detailed human rights provisions that will be acceptable to the governments of States of widely differing cultures, traditions, ideologies, and stages of economic and social development. Agreement on such matters is easier to achieve among governments within the same geographical region, sharing a common history and cultural tradition — a process which the UN encourages and promotes. This is well illustrated by the case of Europe. Less than two years after the adoption of *UDHR*, and inspired by that instrument, the West European Member States of the Council of Europe (CE) had drafted *EHR*, which they signed on 4 November 1950 and which entered into force on 3 September 1953. As at 1 January 1982, it bound the European States listed in Table A, being all those outside the Eastern bloc with the exception of Finland, the Holy See, Liechtenstein, Monaco and San Marino. The English and French texts are equally authentic.

EHR provides, in 18 Articles, for a variety of 'civil and political' rights and freedoms. The State obligation is absolute and immediate, requiring the State Parties to 'secure to everyone within their jurisdiction' the rights and freedoms defined in the Convention.

In its provisions for interpretation, application and enforcement, *EHR* goes much further than *ICPR*. It establishes a permanent Commission (EUCM) and Court (EUCT) of Human Rights, both of which have their seats in Strasbourg,

France (see §28). State Parties may refer to the Commission alleged breaches of the provisions of the Convention by other State Parties. More important, however, where a State Party declares (under *EHR* 25) that it recognizes the competence of the Commission to do so, the Commission may receive 'petitions' from any individual or association claiming to be the victim of a violation by that State Party of the rights set forth in the Convention. The Commission can investigate and report, and it (as well as the State Parties) can refer cases to the Court, provided the State Party concerned has recognized the Court's jurisdiction under *EHR* 46. The Court's judgements are final, and the State Parties undertake to abide by its decisions (see §28).

Five Protocols have since been added to *EHR*, two of which (*P1* and *P4*) include additional rights to be protected.

Since *EHR* entered into force in 1953, EUCM and EUCT have developed a substantial and extensive jurisprudence in the interpretation and application of its provisions, often resulting in changes in the legislation or the administrative arrangements of the State Parties concerned.[2] This jurisprudence is noted in the appropriate sections in Parts II and III below. In addition, recourse to the Commission has led in many cases to 'friendly settlements' between the victim and the State Party, often again involving changes in the State Party's internal arrangements for the future. The accumulated Strasbourg jurisprudence has also affected the attitudes of European and other national courts to human rights questions arising under their domestic constitutions and laws, and some of their decisions also are noted in the appropriate sections in Parts II and III. While none of that jurisprudence is binding on States that are not parties to *EHR*, it may well prove persuasive to other international human rights institutions, such as HRC (§2.4) and the Inter-American Commission and Court (§2.9).

The CE's Committee of Ministers also has certain functions under *EHR* (see §28). However, this has not so far yielded any important jurisprudence; besides, that Committee is not an impartial tribunal composed of independent individuals, but a political body made up of governmental representatives. For both those reasons, its decisions are not considered in the present work.

EHR enjoys the (so far) unique distinction of having been denounced by one of its members — Greece, under its then totalitarian régime, in December 1969. After the fall of that régime, Greece rejoined the Convention in 1974.

§2.6 The European Social Charter (*ESC*)

This instrument is intended to be complementary to *EHR*, as *ICES* is to *ICPR*. It was signed in 1961 and entered into force on 26 February 1965. In Part I, it lists 19 'economic and social' rights; the State Parties' obligation is to 'accept as the aim of their policy, to be pursued by all appropriate means . . . the attainment of conditions in which' those rights 'may be effectively realised'. In Part II, they undertake 'to consider themselves bound by' obligations which they can select from those laid down in 19 corresponding and more detailed Articles, which expand and circumscribe the rights listed in Part I. Some of these extend to 'everyone'; others only to 'workers' or other specified groups.

In Part IV, there are provisions for reports to the Secretary-General of the

---

[2] See, for example, Linke, *The Influence of the European Convention on Human Rights on National European Criminal Proceedings* (1981).

CE, which he forwards to an independent Committee of Experts (EUCE). That Committee's conclusions constitute the independent jurisprudence arising under *ESC*, which is noted in the appropriate sections in Part III below. They are then passed, concurrently, to a sub-committee of the CE's Governmental Social Committee and to the CE's Parliamentary Assembly, and thence finally to the CE's Committee of Ministers (see § 32). The views of those political bodies are not noted in the present work.

An Appendix contains what are in effect reservations in the form of interpretations.

ESC too has had a substantial effect on the domestic laws and practices of its State Parties.

§2.7 The American Declaration of the Rights and Duties of Man (*ADRD*)

In 1948, a few months before *UDHR*, the Organisation of American States (OAS) adopted *ADRD*. This too enumerates, also in 28 Articles, a catalogue of human rights and freedoms (civil, political, economic, social, and cultural, without distinction), differing in a few respects from that of *UDHR*; uniquely (until [*AFR*] thirty-three years later), it adds a catalogue of duties in a further 10 Articles. Its provisions have been used since 1960 by the Inter-American Commission on Human Rights (IACM, see § 29) as the standards to be applied in its work, and continue to be so used for those Member States of the OAS which have not yet become bound by *AMR*. For a brief discussion of the juridical status of *ADRD* in international law, see §6.2.

§2.8 The American Convention on Human Rights (*AMR*)

Drafting and negotiation of this instrument began in 1959, and it was signed ten years later. From then, it took another nine years before it entered into force on 18 July 1978, through the deposit of the eleventh instrument of ratification. The Latin American and Caribbean States which were bound by it on 1 January 1982 are listed in Table A.

AMR sets out, in 25 Articles, a detailed catalogue of (largely) 'civil and political' rights and freedoms. For these, the State obligation is again absolute: the State Parties 'undertake to respect the rights and freedoms recognised herein and to ensure to all persons subject to their jurisdiction the free and full exercise of those rights and freedoms.' In a further Article (26), the State Parties follow the language of *ICES* in undertaking 'to adopt measures ... with a view to achieving progressively, by legislation or other appropriate means, the full realisation of the rights implicit in the economic, social, educational, scientific, and cultural standards' set forth in the revised Charter of the OAS.

Closely following the model of *EHR*, *AMR* provides for interpretation, application, and enforcement by IACM, which has its seat in Washington, DC, USA, and a new Inter-American Court of Human Rights (IACT), having its seat in San José, Costa Rica. Here too, the judgements of the Court are final, and the State Parties undertake to comply with them. But the preconditions of jurisdiction are the converse of those under *EHR*: no special declaration is necessary to render the Commission competent to receive petitions against State Parties from individuals, groups, or non-governmental organisations; but such a declaration *is* required for complaints by one State Party against another (see §29.2).

Apart from its functions under *AMR*, IACM still retains its original competence in respect of all Member States of the OAS, whether or not they are parties to *AMR* (see §29.1). IACM's jurisprudence, arising under both *ADRD* and *AMR*, is noted in the appropriate sections in Parts II and III below.

§2.9 The African Charter on Human and Peoples' Rights ([*AFR*])

This is the fourth and most recent of the regional human rights treaties, It was adopted at a meeting of Heads of State and Government of the Organisation of African Unity (OAU) in Nairobi, Kenya, on 26 June 1981. It has not yet entered into force, but it is included in the present work in the expectation — and the hope — that it will not be too long before it does. Until it has, references to it here are distinguished by square brackets.

[*AFR*] follows tradition in enumerating 'civil and political' rights in 12 of its early Articles. It continues with a catalogue of 'economic, social and cultural' rights in the following four Articles (15-18). The next six Articles (19-24) expand the set of what some commentators call 'third-generation' or 'solidarity' rights — that is, rights not vested in individuals, but in collective groups of individuals, called 'peoples' in [*AFR*] (see §26). From there, [*AFR*] moves to duties: in two Articles (25 and 26) for State Parties, and in three further Articles (27-9) for individuals. [*AFR*] follows *UDHR* and *ADRD* in drawing no distinction between the different categories of rights and duties which it enumerates. However, it breaks new ground in a treaty by imposing (in Article 1) the identical State obligation, absolute and immediate in form, for all of them.

As in the case of the other regional instruments, [*AFR*] creates an independent institution, the African Commission on Human and Peoples' Rights ([AFCM]), to interpret and apply its provisions. But [AFCM] differs from the European and Inter-American institutions in being the only organ of supervision for the Charter — that is, in having no associated Court — and in several other respects, including a possible restriction on the jurisprudence it is allowed to take into account (see §30).

[*AFR*] will come into force (according to Article 63(3)) three months after a simple majority (currently 26) of the OAU Member States has ratified it.

§2.10 Subsidiary Instruments

Both before and since the creation of the UN, States have entered into other international treaties on matters that fall within, or are closely connected with, the field of human rights and fundamental freedoms. These perform a variety of functions, of which the most important for the purposes of the present work are more detailed definitions of the scope of the rights and freedoms guaranteed under the major instruments, and more specific provisions for their implementation. Examples are the Conventions relating to the Status of Refugees (*CR*) and the Status of Stateless Persons (*CS$_1$*) respectively, which contain detailed provisions for the application of the limited 'right of asylum' declared in the major instruments (see §14.5).

There is not space in this book to reprint the texts of all these treaties, let alone to consider them in detail. The most important ones are listed in the List of Instruments immediately following the Table of Contents; where their provisions are relevant they are mentioned in the appropriate cross-reference section, and elsewhere in the section relating to a particular right or freedom, in Parts II and III. Their full texts are available from the UN, and the most important ones are collected together in the UN publication *Human Rights: a Compilation of International Instruments*.

In this field, the International Labour Organisation (ILO) has been exceptionally prolific: there are now in force over 150 international conventions which have been negotiated under its auspices (see §35). The UN Educational, Scientific and Cultural Organisation (UNESCO) has also made a contribution to this body of international law (see §34).

§2.11 The Helsinki Final Act

From July 1973 until July 1975, an inter-governmental Conference on Security and Co-operation in Europe met in Helsinki, Finland, and Geneva, Switzerland in order to negotiate an accord designed to reflect the policy of *détente* — that is, peaceful relations in Europe between the nations of East and West following the Second World War, which had never been terminated by a comprehensive peace treaty. 35 nations participated in that Conference: all the sovereign States of Eastern and Western Europe with the single exception of Albania, as well as the USA and Canada.

The negotiations culminated in a Final Act, signed in Helsinki on 1 August 1975, and composed of a Preamble, ten 'Principles guiding relations between participating States', a large number of detailed provisions arranged in three 'baskets' — respectively concerned with 'Confidence-building measures' in the military field, 'Co-operation in the field of economics, science and technology and of the environment', and 'Co-operation in humanitarian and other fields' — and two other sections respectively entitled 'Questions relating to security and co-operation in the Mediterranean', and 'Follow-up to the Conference'.

The instrument expressly declares that it 'is not eligible for registration under Article 102 of the Charter of the UN'. Accordingly, it imposes no binding obligations under international law, and therefore has no formal legal effect. It is mentioned here only because its political impact has been greater than that of many of the binding treaties themselves — principally because, under one of its final provisions, each of the participating States undertook to publish its text to its own population, and to 'disseminate it and make it known as widely as possible', an obligation which the participating States have in fact widely observed.

Through that publication and dissemination, many people for the first time became aware of the existence of international human rights law, to which the Final Act makes the following references:

Preamble: Recognising the close link between peace and security in Europe and in the world as a whole and conscious of the need for each of them to make its contribution to the strengthening of world peace and security and to the promotion of fundamental rights, economic and social progress and well-being for all peoples;

Principle VII. Respect for human rights and fundamental freedoms, including the freedom of thought, conscience, religion or belief
The participating States will respect human rights and fundamental freedoms, including the freedom of thought, conscience, religion or belief, for all without distinction as to race, sex, language or religion.

They will promote and encourage the effective exercise of civil, political, economic, social, cultural and other rights and freedoms all of which derive from the inherent dignity of the human person and are essential for his free and full development.

Within this framework the participating States will recognise and respect the freedom of the individual to profess and practise, alone or in community with others, religion or belief acting in accordance with the dictates of his own conscience.

The participating States on whose territory national minorities exist will respect the right of persons belonging to such minorities to equality before the law, will afford them the full opportunity for the actual enjoyment of human rights and fundamental freedoms and will, in this manner, protect their legitimate interests in this sphere.

The participating States recognise the universal significance of human rights and fundamental freedoms, respect for which is an essential factor for the peace, justice and well-being necessary to ensure the development of friendly relations and co-operation among themselves as among all States.

They will constantly respect these rights and freedoms in their mutual relations and will endeavour jointly and separately, including in co-operation with the United Nations, to promote universal and effective respect for them.

They confirm the right of the individual to know and act upon his rights and duties in this field.

In the field of human rights and fundamental freedoms, the participating States will act in conformity with the purposes and principles of the Charter of the United Nations and with the Universal Declaration of Human Rights. They will also fulfil their obligations as set forth in the international declarations and agreements in this field, including *inter alia* the International Covenants on Human Rights, by which they may be bound.

Principle X. Fulfilment in good faith of obligations under international law
The participating States will fulfil in good faith their obligations under international law, both those obligations arising from the generally recognised principles and rules of international law and those obligations arising from treaties or other agreements, in conformity with international law, to which they are parties.

In exercising their sovereign rights, including the right to determine their laws and regulations, they will conform with their legal obligations under international law; they will furthermore pay due regard to and implement the provisions in the Final Act of the Conference on Security and Co-operation in Europe.

What is perhaps most significant about those statements, at all events for present purposes, is the fact that *ICES* and *ICPR* did not enter into force until several months *after* the Helsinki Final Act was adopted and signed. The expression 'by which they may be bound' at the end of the last paragraph of Principle VII did not therefore extend to those Covenants at the time of the signature of the Final Act, but acquired that reach, for those participating States which had ratified the Covenants, only early in the following year when they came into force. As will be seen from Table A, those participating States include all the members of the Eastern bloc, as well as 14 others. In addition,

20 of the participating States are bound by *EHR*, and 13 by *ESC*. The only participating States not bound by any of the major international human rights treaties on 1 January 1982 were the Holy See, Liechtenstein, Monaco, San Marino, and the USA.

It is also notable that Principle X expressly calls on the participating States to conform with their obligations under international law (including, therefore, their obligations under international human rights treaties to which they are parties) *in determining their domestic laws and regulations*, notwithstanding that this is still declared to be an exercise of 'their sovereign rights'. In subscribing to the Final Act, therefore, the participating States have expressly recognised a limitation *pro tanto* on the sovereign right to legislate as they please, and have accepted the legitimacy of external scrutiny of their domestic legal and regulatory systems by reference to an objective test of the conformity of those systems with their obligations under international human rights law.[3]

[3] See T. Buergenthal (ed.), *Human Rights, International Law and the Helsinki Accords* (1977).

§3. PARTICIPATION IN
THE INSTRUMENTS

As has already been explained in §1.5, one of the major sources — and, for the purposes of the present work, the most important source — of State obligations under international law consists of agreements concluded between such States, by which they consent to be bound (that is, not merely to make, or join in, declarations[1] of intention or policy). Such agreements may variously describe themselves as conventions, covenants, pacts, etc., but the generic term most commonly used for them today is 'treaties'. (The much wider term 'instruments' is used to describe all categories of documents to which sovereign States have given their assent, including declarations or resolutions that have no binding legal force at the time they are proclaimed, as well as treaties.)

Over time, certain rules have developed to regulate the conclusion of treaties, their entry into force, observance, application, interpretation, amendment, termination, and so on — in short, a general law of contract for agreements between States. Those rules, previously forming part of customary international law, have recently been codified in the form of another treaty: the Vienna Convention on the Law of Treaties, which itself entered into force on 27 January 1980. Although that instrument is expressed not to be retroactive[2] — that is, its provisions apply only to treaties concluded after it has itself entered into force — its provisions very largely reflect the rules of customary international law in this field as they were considered to exist at the time of its own conclusion. It therefore furnishes the most convenient source for the rest of this section, which is intended to summarize briefly how international treaties (such as those concerned with human rights law) come into existence and effect, and what are their incidents in international law.

§3.1 Negotiation and adoption

The first stage in the creation of any international instrument is the negotiation of a text with which the State Parties concerned are willing to concur. That is often a difficult and protracted process. In earlier days, it was carried out by the emissaries of one negotiating sovereign accredited to the court of another, having '*pleins pouvoirs*' to conduct the negotiations, and therefore described as 'plenipotentiaries'. Today, multilateral instruments are more commonly negotiated in some single forum, which may be a permanent inter-governmental organisation such as the UN or the ILO, or an *ad hoc* inter-governmental conference, such as the conference which led to the conclusion of the Vienna Convention.

Such negotiations generally begin with one or more drafts of the text of

---

[1] However, Declarations may in time come to have binding effect in international law, if they become part of customary law: see §§1.3 and 6.2.2.

[2] See Vienna Convention on the Law of Treaties, Art. 4.

the instrument, each clause of which will be successively amended and modified until the plenipotentiaries representing the negotiating States can agree on it. Throughout that process, the plenipotentiaries will of course seek and obtain instructions from their governments, and there will be successive episodes of consultation, bargaining, and compromise until agreement can be reached on a text which reflects the degree of consensus that can be achieved. The final text is therefore often rather different from the initial one.

At that point, the agreed text is formally *adopted* by the representatives of the negotiating States, and this marks the end of the stage of negotiation.[3] For instruments not intended at that time to become binding treaties — such as the various UN Declarations, of which *UDHR* is the pre-eminent example — adoption by the assembled plenipotentiaries (in the case of the UN, the General Assembly) will be the end of the matter.

For multilateral treaties, it is today the universal practice to retain a record of the successive stages of the formal negotiations, which then forms part of the *travaux préparatoires* (see §5.1).

§3.2 Signature

Most written contracts between private individuals come into force when all the contracting parties have signed them. In the past, that has not often been the case for treaties, since it was usually only after the plenipotentiary had returned to his own court that it was possible for his sovereign to receive a full report, examine the text which the plenipotentiary had negotiated on his behalf, and decide whether in the circumstances then ruling he was willing to consent to be bound by it. Signature therefore tended merely to indicate adoption of the text as authentic, and some further step — variously called ratification, acceptance, or approval[4] — was necessary before a treaty could become binding on the State concerned.

With the better communications available today, signature may now sometimes express the consent of a State to be bound by a treaty, especially when the signatures are appended at a formal 'summit' meeting of Heads of State or of Government. But what precise act brings a treaty into force is nowadays almost always provided ·for in the instrument itself.[5] It may, for example, provide that signature shall signify the consent of a State to be bound by it,[6] or it may provide that that consent shall be signified in some other way, such as the exchange or deposit of instruments of ratification.[7]

§3.3 Ratification

Where signature is *not* an expression of consent to be bound, it signifies at most an expression of intent by the State concerned to become bound by the treaty at some later stage, once certain conditions have been satisfied. Those conditions may be the signature or ratification of the treaty by other States, or some internal acts (such as the sounding of public opinion, or legislation) which the signing State needs to carry out within its domestic jurisdiction in order to be able to comply with the treaty.

---

[3] *Ibid.* Art. 9.   [4] See now *ibid.*, Art. 14.   [5] *Ibid.*, Art. 11.
[6] *Ibid.*, Art. 12.   [7] *Ibid.* Arts. 14 and 16.

In particular, where — as in the case of a human rights treaty — the instrument imposes an obligation on State Parties to comply domestically with certain standards, States with a sufficiently high sense of integrity will frequently sign the instrument soon after they have joined in adopting the text, but delay ratification until they have passed any necessary internal legislation, or made any necessary changes in internal administrative arrangements, to the point where they can be satisfied that their domestic arrangements comply with all the obligations imposed by the treaty.

There are also some countries whose domestic constitutions preclude the Head of State or the government from binding the State by foreign treaties until some other constitutionally established national entity has had an opportunity of considering the treaty and giving its assent to it. A notable example is the USA, whose constitution provides[8] that its President 'shall have power, by and with the advice and consent of the Senate, to make treaties, provided two-thirds of the Senators present concur' — which means, in modern practice, that the President of the USA is free to conclude any foreign treaty, but that the USA cannot become an effective party to it until it has been approved by a two-thirds majority of the Senate. Although such a domestic act of approval is sometimes called a 'ratification', it must not be confused with the subsequent formal ratification of the treaty by the government concerned for the purposes of international law.

Where the treaty itself, or the circumstances in which it was negotiated, so provides, the negotiating States do not become legally bound, at the earliest, until they have ratified it,[9] by the exchange, deposit, or notification of a written instrument.[10]

§3.4 Entry into force

The events which bring a treaty into force — that is, place the State Parties to it under an obligation in international law to observe its provisions — are nowadays usually provided for in the treaty itself.[11] The international human rights law treaties all provide that they will only enter into force when they have been ratified by a specified number of States, and the appropriate instruments of ratification have been deposited with a central depositary such as the Secretary-General of the UN, the CE, the OAS, or the OAU.[12] The depositary is usually required by the treaty to inform all the signatories of every ratification he receives.[13] A brief additional time period may sometimes also be provided, running from the deposit of the last required instrument of ratification: on the expiry of that final period, the treaty will enter into force. (None of these provisions are reprinted in the present work, which is concerned — apart from [AFR] and [CT] — only with treaties that have already entered into force.)

Until that point, of course, the treaty is not in force, and none of the State Parties — not even those who have already ratified it — are bound by it in international law. However, once they have expressed an intention to *become* bound by it when it enters into force (e.g. by signature or ratification), they are then obliged to refrain from acts which would defeat its object and purpose.[14]

---

[8] Art. II, Section 2.   [9] Vienna Convention Art. 14.
[10] *Ibid.*, Art. 16.   [11] *Ibid.*, Art. 24.
[12] See *ibid.*, Art. 76.   [13] See *ibid.*, Art. 77.
[14] See *ibid.*, Art. 18.

When the treaty does come into force, it of course instantly binds all those who have previously ratified it.

For the six principal international human rights treaties, Table 1 shows the dates of adoption and coming into force, following the deposit of the specified number of instruments of ratification.

TABLE 1

Treaty	Date of adoption	Number of ratifications required	Date of entry into force
EHR	4 November 1950	10	3 September 1953
ESC	18 October 1961	5	26 February 1965
ICES	16 December 1966	35	3 January 1976
ICPR	16 December 1966	35	23 March 1976
AMR	22 November 1969	11	18 July 1978
[AFR]	26 June 1981	26	

§3.5 Accession or adherence

Ratification is only suitable for a State which has already signed the adopted text of a treaty — that is, most commonly a State which has taken part in the negotiations leading to the adoption of the text. (Some treaties indeed limit the States which can become parties to them, especially where they have been negotiated in a forum to which only a limited number of States belong, such as the CE, the OAS or the OAU.) But some other treaties provide that any State may become a party to them, whether or not it has taken any part in its negotiation, or signed it before or after it has entered into force. The procedure for adding such later State Parties is nowadays almost invariably laid down in the treaty itself, and usually takes the form of 'accession'[15] or 'adherence' (the terms are effectively synonymous), again most commonly through the deposit of an appropriate written instrument by the State concerned with the depositary authorized by the treaty to receive such instruments.[16]

Upon accession or adherence to a treaty which has already entered into force, the State concerned becomes bound by its provisions exactly as if it had signed and ratified it. So, for example, *ICPR* and *ICES* entered into force, in accordance with their respective provisions, when 35 of their original signatories had ratified them; since then, many more States have become bound by them through further ratifications or accessions. (For the full list as at 1 January 1982, see Table A.)

§3.6 Reservations and interpretations

At any of these stages — that is, signature, ratification, or accession — but not afterwards, a State may express 'reservations' about the treaty, unless the

---

[15] *Ibid.*, Art. 15.
[16] *Ibid.*, Art. 16; see also Arts. 76 and 77.

treaty itself forbids or restricts this.[17] By these, a State may withhold or limit its consent to being bound by some specified provision, or group of provisions, in the treaty, and it is by no means uncommon for State Parties to make such reservations.[18] (The reservations made by State Parties to the major human rights law treaties are set out *in extenso* in Table A.)

Somewhat complicated rules govern the extent to which other State Parties are bound, *vis-à-vis* a State that has made reservations, by a treaty between them. These need not be considered here in any detail. Suffice it to say that the general principle is that of reciprocity: where one State makes a reservation, it is open to other States to say that, to that extent, they will not be bound *vis-à-vis* the reserving State by that part of the treaty by which the reserving State itself will not consent to be bound, but that none of this affects the obligations of non-reserving States towards each other.[19] It should be noted that there is a limit to the extent to which any State may make reservations in respect of a treaty: such reservations must not, either singly or when taken together, be incompatible with the object and purpose of the treaty.[20] In effect, a State will not be allowed, by the use of reservations, to appear to express consent to be bound by a treaty by which it does not in reality intend to be bound at all.

On other occasions, a State Party may declare an 'interpretation' of a treaty at the time of signature, ratification, or accession, by which it expresses its understanding of how certain provisions of the treaty will be applied.[21] Such an 'interpretation' may sometimes amount to a disguised reservation. Where, for example, a ratifying party considers that a particular provision in the treaty is drafted more widely than it cares to accept, it may say that it interprets that provision in a more narrow sense spelt out in the 'interpretation', and will then only be bound by the provision to that extent. That is in reality a reservation, to which the usual rules will apply.

§3.7 Amendment

As with contracts generally, it is always open to all the parties to a treaty to amend it by agreement between them.[22] That will normally involve negotiations between all the parties concerned;[23] in the case of multilateral treaties with many parties, that may take a good deal of time. Some of the international human rights law treaties contain specific provisions about amendment, regulating what procedure should be followed. (These provisions are not reprinted in the present work.)

---

[17] *Ibid.*, Art. 19. Of the major human rights treaties, *ICPR, ICES, ESC,* and [*AFR*] are silent about reservations; *AMR* 75 requires that reservations to that Convention must be 'in conformity with the provisions of' the Vienna Convention; and *EHR* 64 only allows reservations by any State 'in respect of any particular provision of the Convention', and 'to the extent that any law then in force in its territory is not in conformity with the provision'; such reservations 'shall contain a brief statement of the law concerned'. 'Reservations of a general character' are not permitted. For the effect of this Article, see Jacobs, *The European Convention on Human Rights,* 212–14.

[18] For a full discussion of this subject, see P.-H. Imbert, 'Reservations and Human Rights Conventions', 6 *Human Rights Review*, 28.

[19] See Vienna Convention, Arts. 20, 21 and 22, and also the Advisory Opinion of the International Court of Justice on *Reservations to the Genocide Convention*, ICJ Reports 1951, 15.

[21] See I. Sinclair, *The Vienna Convention on the Law of Treaties*, 44.

[22] Vienna Convention, Art. 39.   [23] *Ibid.*, Art. 40.

A common way of amending treaties is by means of an Additional Protocol. This is apt for adding new provisions to an existing treaty, and will be negotiated, adopted, signed, and ratified in the same way as the original treaty. Five Additional Protocols to *EHR* have so far entered into force, though not all the State Parties bound by *EHR* itself have yet become bound by all the Protocols (see Table A).

§3.8 Derogation

Some treaties — among them four of the major international human rights law ones — contain express provisions whereby a State Party may, by a unilateral declaration, in certain prescribed circumstances 'derogate' from some of its obligations under the treaty. There is no general rule allowing for unilateral derogation in internatational law:[24] the procedure is available only where the treaty itself expressly provides for it.

For the detailed provisions for derogation in the treaties considered in the present work, see §11.

§3.9 Denunciation

Again, as in the case of domestic contracts, there is a whole variety of circumstances through which an international treaty may come to an end — as, for example, the consent of the parties, a material breach by one of the parties, supervening impossibility of performance, fundamental change of circumstances, etc.[25] In international treaties, it is also not unusual to provide for 'denunciation' — that is, the unilateral abrogation by a State Party of its obligations under the treaty by some procedure provided for in the treaty itself, most usually a mere written notification either direct to the other parties, or to the central depositary on their behalf. For the detailed provisions in this respect of the treaties considered in the present work, see §12.

Where a treaty contains no express provisions for denunciation, a State Party cannot abrogate its obligations under it by this method unless a right of denunciation is implied by the nature of the treaty, or it is established in some other way that the parties intended to admit this possibility.[26]

---

[24] *Ibid.*, Art. 57.   [25] *Ibid.*, Arts. 59–62.
[26] *Ibid.*, Art. 56.

§4. DOMESTIC EFFECT
OF THE INSTRUMENTS

§4.1 Sources and hierarchies of domestic law

The laws that are treated as having binding force within any particular State, and in support of which the State will make its monopoly of force available, are called its 'domestic' (or sometimes 'national' or 'municipal') laws. For any such law to be accepted as binding, it must have emanated from a source which, under the State's internal legal system, is regarded as competent to create it. There are several possible such sources. One that is (necessarily) always recognized as competent to create laws is the national legislature established under the State's own constitution. Another — especially in countries of the Anglo-Saxon legal tradition, where it is known as 'the common law' — is long-established custom, as consistently declared and upheld by the State's judges. In some States, governmental agencies may have law-making competence in some fields. Modern written constitutions generally specify — sometimes expressly, but more usually by necessary implication — the competent sources of law for the States whose governance they regulate.

As has already been mentioned in §1.2, domestic laws are in many States ranked in a hierarchical order, some laws being treated as superior to others. For example, the legislature may delegate law-making powers in particular fields to other institutions, such as governmental or administrative agencies. The test of whether one law ranks above another in the hierarchy is whether the first can control the content of the second; in the case of delegated legislation, for example, the laws made by the agency will rank below the law which gave the agency the power to make them if their validity depends on whether the agency acted within its delegated powers in making them — that is, if they can be struck down as invalid on being shown to have been made *ultra vires*. Similarly, where the national constitution prescribes limitations for the contents of the laws which the legislature is competent to make, so that any laws which transgress those limits are invalid, the constitution will rank above the legislature's laws in the legal hierarchy.

Domestic human rights laws may be found in any of the ranks of such hierarchies. Most national constitutions now contain catalogues of human rights and fundamental freedoms, and either constrain the national legislature not to enact laws which would infringe these, or require the legislature to ensure their enjoyment and protection by enacting appropriate laws, or both. Detailed provisions for the enjoyment of human rights and the safeguards of fundamental freedoms will then be found in the State's 'ordinary' domestic laws, which in their turn will be supplemented by subsidiary regulations such as delegated legislation.

39

§4.2 International treaties as a source of domestic law

Where a State is a party to an international treaty (such as a human rights treaty) which has entered into force, the question arises whether and how the provisions of that treaty can become part of the State's own domestic law — that is, whether and how the obligations undertaken by the State on the international plane, and formally owed on that plane to the other State Parties to the treaty (though in substance intended to enure for the benefit of the individuals within its domestic jurisdiction) can become transformed into obligations owed directly to those individuals within its own domestic legal system. That question involves the relationship between international and domestic law, which has been the subject of a long-standing debate between two schools of thought among academic writers, who call themselves 'dualists' and 'monists' respectively.

Dualists see the two kinds of law as distinct and separate — arising from different sources, governing different areas and relationships, and different in substance. According to that view, in national courts international law is *inferior* to, and *weaker* than, domestic law. If international law ever becomes part of domestic law, that can only be because domestic law has chosen to incorporate it.

Monists, on the other hand, contend that there is only one system of law, of which international and domestic law are no more than two aspects. They justify this by claiming that both of them govern sets of individuals (States being seen for this purpose as collections of individuals), both are binding, and both are manifestations of a single concept of law. Hence international law is *superior* and *stronger*, as it represents the system's highest rules — jurisdiction on a domestic level being only delegated to States, who cannot avoid being bound to apply international law at the domestic level. So, if domestic law anywhere conflicts with international law, that is the State's fault, and will not excuse the State's obligations.[1]

Viewed on the international plane, the dispute between these two schools of thought is indeed academic. 'Formally . . . international and domestic law as systems can never come into conflict. What may occur is something strictly different, namely a conflict of obligations or an inability for a State on the domestic plane to act in the manner required by international law.'[2] It is well settled that international law will apply to a State regardless of its domestic law, and that a State cannot in the international forum plead its own domestic law, or even its domestic constitution, as an excuse for breaches of its international obligations.[3]

Viewed on the domestic plane, however, the dispute is not merely an academic

---

[1] For a summary of the arguments, see H. Lauterpacht (ed.), *Oppenheim's International Law* (8th ed.), I, 37 ff.

[2] Fitzmaurice, 92 Hague Receuil 5 (1957, II).

[3] See Advisory Opinion on *Exchange of Greek and Turkish Populations*, PCIJ, Series B, No. 10, 20; Advisory Opinion on the *Treatment of Polish Nationals and Other Persons of Polish Origin or Speech in the Danzig Territory*, PCIJ, Series A/B, No. 44, 24; *Free Zones of Upper Savoy and District of Gex Case*, PCIJ, Series A/B No. 46, 167. See also *Alabama Claims Arbitration* (Moore 1 Int. Arb. 445 at 456); and the International Law Commission's Draft Declaration on Rights and Duties of States 1949 (YB ILC 1949, 246; 288), Article 13: 'Every State has a duty to carry out in good faith its obligations arising from treaties and other sources of international law, and it may not invoke provisions in its own constitution or its laws as an excuse for failure to perform this duty.' This formulation was later commended by the UN to its Members in UNGA Resolution 375 (IV).

one, for the two schools of thought lead to very different results. Whether international law forms part of domestic law is a question which, in practice, falls to be determined by the domestic courts of each State. Monists say that it will always form such a part; dualists that it will form part only if the domestic law has expressly or impliedly incorporated it. In fact, many States expressly accept international law as part of their domestic law, leaving academics to debate whether the acceptance was necessary or superfluous. But others do not.

Where international law becomes incorporated in a State's domestic law without the need for specific legislation, those parts of it which are sufficiently explicit to be enforceable by the domestic courts are known as 'self-executing'.[4] Some States provide by their constitutions that certain provisions of international law shall be self-executing. The Constitution of the USA, for example, includes international treaties which bind the USA among the sources of US law.[5] Other countries have gone even further by not only making international law self-executing, but assigning to it a rank in the domestic hierarchy superior to all prior and subsequent legislation. Examples of this are France[6] and the Federal German Republic.[7] But there are other States which do not accept any international law as self-executing,[8] or so accept it only in part.

Where international and domestic law coincide, there is of course no problem. But if they differ — either because international law imposes an obligation on a State which is not reflected in its domestic law, or because obligations imposed by international law and domestic law respectively conflict with each other in a particular case — a domestic court will generally have to apply the following rules:

(1) Where the domestic legal system is founded on a dualist view, and the obligation under international law has not become self-executing under a standing provision of the domestic law, or been expressly re-enacted in that law, the court must follow the domestic law and ignore the international law.[9]

---

[4] Robertson would prefer the phrase 'directly enforceable': see *Human Rights in Europe*, 29.

[5] Article VI, Section 2: 'This Constitution and the laws of the United States which shall be made in pursuance thereof; and all treaties made, or which shall be made under the authority of the United States, shall be the supreme law of the land. . . .'

[6] 1958 Constitution, Article 55: 'Treaties or agreements duly ratified or approved shall, upon their publication, have an authority superior to that of laws, subject, for each agreement or treaty, to its application by the other party.'

[7] Basic Law of 8 May 1949, as amended on 1 January 1966, Article 25: 'The general rules of public international law are an integral part of federal law. They shall take precedence over the laws and shall directly create rights and duties for the inhabitants of the federal territory.'

[8] E.g. the United Kingdom.

[9] This will always be the case, for example, in the United Kingdom, where the legal system is entirely dualist and there are no provisions for self-execution; accordingly, the UK courts are not entitled to take into account even the provisions of international treaties by which the United Kingdom is bound if the UK legislature has not expressly enacted them as part of domestic law. So, for instance, although the House of Lords said in *Waddington* v. *Miah* [1974] 2 All ER 377 that, in the light of *UDHR* 11 and *EHR* 7, 'it is hardly credible that any government department would promote or that Parliament would pass retroactive criminal legislation', Vice-Chancellor Megarry subsequently felt bound to hold, in *Malone* v. *Metropolitan Police Commissioner (No. 2)* [1979] 2 All ER 620, that because 'the Convention [*EHR*] is not law here' he had no jurisdiction to declare that the interception by the police of certain telephone calls violated *EHR* 8, even though on the facts he found it 'impossible to see how English law could be said to satisfy the requirements of the Convention' in this respect.

(2) In any other case, the court must have regard both to international law and to domestic law. If there proves to be a conflict between them, the court must follow any rules of domestic law that prescribe which of them is to prevail.[10]

(3) If there are no such rules, it will probably be because the domestic legal system is founded on the monist view, and so the international law will prevail.

§4.3 Rights, freedoms and duties

There is much theory, both in law and philosophy, about the meanings of these concepts, and about the relationships between them. Different proponents have at different times put forward a number of such theories, and different legal systems have at different times founded themselves on one or more of them.[11]

The international instruments speak of 'rights', 'freedoms', and 'duties', but they are far from pedantic in their usage of these terms, nor do they always distinguish very clearly between 'rights' and 'freedoms'. For example, *ICPR* 17(1) says that 'no one shall be subjected to . . . interference with his privacy, family, home or correspondence,' while *EHR* 8(1) says that 'everyone has the right to respect' for these matters. Again, *ICPR*, *EHR*, and *AMR* all declare 'the right to freedom of' conscience and religion (see §23.3), expression (see §23.4), and (in the first two cases) association (see §24.2); yet the right to freedom from torture, one of the most unqualified of them all, is expressed neither as a right nor even as a freedom: all the earlier instruments here choose the imperative injunction 'no one shall be subjected to torture', while the most recent ([*AFR*]) says that torture 'shall be prohibited'.

The instruments have a good deal less to say about duties than about rights — understandably, since the primary correlative duty for human rights falls upon the State and its public authorities, and this can usually be expressed in a single Article (see §6). But some of the instruments do go further and declare that the individual also owes duties to 'the State', 'the community', 'society', 'others', or to more limited groups such as his family — reflecting in this respect provisions found in some national constitutions, notably those of socialist States. *UDHR* devotes one paragraph of one Article to this; *ADRD* ten Articles; and [*AFR*] three. The other treaties declare no express duties for individuals (except that *ICPR* 19(3) and *EHR* 10(2) both say that the right to freedom of expression carries with it 'duties and responsibilities'). Instead, they adopt a different technique which avoids the need to give legal recognition to abstractions such as 'the community' or 'society': they use general and specific Articles of restriction and limitation to delimit the boundaries of the primary rights they declare, by reference to the rights and interests of other persons (see §8).

Probably wisely, the international instruments do not use language which would only be consistent with one particular theory of legal rights and obligations, since they are designed to set universal standards for many different national legal systems. But in transforming the State obligations which they create into the appropriate provisions of a particular State's domestic laws and regulations, that language must be translated into the categories which will

---

[10] In France and the Federal Republic of Germany, for example, the Constitution assigns superior status to treaty obligations, which must therefore prevail even over the enactments of the legislature.

[11] The same holds true for the allied concepts of 'privileges' and 'immunities'.

have the desired effect there. How that is done will depend on the underlying theory, tacit or expressed, on which the domestic legal system is founded, as well as the domestic realities of the country concerned. The appropriate provisions may take a positive or a negative form; they may be incorporated in the constitution, in ordinary civil, criminal, or administrative laws, or in regulations or other measures. All this is necessarily a matter for each of the State Parties concerned, whose obligation — for example under *ICPR* 2(2) (see §6.3) — is 'to take the necessary steps, in accordance with its constitutional processes . . . to adopt such legislative or other measures as may be necessary to give effect to the rights recognised'.

Whether those measures are in the event sufficient for the purpose is another question, which in the nature of things cannot be left for answer exclusively to the domestic institutions of the State Parties. That is the reason for the establishment, under most of the treaties, of an international institution to supervise its performance, and to interpret, apply, and in some cases enforce its provisions by a form of international judicial review. These are considered further in §5.

§4.4 *'Drittwirkung der Grundrechte'*

In the international treaties, the State obligation is generally expressed as one to 'respect', 'recognize', 'ensure', 'secure', or 'give effect to' the rights and freedoms there defined. A much-debated question is whether this merely obliges the State to refrain from violating those rights and freedoms through its own agents, or whether the State is obliged to go further and take whatever steps may be in its power to prevent others within its jurisdiction from violating them also. To take some concrete examples, would a State Party to a human rights treaty which includes the 'right to life' be fulfilling its obligations if its citizens are being murdered in the streets or in their homes, either because the domestic criminal law is inadequate, or because insufficient resources are being devoted to the police or prison services? Is a State that is bound by treaty to respect 'freedom of association' thereby bound to prevent employers by law from dismissing employees who engage in trade union activities? Is a State that is bound to 'respect private life' bound to enact laws which will give its inhabitants a remedy if privately owned newspapers infringe their privacy?

There is no brief English label for this problem. However, in the Federal Republic of Germany, where it has been much discussed,[12] it is called *'Drittwirkung der Grundrechte'* — literally, 'third party effect of fundamental rights' — and the label *'Drittwirkung'* is therefore convenient for use here.

The general view today is that the treaties do entail a degree of *Drittwirkung*, at least to the extent that their State Parties are bound to provide appropriate domestic legislation, and in some cases also administrative regulation, which will furnish protection from infringement *by anyone* of the rights and freedoms guaranteed by the instruments, and effective remedies if they are infringed. So, for example, EUCM has stated that the provision in *EHR* 2 requiring the right to life to be protected by law enjoins the State not only to refrain from taking life intentionally but, further, to take appropriate steps to safeguard

[12] Because of Art. 25 of the Basic Law (*supra*), which provides that 'the general rules of public international law . . . shall directly create rights and duties for the inhabitants of the federal territory.'

life — for example by reducing as far as possible the risks to life in a voluntary vaccination scheme.[13] And EUCT has held that the right to respect for family life in *EHR* 8 obliges a government to make its courts effectively accessible to anyone who may wish to have recourse to them to obtain a decree of judicial separation,[14] and to act in a manner calculated to allow family ties between near relatives to develop naturally.[15]

In the context of trade unions, EUCT has twice held that *EHR* 11 obliges the State not only itself to refrain from interference with the freedom of association, but to take positive measures to protect the individual's freedom of association against some forms of interference by private interests; if it fails to do that, it may be responsible for the consequences even if — indeed precisely because — those who inflict the interference are not.[16] In that connection, EUCM has said that threats by an employer of dismissal for union activity, or for not joining a specific union,[17] and threats of dismissal or other actions intended to bring about the relinquishment by an employee of the office of shop steward, could in principle raise an issue under *EHR* 11, as this could seriously restrict or impede the lawful exercise of the freedom of association in relation to trade unions.[18] EUCE also has concluded that the State obligation under *ESC* 5 to ensure that 'national law shall not be such as to impair' the freedom to form and join trade unions means that States must protect workers' organizations from any interference on the part of employers.[19]

However, there are limits to the extent of *Drittwirkung*. So, for example, EUCM has said that the protection extended by *EHR* 2 to the right to life cannot be interpreted as imposing on a State a duty to provide personal bodyguards, for an unlimited time, to individuals who fear that their lives may be threatened by illegal organizations.[20] At the same time, IACM has said that, where persons 'disappear' in a State's territory but the government concerned refuses to give any information about them, or about the progress of any investigations aimed at discovering their whereabouts, there is a violation of the rights to life, liberty and security since it may be presumed that agents of the government, or individuals protected or tolerated by it, 'have not been uninvolved' in the acts concerned.[21]

---

[13] *Association X v. United Kingdom* (7154/75) DR 14, 31.
[14] *Airey v. Ireland* (6289/73) Judgment: 2 EHRR 305.
[15] *Marckx v. Belgium* (6833/74) Judgment: 2 EHRR 330.
[16] *National Union of Belgian Police v. Belgium* (4464/70) Judgment: 1 EHRR 578; *James, Young and Webster v. United Kingdom* (7601/76; 7806/76) Judgment: 13 August 1981; see also *Schmidt and Dahlström v. Sweden* (5589/72) Report: 17 July 1974.
[17] *James, Young and Webster v. United Kingdom, supra,* Report: 14 December 1979.
[18] *X v. Ireland* (4125/69) CD 37, 42.
[19] I, 31.
[20] *X v. Ireland* (6040/73) CD 44, 121.
[21] Cases 1702, 1748, and 1755 (Guatemala) AR 1975, 67.

§5. SUPERVISION, INTERPRETATION, APPLICATION, AND ENFORCEMENT

§5.1 International institutions and procedures

Not all the international human rights instruments provide international machinery for their supervision, interpretation, application, or enforcement. Resolutions and Declarations — including *UDHR* and *ADRD* — do not; the six major treaties all do; so do the ILO Conventions and a few of the other subsidiary instruments such as *CD* and CW_1. In addition, there are independent 'communication' (i.e. complaints) procedures to CHR and a UNESCO Committee which are not provided for by any specific treaties (see §§ 31.1 and 34).

Supervision is generally carried out through a reporting procedure, under which the State Parties are required to render reports, on request or at prescribed intervals, to an international institution specified in the treaty, describing the measures they have adopted to comply with their obligations under it. The institution will then consider the reports, and may have power to comment on them, or make recommendations about them. All the major human rights treaties considered in the present work contain some provisions of that kind.

Interpretation of the text of a treaty by an international institution may form part of its comments or recommendations on such 'country reports' under the supervision procedure. But it may also come about where the treaty provides a procedure for its *application*, as in the case of *ICPR, EHR, AMR,* and [*AFR*]. Such a procedure enables the international institution or institutions created by the treaty to consider and determine specific allegations that a particular State Party has not fulfilled its obligations under that treaty, and is violating some right which the treaty protects. There are now (apart from the ILO system) five such institutions: HRC under *ICPR*, EUCM and EUCT under *EHR*, and IACM and IACT under *AMR*. When [*AFR*] comes into force, it will add a sixth in the form of [AFCM].

All these procedures specify who has the requisite *locus standi* to initiate it, what are the preconditions for entertaining it, how the allegations are to be investigated, and what form the determination will take. In some (but not all) cases, the procedure cannot be used unless the State concerned has previously accepted the competence of the institution concerned for that purpose. EUCT and IACT also have competence to give advisory or consultative opinions on request.

The general rules of interpretation for international treaties are now codified in the Vienna Convention on the Law of Treaties. A treaty must be interpreted 'in good faith', in accordance with the 'ordinary meaning' to be given to its terms 'in their context' (unless the parties intended some term to have a special meaning[1]), and 'in the light of its object and purpose'.[2] Supplementary aids to interpretation, such as the *travaux préparatoires*[3] which preceded the adoption

---

[1] Article 31(4).
[2] Article 31(1).
[3] No *travaux préparatoires* have been consulted in the preparation of the present work.

of the text, may only be used if the treaty's meaning would otherwise be left 'ambiguous or obscure', or if the interpretation would otherwise lead 'to a result which is manifestly absurd or unreasonable'.[4]

Enforcement is formally required only for the judgements of EUCT and IACT, and the decisions of the Committee of Ministers of the CE under *EHR* 32, with which all the respective State Parties undertake to comply.

All these provisions are set out, and briefly considered, in Part IV below, and the interpretations and applications already undertaken by those institutions which are independent — that is, whose members sit in a personal capacity and not as governmental representatives — constitute the bulk of the international jurisprudence noted in Parts II and III.

§5.2 Domestic institutions and procedures

ICPR, *EHR*, *AMR*, and [*AFR*] all require their State Parties to provide effective domestic remedies for violations of the rights and freedoms which they protect. The institutions having power to supervise, interpret, apply, and enforce human rights law within individual States will of course vary from country to country, depending on the structure of the domestic legal system concerned. There may, for example, be supervision by a Human Rights Commission or Commissioner. Complaints about violations of human rights may fall within the jurisdiction of the ordinary courts, or they may be reserved to a Supreme or Constitutional Court.

Whether the courts concerned are in fact able to take account of their State's obligations under international human rights treaties will depend on whether those obligations are incorporated in the State's domestic law, either by national enactment or through self-execution (see §4.2). If they are not, the courts will be confined to the interpretation, application, and enforcement of the provisions about human rights to be found in the State's own domestic legal system, either in its constitution or in its ordinary laws. Those provisions in their turn may or may not follow the language of one or more of the international instruments.[5] Whether any particular violation by a particular State of a human right protected by one of the international instruments is capable of redress by domestic legal proceedings will therefore depend on whether —

(1) that right is protected by the domestic law of the State, independently or through incorporation of an appropriate provision of international law;
(2) the domestic legal system affords a procedure for such redress;
(3) the preconditions for that procedure are satisfied.

Failing a domestic remedy, whether redress is available through an international procedure will in turn depend on whether —

(4) the State is a party to a treaty which protects that right;
(5) that treaty provides an appropriate procedure before an international institution;

---

[4] Article 32.
[5] Where they do, past decisions of the superior national courts may furnish an aid to the interpretation of the international texts, and some of these are therefore included in the jurisprudence considered in Parts II and III.

(6) the State has accepted the competence of that institution for that purpose, where the treaty requires this;
(7) the preconditions for that procedure are otherwise satisfied.

In any given case, therefore, there may be several different legal procedures for seeking to vindicate a particular human right in a particular case, or seeking redress for its violation: remedies may be available in both a domestic and an international forum. However, in order to avoid a multiplicity of proceedings, the international treaties generally require that all domestic remedies must be exhausted before the appropriate international procedure may be invoked, and often also that no other international procedure is being invoked at the same time (see Part IV).

§5.3 'International crimes'

As a general rule,[6] States apply their criminal laws only territorially — that is, the courts of a State will only assume jurisdiction over a criminal investigation or prosecution if the acts concerned are alleged to have been committed within its own national territory.[7] The rule derives from the doctrine of national sovereignty: it is not for the courts of one State to judge matters which occur within the territory of another, and which the courts of that State are competent to judge for themselves. The rule is also supported by two practical considerations. First, a State has no facilities to investigate directly what has happened outside its own territory. Secondly, the criminal laws of different States vary a good deal; conduct which is criminal in one State may therefore be perfectly lawful in another, and a State could hardly be expected to punish one of its own citizens for an act which, though criminal when committed somewhere else, would have been lawful had it been committed within its own territory.

Such a rule can of course easily lead to criminal acts going unpunished, even if they offend against the laws of most States, should the perpetrator succeed in escaping from the territory of the State in which he has committed the crime. That problem is dealt with by the practice of 'extradition', under which States agree to return to each other, on request, fugitive suspects for investigation and trial, and fugitive convicts for the service of their sentences. This practice is governed today by a substantial network of bilateral and multilateral extradition treaties, to which many States are parties.[8]

Another problem arose from early times in respect of acts committed outside the territory of *any* State, notably piracy on the high seas. In order to suppress this effectively in the interests of all States engaged in maritime trade, it came to be treated as a crime *iure gentium* — that is, contrary to the laws of all civilized nations, and so triable in any State in whose territory the pirate might be found. Piracy thus became the first crime recognized by the custom

---

[6] There are exceptions: for example, the courts of some States will assume jurisdiction over some crimes committed *by* their own nationals abroad, if they would have been crimes had they been committed within their own national territory; and the courts of some States will assume jurisdiction over serious crimes committed *against* their own nationals abroad.

[7] Which includes, for this purpose, territorial waters, ships flying the national flag, and aircraft on the national register.

[8] The provisions of such treaties differ widely, but they commonly exclude from their ambit both political and fiscal offences, as there variously defined.

of States to be a concern of international law — or, more compendiously but less accurately, an 'international crime'.

Since then, the catalogue of international crimes has expanded. The 'Nürnberg Principle', applied by the *ad hoc* War Crimes Tribunals after the Second World War, added certain 'war crimes' and 'crimes against humanity'. More recently, others have been added by treaty: *CG* (see §14.1.6) has added genocide; *CA* (see §7.0.5) has added *apartheid*; and [*CT*] (see §14.3.7), when it comes into force, will add torture.[9] The detailed provisions of these treaties vary, but their general objective is to prevent a person who commits such crimes from finding a safe haven, by ensuring that a State Party in whose territory he is found will either try and punish him itself — even if the crime was not committed on its territory, but at least if it was committed against its own nationals, or he is himself such a national — or will extradite him to another State where he can be tried and punished.

By other treaties such as *SC*₂ and *CP* (see §18.4.6), States have agreed to use their domestic criminal laws to suppress practices such as the slave trade, servitude, the traffic in persons and the exploitation of prostitution — without, however, extending the territorial application of those laws.

In the absence of any permanent international tribunal having jurisdiction to try and punish crimes wherever and by whomever they are committed, the concept of an 'international crime' may therefore be seen as a hybrid form of the application and enforcement of international law, under which individual States, either by custom or by treaty, will make their domestic institutions available for that purpose.

[6] In *Filartiga* v. *Pena-Irala* 630 F (2nd) 876, the US Federal Court of Appeals for the Second Circuit has already held that official torture is now 'clearly and unambiguously prohibited' by international law. However, that was not a criminal case, but an action brought under s. 1350 of the US Alien Torts Statute which confers jurisdiction on US Federal courts in actions brought by aliens for torts (that is, civil delicts) 'committed in violation of the law of nations'.

Part II

Articles of General Application

§6. THE STATE OBLIGATIONS

§6.1 The UN Charter

§6.1.1 TEXT

UNCH

55. With a view to the creation of conditions of stability and well-being which are necessary for peaceful and friendly relations among nations based on respect for the principle of equal rights and self-determination of peoples, the United Nations shall promote:

(*a*) higher standards of living, full employment, and conditions of economic and social progress and development;
(*b*) solutions of international economic, social, health, and related problems; and international cultural and educational co-operation; and
(*c*) universal respect for, and observance of, human rights and fundamental freedoms for all without distinction as to race, sex, language, or religion.

56. All Members pledge themselves to take joint and separate action in co-operation with the Organization for the achievement of the purposes set forth in Article 55.

§6.1.2 COMMENT

As the constituent statute of an intergovernmental organisation, *UNCH* has the status of a multilateral treaty, imposing on its State Parties binding obligations under international law. One of those obligations — expressly assumed in Article 56 in the form of a 'pledge' — is the obligation to take joint and separate action to achieve the purpose set forth in Article 55(*c*), that is 'universal respect for, and observance of, human rights and fundamental freedoms for all . . .'. The importance of this State obligation has decreased in the measure in which States have ratified and acceded to the later human rights treaties which impose their own, and more specific and detailed, State obligations. But the *UNCH* obligation remains important for the diminishing number of States which, while members of the UN, have not yet become bound by any of these other treaties: for them, it is still the only *treaty* obligation relating to human rights.

The extent of this obligation has in its time been a matter of some debate. In support of a restrictive interpretation, the following main arguments have been advanced:

(1) The obligation is only to 'promote', and not to protect, human rights and fundamental freedoms. Against that, it has been argued that 'the legal duty to promote respect for human rights includes the legal duty to respect them'.[1] It might also be pointed out that, as a matter of construction, the obligation in Article 56 is an obligation to take *action* to *achieve* the purposes set forth in Article 55, and that the word 'promote' in that Article merely introduces those purposes, and does not itself form part of them. The purpose is 'universal respect for, and observance of, human rights and fundamental freedoms,' and it is this — and not its promotion — which the State Parties 'pledge' themselves to take action to achieve.

(2) *UNCH* contains no definition, or catalogue, of the human rights and fundamental freedoms concerned. But that lack cannot deprive the obligation of all meaning;[2] besides, the omission has since been repaired by the adoption of *UDHR*, whose preamble expressly refers back to the *UNCH* obligation, as the agreed and authentic UN catalogue (see §6.2).

(3) The obligation is diminished or even vitiated by *UNCH* 2(7), which provides that 'nothing contained in the present Charter shall authorise the UN to intervene in matters which are essentially within the domestic jurisdiction of any State'. To that argument, the short answer is that Articles 55 and 56 do not require, and need not entail, UN intervention (though Article 56 envisages UN co-operation): the obligation stands on its own.[3]

While debates of that kind were common in the first few years after *UNCH* was adopted, they are seldom heard today: it is now almost universally agreed that the *UNCH* obligation is binding in international law on all the UN's members, and is direct and unqualified.

It should, however, be noted that the non-discrimination catalogue in *UNCH* 55(*c*) is the shortest of all those contained in the international instruments, being limited only to the four factors of race, sex, language, and religion (see §7).

§6.1.3 JURISPRUDENCE

The International Court of Justice has had occasion to consider, albeit *obiter*, the legal effect of *UNCH* 55 and 56, and has stated that they 'bind Member States [of the UN] to observe and respect human rights'.[4] These Articles have also been applied in some countries whose domestic legal systems incorporate international law, or allow it to be taken into account. Both the US Supreme Court[5] and the High Court of Ontario[6], for example, have applied them to attempts to enforce racial discrimination by restrictive covenants relating to the occupation of property, and a US Federal Court of Appeals has applied them in holding that official torture is now clearly and unambiguously prohibited under international law.[7]

---

[1] H. Lauterpacht, *International Law and Human Rights*, 152.

[2] *Ibid.*, 148.

[3] For a more detailed refutation, see *ibid.*, Ch. 10, 166 ff.

[4] Advisory Opinion on *The Legal Consequences of the Continued Presence of South Africa in Namibia*, ICJ Reports 1971, 16.

[5] *Oyama* v. *California* 332 US 633.

[6] *In re Drummond Wren* 4 Ont. Rep. 778; 781.

[7] *Filartiga* v. *Pena-Irala* 630 F (2nd) 876.

§6.2 The Universal Declaration and the American Declaration

§6.2.1 *UDHR*

The juridical status of *UDHR* remains a matter of some controversy. It is plain both from the debates in which it found its genesis and from its Preamble that, at the time of its adoption by the UNGA in 1948, it was not by itself intended to create binding obligations in international law for the UN's Member States. Indeed, the Preamble ends with the following words:

Now, therefore, the General Assembly proclaims this Universal Declaration of Human Rights as a common standard of achievement for all peoples and all nations, to the end that every individual and every organ of society, keeping this Declaration constantly in mind, shall strive by teaching and education to promote respect for these rights and freedoms and by progressive measures, national and international, to secure their universal and effective recognition and observance, both among the peoples of Member States themselves and among the people of territories under their jurisdiction.

Some commentators therefore hold that, however great its moral or political authority, *UDHR* cannot by itself create binding obligations under international law.[8]

However, there is also support for other views. The most radical of these holds that, over the thirty-odd years since its adoption, *UDHR* has acquired the status of *ius cogens* in international law, by reason of the consistent practice of States[9] as well as of international institutions[10] in invoking its provisions as evidence of the content of international law. According to that view, it therefore now forms part of customary international law, and so is binding on all States, whether or not they are members of the UN. Moreover, it is directly applicable in those States whose domestic legal systems automatically incorporate customary international law.[11]

Between these two positions, an intermediate one may be taken. This is that *UDHR* today creates binding obligations for the Member States of the UN, not because it has become part of customary international law, but because they have expressly accepted these obligations. Three independent arguments in support of that position may be summarized as follows:

(1) *UNCH* 55 and 56 create a legal obligation (expressed as a 'pledge') for all the UN's Member States to take action to achieve universal respect for, and observance of, human rights and fundamental freedoms (see §6.1). *UNCH* did not enumerate those rights and freedoms, but *UDHR* does. The Preamble to *UDHR* recites that

[8] For the strongest arguments in support of this position, see H. Lauterpacht, *op. cit.*, Ch. 17, 394 ff.

[9] Between 1958 and 1972, references to *UDHR* were included in 25 new national constitutions and 8 domestic legislative acts: see *UN Action in the Field of Human Rights*, 21-2.

[10] For a list of the occasions on which *UDHR* has been cited by UN entities, see *UN Action in the Field of Human Rights*, 14-18. For references to *UDHR* by the International Court of Justice, see *ibid.*, 22.

[11] In support of this thesis, see for example J. P. Humphrey, 'The Universal Declaration of Human Rights: its history, impact and juridical character' in *Human Rights: 30 Years After the Universal Declaration*, Ch. I, 21 ff.; H. Waldock, ICLQ, Supplementary Publication No. II, 1965, 15.

Member States have pledged themselves to achieve . . . the promotion of universal respect for and observance of human rights and fundamental freedoms

and that

a common understanding of these rights and freedoms is of the greatest importance for the full realisation of this pledge.

The first of these recitals uses the precise words of *UNCH* 55 and 56, and must therefore be taken to refer back to those Articles of the Charter; the second points ahead to the substantive *UDHR* catalogue as the 'common understanding' now reached by the assembled nations as to the rights and freedoms referred to in *UNCH* 55(c); this understanding in its turn will facilitate the 'full realisation' of the pledge in *UNCH* 56 by which the Member States accepted the original obligation.

On that view, therefore, *UDHR* supplies the agreed catalogue which was missing from *UNCH* 55(c); the Member States have retrospectively incorporated this catalogue in that Article, and their obligation under *UNCH* 56 is therefore now an obligation to take action to achieve 'universal respect for, and observance of' the specific human rights and fundamental freedoms authentically enumerated in *UDHR*.

(2) As an alternative to that first argument, *UDHR* now constitutes a legitimate aid for the interpretation of the expression 'human rights and fundamental freedoms' in *UNCH* 55(c). It is a general rule of the interpretation of a treaty in international law to take into account any subsequent practice in the application of the treaty which establishes the agreement of the parties about its interpretation.[12] It has been the consistent practice of States and of the UN itself (whose constituent instrument *UNCH* is) to cite *UDHR* as the agreed catalogue of human rights and fundamental freedoms, often in the specific context of *UNCH* 55(c) — as for example in the Proclamation of Teheran (see below). Accordingly, the expression 'human rights and fundamental freedoms' in that Article must now be interpreted to mean the rights and freedoms enumerated in *UDHR*.[13]

(3) From 22 April to 13 May 1968, a UN International Conference on Human Rights met at Teheran, Iran, 'to review the progress made in the twenty years since the adoption of *UDHR* and to formulate a programme for the future'. Among other things, the representatives of the 84 States there represented adopted a solemn Proclamation containing the following clause:

2. The Universal Declaration of Human Rights states a common understanding of the peoples of the world concerning the inalienable and inviolable rights of all members of the human family and constitutes an obligation for the members of the international community.

Accordingly, if *UDHR* did not then already 'constitute an obligation' for the Member States of the UN, the Proclamation of Teheran made it so.

Although the juridical status of *UDHR* cannot yet be said to be free from doubt, there are therefore today substantial grounds for saying that it now constitutes a binding obligation for Member States of the UN, and some grounds also for saying that it has now become part of customary international law,

---

[12] See now the Vienna Convention on the Law of Treaties, Art. 31(3) (b).

[13] This argument is supported by the dissenting opinion of Judge Tanaka in the *South-West African Cases (Second Phase)*, ICJ Reports 1966, 289-93.

and so binds all States. (The relevance of these considerations is of course confined to those States which have not yet become parties to any of the later human rights treaties.)

§6.2.2 *ADRD*

As in the case of *UDHR*, it was not the intention of the nations which in 1948 adopted *ADRD* that this instrument should create binding obligations for them in international law. Indeed, only a year later the Inter-American Juridical Committee (an official organ of the OAS Council) ruled that 'it is obvious that [*ADRD*] does not create a legal contractual obligation', and that it therefore lacked the status of 'positive substantive law'.[14]

However, here again later events may have affected the juridical status of *ADRD*. Article 5(j) of the Charter of the OAS of 1948[15] declared that 'The American States proclaim the fundamental rights of the individual without distinction as to race, nationality, creed or sex.' Here again, the Charter itself did not define what those 'fundamental rights' were. But when IACM was established, the Statute of that Commission which the OAS Council promulgated in 1960 declared that, 'for the purpose of this Statute, human rights are understood to be those set forth in [*ADRD*]'.[16]

In the years since then, IACM has consistently applied the provisions of *ADRD* as its standards in exercising its functions (see §29.1), both before and after it became a 'principal organ' of the OAS under Article 51 of the revised Charter of 1970. Indeed, the Second Special Inter-American Conference held in Rio de Janeiro, Brazil, in 1965 specifically requested IACM 'to give particular attention . . . to [the] observance of the human rights referred to in Articles I, II, III, IV, XVIII, XXV and XXVI of [*ADRD*]'[17] — a provision which was then also incorporated in the Commission's Statute.[18] Both these provisions relating to *ADRD* remain in IACM's current Statute, adopted by the OAS General Assembly in 1979,[19] after *AMR* entered into force. Even before that event, it was argued that the 1970 revision of the OAS Charter had 'significantly strengthened the normative character' of *ADRD*,[20] and that argument may be even stronger today. (Again, these considerations are relevant only for those Member States of the OAS which have not yet become parties to *ICPR*, *ICES*, or *AMR*.)

---

[14] Report of the Committee to the Inter-American Council of Jurists, 26 September 1949.

[15] Now reproduced as Article 3(j) of the revised Charter of 1970.

[16] Article 2.

[17] Resolution XXII.

[18] Article 9 *bis* (a).

[19] At its ninth regular session in La Paz, Bolivia. For the full text of the Statute, see IACM, *Handbook of Existing Rules pertaining to Human Rights* (OAS, 1980). But IACM has said that *AMR* cannot be used to 'interpret' *ADRD* so as to impose on a Member State of the OAS an international obligation based upon *AMR*, if it has not ratified that treaty: Case 2141 (USA) 6 March 1981.

[20] See T. Buergenthal, 'The Revised OAS Charter and the Protection of Human Rights', [1975] *American Journal of International Law* 828; 835.

§6.3 Absolute and immediate obligations

§6.3.1 TEXTS

ICPR

2 (1) Each State Party to the present Covenant undertakes to respect and to ensure to all individuals within its territory and subject to its jurisdiction the rights recognised in the present Covenant . . .

(2) Where not already provided for by existing legislative or other measures, each State Party to the present Covenant undertakes to take the necessary steps, in accordance with its constitutional processes and with the provisions of the present Covenant, to adopt such legislative or other measures as may be necessary to give effect to the rights recognized in the present Covenant.

EHR

1. The High Contracting Parties shall secure to everyone within their jurisdiction the rights and freedoms defined in Section I of this Convention.

AMR

1 (1) The States Parties to this Convention undertake to respect the rights and freedoms recognized herein and to ensure to all persons subject to their jurisdiction the free and full exercise of those rights and freedoms . . .

(2) For the purposes of this Convention, 'person' means every human being.

2. Where the exercise of any of the rights or freedoms referred to in Article 1 is not already ensured by legislative or other provisions, the States Parties undertake to adopt, in accordance with their constitutional processes and the provisions of this Convention, such legislative or other measures as may be necessary to give effect to those rights or freedoms.

[AFR]

1. The Member States of the Organization of African Unity parties to the present Charter shall recognize the rights duties and freedoms enshrined in this Charter and shall undertake to adopt legislative or other measures to give effect to them.

25. States parties to the present Charter shall have the duty to promote and ensure through teaching, education and publication, the respect of the rights and freedoms contained in the present

Charter and to see to it that these freedoms and rights as well as corresponding obligations and duties are understood.

§6.3.2 CROSS-REFERENCES

Signatures, ratifications, accessions, reservations, and interpretations: See Table A for the State Parties bound by these provisions on 1 January 1982, and any reservations and interpretations notified by them.

Derogation: For the provisions as to derogation in exceptional circumstances under *ICPR, EHR*, and *AMR*, see §11.

Non-discrimination: See §7 for the relevant provisions in these instruments.

Abuse: See §9 for the relevant provisions in these instruments.

Savings: See §10 for the relevant provisions in these instruments.

Restrictions and limitations: See §8 for the general provisions in these instruments.

International supervision, interpretation, application, and enforcement: By HRC under *ICPR* (see §27); by EUCM and EUCT under *EHR* (see §28); by IACM and IACT under *AMR* (see §29); by [AFCM] under [AFR] (see §30).

See also: §6.5 for territorial application; §6.6 for the obligation to provide domestic remedies.

§6.33 COMMENT

These are the Articles in *ICPR, EHR, AMR*, and [AFR] which impose upon their respective State Parties the obligations to secure and respect the human rights and fundamental freedoms defined elsewhere in these treaties. These obligations display two principal features:

(1) they are *absolute* — that is, they are not expressed as being limited either by the resources available to the State, or by reference to the means to be employed in performing them;
(2) they are *immediate* — that is, each State is bound to take the necessary steps to secure the human rights and fundamental freedoms concerned from the moment that the treaty comes into force for that State.

The rights and freedoms concerned are, in each case, those with which the treaty deals — described as 'recognised' in *ICPR* 2 and *AMR* 1(1), 'defined' in *EHR* 1(1), and 'enshrined' in [AFR 1]. Their beneficiaries are defined, in respect of each State Party, as 'all individuals within its territory and subject to its jurisdiction' in *ICPR* 2(1), and all persons 'subject to their jurisdiction' in *EHR* 1 and *AMR* 1(1). [AFR 1] does not define the beneficiaries at all. In no case is the protection limited by reference to any nationality.

The State obligation in *ICPR* is 'to respect and to ensure' those rights and freedoms for those beneficiaries, in *EHR* to 'secure' them, and in [AFR] to 'recognise' them. In *AMR*, the State Parties undertake to 'respect' the rights, and to 'ensure' their 'free and full exercise' to the beneficiaries.

EHR says nothing as to the means by which these obligations are to be fulfilled. *ICPR* 2(2) and *AMR* 2 call for such 'legislative or other measures as may be necessary to give effect' to the rights and freedoms concerned. [*AFR*] omits 'as may be necessary'; in *ICPR*, the form of the obligation is 'to take the necessary steps' to adopt these measures.

[*AFR* 25] adds an additional obligation to 'promote and ensure' respect and understanding for the rights, freedoms, obligations, and duties concerned, through 'teaching, education and publication'.

§6.3.4 JURISPRUDENCE

As long ago as 1925, the Permanent Court of International Justice described as 'self-evident' the principle that 'a State which has contracted valid international obligations is bound to make in its legislation such modifications as may be necessary to ensure the fulfilment of the obligations undertaken',[21] and a State cannot invoke the provisions even of its national constitution with a view to evading its treaty obligations.[22]

HRC has commented that the obligation for State Parties under *ICPR* 2 is not confined to mere respect for human rights, but requires specific activities on their part to enable individuals to enjoy those rights. Constitutional or legislative enactments may not be enough. It is particularly important that individuals should know what their rights are, and that all administrative and judicial authorities should know what obligations their State Party has assumed. *ICPR* should therefore be publicized in all the State Party's official languages, and included in the training of the State's authorities.[23]

Notwithstanding the phrase 'within its territory', HRC has also expressed the view that a State Party is accountable under *ICPR* 2(1) for violations of a person's rights recognized in that Covenant and committed by its agents in the territory of another State, whether with the acquiescence of the government of that State or in opposition to it. It would be unconscionable to permit a State Party to perpetrate violations on the territory of another State which it could not perpetrate on its own territory. 'Subject to its jurisdiction' is not a reference to the place where the violation occurs, but to the relationship between the individual and the State concerned.[24]

EUCM also has stated that 'in certain respects the nationals of a contracting State are within its "jurisdiction" even when domiciled or resident abroad',[25] and that the State Parties' obligation to secure the rights and freedoms set forth in *EHR* extends to 'all persons under their actual authority and responsibility, whether that authority is exercised within their own territory or abroad.'[26]

EUCT has held that a violation of *EHR* 1 follows automatically from, but adds nothing to, a violation of any of the substantive rights and freedoms defined in Section I (that is, Articles 2-18 inclusive) of *EHR*.[27] EUCT has also

---

[21] Avisory Opinion on *Exchange of Greek and Turkish Populations*, PCIJ, Series B, No. 10, 20.

[22] Advisory Opinion on the *Treatment of Polish Nationals and Other Persons of Polish Origin or Speech in the Danzig Territory*, PCIJ, Series A/B, No. 44, 24; cf. the International Law Commissions's draft Declaration on Rights and Duties of States 1949, Art. 13 (YB ILC 1949, 246; 288).

[23] GC 3/13; HRC 36, 109.

[24] *Burgos* v. *Uruguay* (R. 12/52) HRC 36, 176; *de Casariego* v. *Uruguay* (R. 13/56) HRC 36, 185.

[25] *X* v. *Federal Republic of Germany* (1611/62) CD 17, 42; see also *X* v. *Federal Republic of Germany* (1197/61) CD 8, 68.

[26] *Cyprus* v. *Turkey* (6780/74; 6950/75) Report: 10 July 1976.

[27] *Ireland* v. *United Kingdom* (5310/71) Judgment: 2 EHRR 25.

held that, if the proximate cause of a violation of a right defined in *EHR* is an agreement between private interests, but the violation is domestically lawful because the State concerned has failed to observe its obligations under *EHR* 1 to enact appropriate domestic legislation to secure that right, the State's responsibility for the relevant violation is engaged, and it must compensate the victim accordingly.[28]

However, a State is not responsible for the acts or omissions of an independent international tribunal which has its seat, and exercises its functions, within that State's territory, but over which the State has no sovereign power or control; in negotiating the Settlement Conventions or Charters of such tribunals, States are entitled to assume that they will conform to recognized standards of international justice, and failure to insert express provisions requiring the observance of Human Rights Conventions by which the State concerned is bound does not therefore constitute a lack of due diligence on its part.[29] Nor is an activity which is carried on by a State Party only jointly with other States, under an international agreement from which none of them can withdraw unilaterally, which cannot be changed without their unanimous consent or that of their representatives, and which pre-dates *EHR*, 'within the jurisdiction' of that State Party within the meaning of *EHR* 1.[30]

§6.4 Qualified and progressive obligations

§6.4.1 TEXTS

ICES

2 (1) Each State Party to the present Covenant undertakes to take steps, individually and through international assistance and co-operation, especially economic and technical, to the maximum of its available resources, with a view to achieving progressively the full realization of the rights recognized in the present Covenant by all appropriate means, including particularly the adoption of legislative measures.

23. The States Parties to the present Covenant agree that international action for the achievement of the rights recognized in the present Covenant includes such methods as the conclusion of conventions, the adoption of recommendations, the furnishing of technical assistance and the holding of regional meetings and technical meetings for the purpose of consultation and study organized in conjunction with the Governments concerned.

---

[28] *James, Young & Webster* v. *United Kingdom* (7601/76; 7806/77) Judgment: 13 August 1981.
[29] *X* v. *Federal Republic of Germany* (235/56) YB 2, 256.
[30] *Hess* v. *United Kingdom* (6231/73) DR 2, 72.

ESC

Part I

The Contracting Parties accept as the aim of their policy, to be pursued by all appropriate means, both national and international in character, the attainment of conditions in which the following rights and principles may be effectively realized:

Part II

The Contracting Parties undertake, as provided for in Part III, to consider themselves bound by the obligations laid down in the following Articles and paragraphs.

(*App.*: 1. Without prejudice to Article 12, paragraph 4 and Article 13, paragraph 4, the persons covered by Articles 1 to 17 include foreigners only insofar as they are nationals of other Contracting Parties lawfully resident or working regularly within the territory of the Contracting Party concerned, subject to the understanding that these Articles are to be interpreted in the light of the provisions of Articles 18 and 19.

This interpretation would not prejudice the extension of similar facilities to other persons by any of the Contracting Parties.)

Part III

20 (1) Each of the Contracting Parties undertakes:

(*a*) to consider Part I of this Charter as a declaration of the aims which it will pursue by all appropriate means, as stated in the introductory paragraph of that Part;

(*b*) to consider itself bound by at least five of the following Articles of Part II of this Charter: Articles 1, 5, 6, 12, 13, 16 and 19;

(*c*) in addition to the Articles selected by it in accordance with the preceding sub-paragraph, to consider itself bound by such a number of Articles or numbered paragraphs of Part II of the Charter as it may select, provided that the total number of Articles or numbered paragraphs by which it is bound is not less than 10 Articles or 45 numbered paragraphs.

(2) The Articles or paragraphs selected in accordance with sub-paragraphs (*b*) and (*c*) of paragraph 1 of this Article shall be notified to the Secretary-General of the Council of Europe at the time when the instrument of ratification or approval of the Contracting Party concerned is deposited.

(3) Any Contracting Party may, at a later date, declare by notification to the Secretary-General that it considers itself bound by any Articles or any numbered paragraphs of Part II of the Charter which it has not already accepted under the terms of paragraph 1 of this

Article. Such undertakings subsequently given shall be deemed to be an integral part of the ratification or approval, and shall have the same effect as from the thirtieth day after the date of the notification.

(4) The Secretary-General shall communicate to all the signatory Governments and to the Director-General of the International Labour Office any notification which he shall have received pursuant to this Part of the Charter.

(5) Each Contracting Party shall maintain a system of labour inspection appropriate to national conditions.

(*App.*: It is understood that the 'numbered paragraphs' may include Articles consisting of only one paragraph.)

(*App.*: It is understood that the Charter contains legal obligations of an international character, the application of which is submitted solely to the supervision provided for in Part IV thereof.)

33 (1) In member States where the provisions of paragraphs 1, 2, 3, 4 and 5 of Article 2, paragraphs 4, 6 and 7 of Article 7 and paragraphs 1, 2, 3, and 4 of Article 10 of Part II of this Charter are matters normally left to agreements between employers or employers' organizations and workers' organizations, or are normally carried out otherwise than by law, the undertakings of those paragraphs may be given and compliance with them shall be treated as effective if their provisions are applied through such agreements or other means to the great majority of the workers concerned.

(2) In member States where these provisions are normally the subject of legislation, the undertakings concerned may likewise be given, and compliance with them shall be regarded as effective if the provisions are applied by law to the great majority of the workers concerned.

AMR

26. The States Parties undertake to adopt measures, both internally and through international cooperation, especially those of an economic and technical nature, with a view to achieving progressively, by legislation or other appropriate means, the full realization of the rights implicit on the economic, social, educational, scientific, and cultural standards set forth in the Charter of the Organization of American States as amended by the Protocol of Buenos Aires.

§ 6.4.2 CROSS-REFERENCES

Signatures, ratifications, accessions, reservations, and interpretations: See Table A for the State Parties bound by these provisions on 1 January 1982, and any reservations and interpretations notified by them.

Derogation: For the provisions as to derogation in exceptional circumstances under *ESC* and *AMR*, see § 11.

Non-discrimination: See § 7 for the relevant provisions in these instruments.

Abuse: See § 9 for the relevant provisions in these instruments.

Savings: See § 10 for the relevant provisions in these instruments.

Restrictions and limitations: Note the specific provisions in *ESC* 33 and *App.* 1. See § 8 for the general provisions in these instruments, and the principles governing all restriction and limitation clauses.

International supervision, interpretation, application, and enforcement: By IACM and IACT under *AMR* (see § 29); supervision only by ECOSOC under *ICES* (see § 31); by EUCE under *ESC* (see § 32).

See also: § 6.5 for territorial application; § 6.6 for the obligation to provide domestic remedies under *AMR*.

§ 6.4.3 COMMENT

The State obligations under *ICES*, *ESC*, and *AMR* 26 differ in two important respects from those under *ICPR*, *EHR*, *AMR* 1, and [*AFR* 1] (see § 6.3):

(1) They are *qualified* rather than absolute — that is, they are limited (in *ICES*) to the maximum of the resources available to the State Parties, and (in all the three treaties) to 'appropriate means';
(2) They are *progressive* rather than immediate — that is, they call (in *ICES*) for steps to be taken or (in *AMR*) for measures to be adopted 'with a view to achieving progressively the full realisation' of the rights concerned; in the case of *ESC*, the language of Part I is one of accepting policy aims to a similar end, but the opening words of Part II are couched in more immediate language and are followed, at the beginning of each of the substantive Articles in that Part, by an expression such as 'With a view to assuring the effective exercise of' the right concerned.

However, qualified and progressive though they may be, all these are still binding obligations in international law, as *ESC* 20 in particular makes clear. Indeed, even the reservation in *ESC App.*, designed to ensure that the obligations will not be justiciable beyond the supervision procedure laid down in *ESC* Part IV, expressly reaffirms that position.

All three of the treaties mention international collaboration towards their ends, in the case of *ICES* and *AMR* with special reference to the 'economic and technical' fields; *ICES* 23 lists examples of this. Legislation is treated as an 'appropriate means' in all of them: *ESC* 33(2) also makes it a sufficient means in many (but not all) cases, provided that it is applied to 'the great majority of the workers concerned'.

    ESC Part III alone allows its State Parties to select some only of the Articles and paragraphs in Part II by which they are willing to be bound: the Articles so selected, as at 1 January 1982, are shown in Table A.

    Note that, exceptionally, there is a two-year time limit to the particular obligation in *ICES* 14: see §20.

§6.4.4 JURISPRUDENCE

None of the competent independent international institutions has so far expressed any views on the interpretation or application of any of these provisions, but it is noteworthy that EUCE has not so far found any justification for delay in the compliance by any State Party with an obligation under *ESC* by which it has become bound.

§6.5 Territorial application

§6.5.1 TEXTS

UDHR

2.... Furthermore, no distinction shall be made on the basis of the political, jurisdictional or international status of the country or territory to which a person belongs, whether it be independent, trust, non-self-governing or under any other limitation of sovereignty.

ICPR

50. The provisions of the present Covenant shall extend to all parts of federal States without any limitations or exceptions.

ICPR OP

10. The provisions of the present Protocol shall extend to all parts of federal States without any limitations or exceptions.

ICES

28. The provisions of the present Covenant shall extend to all parts of federal States without any limitations or exceptions.

EHR

63 (1) Any State may at the time of its ratification or at any time thereafter declare by notification addressed to the Secretary-General of the Council of Europe that the present Convention shall extend to all or any of the territories for whose international relations it is responsible.

    (2) The Convention shall extend to the territory or territories named in the notification as from the thirtieth day after the receipt of this notification by the Secretary-General of the Council of Europe.

(3) The provisions of this Convention shall be applied in such territories with due regard, however, to local requirements.

(4) Any State which has made a declaration in accordance with paragraph 1 of this Article may at any time thereafter declare on behalf of one or more of the territories to which the declaration relates that it accepts the competence of the Commission to receive petitions from individuals, non-governmental organizations or groups of individuals in accordance with Article 25 of the present Convention.

ESC

34 (1) This Charter shall apply to the metropolitan territory of each Contracting Party. Each signatory Government may, at the time of signature or of the deposit of its instrument of ratification or approval, specify, by declaration addressed to the Secretary-General of the Council of Europe, the territory which shall be considered to be its metropolitan territory for this purpose.

(2) Any Contracting Party may, at the time of ratification or approval of this Charter or at any time thereafter, declare by notification addressed to the Secretary-General of the Council of Europe, that the Charter shall extend in whole or in part to a non-metropolitan territory or territories specified in the said declaration for whose international relations it is responsible or for which it assumes international responsibility. It shall specify in the declaration the Articles or paragraphs of Part II of the Charter which it accepts as binding in respect of the territories named in the declaration.

(3) The Charter shall extend to the territory or territories named in the aforesaid declaration as from the thirtieth day after the date on which the Secretary-General shall have received notification of such declaration.

(4) Any Contracting Party may declare at a later date, by notification addressed to the Secretary-General of the Council of Europe, that, in respect of one or more of the territories to which the Charter has been extended in accordance with paragraph 2 of this Article, it accepts as binding any Articles or any numbered paragraphs which it has not already accepted in respect of that territory or territories. Such undertakings subsequently given shall be deemed to be an integral part of the original declaration in respect of the territory concerned, and shall have the same effect as from the thirtieth day after the date of the notification.

(5) The Secretary-General shall communicate to the other signatory Governments and to the Director-General of the International Labour Office any notification transmitted to him in accordance with this Article.

AMR

29 (1) Where a State Party is constituted as a federal state, the national government of such State Party shall implement all the provisions of the Convention over whose subject matter it exercises legislative and judicial jurisdiction.

(2) With respect to the provisions over whose subject matter the constituent units of the federal state have jurisdiction, the national government shall immediately take suitable measures, in accordance with its constitution and its laws, to the end that the competent authorities of the constituent units may adopt appropriate provisions for the fulfillment of this Convention.

(3) Whenever two or more States Parties agree to form a federation or other type of association they shall take care that the resulting federal or other compact contains the provisions necessary for continuing and rendering effective the standards of this Convention in the new state that is organized.

§6.5.2 CROSS-REFERENCES

State obligation: Absolute and immediate under *ICPR*, *EHR*, and *AMR*: see §6.3. Qualified and progressive under *ICES* and *ESC*: see §6.4. For the juridical status of obligations under *UDHR*, see §6.2.

Signatures, ratifications, accessions, reservations, and interpretations: See Table A for the State Parties bound by these instruments on 1 January 1982, and any reservations and interpretations notified by them.

Derogation: For the provisions as to derogation in exceptional circumstances under *ICPR*, *EHR*, *ESC*, and *AMR*, see §11.

Non-discrimination: See §7 for the relevant provisions in these instruments.

Abuse: See §9 for the relevant provisions in these instruments.

Savings: See §10 for the relevant provisions in these instruments.

Restrictions and limitations: See §8 for the general provisions in these instruments.

International supervision, interpretation, application, and enforcement: By HRC under *ICPR* (see §27); by EUCM and EUCT under *EHR* (see §28); by IACM and IACT under *AMR* (see §29); supervision only by ECOSOC under *ICES* (see §31); by EUCE under *ESC* (see §32). See also §6.6 for the obligation to provide domestic remedies under *UDHR*, *ICPR*, *EHR*, and *AMR*.

§6.5.3 COMMENT

UDHR 2, being part of the non-discrimination Article, emphasizes that the territorial associations of any individual cannot adversely affect his human rights. The other provisions collected here essentially relate to the problems of federal States, and of dependent territories.

Federal States

In federal States, it is the federal government that is responsible for external relations — and is therefore the subject of international law — while it is the authorities of the constituent units in the federation which are often responsible for much of the domestic law and administrative arrangements by which the provisions of the human rights instruments have to be implemented. Conflicts can therefore readily arise if the federal government becomes bound by a treaty, and the authorities of the constituent units (which are not directly bound by it) do not wish to implement its provisions.

The two Covenants make short shrift of this: they simply declare that their provisions 'shall extend to all parts of federal States', leaving it to federal State Parties to carry out that injunction. *AMR* 28 is less absolute: it requires national governments to do what they themselves have power to do, and beyond that only to take 'suitable measures . . . to the end that' the authorities of the constituent units do likewise. *AMR* 28(3) adds a provision for future federations between independent States which are already bound by the Convention.

Dependent territories

EHR and *ESC* were concluded at a time when several of their State Parties still had a number of colonies. Accordingly, both of them contain provisions enabling the State Parties to extend their obligations under the treaties to their colonies if they so wish — 'with due regard, however, to local requirements' in the case of *EHR*.

§6.5.4 JURISPRUDENCE

In *Tyrer* v. *United Kingdom*,[31] *EUCT* considered whether 'due regard . . . to local requirements' in the Isle of Man could justify, under *EHR* 63(3), degrading punishment in the form of judicial birching which would otherwise violate *EHR* 3. In this connection, the Court noted that the system established by *EHR* 63 was primarily designed to meet the fact that, when *EHR* was drafted, there were still certain colonial territories whose state of civilization did not, it was thought, permit the full application of the Convention. However, the Isle of Man was an up-to-date society; it had always been included in the European family of nations, and must be regarded as sharing fully that 'common heritage of political traditions, ideals, freedom and the rule of law' to which the Preamble to *EHR* refers. Accordingly, it was not enough that the local population sincerely believed that judicial corporal punishment was necessary in their island as a deterrent, and to maintain law and order: such beliefs and opinions on their own could not constitute positive and conclusive proof of a 'requirement'.[32]

EUCM has been unable to find any significant social or cultural differences between Guernsey and the United Kingdom which could be relevant to the application of *EHR* 63(3).[33]

---

[31] (5856/72) Judgment: 2 EHRR 1.
[32] And even if such a 'requirement' could be established, it could still not justify degrading punishment which violates *EHR* 3, since that Article is absolute and unqualified, and allows of no derogation even in the event of war or other public emergency: see §14.3.3.
[33] *Wiggins* v. *United Kingdom* (7456/76) DR 13, 40.

§6.6 Provision of domestic remedies

§6.6.1 Texts

UDHR

8. Everyone has the right to an effective remedy by the competent national tribunals for acts violating the fundamental rights granted him by the constitution or by law.

ADRD

XVIII. Every person may resort to the courts to ensure respect for his legal rights. There should likewise be available to him a simple, brief procedure whereby the courts will protect him from acts of authority that, to his prejudice, violate any fundamental constitutional rights.

ICPR

2 (3) Each State Party to the present Covenant undertakes:
(*a*) To ensure that any person whose rights or freedoms as herein recognized are violated shall have an effective remedy, notwithstanding that the violation has been committed by persons acting in an official capacity;
(*b*) To ensure that any person claiming such a remedy shall have his right thereto determined by competent judicial, administrative or legislative authorities, or by any other competent authority provided for by the legal system of the State, and to develop the possibilities of judicial remedy;
(*c*) To ensure that the competent authorities shall enforce such remedies when granted.

EHR

13. Everyone whose rights and freedoms as set forth in this Convention are violated shall have an effective remedy before a national authority notwithstanding that the violation has been committed by persons acting in an official capacity.

AMR

25 (1) Everyone has the right to simple and prompt recourse, or any other effective recourse, to a competent court or tribunal for protection against acts that violate his fundamental rights recognized by the constitution or laws of the state concerned or by this Convention, even though such violation may have been committed by persons acting in the course of their official duties.

(2) The States Parties undertake:

(a) to ensure that any person claiming such remedy shall have his rights determined by the competent authority provided for by the legal system of the state;

(b) to develop the possibilities of judicial remedy; and

(c) to ensure that the competent authorities shall enforce such remedies when granted.

[AFR]

7 (1) Every individual shall have the right to have his cause heard. This comprises:

(a) The right to an appeal to competent national organs against acts violating his fundamental rights as recognized and guaranteed by conventions, laws, regulations and customs in force;

26. States parties to the present Charter shall have the duty to guarantee the independence of the Courts and shall allow the establishment and improvement of appropriate national institutions entrusted with the promotion and protection of the rights and freedoms guaranteed by the present Charter.

§6.6.2 CROSS-REFERENCES

State obligation: Absolute and immediate under *ICPR*, *EHR*, *AMR*, and [*AFR*]: see §6.3. For the juridical status of obligations under *UDHR* and *ADRD*, see §6.2.

Signatures, ratifications, accessions, reservations, and interpretations: See Table A for the State Parties bound by these instruments on 1 January 1982, and any reservations and interpretations notified by them.

Derogation: For the provisions as to derogation in exceptional circumstances under *ICPR*, *EHR*, and *AMR*, see §11.

Non-discrimination: See §7 for the relevant provisions in these instruments.

Abuse: See §9 for the relevant provisions in these instruments.

Savings: See §10 for the relevant provisions in these instruments.

Restrictions and limitations: See §8 for the general provisions in these instruments.

International supervision, interpretation, application, and enforcement: By HRC under *ICPR* (see §27); by EUCM and EUCT under *EHR* (see §28); by IACM and IACT under *AMR* (see §29); by [AFCM] under [*AFR*] (see §30).

See also: §§1.12, 4 and 5.2.

§6.6.3 COMMENT

It is plainly preferable that redress for violations of human rights and fundamental freedoms should be available to victims within their own States, rather than that they should need to resort to international institutions. However, since in the nature of things the most frequent violators of such rights and freedoms will be the governments or other executive or administrative authorities of the State, effective redress can only come through institutions that have the necessary independence and impartiality, such as courts or tribunals.

Except for *ICES* and *ESC*, all the instruments require their State Parties to provide effective domestic remedies for violations. The two Declarations both call for such remedies in the case of violations of rights or freedoms protected by the domestic constitutions, as well as 'legal' rights (*ADRD*) or 'fundamental rights granted by law' (*UDHR*) — which may include international law.

By contrast, the four treaties considered here require effective domestic remedies for violations of the rights and freedoms 'as herein recognised' (*ICPR* 2(3)(*a*)), 'as set forth in this Convention' (*EHR* 13), 'recognised . . . by this Convention' (*AMR* (1)), or 'as recognised and guaranteed by conventions' ([*AFR* 7(1)(*a*)]) — that is, they require that these provisions of *international* human rights law should be directly enforceable within the *domestic* forum.

As to the nature of that forum, *UDHR* specifies 'the competent national tribunals', while *ADRD* simply refers to 'the courts'. *ICPR* 2(3)(*b*) requires 'competent judicial, administrative or legislative authorities, or any other competent authority provided for by the legal system of the State,' but goes on to express a preference for 'judicial remedy'. *EHR* 13 contents itself with 'a national authority', [*AFR*] with 'competent national organs' supported (in Article 26) by 'appropriate national institutions'. Only *AMR* 25(1) insists exclusively on 'a competent court or tribunal', though in Article 25(2)(*b*) it too calls on its State Parties to 'develop the possibilities of judicial remedy'.

Only *AMR* 25(1) and [*AFR* 12(1)(*a*)] require domestic remedies also for violations of fundamental rights recognized by *domestic* law, in the form of 'the constitution or laws of the State concerned' for *AMR*, and 'laws, regulations and customs in force' for [*AFR*]. Only *ADRD* XVIII calls for 'a simple, brief procedure'.

ICPR 2(3)(*c*) and *AMR* 25(2)(*c*) specifically require the State concerned to lend its monopoly of force to the enforcement of the remedies when they are granted.

§6.6.4 JURISPRUDENCE

EHR 13 requires that any individual whose Convention rights and freedoms 'are violated' is to have an effective remedy before a national authority, even where 'the violation has been committed' by persons in an official capacity. In *Klass* v. *Federal Republic of Germany*[34] EUCT observed that this provision, read literally, seems to say that a person is entitled to a national remedy only if a 'violation' has been established. However, a person cannot establish a violation before a national authority unless he is first able to lodge with such an authority a complaint to that effect. Consequently, the Court held, it cannot be a prerequisite for the application of *EHR* 13 that the Convention has in fact been violated. In the Court's view, *EHR* 13 requires that where an individual considers

---

[34] (5029/71) Judgment: 2 EHRR 214.

himself to have been prejudiced by a measure allegedly in breach of the Convention, he should have a remedy before a national authority in order both to have his claim decided and, if appropriate, to obtain redress. Thus, *EHR* 13 must be interpreted as guaranteeing an 'effective remedy before a national authority' to everyone who *claims* that his rights and freedoms under the Convention have been violated.

At one time, EUCM took the view that *EHR* 13 related exclusively to a remedy in respect of a violation of one of the rights and freedoms set forth in the other provisions of the Convention. Where, therefore, EUCM did not find any appearance of a violation of any of the rights or freedoms invoked by an applicant, it considered that there could be no basis for the application of *EHR* 13.[35] However, in *Klass* v. *Federal Republic of Germany*[36] EUCT took a different view, and the precise scope of *EHR* 13 still remains to be settled.[37]

In *Eggs* v. *Switzerland*,[38] EUCM observed that in the case of a violation of the right to liberty and security of the person, it is not possible to exercise the remedy provided by *EHR* 13 in addition to that provided by *EHR* 5(4). Since *EHR* 5(4) guarantees a right to proceedings before a 'court' with the special guarantees of independence and procedure attaching thereto, and not merely before an 'authority' of unspecified status, that provision must be regarded as a *lex specialis* with respect to the general principle of providing an effective remedy for any victim of a violation of the Convention. Having declared admissible the complaint based on *EHR* 5(4), the Commission therefore considered it unnecessary to examine the merits of the question whether the same facts also constituted a violation of the more general principle contained in *EHR* 13.

The 'authority' referred to in *EHR* 13 may not necessarily and in all instances be a judicial authority in the strict sense. Nevertheless, the powers and procedural guarantees an authority possesses are relevant in determining whether the remedy before it is 'effective'.[39] It has been suggested[40] that, as a rule, the factors which go to establish whether a remedy is 'effective' for the purpose of *EHR* 26 would be equally useful when defining the requirements of *EHR* 13. These requirements are as follows:

(1) the remedy must be *accessible*, that is to say that the individual must be in a position to start a procedure which will result in a decision from the relevant authority;

(2) the remedy must be *sufficient*, that is to say that the relevant authority must have the power to redress the alleged violation if it is in fact established;[41]

[35] *X* v. *Austria* (1092/61) CD 9, 37; *X, Y, Z, V and W* v. *United Kingdom* (3325/67) CD 25, 117; *X and Y* v. *Netherlands* (6753/74) DR 2, 118; *Klass* v. *Federal Republic of Germany* (5029/71) Report: 9 March 1977; *X* v. *Austria* (8142/78) DR 18, 88.

[36] *Supra.*

[37] See *Sporrong and Lönnroth* v. *Sweden* (7151-2/75) Report: 8 October 1980 (referred to EUCT).

[38] (7341/76) DR 6, 170. See also *De Wilde, Ooms and Versyp* v. *Belgium* (2832/66; 2835/66; 2899/66) Judgment: 1 EHRR 373.

[39] *Klass* v. *Federal Republic of Germany, supra.*

[40] J. Raymond, 'A Contribution to the Interpretation of Article 13 of the European Convention on Human Rights' 5 *Human Rights Review*, 161.

[41] As, for example in the UK, Adjudicators and Immigration Appeals Tribunals which have statutory powers to review and reverse the Home Secretary's decisions about immigration (*Uppal et al.* v. *United Kingdom* (8244/78) DR 17, 149), but not Boards of Visitors, the Parliamentary Commissioner for Administration, and even the regular Courts, where

(3) the remedy must have some *likelihood of being accepted*; for example, there must not be established precedents against its availability;
(4) the remedy must not be the mere *repetition* of a remedy which has already been used.

In *Klass* v. *Federal Republic of Germany*,[42] EUCT rejected a submission that the concept of an 'effective remedy' presupposes that the person concerned should be placed in a position, by means of subsequent information, to pursue a remedy for any inadmissible encroachment upon his guaranteed right of which he had no independent knowledge. The Court observed that no unrestricted right to notification of surveillance measures can be deduced from *EHR* 13, once secret surveillance has been held to be 'necessary in a democratic society' for any of the purposes mentioned in *EHR* 8. Accordingly, the lack of notification does not, in the circumstances of such a case, entail a breach of *EHR* 13. An 'effective remedy' under *EHR* 13 must mean a remedy that is as effective as it can be, having regard to the restricted scope for recourse inherent in any system of secret surveillance.

EUCM has said that *EHR* 13 does not impose on a State an obligation to create a constitutional remedy,[43] nor that there should be several degrees of jurisdiction.[44] *EHR* 13 does not relate to legislation, and does not guarantee a remedy by which legislation can be controlled for its conformity with the Convention.[45]

IACM has expressed the view that the indefinite prolonging of trials for crimes against public order and state security, which give rise in some instances to deprivation of the freedom of the accused for a longer period than the longest sentence he could receive, is a violation of *ADRD* XVIII.[46]

they have no power in domestic law to determine and redress claims relating to prisoners' correspondence (*Silver et al.* v. *United Kingdom* (5947/72, etc.) Report: 11 October 1980 (referred to EUCT).

[42] *Supra.*
[43] *X* v. *Federal Republic of Germany* (448/59) CD 3; *X* v. *Federal Republic of Germany* (2717/66) CD 29, 1.
[44] *Müller* v. *Austria* (5849/72) DR 1, 46.
[45] *James, Young and Webster* v. *United Kingdom* (7601/76; 7806/77) Report: 14 December 1979. But in the same case, EUCT reserved this point; Judgment: 13 August 1981. Cf. *Sporrong and Lönnroth* v. *Sweden, supra,* n. 37.
[46] AR 1976, 16.

§7. NON-DISCRIMINATION

UDHR

2. Everyone is entitled to all the rights and freedoms set forth in this Declaration, without distinction of any kind, such as race, colour, sex, language, religion, political or other opinion, national or social origin, property, birth or other status.

7. All are equal before the law and are entitled without any discrimination to equal protection of the law. All are entitled to equal protection against any discrimination in violation of this Declaration and against any incitement to such discrimination.

ADRD

11. All persons are equal before the law and have the rights and duties established in this Declaration, without distinction as to race, sex, language, creed or any other factor.

ICPR

2 (1) Each State Party to the present Covenant undertakes to respect and to ensure to all individuals within its territory and subject to its jurisdiction the rights recognized in the present Covenant, without distinction of any kind, such as race, colour, sex, language, religion, political or other opinion, national or social origin, property, birth or other status.

3. The States Parties to the present Covenant undertake to ensure the equal right of men and women to the enjoyment of all civil and political rights set forth in the present Covenant.

26. All persons are equal before the law and are entitled without any discrimination to the equal protection of the law. In this respect, the law shall prohibit any discrimination and guarantee to all persons equal and effective protection against discrimination on any ground such as race, colour, sex, language, religion, political or other opinion, national or social origin, property, birth or other status.

ICES

2 (2) The States Parties to the present Covenant undertake to guarantee that the rights enunciated in the present Covenant will be exercised

72

without discrimination of any kind as to race, colour, sex, language, religion, political or other opinion, national or social origin, property, birth or other status.

(3) Developing countries, with due regard to human rights and their national economy, may determine to what extent they would guarantee the economic rights recognized in the present Covenant to non-nationals.

3. The States Parties to the present Covenant undertake to ensure the equal right of men and women to the enjoyment of all economic, social and cultural rights set forth in the present Covenant.

EHR

14. The enjoyment of the rights and freedoms set forth in this Convention shall be secured without discrimination on any ground such as sex, race, colour, language, religion, political or other opinion, national or social origin, association with a national minority, property, birth or other status.

16. Nothing in Articles 10, 11, and 14 shall be regarded as preventing the High Contracting Parties from imposing restrictions on the political activity of aliens.

ESC

(*App.*: 1. Without prejudice to Article 12, paragraph 4 and Article 13, paragraph 4, the persons covered by Articles 1 to 17 include foreigners only insofar as they are nationals of other Contracting Parties lawfully resident or working regularly within the territory of the Contracting Party concerned, subject to the understanding that these Articles are to be interpreted in the light of the provisions of Articles 18 and 19.

This interpretation would not prejudice the extension of similar facilities to other persons by any of the Contracting Parties.

2. Each Contracting Party will grant to refugees as defined in the Convention relating to the Status of Refugees, signed at Geneva on 28th July, 1951, and lawfully staying in its territory, treatment as favourable as possible, and in any case not less favourable than under the obligations accepted by the Contracting Party under the said Convention and under any other existing international instruments applicable to those refugees.)

AMR

1 (1) The States Parties to this Convention undertake to respect the rights and freedoms recognized herein and to ensure to all persons

subject to their jurisdiction the free and full exercise of those rights and freedoms, without any discrimination for reasons of race, color, sex, language, religion, political or other opinion, national or social origin, economic status, birth, or any other social condition.

(2) For the purposes of this Convention, 'person' means every human being.

[*AFR*]

2. Every individual shall be entitled to the enjoyment of the rights and freedoms recognized and guaranteed in the present Charter without distinction of any kind such as race, ethnic group, colour, sex, language, religion, political or any other opinion, national and social origin, fortune, birth or other status.

18 (3) The State shall ensure the elimination of every discrimination against women.

28. Every individual shall have the duty to respect and consider his fellow beings without discrimination, and to maintain relations aimed at promoting, safeguarding and reinforcing mutual respect and tolerance.

§ 7.0.2 CROSS-REFERENCES

Signatures, ratifications, accessions, reservations, and interpretations: See Table A for the State Parties bound by these instruments on 1 January 1982, and any reservations and interpretations notified by them. For the juridical status of *UDHR* and *ADRD*, see §6.2.

Derogation: For the provisions as to derogation in exceptional circumstances under *ICPR, EHR, ESC*, and *AMR*, see §11.

Abuse: See §9 for the relevant provisions in these instruments.

Savings: See §10 for the relevant provisions in these instruments.

Restrictions and limitations: Note the specific provisions in *ICES* 2(3), *EHR* 16, and *ESC App*. 1. See §8 for the general provisions in these instruments, and the principles governing all restriction and limitation clauses.

International supervision, interpretation, application, and enforcement: By HRC under *ICPR* (see §27); by EUCM and EUCT under *EHR* (see §28); by IACM and IACT under *AMR* (see §29); by [AFCM] under [*AFR*] (see §30); supervision only by ECOSOC under *ICES* (see §31); by EUCE under *ESC* (see §32). See also §6.6 for the obligation to provide domestic remedies under *UDHR, ADRD, ICPR, EHR, AMR*, and [*AFR*].

Subsidiary instruments: CD, CA, CE, CW$_1$, ILO 111 (see §7.0.5); ILO 122 (see §18.1.5); CW$_2$ (see §25.0.5).

See also: §22.2 for recognition, and §22.3 for equality, before the law; §26.2 for the prohibition of advocacy of hatred. There are other non-discrimination catalogues in *ICPR* 4(1) and *AMR* 27(1) (§11); *AMR* 22(8) (§14.5); *UDHR* 16(1) (§17.1); *ICPR* 24(1) (§17.2); and *AMR* 13(5) (§26.2). Specific catalogues also appear in some of the other subsidiary instruments, e.g. *CR* 3 (§14.5); *CS₂* 9 (§22.1); and *ILO 105* 1(*e*) (§18.4.5).

§ 7.0.3 COMMENT

The principle of non-discrimination is fundamental to the concept of human rights. The primary characteristic which distinguishes 'human' rights from other rights is their universality: according to the classical theory, they are said to 'inhere' in every human being by virtue of his humanity alone. It must necessarily follow that no particular feature or characteristic attaching to any individual, and which distinguishes him from others, can affect his entitlement to his human rights, whether in degree or in kind (see §1.10), except where the instruments specifically provide for this for a clear and cogent reason — for example, in restricting the right to vote to adults, or in requiring special protection for women and children. Strictly, therefore, it should not be necessary to include non-discrimination provisions in human rights instruments, let alone to draw up catalogues of grounds on which it is illegitimate to discriminate between individuals in securing or respecting their entitlement to, or their exercise or enjoyment of, the universal human rights.

However, both past and present experience show that a high proportion of violations of the human rights of individuals takes place because those individuals differ in some respect from a conventional norm, and are discriminated against on that ground. Accordingly, all the instruments (other than *ESC*) go to considerable lengths to emphasize the illegitimacy of such discrimination. But the expression in *UDHR* 2, *ICPR* 2(1), and [*AFR* 2] 'without distinction of any kind' — or, in the case of *EHR* 14, 'without discrimination on any ground' — followed in each case by the words 'such as', makes it clear that the catalogue of grounds which follow is given only by way of example. (*ICES* 2(2) and *AMR* 1(1) do not appear to use the language of exemplification.)

While a number of non-discrimination grounds is common to all these catalogues, some others are not. The grounds included in the major instruments are shown in Table 2.

As can be seen from this Table, the principal differences between the catalogues are these:

(1) *UNCH* 55(*c*) only lists four grounds: race, sex, language, and religion. To these, *ADRD* II adds 'or any other factor'.
(2) *ICES* 2(2), *ICPR* 2(1) and 26, and [*AFR* 2] follow the standard catalogue of the twelve grounds set out in *UDHR* 2. *EHR* 14 also adopts this, but adds 'association with a national minority'; [*AFR*] instead adds 'ethnic group'.
(3) *AMR* 1(1) omits 'property' and 'other status' from the standard catalogue, and substitutes 'economic status' and 'any other social condition'; [*AFR* 2] substitutes 'fortune' for 'property'.

What is crucial is the placing, and the unequivocal language, of the non-discrimination Articles in *UDHR*, *ICES*, *ICPR*, *EHR*, *AMR*, and [*AFR*]. These Articles govern *all* the rights declared in the instruments concerned, with the result that whenever any State Party discriminates against any one or more of its citizens in respect of any of these rights it will thereby fail to comply with its obligations under the instrument concerned.

TABLE 2

	UNCH 55(c)	UDHR 2	ADRD II	ICPR 2(1) and 26 / ICES 2(2)	EHR 14	AMR 1(1)	[AFR 2]
Race	○	○	○	○[2]	○	○[3]	○
Colour		○		○[2]	○	○[3]	○
Sex	○	○	○	○[2]	○	○[3]	○
Language	○	○	○	○[2]	○	○[3]	○
Religion	○	○	○[1]	○[2]	○	○[3]	○
Political Opinion		○		○	○		○
Other Opinion		○		○	○	○	○
National origin		○		○	○		○
Social origin		○		○[2]	○	○[3]	○
Property		○		○	○		○[4]
Birth		○		○	○	○	○
Other status		○		○	○	○	○
Economic status						○	
Any other social condition						○	
Association with national minority					○		
Ethnic group							○
Any other factor			○				

Notes:

1. Here called 'creed'.
2. See *ICPR* 4(1) (§ 11) as to derogation.
3. See *AMR* 27(1) (§ 11) as to derogation.
4. Here called 'fortune'.

To all this, *UDHR* 7 and *ICPR* 26 add a positive State obligation to protect individuals from discrimination and from incitement to it. In requiring a legal prohibition of discrimination, and legal guarantees of equal and effective protection against it, *ICPR* 26 may be said to create a separate 'right not to be discriminated against', independent of the other rights and freedoms.

ICPR 3 and *ICES* 3 add a specific provision about equality of the two sexes; [*AFR* 18(3)] about the elimination of discrimination against women.

The only exceptions allowed are in respect of aliens — in *ICES* 2(3) as to their economic rights only, and in *EHR* 16 as to their political activities. There is also an exception for aliens not lawfully resident or working in a country in *ESC*, *App.* 1.

Certain other Articles in some of the instruments contain specific non-discrimination catalogues for the rights they protect: see the cross-references at the end of §7.0.2.

§7.0.4 JURISPRUDENCE

HRC has commented that *ICPR* 3 requires not only measures of protection, but also affirmative action designed to ensure the positive enjoyment of equal rights. This cannot be done simply by enacting laws.[1] HRC has also expressed the view that *ICPR* 2(1) and 3 are both violated whenever a restriction is imposed on a right guaranteed by the Covenant, which in fact results in an adverse distinction, based on sex, in the *enjoyment* of the right concerned. For that purpose, it does not matter whether the restriction could be justified if it were applied without discrimination.[2]

In the *Belgian Linguistic Case*,[3] EUCT examined the scope of *EHR* 14. It observed that this Article has no independent existence, since it relates solely to the rights and freedoms set forth in the Convention.[4] Nevertheless, a measure which appears to conform with the requirements of an Article enshrining a particular right or freedom may yet infringe that Article when read in conjunction with *EHR* 14, if its effect is discriminatory.[5]

In spite of the very general wording of the French version ('*sans distinction aucune*'), *EHR* 14 does not forbid every difference in treatment in the exercise of the rights and freedoms recognized. This version must be read in the light of the more restrictive text of the English version ('without discrimination'). One would reach absurd results were one to give *EHR* 14 an interpretation as wide as that which the French version seems to imply. One would, in effect, be led to judge as contrary to the Convention every one of the many legal or administrative provisions which do not secure to everyone complete equality

---

[1] GC 4/13; HRC 36, 109.

[2] *Aumeeruddy-Cziffra et al.* v. *Mauritius* (R. 9/35) HRC 36, 134.

[3] (1474/62, etc.) Judgment: 1 EHRR 252.

[4] Cf. X v. *Federal Republic of Germany* (86/55) YB 1, 198; *X* v. *Belgium* (95/55) YB 1, 201; *X* v. *Federal Republic of Germany* (165/56) YB 1, 203; *X* v. *Federal Republic of Germany* (436/58) CD 1. But this does not mean that a violation of a specific right or freedom must be found before *EHR* 14 can become operative: *Müller* v. *Austria* (5849/72) Report: DR 3, 25.

[5] *Belgian Linguistic Case, supra.* For example, a person cannot draw from *EHR* P1 2 the right to obtain from the public authorities the creation of a particular kind of educational establishment; nevertheless, a State which has set up such an establishment cannot, in laying down entrance requirements, take discriminatory measures within the meaning of *EHR* 14. See also *Sporrong and Lönnroth* v. *Sweden* (7151-2/75) Report: 8 October 1980 (referred to EUCT).

of treatment in the enjoyment of the rights and freedoms recognized. The competent national authorities are frequently confronted with situations and problems which, because of their inherent differences, call for different legal solutions; moreover, certain legal inequalities tend only to correct factual inequalities. Such an extensive interpretation cannot therefore be accepted.[6]

On the criteria which enable a determination to be made as to whether or not a given difference in treatment concerning one of the rights and freedoms set forth in the Convention contravenes *EHR* 14, EUCT has held that the principle of equality of treatment is violated if the distinction has no 'objective and reasonable' justification. The existence of such a justification must be assessed in relation to the aim and effects of the measure under consideration, regard being had to the principles which normally prevail in democratic societies. A difference of treatment in the exercise of a right laid down in the Convention must not only pursue a legitimate aim: *EHR* 14 is likewise violated when it is clearly established that there is no reasonable relationship of proportionality between the means employed and the aim sought to be realized.[7]

According to EUCM, discrimination contrary to *EHR* 14 is established where the following elements are found to exist in the case concerned:

(1) The facts found disclose a differential treatment; and
(2) The distinction does not have a legitimate aim — that is, it has no objective and reasonable justification, having regard to the aim and effects of the measure under consideration; and
(3) There is no reasonable proportionality between the means employed and the aim sought to be realized.[8]

In assessing whether or not there has been an arbitrary distinction, EUCT has pointed out that it cannot disregard those legal and factual features which characterize the life of the society in the State which has to answer for the measure in dispute. In so doing, the Court cannot assume the role of the competent national authorities, for it would thereby lose sight of the subsidiary nature of the international machinery of collective enforcement established by the Convention. The national authorities remain free to choose the measures which they consider appropriate in those matters which are governed by the Convention. Review by EUCT is confined to the conformity of those measures with the requirements of the Convention.[9]

EUCM and EUCT have now considered *EHR* 14 in conjunction with most of the rights and freedoms defined in *EHR*, namely those relating to ill-treatment (*EHR* 3),[10] forced labour (*EHR* 4),[11] liberty and security (*EHR* 5),[12] fair trial

---

[6] *Belgian Linguistic Case, supra.* See also *McFeeley et al.* v. *United Kingdom* (8317/78) Report: 3 EHRR 161; *Ramesh Presaad Singh* v. *State of Bihar* AIR [1978] SC 327.

[7] *Belgian Linguistic Case, supra.*

[8] *De Geillustreerde Pers N.V.* v. *Netherlands* (5178/71) Report: DR 8, 5.

[9] *Belgian Linguistic Case, supra.*

[10] *X* v. *Denmark* (238/56) YB 1, 205; *3 East African Asians* v. *United Kingdom* (4715/70; 4783/71; 4827/71) DR 13, 17.

[11] *Grandrath* v. *Federal Republic of Germany* (2299/64) Report: 12 December 1966; *X* v. *Federal Republic of Germany* (4653/70) CD 46, 22; *Four Companies* v. *Austria* (7427/76) DR 7, 148; *X* v. *Switzerland* (8500/79) DR 18, 238.

[12] *X* v. *Federal Republic of Germany* (1167/61) CD 12, 70; *X* v. *Federal Republic of Germany* (3266/67) CD 30, 53; *X* v. *Federal Republic of Germany* (3911/69) CD 30, 76; *X* v. *Austria* (4280/69) CD 35, 161; *X* v. *Austria* (4622/70) CD 40, 15; *X* v. *Federal Republic*

(*EHR* 6),[13] retroactive penal laws (*EHR* 7),[14] privacy (*EHR* 8),[15] freedom of conscience (*EHR* 9),[16] freedom of expression (*EHR* 10),[17] freedom of assembly and association (*EHR* 11),[18] marriage (*EHR* 12),[19] property (*EHR* P1 1),[20] education (*EHR* P1 2),[21] and free elections (*EHR* P1 3).[22] EUCM has also said

of Germany (5025/71) CD 39, 95;*Engel et al.* v. *Netherlands* (5100-2/71; 5354/72; 5370/72) Judgment: 1 EHRR 647; *Ireland* v. *United Kingdom* (5310/71) Report: 25 January 1976; Judgment: 2 EHRR 25;*Eggs* v. *Switzerland* (7341/76) DR 6, 170; *Krzycki* v. *Federal Republic of Germany* (7629/76) Report: DR 13, 57; *Agee* v. *United Kingdom* (7729/76) DR 7, 164.
[13] *Isop* v. *Austria* (808/60) CD 8, 80; *Struppat* v. *Federal Republic of Germany* (2804/66) CD 27, 61; *Engel et al.* v. *Netherlands, supra*; *Ireland* v. *United Kingdom, supra*; *X* v. *Austria* (7138/75) DR 9, 50; *Agee* v. *United Kingdom, supra*; *X* v. *Sweden* (7973/77) DR 17, 74.
[14] *X* v. *Federal Republic of Germany* (167/61) CD 12, 70; *Delcourt* v. *Belgium* (2689/65) CD 22, 48; *X* v. *Netherlands* (7721/76) DR 11, 209.
[15] *X* v. *Federal Republic of Germany* (167/56) YB 1, 235; *X* v. *Sweden* (911/60) CD 7, 7; *Belgian Linguistic Case* (1474/62, etc.) Judgment: 1 EHRR 252; *Inhabitants of Les Fourons* v. *Belgium* (2209/64) Report: 30 March 1971; *X* v. *Norway* (2792/66) CD 21, 64; *Van den Berghe* v. *Belgium* (2914/66) CD 28, 62; *X* v. *United Kingdom* (3325/67) CD 25, 117; *X* v. *Austria* (4280/69) CD 35, 161; *X* v. *Belgium* (4372/70) CD 37, 101; *X* v. *Ireland* (5913/72) CD 45, 95; *X* v. *Federal Republic of Germany* (5935/72) DR 3, 46; *X* v. *Netherlands* (6202/73) DR 1, 66; *Marckx* v. *Belgium* (6833/74) Report: 10 December 1977; Judgment: 2 EHRR 330; *X* v. *United Kingdom* (7215/75) Report: DR 19, 66. *Wiggins* v. *United Kingdom* (7456/76) DR 13, 40; *Agee* v. *United Kingdom* (7729/76) DR 7, 164; *Hagmann-Hüsler* v. *Switzerland* (8042/77) DR 12, 202; *X* v. *Switzerland* (8166/78) DR 13, 241, *McFeeley et al.* v. *United Kingdom* (8317/78) Report: 3 EHRR 161; *Uppal et al.* v. *United Kingdom* (8244/78) DR 17, 149; *Dudgeon* v. *United Kingdom* (7525/76) Report: 13 March 1980.
[16] *X* v. *Netherlands* (2065/63) CD 18, 40; *Grandrath* v. *Federal Republic of Germany* (2299/64) Report: 12 December 1966; *Inhabitants of Leeuw-St Pierre* v. *Belgium* (2333/64) CD 16, 58; *X* v. *Italy* (6741/74) DR 5, 83; *Arrowsmith* v. *United Kingdom* (7050/75) Report: DR 19, 5; *X* v. *Denmark* (7567/76) DR 9, 117; *McFeeley et al.* v. *United Kingdom* (8317/78) Report: 3 EHRR 161.
[17] *X* v. *Federal Republic of Germany* (2834/66; 4038/69) CD 35, 29; *Engel et al.* v. *Netherlands, supra*; *De Geillustreerde Pers N.V.* v. *Netherlands* (5178/71) Report: DR 8, 5; *Handyside* v. *United Kingdom* (5493/72) Judgment: 1 EHRR 737; *X* v. *Italy* (6741/74) *supra*; *X, Y and Z* v. *Belgium* (6782-4/74) DR 9, 13; *Arrowsmith* v. *United Kingdom, supra*; *Agee* v. *United Kingdom, supra*.
[18] *National Union of Belgian Police* v. *Belgium* (4464/70) Report: 27 May 1974; Judgment: 1 EHRR 578; *Schmidt and Dahlström* v. *Sweden* (5589/72) Report: 17 July 1974, Judgment: 6 February 1976; *Svenska Lokmannaforbundet* v. *Sweden* (5614/72) Report: 27 May 1974, Judgment: 1 EHRR 617; *X* v. *Sweden* (6094/73) DR 9, 5; *X* v. *Italy* (6741/74) *supra*.
[19] *X* v. *Denmark* (238/56) YB 1, 205.
[20] *Gudmundsson* v. *Iceland* (511/59) CD 4; *X* v. *Federal Republic of Germany* (2717/66) CD 35, 1; *X* v. *Federal Republic of Germany* (4050/69) CD 34, 33; *X* v. *Netherlands* (4130/69) CD 38, 9; *X* v. *United Kingdom* (4288/69) CD 33, 53; *X* v. *Federal Republic of Germany* (4653/70) CD 46, 22; *Handyside* v. *United Kingdom, supra*; *X* v. *Austria* (5593/72) CD 45, 113; *Müller* v. *Austria* (5849/72) Report: DR 3, 25; *X* v. *Ireland* (5913/72) CD 45, 95; *X* v. *Austria* (6087/73) DR 5, 10; *X* v. *Austria* (6163/73) DR 1, 60; *X* v. *Netherlands* (6202/73) DR 1, 66; *Marckx* v. *Belgium, supra*; *Four Companies* v. *Austria, supra*; *X* v. *Federal Republic of Germany* (7694/76) DR 12, 131; *AB and Company AS* v. *Federal Republic of Germany* (7742/76) DR 14, 146; *X* v. *Austria* (7624/76) DR 19, 100; *X* v. *Austria* (8003/77) Report: 3 EHRR 285; *X* v. *Austria* (7987/77) DR 18, 31; *X* v. *Federal Republic of Germany* (8410/78) DR 18, 216; *Wiggins* v. *United Kingdom* (7456/76) DR 13, 40.
[21] *Belgian Linguistic Case, supra*; *Inhabitants of Les Fourons* v. *Belgium, supra*; *Van den Berghe* v. *Belgium, supra*; *X* v. *United Kingdom* (3798/68) CD 29, 74; *X* v. *Belgium* (4372/70) CD 37, 101; *X* v. *Austria* (5492/72) CD 44, 63; *Kjeldsen et al.* v. *Denmark* (5095/71; 5920/72; 5926/72) Report: 21 March 1975; Judgment: 1 EHRR 711; *X* v. *United Kingdom* (7782/77) DR 14, 179; *Church of X* v. *United Kingdom* (3798/68) CD 29, 74.
[22] *W, X, Y and Z* v. *Belgium* (6745-6/74) DR 2, 110; *X* v. *Netherlands* (6573/74) DR 1, 87; *X* v. *United Kingdom* (7566/76) DR 9, 121; *X* v. *Belgium* (8701/79) DR 18, 250.

that differences in the age of consent for homosexual and heterosexual relations, and in the legal provisions governing male and female homosexual behaviour, do not constitute discrimination within the meaning of *EHR* 14.[23]

Among the many decisions of national courts applying similar provisions in their constitutions, the following are some examples of acts which have been held to constitute discrimination:

(1) A requirement that female employees in government foreign service should obtain official permission to marry, and a refusal to appoint female candidates who were already married;[24]

(2) A law making it an offence for an Indian to be intoxicated anywhere outside a reserve, where it is an offence for others only in a public place;[25]

(3) The denial of an import licence to a company because of the political opinions of its two shareholders;[26]

(4) The eviction of Asian stall-holders from a public market because they were not Africans;[27]

(5) The non-renewal and restriction of transport licences for a company having no African shareholders;[28]

(6) The restriction of citizenship to 'persons of negro African descent'.[29]

§7.0.5 SUBSIDIARY INSTRUMENTS

Five subsidiary instruments now in force are concerned exclusively with questions of discrimination.

Racial discrimination

The Convention on the Elimination of all Forms of Racial Discrimination (*CD*) defines[30] 'racial discrimination' as

any distinction, exclusion, restriction or preference based on race, colour, descent, or national or ethnic origins which has the purpose or effect of nullifying or impairing the recognition, enjoyment or exercise, on an equal footing, of human rights and fundamental freedoms in the political, economic, social, cultural and any other field of public life,

but excludes from that definition distinctions drawn between citizens and aliens,[31] and certain kinds of what is now often called 'positive' or 'affirmative' action.[32] The State Parties condemn racial discrimination, and undertake not to practise, sponsor, defend, or support it, and to prohibit it and bring it to an end.[33] 'When the circumstances so warrant', they will undertake positive action in the social, economic, and cultural fields 'for the purpose of guaranteeing . . . the full and equal enjoyment of human rights and fundamental freedoms' for certain racial groups and their members, to ensure their 'adequate development and protection'.[34]

---

[23] *X* v. *United Kingdom* (7215/75) Report: DR 19, 66.
[24] *Muthamma* v. *Union of India* AIR [1979] SC 1868 (Supreme Court of India).
[25] *R* v. *Drybones* (1970) 3 CCC (2nd) 355 (Supreme Court of Canada).
[26] *Camacho & Sons Ltd et al.* v. *Collector of Customs* (1971) 18 WIR 159 (Court of Appeal, West Indian Associated States).
[27] *Madhwa* v. *City Council of Nairobi* [1968] EA 406 (High Court of Kenya).
[28] *Shah Vershi* v. *Transport Licensing Board* [1971] EA 289 (High Court of Kenya).
[29] *Akar* v. *Attorney-General of Sierra Leone* [1969] 3 All ER 384 (Privy Council).
[30] *CD* 1(1).   [31] *CD* 1(2).   [32] *CD* 1(4).
[33] *CD* 2(1).   [34] *CD* 2(2).

Accordingly, the State Parties undertake 'to guarantee the right of everyone, without distinction as to race, colour, or national or ethnic origin, to equality before the law, notably in the enjoyment of' a long list of what are in fact the rights declared in the major international human rights instruments (and considered elsewhere in the present work), with the addition of 'the right to protection by the State against violence or bodily harm, whether inflicted by government officials or by any individual group or institution', 'the right to inherit', 'the right to housing', and 'the right of access to any place or service intended for use by the general public, such as transport, hotels, restaurants, cafés, theatres and parks'.[35] The State Parties are further bound to assure effective domestic remedies, including 'just and adequate reparation or satisfaction' for any acts of racial discrimination which violate human rights and fundamental freedoms contrary to *CD*.[36]

In addition, the State Parties undertake to declare as offences punishable by law

all dissemination of ideas based on racial superiority or hatred, incitement to racial discrimination, as well as all acts of violence or incitement to such acts against any race or group of persons of another colour or ethnic origin, and also the provision of any assistance to racist activities, including the financing thereof,[37]

to 'declare illegal and prohibit organisations, and also organised and all other propaganda activities, which promote and incite racial discrimination',[38] and to 'recognise participation in such organisation or activities as an offence punishable by law'.[39]

The Convention establishes[40] a Committee on the Elimination of Racial Discrimination, with a supervisory function based on biennial reports from the State Parties.[41] The Committee also has jurisdiction to investigate communications from State Parties[42] — and, subject to recognition of its competence by the State Party concerned, from individuals or groups[43] — alleging violations of the Convention by a State Party. The Committee's procedure is confidential, but it may summarize its 'suggestions and recommendations' in its annual report to the UNGA.[44]

The International Convention on the Suppression and Punishment of the Crime of *Apartheid* (*CA*) declares to be 'crimes violating the principles of international law'[45] *apartheid* 'and similar policies and practices of racial segration and discrimination'. It defines[46] *apartheid* as the following 'inhuman acts committed for the purpose of establishing and maintaining domination by one racial group of persons over any other racial group of persons and systematically oppressing them':

(1) 'denial to a member or members of a racial group or groups of the right to life and liberty of person', by various means there specified;
(2) 'deliberate imposition on a racial group or groups of living conditions calculated to cause its or their physical destruction in whole or in part';

---

[35] *CD* 5. [36] *CD* 6. [37] *CD* 4(*a*).
[38] *CD* 4(*b*). [39] *Ibid.* [40] *CD* 8.
[41] *CD* 9. [42] *CD* 11–13. [43] *CD* 14.
[44] *Ibid.* By 1 January 1982, no inter-State complaint had yet been referred to this Committee, nor had it published any views on any individual communication.
[45] See § 5.3. [46] *CA* II.

(3) legislative or other measures 'calculated to prevent a racial group or groups from participation in the political, social, economic and cultural life of the country and the deliberate creation of conditions preventing the full development of such a group or groups, in particular by denying to members of a racial group or groups basic human rights and freedoms', giving examples of these;

(4) 'any measures, including legislative measures, designed to divide the population along racial lines by the creation of separate reserves and ghettos for the members of a racial group or groups, the prohibition of mixed marriages among members of various racial groups, the expropriation of landed property belonging to a racial group or groups or to members thereof';

(5) 'exploitation of the labour of the members of a racial group or groups, in particular by submitting them to forced labour';

(6) 'persecution of organisations and persons, by depriving them of fundamental rights and freedoms, because they oppose *apartheid*'.

International criminal responsibility applies to anyone, 'irrespective of the motive involved', who commits, participates in, directly incites, or conspires in the commission of any of these acts, or who directly abets, encourages, or co-operates in the commission of the crime of *apartheid*.[47] Persons charged with these acts may be tried by a competent tribunal of any of the State Parties that may acquire jurisdiction over them, whether or not they reside in, or are nationals of, the State in which the acts were committed, and the State Parties undertake to adopt the necessary measures to enable that to be done.[48] Such persons may also be tried by an international penal tribunal.[49] For the purposes of extradition, the acts constituting the crime of *apartheid* are not to be considered as political crimes.[50] The State Parties will also take measures to suppress, and prevent any encouragement of, the crime of *apartheid*.[51]

A supervisory function, based on periodic reports by the State Parties, is conferred on a group drawn from CHR.[52]

Discrimination against women

The Convention on the Elimination of all Forms of Discrimination against Women (CW_1) was adopted by the UNGA on 18 December 1979 and entered into force on 3 September 1981. It defines[53] 'discrimination against women' as

any distinction, exclusion or restriction made on the basis of sex which has the effect or purpose of impairing or nullifying the recognition, enjoyment or exercise by women, irrespective of their marital status, on a basis of equality of men and women, of human rights and fundamental freedoms in the political, economic, social, cultural, civil or any other field.

Again, as in the case of *CD*, temporary measures of positive or affirmative action, 'aimed at accelerating *de facto* equality between men and women', or measures aimed at protecting maternity, are not to be considered as discrimination within the meaning of this Convention.[54]

CW_1 imposes[55] on the State Parties an obligation to

take in all fields, in particular in the political, social, economic and cultural

---

[47] *CA* III.   [48] *CA* IV(*b*) and V.   [49] *CA* V.
[50] *CA* VI.   [51] *CA* IV(*a*).   [52] *CA* VII–IX.
[53] CW_1 1.   [54] CW_1 4.   [55] CW_1 3.

fields, all appropriate measures, including legislation, to ensure the full development and advancement of women, for the purpose of guaranteeing them the exercise and enjoyment of human rights and fundamental freedoms on a basis of equality with men.

To that end, the State Parties undertake to adopt a large number of detailed measures in the fields of political and public life, international representation, nationality, education, employment, health care, economic and social life, rural areas, the law, and marriage and family relations.[56] The State Parties will also take all appropriate measures to suppress all forms of traffic in women, and the exploitation of the prostitution of women.[57]

The Convention envisages the establishment of a Committee on the Elimination of Discrimination against Women,[58] composed of independent experts, which will supervise compliance through periodic reports to be submitted by the State Parties,[59] on which the Committee will be able to make 'suggestions and general recommendations' in its annual reports to UNGA through ECOSOC.[60]

Discrimination in employment

The ILO Convention concerning Discrimination in Respect of Employment and Occupation (*ILO 111*) defines[61] 'discrimination' to include

any distinction, exclusion or preference made on the basis of race, colour, sex, religion, political opinion, national extraction or social origin, which has the effect of nullifying or impairing equality of opportunity or treatment in employment or occupation.

However, 'any distinction, exclusion or preference in respect of a particular job based on the inherent requirements thereof shall not be deemed to be discrimination'.[62] For the purpose of the Convention, 'employment' and 'occupation' include access to vocational training, access to employment and to particular occupations, and terms and conditions of employment.[63]

The State Parties undertake 'to declare and pursue a national policy designed to promote, by methods appropriate to national conditions and practice, equality of opportunity and treatment in respect of employment and occupation, with a view to eliminating any discrimination in respect thereof',[64] and to adopt certain specified measures to that end.[65]

There is an exception for 'measures affecting an individual who is justifiably suspected of, or engaged in, activities prejudicial to the State', provided that he has 'the right to appeal to a competent body established in accordance with national practice'.[66] There are savings for other ILO Conventions and Recommendations,[67] and for special measures constituting positive or affirmative action.[68]

---

[56] *CW$_1$* 7–16.
[57] *CW$_1$* 6; cf. *AMR* 6(1) (see §18.4.1), and *CP* (see §18.4.5).
[58] *CW$_1$* 17; this Committee was to be elected in 1982.
[59] *CW$_1$* 18.   [60] *CW$_1$* 21.
[61] *ILO 111* 1(1).   [62] *ILO 111* 1(2).
[63] *ILO 111* 1(3).   [64] *ILO 111* 2.
[65] *ILO 111* 3.   [66] *ILO 111* 4.
[67] *ILO 111* 5(1).   [68] *ILO 111* 5(2).

Discrimination in education

The Convention against Discrimination in Education (*CE*) — the only one of these subsidiary instruments sponsored by UNESCO — defines[69] 'discrimination' to include

any distinction, exclusion, limitation or preference which, being based on race, colour, sex, language, religion, political or other opinion, national or social origin, economic condition or birth, has the purpose or effect of nullifying or impairing equality of treatment in education and in particular:

(*a*) of depriving any person or group of persons of access to education of any type or at any level;

(*b*) of limiting any person or group of persons to education of an inferior standard;

(*c*) . . . of establishing or maintaining separate educational systems or institutions for persons or groups of persons; or

(*d*) of inflicting on any person or group of persons conditions which are incompatible with the dignity of man.

However, subject to certain conditions, separate educational systems or institutions for the two sexes, or for religious or linguistic groups, are not to be deemed to constitute discrimination.[70]

The State Parties undertake to adopt various measures and policies 'in order to eliminate and prevent discrimination' in education,[71] in order 'to promote equality of opportunity and of treatment in the matter of education',[72] and in order to ensure the application of certain principles relating to education.[73] The State Parties will periodically report to UNESCO their efforts to apply *CE*.[74] A Protocol to *CE* establishes a UNESCO Conciliation and Good Offices Commission 'to be responsible for seeking the settlement of any disputes which may arise between State Parties' under this Convention.[75]

---

[69] *CE* 1.   [70] *CE* 2.   [71] *CE* 3.
[72] *CE* 4.   [73] *CE* 5.   [74] *CE* 7.
[75] By 1 January 1982, no such dispute had yet been referred to this Commission.

§8. RESTRICTIONS AND LIMITATIONS

UDHR

29 (1) Everyone has duties to the community in which alone the free and full development of his personality is possible.

(2) In the exercise of his rights and freedoms, everyone shall be subject only to such limitations as are determined by law solely for the purpose of securing due recognition and respect for the rights and freedoms of others and of meeting the just requirements of morality, public order and the general welfare in a democratic society.

ADRD

XXVIII. The rights of man are limited by the rights of others, by the security of all, and by the just demands of the general welfare and the advancement of democracy.

XXIX. It is the duty of the individual so to conduct himself in relation to others that each and every one may fully form and develop his personality.

ICPR

47. Nothing in the present Covenant shall be interpreted as impairing the inherent right of all peoples to enjoy and utilize fully and freely their natural wealth and resources.

ICES

4. The States Parties to the present Covenant recognize that, in the enjoyment of those rights provided by the State in conformity with the present Covenant, the State may subject such rights only to such limitations as are determined by law only in so far as this may be compatible with the nature of these rights and solely for the purpose of promoting the general welfare in a democratic society.

25. Nothing in the present Covenant shall be interpreted as impairing the inherent right of all peoples to enjoy and utilize fully and freely their natural wealth and resources.

EHR

16. Nothing in Articles 10, 11, and 14 shall be regarded as preventing the High Contracting Parties from imposing restrictions on the political activity of aliens.

18. The restrictions permitted under this Convention to the said rights and freedoms shall not be applied for any purpose other than those for which they have been prescribed.

ESC

31 (1) The rights and principles set forth in Part I when effectively realized, and their effective exercise as provided for in Part II, shall not be subject to any restrictions or limitations not specified in those Parts, except such as are prescribed by law and are necessary in a democratic society for the protection of the rights and freedoms of others or for the protection of public interest, national security, public health, or morals.

(2) The restrictions permitted under this Charter to the rights and obligations set forth herein shall not be applied for any purpose other than that for which they have been prescribed.

AMR

30. The restrictions that, pursuant to this Convention, may be placed on the enjoyment or exercise of the rights or freedoms recognized herein may not be applied except in accordance with the laws enacted for reasons of general interest and in accordance with the purpose for which such restrictions have been established.

32 (1) Every person has responsibilities to his family, his community, and mankind.

(2) The rights of each person are limited by the rights of others, by the security of all, and by the just demands of the general welfare, in a democratic society.

[*AFR*]

27 (1) Every individual shall have duties towards his family and society, the State and other legally recognized communities and the international community.

(2) The rights and freedoms of each individual shall be exercised with due regard to the rights of others, collective security, morality and common interest.

§8.0.2 CROSS-REFERENCES

Signatures, ratifications, accessions, reservations, and interpretations: See Table A for the State Parties bound by these instruments on 1 January 1982, and any reservations and interpretations notified by them.

Derogation: For the provisions as to derogation in exceptional circumstances under *ICPR, EHR, ESC*, and *AMR*, see §11.

Non-discrimination: See §7 for the relevant provisions in these instruments.

Abuse: See §9 for the relevant provisions in these instruments.

International supervision, interpretation, application, and enforcement: By HRC under *ICPR* (see §27); by EUCM and EUCT under *EHR* (see §28); by IACM and IACT under *AMR* (see §29); by [AFCM] under [AFR] (see §30); supervision only by ECOSOC under *ICES* (see §31); by EUCE under *ESC* (see §32). See also §6.6 for the obligation to provide domestic remedies under *UDHR, ADRD, ICPR, EHR, AMR*, and [AFR].

See also: All the *specific* restriction and limitation clauses in various Articles in the different instruments, listed, discussed, and tabulated in §8.0.3.

§8.0.3 COMMENT

General provisions

§8.0.1 reproduces only the *general* provisions in the instruments which deal with restrictions and limitations, not the specific ones which are to be found in the Articles defining the particular rights and freedoms to which they apply (see below).

It is a commonplace that virtually[1] no right or freedom can be absolute: its boundaries must be set by the rights and freedoms — and sometimes the interests — of others. These general provisions all reflect that general proposition, but they are formulated in several different ways.

Declarations of duties. UDHR 29(1), *ADRD* XXIX, *AMR* 32(1), and [AFR 27(1)] all declare duties: in *AMR* and [AFR] to the family; in *UDHR* 2 to 'the' community, in *AMR* to 'his' community, and in [AFR] to 'society'; and, in addition, in *AMR* to 'mankind' and in [AFR] to 'the State and other legally recognised communities and the international community'.

Savings for the rights of others. All the instruments except for the two Covenants and *EHR* contain these in a general form. Those in *ADRD* XXVIII and [AFR 27(2)] have no limitations; *AMR* 32(2) limits the saving by the phrase 'in a democratic society'; *UDHR* 29(2) and *ESC* 31(1) include it in the exceptions and limitations which may be 'prescribed by law' and 'in a democratic society'.

Savings for the general interest. ADRD XXVIII and [AFR 27(2)], without limitation, respectively save 'the just demands of the general welfare and the advancement of democracy', and 'common interest'. With the limitation of 'determined

---

[1] There are theoretical exceptions in the freedoms of thought, belief, and opinion, before the resulting ideas or views are expressed or disseminated to others. In the international instruments, there are also some exceptions of choice, such as the freedoms from torture, slavery, and imprisonment for debt, which are declared absolutely, without restriction or limitation of any kind, and not subject to derogation even in the most extreme circumstances.

by' (or 'prescribed by', or 'in accordance with') law — except for *AMR* 'in a democratic society' — *UDHR* 29(2) and *ICES* 4 save 'the general welfare', *ESC* 31(1) 'public interest', and *AMR* 30 'reasons of general interest'.

Savings for specific interests. Both the Covenants save, without limitation, 'the inherent right of all peoples to enjoy and utilise fully and freely their national wealth and resources' (see §26.3). *ADRD* XXVIII and [*AFR* 27(2)], again without limitation, respectively save 'the security of all' and 'collective security', to which [*AFR*] adds 'morality'. With the limitations noted above, *UDHR* 29(2) provides for morality, and *ESC* 31(1) for national security, public health, or morals. *EHR* 16 saves restrictions on the political activity of aliens for three of its Articles (see §§7, 23.4, and 25).

Compatibility of purpose. *ICES* 4 provides that, where the law limits rights declared in the instrument, the limitation must 'be compatible with the nature of these rights'; *EHR* 18 and *ESC* 31(2) say that permitted restrictions 'shall not be applied for any purpose other than those for which they have been pre-scribed', and *AMR* 30 says that they must be applied 'in accordance with the purpose for which [they] have been established'.

Specific provisions

Apart from the general provisions considered in this section, all the treaties contain *specific* provisions in various individual Articles which specify the limitations and restrictions that may be allowed on the *particular* rights or freedoms with which those Articles deal, so in effect circumscribing the bound-aries of those particular rights and freedoms. The rights and freedoms, the Articles concerned, and the sections in which they are to be found in the present work, are shown in Table 3.

It will be seen that specific provisions of this kind affect only nine of the rights and freedoms which the instruments enumerate, and are contained in comparatively few Articles: one only in *ICES*, two in *ESC*, four in [*AFR*], six in *ICPR*, seven in *AMR*, and eight in *EHR* (including *P1* and *P4*).

The general scheme of all these provisions is broadly similar. In each case, the right or freedom is stated first, and the provision for restrictions and limitations is subsidiary to that statement. This provision (in almost all cases) requires that any restrictions or limitations must be prescribed by law (that is, must not be imposed arbitrarily — see §1.11), and must be objectively justified on one or more of certain specified grounds. The form of the justification required (again in almost all cases) is that the restriction or limitation must be shown to be 'necessary', often (though not always) 'in a democratic society', to support or protect some specified objective. The maximum number of such objectives listed in a single exception of this kind is ten (in *EHR* 10(2)), though more usually it is around five or six. The total catalogue from which the lists are drawn contains twenty-one items.

In the result, the extent to which these provisions allow restrictions and limitations on the different rights and freedoms concerned varies greatly, both because of the number of the objectives in the appropriate list, and because of the differing widths of the different objectives. So long as the word 'necessary' appears and is strictly construed, there is scope for a narrow interpretation, especially where it is coupled with the expression 'in a democratic society'.[2] The word 'necessary' is in fact present in the great majority of these provisions,

---

[2] For examples of the interpretation and application of these expressions, see §8.0.4.

TABLE 3

§		Articles
14.4	Freedom of movement	*ICPR* 12(3) *EHR P4* 2 *ESC* 18, 19 *AMR* 22(3),(4) [*AFR* 12(2)]
21	Property	*EHR P1* 1 *AMR* 21(2) [*AFR* 14]
22.4	Fair trial	*ICPR* 14(1) *EHR* 6(1) *AMR* 8(5)
23.2	Privacy	*EHR* 8(2)
23.3	Conscience and religion	*ICPR* 18(3) *EHR* 9(2) *AMR* 12(3) [*AFR* 8]
23.4	Opinion and expression	*ICPR* 19(3) *EHR* 10(2) *AMR* 13(2)
24.1	Assembly	*ICPR* 21 *EHR* 11(2) *AMR* 15 [*AFR* 11]
24.2	Association	*ICPR* 22(2) *EHR* 11(2) *AMR* 16(2)
24.3	Trade unions	*ICPR* 22(2) *ICES* 8(1) *EHR* 11(2)

being absent only in [*AFR*], in most of the Articles protecting the right to property, and in the provisions requiring trials to be held in public (where the restriction is anyway subject to direct judicial control). The expression 'in a democratic society' appears in about half of them. The overall position may be more easily appreciated from Table 4.

TABLE 4

	ICPR	ICES	EHR	ESC	AMR	[AFR]
Restriction must be						
Prescribed by law	12[1] 18 19[1] 21[2] 22	8	8[3] 9 10 11 P1,1[1] P4,2[3]		12 13[4] 15[2] 16[5] 21[5] 22[6]	11[1] 12[1] 14[7]
Necessary	12 18 19 21 22	8	8 9 10 11 P1,1 P4,2	19	12 13 15 16 22	
In a democratic society	14	8	8 9 10 11 P4,2		15 16 22	
Consistent with other protected rights	12				12	
And justified by						
National security	12 14 18 19 21 22	8	8 10 11 P4,2	19	13 15 16 22	11 12
Public safety	12 18		8 9 10 11 P4,2		12 13 15 16 22	11[8]
Public order[9]	12 14 18 19 21 22	8			12 13 15 16 22	
Prevention of disorder			8 10 11 P4,2			
Prevention of crime			8 10 11 P4,2			
Law and order	12 18 19 21 22		6[10] 8[10] 9 10[10] 11 P4,2[10]		12 13 15 16 22	8
[Public] health	12 14[10] 18 19 21 22		8[10] 9 10[10] 11[10] P4,2[10]	19	12 13 15 16 22	11[11] 12
[Public] morals	12 18 19 21 22		8 9 10[15] 11 P4,2	19[12]	12 13[15] 15 16 22	11[13] 12
Rights and freedoms of others	12 18[14] 19[15] 21 22	8	8 9 10 11 P1,1 P4,2	19	12 13 15 16 22	11 12[12]
Public interest			P1,1	19	22	
General interest [of community]			P1,1			14
Public need						14
Public utility or social interest					21	
Territorial integrity			10			
Economic well-being of country			8			
Cogent economic or social reasons				18		
Authority and impartiality of judiciary			10			
Interests of justice	14		6		8	
Interests of juveniles	14		6			
Private lives	14		6			
Confidentiality of information			10			

[1] Here called 'provided by law'.
[2] Here called 'in conformity with law'.
[3] Here called 'in accordance with [the] law'.
[4] Here called 'expressly established by law'.
[5] Here called 'established by law'.
[6] Here called 'pursuant to a law'.
[7] Here called 'in accordance with the provisions of appropriate laws'.
[8] Here called 'the safety of others'.
[9] Often, but not always, also called 'ordre public'.
[10] The word 'public' is omitted in these Articles.
[11] Here called the 'fundamental rights and freedoms of others'.
[12] Here called 'morality'.
[13] Here called 'the ethics of others'.
[14] Here called the 'fundamental rights and freedoms of others'.
[15] Here called the 'rights and reputations' of others.

§8.0.4 JURISPRUDENCE

Interpretation of restriction and limitation clauses

In *Handyside* v. *United Kingdom*,[3] EUCM considered the relationship of a paragraph of restrictions (in that case, *EHR* 10(2)) to the right which it qualifies. The relationship, the Commission said, is clearly that of an exception to the general rule. The general rule is the protection of the freedom; the exception is its restriction. The restriction may not be applied in a sense that completely suppresses the freedom, but only insofar as is necessary for preserving the values which the paragraph exhaustively enumerates and protects. Accordingly, in any given case the Commission must first consider whether or not there has been an interference with the right protected; and, if so, whether or not this interference was justified in the light of the paragraph of restrictions.

All exception clauses must be strictly interpreted, and no other criteria than those mentioned in that clause itself may be the basis of any restriction on the right protected.[4] In *Klass* v. *Federal Republic of Germany*,[5] EUCT stated that *EHR* 8(2), since it provides for an exception to a right guaranteed by the Convention, is to be interpreted narrowly. Powers of secret surveillance of citizens, characterizing as they do the police state, are tolerable under *EHR* only insofar as is strictly necessary for safeguarding the democratic institutions. In *Sunday Times* v. *United Kingdom*,[6] the same Court observed that, unlike the House of Lords in the UK, it was not faced with a choice between two conflicting principles, but with a principle of freedom of expression that is subject to a number of exceptions which must be narrowly interpreted.

'Prescribed by law'

The expression 'prescribed by law' appears in *EHR* 9(2), 10(2), and 11(2), the equivalent in the French text being, in each case, *'prévues par la loi'*. The identical French expression appears in *EHR* 8(2), *EHP P1* 1, and *EHR P4* 2; but in those cases it is rendered in the English text as 'in accordance with the law', 'provided for by law' and 'in accordance with law' respectively. In *Sunday Times* v. *United Kingdom*,[7] EUCT observed that when confronted with versions of a law-making treaty which are equally authentic but not exactly the same, the Court must interpret them in a way that reconciles them as far as possible and is most appropriate in order to realize the aim and achieve the objects of the treaty.

At least two requirements flow from the expression 'prescribed by law'. First, the law must be adequately accessible: the citizen must be able to have an indication of the legal rules applicable to a given case that is adequate in the circumstances.[8] Secondly, a norm cannot be regarded as a 'law' unless it is formulated with sufficient precision to enable the citizen to regulate his conduct: he must be able — if need be with appropriate advice — to foresee, to a degree that is reasonable in the circumstances, the consequences which a given action may entail.[9] In *Arrowsmith* v. *United Kingdom*,[10] EUCM noted that the

---

[3] (5493/72) Report: 30 September 1975.
[4] *Caprino* v. *United Kingdom* (6871/75) DR 12, 14.
[5] (5029/71) Judgment: 2 EHRR 214.
[6] (6538/74) Judgment: 2 EHRR 245.   [7] *Supra.*
[8] Rules about prisoners' correspondence established by unpublished administrative instructions to prison governors cannot therefore be regarded as 'law' for this purpose: *Silver et al.* v. *United Kingdom* (5947/72, etc.) Report: 11 October 1980 (referred to EUCT).
[9] *Sunday Times* v. *United Kingdom, supra.*
[10] (7050/75) Report: DR 19, 5.

requirement of certainty is satisfied when it is possible to determine from the relevant statutory provision what act or omission is subject to criminal liability, even if such determination derives from the courts' interpretation of the provision concerned. Any uncertainty in provisions of the law may create doubts as to whether a restriction is 'prescribed by law'.[11]

EUCM has also said that the phrase 'in accordance with the law' refers not only to the State's domestic law, but also to the Rule of Law, or Principle of Legality, which is common to democratic societies and forms part of the common heritage of the Member States of the CE.[12]

The word 'law' covers not only statute law, but also unwritten law.[13] It includes subordinate legislation[14] and a Royal Decree.[15] The requirement is fulfilled if the 'interference' results from Acts passed by Parliament.[16] The Supreme Court of the Netherlands has held that this expression does not relate only to what Dutch law calls *'lois au sens formel'* or 'laws in the strict sense', that is to say passed by the Crown and the States-General; it relates also to measures enacted by subordinate, local, or regional authorities.[17]

In *Klass* v. *Federal Republic of Germany*[18] (a case relating to the secret surveillance of telephone conversations), EUCT noted that in order for the 'interference' not to infringe *EHR* 8, it must, according to paragraph 2 of that Article, have been 'in accordance with the law'. That requirement was fulfilled in this case, but only because the 'interference' resulted from Acts passed by Parliament, including one Act which had been modified by the Federal Constitutional Court in the exercise of its jurisdiction, and because every individual measure of surveillance had to, and did, comply with the strict conditions and procedures laid down in that legislation.

HRC has expressed the view that the phrase 'in accordance with law' in *ICPR* 13 is a reference to domestic law, which must in turn be compatible with the relevant provisions of the Covenant. But HRC is not qualified to evaluate whether the competent authorities of a State Party have correctly interpreted and applied its domestic law, unless it is established that they acted in bad faith or committed an abuse of power.[19]

'Necessary in a democratic society'

In the context of *ICPR* 19, HRC has expressed the view that, where a state detains a person who claims that he was exercising his freedom of opinion and expression, and the State seeks to justify that detention on the ground that he was engaging in 'subversive activities', the State must explain the scope and meaning of that term before the Committee can judge whether such a restriction was 'necessary' in the sense of *ICPR* 19(3).[20]

In *Handyside* v. *United Kingdom*,[21] EUCM had occasion to consider in

[11] *Ibid.*

[12] *Silver et al.* v. *United Kingdom, supra.*

[13] *Sunday Times* v. *United Kingdom, supra* — in that case, English judge-made law relating to contempt of court.

[14] *X* v. *Switzerland* (7736/76) DR 9, 206.

[15] *De Wilde, Ooms and Versyp* v. *Belgium* (2832/66; 2835/66; 2899/66) Judgment: 1 EHRR 373.

[16] *Klass* v. *Federal Republic of Germany* (5029/71) Judgment: 2 EHRR 214.

[17] Decision of 25 June 1963, Hoge Raad, Netherlands (NJ 1964, 595). See also Decision of 24 January 1967, Hoge Raad, Netherlands (NJ 1967, 760).

[18] *Supra.* Cf. *Malone* v. *United Kingdom* (8691/79) Decision: 13 July 1981.

[19] *Maroufidou* v. *Sweden* (R. 13/58) HRC 36, 160.

[20] *Carballal* v. *Uruguay* (R. 8/33) HRC 36, 125.

[21] (5493/72) Report: 30 September 1975.

detail the scope of the expression 'necessary in a democratic society'. According to the Commission, the models of a 'democratic society' in the sense of *EHR* are the Member States of the CE. The questions which then fall to be considered are the needs or objectives of a democratic society in relation to the right or freedom concerned; without a notion of such needs, the limitations essential to support them cannot be evaluated. For example, freedom of expression is based on the need of a democratic society to promote the individual self-fulfilment of its members, the attainment of truth, participation in decision-making, and the striking of a balance between stability and change. The aim is to have a pluralistic, open, tolerant society. This necessarily involves a delicate balance between the wishes of the individual and the utilitarian 'greater good of the majority'. But democratic societies approach this problem from the standpoint of the importance of the individual, and the undesirability of restricting his or her freedom. However, in striking the balance, certain controls on the individual's freedom of expression may, in appropriate circumstances, be acceptable in order to respect the sensibilities of others. In this context, freedom of expression is commonly subject in a democratic society to laws importing restrictions considered necessary to prevent seditious, libellous, blasphemous, or obscene publications. Indeed, the legal codes of all the Member States of the CE contain legislation restricting in one way or another the right to freedom of expression, in the context of indecent, obscene, or pornographic objects and literature. This can be regarded as a clear indication of the need for such legislation in a democratic society.[22]

While the adjective 'necessary' is not synonymous with 'indispensable' (cf., in *EHR* 2(2) and 6(1), the words 'absolutely necessary' and 'strictly necessary' and, in *EHR* 15(1), the phrase 'to the extent strictly required by the exigencies of the situation'), neither has it the flexibility of such expressions as 'admissible', 'ordinary' (cf. *EHR* 4(3)), 'useful' (cf. the French text of *EHR P1* 1(1)), 'reasonable' (cf. *EHR* 5(3) and 6(1)), or 'desirable'. The notion 'necessary' implies the existence of a 'pressing social need' which may include the 'clear and present danger' test (as developed by the US Supreme Court), and must be assessed in the light of the circumstances of a given case;[23] it is for the national authorities to make the initial assessment of the reality of the pressing social need implied by the notion of 'necessity' in this context.[24]

The hallmarks of a 'democratic society' are pluralism, tolerance, and broad-mindedness. Although individual interests must on occasion be subordinated to those of a group, democracy does not simply mean that the views of a majority must always prevail: a balance must be achieved which ensures the fair and proper treatment of minorities and avoids any abuse of a dominant position.[25]

To assess whether the interference complained of was based on 'sufficient' reasons which rendered it 'necessary in a democratic society', account must be taken of any public interest aspect of the particular case. It is not enough that

---

[22] *Ibid.*, paras. 145-51. The matter has also been considered in *X* v. *United Kingdom* (7215/75) Report: DR 19, 66; *Klass* v. *Federal Republic of Germany* (5029/71) Judgment: 2 EHRR 214; *James, Young and Webster* v. *United Kingdom* (7601/76; 7806/77) Judgment: 13 August 1981; and *Dudgeon* v. *United Kingdom* (7525/76) Judgment: 22 October 1981.

[23] *Arrowsmith* v. *United Kingdom* (7050/75) Report: DR 19, 5.

[24] *Handyside* v. *United Kingdom, supra*; *Sunday Times* v. *United Kingdom* (6538/74) Judgment: 2 EHRR 245. See also *Golder* v. *United Kingdom* (4451/70) Judgment: 1 EHRR 524; *James, Young and Webster* v. *United Kingdom, supra*; and below, 'The doctrine of governmental "margin of appreciation".'

[25] *James, Young and Webster* v. *United Kingdom, supra.*

the interference involved belongs to that class of the exceptions listed in the appropriate Article of *EHR* which has been invoked; neither is it enough that the interference was imposed because its subject-matter fell within a particular category or was caught by a legal rule formulated in general or absolute terms: the Court has to be satisfied that the interference was 'necessary', having regard to the facts and circumstances prevailing in the specific case before it. For instance, in *Sunday Times* v. *United Kingdom*,[26] EUCT noted that the thalidomide tragedy was a matter of undisputed public concern; that fundamental issues concerning protection against and compensation for injuries resulting from scientific developments were raised; and that the families of numerous victims of the tragedy had a vital interest in knowing all the underlying facts and the various possible solutions. In those circumstances, the Court held that the interference complained of did not correspond to a social need (namely, maintaining the authority of the judiciary) sufficiently pressing to outweigh the public interest in freedom of expression; accordingly, the restraint was not necessary in a democratic society.[27]

The principle of proportionality

The principle of proportionality is inherent in the adjective 'necessary'. This means, among other things, that every 'formality', 'condition', 'restriction', or 'penalty' imposed must be proportionate to the legitimate aim pursued.[28] This principle is one of the factors to be taken into account when assessing whether a measure of interference is 'necessary'.[29] In *Sunday Times* v. *United Kingdom*,[30] EUCT formulated the question thus: does the interference complained of correspond to a 'pressing social need'; is it proportionate to the legitimate aim pursued; are the reasons given by the national authorities to justify it relevant and sufficient under the paragraph of restrictions?

Interpreting *EHR* 14 in the *Belgian Linguistic Case*,[31] EUCT held that a difference of treatment in the exercise of a right laid down in *EHR* must not only pursue a legitimate aim: *EHR* 14 is likewise violated when it is clearly established that there is no reasonable relationship of proportionality between the means employed and the aim sought to be realized.

HRC has also applied the principle of proportionality, in expressing the view that a measure as harsh as the deprivation of all political rights for a period of 15 years needs to be specifically justified in each individual case,[32] and that its general application to all persons who had stood as candidates for certain political groups in certain past elections therefore constituted a violation of *ICPR* 25.[33]

'National security'

In *Klass* v. *Federal Republic of Germany*,[34] EUCT held to be justified a law which permitted the secret surveillance of mail, post, and telecommunications,

---

[26] *Supra.*

[27] Cf. *James, Young and Webster* v. *United Kingdom, supra.*

[28] *Handyside* v. *United Kingdom, supra.* See also *Arrowsmith* v. *United Kingdom, supra; De Becker* v. *Belgium* (214/56) Report: 21 August 1961; Judgment: 1 EHRR 43.

[29] *Rassemblement Jurassien and Unité Jurassienne* v. *Switzerland* (8191/78) DR 17, 93.

[30] See also *James, Young and Webster* v. *United Kingdom, supra; Dudgeon* v. *United Kingdom, supra,* n. 22.

[31] (1474/62, etc.) Judgment: 1 EHRR 252. See also *Marckx* v. *Belgium* (6833/74) Report: 10 December 1977.

[32] *Pietraroia* v. *Uruguay* (R. 10/44) HRC 36, 153.   [33] See §25.0.4.

[34] (5029/71) Judgment: 2 EHRR 214. See also *A, B, C and D* v. *Federal Republic of Germany* (8290/78) DR 18, 176.

because that law defined precisely, and thereby limited, the purposes for which surveillance might be imposed — namely, to protect against 'imminent dangers threatening the free democratic constitutional order', 'the existence or security of the Federation or of a *Land*', 'the security of the [allied] armed forces' stationed on the territory of the Republic, or the security of 'the troops of one of the Three Powers stationed in the *Land* of Berlin'. Accordingly, the law was designed to safeguard national security and/or to prevent disorder or crime, within the meaning of *EHR* 8(2).

A law prohibiting activities aimed at the reintroduction of National Socialism may also be justified on the ground of national security.[35]

'Public safety'

EUCM has also accepted 'public safety' as a justification for the law prohibiting activities aimed at the reintroduction of National Socialism,[35] as well as for a law punishing the distribution of material to servicemen seeking to persuade them to disobey their orders.[36] The Supreme Court of India has said that 'public safety' may be taken to denote the safety or security of the State.[37]

'Public order'

EUCM has also accepted 'public order' as a justification for the law punishing the distribution of material to servicemen seeking to persuade them to disobey their orders,[36] as well as for the refusal to allow a prisoner to grow a beard which would have made him more difficult to identify, and the refusal to allow him a prayer chain.[38] The protection of public order may also justify limitations on the right to hold religious services on a public highway, at all events in a country containing religious divisions.[39]

The Supreme Court of India has said that the contravention of law always affects order, but before it can be said to affect *public* order it must affect the community or the public at large. One has to imagine three concentric circles, the largest representing 'law and order', the next representing 'public order', and the smallest representing 'security of the State'. An act may affect law and order but not public order, just as an act may affect public order but not the security of the State.[40] 'Public order' includes acts which disturb public tranquillity and are breaches of the peace, but not acts which only disturb the serenity of others.[41]

The Supreme Court of Jamaica has held that the interests of public order require that persons should serve on juries even if they have conscientious objections to taking part in judging others.[42]

'Prevention of disorder or crime'

The words 'disorder *or* crime' are alternative grounds of justification.[43]

The concept of 'order', as envisaged by this provision, refers not only to

---

[35] *X* v. *Austria* (1747/62) CD 13, 42.

[36] *X* v. *United Kingdom* (6084/73) DR 3, 62.

[37] *Brij Bhushan* v. *State of Delhi* [1950] SCR 605.

[38] *X* v. *Austria* (1753/63) CD 16, 20.

[39] Decision of 19 January 1962, Hoge Raad, Netherlands (NJ 1962, 417).

[40] *Lohia* v. *State of Bihar* [1966] 1 SCR 709.

[41] *Madhu Limaye* v. *Sub-Divisional Magistrate, Monghyr* [1971] 2 SCR 711.

[42] *Re Eric Darien* (1974) 22 WIR 323.

[43] *Engel et al.* v. *Netherlands* (5100-2/71; 5354/72; 5370/72) Report: 19 July 1974; Judgment: 1 EHRR 647.

public order or '*ordre public*' within the meaning of *EHR* 6(1) and 9(2) and *P4* 2(3): it also covers the order that must prevail within the confines of a specific social group. This is so, for example, when, as in the case of the armed forces, disorder in that group can have repercussions on order in society as a whole.[44]

In *Engel et al.* v. *Netherlands*,[45] EUCM considered the interpretation of the word 'disorder' in relation to a serviceman's writings which were directed to, and took effect in, only a segment of society at a particular place and time. The Commission observed that it would not be reasonable to hold that only the prevention of disorder in society as a whole could justify a measure interfering with his freedom of expression. For it is only in relation to the particular circumstances prevailing at the place and time of the application of the measures complained of that their justification can be examined on the ground of a need to prevent disorder. Therefore, although the writings in question, if examined in isolation, could perhaps not be regarded as being normally likely to cause disorder in the armed forces, they could reasonably be regarded as writings which were giving rise to disturbances if examined against the background of the particular situation prevailing in the armed forces at the time and place of their publication and distribution; accordingly, the interference was justified as having been necessary for the prevention of disorder in the armed forces.

EUCM has also accepted the prevention of disorder or crime as a ground justifying the recording of telephone conversations,[46] placing a juvenile under observation as part of a judicial investigation concerning him,[47] and, in the case of convicted prisoners, their surveillance and search by prison warders, their removal from association with other prisoners, the requirement to wear prison uniform, restrictions on family visits,[48] and restrictions on correspondence.[49]

'*Protection of health or morals*'

This term covers not only the protection of the general health or morals of the community as a whole, but also the protection of the health or morals of its individual members. Furthermore, the term necessarily includes the psychological as well as the physical well-being of individuals and, where a child is concerned, its mental stability and its freedom from serious psychic disturbance.[50] The term refers primarily to the protection of the moral ethos of society, and *EHR* (*EHR* 8 and 9 in particular) preserves to the individual an area of strictly private morality in which the State may not interfere. That is not to say that some interferences in 'private life' may not be 'necessary' for the purpose of protecting the morals of society, but only if they can be justified by a pressing social need in a democratic society — that is, one that is plural, tolerant, and broadminded. Because exception clauses must be narrowly interpreted, they cannot allow a majority an unqualified right to impose its standards of private sexual morality on the whole of society.[51]

[44] *Ibid.* See also *Arrowsmith* v. *United Kingdom* (7050/75) Report: DR 19, 5.
[45] *Supra.*
[46] *A, B, C and D* v. *Federal Republic of Germany* (8290/78) DR 18, 176.
[47] *X* v. *Switzerland* (8500/79) DR 18, 238.
[48] *McFeeley et al.* v. *United Kingdom* (8317/78) Report: 3 EHRR 161.
[49] *Silver et al.* v. *United Kingdom* (5947/72, etc.) Report: 11 October 1980 (referred to EUCT).
[50] *X* v. *Sweden* (911/60) CD 7, 7; *X* v. *United Kingdom* (5608/72) CD 44, 66; *X* v. *Federal Republic of Germany* (2699/65) CD 26, 33.
[51] *Dudgeon* v. *United Kingdom* (7525/76) Report: 13 March 1980.

In *Handyside* v. *United Kingdom*,[52] EUCM noted that it is impossible to impose uniform standards of morality on the Member States of the CE, but that the moral standards prevailing in the country in question must be considered in order to determine whether the action taken was necessary to protect those standards. In the same case, EUCT observed that it is not possible to find in the domestic law of the Member States a uniform European conception of morals. The view taken by their respective laws of the requirements of morals varies from time to time and from place to place, especially in our era which is characterized by a rapid and far-reaching evolution of opinions on the subject. By reason of their direct and continuous contact with the vital forces of their countries, State authorities are in principle in a better position than the international judge to give an opinion on the exact content of these requirements, as well as on the 'necessity' of a 'restriction' or 'penalty' intended to meet them.[53]

Nonetheless, EUCT has since relied on the toleration, under the laws of many of the CE's Member States, of private homosexual conduct between consenting male adults as a ground for holding that it was not 'necessary' to penalize it in Northern Ireland, notwithstanding the respondent government's assessment of the state of public opinion on the matter in the Province.[54]

EUCM has also accepted the protection of health as a justification for requiring all motor-cyclists to wear a crash helmet, including those whose religion requires them to wear a turban,[55] and for requiring farmers to belong to a health service as a condition of owning cattle, in order to prevent tuberculosis.[56]

'Protection of the rights and freedoms of others'

Neither EUCM nor EUCT has yet authoritatively defined this expression. However, the 'rights and freedoms' concerned do not appear to be limited to the other 'human' rights defined in *EHR*.[57] Among other cases,[58] and often together with other grounds, the concept has been applied to justify the following interferences with rights and freedoms protected by different Articles of *EHR*:

(1) A conviction for activities aimed at the reintroduction of National Socialism;[59]
(2) A prosecution for distributing material to servicemen seeking to persuade them to disobey their orders;[60]
(3) The prohibition of homosexual acts between male persons under 21;[61]

---

[52] *Supra.* Cf. *X* v. *United Kingdom* (7215/75) DR 19, 66.
[53] Judgment: 1 EHRR 737. See also *X, Y and Z* v. *Belgium* (6782–4/74) DR 9, 13; Decision of 30 January 1968, Hoge Raad, Netherlands (NJ 1968, 199).
[54] *Dudgeon* v. *United Kingdom*, Judgment: 22 October 1981.
[55] *X* v. *United Kingdom* (7992/77) DR 14, 234.
[56] *X* v. *Netherlands* (1068/61) YB 5, 278; cf. *Deklerck* v. *Belgium* (8307/78) DR 21, 116 for restrictions on the public sale of spirits.
[57] See A. M. Connelly, 'The Protection of the Rights of Others' 5 *Human Rights Review* 117.
[58] See also *X* v. *United Kingdom* (7215/75) Report: DR 19, 66; *X* v. *Switzerland* (8257/78) DR 13, 248; *X* v. *United Kingdon* (8065/77) DR 14, 246; *X* v. *United Kingdom* (5712/72) CD 46, 112; *De Wilde, Ooms and Versyp* v. *Belgium* (2832/66, etc.) Judgment: 1 EHRR 373; *X* v. *United Kingdom* (6886/75) DR 5, 100; *De Becker* v. *Belgium* (214/56) Report: 21 August 1961; Judgment: 1 EHRR 43.
[59] *X* v. *Austria* (1747/62) CD 13, 42.
[60] *X* v. *United Kingdom* (6084/73) DR 3, 62.
[61] *Dudgeon* v. *United Kingdom* (7525/76) Report: 13 March 1980.

(4) The eviction of a person from his home under a housing control law aimed at preventing over-population which would be harmful to the economy;[62]
(5) Failure to give a husband a right to be consulted on, or to seize the authorities of, the question of a proposed termination of pregnancy by his wife;[63]
(6) A compulsory medical test to determine paternity;[64]
(7) A conviction for withholding a wanted minor from the police;[65]
(8) The grant of the custody of a child to one parent in preference to another;[66] likewise, the grant of 'care and control' to a mother which prevented the father from bringing the child up in his home country;[67]
(9) Compulsory motor insurance designed to safeguard the victims of motor accidents;[68]
(10) The refusal to allow a prisoner a book which, though religious and philosophical in character, contained a chapter dedicated to the martial arts;[69]
(11) The refusal to forward to the President's Office a letter accusing a judge of bias, and both him, counsel, and witnesses of misconduct, in an allegedly 'rigged' trial;[70] but not the refusal to allow a prisoner to correspond with a solicitor with a view to suing a prison officer for libel.[71]

'Maintaining the authority and impartiality of the judiciary'

The expression 'authority and impartiality of the judiciary', which appears in *EHR* 10(2), has to be understood in the context of *EHR* as a whole. For this purpose, account must be taken of the central position occupied by *EHR* 6, which reflects the fundamental principle of the Rule of Law. The term 'judiciary' (*'pouvoir judiciaire'*) comprises the machinery of justice or the judicial branch of government, as well as the judges in their official capacity. The phrase 'authority of the judiciary' includes, in particular, the notion that the courts are, and are accepted by the public at large as being, the proper forum for the ascertainment of legal rights and obligations and the settlement of disputes relating thereto; further, that the public at large has respect for and confidence in the courts' capacity to fulfil that function. The majority of the categories of conduct covered by the law of contempt of court relate either to the position of the judges or to the functioning of the courts and of the machinery of justice: 'maintaining the authority and impartiality of the judiciary' is therefore one purpose of that law.[72]

In *Sunday Times* v. *United Kingdom*,[73] EUCT observed that the institution of contempt of court is peculiar to common-law countries, and has no equivalent in many other Member States of the CE. The reason for the insertion of the words 'maintaining the authority and impartiality of the judiciary' would

---

[62] *Wiggins* v. *United Kingdom* (7456/76) DR 13, 40.
[63] *X* v. *United Kingdom* (8416/78) DR 19, 244. See also Decision of 31 October 1980, Conseil d'Etat, France, 6 *Human Rights Review* 75.
[64] *X* v. *Austria* (8278/78) DR 18, 154.
[65] *X and Y* v. *Netherlands* (6753/74) DR 2, 118.
[66] *X* v. *Federal Republic of Germany* (2699/65) CD 26, 33.
[67] *X* v. *United Kingdom* (5608/72) CD 44, 66.
[68] *X* v. *Netherlands* (2988/66) CD 23, 137.
[69] *X* v. *United Kingdom* (6886/75) DR 5, 100.
[70] *X* v. *Ireland* (3717/68) CD 31, 96.
[71] *Golder* v. *United Kingdom* (4451/70) Judgment: 1 EHRR 524.
[72] *Sunday Times* v. *United Kingdom* (6538/74) Judgment: 2 EHRR 245.
[73] *Ibid.*

have been to ensure that the general aims of such a law should be considered legitimate aims under *EHR* 10(2), but not to make that particular law the standard by which to assess whether a given measure was 'necessary'.

'"Public" or "general" interest'

'Public' or 'general' interest (in *EHR P1* 1 and *P4* 2) is wider in scope than 'necessary in a democratic society'. Clearly the public or general interest encompasses measures which would be preferable or advisable, and not only essential, in a democratic society. Nonetheless, it is the duty of EUCM to review, in individual cases, the actions of Member States purporting to be in the public or general interest, in order to establish that they have acted reasonably and in good faith.[74]

'The economic well-being of the country'

EUCM has found justified on this ground a *prima facie* violation of *EHR* 8 in the form of the eviction of a person from what had, until his wife left him, been his home, under a housing control law having the legitimate aim of preventing over-population harmful to the economy.[75]

The doctrine of governmental 'margin of appreciation'

This doctrine was first applied by EUCM in *Greece* v. *United Kingdom*.[76] In that case it was alleged that the respondent government had failed to satisfy the conditions required by *EHR* 15 when it invoked that Article and derogated from its obligations under the Convention in respect of Cyprus. The respondent government maintained that at the time of the derogation there existed in Cyprus a public emergency threatening the life of the nation, due to repeated acts of violence aimed at the subversion of the lawful government of Cyprus. In that context, EUCM laid down the following principle:

The Commission always has the competence and the duty under Article 15 to examine and pronounce upon a government's determination of the existence of a public emergency threatening the life of the nation for the purpose of that Article; but some discretion and some margin of appreciation must be allowed to a government in determining whether there exists a public emergency which threatens the life of the nation and which must be dealt with by exceptional measures derogating from its normal obligations under the Convention.[77]

In *Lawless* v. *Ireland*,[78] the President of EUCM explained the meaning and rationale of this doctrine to EUCT in the following terms:

The concept behind this doctrine is that Article 15 has to be read in the context of the rather special subject matter with which it deals: the responsibilities of a government for maintaining law and order in times of war or public emergency threatening the life of the nation. The concept of the margin of appreciation is that a government's discharge of these responsibilities is essentially a delicate

---

[74] *Handyside* v. *United Kingdom* (5493/72) Report: 30 September 1975. See also *A, B, C and D* v. *United Kingdom* (3039/67) CD 23, 66; *Sporrong and Lönnroth* v. *Sweden* (7151-2/75) Report: 8 October 1980 (referred to EUCT); *X* v. *Austria* (8003/77) Report: 3 EHRR 285.

[75] *Wiggins* v. *United Kingdom* (7456/76) DR 13, 40.

[76] (176/56) YB 2, 182.

[77] Report: 19 December 1959; for a discussion of its interpretation of *EHR* 15, see *Lawless* v. *Ireland* (332/57) 1 EHRR 15.

[78] *Supra.*

problem of appreciating complex factors and of balancing conflicting considerations of the public interest; and that, once the Commission or the Court is satisfied that the government's appreciation is at least within the margin of the powers conferred by Article 15, then the interest which the public itself has in effective government and in the maintenance of order justifies and requires a decision in favour of the legality of the government's appreciation.[79]

In *Ireland* v. *United Kingdom*,[80] EUCT itself expressed the doctrine as follows:

It falls in the first place to each contracting State with its responsibility for 'the life of [its] nation', to determine whether that life is threatened by a 'public emergency' and, if so, how far it is necessary to go in attempting to overcome the emergency. By reason of their direct and continuous contact with the pressing needs of the moment, the national authorities are in principle in a better position than the international judge to decide both on the presence of such an emergency and on the nature and scope of derogation necessary to avert it. In this matter Article 15(1) leaves those authorities a wide margin of appreciation.

Nevertheless, the States do not enjoy an unlimited power in this respect. The Court, which, with the Commission, is responsible for ensuring the observance of the State's engagements (Article 19), is empowered to rule on whether the States have gone beyond the 'extent strictly required by the exigencies' of the crisis. The domestic margin of appreciation is thus accompanied by a European supervision.[81]

But EUCM has also applied the doctrine to other Articles, particularly those which incorporate clauses of exception and limitation. In *X* v. *Sweden*,[82] an application brought by a parent who had been denied custody of his child in divorce proceedings, the Commission observed that the exceptions and limitations in *EHR* 8(2) to the right to respect for family life 'left a considerable measure of discretion to the domestic courts in taking into account, when deciding on questions of access to the children, factors in the case which might appear to them to be critical for the protection of the health and morals of the child.'[83] In *X* v. *Netherlands*,[84] EUCM said that, in regard to the exceptions and limitations mentioned in *EHR* 9(2) to the right to freedom of thought, conscience, and religion, 'a considerable measure of discretion is left to national Parliaments in appreciating the vital interests of the community'. In *Iversen* v. *Norway*,[85] a dentist who had been required to perform obligatory public dental service invoked *EHR* 4. By a majority of six to four, EUCM rejected

[79] Publications of the Court, Series, B, *Lawless case*, 1960–1, 408.
[80] (5310/71) Judgment: 2 EHRR 25.
[81] *Ibid.* See also *Denmark, Norway, Sweden and Netherlands* v. *Greece* (3321–3/67; 3344/67) Report: YB 12 *bis*; and particularly the dissenting opinion of Mr Susterhenn in which he explained his understanding of the doctrine of margin of appreciation as follows: 'In the examination of the question whether or not there is a threat to the life of the nation, the right of decision lies with the responsible government within the limits of its *bona fide* discretion. In its review of this decision, the Commission is not entitled to put itself in the position of the responsible government and assume the functions of a sort of super-government. The Commission has rather to examine whether the respondent government in exercising its discretion has not manifestly behaved in an unreasonable or even arbitrary manner.' (At 87.)
[82] (911/60) CD 7, 7.
[83] See also *X* v. *Netherlands* (1449/62) CD 10, 1; *X* v. *Denmark* (1329/62) CD 9, 28.
[84] (1068/61) YB 5, 278.
[85] (1468/62) CD 12, 80.

the application as inadmissible. Four of the majority were of the view that the service required of the applicant was manifestly not forced or compulsory labour. The two others, however, (whose votes were decisive) were of the view that the service fell within one of the exceptions in *EHR* 4(3)(c) to the prohibition of forced labour, in that it was reasonably required as an emergency service. They observed that —

The Commission has frequently held that, although a certain margin of appreciation should be given to a government in determining the existence of a public emergency within the meaning of Article 15 in its own country, the Commission has the competence and the duty to examine and pronounce upon the consistency with the Convention of a government's determination of this question. In the analogous circumstances of the present case, the Commission cannot question the judgment of the Norwegian government and Parliament as to the existence of an emergency, as there is evidence before the Commission showing reasonable grounds for such judgment.[86]

In *A, B, C and D* v. *United Kingdom*,[87] EUCM applied the doctrine to the deprivation of property (in the form of a compulsory acquisition by the State of the applicants' debenture stock) in the context of the right to the peaceful enjoyment of possessions under *EHR P1* 1.

In *Engel et al.* v. *Netherlands*,[88] EUCT applied the doctrine to *EHR* 10(2) (which restricts and limits the right to freedom of expression) by holding that this too leaves a margin of appreciation to the contracting States. This margin is given both to the domestic legislator ('prescribed by law') and to the bodies, judicial amongst others, that are called upon to interpret and apply the laws in force. In *Handyside* v. *United Kingdom*[89] (which was also concerned with restrictions on freedom of expression) EUCT applied the doctrine as stated in *Ireland* v. *United Kingdom*[90] by observing that —

[*EHR* 10(2)] does not give the contracting States an unlimited power of appreciation. The Court, which, with the Commission, is responsible for ensuring the observance of those States' engagements (Article 19), is empowered to give the final ruling on whether a 'restriction' or 'penalty' is reconcilable with freedom of expression as protected by Article 10. The domestic margin of appreciation thus goes hand in hand with a European supervision. Such supervision concerns both the aim of the measure challenged and its 'necessity'; it covers not only the basic legislation but also the decision applying it, even one given by an independent court.[91]

EUCT has also applied the doctrine to the right to liberty and security of person under *EHR* 5. In both *Winterwerp* v. *Netherlands*[92] and *X* v. *United*

---

[86] *Ibid.*, at 108.
[87] (3039/67) CD 23, 66. See also *Sporrong and Lönnroth* v. *Sweden* (7151-2/75) Report: 8 October 1980 (referred to EUCT); *X* v. *Austria* (8003/77) Report: 8 October 1980 (referred to EUCT); *X* v. *Austria* (8003/77) Report: 3 EHRR 285.
[88] (5100-2/71; 5354/72; 5370/72) Judgment: 1 EHRR 647. See also *X* v. *Austria* (1747/62) CD 13, 42; *X* v. *Austria* (753/60) CD 4; *X* v. *Federal Republic of Germany* (1167/61) CD 12, 70.
[89] (5493/72) Judgment: 1 EHRR 737.
[90] *Supra.*
[91] Paragraph 49.
[92] (6301/73) Judgment: 2 EHRR 387.

Kingdom,[93] the Court prescribed the minimum conditions required for the 'lawful detention of a person of unsound mind' under *EHR* 5(1)(*e*), adding

Whilst the Court undoubtedly has the jurisdiction to verify the fulfilment of these conditions in a given case, the logic of the system of safeguard established by the Convention places limits on the scope of this control; since the national authorities are better placed to evaluate the evidence adduced before them, they are to be recognised as having a certain discretion in the matter and the Court's task is limited to reviewing under the Convention the decisions they have taken.

In *Sunday Times* v. *United Kingdom*,[94] EUCT again pointed out, in the context of the right to freedom of expression, that the Court's supervision is not limited to ascertaining whether a respondent State has exercised its discretion reasonably, carefully, and in good faith. Even a contracting State so acting remains subject to the Court's control as regards the compatibility of its conduct with the engagements it has undertaken under the Convention. The Court further observed that

The scope of the domestic power of appreciation is not identical as regards each of the aims listed in Article 10(2). The *Handyside* case concerned the 'protection of morals'. The view taken by the contracting States of the 'requirements of morals', observed the Court, 'varies from time to time and from place to place, especially in our era', and 'State authorities are in principle in a better position than the international judge to give an opinion on the exact content of these requirements.' Precisely the same cannot be said of the far more objective notion of the 'authority' of the judiciary. The domestic law and practice of the contracting States reveal a fairly substantial measure of common ground in this area. This is reflected in a number of provisions of the Convention, including Article 6, which have no equivalent as far as 'morals' are concerned. Accordingly, here a more extensive European supervision corresponds to a less discretionary power of appreciation.

In *Rassemblement Jurassien and Unité Jurassienne* v. *Switzerland*,[95] EUCM repeated that *EHR* allowed the contracting States a margin of appreciation in applying restrictions to a protected right: it was primarily up to their authorities to judge whether there really is the 'imperative social requirement' which is implied by the concept of necessity. In the context of the right of peaceful assembly under *EHR* 11, that margin is fairly broad once the authority is confronted with a foreseeable danger affecting public safety and order and must decide, often at short notice, what means to employ to prevent it.

HRC has expressed the view that, while it is competent to evaluate whether a provision of a State's domestic law is compatible with *ICPR*, it is not qualified to evaluate whether in a given case the competent authorities of that State have correctly interpreted and applied that law, unless it is established that they have acted in bad faith or abused their power.[96]

---

[93] (6998/75) Judgment: 5 November 1981.
[94] (6538/74) Judgment: 2 EHRR 245.
[95] (8191/78) DR 17, 93.
[96] *Maroufidou* v. *Sweden* (R. 13/58) HRC 36, 160. Nor is it HRC's function to determine whether a domestic court has erred in fact, or to review its application of domestic law, but only to determine whether the relevant provisions of *ICPR* have been observed: *Pinkney* v. *Canada* (R. 7/27), published 14 December 1981.

The doctrine of 'inherent' limitations

In a series of decisions some years ago,[97] EUCM appeared to take the view that certain restrictions (particularly on correspondence) imposed on convicted prisoners and other detainees could be justified, not because they fell within a specific exception or limitation listed in the appropriate Article of *EHR*, but because such a restriction was an 'inherent' feature of the punishment of imprisonment.[98] EUCT has never applied such a doctrine. In EUCM's more recent decisions and reports, the justification for such restrictions has been founded on one or more of the specific exceptions or limitations set out in the paragraph of exceptions to the relevant Article, especially the 'prevention of disorder or crime'.[99] At the same time, EUCM now appears to take the view that there may be an 'implied limitation' on the right to life in favour of the life or health of another.[100]

Compatibility of purpose

EHR 18, like *EHR* 14, does not have an autonomous role. It can only be applied in conjunction with other Articles of the Convention. There may however be a violation of *EHR* 18 in conjunction with another Article, even though there is no violation of that Article taken alone. Furthermore, a violation of *EHR* 18 can only arise when the right or freedom concerned is subject to 'restrictions permitted under this Convention'. For instance, *EHR* 5(1) guarantees 'the right to liberty and security of person'. The right to 'security of person' is guaranteed in absolute terms: there can therefore be no violation of *EHR* 18 in conjunction with that right alone. But the right to 'liberty' may be restricted in accordance with sub-paragraphs (*a*) to (*f*) of *EHR* 5(1); there may, therefore, be a violation of *EHR* 18 in conjunction with that right.[101]

---

[97] See *X* v. *Federal Republic of Germany* (1860/63) CD 18, 47; *De Courcy* v. *United Kingdom* (2749/66) CD 24, 93; *X* v. *Federal Republic of Germany* (4104/69) CD 34, 38; *X* v. *Federal Republic of Germany* (2795/66) CD 30, 23; *X* v. *Federal Republic of Germany* (3819/68) CD 32, 23; *X* v. *Luxembourg* (4144/69) CD 33, 27; *Huber* v. *Austria* (4517/70) CD 38, 90.

[98] In support of such a doctrine, see Fawcett, *The Application of the European Convention on Human Rights*, 69; for a critique of it, see Jacobs, *The European Convention on Human Rights*, 198–201.

[99] *McFeeley et al.* v. *United Kingdom* (8317/78) Report: 3 EHRR 161; *Silver et al.* v. *United Kingdom* (5947/72, etc.) Report: 11 October 1980 (referred to EUCT).

[100] *X* v. *United Kingdom* (8416/78) DR 19, 244.

[101] *Kamma* v. *Netherlands* (4771/71) Report: DR 1, 4. See also *Engel et al.* v. *Netherlands* (5100-2/71; 5354/72; 5370/72) Report: 19 July 1974. Jacobs states that *EHR* 18 is directed against *détournement de pouvoir*, or abuse of (otherwise legitimate) power by national authorities: see *The European Convention on Human Rights*, 202–4.

§9. ABUSE

UDHR

29 (3) These rights and freedoms may in no case be exercised contrary to the purposes and principles of the United Nations.

30. Nothing in this Declaration may be interpreted as implying for any State, group or person any right to engage in any activity or to perform any act aimed at the destruction of any of the rights and freedoms set forth herein.

ICPR

5 (1) Nothing in the present Covenant may be interpreted as implying for any State, group or person any right to engage in any activity or to perform any act aimed at the destruction of any of the rights or freedoms recognized herein, or at their limitation to a greater extent than is provided for in the present Covenant.

ICES

5 (1) Nothing in the present Covenant may be interpreted as implying for any State, group or person any right to engage in any activity or to perform any act aimed at the destruction of any of the rights or freedoms recognized herein, or at their limitation to a greater extent than is provided for in the present Covenant.

EHR

17. Nothing in this Convention may be interpreted as implying for any State, group or person any right to engage in any activity or perform any act aimed at the destruction of any of the rights and freedoms set forth herein or at their limitation to a greater extent than is provided for in the Convention.

AMR

29. No provision of this Convention shall be interpreted as:
(*a*) permitting any State Party, group, or person to suppress the enjoyment or exercise of the rights and freedoms recognized in

this Convention or to restrict them to a greater extent than is provided for herein;

§9.0.2 CROSS-REFERENCES

Signatures, ratifications, accessions, reservations, and interpretations: See Table A for the State Parties bound by these instruments on 1 January 1982, and any reservations and interpretations notified by them.

Derogation: For the provisions as to derogation in exceptional circumstances under *ICPR*, *EHR*, and *AMR*, see §11.

Non-discrimination: See §7 for the relevant provisions in these instruments.

Savings: See §10 for the relevant provisions in these instruments.

Restrictions and limitations: See §8 for the general provisions in these instruments, and the principles governing all restriction and limitation clauses.

International supervision, interpretation, application, and enforcement: By HRC under *ICPR* (see §27); by EUCM and EUCT under *EHR* (see §28); by IACM and IACT under *AMR* (see §29); supervision only by ECOSOC under *ICES* (see §31). See also §6.6 for the obligation to provide domestic remedies under *UDHR*, *ICPR*, *EHR*, and *AMR*.

§9.0.3 COMMENT

The purpose of all these provisions is to prevent the abuse, either by States or by their inhabitants, of any one of the human rights or freedoms declared in the relevant instrument for the purpose of prejudicing one or more of the others.

The language used for that purpose in *UDHR* 30 is adopted by *ICPR* 5(1), *ICES* 5(1), and *EHR* 17, with the addition of expressions appropriate to prevent illegitimate 'limitation' of other rights in addition to their 'destruction'. *AMR* 29(a) directs its language instead against attempts to 'suppress the enjoyment or exercise', or to 'restrict', the other rights. *UDHR* 29(3) alone prohibits abuse 'contrary to the purposes and principles of the UN'.

§9.0.4 JURISPRUDENCE

EHR 17 is designed to safeguard the rights listed in the Convention by protecting the free operation of democratic institutions. In *German Communist Party v. Federal Republic of Germany*,[1] EUCM quoted from the Convention's *travaux préparatoires* the statement that the object of this provision was to prevent adherents to totalitarian doctrines from exploiting the rights guaranteed by the Convention for the purpose of destroying human rights. On that ground, the Commission rejected the applicant's complaint that, contrary to *EHR* 9, 10, and 11, the Federal German Constitutional Court had dissolved the Party and ordered the confiscation of its property. EUCM observed that the avowed aim of the applicant, according to its own declarations, was to establish a Communist society by means of a proletarian revolution and the 'dictatorship' of the pro-

---

[1] (250/57) YB 1, 222. See also *Retimag S.A.* v. *Federal Republic of Germany* (712/60) CD 8, 29.

letariat. Consequently, even if it sought power by solely constitutional methods, recourse to a dictatorship was inevitable; this was incompatible with *EHR* because it would entail the suppression of a number of the rights and freedoms which *EHR* guaranteed. EUCM has applied similar reasoning to advocates of racial discrimination.[2]

In *Lawless* v. *Ireland*,[3] EUCM explained that, to achieve the purpose of *EHR* 17, there was no need to deprive a person of all the rights and freedoms guaranteed in the Convention. *EHR* 17 covered essentially those rights (e.g. those protected by *EHR* 9, 10, and 11) which, if invoked, would enable him to engage in the activities referred to in that provision.[4] In affirming this view, EUCT observed that the purpose of *EHR* 17 was to make it impossible for groups or individuals to derive from the Convention a right to engage in or perform any act aimed at destroying any of the rights and freedoms set forth in the Convention. No one may therefore take advantage of the provisions of the Convention to perform acts aimed at destroying the aforesaid rights and freedoms. However, *EHR* 17, which is negative in scope, cannot be construed *a contrario* as depriving a physical person of the fundamental individual rights guaranteed in *EHR* 5 and 6.[5]

In *X* v. *United Kingdom*,[6] EUCM had regard to *EHR* 17 in holding that a State cannot substitute disciplinary proceedings for criminal ones with the object of depriving an offender of the protection of *EHR* 6. However, where disciplinary proceedings are taken to deal with an offence which is both disciplinary and criminal, there may be factors which should be taken into account as indicating that this was not the State's object. Such factors would include that —

(1) the proceedings are already prescribed by law;
(2) any penalty imposed as a result of the proceedings is directly connected with, and contributes to, the proper functioning of the administration concerned, and is not disproportionate in nature or severity;
(3) the proceedings are conducted fairly, the minimum standards prescribed by *EHR* 6(3) being observed;
(4) an appeal from the finding lies to an independent tribunal.

HRC has relied on *ICPR* 5(1) to reject an argument that a State Party was not accountable for violations of human rights perpetrated by its agents outside its own territory.[7]

---

[2] *Glimmerveen and Hagenbeeck* v. *Netherlands* (8348/89; 8406/78) DR 18, 187.
[3] (322/57) Report: 19 December 1959.
[4] See also *Glimmerveen and Hagenbeeck* v. *Netherlands, supra.*
[5] *Lawless* v. *Ireland* (322/57) Judgment: 1 EHRR 15.
[6] (5916/72) CD 46, 165. See also *Mrs X* v. *Netherlands* (5763/72) CD 45, 76.
[7] *Burgos* v. *Uruguay* (R. 12/52) HRC 36, 176; *de Casariego* v. *Uruguay* (R. 13/56) HRC 36, 185.

§10. SAVINGS

ICPR

5 (2) There shall be no restriction upon or derogation from any of the fundamental human rights recognized or existing in any State Party to the present Covenant pursuant to law, conventions, regulations or custom on the pretext that the present Covenant does not recognize such rights or that it recognizes them to a lesser extent.

46. Nothing in the present Covenant shall be interpreted as impairing the provisions of the Charter of the United Nations and of the constitutions of the specialized agencies which define the respective responsibilities of the various organs of the United Nations and of the specialized agencies in regard to the matters dealt with in the present Covenant.

ICES

5 (2) No restriction upon or derogation from any of the fundamental human rights recognized or existing in any country in virtue of law, conventions, regulations or custom shall be admitted on the pretext that the present Covenant does not recognize such rights or that it recognizes them to a lesser extent.

24. Nothing in the present Covenant shall be interpreted as impairing the provisions of the Charter of the United Nations and of the constitutions of the specialized agencies which define the respective responsibilities of the various organs of the United Nations and of the specialized agencies in regard to the matters dealt with in the present Covenant.

EHR

60. Nothing in this Convention shall be construed as limiting or derogating from any of the human rights and fundamental freedoms which may be ensured under the laws of any High Contracting Party or under any other agreement to which it is a Party.

61. Nothing in this Convention shall prejudice the powers conferred on the Committee of Ministers by the Statute of the Council of Europe.

ESC

32. The provisions of this Charter shall not prejudice the provisions of domestic law or of any bilateral or multilateral treaties, conventions or agreements which are already in force, or may come into force, under which more favourable treatment would be accorded to the persons protected.

ESC App.

2. Each Contracting Party will grant to refugees as defined in the Convention relating to the Status of Refugees, signed at Geneva on 28th July, 1951, and lawfully staying in its territory, treatment as favourable as possible, and in any case not less favourable than under the obligations accepted by the Contracting Party under the said Convention and under any other existing international instruments applicable to those refugees.

AMR

29. No provision of this Convention shall be interpreted as:
(*b*) restricting the enjoyment or exercise of any right or freedom recognized by virtue of the laws of any State Party or by virtue of another convention to which one of the said states is a party;
(*c*) precluding other rights or guarantees that are inherent in the human personality or derived from representative democracy as a form of government; or
(*d*) excluding or limiting the effect that the American Declaration of the Rights and Duties of Man and other international acts of the same nature may have.

31. Other rights and freedoms recognized in accordance with the procedures established in Articles 76 and 77 may be included in the system of protection of this Convention.

§ 10.0.2 CROSS-REFERENCES

Signatures, ratifications, accessions, reservations, and interpretations: See Table A for the State Parties bound by these instruments on 1 January 1982, and any reservations and interpretations notified by them.

Derogation: For the provisions as to derogation in exceptional circumstances under *ICPR, EHR, ESC*, and *AMR*, see § 11.

Non-discrimination: See § 7 for the relevant provisions in these instruments.

Abuse: See § 9 for the relevant provisions in these instruments.

Restrictions and limitations: See § 8 for the general provisions in these instruments.

International supervision, interpretation, application, and enforcement: By HRC under *ICPR* (see §27); by EUCM and EUCT under *EHR* (see §28); by IACM and IACT under *AMR* (see §29); supervision only by ECOSOC under *ICES* (see §31); by EUCE under *ESC* (see §32). See also §6.6 for the obligation to provide domestic remedies under *ICPR, EHR,* and *AMR.*

See also: §14.5.5 for a summary of the provisions of *CR.*

§10.0.3 COMMENT

All these provisions are designed to preserve past, present, and future measures or arrangements other than those entered into pursuant to the instrument concerned, where those measures or arrangements do not conflict because they are not *in pari materia,* or because they protect human rights better than the instrument itself requires.

§10.0.4 JURISPRUDENCE

None of the competent independent international institutions has so far expressed any views on the interpretation or application of any of these provisions.

§11. DEROGATION

ICPR

4 (1) In time of public emergency which threatens the life of the nation and the existence of which is officially proclaimed, the State Parties to the present Covenant may take measures derogating from their obligations under the present Covenant to the extent strictly required by the exigencies of the situation, provided that such measures are not inconsistent with their other obligations under international law and do not involve discrimination solely on the ground of race, colour, sex, language, religion or social origin.

(2) No derogation from Articles 6, 7, 8 (paragraphs 1 and 2), 11, 15, 16 and 18 may be made under this provision.

(3) Any State Party to the present Covenant availing itself of the right of derogation shall immediately inform the other States Parties to the present Covenant, through the intermediary of the Secretary-General of the United Nations, of the provisions from which it has derogated and of the reasons by which it was actuated. A further communication shall be made, through the same intermediary, on the date on which it terminates such derogation.

EHR

15 (1) In time of war or other public emergency threatening the life of the nation any High Contracting Party may take measures derogating from its obligations under this Convention to the extent strictly required by the exigencies of the situation, provided that such measures are not inconsistent with its other obligations under international law.

(2) No derogation from Article 2, except in respect of deaths resulting from lawful acts of war, or from Articles 3, 4 (paragraph 1) and 7 shall be made under this provision.

(3) Any High Contracting Party availing itself of this right of derogation shall keep the Secretary-General of the Council of Europe fully informed of the measures which it has taken and the reasons therefor. It shall also inform the Secretary-General of the Council of Europe when such measures have ceased to operate and the provisions of the Convention are again being fully executed.

ESC

30 (1) In time of war or other public emergency threatening the life of the nation any Contracting Party may take measures derogating from its obligations under this Charter to the extent strictly required by the exigencies of the situation, provided that such measures are not inconsistent with its other obligations under international law.

(2) Any Contracting Party which has availed itself of this right of derogation shall, within a reasonable lapse of time, keep the Secretary-General of the Council of Europe fully informed of the measures taken and of the reasons therefor. It shall likewise inform the Secretary-General when such measures have ceased to operate and the provisions of the Charter which it has accepted are again being fully executed.

(3) The Secretary-General shall in turn inform other Contracting Parties and the Director-General of the International Labour Office of all communications received in accordance with paragraph 2 of this Article.

(*App.* The term 'in time of war or other public emergency' shall be so understood as to cover also the *threat* of war.)

AMR

27 (1) In time of war, public danger, or other emergency that threatens the independence or security of a State Party, it may take measures derogating from its obligations under the present Convention to the extent and for the period of time strictly required by the exigencies of the situation, provided that such measures are not inconsistent with its other obligations under international law and do not involve discrimination on the ground of race, color, sex, language, religion, or social origin.

(2) The foregoing provision does not authorize any suspension of the following articles: Article 3 (Right to Juridical Personality), Article 4 (Right to Life), Article 5 (Right to Humane Treatment), Article 6 (Freedom from Slavery), Article 9 (Freedon from Ex Post Facto Laws), Article 12 (Freedom of Conscience and Religion), Article 17 (Rights of the Family), Article 18 (Right to a Name), Article 19 (Rights of the Child), Article 20 (Right to Nationality), and Article 23 (Right to Participate in Government), or of the judicial guarantees essential for the protection of such rights.

(3) Any State Party availing itself of the right of suspension shall immediately inform the other States Parties, through the Secretary General of the Organization of American States, of the provisions the application of which it has suspended, the reasons that gave rise

to the suspension, and the date set for the termination of such suspension.

§11.0.2 CROSS-REFERENCES

Signatures, ratifications, accessions, reservations, and interpretations: See Table A for the State Parties bound by these instruments on 1 January 1982, and any reservations and interpretations notified by them.

Non-discrimination: Note the specific provisions in *ICPR* 4(1) and *AMR* 27(1). See §7 for the other provisions in these instruments.

Abuse: See §9 for the relevant provisions in these instruments.

Savings: See §10 for the relevant provisions in these instruments.

Restrictions and limitations: See §8 for the general provisions in these instruments, and the principles governing all restriction and limitation clauses.

International supervision, interpretation, application, and enforcement: By HRC under *ICPR* (see §27); by EUCM and EUCT under *EHR* (see §28); by IACM and IACT under *AMR* (see §29); supervision only by EUCE under *ESC* (see §32). See also §6.6 for the obligation to provide domestic remedies under *ICPR*, *EHR*, and *AMR*.

Subsidiary instruments: See §11.0.5 for the effect of international humanitarian law.

§11.0.3 COMMENT

UDHR and *ADRD* say nothing about war or public emergency, and neither *ICES* nor [*AFR*] contains any provisions for derogation.

The language of the four treaties considered here differs in several respects.

Occasions for derogation

(1) Only *ICPR* does not mention 'war';
(2) The two European treaties and *ICPR* 4(1) all use the expression 'public emergency which threatens the life of the nation'; *AMR* 27(1) instead speaks of 'public danger, or other emergency that threatens the independence or security of a State Party';
(3) *ICPR* 4(1) alone requires the existence of the public emergency to be 'officially proclaimed'.

Extent of derogation

(1) All the four treaties limit the extent of derogation measures to those 'strictly required by the exigencies of the situation'; *AMR* 27(1) alone also limits, by the same test, the period of time during which those measures may remain in force;
(2) Under all the four treaties, the derogation measures must not entail breaches of the State Parties' other obligations under international law;
(3) *ICPR* and *AMR* (but not the European treaties) prohibit derogation measures which discriminate on one or more of a restricted number of six grounds —

race, colour, sex, language, religion, or social origin — out of the *UDHR* 'standard catalogue' of twelve (see §7), so allowing measures which, for example, discriminate on grounds of political opinion or property;

(4) There is nothing in *ESC* 30 to prevent any derogation from extending to any of the rights declared in that Charter; for the other treaties, the rights and freedoms from which no derogation may take place in any circumstances are shown in Table 5.

TABLE 5

See §		ICPR 4(2)	EHR 15(2)	AMR 27(2)
14.1	Life	○	○[1]	○
14.2	Imprisonment for debt	○		
14.3	Torture and other ill-treatment	○	○	○
18.4	Slavery and servitude[2]	○	○	○
22.5	Retroactive penal laws	○	○	○
22.2	Recognition before the law	○		○
23.3	Conscience and religion	○		○
17.1	Marriage and family			○
17.2	Children			○
23.1	Name			○
22.1	Nationality			○
25	Participation in government			○

Notes:

[1] Except for deaths resulting from lawful acts of war.

[2] But not forced or compulsory labour — in the case of *AMR*, by the operation of Art. 6(3)(*c*), 'in time of danger or calamity that threatens the existence or the well-being of the community'.

Notification of derogation

All four treaties require derogations to be notified to their respective depositaries. What must be notified, in the case of *ICPR* 4(3) and *AMR* 27(3), are the provisions in the treaty from which the notifying State has derogated (or, in the case of *AMR*, 'the application of which it has suspended'); in the case of the two European treaties, the measures which the State Party has taken. Under *ICPR* and *AMR*, this notification must be given 'immediately'; under *ESC* 30(2) 'within a reasonable lapse of time'. *EHR* 15(3) says nothing expressly about the timing. All four treaties require the notification to include the reasons for the derogation. *AMR* 27(3) requires the original notification to include 'the date set for the termination' of the derogation; the other three treaties call for a further notification when the derogation has come to an end.

None of the treaties makes it clear whether failure to notify invalidates the derogation, or is no more than a breach of a formal obligation.

§11.0.4 JURISPRUDENCE

'Public emergency threatening the life of the nation'

HRC has commented that measures taken under *ICPR* 4 are of an exceptional and temporary nature, and may only last as long as the life of the nation is threatened. In times of emergency, the protection of human rights becomes all the more important — particularly those rights from which no derogations can be made.[1]

In *Lawless* v. *Ireland*,[2] EUCT observed that the natural and customary meaning of the words 'public emergency threatening the life of the nation' is sufficiently clear; they refer to an exceptional situation of crisis or emergency which affects the whole population and constitutes a threat to the organized life of the community of which the State is composed. In *Denmark, Norway, Sweden and Netherlands* v. *Greece*,[3] EUCM distinguished four separate elements in this definition, namely:

(1) The public emergency must be actual and imminent.
(2) Its effects must involve the whole nation.
(3) The continuance of the organized life of the community must be threatened.
(4) The crisis or danger must be exceptional, in that the normal measures or restrictions permitted by *EHR* for the maintainance of public safety, health, and order are plainly inadequate.

It falls in the first place to each government, with its responsibility for 'the life of the nation', to determine whether that life is threatened by a 'public emergency'.[4] However, as EUCM pointed out in *Greece* v. *United Kingdom*,[5] although some discretion and some 'margin of appreciation' must be allowed to a government in determining whether there exists a public emergency threatening the life of the nation which must be dealt with by exceptional measures derogating from its normal obligations under *EHR*, the Commission always has the competence and the duty under *EHR* 15 to examine and pronounce upon a government's determination of the existence of such an emergency.

In *Lawless* v. *Ireland*,[6] EUCT adopted the doctrine of the margin of appreciation, but confirmed that it is for the Court to determine whether the conditions laid down in *EHR* 15 for the exercise of the exceptional right of derogation have been fulfilled; as the Court later put it in *Ireland* v. *United Kingdom*,[7] 'the domestic margin of appreciation is [thus] accompanied by a European supervision'.

Applying these principles in *Lawless* v. *Ireland*,[8] EUCT held that the existence on 5 July 1957 of a 'public emergency threatening the life of the nation' had been reasonably deduced by the respondent government from a combination of several factors: namely, the existence in its territory of a secret army (the IRA) engaged in unconstitutional activities and using violence to attain its purposes; the fact that this army was also operating outside its territory, thus seriously jeopardizing the relations of the Republic of Ireland with its neighbour; and the steady and alarming increase in terrorist activities from the autumn of 1956 and

---

[1] GC 5/13, HRC 36, 110.
[2] (322/57) Judgment: 1 EHRR 15.
[3] (3321–3/67; 3344/67) Report: 5 November 1969.
[4] *Ireland* v. *United Kingdom* (5310/71) 2 EHRR 25.
[5] (176/56) Report unpublished, but its interpretation of *EHR* 15 is discussed in *Lawless* v. *Ireland, supra.*
[6] *Supra.*
[7] *Supra.*
[8] *Supra.* See also *X* v. *Ireland* (493/59) CD 7, 85, where EUCM found that the respondent government must be considered to have had sufficient grounds for considering that the public emergency still subsisted in February 1958. In *Ireland* v. *United Kingdom, supra,* the applicant government did not contest the existence of a public emergency at all material times.

throughout the first half of 1957. By contrast, in *Denmark, Norway, Sweden and Netherlands* v. *Greece*[9] EUCM expressed the opinion that there was not in Greece on 21 April 1967 a public emergency threatening the life of the nation, despite three factors which had been adduced by the 'Government of the Colonels' which had seized power by military force and overthrown the legitimate government: namely, the threat of a Communist take-over of the government by force; the state of public order; and the constitutional crisis immediately preceding the general election due to be held in May 1967.

'Strictly required by the exigencies of the situation'

In *Lawless* v. *Ireland*,[10] EUCT held that a law which provided for detention without trial, subject to certain safeguards announced by the respondent government,[11] appeared to be a measure strictly required by the exigencies of the situation within the meaning of *EHR* 15. In so doing, it had regard to the fact that the application of the ordinary law had proved unable to check the growing danger which threatened the State; that the ordinary criminal courts, and even the special criminal courts and the military courts, could not succeed in restoring peace and order; and that the assembling of the necessary evidence to convict persons involved in activities of the IRA and its splinter groups was meeting with great difficulties caused by the military, secret, and terrorist character of those groups, and the fear they created among the population.

In *Ireland* v. *United Kingdom*,[12] where the respondent government sought justification for certain measures introduced in derogation of *EHR* 5 by referring to the security situation in Northern Ireland at the relevant times, EUCM observed that justification under *EHR* 15 does not follow automatically from a high level of violence. There must be a link between the facts of the emergency on the one hand, and the measures chosen to deal with it on the other. Moreover, the obligations under *EHR* do not entirely disappear; they can only be suspended or modified 'to the extent strictly required'. Noting that EUCT had, in *Lawless* v. *Ireland*,[13] stressed the importance of certain safeguards applicable under the legislation contested in that case, the Commission observed that it does not follow that exactly these or similar safeguards (e.g. parliamentary control) are necessarily required in every other public emergency. The State facing the emergency must choose its means and prescribe its safeguards against abuse, subject to the terms of *EHR* 15 and the control machinery under the Convention. In this case, both the Commission and the Court held that, in imposing extra-judicial deprivation of liberty, the respondent Government had not exceeded the 'extent strictly required' referred to in *EHR* 15.[14]

---

[9] *Supra.* On the first point, it did not find that the evidence adduced showed that a displacement of the lawful government by force of arms by the Communists and their allies was imminent on 21 April 1967. On the second point, the picture of strikes and work stoppages in Greece at that time did not differ markedly from that in many other European countries over a similar period. On the third point, it did not agree that there was an imminent threat of such political instability and disorder that the organized life of the community could not be carried on.

[10] *Supra.*

[11] That it would release any person who would undertake to observe the law and refrain from unlawful activities, each person arrested being informed immediately after his arrest that he would be released following such an undertaking.

[12] *Supra.*

[13] *Supra.*

[14] (5310/71) Report: 25 January 1976; Judgment: 1 EHRR 25. EUCT observed that while the incorporation, from the start, of more satisfactory judicial or at least administrative

It is, in the first place, for the government concerned to determine how far it is necessary to go in attempting to overcome the emergency. In this matter, *EHR* 15 leaves national authorities a wide margin of appreciation. Nevertheless, States do not enjoy an unlimited power in this respect. EUCT which, with EUCM, is responsible for ensuring the observance of the States' engagements (*EHR* 19) is empowered to rule on whether States have gone beyond the 'extent strictly required by the exigencies' of the crisis. The domestic margin of appreciation is thus accompanied by a European supervision. To decide this question, EUCT must enquire into the necessity for, on the one hand, deprivation of liberty contrary to *EHR* 5 (if that be the derogation) and, on the other hand, the failure of guarantees to attain the level established by paragraphs 2 to 4 of that Article.[15] However, in deciding the question, EUCT has stressed that it is not the Court's function to substitute for the government's assessment any other assessment of what might be the most prudent or most expedient policy to combat terrorism. The Court must do no more than review the lawfulness, under *EHR*, of the measures adopted by that government. For this purpose, the Court must arrive at its decision in the light, not of a purely retrospective examination of the efficacy of those measures, but of the conditions and circumstances reigning when they were originally taken and subsequently applied.

In the view of IACM, the declaration of a state of emergency or a state of siege cannot serve as a pretext for the indefinite detention of individuals without any charge, or for delaying their trials even beyond the longest sentences they could receive.[16]

'Shall keep the Secretary-General . . . fully informed of the measures which it has taken and of the reasons therefor'

In *Lawless* v. *Ireland*,[17] EUCT held that a letter sent by the Irish Government to the Secretary-General of the CE on 20 July 1957 informing him that Part II of the Offences against the State (Amendment) Act 1940 had been brought into force on 8 July 1957 (to which letter copies of the Irish Government's Proclamation on the subject and of the Act itself were attached) was a sufficient notification for the purposes of *EHR* 15(3), since it said that this was 'considered necessary to prevent the commission of offences against public peace and order and to prevent the maintaining of military or armed forces other than those authorised by the Constitution'. But in *Denmark, Norway, Sweden and Netherlands* v. *Greece*,[18] EUCM considered that the respondent government's notice of derogation did not comply adequately with the requirements of *EHR*

---

guarantees would certainly have been desirable, it would be unrealistic to isolate the first from the later phases. 'When a State is struggling against a public emergency threatening the life of the nation, it would be rendered defenceless if it were required to accomplish everything at once, to furnish from the outset each of the safeguards reconcilable with the priority requirements for the proper functioning of the authorities and for restoring peace within the Community. The interpretation of [*EHR* 15] must leave a place for progressive adaptations.'

[15] *Ireland* v. *United Kingdom*, Judgment, *supra*. The Court is not bound under *EHR*, or under the general principles applicable to international tribunals, by strict rules of evidence. In order to satisfy itself, the Court is entitled to rely on evidence of every kind, including (insofar as it deems them relevant) documents or statements emanating from governments, be they respondent or applicant, or from their institutions or officials: *ibid.*

[16] AR 1976, 16.

[17] *Supra*. See also *Ireland* v. *United Kingdom* (5310/71) Report: 25 January 1976.

[18] (3321–3/67; 3344/67) Report: 5 November 1969. The question was, however, secondary since EUCM had concluded that, in its view, there did not exist a public emergency threatening the life of the nation.

15(3), since the reasons for the measures of derogation had not been communicated until more than four months after they were first taken. EUCT has stressed that communication without delay is an element in the sufficiency of information, although this is not expressly stated in *EHR* 15(3).[19]

In *Cyprus* v. *Turkey*,[20] EUCM observed that *EHR* 15(3) requires some formal and public act of derogation, such as a declaration of martial law or state of emergency, and that, where (apart from not informing the Secretary-General) the government concerned proclaimed no such act although it was not in the circumstances prevented from doing so, *EHR* 15 cannot be invoked. But EUCT has rejected an argument that a derogation duly notified to the Secretary-General could not be enforced against persons within the jurisdiction of the State concerned in respect of a period before that derogation was first made public in that State. *EHR* 15(3) requires only that the Secretary-General be informed of the measures of derogation taken; it does not oblige the State concerned to promulgate the notice of derogation within the framework of its municipal laws.[21]

The information communicated to the Secretary-General by a State Party in pursuance of *EHR* 15(3) must be communicated by him as soon as possible to the other States Parties and to EUCM.[22] This information is now also communicated to EUCT, the Chairman of the Committee of Ministers, and the President of the Parliamentary Assembly.

HRC has expressed the view that a Note addressed to the UN Secretary-General, expressed to be delivered under *ICPR* 4(3) but doing no more than stating that an emergency situation in the country concerned was 'a matter of universal knowledge', containing no factual details, and making no attempt to indicate the nature or scope of derogations or to show that they were strictly necessary, could not evade that State's obligations under *ICPR*. While every State has the sovereign right to declare a state of emergency, it is the function of HRC under *ICPR OP* to see to it that the State Parties to *ICPR* live up to their commitments. Failing full and comprehensive information under *ICPR* 4(3) and *ICPR OP* 4(2), HRC cannot conclude that valid reasons exist to legitimize a departure from the normal legal régime prescribed by *ICPR*.[23]

§11.0.5 SUBSIDIARY INSTRUMENTS

Even if there is a war or a public emergency threatening the life of the nation, and the government concerned exercises its power of derogation to the maximum permissible extent, that cannot suspend all human rights. First, there are several rights from which no derogation of any kind is allowed in any circumstances (see §11.0.3). Secondly, the extent of any suspension must be confined to what is 'strictly required by the exigencies of the situation', a matter which is subject to the objective supervision of the competent independent international institutions (see §11.0.4).

But in times of armed conflict, both international and non-international, there also comes into operation another branch of international law known as 'humanitarian law', designed to limit the suffering of both combatants and

---

[19] *Lawless* v. *Ireland, supra.*
[20] (6780/74; 6950/75) Report: 10 July 1976.
[21] *Lawless* v. *Ireland, supra.*
[22] Resolution (56) 16, adopted by the Committee of Ministers in September 1956.
[23] *Silva et al.* v. *Uruguay* (R. 8/34) HRC 36, 130.

non-combatants. It is comprised in a number of treaties promoted by the Red Cross movement, and now ratified by many States: the Hague Conventions of 1899[24] and 1907,[25] the Geneva Protocol of 1925,[26] the four Geneva Conventions of 1949,[27] and the additional Protocols I and II to the latter, adopted in 1977.[28] Although strictly outside the scope of the present work, several of these provisions[29] seek to protect what are in fact some of the classic human rights in the situations of armed conflict to which the relevant treaties apply — provided of course that they have been ratified without any relevant reservation by the State concerned. It may therefore be said that, at all events in modern international law, Cicero's cynical maxim *'silent enim leges inter arma'* no longer applies.

[24] 'With respect to the Laws and Customs of War on Land.'

[25] 'Respecting the Laws and Customs of War on Land.'

[26] 'For the Prohibition of the Use in War of Asphyxiating, Poisonous or Other Gases, and of Bacteriological Methods of Warfare.'

[27] 'For the Amelioration of the Conditions of the Wounded and Sick in Armed Forces in the Field', 'for the Amelioration of the Conditions of Wounded, Sick and Shipwrecked Members of Armed Forces at Sea', 'relative to the Treatment of Prisoners of War', and 'relative to the Protection of Civilian Persons in Time of War' respectively.

[28] Relating, respectively, to the Protection of Victims of International, and Non-International, Armed Conflicts.

[29] Especially Articles 75, 76, 77 of Protocol I, and Articles 4, 5, and 6 of Protocol II.

§12. DENUNCIATION

§12.0.1 TEXTS

ICPR OP

12 (1) Any State Party may denounce the present Protocol at any time by written notification addressed to the Secretary-General of the United Nations. Denunciation shall take effect three months after the date of receipt of the notification by the Secretary-General.

(2) Denunciation shall be without prejudice to the continued application of the provisions of the present Protocol to any communication submitted under Article 2 before the effective date of denunciation.

EHR

65 (1) A High Contracting Party may denounce the present Convention only after the expiry of five years from the date on which it became a Party to it and after six months' notice contained in a notification addressed to the Secretary-General of the Council of Europe, who shall inform the other High Contracting Parties.

(2) Such a denunciation shall not have the effect of releasing the High Contracting Party concerned from its obligations under this Convention in respect of any act which, being capable of constituting a violation of such obligations, may have been performed by it before the date at which the denunciation became effective.

(3) Any High Contracting Party which shall cease to be a Member of the Council of Europe shall cease to be a Party to this Convention under the same conditions.

(4) The Convention may be denounced in accordance with the provisions of the preceding paragraphs in respect of any territory to which it has been declared to extend under the terms of Article 63.

ESC

37 (1) Any Contracting Party may denounce this Charter only at the end of a period of five years from the date on which the Charter entered into force for it, or at the end of any successive period of two years, and, in each case, after giving six months' notice to the Secretary-General of the Council of Europe, who shall inform the other Parties and the Director-General of the International Labour

Office accordingly. Such denunciation shall not affect the validity of the Charter in respect of the other contracting Parties provided that at all times there are not less than five such Contracting Parties.

(2) Any Contracting Party may, in accordance with the provisions set out in the preceding paragraph, denounce any Article or paragraph of Part II of the Charter accepted by it provided that the number of Articles or paragraphs by which this Contracting Party is bound shall never be less than 10 in the former case and 45 in the latter and that this number of Articles or paragraphs shall continue to include the Articles selected by the Contracting Party among those to which special reference is made in Article 20, paragraph 1, sub-paragraph (*b*).

(3) Any Contracting Party may denounce the present Charter or any of the Articles or paragraphs of Part II of the Charter, under the conditions specified in paragraph 1 of this Article, in respect of any territory to which the said Charter is applicable by virtue of a declaration made in accordance with paragraph 2 of Article 34.

AMR

78 (1) The States Parties may denounce this Convention at the expiration of a five-year period starting from the date of its entry into force and by means of notice given one year in advance. Notice of the denunciation shall be addressed to the Secretary-General of the Organization, who shall inform the other States Parties.

(2) Such a denunciation shall not have the effect of releasing the State Party concerned from the obligations contained in this Convention with respect to any act that may constitute a violation of those obligations and that has been taken by that state prior to the effective date of denunciation.

§12.0.2 CROSS-REFERENCES

Signatures, ratifications, accessions, reservations, and interpretations: See Table A for the State Parties bound by these instruments on 1 January 1982, and any reservations and interpretations notified by them.

§12.0.3 COMMENT

Neither *ICPR* nor *ICES* provides for denunciation.[1]

The use of the word 'at' rather than 'after' in *AMR* 78(1) seems to indicate that this treaty can only be denounced once, on the fifth anniversary of its entry

---

[1] Accordingly, under the general rules of international law, now reflected in Art. 56(1) of the Vienna Convention on the Law of Treaties, no denunciation of these instruments

into force. *ESC* can also be denounced on the same occasion, and again on every second anniversary after that. By contrast, any State Party may denounce *EHR* at any time after it has been a party to it for five years or more.

For *AMR*, the necessary notice of denunciation is 12 months; for *EHR* and *ESC* 6 months. In all three cases, the notice must be addressed to the depositary of the instrument. For both *EHR* and *AMR*, denunciation cannot affect retro-actively any violations which the denouncing State may have committed before the denunciation becomes effective. *ESC* has no comparable provision. Both *EHR* 65(4) and *ESC* 37(3) afford State Parties the opportunity of denouncing in respect of specified dependent territories only. In the case of *EHR* 65(3) alone, the termination of membership of the CE automatically determines membership of *EHR* 'under the same conditions'. *ESC* 37(2) alone allows partial denunciations, but subject to conditions ensuring that the minimum obligations required by the treaty continue to subsist for the State Parties concerned.

§12.0.4 JURISPRUDENCE

None of the competent independent international institutions has so far expressed any views on the interpretation or application of any of these provisions.

is possible unless either it is established that the parties intended to admit that possibility, or the nature of the treaty may imply a right of denunciation. Neither of these circumstances appears to apply to *ICPR* or *ICES*.

Part III

The Rights and Freedoms Guaranteed

§13. CLASSIFICATION OF THE RIGHTS AND FREEDOMS

Between them, the international instruments enumerate somewhere between forty and fifty distinct rights and freedoms. As with any other set of distinguishable concepts, the members of this one can be classified in a variety of different ways, by reference to some one or more of their respective features.

The most obvious distinction, and the one most frequently followed, is that of the titles of two of the instruments themselves: on the one hand, the 'civil and political' rights and freedoms enumerated in *ICPR, EHR*, and most of *AMR*; and, on the other, the 'economic, social and cultural' rights dealt with in *ICES* and *ESC*. That distinction has the useful merit that it largely coincides with the distinction between rights for which the correlative state obligation is absolute and immediate, and rights for which it is qualified and progressive. But even by that test the distinction is not entirely continent, for some of the rights attract both these classes of State obligation. The right to form and join trade unions, for example, is protected by both *ICPR* 22(1) and *ICES* 8(1)(*a*), and by both *EHR* 11(1) and *ESC* 5. Similarly, *ICPR* 23(1) and *ICES* 10(1), and *EHR* 12 and *ESC* 16, all provide for protection of the family. Besides, both the oldest instrument (*UDHR*) and the youngest ([*AFR*]) draw no distinction of this kind, and indeed [*AFR*] submits rights in all these categories to the identical form of State obligation.

In support of such a primary distinction, however, it is often argued that the division between the two groups of instruments reflects some substantive differences between the two categories of right which they enumerate. Some take the view, for example, that civil and political rights are 'individual' or 'personal', whereas economic, social and cultural rights are 'collective' or 'social'. But on closer examination that proves not to be the case, either formally or in substance. With the exception of a very few rights ascribed to 'peoples' or 'minorities' (see §26), the instruments consistently attribute the rights they declare to 'every person', 'everyone' or 'every individual': in both the categories, virtually all the rights are expressed as rights of individuals. At the same time, it is difficult to conceive how most of the rights in either category could usefully be exercised in total isolation from other individuals: even the right to freedom of expression — one of the classical 'civil and political' rights — presupposes at least one other person to whom opinions, information, and ideas may be expressed. Before the arrival of Man Friday, Robinson Crusoe would have found few occasions to claim any of his human rights. In that sense, all human rights are social rights.

Another ground sometimes prayed in aid for the same distinction is that the realization of economic, social and cultural rights requires programmes of positive action by the State; those rights are therefore said to be 'costly', whereas civil and political rights are said to be 'cost-free' because they are, in essence, claims for non-intervention. But this proposition too fails to stand up to closer examination. States require no costly programmes in order to comply with their obligations to ensure 'equal opportunity for everyone to be promoted in his employment to an appropriate higher level, subject to no considerations other than those of seniority and competence' (*ICES* 7(*c*)), 'the right of trade unions to establish national federations' (*ICES* 8(1)(*b*)), or 'the right of everyone to take part in cultural life' (*ICES* 15(1)(*a*)). On the other hand, some of the civil and political rights are decidedly costly to implement: liberty and security, arrest and detention, the rights of accused persons and the provision of fair trials all require substantial expenditure by the State in training and maintaining competent police forces, a responsible public prosecution service, and a competent, independent, and impartial judiciary — as well as providing, where necessary, free legal assistance and court interpreters.

But this conventional distinction also presents a more insidious problem, because it reflects a line of cleavage between two antithetical political orientations or ideologies, which describe themselves as 'liberal' and 'socialist', and each other as 'bourgeois' and 'communist', respectively. Advocates of each of these political and economic systems are apt to distinguish between the two classes of right not only in formal and functional description, but also in importance, attaching greater weight to one or the other class according to their respective ideological positions.[1]

In fact, the instruments themselves say nothing about their own ranking in any hierarchical order, or which of them is to prevail in the case of any conflicts between their respective provisions. The early *UDHR* and *ADRD* made no attempts at classification: they enumerated all the rights and freedoms in unqualified form, without headings or other distinction. The subsequent allocation of these rights to separate instruments — *ICPR* and *ICES*, and *EHR* and *ESC* — was the result of diplomatic negotiations between the governments represented at the drafting sessions, and in the case of the two UN Covenants reflects a compromise between the positions respectively adopted by groups of governments of antithetical political orientation. Yet the UNGA continues to confirm that all human rights form an indivisible whole;[2] and [*AFR*] in fact brings them all together again in a single instrument, and subject to a single and comprehensive State obligation.

Once the instruments have entered into force, all the rights and freedoms which they define enure to the benefit of all the persons whom they specify, against all the States which have become bound by them, regardless of their political or economic colour. In matters of practical application, therefore, lawyers should be concerned only with the meaning and effect of the right defined in each relevant Article, in the context of the correlative State obligation and the other Articles of general application, and not with any political ideology from which that right may have had its historical origin — let alone with the diplomatic motives which may have operated on the negotiating State Parties in including a particular Article in one instrument rather than another. For that reason, the present work does not adopt any classification by reference to the different instruments in which the rights are enumerated.

There are, of course, many other ways in which these rights and freedoms might be classified. For instance, there is a substantial body of theory about the difference between 'positive' and 'negative' rights, the positive right to life being for example contrasted with the negative freedom from torture. However, on analysis such differences in formulation prove more often to flow from the

[1] In their most extreme form, these two positions are respectively caricatured by the slogans 'Human rights begin at the police station', and 'Human rights begin after breakfast'.
[2] See, for example, UNGA Resolution 32/130, 16 December 1977.

exigencies of language rather than from any difference of substance (see also §4.3).

Again, some rights (such as freedom from arbitrary arrest or detention under *ICPR* 9) are derogable in times of national emergency, and others (such as freedom from torture and slavery under *ICPR* 7 and 8(1), freedom from imprisonment for debt under *ICPR* 11, and all the rights enumerated in *ICES* and [*AFR*]) are not. Similarly, some of the rights and freedoms (especially in *EHR*) are qualified by specific restriction and limitation clauses, while many others are not so qualified. Distinctions could also be drawn between rights which are attributed to 'everyone', and others which are allotted only to the members of some groups of human beings, such as workers, mothers, children, or prisoners.

Though distinctions of that kind have much theoretical interest, they have little practical utility. Accordingly, the present work makes no attempt to classify the different rights and freedoms in accordance with any distinction founded on theoretical considerations, let alone to rank them in any order which might reflect value judgments about their relative importance. Instead, and regardless of the instruments in which they appear or of any sequence followed within those instruments, they are arranged here in a sequence designed to be purely functional, and to facilitate ease of reference.

That sequence is necessarily arbitrary, and emphatically does not reflect any ranking order. Instead it reflects, if anything, the developing perceptions of those whose rights stand in need of protection, beginning with the most simple and concrete (physical integrity, standard of living, health, etc.) and ending with the most complex and abstract (political activities). No special merit is claimed for this ordering: it is used only for the convenience of the reader. The international canon of rights and freedoms itself neither makes nor implies any judgment as to the relative importance of the different rights: each right is dealt with independently of every other, in no particular order — and indeed the ordering of the same rights varies between different instruments *in pari materia*.

What concerns the student or practitioner is to be able to find and analyse all the texts which define a particular right, to establish what the State obligations are in relation to it, to see whether it is derogable and to what extent it may legitimately be restricted or limited, and to discover what light has so far been cast on its interpretation or application by independent international institutions or superior national courts. That is the material which this Part of the present work therefore attempts to provide.

§14. PHYSICAL INTEGRITY

§14.1 Life

§14.1.1 TEXTS

UDHR

3. Everyone has the right to life . . .

ADRD

I. Every human being has the right to life . . .

ICPR

6 (1) Every human being has the inherent right to life. This right shall be protected by law. No one shall be arbitrarily deprived of his life.

(2) In countries which have not abolished the death penalty, sentence of death may be imposed only for the most serious crimes in accordance with the law in force at the time of the commission of the crime and not contrary to the provisions of the present Covenant and to the Convention on the Prevention and Punishment of the Crime of Genocide. This penalty can only be carried out pursuant to a final judgement rendered by a competent court.

(3) When deprivation of life constitutes the crime of genocide, it is understood that nothing in this article shall authorize any State Party to the present Covenant to derogate in any way from any obligation assumed under the provisions of the Convention on the Prevention and Punishment of the Crime of Genocide.

(4) Anyone sentenced to death shall have the right to seek pardon or commutation of the sentence. Amnesty, pardon or commutation of the sentence of death may be granted in all cases.

(5) Sentence of death shall not be imposed for crimes committed by persons below eighteen years of age and shall not be carried out on pregnant women.

(6) Nothing in this article shall be invoked to delay or to prevent the abolition of capital punishment by any State Party to the present Covenant.

EHR

2 (1) Everyone's right to life shall be protected by law. No one shall be deprived of his life intentionally save in the execution of a sentence of a court following his conviction of a crime for which this penalty is provided by law.

(2) Deprivation of life shall not be regarded as inflicted in contravention of this Article when it results from the use of force which is no more than absolutely necessary:

(*a*) in defence of any person from unlawful violence;

(*b*) in order to effect a lawful arrest or to prevent the escape of a person lawfully detained;

(*c*) in action lawfully taken for the purpose of quelling a riot or insurrection.

AMR

4 (1) Every person has the right to have his life respected. This right shall be protected by law, and, in general, from the moment of conception. No one shall be arbitrarily deprived of his life.

(2) In countries that have not abolished the death penalty, it may be imposed only for the most serious crimes and pursuant to a final judgment rendered by a competent court and in accordance with a law establishing such punishment, enacted prior to the commission of the crime. The application of such punishment shall not be extended to crimes to which it does not presently apply.

(3) The death penalty shall not be reestablished in states that have abolished it.

(4) In no case shall capital punishment be inflicted for political offenses or related common crimes.

(5) Capital punishment shall not be imposed upon persons who, at the time the crime was committed, were under 18 years of age or over 70 years of age; nor shall it be applied to pregnant women.

(6) Every person condemned to death shall have the right to apply for amnesty, pardon, or commutation of sentence, which may be granted in all cases. Capital punishment shall not be imposed while such a petition is pending decision by the competent authority.

[*AFR*]

4. Human beings are inviolable. Every human being shall be entitled to respect for his life and the integrity of his person. No one may be arbitrarily deprived of this right.

§14.1.2 CROSS-REFERENCES

State obligation: Absolute and immediate under *ICPR, EHR, AMR*, and [*AFR*]: see §6.3. For the juridical status of obligations under *UDHR* and *ADRD*, see §6.2.

Signatures, ratifications, accessions, reservations, and interpretations: See Table A for the State Parties bound by these provisions on 1 January 1982, and any reservations and interpretations notified by them.

Derogation: Non-derogable in any circumstances: see §11.

Non-discrimination: No discrimination of any kind is allowed in respect of this right: see §7 for the relevant provisions in the instruments.

Abuse: See §9 for the relevant provisions in these instruments.

Savings: See §10 for the relevant provisions in these instruments.

Restrictions and limitations: Note the specific provisions in *EHR* 2(2). See §8 for the general provisions in these instruments, and the principles governing all restriction and limitation clauses.

International supervision, interpretation, application, and enforcement: By HRC under *ICPR* (see §27); by EUCM and EUCT under *EHR* (see §28); by IACM and IACT under *AMR* (see §29); by [AFCM] under [*AFR*] (see §30). See also §6.6 for the obligation to provide domestic remedies under *UDHR, ADRD, ICPR, EHR, AMR*, and [*AFR*].

Subsidiary instruments: *CG* (see §14.1.6).

See also: § 14.2 for lawful arrest and detention; §22.5 for retroactive penal laws.

§14.1.3 COMMENT

As human rights can only attach to living human beings, one might expect the right to life itself to be in some sense primary, since none of the other rights would have any value or utility without it. But the international instruments do not in fact accord it any formal primacy: on the contrary, *ICPR, EHR*, and *AMR* all contain qualifications rendering the right less than absolute, and allowing human life to be deliberately terminated in certain specified cases. [*AFR*] too prohibits only the 'arbitrary' deprivation of the right to respect for life.

The right to life thus stands in marked contrast to some of the other rights protected by the same instruments: for example, the freedom from torture and other ill-treatment (see §14.3) and the freedom from slavery and servitude (see §18.4) are both absolute, and subject to no exceptions of any kind. It may therefore be said that international human rights law assigns a higher value to the quality of living as a process, than to the existence of life as a state. This reflects a similar apparent anomaly found in many national legal systems, which award higher measures of compensation for the suffering of pain or long-term debilitating injuries (e.g. as the result of some avoidable accident) than for death caused in similar circumstances. From the point of view of the person concerned, the law tends to regard acute or prolonged suffering (at all events in cases where it is inflicted by others, and so is potentially avoidable) as a greater evil than death, which is ultimately unavoidable for everyone.

Both the Declarations (*UDHR* 3 and *ADRD* I) explicitly declare a 'right to life'. But only one of the treaties (*ICPR* 6(1)) does likewise, adding the adjective 'inherent'.[1] *EHR* 2(1) does not declare the right, but presupposes its existence by stipulating (in common with *ICPR* and *AMR*) that it 'shall be protected by law'. *AMR* 4(1) and [*AFR* 4] differ from the other instruments in defining the right as one to have life respected.

All the treaties other than [*AFR*] expressly save the death penalty. Beyond that, *ICPR* 6(1), *AMR* 4(1), and [*AFR* 4] prohibit 'arbitrary' deprivation of life; *EHR* 2(1) differs in prohibiting 'intentional' killing, and in specifying (in addition to the death penalty), three further and distinct exceptions to that prohibition. Both *ICPR* and *AMR* restrict the death penalty to 'the most serious crimes', require it to be imposed only by a 'final judgment' of a 'competent court' in accordance with non-retroactive laws (see §22.5), confer a right to seek 'pardon or commutation of the sentence', and provide that amnesty, pardon, or commutation 'may be granted in all cases'. Both these treaties also prohibit the imposition of the death sentence on persons who were below the age of 18 at the time of commission of the crime, and its execution on pregnant women.

But *AMR* goes further than *ICPR* in several respects connected with the death penalty. It expressly confers a right to seek 'amnesty' as well as pardon or commutation of sentence, and prohibits the imposition of capital punishment while any petition for such relief is pending decision; in addition to persons under 18, it also exempts persons over 70; it prohibits capital punishment for 'political offences or related common crimes'; and it seeks to encourage progressive reduction of the death penalty by prohibiting its extension to new crimes, or its re-establishment once it has been abolished. *ICPR* 6(2) appears to exhibit a bias in favour of abolition, reinforced by the provision (in Article 6(6)) that 'nothing in this Article shall be invoked to delay or prevent' it.[2] *EHR* is silent on all these matters; for the death penalty to be legitimately carried out, it is enough for it to have been imposed by a court, following conviction of a crime for which it is provided by law.

ICPR 6(2) and (3) expressly save *CG* (see §14.1.6); neither *EHR*, *AMR*, nor [*AFR*] mention it.

Only *AMR* addresses the question of when life begins: Article 4(1) requires the protection of the law 'in general, from the moment of conception'. (Note that *CG* 2 includes in the definition of genocide measures intended to prevent births within a national, ethnic, racial, or religious group.)

§14.1.4 HISTORY

The earliest national statute prohibiting the arbitrary deprivation of life is probably the English Magna Carta of 1215, which provides that

No freeman shall be taken or imprisoned, or be disseised of his freehold, or liberties, or free customs, or be outlawed, or exiled, or any other wise destroyed; nor will we pass upon him, nor condemn him, but by the lawful judgment of his peers, or by the law of the land.[3]

---

[1] As to 'inherence', see the Decision of 16 January 1964, BVwG, Federal Republic of Germany, CDNC 2, 4.

[2] The UNGA is currently considering the idea of elaborating a second Optional Protocol to *ICPR*, aiming at the abolition of the death penalty: see Decision 35/437 of 15 December 1980.

[3] Ch. 26 in the version confirmed by King Edward I in 1297; 6 Halsbury's Statues (3rd ed.) 401.

The same principle found expression in 1791 in the Fifth (and later the Fourteenth) Amendment to the US Constitution which provided that 'No person shall be . . . deprived of life . . . without due process of law.'

Later national constitutions and bills of rights have modelled themselves either on the US Constitution or on one or other of the international or regional instruments.

§14.1.5 JURISPRUDENCE

'Right to life'

IACM has expressed the view that 'the use of abortion to help solve economic and subsistence problems resulting from the population explosion would be a manifest and grave violation of human rights.'[4]

In 1960, the question whether human rights were fully applicable to the human embryo from the time of conception was specifically posed in an application to EUCM directed against a Norwegian law which legalized the termination of pregnancy under certain conditions. The Commission, however, left the question unanswered on that occasion, on the ground that the applicant did not claim to be a victim of the law concerned, and that it was not competent to examine the question *in abstracto*.[5] However, in *Brüggeman and Scheuten* v. *Federal Republic of Germany*,[6] the Commission found that a German law which prohibited the termination of a pregnancy merely because it was unwanted did not violate the right to respect for private life under *EHR* 8. And in an application in 1979, EUCM expressed some doubt whether the word 'everyone' in *EHR* 2(1) could apply to an unborn child; even if the right to life were secured to a foetus from conception, the Commission considered that it would be subject to an implied limitation allowing the pregnancy to be terminated in order to protect the mother's life or health.[7] Several courts in Europe,[8] and the Court of Appeal in New Zealand,[9] have likewise held that an induced miscarriage in the first trimester of pregnancy, in order to preserve the health of the mother from a real and substantial risk of serious harm, does not violate the right to life.

The question whether the right to life implies the right to reproduce life has also not yet been pronounced upon authoritatively. In an unpublished decision,[10] EUCM has stated that an operation for sterilization might, in certain circumstances, involve an infringement of the right to life.[11]

'Protected by law'

In a series of decisions, EUCM has sought to determine the extent to which the law could be called upon to protect the right to life. In *X* v. *Ireland*,[12] it

---

[4] AR 1971, 33. But the decision of a court reversing the conviction of a medical practitioner for terminating a pregnancy does not violate *ADRD* I: Case 2141 (USA) 6 March 1981.
[5] *X* v. *Norway* (867/60) CD 6, 34.   [6] (6959/75) Report: DR 10, 100.
[7] *X* v. *United Kingdom* (8416/78) DR 19, 244.
[8] Decision of 11 October 1974, VfGH, Austria (EuGRZ 1975, 74); Decision of 15 January 1975, Conseil Constitutionnel, France (EuGRZ 1975, 54); Decision of 18 February 1975, Corte Constituzionale, Italy (EuGRZ 1975, 162).
[9] *R.* v. *Woolnough* [1977] 2 NZLR 508.
[10] (1287/61) unpublished, but referred to in Jacobs, *The European Convention on Human Rights*, 22.
[11] See also the English case of *Re D (a minor)* [1976] 1 All ER 326, which held that a sterilization operation was one which involved the deprivation of a basic human right, i.e. the right of a woman to reproduce.
[12] (6040/73) CD 44, 121.

held that *EHR* 2 cannot be interpreted as imposing a duty on a State to provide personal bodyguards, at least for an indefinite period, to individuals who fear that their lives may be threatened by illegal organizations. But *EHR* 2 may be invoked by a person in proceedings which seek to evict him from his house on the ground that, having regard to his state of health, eviction may endanger his life.[13] In *X* v. *United Kingdom*,[14] a prisoner alleged that his prison staff had 'a license to kill' and that his life was therefore in danger. The respondent government, while denying the allegation, pointed out that, in English law, the life of a prisoner was protected by the ordinary law of homicide. The Commission rejected that particular application, but in *Simon-Herold* v. *Austria*[15] it declared admissible (without determining the merits) a prisoner's complaint that his prison conditions and the negligence of his prison officers resulted in pneumonia, paralysis of one arm and the loss of more than 16 kg. in weight, in violation of his right to life.

In the context of the rights to life, liberty, and security protected by *ADRD* I, IACM has said that

the Commission is concerned with the view that the government is responsible only for violations committed by its officials or agents and that it could remain with its arms crossed in the face of attacks on these rights that are the result of armed struggle between enemy factions. The duty of the State is to guarantee the security of the population, and it would be failing in this duty, both by action and by omission. The State cannot remain indifferent in such a fundamental matter, and it must do everything in its power to effectively protect these rights.[16]

In *Association X* v. *United Kingdom*,[17] EUCM stated that the phrase 'shall be protected by law' enjoins the State not only to refrain from taking life intentionally but, further, to take appropriate steps to safeguard life. In that case, the Commission held that a State sufficiently complied with its obligation to protect life under *EHR* 2 if it established a system of control and supervision to reduce as much as possible the number of fatalities that could occur in the context of a voluntary vaccination scheme, whose sole purpose was to protect the health of society by eliminating an infectious disease.[18] In *Cyprus* v. *Turkey*,[19] EUCM found that the killing of Cypriot civilians by Turkish soldiers commanded by an officer in activities unconnected with any war contravened *EHR* 2.

IACM has said that, where individuals have 'disappeared' but the government concerned refuses to provide any information about them, or about the progress of any investigations aimed at determining their whereabouts, it is legitimate to presume that *ADRD* I has been violated, and that agents of the government,

---

[13] *X* v. *Federal Republic of Germany* (5207/71) CD 39, 99.

[14] (4203/69) CD 34, 48.

[15] (4340/69) CD 38, 18. This case was settled; see Report: 19 December 1972.

[16] AR 1976, 19.

[17] (7154/75) DR 14, 31.

[18] For conduct not amounting to a violation of the right to life, see also *X*. v. *Belgium* (2758/66) CD 30, 11: accidental shooting by a constable dealing with a riot; Decision of 17 June 1977, VfGH, Austria (JB 1978, 311): use of firearms to arrest a man who had crossed a police road block by force; Decision of 19 July 1976, BGer, Switzerland (750/76): insanitary conditions of prison cell; Decision of 16 October 1977, BVfG, Federal Republic of Germany (1 BvQ 5/77): refusal to release terrorist prisoners in order to save life of kidnapped person.

[19] (6780/74; 6950/75) Report: 10 July 1976.

or individuals protected or tolerated by it, 'have not been uninvolved' in the violation.[20]

'Deprived of life'

The question whether euthanasia would be considered as the arbitrary (or intentional) deprivation of life has not yet been pronounced upon in Strasbourg. It involves the further complicated question how far the consent of a victim may authorize what would otherwise be unlawful. Jacobs[21] is of the view that, in principle, the fundamental character of the right to life and the element of public interest would exclude the possibility of any form of waiver. Two German courts have differed on this question.[22]

In *Munn* v. *Illinois*,[23] a case decided by the US Supreme Court, Field, J stated, *obiter*, that the expression 'deprived of life' should not be construed to refer only to the extreme case of death. He added:

By the term 'life' as here used [Fourteenth Amendment to the US Constitution], something more is meant than mere animal existence. The inhibition against its deprivation extends to all those limbs and faculties by which life is enjoyed. The prohibition equally prohibits the mutilation of the body by the amputation of an arm or leg, or the putting out of an eye, or the destruction of any other organ of the body through which the soul communicates with the outer world. The deprivation not only of life, but of whatever God has given to every one with life, for its growth and enjoyment, is prohibited by the provision in question, if its efficacy be not frittered away by judicial decision.[24]

However, the Constitutional Court of the Federal Republic of Germany has held that it would not be legitimate to stretch the concept of the right to life to include the free development of the personality.[25]

§14.1.6 SUBSIDIARY INSTRUMENTS

The Convention on the Prevention and Punishment of the Crime of Genocide (CG)[26] creates a new 'crime under international law'[27] in the form of 'genocide', which it defines[28] as

any of the following acts committed with intent to destroy, in whole or in part, a national, ethnical, racial or religious group, as such:

---

[20] Cases 1702, 1748, and 1755 (Guatemala) AR 1975, 67.

[21] *Op. cit.*, 22.

[22] Decision of 8 October 1959, VwG Bremen (NJW 1960, 400) and Decision of 16 January 1964, BVwG, Federal Republic of Germany, *supra*, n. 1.

[23] 94 US 133.

[24] *Ibid.*, at 142. This definition receives support from *CG* 2: see §14.1.6. But cf. Blackstone's Commentaries 1, 134: deprivation means total loss (as distinguished from restriction or partial control).

[25] Decision of 10 May 1957, BVfG, Federal Republic of Germany (E/BVfG 6, 389).

[26] The International Court of Justice has said that 'the principles underlying [this] Convention are principles which are recognised by civilised nations as binding on States, even without any conventional obligation', i.e. that they already form part of customary international law: Advisory Opinion on *Reservations to the Genocide Convention*, ICJ Reports 1951, 23.

[27] 'Whether committed in time of peace or in time of war': *CG* I; see also §5.3.

[28] *CG* II.

(*a*) killing members of the group;
(*b*) causing serious bodily or mental harm to members of the group;
(*c*) deliberately inflicting on the group conditions of life calculated to bring about its physical destruction in whole or in part;
(*d*) imposing measures intended to prevent births within the group;
(*e*) forcibly transferring children of the group to another group.

As well as genocide itself, *CG* also declares to be punishable conspiracy, direct and public incitement, and attempt to commit genocide, as well as complicity in genocide.[29]
The Convention provides that persons charged with any of the crimes punishable under it may be tried by a competent tribunal of the State where the act was committed, or by an international penal tribunal having jurisdiction accepted by a State Party.[30] For the purposes of extradition, these crimes shall not be considered as political crimes.[31] All persons guilty of these crimes are to be punished, 'whether they are constitutionally responsible rulers, public officials or private individuals,'[32] and the State Parties are bound to enact the necessary legislation to give effect to the Convention, and to provide effective penalties.[33]

§14.2 Liberty and security; arrest and detention

§14.2.1 TEXTS

UDHR

3. Everyone has the right to ... liberty and security of person.

9. No one shall be subjected to arbitrary arrest or detention ...

ADRD

I. Every human being has the right to ... liberty and the security of his person.

XXV. No person may be deprived of his liberty except in the cases and according to the procedures established by pre-existing law.

No person may be deprived of liberty for nonfulfilment of obligations of a purely civil character.

Every individual who has been deprived of his liberty has the right to have the legality of his detention ascertained without delay by a court, and the right to be tried without undue delay, or otherwise, to be released.

ICPR

9 (1) Everyone has the right to liberty and security of person. No one shall be subjected to arbitrary arrest or detention. No one shall

[29] *CG* III.   [30] *CG* VI.   [31] *CG* VII.   [32] *CG* IV.   [33] *CG* V.

be deprived of his liberty except on such grounds and in accordance with such procedure as are established by law.

(2) Anyone who is arrested shall be informed, at the time of arrest, of the reasons for his arrest and shall be promptly informed of any charges against him.

(3) Anyone arrested or detained on a criminal charge shall be brought promptly before a judge or other officer authorized by law to exercise judicial power and shall be entitled to trial within a reasonable time or to release. It shall not be the general rule that persons awaiting trial shall be detained in custody, but release may be subject to guarantees to appear for trial, at any other stage of the judicial proceedings, and, should occasion arise, for execution of the judgment.

(4) Anyone who is deprived of his liberty by arrest or detention shall be entitled to take proceedings before a court, in order that that court may decide without delay on the lawfulness of his detention and order his release if the detention is not lawful.

(5) Anyone who has been the victim of unlawful arrest or detention shall have an enforceable right to compensation.

10 (2)

(*a*) Accused persons shall, save in exceptional circumstances, be segregated from convicted persons and shall be subject to separate treatment appropriate to their status as unconvicted persons;

(*b*) Accused juvenile persons shall be separated from adults and brought as speedily as possible for adjudication.

(3) The penitentiary system shall comprise treatment of prisoners the essential aim of which shall be their reformation and social rehabilitation. Juvenile offenders shall be segregated from adults and be accorded treatment appropriate to their age and legal status.

EHR

11. No one shall be imprisoned merely on the ground of inability to fulfil a contractual obligation.

5 (1) Everyone has the right to liberty and security of person.

No one shall be deprived of his liberty save in the following cases and in accordance with a procedure described by law:

(*a*) the lawful detention of a person after conviction by a competent court;

(*b*) the lawful arrest or detention of a person for non-compliance with the lawful order of a court or in order to secure the fulfilment of any obligation prescribed by law;

(*c*) the lawful arrest or detention of a person effected for the purpose of bringing him before the competent legal authority on reasonable suspicion of having committed an offence or when it is reasonably considered necessary to prevent his committing an offence or fleeing after having done so;

(*d*) the detention of a minor by lawful order for the purpose of educational supervision or his lawful detention for the purpose of bringing him before the competent legal authority;

(*e*) the lawful detention of persons for the prevention of the spreading of infectious diseases, of persons of unsound mind, alcoholics or drug addicts, or vagrants;

(*f*) the lawful arrest or detention of a person to prevent his effecting an unauthorized entry into the country or of a person against whom action is being taken with a view to deportation or extradition.

(2) Everyone who is arrested shall be informed promptly, in a language which he understands, of the reasons for his arrest and of any charge against him.

(3) Everyone arrested or detained in accordance with the provisions of paragraph 1 (*c*) of this Article shall be brought promptly before a judge or other officer authorized by law to exercise judicial power and shall be entitled to trial within a reasonable time or to release pending trial. Release may be conditioned by guarantees to appear for trial.

(4) Everyone who is deprived of his liberty by arrest or detention shall be entitled to take proceedings by which the lawfulness of his detention shall be decided speedily by a court and his release ordered if the detention is not lawful.

(5) Everyone who has been the victim of arrest or detention in contravention of the provisions of this Article shall have an enforceable right to compensation.

EHR P4

1. No one shall be deprived of his liberty merely on the ground of inability to fulfil a contractual obligation.

AMR

7 (1) Every person has the right to personal liberty and security.

(2) No one shall be deprived of his physical liberty except for the reasons and under the conditions established beforehand by the constitution of the State Party concerned or by a law established pursuant thereto.

(3) No one shall be subject to arbitrary arrest or imprisonment.

(4) Anyone who is detained shall be informed of the reasons for his detention and shall be promptly notified of the charge or charges against him.

(5) Any person detained shall be brought promptly before a judge or other officer authorized by law to exercise judicial power and shall be entitled to trial within a reasonable time or to be released without prejudice to the continuation of the proceedings. His release may be subject to guarantees to assure his appearance for trial.

(6) Anyone who is deprived of his liberty shall be entitled to recourse to a competent court, in order that the court may decide without delay on the lawfulness of his arrest or detention and order his release if the arrest or detention is unlawful. In States Parties whose laws provide that anyone who believes himself to be threatened with deprivation of his liberty is entitled to recourse to a competent court in order that it may decide on the lawfulness of such threat, this remedy may not be restricted or abolished. The interested party or another person in his behalf is entitled to seek these remedies.

(7) No one shall be detained for debt. This principle shall not limit the orders of a competent judicial authority issued for nonfulfillment of duties of support.

5 (3) Punishment shall not be extended to any person other than the criminal.

(4) Accused persons shall, save in exceptional circumstances, be segregated from convicted persons, and shall be subject to separate treatment appropriate to their status as unconvicted persons.

(5) Minors while subject to criminal proceedings shall be separated from adults and brought before specialized tribunals, as speedily as possible, so that they may be treated in accordance with their status as minors.

(6) Punishments consisting of deprivation of liberty shall have as an essential aim the reform and social readaptation of the prisoners.

[*AFR*]

6. Every individual shall have the right to liberty and to security of his person. No one may be deprived of his freedom except for reasons and conditions previously laid down by law. In particular, no one may be arbitrarily arrested or detained.

7 (2) Punishment is personal and can be imposed only on the offender.

§14.2.2 CROSS-REFERENCES

State obligation: Absolute and immediate under *ICPR, EHR, AMR,* and [*AFR*]: see §6.3. For the juridical status of obligations under *UDHR* and *ADRD*, see §6.2.

Signatures, ratifications, accessions, reservations, and interpretations: See Table

A for the State Parties bound by these provisions on 1 January 1982, and any reservations and interpretations notified by them.

Derogation: Except for *ICPR* 11, all these rights and freedoms are derogable in exceptional circumstances under *ICPR*, *EHR*, and *AMR*: see §11.

Non-discrimination: No discrimination of any kind is allowed in respect of these rights: see §7 for the relevant provisions in the instruments.

Abuse: See §9 for the relevant provisions in these instruments.

Savings: See §10 for the relevant provisions in these instruments.

Restrictions and limitations: Note the specific provisions in *ICPR* 10(2)(*a*), *EHR* 5(1), and *AMR* 7(7) and 5(4). See §8 for the general provisions in these instruments, and the principles governing all restriction and limitation clauses.

International supervision, interpretation, application, and enforcement: By HRC under *ICPR* (see §27). by EUCM and EUCT under *EHR* (see §28); by IACM and IACT under *AMR* (see §29); by [AFCM] under [*AFR*] (see §30). See also §6.6 for the obligation to provide domestic remedies under *UDHR*, *ADRD*, *ICPR*, *EHR*, *AMR*, and [*AFR*].

Subsidiary instruments: UN Standard Minimum Rules for the Treatment of Prisoners, CE Standard Minimum Rules for the Treatment of Prisoners; UN Code of Conduct for Law Enforcement Officials; [UN Body of Principles for the Protection of All Persons under any Form of Detention or Imprisonment].

See also: §14.3 for treatment of prisoners; §22.3 for equality before the law; §22.4 for the right to a fair trial; §22.5 for retroactive penal laws; §22.6 for the rights of accused persons; §22.7 for remedies for miscarriages of justice.

§14.2.3 COMMENT

The rights protected by these Articles fall into a number of distinct but related categories.

The right to liberty and security of person

Although, as a matter of language, all the instruments protect these two rights jointly in virtually identical terms, they have been interpreted as being separate and independent rights.[1]

Freedom from arbitrary arrest and detention

UDHR 9, *ICPR* 9(1), *AMR* 7(3), and [*AFR* 6] all protect this freedom explicitly; *EHR* does not mention it in terms, but it has been held to be implied in *EHR* 5(1);[2] it is also missing from *ADRD*.

Deprivation of liberty to be only on grounds, and by procedures, established (or prescribed) by law

This is, in essence, the positive equivalent of the negative proposition that arrest and detention shall not be arbitrary. In one form or another, all the instruments except *UDHR* provide for it. *ADRD* XXV requires the law to be

---

[1] See *Kamma* v. *Netherlands* (4771/71) Report: DR 1, 4; see also *Engel et al.* v. *Netherlands* (5100–2/71; 5354/72; 5370/72) Report: 19 July 1974.
[2] *Winterwerp* v. *Netherlands* (6301/73) Judgment: 2 EHRR 387.

'pre-existing' and [*AFR* 6] 'previously laid down'; *AMR* 7 in addition requires it to be constitutional. *EHR* 5(1) is unique in that it specifies exhaustively what the *grounds* of deprivation of liberty may be, and thereby effectively forbids arrest or detention on any other grounds, even if prescribed by law.

The right to be informed of the reasons for arrest, and of any charges

ICPR 9(2), *EHR* 5(2), and *AMR* 7(4) all contain this requirement. *ICPR* alone specifies that the reasons for the arrest must be given 'at the time of arrest'; *ICPR* and both the other treaties require the notification of the charges to be given 'promptly', and that word also governs the giving of the reasons for the arrest in *EHR*, but not in *AMR*. *EHR* 5(2) alone expressly requires the information to be given *on the occasion of the arrest* in a language which the person arrested understands; both *EHR* 6(3)(*a*) and *ICPR* 14(3)(*a*) contain this requirement in respect of the subsequent legal proceedings (see §22.6).

The right to judicial control of arrest and detention

All the instruments except *UDHR* and [*AFR*] guarantee this right. *ICPR* 9(3), *EHR* 5(3), and *AMR* 7(5) all require persons arrested or detained to be brought 'promptly' before a judge or judicial officer, and to be either tried 'within a reasonable time' or released, if necessary subject to guarantees to appear for trial.[3] (*ADRD* XXV only requires trial 'without undue delay'.) *ICPR* and *EHR* confine these requirements to arrest on criminal charges; *ADRD* and *AMR* do not. *ICPR* 9(3) alone expressly provides that 'it' shall not be the general rule that persons awaiting trial shall be detained in custody'.

The right to test the legality of arrest or detention

ADRD XXV, *ICPR* 9(4), *EHR* 5(4), and *AMR* 7(6) all prescribe that the person deprived of his liberty shall have the opportunity of testing the legality of that deprivation by judicial proceedings in the nature of *habeas corpus* or *recurso de amparo*, but in the case of *ICPR* and *EHR* only where the deprivation takes the form of arrest or detention. *EHR* requires the court's decision to be given 'speedily'; the other instruments prefer the phrase 'without delay'. All these treaties require the person's release if the deprivation is unlawful. *AMR* requires the court to be 'competent', and prohibits State Parties which already have provisions for anticipatory or protective *amparo* from restricting or abolishing them. Only *AMR* says in terms that the remedy may be sought by other persons on the applicant's behalf.

Compensation for unlawful arrest or detention

Only *ICPR* 9(5) and *EHR* 5(5) prescribe an enforceable right to this, in the case of *ICPR* whenever the arrest or detention has been 'unlawful', and in the case of *EHR* when it has been in contravention of the provisions of *EHR* 5.

Conditions of detention

Only *ICPR* 10 and *AMR* 5 contain provisions about these. Both require convicted prisoners to be segregated from each other 'save in exceptional circumstances', and the 'separate treatment' of unconvicted persons appropriate to their status as such. These Articles likewise require unconvicted juveniles to be

---

[3] Note that, except in the case of *ICPR*, there is an independent right for all trials — not only criminal ones, and not only for persons held in detention — to take place 'within a reasonable time', as part of the right to a fair trial: see §22.4.

separated from adults, and to be tried speedily — in the case of *AMR* only, 'before specialized tribunals'. *ICPR* also requires the segregation of convicted juveniles from adults, and treatment for them 'appropriate to their age and legal status'. Both these treaties require prison régimes to have as their 'essential aim' the reform and social rehabilitation of the prisoners (see also § 14.3.5).

Freedom from civil imprisonment

All the instruments other than *UDHR* and [*AFR*] provide for this. *ADRD* XXV extends the protection to 'nonfulfilment of obligations of a purely civil character', *ICPR* 11 and *EHR P4* 1 to 'inability to fulfil a contractual obligation', and *AMR* 7(7) simply to 'debt', other than 'nonfulfilment of duties of support'. In the case of *ICPR* only, this freedom is non-derogable.

No one other than the criminal to be punished

Only *AMR* 5(3) and [*AFR* 7(2)] contain this express provision.

§14.2.4 HISTORY

Liberty of the person is one of the oldest concepts to be protected by national laws. As long ago as 1215, the English Magna Carta provided that

no freeman shall be taken or imprisoned . . . but . . . by the law of the land.[4]

By the end of the eighteenth century, 'liberty' (by then a much more extended concept) had become one of the three highest values to be defended, being coupled with equality and fraternity in the French Revolution, and with life and either property or the pursuit of happiness in the American one. And in 1789, the French *déclaration des droits de l'homme et du citoyen* also contained, in Article 7, a provision that 'no one shall be accused, arrested or imprisoned, save in the cases determined by law, and according to the forms which it has prescribed.'

But none of the earlier national constitutions contains the detailed provisions now found in the international treaties. For instance, the US Constitution merely declares that no person shall be 'deprived of . . . liberty . . . without due process of law'. Similarly, the Canadian Bill of Rights of 1960 recognizes and declares that 'there have existed and shall continue to exist without discrimination . . . the right of the individual to . . . liberty [and] security of person . . . , and the right not to be deprived thereof except by due process of law.' The Constitution of India, in Article 21, states that 'no person shall be deprived of his . . . personal liberty except according to procedure established by law.'

Some of the more recent national constitutions, however, have adopted more detailed provisions similar to those contained in the international treaties.

§14.2.5 JURISPRUDENCE

'Liberty and security of person'

The expression 'liberty and security of person' has been considered several times in Strasbourg. In *Guzzardi* v. *Italy*,[5] EUCT expressed the view that in proclaiming

---

[4] Ch. 26 in the version confirmed by King Edward I in 1297; 6 Halsbury's Statutes (3rd ed.) 401.

[5] (7367/76) Judgment: 3 EHRR 333.

the 'right to liberty', *EHR* 5 was contemplating the physical liberty of the person, and in *Arrowsmith* v. *United Kingdom*,[6] EUCM observed that 'personal liberty' means primarily freedom from arrest and detention. In *X* v. *United Kingdom*,[7] EUCM also considered that the expression 'liberty and security of person' must be read as a whole and that 'security', being therefore understood in the context of 'liberty', means only physical security, that is freedom from arbitrary arrest and detention.

IACM has consistently treated the application of torture as a violation of the right to security of person under *ADRD* I.[8] It has also held that this right is violated where a Minister of the Interior sends a message to a man for whose arrest a warrant has been issued saying, on behalf of the National Guard, that if he surrenders to the warrant 'they were not guaranteeing his life.'[9] IACM has further held that *ADRD* I is violated where persons 'disappear' within the territory of a State, but the government concerned refuses to provide any information about them, or about the progress of any investigations aimed at determining their whereabouts, since it may be presumed in these circumstances that agents of the government, or individuals protected or tolerated by it, have 'not been uninvolved' in the acts concerned.[10]

In the United States[11] and in India,[12] the concept of 'liberty' has received a far more expansive interpretation. Supreme Courts in both countries have rejected the view that liberty denotes merely freedom from bodily restraint,[13] and have held that it encompasses those rights and privileges which have long been recognized as being essential to the orderly pursuit of happiness by free men. In *Board of Regents* v. *Roth*,[14] the US Supreme Court observed that 'liberty' is a 'broad and majestic term', which is among the constitutional concepts purposely left to gather meaning from experience and which relate to the whole domain of social and economic facts, subject to change in a society that is not stagnant. In *Kharak Singh* v. *State of Uttar Pradesh*,[15] the Indian Supreme Court observed that the right of personal liberty in the Indian Constitution is

[6] (7050/75) Report: DR 19, 5.

[7] (5877/72) CD 45, 90. In that case the Commission declared inadmissible a complaint that X had been photographed by the police against her will after being arrested during a demonstration against the South African government's *apartheid* policy, that the police had refused to destroy the photographs or hand them over to her, and that this conduct constituted an infringement of her rights under *EHR* 5. See also *35 East African Asians* v. *United Kingdom* (4626/70) DR 13, 5; *3 East African Asians* v. *United Kingdom* (4715/70; 4783/71; 4827/71) DR 13, 17; *X and Y* v. *United Kingdom* (5302/71) CD 44, 29; *Agee* v. *United Kingdom* (7729/76) DR 7, 164. The (equally authentic) French text of *EHR* 5 specifies '*sécurité*' without any limitation to 'of person', so leaving it open whether liberty and security are to be treated as distinct.

[8] See its Annual Reports, *passim*.

[9] Case 2509 (Panama) AR 1979/80, 63.

[10] Cases 1702, 1748, and 1755 (Guatemala) AR 1975, 67.

[11] '[No person shall] be deprived of life, liberty or property, without due process of law': Fifth Amendment to the US Constitution.

[12] 'No person shall be deprived of his life or personal liberty except according to procedure established by law': Article 21, Constitution of India.

[13] See, for USA, *Allgeyer* v. *Louisiana* 165 US 578; *Williams* v. *Fears* 179 US 270; *Booth* v. *Illinois* 184 US 425; *Meyer* v. *Nebraska* 262 US 390; *Board of Regents* v. *Roth* 408 US 564; and for India, *Maneka Gandhi* v. *Union of India and another* [1978] SCR 312; *Cooper* v. *Union of India* [1971] 1 SCR 512, overruling on this point *Gopalan* v. *State of Madras* [1950] SCR 88; *Kharak Singh* v. *State of Uttar Pradesh et al.* [1964] 1 SCR 332.

[14] *Supra.*

[15] *Supra.*

the right of an individual to be free from restrictions or encroachments on his person, whether they are directly imposed or indirectly brought about by calculated measures.[16] In *Maneka Gandhi* v. *Union of India and another*,[17] the same Court held that the expression 'personal liberty' is of the widest amplitude and includes within its ambit the right to travel abroad.

Although the US Supreme Court has never attempted to define the term 'liberty' with exactness, it has, in a series of judgments, extended its meaning to include a wide variety of interests. These include the right to a fair trial,[18] freedom to worship,[19] freedom of speech,[20] freedom of association,[21] liberty of thought,[22] the right to privacy,[23] freedom to contract,[24] liberty to pursue any livelihood or lawful vocation,[25] the right to work for a living in the common occupations of the community,[26] the right to acquire useful knowledge,[27] liberty of parents and guardians to direct the upbringing and education of children under their control,[28] freedom of personal choice in matters of marriage and family life,[29] the right to live and work where one wills,[30] the right to move from one place to another,[31] and the right to travel abroad.[32]

Similarly, the Supreme Court of India has held that even lawful imprisonment does not spell farewell to all fundamental rights. A prisoner retains all the rights

[16] Per Subha Rao, J in a minority opinion which, in view of *Maneka Ghandi* v. *Union of India and another, supra,* may now be considered to be the authorative view.

[17] *Supra.* See also *Satwant Singh Sawhney* v. *Ramarathnam et al.* [1967] 3 SCR 525.

[18] *Estelle* v. *Williams* 425 US 501.

[19] *Meyer* v. *Nebraska, supra,* n. 13; *Cantwell* v. *Connecticut* 310 US 296; *Gibson* v. *Florida Legislative Investigation Committee* 372 US 539; *School District of Abington Township* v. *Schempp* 374 US 203; *Board of Regents* v. *Roth, supra,* n. 13.

[20] *Gitlow* v. *New York* 268 US 652; *Stromberg* v. *California* 283 US 359; *Near* v. *Minnesota* 283 US 697; *Lovell* v. *Griffin* 303 US 444; *Taylor* v. *Mississippi* 319 US 583; *Joseph Bursteyn, Inc.* v. *Wilson* 343 US 495; *Staub* v. *Baxley* 355 US 313; *NAACP* v. *Alabama* 357 US 449; *Smith* v. *California* 361 US 147.

[21] *New York ex rel. Bryant* v. *Zimmerman* 278 US 63; *Gibson* v. *Florida Legislative Investigation Committee, supra.*

[22] *Hughes* v. *Superior Court of Californa* 339 US 460.

[23] *Roe* v. *Wade* 410 US 113; *Paris Adult Theatre I* v. *Slaton* 413 US 49; *Wolf* v. *Colorado* 383 US 25.

[24] *Patterson* v. *Bark Eudora* 190 US 169; *Allgeyer* v. *Louisiana, supra,* n. 13; *Addyston Pipe & Steel Co.* v. *United States* 175 US 211; *Williams* v. *Fears, supra,* n. 13; *Booth* v. *Illinois, supra,* n. 13; *Northwestern Nat. Life Ins. Co.* v. *Riggs* 203 US 243; *Muller* v. *Oregon* 208 US 412; *Chicago B & Q.R. Co.* v. *McGuire* 219 US 549; *Hall* v. *Geiger-Jones Co.* 242 US 539; *New York Life Ins. Co.* v. *Dodge* 246 US 357; *Adkins* v. *Children's Hospital of Dist. of Columbia* 261 US 525; *Meyer* v. *Nebraska, supra,* n. 13; *Highland* v. *Russell Car & Snow Plow Co.* 279 US 253; *Hardware Dealers Mut. Fire Ins. Co.* v. *Glidden Co.* 284 US 151; *Advance-Rumely Thresher Co.* v. *Jackson* 287 US 283; *Bayside Fish Flour Co.* v. *Gentry* 297 US 422; *Board of Regents* v. *Roth, supra,* n. 13.

[25] *Allgeyer* v. *Louisiana, supra,* n. 13; *Addyston Pipe & Steel Co.* v. *United States, supra,* n. 24; *Williams* v. *Fears, supra,* n. 24; *Booth* v. *Illinois, supra,* n. 13; *Northwestern Nat. Life Ins. Co.* v. *Riggs, supra,* n. 24; *Meyer* v. *Nebraska, supra,* n. 13; *Board of Regents* v. *Roth, supra,* n. 13; *Greene* v. *McElroy* 360 US 474; *United States* v. *Robel* 389 US 258.

[26] *Traux* v. *Raich* 239 US 33; *Re Griffiths* 413 US 717.

[27] *Meyer* v. *Nebraska, supra,* n. 13; *Board of Regents* v. *Roth, supra,* n. 13; *Bolling* v. *Sharpe* 347 US 497.

[28] *Pierce* v. *Society of Sisters* 268 US 510.

[29] *Meyer* v. *Nebraska, supra.* n. 13. *Loving* v. *Virgina* 388 US 1; *Board of Regents* v. *Roth, supra,* n. 13; *Cleveland Board of Education* v. *La Fleur* 414 US 632.

[30] *Allgeyer* v. *Louisiana, supra,* n. 13; *Williams* v. *Fears, supra,* n. 24.

[31] *Booth* v. *Illinois, supra,* n. 13; *Jacobson* v. *Massachusetts* 197 US 11.

[32] *Kent* v. *Dulles* 357 US 116; *Aptheker* v. *Secretary of State* 378 US 500; *Zemel* v. *Rusk* 381 US 1; *United States* v. *Laub et al.* 385 US 475.

enjoyed by a free citizen except only those 'necessarily' lost as an incident of imprisonment.[33]

Both in the USA and in India, the Supreme Courts have held that the fact that some of these rights may have been separately entrenched in a Bill of Rights or in a Constitution will not detract from the wide meaning to be attributed to the concept of 'liberty'.[34]

'Deprived of his liberty'

In order to determine whether a person has been deprived of his liberty, account must be taken of a whole range of criteria such as the type, duration, effects, and manner of implementation of the measure in question.[35] In *Guzzardi* v. *Italy*,[36] EUCM and EUCT both examined the question whether the compulsory residence of the applicant on an island involved a deprivation of his liberty. The Commission attached particular significance to the small size of the area where he was confined, the almost permanent supervision to which he was subject, the all but complete impossibility for him to make social contacts, and the length of his enforced stay on the island, and concluded that he had suffered a deprivation of his liberty. The Court, while emphasizing that it was not possible to speak of 'deprivation of liberty' on the strength of any one of these features taken individually,[37] agreed that taken cumulatively and in combination it was. In *Kharak Singh* v. *State of Uttar Pradesh*[38] the Supreme Court of India held that domiciliary visits at night by police officers, as a form of surveillance, constituted a deprivation of liberty.

A disciplinary penalty or measure which would unquestionably be deemed a deprivation of liberty were it to be applied to a civilian may not possess this characteristic when imposed upon a serviceman. Nevertheless, such penalty or measure may conflict with the right to liberty when it takes the form of restrictions that clearly deviate from the normal conditions of life within the armed forces.[39] Accordingly, 'strict arrest' which entailed solitary confinement in a cell during the entire period of the punishment, and 'service in a disciplinary unit' for periods of three to six months during which the persons concerned were not permitted to leave the establishment, and spent the nights in solitary confinement, were both regarded by EUCT as deprivations of liberty.[40] However, since the normal conditions of life in prison — contrary to the normal conditions of military life — do constitute deprivation of liberty regardless of the freedom of action which a prisoner may enjoy within the prison, disciplinary measures applied to a prisoner, such as isolation and suppression of leave, will not be considered as constituting deprivations of liberty because such measures are only modifications of the conditions of lawful detention.[41]

The difference between deprivation of, and restriction upon, liberty is merely

---

[33] *Sobraj* v. *Superintendent, Central Jail, Tihar* AIR [1978] SC 1514.

[34] *Paul* v. *Davies* 424 US 693; *Maneka Ghandi* v. *Union of India and another, supra,* n. 13.

[35] *Guzzardi* v. *Italy* (7367/76) Report: 7 December 1978; Judgment: 3 EHRR 333.

[36] *Supra.*

[37] The Commission was also of the view that the mere fact of having to reside within the limits of a specified area did not in itself necessarily amount to a deprivation of liberty.

[38] [1964] 1 SCR 332.

[39] *Engel et al.* v. *Netherlands* (5100/71, etc.) Judgment: 1 EHRR 647. See also *Eggs* v. *Switzerland* (7341/76) Report: DR 15, 35.

[40] *Ibid.*

[41] *X* v. *Switzerland* (7754/77) DR 11, 216.

one of degree or intensity, and not one of nature or substance.[42] The compulsory taking of a blood sample is a deprivation of liberty, however short.[43]

'Grounds established by law'

HRC has expressed the view that the forcible abduction of a person from one State to another by the agents of that other State constitutes an 'arbitrary arrest and detention' within the meaning of *ICPR* 9(1).[44]

Only *EHR* specifically, and restrictively, enumerates the grounds on which a person may lawfully be deprived of his liberty, and many cases have been decided about these grounds by the Strasbourg institutions. They are taken here in the order in which they appear in *EHR* 5(1). The word 'lawful' appears in all of them: as to this, EUCM has said that the arrest or detention must conform with the provisions of the applicable domestic law,[45] and EUCT has added that 'no detention that is arbitrary can ever be regarded as "lawful"'.[46]

(a) *The lawful detention of a person after conviction by a competent court.* There cannot be a 'conviction' unless it has been established in accordance with the law that there has been an offence — either criminal or, if appropriate, disciplinary.[47] Moreover, since 'conviction' implies a finding of guilt, detention as a preventive security measure would fall outside the scope of this provision.[48] What is required is that the actual detention should be preceded by a decision on the validity of charges or complaints, taken by a competent court in conformity with national legislation. However, *EHR* 5(1)(*a*) applies to all sentences imposing deprivation of liberty imposed by a competent court, whatever the legal nature of the offence, and however the domestic law classifies the deprivation, provided that it constitutes a sanction imposed by the court for a type of behaviour, or a situation, which infringes the law and threatens public order. It can therefore extend to certain security, preventive or social protection measures applied to recidivists or habitual offenders in addition, or as an alternative, to the main sentence of imprisonment, including detention in a special institution or work camp.[49]

The concept 'court' applies to an organ which can be said, because of the way it is organized, to have a judicial character in that it is independent of the Executive and of the parties to the case; it must also offer adequate procedural guarantees.[50] The appointment procedure cannot itself affect the independence of a judge. To be independent, a judge does not necessarily have to be appointed for life. Nor need he be irremovable in law, in the sense that he cannot be transferred to a new post without his consent. The essential features are that he should enjoy a certain degree of stability, albeit only for a specified period; that he is not subject to any authority in the exercise of his duties as a judge;

---

[42] *Guzzardi* v. *Italy, supra,* n. 35. See also *Engel et al.* v. *Netherlands* (5100/71, etc.) Report: 19 July 1974.

[43] *X* v. *Austria* (8278/78) DR 18, 154.

[44] *Burgos* v. *Uruguay* (R. 12/52) HRC 36, 176; *de Casariego* v. *Uruguay* (R. 13/56) HRC 36, 185.

[45] *Caprino* v. *United Kingdom* (6871/75) DR 12, 14.

[46] *Winterwerp* v. *Netherlands* (6301/73) Judgment: 2 EHRR 387; *X* v. *United Kingdom* (6998/75) Judgment: 5 November 1981.

[47] *Engel et al.* v. *Netherlands,* Judgment, *supra,* n. 39. See also *Eggs* v. *Switzerland, supra,* n. 39.

[48] *Guzzardi* v. *Italy, supra,* n. 35.

[49] *Van Droogenbroek* v. *Belgium* (7906/77) Report: 9 July 1980 (referred to EUCT).

[50] *Eggs* v. *Switzerland, supra,* n. 39.

and that all his duties guarantee an impartial attitude on his part.[51] Accordingly, while a Supreme Military Court may constitute a court from the organisational point of view,[52] a chief military prosecutor would not.[53]

Where a convicted person was first lawfully detained and then conditionally released and, several years later, returned to a detention centre by order of an administrative authority, EUCM considered that the detention was lawful since it was a continuation of the original detention ordered by a competent court, even though reactivated by new acts: the means of execution of a detention ordered by such a court may be left to the decision of an administrative authority.[54] But the renewed deprivation of liberty may be subject to renewed judicial control under *EHR* 5(4): see below.

EHR 5(1)(*a*) does not require a 'lawful' conviction, but only speaks of 'lawful' detention. A court's decision setting aside a conviction does not therefore retroactively affect the lawfulness of the detention which followed that conviction.[55] Where national law provides that the execution of a sentence may begin only after the conviction has become *res judicata*, i.e. after the dismissal of any appeal that may be brought, it is not clear whether the detention served while an appeal is pending can be considered as detention following conviction within the meaning of *EHR* 5(1)(*a*). EUCT appears to take the view that it can,[56] EUCM that it cannot.[57]

(*b*) *The lawful arrest or detention of a person for non-compliance with the lawful order of a court or in order to secure the fulfilment of any obligation prescribed by law.* The words 'secure the fulfilment of any obligation prescribed by law' concern only cases where the law permits the detention of a person to compel him to fulfil a specific and concrete obligation which he has until then failed to satisfy. A wider interpretation would entail consequences incompatible with the notion of the Rule of Law. It would justify, for example, administrative internment meant to compel a citizen to discharge, in relation to any point whatever, his general duty of obedience to the law.[58] Accordingly, the obligation to maintain discipline in the army would be outside the scope of this provision.[59] So would arrest or detention for the prevention of offences against the public peace and public order, or against the security of the state.[60]

(*c*) *The lawful arrest or detention of a person effected for the purpose of bringing him before the competent legal authority on reasonable suspicion of having committed an offence or when it is reasonably considered necessary to prevent his committing an offence or fleeing after having done so.* In *Lawless v. Ireland*,[61]

---

[51] *Ibid.*
[52] *Engel et al.* v. *Netherlands*, Judgment, *supra*, n. 39.
[53] *Eggs* v. *Switzerland*, *supra*, n. 39.
[54] *Christinet* v. *Switzerland* (7648/76) Report: DR 17, 35; cf. *Van Droogenbroek* v. *Belgium*, *supra*, n. 49; see also *X* v. *Austria* (2742/66) CD 19, 95; *X* v. *Austria* (7034/75) DR 10, 146.
[55] *Krzycki* v. *Federal Republic of Germany* (7629/76) Report: DR 13, 57.
[56] *Wemhoff* v. *Federal Republic of Germany* (2122/64) Judgment: 1 EHRR 55.
[57] *X* v. *Federal Republic of Germany* (3911/69) CD 30, 76.
[58] *Engel et al.* v. *Netherlands*, Judgment, *supra*, n. 39.
[59] *Ibid.* See also *Eggs* v. *Switzerland*, *supra*, n. 39.
[60] *Lawless* v. *Ireland* (332/57) Report: 19 December 1959. See also Judgment: 1 EHRR 15.
[61] *Ibid.*

EUCT considered the question whether the expression 'effected for the purpose of bringing him before the competent legal authority' qualifies only the words 'on reasonable suspicion of having committed an offence', or also the words 'when it is reasonably considered necessary to prevent his committing an offence'. It held that the expression qualifies every category of arrest or detention there referred to. Accordingly, deprivation of liberty is permitted by this provision only when it is effected for the purpose of bringing the person arrested or detained before the competent legal authority, irrespective of whether he is a person who is reasonably suspected of having committed an offence, or a person whom it is reasonably considered necessary to restrain from committing an offence, or from absconding after having committed one. Under *EHR* 5(3), everyone arrested or detained in any of these circumstances must in any event be brought before a judge, for the purpose either of examining the question of deprivation of liberty, or of deciding on the merits.

The Greek Council of State has held that *EHR* 5 does not permit the deprivation of liberty entailed by the removal from a specific locality of persons suspected of having committed acts endangering public order, or public peace and safety.[62]

EHR 5(1)(*c*) does not stipulate that an arrest can only be effected on the authority of a warrant issued by a judge. Read with *EHR* 5(3), it merely requires that the person arrested or detained should be brought promptly before a judge.[63] Nor is it necessary in order to justify arrest or detention that the reality and nature of the offences alleged should be definitely proved, since that is the purpose of the process of investigation, and detention is designed to allow this process to continue unhindered.[64] Where a person is arrested on the ground of the existence of 'reasonable suspicion' that he 'has committed an offence', the persistence of such a suspicion is a necessary condition for the validity of his continued detention,[65] but ceases to become a sufficient condition after a certain lapse of time.[66]

The Supreme Court of Nova Scotia has held that a person stopped by a police officer for a 'spot check' while driving on a highway, and required to 'accompany' the officer in order to take a breathalyser test, has been 'detained' within the meaning of the Canadian Bill of Rights.[67]

The phrase 'reasonably considered necessary to prevent his committing an offence' does not contemplate a policy of general prevention directed against an individual, or a category of individuals, who present a danger because of their continuing propensity to crime. It does no more than afford the State a means of preventing a concrete and specific offence.[68]

A person's high degree of mobility, the fact that he had no fixed abode, and his flight to another country after having committed an offence, have been considered sufficient grounds by EUCM to justify his detention on the basis that it was reasonably necessary to do so in order to prevent him from fleeing before he was brought to trial.[69] EUCT has said that the danger of absconding

---

[62] Decision of 5 December 1960, No. 35/1961.

[63] *X* v. *Austria* (7755/77) DR 9, 210.

[64] *Bonnechaux* v. *Switzerland* (8224/78) Report: 3 EHRR 259; *Schertenleib* v. *Switzerland* (8329/78) DR 17, 180.

[65] *Stögmüller* v. *Austria* (1602/62) Judgment: 1 EHRR 155.

[66] *Schertenleib* v. *Switzerland, supra.*

[67] *R* v. *MacDonald* (175) 22 CCC (2nd) 350.

[68] *Guzzardi* v. *Italy, supra,* n. 35.

[69] *X* v. *Federal Republic of Germany* (7680/76) DR 9, 190.

must be assessed on the basis of a number of considerations. Factors such as the character of the person concerned, his morals, his home, his occupation, his assets, his family ties, and all kinds of links with the country in which he is being prosecuted, may either confirm the existence of a danger of flight or make it appear so small that it cannot justify detention pending trial.[70] In order for a danger of absconding to exist, there must be a whole set of circumstances, particularly the heavy sentence to be expected, or the accused's particular distaste of detention, or the lack of well-established ties in the country, which give reason to suppose that the consequences and hazards of flight will seem to him to be a lesser evil than continued imprisonment.[71]

(d) *The detention of a minor by lawful order for the purpose of educational supervision or his lawful detention for the purpose of bringing him before the competent legal authority;*[72] *and*

(e) *The lawful detention of persons for the prevention of the spreading of infectious diseases, of persons of unsound mind, alcoholics or drug addicts, or vagrants.* Deprivation of liberty in accordance with these provisions must fulfil three conditions: it must result from a procedure prescribed by law, be based on a legal provision, and satisfy the relevant material criteria cited therein. So, where a code of criminal procedure so provides, a juvenile who has been arrested in connexion with thefts and traffic offences, and who has failed to benefit from previous educative measures, may be detained in an observation centre on the orders of the competent legal authorities (the public prosecutor and the president of the court) in order that the authorities may obtain a better understanding of his personality. The fact that the detention lasted for eight months before the required medical and psychological reports were made was not of itself enough to cast doubt on the purpose of the detention, or its conformity with *EHR* 5(1)(d).[73]

In *Winterwerp* v. *Netherlands*[74] EUCT specified three minimum conditions before there could be a 'lawful detention of a person of unsound mind': except in emergency cases, a true mental disorder must be reliably established before a competent authority on the basis of objective medical expertise; the mental disorder must be of a kind or degree warranting compulsory medical confinement; and the validity of continued confinement must depend on the persistence of such a disorder. However, in *X* v. *United Kingdom*[75] EUCT explained that the 'objective medical expertise' need not in all conceivable cases be obtained before, rather than after, the confinement of the person concerned: where an emergency required the immediate confinement of a person capable of presenting a danger to others, it would be impracticable to require a thorough medical examination before arrest or detention.

---

[70] *Neumeister* v. *Austria* (1936/63) Judgment: 1 EHRR 91.

[71] *Stögmüller* v. *Austria, supra,* n. 65.

[72] Jacobs mentions several instances of the application of this provision under English law. He points out that there is no requirement that the order should be that of a court. However, the person subject to the order will be entitled under *EHR* 5(4) to take proceedings by which the lawfulness of his detention can be decided speedily by a court, and his release ordered if the detention is not lawful. *The European Convention on Human Rights,* 54.

[73] *X* v. *Switzerland* (8500/79) DR 18, 238.

[74] (6301/73) Judgment: 2 EHRR 387; see also *X* v. *United Kingdom* (6998/75) Report: 16 July 1980.

[75] (6998/75) Judgment: 5 November 1981. See also *Luberti* v. *Italy* (9019/80) Decision: 7 July 1981; *Barclay-Maguire* v. *United Kingdom* (9117/80) Decision: 17 December 1981.

In *De Wilde, Ooms and Versyp* v. *Belgium*,[76] EUCT considered that the definition of the term 'vagrant' in Article 347 of the Belgian Criminal Code ('Vagrants are persons who have no fixed abode, no means of subsistence and no regular trade or profession') corresponded closely to the ordinary meaning of that term. But in *Guzzardi* v. *Italy*,[77] it declined to extend the meaning to include 'a person whose character is socially dangerous and whose manner of life causes alarm', observing that this provision was intended to permit the deprivation of liberty of socially maladjusted persons not only because they might be considered as occasionally dangerous to public safety, but also because their own interests might necessitate their detention.

(f) The lawful arrest or detention of a person to prevent his effecting an unauthorized entry into the country or of a person against whom action is being taken with a view to deportation or extradition. 'Lawful' in this context, as in the other sub-paragraphs of *EHR* 5(1), means that the arrest or detention must be lawful under the applicable domestic law,[78] but the lawfulness of the deportation order itself is not a prerequisite for conformity with *EHR* 5(1)(*f*).[79]

The question whether the detention is *necessary* to secure deportation must be examined separately from the *lawfulness* of the detention. Although *EHR* 5(1)(*f*) does not expressly refer to necessity, it is implied in the character of this provision as an exception clause that it must be strictly interpreted, and that no criteria other than those mentioned in it may be the basis of any restriction of the right to liberty and security of person. Accordingly, the detention of a proposed deportee can only be justified under this provision if it is related to the deportation proceedings and is for no other purpose. It may, for example, not be used as a substitute for detention pending trial, or for any other form of detention which would have been open to the authorities but which they have chosen not to use.[80] On the other hand, the language used in *EHR* 5(1)(*f*) does not make it a condition for the detention of a proposed deportee that a deportation order be already in force against him. It suffices that 'action is being taken [against him] with a view to deportation' or, according to the French text, that '*une procédure d'expulsion . . . est en cours*'. This can only mean that the eventual outcome of the deportation proceedings is irrelevant for the justification of the detention, provided that a lawful deportation procedure has been instituted and is being seriously pursued.[81]

Detention for the purpose of deportation may not be prolonged indefinitely: indeterminate detention cannot be considered a provisional measure for the purpose of ensuring that deportation takes place.[82]

'Procedure prescribed (or established) by law'

In *Winterwerp* v. *Netherlands*,[83] EUCT said that the words 'in accordance with a procedure prescribed by law' essentially referred back to domestic law. They state the need for compliance with the relevant procedure under that law. However, the domestic law must itself be in conformity with the provisions of *EHR*,

---

[76] (2832/66; 2835/66; 2899/66) Judgment: 1 EHRR 373.
[77] *Supra*, n. 35.
[78] *Caprino* v. *United Kingdom* (6871/75) DR 12, 14.
[79] *Ibid*., Report: 17 July 1980.
[80] *Ibid*., DR 12, 14.
[81] *Ibid*.
[82] Decision of 10 March 1965, AG Köln (5. XIV 691 B).
[83] *de Bouton* v. *Uruguay* (R. 9/37) HRC 36, 143.

including the general principles expressed or implied therein. The notion under-lying the term in question is one of fair and proper procedure. (Although the English text has '*a* procedure prescribed by law', the French text speaks of '*les voies légales*'.)

HRC has expressed the view that *ICPR* 9(1) was violated where persons continued to be detained for a month,[84] six weeks,[85] several months,[86] and in another case nearly a year,[87] after a judge had ordered their conditional release; likewise, where a person was not released until five months after his sentence had been fully served.[88]

Neither HRC nor IACM has yet had occasion to consider the import of the word 'established' in this context. However, in 1959 the Indian Supreme Court held, in *Gopalan* v. *State of Madras*,[89] that 'procedure established by law' does not mean any procedure which may be prescribed by a competent legislature, but the ordinary well-established criminal procedure sanctioned by the Criminal Procedure Code. At that time, the Court would not go so far as to hold that 'procedure established by law' must include what a minority opinion described as:

the four principles of elementary justice which inhere in and are at the root of all civilised systems of law, and which have been stated by the American Courts and jurists as consisting of (1) notice, (2) opportunity to be heard, (3) impartial tribunal and (4) orderly course of procedure. These four principles are really different aspects of the same right, namely the right to be heard before one is condemned. Hence, the words 'procedure established by law', whatever its exact meaning may be, must necessarily include the principle that no person shall be condemned without hearing by an impartial tribunal.[90]

But nearly thirty years later, the same Court held that a procedure which deals with the modalities of regulating, restricting, or even rejecting a funda-mental right has to be fair, not foolish; carefully designed to effectuate, not to subvert, the substantive right itself. Thus understood, 'procedure' must rule out anything arbitrary, freakish, or bizarre. This quality of fairness in the process is emphasized by the strong word 'established' which means 'settled firmly', not wantonly or whimsically. Accordingly, the Court held that a procedure pre-scribed by law for impounding a passport would be right, fair, and just, and would not suffer from the vice of arbitrariness or unreasonableness, only if the *audi alterem partem* rule was held to be incorporated in the relevant law by necessary implication.[91]

The right to be informed of the reasons for arrest, and of any charges

The purpose of this requirement is to inform the detained person adequately of the reasons for his arrest, so that he may judge the lawfulness of the measure and take steps to challenge it if he sees fit.[92] The Supreme Court of Ceylon has said that liberty is a sacred right, and the least that a police officer who

---

[84] *Ramirez* v. *Uruguay* (R. 1/4) HRC 35, 121.
[85] *Carballal* v. *Uruguay* (R. 8/33) HRC 36, 125.
[86] *Ambrosini* v. *Uruguay* (R. 1/5) HRC 34, 124.
[87] *Perdomo and de Lanza* v. *Uruguay* (R. 2/8) HRC 35, 111.
[88] (6301/73) Judgment: 2 EHRR 387.
[89] [1950] SCR 88.
[90] *Ibid.*, per Fazil Ali, J.
[91] *Maneka Gandhi* v. *Union of India and another* [1978] SCR 312.
[92] On that ground, EUCT has said that this requirement would follow in any event from *EHR* 5(4): *X* v. *United Kingdom* (6998/75) Judgment: 5 November 1981.

interferes with it can do is to inform the person concerned of the reasons for his arrest.[93] If he arrests a man without a warrant on a mere 'unexpressed suspicion' that a particular cognizable offence has been committed, he will be guilty of assault and wrongful confinement unless the circumstances are such that the man must know the general nature of the offence for which he is being detained, or himself produces a situation which makes it impossible in practice to inform him.[94]

EUCM has said that this information is not required to be given in writing.[95] Nor is it required to be conveyed in any special form.[96] An oral statement by the examining magistrate to the person arrested saying that 'You are accused of corruption' would suffice.[97] Nor is it necessary that a complete description of all the charges should be given to the accused person at the moment of his arrest.[98] Information in general terms of the reasons for the arrest and of the charges against him may suffice.[99] The required information may be conveyed by reading out the warrant of arrest.[100] In *Neumeister* v. *Austria*,[101] EUCM found that, prior to his arrest, the applicant had been interrogated in detail by the investigating judge on several days and had also been confronted with another suspect. In the circumstances, the Commission observed that the applicant must have been fully aware of the reasons for his arrest and the nature of the charges against him.

The right to be informed of the reasons for arrest arises on the initial arrest. Thus, there is no duty to keep the detainee constantly informed. However, EUCM has said that if the grounds for detention change, or if new relevant facts arise concerning the detention, the detainee has a right to this further information because new reasons may call for a modified or new defence. Therefore, if a person is rearrested after a significant period of conditional release, the new arrest must be motivated in accordance with this provision.[102]

In the application of this requirement to mental health patients, EUCM has said that the amount of detail and type of information to be disclosed to the detainee would depend on the circumstances of the particular case. However, if the patient is incapable of receiving proper information, the relevant details must be given to those persons who represent his interests, such as a

---

[93] *The Queen* v. *Guanaseeha Thero et al.* 73 NLR 154.

[94] *Corea* v. *The Queen* 55 NLR 457.

[95] *X* v. *Netherlands* (1211/61) CD 9, 46. But where the Constitution requires it to be given in writing, it must be given with sufficient particularity to enable the person detained to know what is alleged against him, and to make adequate representations: *In the matter of Simon Kapepwe* [1972] ZR 248 (Court of Appeal, Zambia); *Herbert* v. *Phillips and Sealey* (1967) 10 WIR 435 (Court of Appeal, West Indian Associated States). Cf. *Bhawarlal Garashmalji* v. *State of Tamil Nadu* AIR [1979] SC 541 (Supreme Court of India).

[96] *X* v. *Netherlands* (2621/65) CD 19, 100.

[97] *X* v. *Belgium* (1103/61) CD 8, 113. See also Decision of 22 October 1975, OLG Bayern (NJW 1976, Heft 115, 483); Decision of 14 December 1976, OLG Bayern (Bay. VB 1977, Heft 1, 24). The Privy Council has held that the failure of a judge to inform the appellant of the nature of the contempt charged before committing him to prison constituted a deprivation of liberty without due process of law: *Maharaj* v. *Attorney-General of Trinidad and Tobago (No. 2)* [1978] 2 All ER 670.

[98] *X* v. *United Kingdom* (4220/69) CD 37, 51. Under English law, an arrest will not be lawful if the suspect is not told at the time that he is suspected of a specific offence for which he can lawfully be arrested: *Christie* v. *Leachinsky* [1945] 2 All ER 395.

[99] *Nielsen* v. *Denmark* (343/57) YB 2, 412.

[100] *X* v. *Federal Republic of Germany* (1216/61) CD 11, 1.

[101] (1936/63) YB 7, 224.

[102] *X* v. *United Kingdom* (6998/75) Report: 16 July 1980. See also Judgment: 5 November 1981.

lawyer or guardian. The responsibility of informing the patient or his representative would usually fall on the medical officers concerned, and this obligation should be discharged promptly, that is at the latest on arrival at the hospital.[103]

EHR 5(2) specifically requires this information to be conveyed to the person arrested in a language which he understands. In *Delcourt* v. *Belgium*,[104] EUCM found that the requirement had been complied with where, although the warrant of arrest had been drawn up in Flemish, the applicant had been interrogated by the examining judge in French, which was a language he understood.[105]

HRC has expressed the view that *ICPR* 9(2) is violated where a person is not charged until nine months after his arrest.[106]

Judicial control of arrest and detention

1. The right to be brought promptly before a judge or a judicial officer. The phrase 'officer authorised by law to exercise judicial power' has three components. The second ('authorised by law to exercise') does not give rise to any difficulty. The first ('officer') and third ('judicial power') have to be considered together. In providing that an arrested person shall be brought promptly before a 'judge' or 'other officer', the State has been left a choice between two categories of authority. It is implicit in such a choice that these categories are not identical. However, the fact that they are mentioned in the same phrase presupposes that they fulfil similar functions. The existence of a certain analogy between 'judge' and 'officer' is thus clearly recognized. On the other hand, the exercise of 'judicial power' is not necessarily confined to adjudicating on legal disputes. In many States, officers ('*magistrats*') and even judges exercise such power without adjudicating; for example, members of the prosecuting authorities and investigating judges.[107]

In *Schiesser* v. *Switzerland*,[108] EUCT considered that while the 'officer' is not identical with the 'judge', he must nevertheless have some of the latter's attributes, that is to say he must satisfy certain conditions each of which constitutes a guarantee for the person arrested. The first is independence of the Executive (notably, of the prosecutor) and of the parties. This does not mean that the 'officer' may not be to some extent subordinate to other judges or officers, provided that they themselves enjoy a similar independence. The second is the obligation of himself hearing the individual brought before him. The third is the obligation of reviewing the circumstances militating for and against detention: of deciding, by reference to legal criteria, whether there are reasons to justify detention, and of ordering release if there are not. Applying these criteria, the Court held in that case that the District Attorney in Zurich was a '*magistrat habilité par la loi à exercer des fonctions judiciaires*'.[109]

The requirement that the person detained should be brought promptly before

---

[103] *Ibid.*

[104] (2689/65) CD 22, 48.

[105] See also Decision of 11 October 1972, Corte Suprema di Cassazione, Italy (No. 6588), where it was held that the information must be given in a language which the accused understands, but not necessarily that of the ethnic group to which he belongs.

[106] *de Massera* v. *Uruguay* (R. 1/5) HRC 34, 124; see also *Carballal* v. *Uruguay* (R. 8/33) HRC 36, 125; *Pietraroia* v. *Uruguay* (R. 10/44) HRC 36, 153.

[107] *Schiesser* v. *Switzerland* (7710/76) Judgment: 2 EHRR 417; see also Report: 9 March 1978.

[108] *Supra.*

[109] See also Decision of 14 July 1976, BGer, Switzerland (PE 2/76 he); Decision of 3 November 1976, BGer, Switzerland (see YB 20, 801).

a judge or other officer exercising judicial functions is concerned only with the suspect's first examination after arrest or detention, and not with the criminal preliminary enquiry proper. This appearance must also be clearly distinguished from proceedings to decide the *lawfulness* of his detention as prescribed by *EHR* 5(4). The object of this first examination is to give the arrested person an opportunity of exculpating himself as soon as possible. In the circumstances, the Federal Court of Switzerland has held that the suspect should be brought before the authority in person, and that the latter should not be content with merely written proceedings.[110]

As to 'promptness', HRC has expressed the view that *ICPR* 9(3) is violated where a person is only brought before a judge a month after his arrest, during which time he has been held incommunicado and has had no access to any lawyer.[111]

2. The right to trial within a reasonable time if not released. EHR 5 is concerned only with the rights of detained persons. Accordingly, it ceases to apply once a person is provisionally released. After that, a State Party's obligation to bring him to trial 'within a reasonable time' ceases under *EHR* 5, though it continues under *EHR* 6 (see §22.4).[112]

The word 'trial' in this context refers not just to the commencement of proceedings before a court, but to the whole of those proceedings. The words 'entitled to trial' are not necessarily to be equated with 'entitled to be brought to trial'. Therefore the period of detention which begins with a person's arrest ends, for this purpose, on the date on which he is convicted or acquitted at first instance.[113] But where the domestic law prescribes a specific period within which the trial of a detained person must begin, he is entitled to be released on bail if he has not been brought to trial before that period has expired. 'The liberty of the subject is not a slogan' . . . but is a valuable right of a citizen, and the courts must be vigilant in ensuring that it is not unprofitably thwarted.'[114]

EUCM has said that the term 'reasonable time', in this context, must be determined in the light of the concrete facts of each case. In a number of cases,[115] it has listed and discussed various elements as being relevant to the evaluation of the circumstances in a given case. The Commission at first took the view that, in any particular case, the conclusion would depend upon an evaluation of all these elements. Some of them might point to the conclusion that the length of detention was within reasonable limits, whereas other elements might indicate the contrary. The conclusion would then depend on their relative importance. This did not exclude the possibility that, in some cases, one single element could be

---

[110] Decision of 3 November 1976, *supra*.

[111] *Motta* v. *Uruguay* (R. 2/11) HRC 35, 132; *a fortiori* where the period is even longer: see *Carballal* (4 months), *Touròn* (6 months), *de Bouton* (6 months), *Weinberger* (10 months), all v. *Uruguay* in HRC 36.

[112] *X* v. *United Kingdom* (8233/78) Report: 3 EHRR 271.

[113] *Wemhoff* v. *Federal Republic of Germany* (2122/64) Judgment: 1 EHRR 55. This interpretation is supported by the French text, which has '*pendant la procédure*'. But see, *per contra*, *X* v. *Federal Republic of Germany* (3911/69) CD 30, 76.

[114] *Premasiri* v. *Attorney-General* 70 NLR 193, per T. S. Fernando, ACJ at 199 (Supreme Court of Ceylon).

[115] *Wemhoff* v. *Federal Republic of Germany* (2122/64) Report: 1 April 1966; *Neumeister* v. *Austria* (1936/63) Report: 27 May 1966; *Stögmüller* v. *Austria* (1602/62) Report: 9 February 1967; *Matznetter* v. *Austria* (2178/64) Report: 4 April 1967; *Ringeisen* v. *Austria* (2614/65) YB 15, 678.

of decisive importance, even though other elements might indicate a different conclusion.

However, EUCT has felt unable to adopt this method. It has pointed out that national judicial authorities do not simply have a choice between two obligations, namely that of conducting the proceedings until judgment within a reasonable time, or that of releasing the accused pending trial, if necessary against certain guarantees. On the contrary, national courts are required to determine, in the light of the fact of the detention of the person being prosecuted, whether the time that has elapsed, for whatever reason, before judgment is passed has at some stage exceeded a reasonable limit — that is to say, whether it has imposed a greater sacrifice than could, in the circumstances, reasonably be expected of a person presumed to be innocent. In other words, it is the provisional detention of the accused person which must not be prolonged beyond a reasonable time.[116] Accordingly, in the view of the Court, there are two principal questions which must be examined when deciding upon the reasonableness of any period of detention on remand. First, the Commission must determine whether the reasons given by the national authorities to justify continued detention are relevant and sufficient to show that the detention was not unreasonably prolonged, and thus contrary to *EHR* 5(3). Secondly, the Commission must determine whether or not — even assuming that there was a good cause not to release the applicant pending trial — the national judicial authorities have conducted the case in a manner which unreasonably prolonged the detention on remand, thus imposing on the applicant a greater sacrifice in the interest of public order than could normally be expected of a person presumed to be innocent.

To answer the first of these questions, the following reasons may, in appropriate cases, be considered relevant and sufficient:

(*a*) the danger of absconding;[117]
(*b*) the danger of repetition of the offence;[118]
(*c*) the danger of suppression of evidence.[119]

To determine whether the authorities have displayed the special diligence which is required in the case of a detained person, a court may take account of the exceptional complexity of the case[120] and, in an appropriate case, the conduct of the detained person himself.[121]

---

[116] *Wemhoff* v. *Federal Republic of Germany*, Judgment: 1 EHRR 55; *Neumeister* v. *Austria*, Judgment: 1 EHRR 91.

[117] *Ibid.*; *Stögmüller* v. *Austria*, Judgment: 1 EHRR 155; *Matznetter* v. *Austria*, Judgment: 1 EHRR 198. See also *Haase* v. *Federal Republic of Germany* (7412/76) Report: DR 11, 78; *X* v. *Federal Republic of Germany* (7680/76) DR 9, 190; *Monika Berberich* v. *Federal Republic of Germany* (5874/72) CD 46, 146; *Jentzsch* v. *Federal Republic of Germany* (2604/65) Report: 6 October 1970; *X* v. *Federal Republic of Germany* (3994/69) CD 33, 15; *X* v. *United Kingdom* (3868/68) CD 34, 10; *X* v. *Federal Republic of Germany* (3637/68) CD 31, 51; *Rosenbaum* v. *Federal Republic of Germany* (3376/67) CD 29, 31; *Levy* v. *Federal Republic of Germany* (6066/73) Report: 9 July 1975.

[118] *Matznetter* v. *Austria*, Judgment, *supra*; *Stögmüller* v. *Austria*, Judgment, *supra*.

[119] *Wemhoff* v. *Federal Republic of Germany*, Judgment, *supra*; *Matznetter* v. *Austria*, Judgment, *supra*; *X* v. *Federal Republic of Germany* (3637/68) *supra*; *Rosenbaum* v. *Federal Republic of Germany*, *supra*; cf. *X* v. *Netherlands* (4962/71) CD 40, 42; *Costas Tsirides* v. *The Police* [1973] 2 CLR 204 (Court of Appeal, Cyprus).

[120] *Levy* v. *Federal Republic of Germany*, *supra*.

[121] *X* v. *Federal Republic of Germany* (6541/74) DR 3, 86; *Levy* v. *Federal Republic of Germany*, *supra*; an accused person cannot automatically be held responsible for any prolongation of the proceedings while he is in detention, merely because he has availed

The Belgian Cour de Cassation has held that the continued detention of an accused person cannot be justified under *EHR* 5(3) once his case has been investigated if no definite, or even probable, date has been fixed for his appearance before the court dealing with the case.[122]

HRC has expressed the view that *ICPR* 9(3) was violated where, within a period of nine months between a person's arrest and his escape from detention, he was brought before a military judge on three occasions, but no steps were taken either to commit him for trial or to release him;[123] likewise, where the periods of detention between arrest and trial were 18,[124] 21,[125] 22[126], and 26[127] months, and in one case three-and-a-half years.[128]

IACM has said that where security measures under a state of emergency or a state of siege, which authorize the indefinite detention of individuals without charge, are extended beyond a reasonable time 'they become true and serious violations of the right to freedom'.[129]

3. Release pending trial. If the only remaining reason for continued detention is the fear that the accused will abscond and thereby subsequently avoid appearing for trial, his release pending trial must be ordered if it is possible to obtain from him guarantees that will ensure such appearance.[130] However, the right to be released on bail only exists if it can be ensured that the security is in fact sufficient to neutralize the ground for detention — in other words, if one can be sure that the accused will be deterred from absconding by the prospect of losing or not being repaid the amount of the bail.[131] The object of bail is not to make good the damage done, but to secure the appearance of the suspect for trial. The amount of bail must therefore be fixed with regard to the resources and circumstances of the person concerned.[132]

The right to test the legality of arrest or detention before a court

EHR 5(4) is a separate provision which can be infringed independently of the other provisions of *EHR* 5:[133] where no remedy exists at all, this provision will

---

himself of the rights to which he is entitled. However, in the present cases, the applicants had availed themselves excessively, if not abusively, of certain legal possibilities, which could not have failed to extend the periods they spent in detention in a manner they could have foreseen. *X* v. *Federal Republic of Germany* (3637/68) *supra*: regardless of the question whether or not an accused person is, in principle, entitled to avail himself of all possibilities that are at his disposal under the applicable procedural law to prevent him from being committed for trial, he must bear the consequences as to any resultant prolongation of the investigation.

[122] Decision of 20 March 1972 (Cassation, 2nd Chamber, No. 6401).

[123] *Sequeira* v. *Uruguay* (R. 1/6) HRC 35, 127.

[124] *Burgos* v. *Uruguay* (R. 12/52) HRC 36, 176.

[125] *Perdomo and de Lanza* v. *Uruguay* (R. 2/8) HRC 35, 111.

[126] *Ambrosini* v. *Uruguay* (R. 1/5) HRC 34, 124; *Massera* v. *Uruguay*, (R. 1/5) HRC 34, 124.

[127] *de Massera* v. *Uruguay* (R. 1/5) HRC 34, 124.

[128] *Weinberger* v. *Uruguay* (R. 7/28) HRC 36, 114. See also *Antonaccio* v. *Uruguay* (R. 14/63) published 14 December 1981.

[129] AR 1976, 16.

[130] *Wemhoff* v. *Federal Republic of Germany*, Judgment, *supra*, n. 113.

[131] Decision of 3 November 1976, BGer, Switzerland (see YB 20, 801).

[132] *Ibid.*; see also *Neumeister* v. *Austria*, Judgment, *supra*, n. 116; *X* v. *United Kingdom* (4225/69) CD 33, 34.

[133] *Van Droogenbroek* v. *Belgium* (7906/77) Report: 9 July 1980.

be violated even though there may be no indications that the detention is unlawful.[134] It is a strict requirement, designed to safeguard the liberty of the individual and to prevent arbitrary measures of detention. To comply with it, the procedure must be able to cover the substantive grounds for the detention, though the court concerned need not have unlimited powers of review. The extent of the review may vary according to the grounds for the deprivation of liberty: the court under *EHR* 5(4) does not have to review the correctness of a criminal conviction under *EHR* 5(1)(*a*), nor the lawfulness of a deportation order under *EHR* 5 (1)(*f*), but it must be able to ascertain whether a person is of unsound mind under *EHR* 5(1)(*e*).[135]

The term 'court' implies that the authority called upon to decide the question must possess a judicial character, that is to say be independent both of the Executive and of the parties to the case.[136] The judicial proceedings need not always be attended by the same guarantees as those required for civil or criminal litigation. Nevertheless, it is essential that the person concerned should have access to a court and the opportunity to be heard either in person or, where necessary, through some form of representation.[137] Though the court need not be a court of law of the classic kind, integrated within the standard judicial machinery of the country, it must offer the guarantees — appropriate to the kind of deprivation of liberty in question — of a judicial procedure, the forms of which may vary from one domain to another. But tribunals which only have advisory functions, cannot 'decide' the lawfulness of the detention, and cannot order release if it is unlawful, cannot be considered as 'courts' within the meaning of *EHR* 5(4), even if they have the necessary independence and offer sufficient procedural safeguards.[138]

When the prosecuting authority alone was heard, in the absence of the accused or his legal representative, EUCT agreed that the procedure was contrary to the principle of 'equality of arms'. However, it found that this principle, though included in the notion of fair trial (*procès équitable*), was not applicable to the examination of requests for *provisional* release.[139]

EHR 5(4) requires the court's decision to be given 'speedily'. In *Christinet v. Switzerland*,[140] EUCM observed that the concept 'speedily' cannot be defined in the abstract, but must be assessed in the light of the circumstances of the particular case. In that case, a delay of ten days was held to be within the law, while in *Engel et al. v. Netherlands*,[141] the Commission considered that a period of one month went beyond the limits inherent in the concept of a speedy decision.

In *De Wilde, Ooms and Versyp v. Belgium*,[142] EUCT raised the question

---

[134] *Caprino* v. *United Kingdom* (6871/75) Report: 17 July 1980.

[135] *Ibid.*; see also *X* v. *United Kingdom* (6998/75) Judgment: 5 November 1981.

[136] *Neumeister* v. *Austria*, Judgment, *supra*, n. 116; see also *Engel et al.* v. *Netherlands*, Report: 19 July 1974; *X* v. *United Kingdom* Judgment, *supra*.

[137] *Winterwerp* v. *Netherlands* (6301/73) Judgment: 2 EHRR 387; see also *X* v. *Belgium* (858/60) CD 6, 5.

[138] *X* v. *United Kingdom*, Judgment, *supra*.

[139] *Neumeister* v. *Austria*, Judgment, *supra*, n. 116; cf. *Köplinger* v. *Austria* (1850/63) CD 19, 71.

[140] (7648/76) Report: DR 17, 35.

[141] (5100/71, etc.) Report: 19 July 1974. See also *X and Y* v. *Sweden* (7376) DR 7, 123; *X* v. *Belgium* (6692/74) DR 2, 108; *X* v. *Federal Republic of Germany* (4833/71) CD 38, 130.

[142] (2832/66; 2835/66; 2899/66) Judgment: 1 EHRR 373. See also *X* v. *Federal Republic of Germany* (4833/71) *supra*; *De Courcy* v. *United Kingdom* (3457/68) CD 29, 50.

whether *EHR* 5(4) requires that two authorities should deal with the cases falling under it; that is, one which orders the detention, and a second, having the attributes of a court, which examines the lawfulness of this measure on the application of the person concerned. Or, as against this, was it enough that the detention should be ordered by an authority which had the elements inherent in the concept of a 'court'? The Court was of the opinion that where the decision depriving a person of his liberty was one taken by an administrative body, there was no doubt that the State was obliged to make available to the person detained a right of recourse to a court; but there was nothing to indicate that the same applied when the decision was made by a court at the close of judicial proceedings. In the latter case, the supervision required was incorporated in the decision itself. The Court concluded that the intervention of one organ satisfies *EHR* 5(4), but only if the procedure followed has a judicial character and gives to the individual concerned guarantees appropriate to the kind of deprivation of liberty in question.

However, this reasoning does not apply where the detention, though originally ordered by a court at the close of judicial proceedings, is of indefinite duration or may be renewed at later stages by administrative decisions alone. For example, in *Winterwerp* v. *Netherlands*[143] EUCT observed that special procedural safeguards may be called for in order to protect the interests of persons who, on account of their mental disability, are not fully capable of acting for themselves. In that case, the Court found that the various decisions ordering or authorizing the applicant's detention had issued from bodies which either did not possess the characteristics of a 'court' or, alternatively, failed to furnish the guarantees of judicial procedure required by *EHR* 5(4); neither did the applicant have access to a 'court' or the benefits of such guarantees when his requests for discharge were examined. EUCT took the view that it would be contrary to the object and purposes of *EHR* 5 to interpret paragraph 4 as making the detention of persons of unsound mind immune from subsequent review of its lawfulness, merely because the initial decision had issued from a court. In such cases, judicial review of lawfulness should be available at 'reasonable intervals'.

In *X* v. *United Kingdom*,[144] EUCT explained that the scope of the periodic judicial control of the lawfulness of the continued detention of persons of unsound mind need not empower the court of review, on all aspects of the case, to substitute its own discretion for that of the decision-making authority. But the review must be wide enough to bear on the essential conditions for the lawfulness of the detention under *EHR*, and especially on the questions whether the patient's disorder still persisted, and whether the administrative authority was entitled to think that his continued compulsory confinement was necessary in the interests of public safety. Accordingly, *habeas corpus* proceedings will not satisfy the requirements of *EHR* 5(4) in such cases if they can only test the formal legality of the detention, and can only investigate whether the detaining authority misused its powers by acting in bad faith, or capriciously, or for a wrongful purpose, or whether the decision was not supported by any evidence, or could not have been reached by any reasonable person in the circumstances, but when those proceedings cannot review the grounds or merits of the decision itself because these are exclusively a matter for the determination of the authority concerned.

[143] *Winterwerp* v. *Netherlands*, Judgment, *supra*, n. 137.
[144] Judgment, *supra*, n. 135.

EUCM has applied similar considerations not only to the detention of persons of unsound mind,[145] but also to the detention of persons convicted of criminal offences who may be recalled into detention again at a later stage by the mere decision of an administrative authority. In *Van Droogenbroek* v. *Belgium*,[146] the applicant was sentenced to two years' imprisonment for theft by a competent court, which found that he was a recidivist and accordingly also placed him 'at the government's disposal' for ten years. Distinguishing EUCT's judgment in *De Wilde, Ooms and Versyp* v. *Belgium*,[147] the Commission considered that, although the detention had originally been ordered by a court at the close of judicial proceedings which left its execution to the Executive, the high degree of its indeterminacy, and the fact that the social danger justifying it may over such a long period cease to exist, required judicial control under *EHR* 5(4) of its subsequent execution at 'reasonable intervals'.

In a similar case, where the domestic law empowered the Executive to recall a prisoner whose sentence had been suspended or remitted but, while authorizing his arrest in such a case without warrant, required his remand by a court to serve the unexpired portion of his sentence, the Supreme Court of Ceylon said that, where such a person had been arrested but not so remanded, his detention in prison was unlawful, and his escape from prison could not constitute the offence of escaping from lawful custody. The requirement for a remand was not a mere formality: the person arrested might be able to show cause against it.[148]

HRC has expressed the view that *ICPR* 9(4) is violated where, under a decree providing for 'prompt security measures', persons may be arrested on grounds of 'a grave and imminent danger to security and public order' and no remedies in the nature of *habeas corpus* are available to them.[149]

Compensation for unlawful arrest or detention

A 'fault' on the part of the State authorities in the exercise of their functions is not essential for the establishment of a right to compensation under *EHR* 5(5). On the contrary, it is the objective breach of the conditions for detention laid down in the international and domestic law which in itself establishes a right to compensation.[150]

The right to compensation covers material and moral damages;[151] not only 'satisfaction', but real 'compensation'.

EHR 5(5) is not a *lex specialis* in relation to *EHR* 50. Once EUCT has found a violation of *EHR* 5, the victim need not wait until the respondent government has failed to compensate him under *EHR* 5(5), and then launch a fresh application to EUCM: the Court can adjudicate the claim for compensation as part of

---

[145] *X* v. *Belgium* (6839/74) DR 3, 139; *Winterwerp* v. *Netherlands* (6301/73) Report: 15 December 1977; *Luberti* v. *Italy* (9019/80) Decision: 7 July 1981; *Barclay-Maguire* v. *United Kingdom* (9117/80) Decision: 17 December 1981.

[146] (7906/77) Report: 9 July 1980.

[147] Judgment, *supra*, n. 142.

[148] *Kolugala* v. *Superintendent of Prisons* 66 NLR 412.

[149] *Valcada* v. *Uruguay* (R. 2/9) HRC 35, 107; *Perdomo and de Lanza* v. *Uruguay* (R. 2/8) HRC 35, 111; *Ramirez* v. *Uruguay* (R. 1/4) HRC 35, 121; *Sequeira* v. *Uruguay* (R. 1/6) HRC 35, 127; *Motta* v. *Uruguay* (R. 2/11) HRC 35, 132; followed in five further cases against Uruguay reported in HRC 36.

[150] Decision of 31 January 1965, BG, Federal Republic of Germany (NJW 1966, 1021).

[151] *Ibid.*; see also *Huber* v. *Austria* (6821/74) DR 6, 65. For computation of the 'redress' to which a barrister was entitled when he had been unlawfully committed to prison for seven days for contempt of court, see *Re Ramesh L. Maharaj* (No. 974 of 1975, High Court of Trinidad and Tobago).

the proceedings already before it and, in so doing, it will take into account the rule of substance which *EHR* 5(5) contains.[152]

Freedom from civil imprisonment

According to the *Explanatory Reports on the Second to Fifth Protocols to the European Convention* (Strasbourg, 1971), the obligation concerned must arise out of contract; the prohibition does not apply to obligations arising from legislation in public or private law. Nor does the prohibition apply if a debtor acts with malicious or fraudulent intent; or if a person deliberately refuses to fulfil an obligation, irrespective of his reasons therefor; or if his inability to meet a commitment is due to negligence. In these circumstances, the failure to fulfil a contractual obligation may legitimately constitute a criminal offence.[153]

§14.3 Torture and other ill-treatment

§14.3.1 TEXTS

UDHR

5. No one shall be subjected to torture or to cruel, inhuman or degrading treatment or punishment.

ADRD

XXV. Every individual who has been deprived of his liberty has the right . . . to humane treatment during the time he is in custody.

XXVI. Every person accused of an offense has the right . . . not to receive cruel, infamous or unusual punishment.

ICPR

7. No one shall be subjected to torture or to cruel, inhuman or degrading treatment or punishment. In particular, no one shall be subjected without his free consent to medical or scientific experimentation.

10 (1) All persons deprived of their liberty shall be treated with humanity and with respect for the inherent dignity of the human person.

EHR

3. No one shall be subjected to torture or to inhuman or degrading treatment or punishment.

---

[152] *Neumeister* v. *Austria* (No. 2) Judgment: 1 EHRR 136.
[153] See also *X* v. *Federal Republic of Germany* (5025/71) CD 39, 95.

AMR

5 (2) No one shall be subjected to torture or to cruel, inhuman, or degrading punishment or treatment. All persons deprived of their liberty shall be treated with respect for the inherent dignity of the human person.

[*AFR*]

5. . . . All forms of exploitation and degradation of man, particularly . . . torture, cruel, inhuman or degrading punishment and treatment shall be prohibited.

§14.3.2 CROSS-REFERENCES

State obligation: Absolute and immediate under *ICPR, EHR, AMR*, and [*AFR*]: see §6.3. For the juridical status of obligations under *UDHR* and *ADRD*, see §6.2.

Signatures, ratifications, accessions, reservations, and interpretations: See Table A for the State Parties bound by these provisions on 1 January 1982, and any reservations and interpretations notified by them.

Derogation: Non-derogable in any circumstances: see §11.

Non-discrimination: No discrimination of any kind is allowed in respect of these rights or freedoms: see §7 for the relevant provisions in the instruments.

Abuse: See §9 for the relevant provisions in these instruments.

Savings: See §10 for the relevant provisions in these instruments.

Restrictions and limitations: None.

International supervision, interpretation, application, and enforcement: By HRC under *ICPR* (see §27); by EUCM and EUCT under *EHR* (see §28); by IACM and IACT under *AMR* (see §29); by [*AFCM*] under [*AFR*] (see §30). See also §6.6 for the obligation to provide domestic remedies under *UDHR, ADRD, ICPR, EHR, AMR*, and [*AFR*].

Subsidiary instruments: [*CT*] (see §14.3.7); UN Standard Minimum Rules for the Treatment of Prisoners; CE Standard Minimum Rules for the Treatment of Prisoners; UN Code of Conduct for Law Enforcement Officials; [UN Body of Principles for the Protection of All Persons under any Form of Detention or Imprisonment]; [UN Code of Medical Ethics].

See also: §22.6 for the specific provision in *AMR* 8(3) as to confessions made under coercion.

§14.3.3 COMMENT

The wording of the principal prohibition is identical in *UDHR* and *ICPR*. *EHR* omits the word 'cruel',[1] and *AHR* and [*AFR*] reverse the order of 'treatment'

---

[1] Robertson attaches no importance to this omission, on the ground that 'the sense of "cruel" is equally covered by "inhuman"'. See *Human Rights in Europe*, 38.

and 'punishment'. *ADRD* confines itself to accused persons, makes no specific mention of torture,[2] and is also unique in its use of the terms 'infamous' and 'unusual', and its omission of 'treatment'. [*AFR*] alone uses the formulation 'shall be prohibited'.

Because of the use of disjunctive 'ors', the principal prohibition appears to extend to seven (in the case of *EHR*, five) distinct modes of conduct:

(1) torture;
(2) cruel treatment;
(3) cruel punishment;
(4) inhuman treatment;
(5) inhuman punishment;
(6) degrading treatment;
(7) degrading punishment.

However, the prohibition extends equally to all these, and in all cases the State obligation is absolute, non-derogable and unqualified.[3] All that is therefore required to establish a violation of the relevant Article is a finding that the State concerned has failed to comply with its obligation in respect of any one of these modes of conduct: no questions of justification can ever arise.

The wording of *ICPR* 10(1) and *AHR* 5(2) is identical, except that the latter omits the requirement to treat prisoners 'with humanity'. No comparable provision appears in *EHR* or [*AFR*].

§14.3.4 HISTORY

The first appearance of the wording of the main prohibition comes in the English Bill of Rights of 1688.[4] After reciting a catalogue of grievances, including that 'of late years . . . illegal and cruel punishments [have been] inflicted', that statute goes on to declare, 'for the vindicating and asserting of [Parliament's] ancient rights and liberties', *inter alia* that 'cruel and unusual punishment' ought not to be inflicted.

A century later, the French *déclaration des droits de l'homme et du citoyen* of 1789 provided that 'the law should impose only such penalties as are absolutely and evidently necessary'. The Eighth Amendment to the US Constitution (forming part of that nation's Bill of Rights) two years later reverted to the English precedent, providing that 'cruel and unusual punishments' should not be inflicted. Section 2 of the Canadian Bill of Rights 1960 provides that no law shall be construed or applied so as to impose, or authorize the imposition of, 'cruel and unusual treatment or punishment'. Neither of these enactments specifically mentions torture, or inhuman or degrading treatment or punishment.

---

[2] IACM has consistently treated the application of torture as a violation of the right to personal security under *ADRD* I: see its Annual Reports, *passim*.

[3] So held for *EHR* by both EUCM and EUCT in *Ireland* v. *United Kingdom* (5310/71) Report: 25 January 1976; Judgment: 2 EHRR 25. IACM has also stated that emergency situations cannot justify the application of torture: AR 1976, 16. In *Tyrer* v. *United Kingdom* (Judgment: 2 EHRR 1), EUCT pointed out that, *a fortiori*, a degrading punishment which violates *EHR* 3 cannot be justified under the Convention even if it could be conclusively demonstrated that law and order could not be maintained without it.

[4] Formally entitled 'An Act Declaring the Rights and Liberties of the Subject and Settling the Succession of the Crown'.

National constitutions adopted since 1948, both in the British Commonwealth and elsewhere, tend to follow the wording of *UDHR*.

§ 14.3.5 JURISPRUDENCE

'Torture'

There have been several attempts to define the expression 'torture'. The UNGA has defined it as follows:

Torture means any act by which severe pain or suffering, whether physical or mental, is intentionally inflicted by or at the instigation of a public official on a person for such purposes as obtaining from him or a third person information or confession, punishing him for an act he has committed, or intimidating him or other persons. It does not include pain or suffering arising only from, inherent in or incidental to, lawful sanctions to the extent consistent with the Standard Minimum Rules for the Treatment of Prisoners.

The UNGA added that —

Torture constitutes an aggravated and deliberate form of cruel, inhuman or degrading treatment or punishment.[5]

The definition in the current draft of the Convention on the Elimination of Torture ([*CT*]) reads:

Torture means any act by which severe pain or suffering, whether physical or mental, is intentionally inflicted on a person for such purposes as obtaining from him or a third person information or a confession, punishing him for an act he or a third person has committed or is suspected of having committed, or intimidating or coercing him or a third person, or for any reason based on discrimination of any kind, when such pain or suffering is inflicted by or at the instigation of or with the consent or acquiescence of a public official or other person acting in an official capacity. It does not include pain or suffering arising only from, inherent in or incidental to lawful sanctions.[6]

Although any distinctions between torture, inhuman and degrading treatments or punishments are academic in the sense that all of them are equally prohibited by the international instruments, EUCM and EUCT have more than once discussed the relationships between them. In *Denmark, Norway, Sweden and the Netherlands* v. *Greece* EUCM said that 'all torture must be inhuman and degrading treatment, and inhuman treatment also degrading'[7] and added that —

the word 'torture' is often used to describe inhuman treatment which has a purpose, such as the obtaining of information or confessions, or the infliction of punishment, and it is generally an aggravated form of inhuman treatment.[8]

---

[5] Declaration on the Protection of All Persons from being Subjected to Torture and Other Cruel, Inhuman or Degrading Treatment or Punishment, adopted unanimously on 9 December 1975 (Resolution 3452 (XXX)).

[6] Report of the Working Group on a Draft Convention against Torture and Other Cruel, Inhuman or Degrading Treatment or Punishment (E/CN.4/L 1576) of 6 March 1981.

[7] (3321-3/67; 3344/67) Report: YB 12 *bis*.

[8] *Ibid*. This definition was adopted by the Court of Criminal Appeal of Northern Ireland in *R* v. *McCormick et al.* [1977] 4 NIJB 105.

In *Ireland* v. *United Kingdom*, EUCM and EUCT both found that the conduct there established against the British security forces in Northern Ireland constituted inhuman and degrading treatment, but disagreed on the question whether it also constituted torture. EUCM adopted its earlier definition of torture as 'an aggravated form of inhuman treatment' and found that the conduct established (as to which, see below) satisfied that test.[9] But a majority of EUCT instead defined torture as 'deliberate inhuman treatment causing very serious and cruel suffering' and held that the conduct established did not occasion suffering of the paticular intensity and cruelty implied by the word 'torture' as so understood.[10] While agreeing that torture was an aggravated form of inhuman treatment, EUCT differed from EUCM in regard to the degree of severity required to constitute torture.[11]

There have also been differences of judicial opinion on whether the motive with which the conduct is carried out has any relevance to the question whether it constitutes torture. The decisions of both EUCM and EUCT seem to indicate that the existence of an objective such as the obtaining of information or confession is a necessary ingredient.[12] However, in his dissenting opinion in *Ireland* v. *United Kingdom*,[13] Judge Fitzmaurice said:

the motivation of the alleged treatment — e.g. that it has the, in itself, legitimate object of obtaining information — is rendered irrelevant by the unconditional wording of Article 3. Torture is torture, whatever its purpose, if inflicted compulsorily.[14]

Among the physical brutalities which EUCM has found to amount to torture are '*falanga*' or '*bastinado*' (beating of the feet with a wooden or metal stick or bar which makes no skin lesions and leaves no permanent and recognisable marks, but causes intense pain and swelling of the feet), the application of electric shock, the placing of a metal clamp on the head which is then screwed into both sides of the temples, pulling out of hair from the head or pubic region, kicking of the male genital organs, dripping water on the head, intense noises to prevent sleep, introduction of a stick into the rectum, burning with cigarettes, burial up to the head, insertion of pins under nails, being hung up head downwards over a fire, having one's hands manacled behind the back for several days, or being kept handcuffed for a prolonged period.[15]

Torture may also be constituted by the infliction of mental suffering through the creation of a state of anguish and stress by means other than bodily assault. As Judge Evrigenis observed in *Ireland* v. *United Kingdom*,[16]

---

[9] (5310/71) Report: 25 January 1976.

[10] Judgment: 2 EHRR 25.

[11] But four members of the Court (Judges Zekia, O'Donoghue, Evrigenis, and Matscher) dissented from this approach, arguing that the notion of torture which emerged from the judgment was too limited.

[12] *Denmark et al.* v. *Greece, supra*, n. 5; *Ireland* v. *United Kingdom, supra*.

[13] *Supra*.

[14] A similar view has been expressed by the Court Martial of Liège in its Decision of 20 November 1972 (Journal des Tribunaux, 3 March 1973, 148). But in *The State* v. *John Frawley* [1976] IR 365, the High Court of Ireland has taken the opposite view, in holding that restraints used on a prisoner to eliminate or diminish the possibility of his harming himself could not constitute torture, since that entire concept 'must be construed as being not only evil in its consequences but evil in its purpose as well'.

[15] *Denmark et al.* v. *Greece, supra*. See also the Annual Reports of IACM, *passim*, and many of HRC's Uruguay cases, for descriptions of similar horrific practices.

[16] *Supra*.

Torture can be practised — and indeed is practised — by using subtle techniques developed in multidisciplinary laboratories which claim to be scientific. By means of new forms of suffering that have little in common with the physical pain caused by conventional torture it aims to bring about, even if only temporarily, the disintegration of an individual's personality, the shattering of his mental and psychological equilibrium and the crushing of his will.[17]

In *Denmark et al.* v. *Greece*,[18] EUCM said that solitary confinement, isolation in a police cell without food, water, or access to toilets, mock executions, threats to throw a person out of a window, the use of insulting language, rubbing the head with vomit, being forced to strip naked, and being compelled to be present at the torture or inhuman or degrading treatment of relatives or friends, all constitute torture because they are forms of intimidation and humiliation designed to destroy an individual's will and conscience.

Conditions of detention may sometimes amount to torture. For instance, in *Denmark et al.* v. *Greece*, overcrowded detention quarters, a lack of proper washing facilities, absence of heating in winter, lack of hot water, poor lavatory facilities, unsatisfactory dental treatment, close restriction of letters and visits, and the extreme manner of separating detainees from their families, were considered, in combination, to constitute torture.

The techniques of sensory deprivation which came under scrutiny in the case of *Ireland* v. *United Kingdom* appear to mark the boundary, having been considered, in combination, to constitute torture by EUCM, but found to fall short of it by a majority of EUCT. These techniques consisted of

(1) *wall-standing*: forcing the detainees to remain for periods of some hours in a 'stress position', described by those who underwent it as being spread-eagled against the wall, with the fingers put high above the head against the wall, the legs spread apart and the feet back, causing them to stand on their toes with the weight of the body mainly on the fingers;
(2) *hooding*: putting a black or navy blue bag over the detainees' heads and, at least initially, keeping it there all the time except during interrogation;
(3) *subjection to noise*: pending their interrogations, holding the detainees in a room where there was a continuous loud and hissing noise;
(4) *deprivation of sleep*: pending their interrogation, depriving the detainees of sleep;
(5) *deprivation of food and drink*: subjecting the detainees to a reduced diet pending interrogation.[19]

IACM has said that 'disappearances' — that is, the systematic denial by governments of the detention of individuals, when they have in fact been detained by police or military authorities — are not only cruel and inhuman, but constitute

[17] Separate Opinion. In the same case, Judge Zekia observed in his Separate Opinion that it was permissible, in ascertaining whether or not torture or inhuman treatment had been committed, to apply not only an objective test, but also a subjective one. He referred to the example — not alleged in the case under consideration — of a mother who, for purposes of interrogation, is separated from her suckling baby by being kept in an adjoining room; the baby, because of hunger, starts yelling for hours within the hearing of the mother, who is not allowed to attend it. He was of the view that the mother by being agonized, and the baby by being deprived of the urgent attention of the mother, would both have been subjected to inhuman treatment although neither would have been assaulted.

[18] *Supra*.

[19] See Report and Judgment, *supra*.

'a true form of torture for the victims' family and friends, because of the un-certainty they experience as to the fate of the victim and because they feel powerless to provide legal, moral and material assistance.'[20]

A US Federal Court of Appeals has held that, independently of any treaty obligations, official torture is clearly and unambiguously prohibited by custom-ary international law.[21]

'Cruel treatment'

The word 'cruel' does not appear in *EHR* 3, and neither HRC nor IACM or IACT has yet had occasion to consider it in relation to *ICPR* 7 or *AMR* 5(2), where it does appear. In turn, the word 'treatment' does not appear in either the English or the US Bill of Rights, and the Canadian Bill of Rights (where it does appear) has not so far been successfully invoked in this respect.[22] For these reasons, there is as yet no international, or English or North American national con-stitutional, jurisprudence on the interpretation or application of the expression 'cruel treatment'.

'Cruel punishment'

For similar reasons, there is so far no international jurisprudence on the inter-pretation or application of the expression 'cruel punishment'. But this expression is found in both the Eighth Amendment to the US Constitution and the English and Canadian Bills of Rights, and has been interpreted and applied by the superior courts of at least two of these countries. From those decisions, the following propositions may be extracted.

A punishment was originally considered cruel if it involved torture or a lingering death.[23] For instance, burning at the stake, quartering, the rack and thumbscrew, and in some circumstances solitary confinement were classical forms of cruel punishment.[24] But the US Supreme Court observed in 1910 that the Eighth Amendment is progressive and does not merely prohibit the cruel punishments known in 1688 and 1787, but may acquire wider meaning as public opinion becomes enlightened by humane justice.[25] Accordingly, it has

---

[20] AR 1977, 26.

[21] *Filartiga* v. *Pena-Irala* 630 F (2nd) 876.

[22] The following conduct has been held in Canada not to constitute cruel treatment: the denial of a certificate of citizenship: *Dowhopoluk* v. *Martin* [1972] 1 OR 311; the carrying out, by order of a court and contrary to the wishes of the patient, of a surgical operation by competent and qualified persons and under general anaesthetic: *Re Laporte and the Queen* (1972) 8 CCC (2nd) 343; administrative segregation as practised at the British Columbia penitentiary: *R* v. *Bruce et al.* (1977) 36 CCC (2nd) 158; an indeterminate sentence of imprisonment: *R* v. *Buchler* (1970) 2 CCC (2nd) 4.

[23] Therefore, shooting as a mode of executing the death sentence was not considered cruel: *Wilkerson* v. *Utah* 99 US 130. Nor was electrocution: *In Re Kemmler* 136 US 436. Proceeding with the execution of a sentence of death after an accidental failure of electrical equipment had rendered a previous attempt unsuccessful was also held not to be cruel: *Louisiana* v. *Resweber* 329 US 459, but see the dissenting opinion of Burton, J (with which three other justices concurred) that 'instantaneous death should be distinguished from death by instalments'.

[24] *Robinson* v. *California* 370 US 660 at 675, per Douglas, J.

[25] *Weems* v. *United States* 217 US 349. See also *Trop* v. *Dulles* 356 US 86, which held that the Eighth Amendment must draw its meaning from the evolving standards of decency that mark the progress of a maturing society; and the observations of Burger, CJ in *Furman* v. *Georgia* 408 US 238 at 382, that a punishment is inordinately cruel chiefly as perceived by the society so characterizing it. For *EHR*, see the statement of EUCT in *Tyrer* v. *United Kingdom* (Judgment: 2 EHRR 1) that the European Convention is a living instrument which must be interpreted in the light of present-day conditions.

been held that punishment for crime should be graduated and proportioned to the offence. A sentence of twelve years' imprisonment, in chains, at hard and painful labour, with the automatic loss of many basic civil rights and subjection to lifetime surveillance, for the offence of falsifying an official document is excessive and out of all proportion to the offence, and is therefore cruel.[26] So too, the death penalty for the rape of an adult woman.[27]

A punishment which does not accord with the dignity of man is cruel. Into this category would fall the use of denationalization as a punitive measure.[28] in so deciding, the US Supreme Court observed that —

There may be involved no physical mistreatment, no primitive torture. There is instead the total destruction of the individual's status in organised society. It is a form of punishment more primitive than torture, for it destroys for the individual the political existence that was centuries in the development. The punishment strips the citizen of his status in the national and international political community.[29]

The punishment of a status — such as, for instance, addiction to the use of narcotics — is cruel since it involves punishment for a mere propensity, a desire to commit an offence.[30] Dealing with a Californian statute which made the status of narcotic addiction a criminal offence for which the offender could be prosecuted 'at any time before he reforms', Douglas, J said, 'If addicts can be punished for their addiction, then the insane can also be punished for their insanity. Each has a disease and each must be treated as a sick person.'[31]

A punishment is cruel if it makes no measurable contribution to acceptable goals, and hence is nothing more than the purposeless and needless imposition of pain and suffering. Among the criteria to be considered are whether the permissible aims of punishment — such as deterrence, isolation, and rehabilitation — can be achieved as effectively by punishing an offence less severely; and whether, if such aims can be so achieved, the imposition of a more severe punishment constitutes unnecessary cruelty.[32] In *Furman* v. *Georgia*,[33] it was held that

---

[26] *Weems* v. *United States, supra.* See also the *obiter dictum* in *O'Neil* v. *Vermont* 144 US 323 — where sentence of 54 years' imprisonment was imposed for 307 offences of illegally selling intoxicating liquor — that it does not alter its character as cruel that for each distinct offence there is a small punishment if, when they are brought together and one punishment for the whole is inflicted, it becomes one of excessive severity. This approach was, in essence, later adopted by the Court in *Howard* v. *Fleming* 191 US 126. For cases where punishments imposed were held not to be cruel, see *Badders* v. *United States* 240 US 390; *McDonald* v. *Massachusetts* 180 US 311; *Graham* v. *West Virginia* 224 US 616; *R.* v. *Buckler* (1970) 2 CCC (2nd) 4; *R* v. *Shand* (1976) 30 CCC (2nd) 23.

[27] *Coker* v. *Georgia* 433 US 584.

[28] *Trop* v. *Dulles* 356 US 86. See also the observations of Brennan, J in *Furman* v. *Georgia* (*supra*, at 367) that the State, even as it punishes, must treat its members with respect for their intrinsic worth as human beings. He expressed the view that classical forms of torture were condemned by history not merely because of the acute pain involved; they treated members of the human race as non-humans, as objects to be toyed with and discarded. They were thus inconsistent with the fundamental premise that even the vilest criminal remained a human being possessed of common human dignity.

[29] *Ibid.*, at 101.

[30] *Robinson* v. *California* 370 US 660.

[31] *Ibid.*, at 674. Cf. *Powell* v. *Texas* 392 US 514, where it was held that there was a substantial difference between a status and a condition, and that the punishment of a person, not for being a chronic alcoholic, but for being in public while drunk on a particular occasion, is not the punishment of a 'status'.

[32] This principle was first enunciated in the dissenting opinions of Goldberg, Douglas and Brennan, JJ in *Rudolph* v. *Alabama* 375 US 889.

[33] 408 US 238.

the imposition of the death penalty was not necessary as a means of stopping convicted individuals from committing further crimes; that there was no reason to believe that the death penalty as then administered was necessary either to deter the commission of capital crimes or to protect society; that it could not be concluded that death served the purpose of retribution more effectively than imprisonment; and that it was likely that the death penalty could not be shown to be serving any penal purpose which could not be served equally well by some less severe punishment. However, the US Supreme Court has since held that the death penalty does not, in all circumstances, constitute cruel punishment.[34]

A punishment is cruel when it is imposed under sentencing procedures that create a substantial risk that it may be inflicted in an arbitrary and capricious manner. The US Supreme Court has held that the death penalty suffers from this disability where the law enables it to be selectively applied,[35] as well as where the law makes its imposition mandatory.[36]

'Inhuman treatment'

In *Denmark et al.* v. *Greece*,[37] EUCM stated that the notion of inhuman treatment covers at least such treatment as deliberately causes severe suffering, mental or physical, which in the particular situation is unjustifiable. However, in its report in *Ireland* v. *United Kingdom*,[38] the Commission noted that its use of the term 'unjustifiable' had given rise to some misunderstanding, and explained that it did not have in mind the possibility that there could be a justification for the infliction of inhuman treatment.[39]

Treatment must attain a minimum level of severity if it is to fall within the scope of the term 'inhuman'. The assessment of this minimum is, in the nature of things, relative; it depends on all the circumstances of the case, such as the duration of the treatment, its physical or mental effects and, in some cases, the sex, age and state of health of the victim.[40] For instance, EUCM has found that securing a prisoner by fastening one hand and one foot in the same handcuffs while he was being transported from one place to another could constitute inhuman treatment.[41]

All methods of interrogation which go beyond the mere asking of questions may bring some pressure on the person being interrogated, but they cannot, by that fact alone, be classified as inhuman.[42] EUCM has noted that there may sometimes be a certain roughness of treatment in the form of slaps or blows

---

[34] *Gregg* v. *Georgia* 428 US 153; *Proffitt* v. *Florida* 428 US 242; *Jurek* v. *Texas* 428 US 262; *Woodson* v. *North Carolina* 428 US 280; *Coker* v. *Georgia* 433 US 584. For Canada, see *R* v. *Miller* (1975) 24 CCC (2nd) 401.

[35] *Furman* v. *Georgia, supra*, n. 25; *Woodson* v. *North Carolina, supra*.

[36] *Stanislaus Roberts* v. *Louisiana* 428 US 325; *Roberts* v. *Louisiana* 431 US 633.

[37] (3321-3/67, 3344/67) Report: YB 12 *bis.*

[38] (5310/71) Report: 25 January 1976.

[39] Jacobs suggests that there could be treatment which, while being justifiable in some circumstances, may in different circumstances be unlawful. A penalty which might be justified for a serious crime could constitute inhuman treatment or punishment if imposed for a petty offence: *The European Convention on Human Rights*, 28. But what EUCM may have had in mind was that the infliction of *suffering* may on occasions be justifiable — e.g. in the case of surgery voluntarily, or necessarily, undergone.

[40] *Ireland* v. *United Kingdom* (5310/71) Judgment: 2 EHRR 25. See also the observations of Judge Zekia on the effects of identical treatment on an elderly sick man and a young athlete, *ibid.*

[41] *Wiechert* v. *Federal Republic of Germany* (1404/62) CD 15, 15.

[42] *Ireland* v. *United Kingdom*, Report: *supra*. See also *Kamma* v. *Netherlands* (4771/71) CD 42, 22.

of the hand on the head or face which is often tolerated and accepted by detainees as being neither cruel nor excessive.[43] Similarly, deprivation of sleep or restrictions on diet, if considered separately, may not as such constitute inhuman treatment.[44] However, the combined application of several techniques which are designed to cause severe mental and physical stress on a person, in order to obtain information from him, would constitute inhuman treatment.[45]

The deportation or extradition of a person may constitute inhuman treatment if there are substantial grounds to fear that such a step might expose the person concerned to torture or to cruel, inhuman, or degrading treatment or punishment in the State to which he is to be sent,[46] or where there are adequate medical grounds for the assumption that such a measure might, owing to the mental state of the person concerned, lead to serious damage to health or the danger of suicide.[47] But in a number of cases,[48] deportation or extradition has been held not to amount to inhuman treatment.

Solitary confinement of a person under interrogation or awaiting trial, having regard to its strictness, its duration and the end pursued, may constitute inhuman treatment.[49] Similarly, where a prisoner suffers any physical harm or is caused mental suffering in consequence of such confinement.[50] However, other situations in which convicted prisoners find themselves do not necessarily give rise to any such issue.[51]

---

[43] *Denmark et al.* v. *Greece, supra.* But cf. the acts of violence used by the British security forces on detainees in Northern Ireland, which *were* held to constitute inhuman treatment both by the Commission and the Court in *Ireland* v. *United Kingdom, supra.*

[44] *Ireland* v. *United Kingdom*, Report, *supra.*

[45] *Ibid.*; see also Judgment, *supra.* For a description of the techniques concerned, see above.

[46] *X* v. *Belgium* (984/61) CD 5, 39; *X* v. *Federal Republic of Germany* (1465/62) CD 9, 63; *X* v. *Federal Republic of Germany* (1802/63) CD 10, 26; *X* v. *Austria and Yugoslavia* (2143/64) CD 14, 15; *X* v. *Federal Republic of Germany* (3040/67) CD 22, 133; *Becker* v. *Denmark* (7011/75) DR 4, 215; *X* v. *Federal Republic of Germany* (7216/75) DR 5, 137; *Lynas* v. *Switzerland* (7317/75) DR 6, 141; Decision of 2 September 1955, VwG Stuttgart (ÖVw 1956, 381); Decision of 13 September 1955, OVwG Münster (ÖVw 1956, 381); Decision of 10 January 1956, VwG Württemberg/Baden (VwRS 8, 859); Decision of 27 September 1960, OVwG Berlin (see YB 3, 638).

[47] *Brückmann* v. *Federal Republic of Germany* (6242/73) CD 46, 202.

[48] See *X* v. *Netherlands* (1983/63) CD 18, 19: possibility of being sentenced to a longer term of imprisonment than could be imposed in the country in which the applicant is resident; *X* v. *Federal Republic of Germany* (4162/69) CD 32, 87; *X* v. *Denmark* (7465/76) DR 7, 153: likelihood of being prosecuted for offences which were considered criminal acts in all CE countries; *X* v. *Federal Republic of Germany* (4314/69) CD 32, 96: obligation to perform military service or suffer imprisonment for failure to do so; *X* v. *Federal Republic of Germany* (6315/73) DR 1, 73: possible act of a third country to which applicant may ultimately be sent; *X* v. *Federal Republic of Germany* (7334/76) DR 5, 154; Decision of 27 September 1960, OVwG Berlin (see YB 3, 638): criminal prosecution for desertion from the army; *Agee* v. *United Kingdom* (7729/76) DR 7, 164: the act of deportation itself; Decision of 6 November 1953, VwG Stuttgart (ÖVw 1954, 223); Decision of 15 December 1955, BVwG (E/BVwG 3, 58): expulsion of a married man if his wife has the possibility of following him.

[49] *De Courcy* v. *United Kingdom* (2749/66) CD 24, 93; *Wemhoff* v. *Federal Republic of Germany* (3448/67) CD 30, 56; *X* v. *United Kingdom* (4203/69) CD 34, 48; *Bonzi* v. *Switzerland* (7854/77) DR 12, 185; *Krause* v. *Switzerland* (7986/77) DR 13, 73; *Kröcher and Möller* v. *Switzerland* (8463/78) Decision: 9 July 1981; Decision of 13 June 1963, OLG Hamburg (NJW 1963, 1840).

[50] Decision of 16 October 1964, OLG Hamburg (NJW 1965, 357)

[51] *Ensslin, Baader and Raspe* v. *Federal Republic of Germany* (7572/76; 7586-7/76) DR 14, 64: segregation of prisoner in order to prevent risk of escape, attack or disturbance of prison community and to protect prisoner from fellow prisoners; Decision of 9 December 1965, KG Berlin (NJW 1966, 1088): treatment designed to enable detainee to maintain

'Inhuman punishment'

Apart from the dictum of EUCT, in *Tyrer* v. *United Kingdom*,[52] that the suffering occasioned must attain a particular level before a punishment can be classified as 'inhuman',[53] there is as yet no international or national constitutional jurisprudence on the interpretation or application of the expression 'inhuman punishment'. The European Committee on Crime Problems has, however, declared that life imprisonment without any hope of release is inhuman.[54]

'Degrading treatment'

In *Denmark et al.* v. *Greece*,[55] EUCM defined 'degrading treatment' as treatment which grossly humiliates an individual or drives him to act against his will or conscience. EUCT applied a similar test when it held that the five techniques used by the British security forces in the interrogation of suspects in Northern Ireland (see above) were degrading, 'since they were such as to arouse in their victims feelings of fear, anguish and inferiority capable of humiliating and debasing them and possibly breaking their physical or moral resistance'.[56]

Rejecting a submission that the expression 'degrading treatment' should be interpreted as referring to physical acts only, EUCM found in *Patel et al.* v. *United Kingdom*,[57] that the general purpose of the prohibition of degrading

his physical and mental health; *X* v. *Austria* (462/59) CD 1: additional punishment of five days' strict arrest; *X* v. *Federal Republic of Germany* (2413/65) CD 23, 1: obligation to work for low wages; *Kiss* v. *United Kingdom* (6224/73) DR 7, 55; *X and Y* v. *Switzerland* (7289/75; 7349/76) DR 9, 57: withholding of access to a particular medical expert if there is a possibility of obtaining medical treatment elsewhere; *X* v. *Belgium* (6337/73) DR 3, 83: use of barred yard for exercise; *X* v. *United Kingdom* (6564/74) DR 2, 105: deprivation of conjugal rights and of the adequate exercise of parental rights; *Eggs* v. *Switzerland* (7341/76) DR 6, 170; *X* v. *Federal Republic of Germany* (7408/76) DR 10, 221: non-compliance with certain provisions of the Minimum Rules for the Treatment of Prisoners; *Kotalla* v. *Netherlands* (7994/77) DR 14, 238: continued imprisonment of sick prisoner provided he receives necessary medical care; an expectation of release from prison which does not materialize.

[52] (5856/72) Judgment: 2 EHHR 1. Both the Commission (Report: 14 December 1976) and the Court proceeded on the basis that judicial birching did not constitute an 'inhuman' punishment.

[53] See also the dictum in the Decision of 10 June 1963 of OLG Köln (NJW 1963, 1748) that a penalty or measure is inhuman if it wounds a man's soul and tramples on his human dignity. In that case, the Court held that in less serious cases of perjury, the permanent loss of capacity to take an oath, as provided for in section 161 of the Federal German Penal Code, constitutes inhuman punishment. The Supreme Court of Sri Lanka has held that the mandatory forfeiture of all the offender's movable and immovable property, and the mandatory removal of his name from any professional register, for any contravention (irrespective of its gravity) of any of the provisions of an Essential Public Services measure 'savours of cruelty' and is therefore unconstitutional: *Wickremanayake* v. *The State*, Hansard, 2 October 1979, 407. On the question whether the death penalty in Southern Rhodesia constitutes inhuman or degrading punishment, see the judgment of the Judicial Committee of the Privy Council in *Runyowa* v. *The Queen* [1966] 1 All ER 633.

[54] General Report on the Treatment of Long-Term Prisoners, prepared by Sub-Committee XXV of the European Committee on Crime Problems in 1975. This report was cited in *Kotalla* v. *Netherlands, supra*. Cf. Decision of 27 February 1976, Court of Appeal, The Hague (8 NYIL, January 1978): a prison sentence of unlimited duration is not in itself inhuman; and *R* v. *Buckler* (1970) 2 CCC (2nd) 4: a sentence of preventive detention for an indeterminate period is not cruel.

[55] *Supra*, n. 37.

[56] *Ireland* v. *United Kingdom*, Judgment, *supra*, n. 40.

[57] The *'East African Asians case'* (4403–19/70 etc.) CD 36, 92; Report: 3 EHRR 76. By Resolution DH(77) 2, the CE's Committee of Ministers later resolved that, in the light of

treatment was to prevent interferences with the dignity of man of a particular serious nature. Accordingly, any act which lowers a person in rank, position, reputation, or character can be regarded as 'degrading treatment' if it reaches a certain level of severity, and 'publicly to single out a group of persons for differential treatment on the basis of race might, in certain circumstances, constitute a special form of affront'.[58] In that case, the Commission found that recent British immigration laws discriminated against certain sections of British citizens on the grounds of their colour or race, and said that such racial discrimination amounted to degrading treatment.[59]

EUCM has also decided that an issue of degrading treatment could arise on the refusal of a State's authorities to give formal recognition to an individual's change of sex,[60] or on a State's failure to issue a nomadic group with aliens' passports or other documents of identity,[61] or on prolonged solitary confinement,[62] or denial of exercise,[63] to prisoners whether convicted or on remand. The Austrian Constitutional Court has held that the unnecessary application of physical force in escorting an arrested man to the police station constitutes degrading treatment.[64]

Treatment has also been held not to be degrading in a number of cases.[65]

'Degrading punishment'

For punishment to be degrading, the humiliation and debasement involved must attain a particular level and must, in any event, be other than the usual element of humiliation involved in judicial punishment.[66] The assessment is,

---

the measures subsequently adopted by the respondent Government, no further action was called for on the violations which EUCM had found to have taken place.

[58] *Ibid.*

[59] Cf. *X & Y* v. *United Kingdom* (5302/71) CD 44, 29, where EUCM found that delay in processing applications to enter the United Kingdom made by two British citizens of Asian origin did not constitute degrading treatment where the only consequence of such a delay was the risk that they might lose some of their assets. See also *3 East African Asians* v. *United Kingdom* (4715/70; 4783/71; 4827/71) DR 13, 17, which concerned British protected persons.

[60] *X* v. *Federal Republic of Germany* (6699/74) DR 11, 16.

[61] *48 Kalderas' Gypsies* v. *Federal Republic of Germany and Netherlands* (7823–4/77) DR 11, 221.

[62] *Reed* v. *United Kingdom* (7630/76) DR 19, 113; Report: 17 December 1981.

[63] *McFeeley et al.* v. *United Kingdom* (8317/78) Report: 3 EHRR 161.

[64] Decision of 6 October 1977 (JB 1978, 312).

[65] *X* v. *Austria* (2291/64) CD 24, 20: taking a person through the town wearing handcuffs and convict's dress; *X* v. *United Kingdom* (3973/69) CD 32, 70: classification of a person, who was subsequently acquitted, as a 'Category A' prisoner on the basis of his conviction for murder; *X* v. *Netherlands* (7602/76) DR 7, 161: obligation to accept whatever job is offered (including a job to which social discredit may be attached) in order to profit from unemployment benefits; *X* v. *Belgium* (7697/76) DR 9, 194: release of a person from prison without any resources or employment; *Agee* v. *United Kingdom* (7729/76) DR 7, 164: a statement made in Parliament by a Minister giving reasons for the deportation of an alien; *X* v. *Austria* (8142/78), DR 18, 88: a confidential mother-tongue census designed to discover the languages spoken by citizens; *Campbell and Cosans* v. *United Kingdom* (7511/76; 7743/76) Report: 16 May 1980 (referred to EUCT): the mere fact that the applicants' children attended an educational system providing for physical chastisement; *McFeeley et al.* v. *United Kingdom, supra*: having to wear prison uniform, or to work, in prison; restricted diet, cellular confinement, and the loss of remission of sentence for diciplinary offences there; close-body searches; or the combination of all these; *X* v. *Federal Republic of Germany* (8518/79) DR 20, 193: the forced administration of medicines, subject to judicial control, to a mentally abnormal prisoner in a psychiatric hospital.

[66] *Tyrer* v. *United Kingdom*, Judgment, *supra*, n. 52.

in the nature of things, relative; it depends on all the circumstances and, in particular, on the nature and context of the punishment itself and the manner and method of its execution.[67] In *Tyrer* v. *United Kingdom*,[68] EUCM found that birching as a punishment, ordered by a court and administered as provided for in the Isle of Man, is an assault on human dignity which humiliates and disgraces the offender without any redeeming social value. (It also degrades all others who take part in the procedure: the police, the offender's parents, and the attending doctor.) Confirming the finding of 'degrading punishment', the majority of EUCT declared:

The very nature of judicial corporal punishment is that it involves one human being inflicting physical violence on another human being. Furthermore, it is institutionalised by law, ordered by the judicial authorities of the State and carried out by the police authorities of the State. Thus, although the applicant did not suffer any severe or long-lasting physical effects, his punishment — whereby he was treated as an object in the power of the authorities — constituted an assault on precisely that which it is one of the main purposes of [*EHR* 3] to protect, namely a person's dignity and physical integrity.[69]

Publicity may be a relevant factor in assessing whether a punishment is degrading. But the absence of publicity will not necessarily prevent a punishment from being so classified. It may well suffice that the victim is humiliated in his own eyes, even if not in the eyes of others.[70]

A punishment does not lose its degrading character merely because it is believed to be, or actually is, an effective deterrent or aid to crime control.[71] Nor does the fact that one penalty may be preferable to, or have less adverse effects or be less serious than, another penalty, of itself mean that the first penalty is not degrading.[72]

A penalty which is not proportionate to the offence is degrading.[73] Federal German national courts have held that the deprivation of civic rights as a punitive measure for a comparatively light offence constitutes degrading punishment.[74]

Treatment of prisoners

HRC has expressed the view that imprisonment 'in conditions seriously detrimental to a prisoner's health' constitutes violations of *ICPR* 7 and 10(1);[75] so

---

[67] *Ibid.*

[68] Report: 14 December 1976.

[69] Judgment, *supra*. On the practice in schools of applying corporal punishment as a disciplinary measure, see *Campbell* v. *United Kingdom* (7511/76) DR 12, 49; *Cosans* v. *United Kingdom* (7743/76) DR 12, 140; Report (on both applications): 16 May 1980 (referred to EUCT).

[70] *Tyrer* v. *United Kingdom*, Judgment, *supra*.

[71] *Ibid.*

[72] *Ibid.*

[73] Decision of 14 July 1971, BG, Federal Republic of Germany (NJW 1971, 20). See also Decision of 25 January 1963, AG Wiesbaden (NJW 1963, 967): 'The words "inhuman or degrading" are to be understood as equivalent not to "cruel and crushing" but to "disproportionate and unreasonably prejudicial to the personal rights of the individual" . . . Article 3 [of *EHR*] embodies the very relevant and universally binding principle of the necessity for a reasonable relation between the quantity of guilt and opprobriousness of the crime on the one hand and the punishment to be inflicted, together with its secondary consequences, on the other.'

[74] *Ibid.* See also Decision of 4 October 1967, AG Berlin-Tiergarten (NJW 1968, 61); Decision of 10 June 1963, OLG Köln NJW 1963, 1748).

[75] *Ambrosini et al.* v. *Uruguay* (R. 1/5) HRC 34, 124.

does maltreatment in prison as a result of which, after release, one of a prisoner's legs is several centimetres shorter than the other;[76] so does being kept, for most of the time during several months, blindfolded and with his hands tied together,[77] especially where this results in the paralysis of one arm, leg injuries, infected eyes, and a substantial loss of weight.[78] *ICPR* 10(1) is also violated where prisoners are held incommunicado for periods between three and ten months, and denied visits by any members of their family.[79]

EHR contains no provision equivalent to *ICPR* 10(1): cases about the treatment of prisoners are generally considered at Strasbourg in the context of the prohibitions of 'inhuman or degrading treatment or punishment' in *EHR* 3 (see above). *AMR* 5(2) does have such a provision, but no case on it has yet come before IACM or IACT.

§14.3.6 EVIDENCE

In *Denmark et al.* v. *Greece*,[80] EUCM noted that there are certain inherent difficulties in the proof of allegations of torture or cruel, inhuman or degrading treatment or punishment:

First, a victim or a witness able to corroborate his story might hesitate to describe or reveal all that has happened to him for fear of reprisals upon himself or his family. *Secondly*, acts of torture or ill-treatment by agents of the police or armed services would be carried out as far as possible without witnesses and perhaps without the knowledge of higher authority. *Thirdly*, where allegations of torture or ill-treatment are made, the authorities, whether the police or armed services or the Ministers concerned, must inevitably feel that they have a collective reputation to defend, a feeling which would be all the stronger in those authorities that had no knowledge of the activities of the agents against whom the allegations are made. In consequence, there may be reluctance of higher authority to admit, or allow inquiries to be made into, facts which might show that the allegations are true. *Lastly*, physical traces of torture or ill-treatment may with lapse of time become unrecognisable, even by medical experts, particularly where the form of torture itself leaves little external marks.

In *Ireland* v. *United Kingdom*,[81] while EUCT held that the standard of proof should be 'beyond reasonable doubt', it observed that such proof may follow from the co-existence of sufficiently strong, clear, and concordant inferences or of similar unrebutted presumptions of fact.

HRC has expressed the view that where specific allegations of torture and ill-treatment are made, and the respondent government merely dismisses them as 'not worthy of any further comment', giving no specific response or any

---

[76] *Ibid.*
[77] *Carballal* v. *Uruguay* (R. 8/33) HRC 36, 125.
[78] *Weinberger* v. *Uruguay* (R. 7/28) HRC 36, 114. Denial of medical treatment is also a violation of *ICPR* 10(1): *Antonaccio* v. *Uruguay* (R. 14/63) published 14 December 1981.
[79] *Ambrosini et al.* v. *Uruguay* (R 1/5) HRC 34, 124; *Pietraroia* v. *Uruguay* (R. 10/44) HRC 36, 153; *de Casariego* v. *Uruguay* (R. 13/56) HRC 36, 185. But *ICPR* 10(2)(a) (see §14.2.1) is not violated where convicted prisoners work as food servers and cleaners in the remand area of a prison, provided that contacts between the two classes of prisoners are kept strictly to a minimum necessary for the performance of these tasks: *Pinkney* v. *Canada* (R. 7/27) published 14 December 1981.
[80] (3321–3/67; 3344/67) Report: 25 January 1976.
[81] (5310/71) Judgment: 2 EHRR 25.

indication that it has even investigated them, 'the Committee cannot but draw appropriate conclusions on the basis of the information before it'.[82] It can form its views on 'facts which have not been contradicted by the State Party'.[83] Where the complainant has given adequate particulars of the acts concerned, including the names of their alleged perpetrators, 'a refutation of these allegations in general terms is not sufficient: the State Party should have investigated the allegations in accordance with its laws and its obligations under the Covenant and the Optional Protocol'[84], 'and brought to justice those found to be responsible'.[85]

IACM too routinely makes findings of torture against respondent governments on evidence which, when it is communicated to them, they do not contradict, or merely deny in general terms, or fail to investigate.[86]

§14.3.7 SUBSIDIARY INSTRUMENTS

Some of the draft Articles of a new Convention on the Elimination of Torture [*CT*] have not yet been agreed, and its text has therefore not yet been adopted. The Convention is designed to supply the definition of 'torture' which is missing from the major instruments,[87] and to impose on each of its State Parties obligations

(1) to ensure that neither torture, nor other cruel, inhuman or degrading treatment or punishment, will take place within its jurisdiction;

(2) to take all available measures to prevent any such acts from being perpetrated there; to provide an enforceable right to compensation if they are; and to make statements obtained by means of them inadmissible in evidence;

(3) not to expel, return, or extradite anyone to a State where there are substantial grounds for believing that there is a danger that such acts will be perpetrated on him there;

(4) to bring the prohibition to the attention of its law enforcement personnel, other public officials, and relevant medical personnel;

(5) to keep its interrogation methods and practices, and its arrangements for the custody and treatment of detained persons, under systematic review to the same end;

(6) to ensure that all acts of torture (including participation, complicity, incitement and attempt) are offences under its criminal law, punishable by severe penalties;

(7) to establish jurisdiction over such offences whenever they are committed in its territory, or by or against its nationals;

(8) to try, or to extradite to a State where he can be tried, any alleged offender — regardless of his or the victim's nationality — who is found to be present in its territory.

---

[82] *Perdomo and de Lanza* v. *Uruguay* (R. 2/8) HRC 35, 111; cf. *de Bouton* v. *Uruguay* (R. 9/37) HRC 36, 143.

[83] *Ambrosini et al.* v. *Uruguay* (R. 1/5) HRC 34, 124; *Sequeira* v. *Uruguay* (R. 1/6) HRC 35, 127.

[84] *Ramirez* v. *Uruguay* (R. 1/4) HRC 35, 121; *Motta* v. *Uruguay* (R. 2/11) HRC 35, 132; *Carballal* v. *Uruguay* (R. 8/33) HRC 36, 125; *Burgos* v. *Uruguay* (R. 12/52) HRC 36, 176. Cf. *Pinkney* v. *Canada* (R. 7/27), *supra*, where the respondent government *had* investigated the allegations of maltreatment, and HRC declined to uphold them although it had initially declared them to be admissible.

[85] *Motta* v. *Uruguay, supra.*

[86] See its Annual Reports, *passim.*

[87] See n. 6, *supra.*

Two options are under discussion for the international supervision of these provisions. One is to confer that task upon HRC. The other, in the form of a draft Optional Protocol, would establish a new International Committee which would have power to visit all places of detention subject to a State Party's jurisdiction, and to report and make recommendations (initially confidential, but publishable in the event of subsequent disagreement) as a result.[88]

Both the UN and the CE have adopted Standard Minimum Rules for the Treatment of Prisoners; there is also a UN Code of Conduct for Law Enforcement Officials, a Draft UN Body of Principles for the Protection of All Persons under any Form of Detention or Imprisonment, and a Draft UN Code of Medical Ethics.

§14.4 Freedom of movement

§14.4.1 TEXTS

UDHR

9. No one shall be subjected to arbitrary . . . exile.

13 (1) Everyone has the right to freedom of movement and residence within the borders of each state.

(2) Everyone has the right to leave any country, including his own, and to return to his country.

ADRD

VIII. Every person has the right to fix his residence within the territory of the state of which he is a national, to move about freely within such territory, and not to leave it except by his own will.

ICPR

12 (1) Everyone lawfully within the territory of a State shall, within that territory, have the right to liberty of movement and freedom to choose his residence.

(2) Everyone shall be free to leave any country, including his own.

(3) The above-mentioned rights shall not be subject to any restrictions except those which are provided by law, are necessary to protect national security, public order (*ordre public*), public health or morals or the rights and freedoms of others, and are consistent with the other rights recognized in the present Covenant.

(4) No one shall be arbitrarily deprived of the right to enter his own country.

[88] See *Torture: How to Make the International Convention Effective*, International Commission of Jurists and Swiss Committee against Torture (2nd ed., 1980).

13. An alien lawfully in the territory of a State Party to the present Covenant may be expelled therefrom only in pursuance of a decision reached in accordance with law and shall, except where compelling reasons of national security otherwise require, be allowed to submit the reasons against his expulsion and to have his case reviewed by, and be represented for the purpose before, the competent authority or a person or persons especially designated by the competent authority.

EHR P4

2 (1) Everyone lawfully within the territory of a State shall, within that territory, have the right to liberty of movement and freedom to choose his residence.

(2) Everyone shall be free to leave any country, including his own.

(3) No restrictions shall be placed on the exercise of these rights other than such as are in accordance with law and are necessary in a democratic society in the interests of national security or public safety, for the maintenance of *ordre public*, for the prevention of crime, for the protection of health or morals, or for the protection of the rights and freedoms of others.

(4) The rights set forth in paragraph 1 may also be subject, in particular areas, to restrictions imposed in accordance with law and justified by the public interest in a democratic society.

3 (1) No one shall be expelled, by means either of an individual or of a collective measure, from the territory of the State of which he is a national.

(2) No one shall be deprived of the right to enter the territory of the State of which he is a national.

4. Collective expulsion of aliens is prohibited.

ESC

I, (18) The nationals of any one of the Contracting Parties have the right to engage in any gainful occupation in the territory of any one of the others on a footing of equality with the nationals of the latter, subject to restrictions based on cogent economic or social reasons.

II, 18. With a view to ensuring the effective exercise of the right to engage in a gainful occupation in the territory of any other Contracting Party, the Contracting Parties undertake:

(1) to apply existing regulations in a spirit of liberality;

(2) to simplify existing formalities and to reduce or abolish chancery dues and other charges payable by foreign workers or their employers;

175

    (3) to liberalize, individually or collectively, regulations governing the employment of foreign workers;

and recognize:

    (4) the right of their nationals to leave the country to engage in a gainful occupation in the territories of the other Contracting Parties.

(*App.* It is understood that these provisions are not concerned with the question of entry into the territories of the Contracting Parties and do not prejudice the provisions of the European Convention on Establishment, signed at Paris on 13th December 1955.)

I, (19) Migrant workers who are nationals of a Contracting Party and their families have the right to protection and assistance in the territory of any other Contracting Party.

II, 19. With a view to ensuring the effective exercise of the right of migrant workers and their families to protection and assistance in the territory of any other Contracting Party, the Contracting Parties undertake:

    (1) to maintain or to satisfy themselves that there are maintained adequate and free services to assist such workers, particularly in obtaining accurate information, and to take all appropriate steps, so far as national laws and regulations permit, against misleading propaganda relating to emigration and immigration;

    (2) to adopt appropriate measures within their own jurisdiction to facilitate the departure, journey and reception of such workers and their families, and to provide, within their own jurisdiction, appropriate services for health, medical attention and good hygienic conditions during the journey;

    (3) to promote co-operation, as appropriate, between social services, public and private, in emigration and immigration countries;

    (4) to secure for such workers lawfully within their territories, insofar as such matters are regulated by law or regulations or are subject to the control of administrative authorities, treatment not less favourable than that of their own nationals in respect of the following matters:

        (*a*) remuneration and other employment and working conditions;

        (*b*) membership of trade unions and enjoyment of the benefits of collective bargaining;

        (*c*) accommodation;

    (5) to secure for such workers lawfully within their territories

treatment not less favourable than that of their own nationals with regard to employment taxes, dues or contributions payable in respect of employed persons;

(6) to facilitate as far as possible the reunion of the family of a foreign worker permitted to establish himself in the territory;

(*App.* For the purpose of this provision, the term 'family of a foreign worker' is understood to mean at least his wife and dependent children under the age of 21 years.)

(7) to secure for such workers lawfully within their territories treatment not less favourable than that of their own nationals in respect of legal proceedings relating to matters referred to in this Article;

(8) to secure that such workers lawfully residing within their territories are not expelled unless they endanger national security or offend against public interest or morality;

(9) to permit, within legal limits, the transfer of such parts of the earnings and savings of such workers as they may desire;

(10) to extend the protection and assistance provided for in this Article to self-employed migrants insofar as such measures apply.

AMR

22 (1) Every person lawfully in the territory of a State Party has the right to move about in it and to reside in it subject to the provisions of the law.

(2) Every person has the right to leave any country freely, including his own.

(3) The exercise of the foregoing rights may be restricted only pursuant to a law to the extent necessary in a democratic society to prevent crime or to protect national security, public safety, public order, public morals, public health, or the rights or freedoms of others.

(4) The exercise of the rights recognized in paragraph 1 may also be restricted by law in designated zones for reasons of public interest.

(5) No one can be expelled from the territory of the state of which he is a national or be deprived of the right to enter it.

(6) An alien lawfully in the territory of a State Party to this Convention may be expelled from it only pursuant to a decision reached in accordance with law.

(9) The collective expulsion of aliens is prohibited.

[*AFR*]

12 (1) Every individual shall have the right to freedom of movement and residence within the borders of a State provided he abides by the law.

(2) Every individual shall have the right to leave any country including his own, and to return to his country. This right may only be subject to restrictions provided for by law for the protection of national security, law and order, public health or morality.

(4) A non-national legally admitted in a territory of a State Party to the present Charter, may only be expelled from it by virtue of a decision taken in accordance with the law.

(5) The mass expulsion of non-nationals shall be prohibited. Mass expulsion shall be that which is aimed at national, racial, ethnic or religious groups.

§14.4.2 CROSS-REFERENCES

State obligation: Absolute and immediate under *ICPR, EHR, AMR*, and [*AFR*]: see §6.3. Qualified and progressive under *ESC*: see §6.4. For the juridical status of obligations under *UDHR* and *ADRD*, see §6.2.

Signatures, ratifications, accessions, reservations, and interpretations: See Table A for the State Parties bound by these provisions on 1 January 1982, and any reservations and interpretations notified by them.

Derogation: Non-derogable in any circumstances under [*AFR*]; derogable in exceptional circumstances under *ICPR, EHR, ESC*, and *AMR*: see §11.

Non-discrimination: No discrimination of any kind is allowed in respect of these rights or freedoms: see §7 for the relevant provisions in the instruments.

Abuse: See §9 for the relevant provisions in these instruments.

Savings: See §10 for the relevant provisions in these instruments.

Restrictions and limitations: Note the specific provisions in *ICPR* 12(3), *EHR P4* 2(3) and (4), *AMR* 22(3) and (4), and [*AFR* 12(2)]. See §8 for the general provisions in these instruments, and the principles governing all restriction and limitation clauses.

International supervision, interpretation, application and enforcement: By HRC under *ICPR* (see §27); by EUCM and EUCT under *EHR* (see §28); by IACM and IACT under *AMR* (see §29); by [AFCM] under [*AFR*] (see §30); supervision only by EUCE under *ESC* (see §32). See also §6.6 for the obligation to provide domestic remedies under *UDHR, ADRD, ICPR, EHR, AMR*, and [*AFR*].

§14.4.3 COMMENT

As defined in these instruments, freedom of movement falls into six distinct categories:

(1) freedom to choose a residence within the territory of a State;
(2) freedom to move about within the borders of a State;
(3) freedom to leave a State;
(4) freedom to enter a State;
(5) freedom from expulsion from a State;
(6) freedom from exile.

These six freedoms are subject to quite different incidents. The first two — freedom to choose (or, in the case of *ADRD*, 'fix') one's residence and move about within a single State territory — are treated together in all the instruments. Only *ADRD* VIII confines them to 'nationals'; *ICPR, EHR P4*, and *AMR* limit them to persons 'lawfully within the territory', but draw no distinction between nationals and aliens. *AMR* 22(1) alone adds the phrase 'subject to the provisions of the law'; [*AFR* 12(1)] instead adds a proviso that 'he abides by the law'. The third freedom — to leave any country 'including his own' — appears almost identically in all the instruments.

ICPR, EHR P4, and *AMR* — unlike the Declarations — allow restrictions for each of these three freedoms. [*AFR*] allows them only for the third. In each case, the restriction must be 'provided by' (*ICPR* and [*AFR*]), 'in accordance with' (*EHR P4*), or 'pursuant to' (*AMR*) law — and, in the latter two cases only, 'necessary in a democratic society'. (*ICPR* instead requires consistency with the other rights recognized in it.) The only objectives of the restrictions common to all four of these treaties are national security and public order ('law and order' in the case of [*AFR*]). *ICPR* and the two Conventions add the rights and freedoms of others. *ICPR* 12(3), *AMR* 22(3), and [*AFR* 12(2)] add public health and public morals; *AMR* and *EHR P4* add public safety, and *EHR P4* is the only one to reserve 'the prevention of crime' as well. *AMR* and *EHR P4* also allow, in the case of the first two freedoms only, an additional restriction in favour of 'the public interest' for 'designated zones' or 'particular areas', but in the case of *EHR P4* again only if 'imposed in accordance with law' and justified in 'a democratic society'.

The fourth freedom — to enter (or, in the case of *UDHR*, return to) a State — differs profoundly from the first three, in that it is confined throughout to nationals of the State concerned. Nowhere in any international human rights treaty has any State accepted any express obligation to allow aliens to enter its territory. But for nationals, the freedom to enter is absolute and not subject to any restrictions — except that *ICPR* 12(4) alone requires that they should not be 'arbitrarily' deprived of it, and that [*AFR*] uniquely subjects it to the same exceptions as the freedom to leave. (*ADRD* VIII omits it altogether.)

As for expulsion, only *EHR P4* 3(1) and *AMR* 22(5) even contemplate it as a possibility for nationals, and proceed to forbid it for that case without any qualification. But *ICPR, EHR P4, AMR*, and [*AFR*] all allow the expulsion of aliens: *EHR P4* 4 only requires that it shall not be 'collective';[1] *AMR* 22(9) and [*AFR* 12(5)] contain the same prohibition, but (in *AMR* 22(6) and [*AFR* 12(4)] respectively) also require that, in the case of individuals, it may only take place pursuant to a decision taken 'in accordance with [the] law'. *ICPR* 13 calls, in such cases, for two additional safeguards: the opportunity for the alien to submit reasons against his expulsion, and to have his case competently reviewed

---

[1] Robertson explains that the omission of any mention of individual expulsion here is principally because there is already a provision on the subject in Article 3 of the European Convention on Establishment of 13 December 1955; *Human Rights in Europe*, 133.

— 'except where compelling reasons of national security otherwise require'. But those safeguards are only available to aliens 'lawfully in the territory'; there is no protection here of any kind against the expulsion of unlawful immigrants — not even in the case of refugees (but see §14.5.5).

As for exile, that is necessarily an infringement of the first freedom if it is internal, and of the fifth if it is external. Only *UDHR* 9 mentions it separately, and prohibits it only if it is 'arbitrary'.

The detailed provisions in *ESC* relate entirely to 'migrant workers' — that is, nationals of one of the State Parties working within the territories of one of the others. These provisions are designed to relieve migrant workers of at least some part of the handicaps from which, as aliens competing with native workers, they might otherwise suffer.

§14.4.4 HISTORY

The right to freedom of movement was legally recognized as early as 1215 in the English Magna Carta, in the following terms:

It shall be lawful to any person, for the future, to go out of our Kingdom, and to return, safely and securely, by land or by water, saving his allegiance to us, unless it be in time of war, for some short space, for the common good of the Kingdom: excepting prisoners and outlaws, according to the law of the land, and of the people of the nation at war against us, and Merchants who shall be treated as it is said above.[2]

This right, however, does not appear to have been specifically provided for in any of the older national constitutions. There is no reference to it in either the French *déclaration des droits de l'homme et du citoyen* of 1789, or the American Bill of Rights of 1791. However, in a series of judgments beginning in the nineteenth century, the US Supreme Court has held that freedom to travel throughout the United States, which includes the freedom to enter and abide in any State in the Union, is one of the rights and privileges of national citizenship,[3] and that freedom to travel abroad is an attribute of 'personal liberty' which is guaranteed to every person (i.e. not only US citizens) in the Fifth and Fourteenth Amendments.[4]

In India, where the 1949 Constitution recognizes the right of every citizen to move freely throughout its territory and to reside and settle in any part of it, the Supreme Court has held that the right to travel abroad, though not specifically provided for, is implied in the right to personal liberty of which a person may not be deprived except according to a procedure established by law.[5]

More recent national constitutions have tended to adopt the terminology of *ICPR*.

---

[2] Ch. 42 in the version confirmed by King Edward I in 1297; 6 Halsbury's Statutes (3rd ed.) 401.
[3] *Aptheker* v. *Secretary of State* 378 US 500; *United States* v. *Guest* 383 US 745; *Shapiro* v. *Thompson* 394 US 618; *Griffin* v. *Breckenridge* 403 US 88; *Dunn* v. *Blumstein* 405 US 330.
[4] *Kent* v. *Dulles* 357 US 116. See also *Aptheker* v. *Secretary of State, supra*; *Zemel* v. *Rusk* 381 US 1, at 23.
[5] *Maneka Gandhi* v. *Union of India and another* [1978] SCR 312; *Satwant Singh Sawhney* v. *Ramarthnam et al.* [1967] 3 SCR 525.

§14.4.5 JURISPRUDENCE

Freedom of movement within a State

HRC has indicated that among restrictions justifiable under *ICPR* 12(3), on the freedom of choice of residence protected by *ICPR* 12(1), might be restrictions on the categories of persons entitled to live on a tribal reserve, for the purpose of protecting the resources and preserving the identity of the tribe.[6]

In *Kharak Singh* v. *State of Uttar Pradesh et al.*,[7] the Supreme Court of India examined the question whether the placing of a person under surveillance[8] restricted his right 'to move freely throughout the territory of India'. The majority view was that the right to 'move' denoted nothing more than a right of locomotion, and that in the context the adverb 'freely' would only connote that the freedom to move is without restriction and absolute, i.e. to move wherever one likes, whenever one likes and however one likes, subject of course to any valid law. The Court observed that by a knock at the door or by a man being roused from his sleep, his locomotion was not impeded or prejudiced in any way. Rejecting a submission that the knowledge or apprehension that the police were on the watch for the movements of the petitioner might induce a psychological inhibition against his movements, the majority held that the freedom guaranteed had reference to something tangible and physical, and not to the imponderable effect on the mind of a person which might guide his action in the matter of his movement or locomotion.

The minority view was expressed by Subha Rao, J in the following terms:

Mere movement unobstructed by physical restriction cannot in itself be the object of a person's travel. A person travels ordinarily in quest of some objective. He goes to a place to enjoy, to do business, to meet friends, to have secret and intimate consultations with others and to do many other things. If a man is shadowed, his movements are obviously constricted. He can move physically, but it can only be a movement of automation. How could a movement under the scrutinising gaze of the policeman be described as a free movement? The whole country is his jail. The freedom of movement [guaranteed] therefore must be a movement in a free country, i.e. in a country where he can do whatever he likes, speak to whomever he wants, meet people of his own choice without any apprehension, subject of course to the law of social control. The petitioner under the shadow of surveillance is certainly deprived of his freedom. He can move physically, but he cannot do so freely, for all his activities are watched and noted. The shroud of surveillance cast upon him perforce engenders inhibitions in him and he cannot act freely as he would like to.[9]

In view of subsequent pronouncements by the Court adopting a more liberal approach to interpretation,[10] that minority view may probably now be regarded as a correct statement of the Indian law.

[6] *Lovelace* v. *Canada* (R. 6/24) HRC 36, 166.

[7] [1964] 1 SCR 332.

[8] The surveillance involved secret picketing of the house or approaches to the house, domiciliary visits at night, periodical inquiries by police officers into repute, habits, association, income, expenses, and occupation, the reporting by constables of movements and absences from home, the verification of movements and absences by means of inquiry slips, and the collection and recording on a history sheet of all information bearing on conduct: ibid.

[9] *Ibid.*, at 360.

[10] See *Cooper* v. *Union of India* [1971] 1 SCR 512; *Maneka Gandhi* v. *Union of India and another, supra*, n. 5.

In *Shapiro* v. *Thompson*,[11] the US Supreme Court held that a statute which classified indigent resident families in a State into two categories — those who resided a year or more in the State and were thus eligible for welfare assistance, and those who had resided less than a year in the State and were thus ineligible for assistance — was in violation of a person's basic constitutional right to travel freely from one State to another. A similar conclusion was reached in *Dunn* v. *Blumstein*, where the Court examined the validity of durational residence voting requirements.[12] But in *Zemel* v. *Rusk*, Warren, CJ of the US Supreme Court observed that freedom of movement within a country does not mean that movement into areas ravaged by flood, fire, or pestilence can be guaranteed, if it can be demonstrated that unlimited travel to such areas would directly and materially interfere with the safety and welfare of the area, or of the nation as a whole.[13]

The Supreme Court of Cyprus has held that a regulation which restricts the circulation of private motor vehicles, according to their registration numbers, to alternate weekends restricts the 'right to move freely throughout the territory of the Republic', since public transport was inadequate at weekends, few citizens could afford to own two motor cars or to use taxis, and the distances could not reasonably be covered on foot.[14]

Freedom to choose a residence within a State

The freedom to choose a residence was successfully invoked in the German courts by a Turkish national residing in Berlin for employment purposes when, for the first time, his indefinite residence permit issued under the Aliens Act by the Commissioner of Police was stamped: 'Not authorised to take up residence in the districts of Kreuzberg, Tiergarten or Wedding.'[15]

In India, an Indian citizen successfully contended that section 7 of the Influx from Pakistan (Control) Act 1949, under which his removal from his own country could be ordered by the government if he returned from a visit to Pakistan with an invalid or defective permit, was in conflict with his right 'to reside and settle in any part of the territory of India'.[16]

Freedom to leave a country

IACM has expressed the view that 'no State has the right to prevent an individual from leaving the country, except when that individual is accused of a common crime.' Although States have the right to require administrative formalities to be completed before departure, the imposition of prison sentences from six months to three years for failure to comply with such formalities 'appears to be excessive'.[17] IACM has also expressed the view that, where a State prevents an

---

[11] *Supra*, n. 3.

[12] *Supra*, n. 3. See also *United States* v. *Guest, supra*, n. 3, which dealt with interference with a person's right to move freely on highways and other instrumentalities of interstate commerce.

[13] *Supra*, n. 4, at 15.

[14] *Elia* v. *The Police* [1980] 2 CLR 118.

[15] Decision of 26 August 1977, VwG Berlin, (NJW 1978, 68). But contrast the decision of the European Court of Justice (established under the Treaty of Rome) in *Rutili* v. *Minister of Interior, France* [1975] ECR 1219, which does not seem to accord with *EHR P4* 2(1) and *EHR* 14.

[16] *Ebrahim Vazir Mavat* v. *State of Bombay and others* [1954] SCR 933.

[17] 6 Cuba 9.

alien from returning to his own country, that constitutes a violation of *ADRD* VIII.[18]

Under *EHR P4*, the freedom to leave a country is not available to a person who is lawfully detained in that country.[19]

Originally, a passport was a document identifying a citizen, requesting foreign powers to allow its bearer to enter and pass freely and safely, and recognizing the right of the bearer to the protection and good offices of his own country's diplomatic and consular officers. Today, however, another crucial function is control over exit.[20]

In India, in the absence of a law regulating the issue of passports, the Supreme Court has held that the refusal of a passport by the Executive, acting in its discretion, was a violation of the citizen's right to leave his country.[21]

In the United States, the Supreme Court has, in a series of cases, been called upon to interpret and apply an Act of Congress in the following terms:

The Secretary of State may grant and issue passports . . . under such rules as the President shall designate and prescribe for and on behalf of the United States, and no other person shall grant, issue or verify such passports.[22]

In *Kent* v. *Dulles*,[23] the petitioner, an American citizen, applied for a passport to visit England and to attend a meeting in Helsinki, Finland, of an organization known as the World Council of Peace. His request was denied on the grounds: (*a*) that he was a Communist and (*b*) that he had had 'a consistent and prolonged adherence to the Communist Party line'. The Court held that —

(1) the citizen's right of exit can be regulated only pursuant to the law-making functions of the Congress, and if that power is delegated, the standards must be adequate to pass scrutiny by the accepted tests;
(2) all delegated powers that curtail or dilute activities such as travel will be construed narrowly;
(3) an intention to give the Secretary of State an unbridled discretion to grant or withhold a passport will not be imputed to the Congress, having regard to previous administrative practice under which a passport was denied only in a situation involving either citizenship or criminal activity;
(4) the Secretary of State has no authority to withhold a passport from a citizen because of his beliefs and associations.

In *Aptheker* v. *Secretary of State*,[24] the Court held that section 6 of the Subversive Activities Control Act, which forbade members of Communist organizations 'to apply for, use, or attempt to use, a passport', too broadly and indiscriminately restricted a citizen's right to travel. The Court emphasized that, in the absence of war, there was no way in which a citizen could be prevented from travelling within or without the country, unless there was power to detain him. Pointing out that being a Communist was not a crime, the Court explained that if the argument was that travel might increase the likelihood of illegal

---

[18] Case 1742 (Cuba) AR 1975, 37.
[19] *X* v. *Federal Republic of Germany* (3962/69) CD 32, 68; *X* v. *Federal Republic of Germany* (4256/69) CD 37, 67; *X* v. *Federal Republic of Germany* (7680/76) DR 9, 190.
[20] *Kent* v. *Dulles, supra*, n. 4 at 120; *United States* v. *Laub et al.* 385 US 475.
[21] *Satwant Singh Sawhney* v. *Ramarathnam, supra*, n. 5; cf. the *obiter dictum* of T. S. Fernando, J. of the Supreme Court of Ceylon in *In re Ratnagopal* 70 NLR 409.
[22] The Passport Act of July 3, 1926; 44 Stat 887, 22 USC s. 211a.
[23] *Supra*, n. 4.   [24] *Supra*, n. 3.

events happening, 'so does being alive'. In such an event, the illegal act can of course be punished; but the right remains sacrosanct.

In *Zemel* v. *Rusk*,[25] the petitioner complained that his application to the State Department to have his passport validated for travel to Cuba as a tourist had been denied. The question was raised whether the Secretary of State had the authority to impose area restrictions on travel. Warren, CJ, expressing the majority opinion, held that in the light of administrative practice before the enactment of the Passport Act, the answer should be in the affirmative. Three dissenting judgments were, however, delivered. The same question was raised again, but in a different context, in *United States* v. *Laub et al.*[26] Acquitting several defendants who had been charged with recruiting and arranging the travel to Cuba of American citizens whose passports, although otherwise valid, were not specifically validated for travel to that country, the Court unanimously held that area restrictions upon the use of an otherwise valid passport were not criminally enforceable.

In *Maneka Gandhi* v. *Union of India*,[27] the Indian Supreme Court held that the *audi alterem partem* rule must be regarded as incorporated in the Passport Act by necessary implication, since any procedure which dealt with the modalities of regulating, restricting, or even rejecting a fundamental right has to be fair, not 'arbitrary, freakish or bizarre'. Accordingly, the passport authority may proceed to impound a passport without any prior intimation, but as soon as the order impounding the passport is made, an opportunity for a hearing, remedial in aim, should be given to the person concerned so that he may present his case and controvert that of the passport authority, point out why his passport should not be impounded, and have the order impounding it recalled.

An attempt in Ceylon to impose additional restrictions on the freedom to travel was effectively stifled by the Supreme Court of that country. In 1964, the immigration authorities insisted on 'clearance' from the Ministry of Defence and External Affairs before a person holding a valid passport, the necessary visas, and a ticket could be permitted to leave the country. The General Secretary of the Ceylon United Nations Association applied for 'clearance' to visit Kuala Lumpur to attend a meeting of his Association's parent body, and was notified that the clearance required could not be granted. He appealed to the Supreme Court, which insisted that this 'illegal requirement' should be withdrawn forthwith.[28]

IACM has stated that the refusal to issue a passport to a State's own national constitutes a violation of *ADRD* VIII.[29]

Exile, or denial of entry, for nationals

IACM has expressed the opinion that domestic laws which empower a government to exile individuals (be they foreigners or nationals) from the country 'when the supreme interests of the security of the State so require', or to prohibit such individuals from entering the country when they perform certain acts or, in the opinion of the government, 'constitute a danger to the State', are contrary to *ADRD* VIII, *AMR* 22, and *ICPR* 12.[30] Both as general

---

[25] *Supra*, n. 4.   [26] 385 US 475.   [27] *Supra*, n. 5.
[28] *Aseerwatham* v. *Permanent Secretary, Ministry of Defence and External Affairs et al.*, 6 *J. International Commission of Jurists* 319; see also *Gooneratne* v. *Permanent Secretary, Ministry of Defence and External Affairs et al.*, ibid. 320.
[29] AR 1976, 16.   [30] AR 1977, 86–7; 88.

propositions,[31] and in a series of cases, IACM has also said that the individual exile of nationals,[32] and the denial of entry to their own countries,[33] constitute violations of their rights under *ADRD* VIII. That provision is also violated where a national is forced to flee from his country because he has received a message from the Minister of the Interior to the effect that, if he surrenders to a warrant which has been issued for his arrest, the National Guard 'were not guaranteeing his life'.[34]

Expulsion of aliens

'Expulsion' must be distinguished from 'extradition'. Expulsion is the execution of an order to leave the country without being left the possibility of returning later, while extradition means the transfer of a person from one jurisdiction to another for the purpose of standing trial,[35] or for the execution of a sentence imposed upon him.[36]

HRC has expressed the view that, where an alien is expelled in accordance with the procedures laid down by a State's domestic law, it is not for the Committee to evaluate whether the competent authorities of that State have correctly interpreted and applied that law, unless it is established that they have acted in bad faith or abused their power.[37]

In *Becker* v. *Denmark*,[38] EUCM explained that 'collective expulsion of aliens' means any measure of the competent authority compelling aliens as a group to leave the country, where such a measure is not taken after, and on the basis of, a reasonable and objective examination of the particular case of each individual alien of the group.

European migrant workers

In the course of the supervision procedure under *ESC* (see §32), EUCE has given the following interpretations of the relevant provisions of *ESC* 18 and 19:

Article 18 applies only to nationals of the State Parties bound by *ESC*, and not to other foreigners.[39] The obligations in this Article are not concerned with entry into the territories of the State Parties, but only with the pursuit of a gainful occupation in those territories.[40] The expression 'subject to restrictions based on cogent economic or social reasons' in *ESC* I, (18) is to be construed as a limitation, and the burden is upon the State Party concerned to show that such reasons exist, and that they justify the restrictions concerned.[41] A regulation which *de iure* or *de facto* restricts an authorization to engage in a gainful occupation to a specific post for a specific employer is not consistent with this Article. Economic or social reasons might justify restricting the employment of aliens to specific types of jobs in certain occupational or geographical sectors, but not the obligation to remain in the employment of a specific enterprise.[42] Nor would they justify the systematic refusal of a work permit to a foreign

---

[31] AR 1976, 16; AR 1978, 132.

[32] Cases 2719, 2723, and 2760 (Bolivia) AR 1978, 54; 62; 75.

[33] Cases 3411-16, 3418-19, 3428, 3434-6, 3440-4, 3446, 3498 and 3548 (Chile) AR 1978, 83 ff. EUCM has said that, even where a State Party has not ratified *EHR P4* and is therefore not bound under that treaty to admit its nationals to its own territory, the discriminatory denial of the right of entry to nationals of one particular race could constitute 'degrading treatment' within the meaning of *EHR* 3 (see §14.3): *Patel et al.* v. *United Kingdom* (4403/70, etc.) CD 36, 92; Report: 3 EHRR 76.

[34] Case 2509 (Panama) AR 1979/80, 63.

[35] *Brückman* v. *Federal Republic of Germany* 6242/73 CD 46,202.

[36] *X* v. *Austria* (6189/73) CD 46, 214.

[37] *Maroufidou* v. *Sweden* (R. 13/58) HRC 36, 160. [38] (7011/75) DR 4, 215.

[39] I, 79. [40] II, 60. [41] II, 60. [42] II, 60.

national who had entered the territory of the State Party concerned without having obtained a work permit beforehand.[43]

'Liberal' regulations should normally make it possible for the foreign worker gradually to have access to activities other than those he was authorized to engage in when entering the host country, and to be perfectly free to do so after a certain period of residence or of activity in his occupation. The letter and spirit of the Article mean that, in each State Party, the situation of nationals of other State Parties should gradually become as far as possible like that of its own nationals.[44] Where a foreign worker who has completed five years' occupational activity in the country is entitled to a valid permit without geographical or occupational restrictions, the obligations under the Article are fulfilled.[45] But where geographical restrictions are imposed on migrant workers in their choice of residence, the obligations are not fulfilled.[46] Nor are they where foreigners may not apply for a vacancy if there is an applicant of local nationality.[47]

Article 19, like Article 18, applies only to nationals of State Parties to *ESC*, and not to other foreigners.[48] However, unlike Article 18, it goes beyond merely guaranteeing equality of treatment as between foreign and national workers: recognizing that migrants are in fact handicapped, it requires the institution by the State Parties of measures which are more favourable and more positive to this category of persons than to their own nationals.[49]

Article 19, paragraph (1) applies both to the nationals of any given State Party who are located in the territory of another, or who wish to go there, and to any nationals of a State who are moving out of it or wish to do so.[50]

Article 19, paragraph (2). Except where the general measures taken to facilitate the departure, travel, and reception of travellers are of an exceedingly high standard, the satisfaction of the obligation arising under this paragraph normally involves the taking of special measures for the benefit of migrant workers.[51] The 'reception' must be provided at the time of arrival and the period immediately following, that is to say during the weeks in which immigrant workers and their families find themselves in a particularly difficult position.[52]

Article 19, paragraph (3). The words 'as appropriate' in this paragraph do not apply to the obligation as such, but to the ways of implementing it: co-operation must be promoted 'as appropriate' either between public services or between private services, or between both of them, depending on the structure of the social services in the countries concerned.[53]

Article 19, paragraph (4). It is not enough for a government to prove that no discrimination exists in law alone: it is obliged to prove in addition that no discrimination is practised in fact.[54] A State Party in which alien workers may only be granted public housing if they have lived there for seven years fails to meet its obligation under this paragraph.[55] Even where there are social problems due to overcrowding, the number of migrant workers is small and the situation in respect of housing therefore trivial, a residential qualification of

---

[43] II, 83.
[44] II, 60.
[45] III, 84.
[46] V, 119.
[47] VI, 110.
[48] I, 81.
[49] I, 81.
[50] I, 82.
[51] III, 88.
[52] IV, 115.
[53] III, 90.
[54] III, 92
[55] II, 68; VI, 122; cf. *Shapiro* v. *Thompson, supra,* n. 3.

five years for the provision of publicly financed accommodation in respect of any person who was not born within the State fails to satisfy the requirements of this paragraph.[56]

Article 19, paragraph (6). Where the word 'worker' is used in *ESC* it applies equally to female workers as to male ones, except where the context demands a different interpretation. Accordingly, the expression 'family of a foreign worker' in this paragraph — when taken in conjunction with the definition of that expression in the Appendix — includes the children (but not the husband) of a female worker.[57]

Where foreigners employed on domestic work are not entitled to be reunited with their spouses and children, the obligation under this paragraph is not fulfilled. Nor is it where the child of a migrant worker travelling with its parents is liable to be refused permission to remain if it suffers from some disability which calls for special care and treatment, and the financial situation of the parents is such that recourse to a public institution will be involved,[58] unless the only effect of the regulation would be to put obstacles in the way of foreign workers taking up employment in the country with the sole aim of obtaining the benefits of the country's health services for their sick or disabled children.[59]

The obligation under this paragraph is also not met if, by the terms of a regulation in force, permission for members of the family to join a migrant worker can be given only if he has been living in the State for at least three years, even if this rule is not always applied to the letter and residents' permits are in many cases granted to the families of migrant workers at the end of the first year.[60]

The obligation under this paragraph includes a requirement to take special steps to aid foreign workers to find accommodation, unless conditions on the housing market are such that no steps are necessary.[61] Where foreign workers cannot apply for family housing as long as they are living alone in the country, and cannot obtain permission for their families to join them in that country unless they have suitable accommodation to house them, the obligation under this paragraph is not fulfilled.[62]

Article 19, paragraph (8). For the purpose of this paragraph, 'lawfully residing within their territories' means being in possession of all papers legally required by the country of residence for regular residents — including, if need be, a resident's permit and a work permit.[63] Where legislation enables a person to be deported on the sole ground of membership of another deported person's family, the obligation under this paragraph is not satisfied, since the persons to be so deported might themselves be lawfully resident foreign workers.[64] The expulsion of migrant workers on the grounds of mental or any other sickness would constitute a violation of this provision, except in the case of refusal of treatment.[65] For this purpose, the expression 'public interest' in the paragraph does not include 'public health'.[66] Unless there is a right of appeal to an independent body against a deportation order, even on the grounds of national security, public interest, or public morality, the obligation under this paragraph

[56] IV, 123.
[57] IV, 124.
[58] I, 85.
[59] III, 97.
[60] II, 69.
[61] III, 94.
[62] V, 136.
[63] II, 197.
[64] IV, 130.
[65] IV, 130.
[66] V, 138; VI, 127.

is not satisfied. There must be appropriate guarantees against arbitrary decisions in such cases.[67]

Article 19, paragraph (9). The expression 'within legal limits' in this paragraph does not permit a State Party to place any obstacle in the way of transferring a reasonable amount of earnings and savings, having regard to the situation of the migrant and his family.[68] It is not enough that migrant workers are treated equally with the nationals of the State Party concerned: if substantial restrictions are imposed on the transfer of money by those nationals, more generous arrangements must be made for foreign workers within the territory.[69]

§14.5 Asylum

§14.5.1 TEXTS

UDHR

14 (1) Everyone has the right to seek and to enjoy in other countries asylum from persecution.

(2) This right may not be invoked in the case of prosecutions genuinely arising from non-political crimes or from acts contrary to the purposes and principles of the United Nations.

ADRD

XXVII. Every person has the right, in case of pursuit not resulting from ordinary crimes, to seek and receive asylum in foreign territory, in accordance with the laws of each country and with international agreements.

AMR

22 (7) Every person has the right to seek and be granted asylum in a foreign territory, in accordance with the legislation of the state and international conventions, in the event he is being pursued for political offenses or related common crimes.

(8) In no case may an alien be deported or returned to a country, regardless of whether or not it is his country of origin, if in that country his right to life or personal freedom is in danger of being violated because of his race, nationality, religion, social status, or political opinions.

[AFR]

12 (3) Every individual shall have the right, when persecuted, to seek and obtain asylum in other countries in accordance with the laws of those countries and international conventions.

---

[67] I, 86; V, 139; VI, 128.   [68] I, 86.   [69] IV, 121.

23 (2) For the purpose of strengthening peace, solidarity and friendly relations, States parties to the present Charter shall ensure that:

(*a*) any individual enjoying the right of asylum under Article 12 of the present Charter shall not engage in subversive activities against his country of origin or any other State party to the present Charter;

§14.5.2 CROSS-REFERENCES

State obligation: Absolute and immediate under *AMR* and [*AFR*]: see §6.3. For the juridical status of obligations under *UDHR* and *ADRD*, see §6.2.

Signatures, ratifications, accessions, reservations, and interpretations: See Table A for the State Parties bound by these provisions on 1 January 1982, and any reservations and interpretations notified by them.

Derogation: Non-derogable in any circumstances under [*AFR*]; derogable in exceptional circumstances under *AMR*: see §11.

Non-discrimination: No discrimination of any kind is allowed in respect of these rights or freedoms: see §7 for the relevant provisions in the instruments. But note the restricted non-discrimination catalogue in *AMR* 22(8).

Abuse: See §9 for the relevant provisions in these instruments.

Savings: See §10 for the relevant provisions in these instruments.

Restrictions and limitations: Note the specific provisions in [*AFR* 23(2)(*a*)]; see §8 for the general provisions in these instruments, and the principles governing all restriction and limitation clauses.

International supervision, interpretation, application, and enforcement: By IACM and IACT under *AMR* (see §29); by [*AFCM*] under [*AFR*] (see §30). See also §6.6 for the obligation to provide domestic remedies under *UDHR*, *ADRD*, *AMR*, and [*AFR*].

Subsidiary instruments: CR, CS_1 (see §14.5.5).

§14.5.3 COMMENT

Although a right of asylum is declared in both the Declarations, *AMR* and [*AFR*] are the only treaties that include it: both *ICPR* and *EHR*[1] are silent on the matter.

All four instruments seek to restrict the right to persons who are not ordinary fugitives from justice. *AMR* positively confines it to pursuit for 'political offences or related common crimes'; *UDHR* negatively excludes prosecution for 'non-political crimes', and for 'acts contrary to the purposes and principles of the UN'. *ADRD* excludes pursuit resulting from 'ordinary crimes'. None of the instruments attempts any definition of these concepts: *UDHR*'s use of the word 'genuinely' appears to envisage an objective test; *ADRD* and *AMR* refer the question to the domestic laws of the nations concerned, and to international

---

[1] But see Resolution (67) 14 of the CE's Council of Ministers on Asylum to Persons in Danger of Persecution: YB 10, 104.

agreements, of which two (CR and CS_1) are in force (see §14.5.5). [AFR]'s use of the word 'persecuted' is presumably to be taken in contradistinction to 'prosecuted'.

The right to 'seek' asylum is common to all four instruments; $UDHR$ adds a right to 'enjoy' it, $ADRD$ to 'receive' it, AMR to 'be granted' it, and [AFR] to 'obtain' it.

Only AMR 22(8) contains an express prohibition of *refoulement* (as there defined), though this is confined to apprehended violations of only two rights — those to life (see §14.1) and to personal freedom (see §14.2) — and only to part of the discrimination catalogue (see §7). In that treaty, *refoulement* appears, by omission, to be legitimate if there is danger of violations of other rights, or for other reasons (e.g. because of the deportee's colour, sex, language, or birth). Although EHR contains no express provision on this subject, EUCM has stated[2] that an issue can arise under EHR 3 (see §14.3) if a person is liable to suffer inhuman treatment in the country to which he is expelled.

The provision in [ARF 23(2)(a)] is unique.

§14.5.4 JURISPRUDENCE

IACM has expressed the view that the failure of a State to provide safe conduct, for months on end, out of its territory to persons who had sought and received asylum at a foreign embassy constitutes a violation of $ADRD$ XXVII. In the Commission's view, the purpose of territorial and diplomatic asylum is to safeguard the freedom, safety, and physical integrity of individuals, and the prolonged confinement of an individual in a place protected by diplomatic immunity constitutes a violation of his freedom in asylum, and so becomes a form of excessive punishment.[3]

Apart from that, there is as yet no international jurisprudence on the interpretation or application of this right.[4] One case declared admissible by the European Commission may, however, be noted. Lieutenant-Colonel Amekrane, an officer in the Moroccan Air Force, arrived in Gibraltar by helicopter on the day that an attempt to assassinate the King of Morocco had failed, and sought political asylum. This was refused. On the following day, at the request of the Moroccan authorities, he was sent back in a Moroccan Air Force plane to Morocco, where he was tried and executed. An application by his widow alleging violations by the United Kingdom government of EHR 3, 5(4) and 8 was declared admissible, but no adjudication took place as the case was concluded by a friendly settlement: the respondent government, without admitting any violation of EHR, agreed to make a payment of £37,500 to the applicant and her two children.[5]

In effect, by operating EHR 3 extra-territorially, EUCM could create a right of asylum, or at least a right to *non-refoulement*.

§14.5.5 SUBSIDIARY INSTRUMENTS

Two international Conventions now in force have some relevance to the right of asylum, though neither of them in fact guarantees it, either expressly or by necessary implication.

[2] See the cases noted to §14.3, nn. 46 and 47.   [3] Argentina 177.
[4] But Judge Azevedo, in a dissenting opinion in the International Court of Justice, referred to $UDHR$ 14 in the *Colombian-Peruvian Asylum Case*: ICJ Reports 1950, 339.
[5] *Amekrane* v. *United Kingdom* (5961/72) Report: 19 July 1974.

The Convention Relating to the Status of Refugees (*CR*) requires its contracting States to accord to refugees within their territories rights not less favourable than those enjoyed by aliens generally — without discrimination as to race, religion, or country of origin[6] — as well as a number of additional rights there set out. A refugee is defined[7] as a person who

owing to well-founded fear of being persecuted for reasons of race, religion, nationality, membership of a particular social group or political opinion, is outside the country of his nationality and is unable, or owing to such fear, is unwilling to avail himself of the protection of that country; or who, not having a nationality and being outside the country of his former habitual residence, is unable or, owing to such fear, is unwilling to return to it

and a person may lose the status of a refugee in a number of different ways.[8]

The Convention Relating to the Status of Stateless Persons (*CS₁*) contains almost identical provisions for the benefit of stateless persons, defined[9] as 'a person who is not considered as a national by any State under the operation of its law'.

Both *CR* and *CS₁* expressly, and in almost identical terms, provide[10] that they shall not apply to persons with respect to whom there are serious reasons for considering that

(a) they have committed a crime against peace, a war crime, or a crime against humanity, as defined in the international instruments drawn up to make provisions in respect of such crimes;
(b) they have committed a serious non-political crime outside the country of their residence prior to their admission to that country;
(c) they have been guilty of acts contrary to the purposes and principles of the United Nations.

Though neither of these Conventions guarantees a right of asylum as such — that is, they do not impose any obligation on the contracting States to allow such persons to enter their territories in the first place — each of them extends substantial protection to the classes of person with whom they deal against expulsion from the territory once they are there. Neither refugees[11] nor stateless persons[12] *lawfully* in the territory of a contracting State may be expelled 'save on grounds of national security or public order', and then only subject to safeguards including 'a decision reached in accordance with due process of law', a right to submit evidence to clear themselves, a right of appeal, and a reasonable period in which to seek lawful admission elsewhere. These safeguards, except the last one, are essentially those prescribed by *ICPR* 13 (see §14.4)

The protection for refugees goes yet further. Though they may be expelled if they have gained illegal entry, they may not be otherwise penalized provided they have come directly from the country from which they have fled, and that they present themselves to the authorities without delay and show good cause for their illegal entry.[13] Moreover, *CR* prohibits the *refoulement* of refugees in terms very similar to those of *AMR* 22(8), unless there are reasonable grounds for regarding them as a danger to the security of the host country or, because of a conviction of a particularly serious crime, a danger to the community of that country.[14]

---

[6] *CR* 3.   [7] By *CR* 1A(2).   [8] *CR* 1C.
[9] By *CS₁* 1(1).   [10] *CR* 1F; *CS₁* 1(2)(iii).   [11] *CR* 32.
[12] *CS₁* 31.   [13] *CR* 31.   [14] *CR* 33.

The UNGA has adopted a Declaration on Territorial Asylum,[15] which recommends all States to grant asylum in proper cases, to respect asylum granted by others, to collaborate in lightening the burden of asylum for States in difficulties, and to avoid *refoulement*. But a draft Convention on this subject has not yet been adopted.

The UN has established a special officer — the UN High Commissioner for Refugees, with an office and staff in Geneva, Switzerland — to protect and help refugees in their plight.

---

[15] Resolution 2312 (XXII) of 14 December 1967.

§15. STANDARD OF LIVING

UDHR

25 (1) Everyone has the right to a standard of living adequate for the health and well-being of himself and of his family, including food, clothing, housing and medical care and necessary social services, and the right to security in the event of unemployment, sickness, disability, widowhood, old age or other lack of livelihood in circumstances beyond his control.

ICES

11 (1) The States Parties to the present Covenant recognize the right of everyone to an adequate standard of living for himself and his family, including adequate food, clothing and housing, and to the continuous improvement of living conditions. The States Parties will take appropriate steps to ensure the realization of this right, recognizing to this effect the essential importance of international co-operation based on free consent.

(2) The States Parties to the present Covenant, recognizing the fundamental right of everyone to be free from hunger, shall take, individually and through international co-operation, the measures, including specific programmes, which are needed:

(a) To improve methods of production, conservation and distribution of food by making full use of technical and scientific knowledge, by disseminating knowledge of the principles of nutrition and by developing or reforming agrarian systems in such a way as to achieve the most efficient development and utilization of natural resources;

(b) Taking into account the problems of both food-importing and food-exporting countries, to ensure an equitable distribution of world food supplies in relation to need.

§15.0.2. CROSS-REFERENCES

State obligation: Qualified and progressive under *ICES*: see §6.4. For the juridical status of obligations under *UDHR*, see §6.2.

Signatures, ratifications, accesssions, reservations, and interpretations: See Table A for the State Parties bound by these provisions on 1 January 1982, and any reservations and interpretations notified by them.

Derogation: Non-derogable in any circumstances.

Non-discrimination: No discrimination of any kind (except against non-nationals, for developing countries only, under *ICES*) is allowed in respect of these rights: see §7 for the relevant provisions in these instruments.

Abuse: See §9 for the relevant provisions in these instruments.

Savings: See §10 for the relevant provisions in these instruments.

Restrictions and limitations: See §8 for the general provisions in these instruments.

International supervision, interpretation, application and enforcement: Supervision only by ECOSOC under *ICES* (see §31). See also §6.6 for the obligation to provide domestic remedies under *UDHR*.

Subsidiary instruments: The UN specialized agency primarily competent in the field of *ICES* 11(2) is the Food and Agriculture Organisation, but no relevant treaties have so far been proposed.

See also: §18.2 for other references to standards of living in *UDHR*, *ADRD*, *ICES*, and *ESC*.

§15.0.3. COMMENT

UDHR 25 (1) links 'standard of living' not only to the factors of food, clothing, and housing which form the specific subject-matter of *ICES* 11, but also to health, medical care, social services, and security which are dealt with separately in the treaties, and in the present work (see §§16 and 19).

ICES 11(1) goes beyond *UDHR* 25(1) in recognizing a right to 'the continuous improvment of living conditions', and not merely to a stable condition of 'well-being'. *ICES* 11(2) then lists a variety of measures to be undertaken in order to achieve freedom from hunger.

ESC provides 'a decent standard of living' as the object of the right to fair remuneration for workers: this is considered under the heading of 'pay and conditions of work' in §18.2.

[*AFR*] has not comparable provisions.

§15.0.4 JURISPRUDENCE

The provisions of *ICES* 11 have not yet been authoritatively interpreted or applied in the course of the international supervision procedure laid down in that Covenant (see §31). However, EUCE has interpreted the expression 'a decent standard of living' under the supervision procedure for *ESC* in the context of the right of workers to a fair remuneration: see §18.2.4.

§16. HEALTH

UDHR

25 (1) Everyone has the right to a standard of living adequate for the health and well-being of himself and of his family, including food, clothing, housing and medical care and necessary social services. . .

ADRD

XI. Every person has the right to the preservation of his health through sanitary and social measures relating to food, clothing, housing and medical care, to the extent permitted by public and community resources.

ICES

12 (1) The States Parties to the present Covenant recognize the right of everyone to the enjoyment of the highest attainable standard of physical and mental health.

(2) The steps to be taken by the States Parties to the present Covenant to achieve the full realization of this right shall include those necessary for:

(a) The provision for the reduction of the stillbirth-rate and of infant mortality and for the healthy development of the child;

(b) The improvement of all aspects of environmental and industrial hygiene;

(c) The prevention, treatment and control of epidemic, endemic, occupational and other diseases;

(d) The creation of conditions which would assure to all medical service and medical attention in the event of sickness.

ESC

I, (11) Everyone has the right to benefit from any measures enabling him to enjoy the highest possible standard of health attainable.

II, 11. With a view to ensuring the effective exercise of the right to protection of health, the Contracting Parties undertake, either directly or in co-operation with public or private organizations, to take appropriate measures designed *inter alia:*

(1) to remove as far as possible the causes of ill-health;
(2) to provide advisory and educational facilities for the promotion of health and the encouragement of individual responsibility in matters of health;
(3) to prevent as far as possible epidemic, endemic and other diseases.

[*AFR*]

16 (1) Every individual shall have the right to enjoy the best attainable state of physical and mental health.

(2) State Parties to the present Charter shall take the necessary measures to protect the health of their people and to ensure that they receive medical attention when they are sick.

§16.0.2 CROSS-REFERENCES

State obligation: Absolute and immediate under [*AFR*]: see §6.3. Qualified and progressive under *ICES* and *ESC*: see §6.4. For the juridical status of obligations under *UDHR* and *ADRD*, see §6.2.

Signatures, ratifications, accessions, reservations, and interpretations: see Table A for the State Parties bound by these provisions on 1 January 1982, and any reservations and interpretations notified by them.

Derogation: Non-derogable in any circumstances under *ICES* and [*AFR*]; derogable in exceptional circumstances under *ESC*: see §11.

Non-discrimination: No discrimination of any kind is allowed in respect of these rights; see §7 for the relevant provisions in the instruments.

Abuse: See §9 for the relevant provisions in these instruments.

Savings: See §10 for the relevant provisions in these instruments.

Restrictions and limitations: See §8 for the general provisions in these instruments.

International supervision, interpretation, application, and enforcement: By [*AFCM*] under [*AFR*] (see §30); supervision only by ECOSOC under *ICES* (see §31), and by EUCE under *ESC* (see §32).

Subsidiary instruments: The UN specialized agency primarily competent in this field is the World Health Organisation, but no relevant treaties have so far been proposed. There is, however, a large number of ILO Conventions relating to occupational safety and health.

See also: §19 for further references to medical assistance in *ESC* 13.

§16.0.3 COMMENT

Only *UDHR* expressly links health to the standard of living; all the other instruments treat it as an independent right. *ICES* alone mentions both 'physical' and 'mental' health.

Both *ICES* and *ESC* define the right in terms of the 'highest' standard of health 'attainable'; [*AFR*] calls it the 'best attainable state'; *ESC* the highest 'possible' standard attainable. The *ICES* right is to the 'enjoyment' of that standard; so is that in [*AFR*]; the right in *ESC* I, (11) is confined to the right 'to benefit from any measures enabling him' to enjoy that standard. The State obligation to provide such measures is imposed by *ESC* II, 11, rather than by the corresponding paragraph in Part I.

The measures to be taken in support of the right differ in several respects between *ICES*, *ESC* and [*AFR*]:

(1) *ICES* 12(2) and [*AFR* 16(2)] require the taking of steps which are 'necessary' to achieve the purposes there listed; *ESC* II, 11 only calls for 'appropriate' measures 'designed' to achieve its stated aims;
(2) The only purpose common to both *ICES* and *ESC* is the 'prevention' of epidemic, endemic, and other diseases, to which *ICES* 12(2) (*c*) adds 'occupational' ones;
(3) *ESC* II, 11 goes further than *ICES* 12(2) in calling for measures designed to 'remove as far as possible the causes of ill-health';
(4) *ESC* (but not *ICES*) calls for advice and education to promote health and encourage individual responsibility for health;
(5) *ICES* (but not *ESC*) refers specifically both to the health of children and to hygiene, and calls for the installation of medical services and medical attention, following *UDHR* in this respect;
(6) [*AFR*] instead simply calls for the protection of people's health, and for medical attention when they are sick.

Note that *ESC* I, (11) extends to 'everyone', and not only to workers.

§16.0.4 JURISPRUDENCE

The provisions of *ICES* 12 have not yet been authoritatively interpreted or applied in the course of the international supervision procedure laid down in that Covenant (see §31).

Under the supervision procedure for *ESC* (see §32), EUCE has concluded that a country bound by that Charter should be considered as fulfilling its obligations under Article 11 if it can provide evidence of the existence of a medical and health system comprising the following elements:

(1) Public health arrangements making generally available medical and para-medical practitioners and adequate equipment consistent with meeting its main health problems. Such arrangements must ensure —
   (*a*) proper medical care for the whole population;
   (*b*) the prevention and diagnosis of disease.
(2) Special measures to protect the health of mothers, children, and old people.
(3) General measures aimed in particular at the prevention of air and water pollution, protection from radio-active substances, noise abatement, food control, environmental hygiene, and the control of alcoholism and drugs.
(4) A system of health education.
(5) Measures such as vaccination, disinfection, and the control of epidemics, providing the means of combating epidemic and endemic diseases.

(6) The bearing by collective bodies of all, or at least a substantial part, of the cost of the health services.[1]

IACM has said that the decision of a court reversing the conviction of a medical practitioner for terminating a pregnancy does not violate *ADRD* XI.[2]

[1] I, 59.
[2] Case 2141 (USA) 6 March 1981.

§17. FAMILY

§17.1 Marriage and family

§17.1.1 TEXTS

UDHR

16 (1) Men and women of full age, without any limitation due to race, nationality or religion, have the right to marry and to found a family. They are entitled to equal rights as to marriage, during marriage and at its dissolution.

(2) Marriage shall be entered into only with the free and full consent of the intending spouses.

(3) The family is the natural and fundamental group unit of society and is entitled to protection by society and the State.

ADRD

VI. Every person has the right to establish a family, the basic element of society, and to receive protection therefor.

ICPR

23 (1) The family is the natural and fundamental group unit of society and is entitled to protection by society and the State.

(2) The right of men and women of marriageable age to marry and to found a family shall be recognized.

(3) No marriage shall be entered into without the free and full consent of the intending spouses.

(4) States Parties to the present Covenant shall take appropriate steps to ensure equality of rights and responsibilities of spouses as to marriage, during marriage and at its dissolution. In the case of dissolution, provision shall be made for the necessary protection of any children.

ICES

10. The States Parties to the present Covenant recognize that:

(1) The widest possible protection and assistance should be accorded to the family, which is the natural and fundamental group unit of society, particularly for its establishment and while it is responsible for the care and education of dependent children. Marriage must be entered into with the free consent of the intending spouses.

ESC

I, (16) The family as a fundamental unit of society has the right to appropriate social, legal and economic protection to ensure its full development.

II, 16. With a view to ensuring the necessary conditions for the full development of the family, which is a fundamental unit of society, the Contracting Parties undertake to promote the economic, legal and social protection of family life by such means as social and family benefits, fiscal arrangements, provision of family housing, benefits for the newly married, and other appropriate means.

AMR

17 (1) The family is the natural and fundamental group unit of society and is entitled to protection by society and the state.

(2) The right of men and women of marriageable age to marry and to raise a family shall be recognized, if they meet the conditions required by domestic laws, insofar as such conditions do not affect the principle of nondiscrimination established in this Convention.

(3) No marriage shall be entered into without the free and full consent of the intending spouses.

(4) The States Parties shall take appropriate steps to ensure the equality of rights and the adequate balancing of responsibilities of the spouses as to marriage, during marriage, and in the event of its dissolution. In case of dissolution, provision shall be made for the necessary protection of any children solely on the basis of their own best interests.

[*AFR*]

18 (1) The family shall be the natural unit and basis of society. It shall be protected by the State.

(2) The State shall have the duty to assist the family which is the custodian of morals and traditional values recognized by the community.

27 (1) Every individual shall have duties towards his family . . .

29. The individual shall also have the duty:

(1) To preserve the harmonious development of the family and to work for the cohesion and respect of the family, to respect his parents at all times, to maintain them in case of need.

§17.1.2 CROSS-REFERENCES

State obligation: Absolute and immediate under *ICPR, EHR, AMR*, and [*AFR*]: see §6.3. Qualified and progressive under *ICES* and *ESC*: see §6.4. For the juridical status of obligations under *UDHR* and *ADRD*, see §6.2.

Signatures, ratifications, accessions, reservations, and interpretations: See Table A for the State Parties bound by these provisions on 1 January 1982, and any reservations and interpretations notified by them.

Derogation: Non-derogable in any circumstances under *ICES, AMR*, and [*AFR*]; derogable in exceptional circumstances under *ICPR, EHR*, and *ESC*: see §11.

Non-discrimination: No discrimination of any kind (except against non-nationals, for developing countries only, under *ICES*) is allowed in respect of these rights or freedoms: see §7 for the relevant provisions in the instruments. Note also the specific provisions in *UDHR* 16(1) and *AMR* 17(2).

Abuse: See §9 for the relevant provisions in these instruments.

Savings: See §10 for the relevant provisions in these instruments.

Restrictions and limitations: see §8 for the general provisions in these instruments.

International supervision, interpretation, application, and enforcement: By HRC under *ICPR* (see §27); by EUCM and EUCT under *EHR* (see §28); by IACM and IACT under *AMR* (see §29); by [AFCM] under [*AFR*] (see §30); supervision only by ECOSOC under *ICES* (see §31); by EUCE under *ESC* (see §32). See also §6.6 for the obligation to provide domestic remedies under *UDHR, ADRD, ICPR, EHR, AMR*, and [*AFR*].

Subsidiary instruments: *CM* (see §17.1.5).

See also: §17.2 for the right of children to protection; §23.2 for the right to respect for family life.

§17.1.3 COMMENT

Six distinct rights are enumerated in these Articles.

The right to marry, and the right to found a family

ADRD does not expressly mention the right to marry, and speaks of 'establishing' a family; *AMR* instead speaks of 'raising' one. Otherwise, the language in all the instruments is identical. In *UDHR*, the right accrues with 'full' age; in *ICPR, EHR*, and *AMR* with 'marriageable' age. *EHR* envisages the existence of 'national laws', *AMR* of 'domestic laws' which may impose conditions, provided these are not discriminatory. *UDHR* also forbids discrimination in this instance as to race, nationality, or religion, but not as to any other factor. [*AFR*] does not mention this right.

The right not to marry without full and free consent

This is specified in almost identical terms in *UDHR* 16(2), *ICPR* 23(3), *ICES* 10(1), and *AMR* 17(3), but is not explicitly mentioned in either *EHR* or [*AFR*].

Equal rights to, in, and after marriage

UDHR 16(1) says that men and women are 'entitled' to this equality of rights; ICPR 23(4) and AMR 17(4) require the State Parties to take 'appropriate steps to ensure' it. Neither EHR nor [AFR] mention it in terms. AMR alone adds 'the adequate balancing of responsibilities'.

The family's right to protection

UDHR 16(3), ICPR 23(1), ICES 10(1), and AMR 17(1) all declare that the family is 'the natural and fundamental group unit of society'. ADRD VI calls it 'the basic element', ESC 'a fundamental unit', and [AFR] 'the natural unit and basis'. All the instruments except EHR call for its protection: in the case of UDHR, ICPR, and AMR 'by society and the State'; in the case of [AFR], 'by the State'. ICES and [AFR] call for assistance as well as protection; ESC qualifies the protection as 'appropriate social, legal and economic' protection 'to ensure its full development', and is alone in giving specific examples of what are in fact forms of assistance. Only [AFR] adds individual duties to the family.

The right of children to protection

ICES mentions the care and education of dependent children in the context of protection and assistance for the family; ICPR 23(4) and AMR 17(4) call for the protection of children after the dissolution of their parents' marriage, in the case of AMR 'solely on the basis of their own best interests'.

§17.1.4 JURISPRUDENCE

The right to marry

HRC has expressed the view that an unmarried female national of a State is not a victim of a violation of her right to marry under ICPR 23(2) merely because the domestic law of that State entitles it to restrict access to, and remove from, its territory the alien husbands of female nationals, but not the alien wives of male nationals.[1]

In *Van Oosterwijck* v. *Belgium*,[2] a transsexual, who had undergone medical treatment and assumed the external physical form of the masculine sex, complained that he was unable to exercise his right to marry because the respondent government had failed to authorize the rectification of his birth certificate which still described him as a female. EUCM observed that transsexualism raises relatively new and complex questions to which States must find solutions compatible with respect for fundamental rights. By raising, in advance of any application to marry, an indirect objection based merely on the statements in the birth certificate and the general theory of the rectification of civil status certificates without examining the matter more thoroughly, the government had failed in this case to recognize the applicant's right to marry. However, EUCT subsequently held that the applicant had failed to exhaust all the available domestic remedies before applying under EHR, and accordingly refused to investigate the merits of the case.[3]

[1] *Aumeeruddy-Cziffra* v. *Mauritius* (R. 9/35) HRC 36, 134.
[2] (7654/76) Report: 1 March 1979.
[3] Judgment: 3 EHRR 557.

In *Hamer* v. *United Kingdom*,[4] EUCM observed that the position of a convicted person serving a prison sentence was not necessarily comparable with that of a person who, voluntarily or otherwise, is placed in circumstances which make it impossible for him to marry (e.g. a soldier on active service or a sailor at sea). Nor is it analogous to that of a person such as a priest who decides, for religious or other reasons, not to exercise his right to marry. A prisoner may wish to marry, notwithstanding that he is deprived of his liberty. It should therefore be possible for the authorities to permit his marriage either by allowing him to be escorted out of prison or by making provisions for a marriage within the prison.

The right to found a family

Under *EHR* the capacity to procreate is not an essential condition of marriage; nor is procreation an essential purpose of marriage. Therefore, even if a person lacks the capacity to procreate, he is still entitled to exercise his right to marry.[5]

A family may be founded by the adoption of children.[6] But while *EHR* 12 implicitly guarantees a right to procreate children, it does not as such guarantee a right to adopt or otherwise integrate into a family a child which is not the natural child of the couple concerned. It is left to national laws to determine whether, and subject to what conditions, the exercise of such a right should be permitted.[7] Nor does *EHR* 12 guarantee the right to have children born out of wedlock. It foresees the right to marry and to found a family as one single right. It recognizes the right of men and women at the age of consent to found a family, that is to have children. The existence of a couple is fundamental. The adoption of an adolescent by an unmarried person cannot therefore lead to the existence of a family life.[8]

Although the right to found a family is an absolute right in the sense that *EHR* 12 provides no express restrictions, this does not mean that a person must at all times be given the actual possibility to procreate his descendants. The situation of a lawfully convicted person detained in prison falls under his own responsibility.[9]

English and French courts have both held that a husband has no enforceable right to prevent his wife from having her pregnancy lawfully terminated,[10] and EUCM has supported that view.[11]

---

[4] (7114/75) DR 10, 1974. See also *X and Y* v. *Switzerland* (8166/78) DR 13, 241; *Draper* v. *United Kingdom* (8186/78), unreported. In both the *Draper* and the *Hamer* cases, the CE's Committee of Ministers decided (by Resolutions DH (81) 4 and 5 respectively) to take no further action in the light of the respondent government's change of practice.

[5] *Van Oosterwijck* v. *Belgium* (7654/76) Report, *supra*.

[6] Ibid.

[7] *X and Y* v. *United Kingdom* (7229/75) DR 12, 32.

[8] *X* v. *Belgium and Netherlands* (6482/74) DR 7, 75.

[9] *X* v. *United Kingdom* (6564/74) DR 2, 105. But see *Hamer* v. *United Kingdom* (7114/75) DR 10, 174: a prisoner's ability to exercise his right to marry whilst he is deprived of his liberty may be a matter within the control of the State, similar to his ability to exercise other rights such as access to the courts under *EHR* 6, and not dependent solely on the factual circumstances in which he is placed.

[10] *Paton* v. *British Pregnancy Advisory Service Trustees* [1978] 2 All ER 987; Decision of 31 October 1980, Conseil d'Etat, France, 6 *Human Rights Review* 75.

[11] *X* v. *United Kingdom* (8416/78) DR 19, 244.

'According to the national laws'

In order to exercise his right to marry, a person must respect the formal rules laid down by the relevant national law. For example, he must obtain the required permission, publish the specified notices and appear before the competent authority. He may also have to observe the substantive rules laid down by law in accordance with generally recognized principles, such as impediments due to close relationship.[12] But while regulating the exercise of the right to marry, national law must not interfere with the substance of the right itself — that is, it may not deprive a person or a category of persons altogether of the freedom to exercise this right;[13] even hindering its effective exercise may amount to a breach of *EHR* 12,[14] However, a clause in an employment contract forbidding policemen to marry for two years does not contravene *EHR* 12, so long as the domestic *law* does not prevent them from marrying during that time.[15]

The family's right to protection

HRC has expressed the view that the 'protection' under *ICPR* 23(1) which a State can afford to the family may vary from country to country and depend on different social, economic, political, and cultural conditions and traditions. But *ICPR* 2(1), 3, and 26 all require that such protection must be equal, that is to say not discriminatory, for example on the basis of sex. Accordingly, where a State's laws enable it to restrict access to, and expel from, its territory the alien husbands of its female nationals but not the alien wives of its male nationals, the wives of such alien husbands are the victims of a violation of *ICPR* 2(1), 3, and 26 in conjunction with their rights under *ICPR* 23(1).[16]

The provisions of *ICES* 10 have not yet been authoritatively interpreted or applied in the course of the international supervision procedure laid down in that Covenant (see §31).

Under the supervision procedure for *ESC* (see §32), EUCE has concluded that the State obligation under *ESC* 16 is one to implement a true family policy, intended to operate in those fields where the needs of families become particularly pressing because of the restricted means they have available to meet them.[17] Where women increasingly participate in the labour market, an adequate number of day-care institutions for children, especially facilities for parents of sick children, must be provided.[18] A provision according to which a couple is entitled to certain social security payments only if the *man* is in full-time work could be considered as incompatible with the principle of equality of treatment between men and women.[19]

---

[12] *Van Oosterwijck* v. *Belgium* (7654/76) Report: 1 March 1979; *X* v. *Federal Republic of Germany* (6167/73) DR 1, 64. See also: Decision of 4 May 1971, BVfG, Federal Republic of Germany (NJW 1971, 1509; 2121): foreigners who intend to marry are not obliged to comply with the same formalities for the conclusion of the marriage as those which are formally required of nationals.
[13] *Van Oosterwijck* v. *Belgium, supra.*
[14] *Hamer* v. *United Kingdom* (7114/75) DR 10, 174.
[15] Decision of 22 February 1962, BVwG, Federal Republic of Germany (NJW 1962, 1532).
[16] *Aumeeruddy-Cziffra* v. *Mauritius* (R. 9/35) HRC 36, 134.
[17] I, 75.
[18] IV, 101.
[19] V, 110.

Equality of spouses

HRC has expressed the view that an unmarried female national of a State is not a victim of a violation of her right to the equality of spouses under *ICPR* 23(4) merely because the domestic law of that State entitles it to restrict access to, and remove from, its territory the alien husbands of female nationals, but not the alien wives of male nationals.[20]

However, IACM has expressed the view that there is a violation of *AMR* 17(4) where the domestic law of a State allows a husband to divorce his wife on the simple ground of adultery, whereas his own adultery is only a ground for divorce at his wife's suit if she proves, in addition, that it was accompanied by 'public scandal' or 'abandonment of the woman'.[21]

§17.1.5 SUBSIDIARY INSTRUMENTS

The Convention on Consent to Marriage, Minimum Age for Marriage and Registration of Marriages (*CM*) provides that its State Parties shall specify a minimum age for marriage by legislation, from which a competent authority can only dispense 'for serious reasons, in the interest of the intending spouses';[22] that all marriages shall require the 'full and free consent of both parties', after 'due publicity', and in the presence of a competent authority (though, in exceptional circumstances, only one party need be present at the ceremony);[23] and that the competent authority shall register all marriages in an official register.[24]

§17.2 Mothers and children

§17.2.1 TEXTS

UDHR

25 (2) Motherhood and childhood are entitled to special care and assistance. All children, whether born in or out of wedlock, shall enjoy the same social protection.

ADRD

VII. All women, during pregnancy and the nursing period, and all children have the right to special protection, care and aid.

XXX. It is the duty of every person to aid, support, educate and protect his minor children, and it is the duty of children to honor their parents always and to aid, support and protect them when they need it.

---

[20] *Aumeeruddy-Cziffra* v. *Mauritius, supra.*
[21] El Salvador 160.
[22] *CM* 2.
[23] *CM* 1.
[24] *CM* 3.

ICPR

24 (1) Every child shall have, without any discrimination as to race, colour, sex, language, religion, national or social origin, property or birth, the right to such measures of protection as are required by his status as a minor, on the part of his family, society and the State.

(2) Every child shall be registered immediately after birth and shall have a name.

(3) Every child has the right to acquire a nationality.

ICES

10. The States Parties to the present Covenant recognise that:

(2) Special protection should be accorded to mothers during a reasonable period before and after childbirth. During such period working mothers should be accorded paid leave or leave with adequate social security benefits.

(3) Special measures of protection and assistance should be taken on behalf of all children and young persons without any discrimination for reasons of parentage or other conditions. Children and young persons should be protected from economic and social exploitation. Their employment in work harmful to their morals or health or dangerous to life or likely to hamper their normal development should be punishable by law. States should also set age limits below which the paid employment of child labour should be prohibited and punishable by law.

ESC

I, (7) Children and young persons have the right to a special protection against the physical and moral hazards to which they are exposed.

(8) Employed women, in case of maternity, and other employed women as appropriate, have the right to a special protection in their work.

(17) Mothers and children, irrespective of marital status and family relations, have the right to, appropriate social and economic protection.

II, 7. With a view to ensuring the effective exercise of the right of children and young persons to protection, the Contracting Parties undertake:

(1) to provide that the minimum age of admission to employment shall be 15 years, subject to exceptions for children employed in prescribed light work without harm to their health, morals or education;

(2) to provide that a higher minimum age of admission to employment shall be fixed with respect to prescribed occupations regarded as dangerous or unhealthy;

(3) to provide that persons who are still subject to compulsory education shall not be employed in such work as would deprive them of the full benefit of their education;

(4) to provide that the working hours of persons under 16 years of age shall be limited in accordance with the needs of their development, and particularly with their need for vocational training;

(5) to recognize the right of young workers and apprentices to a fair wage or other appropriate allowances;

(6) to provide that the time spent by young persons in vocational training during the normal working hours with the consent of the employer shall be treated as forming part of the working day;

(7) to provide that employed persons of under 18 years of age shall be entitled to not less than three weeks' annual holiday with pay;

(8) to provide that persons under 18 years of age shall not be employed in night work with the exception of certain occupations provided for by national laws or regulations;

(*App.*: It is understood that a Contracting Party may give the undertaking required in this paragraph if it fulfils the spirit of the undertaking by providing by law that the great majority of persons under 18 years of age shall not be employed in night work.)

(9) to provide that persons under 18 years of age employed in occupations prescribed by national laws or regulations shall be subject to regular medical control;

(10) to ensure special protection against physical and moral dangers to which children and young persons are exposed, and particularly against those resulting directly or indirectly from their work.

II, 8. With a view to ensuring the effective exercise of the right of employed women to protection, the Contracting Parties undertake:

(1) to provide either by paid leave, by adequate social security benefits or by benefits from public funds, for women to take leave before and after childbirth up to a total of at least 12 weeks;

(2) to consider it as unlawful for an employer to give a woman notice of dismissal during her absence on maternity leave or

to give her notice of dismissal at such a time that the notice would expire during such absence;

(3) to provide that mothers who are nursing their infants shall be entitled to sufficient time off for this purpose;

(4) (*a*) to regulate the employment of women workers on night work in industrial employment;

    (*b*) to prohibit the employment of women workers in underground mining, and, as appropriate, on all other work which is unsuitable for them by reason of its dangerous, unhealthy, or arduous nature.

II, 17. With a view to ensuring the effective exercise of the right of mothers and children to social and economic protection, the Contracting Parties will take all appropriate and necessary measures to that end, including the establishment or maintenance of appropriate institutions or services.

AMR

17 (5) The law shall recognize equal rights for children born out of wedlock and those born in wedlock.

19. Every minor child has the right to the measures of protection required by his condition as a minor on the part of his family, society, and the state.

[*AFR*]

18 (3) The State shall . . . ensure the protection of the rights of the woman and the child as stipulated in international declarations and conventions.

§17.2.2 CROSS-REFERENCES

State obligation: Absolute and immediate under *ICPR, AMR,* and [*AFR*]: see §6.3. Qualified and progressive under *ICES* and *ESC*: see §6.4. (Note that *ESC* 33 applies to paragraphs (4), (6), and (7) of *ESC* II, 7.) For the juridical status of obligations under *UDHR* and *ADRD*, see §6.2.

Signatures, ratifications, accessions, reservations, and interpretations: see Table A for the State Parties bound by these provisions on 1 January 1982, and any reservations and interpretations notified by them.

Derogation: Non-derogable in any circumstances under *ICES, AMR,* and [*AFR*]; derogable in exceptional circumstances under *ICPR* and *ESC*: see §11.

Non-discrimination: No discrimination of any kind (except against non-nationals , for developing countries only, under *ICES*) is allowed in respect of these rights: see §7 for the relevant provisions in the instruments. Note also the specific provisions in *ICPR* 24(1) and *ICES* 10(3).

Abuse: See §9 for the relevant provisions in these instruments.

Savings: See §10 for the relevant provisions in these instruments.

Restrictions and limitations: See §8 for the general provisions in these instruments, and the principles governing all restriction and limitation clauses.

International supervision, interpretation, application, and enforcement: By HRC under *ICPR* (see §27); by IACM and IACT under *AMR* (see §29); by [AFCM] under [*AFR*] (see §30); supervision only by ECOSOC under *ICES* (see §31); by EUCE under *ESC* (see §32). See also §6.6 for the obligation to provide domestic remedies under *UDHR, ADRD, ICPR, AMR*, and [*AFR*].

Subsidiary instruments: Many ILO Conventions relating to the employment of women, children, and young persons are in force.

See also: §16 as to infant health in *ICES* 12(2) (*a*); § 7.1 as to the protection of children on dissolution of their parents' marriage in *ICPR* 23(4) and *AMR* 17(4); §22.1 for the right to a nationality; §23.1 for a child's right to a name in *ICPR* 24(2); §23.2 for respect for family life.

§17.2.3 COMMENT

The general proposition in *UDHR* 25(2) — 'motherhood and childhood are entitled to special care and assistance' — is taken up and developed in some of the later instruments. (*ADRD* restricts motherhood to 'pregnancy and the nursing period', and adds reciprocal duties between parents and children.)

Mothers

Neither *ICPR, EHR, AMR*, or [*AFR*] contains any provision about motherhood. *ICES* 10(2) and *ESC* I, (8) require 'special protection' for working mothers, *ICES* in the form of leave with pay or adequate social security benefits, and *ESC* II, 8 in this and four other specific respects. *ESC* I, (17) calls, in addition, for 'appropriate social and economic protection' for all mothers and children. [*AFR* 18(3)] calls for protection of 'the rights of the woman', 'as stipulated in international declarations and conventions'.[25]

Children

Both *ICPR* 24(1) and *AMR* 19 give children the right to the measures of protection they 'require', and *ICPR* 24(2) and (3) add specific rights to registration at birth, a name, and a nationality. *ICES* 10(3) is especially concerned to protect them from 'economic and social exploitation', and to safeguard their health, morals, life, and normal development. *ESC* I, (7) calls for special protection against 'the physical and moral hazards to which they are exposed', and lists ten specific forms of such protection in relation to their employment in the corresponding Article in Part II. [*AFR* 18(3)] calls simply for protection of 'the rights of the child', 'as stipulated in international declarations and conventions'.[26]

Only *UDHR* 25(2) and *AMR* 17 (5) expressly call for equal treatment for children born in and out of wedlock, *UDHR* in the field of 'social protection',

[25] See CW_1 and CW_2: §8.0.5.
[26] There is an international Declaration of the Rights of the Child (UNGA Resolution 1386 (XIV), 20 November 1959), but so far no specific convention.

AMR in requiring the law to recognize 'equal rights' for them. However, this equality also follows implicitly from the requirement not to discriminate, in *ICPR* 24(1) as to 'birth', in *ICES* 10(3) 'for reasons of parentage', and in *ESC* I, (17) from the expression 'irrespective of marital status and family relations'.

There are no equivalent provisions in *EHR*.

§17.2.4 JURISPRUDENCE

The provisions of *ICES* 10 have not yet been authoritatively interpreted or applied in the course of the international supervision procedure laid down in that Covenant (see §31), and HRC has not yet had occasion to express any views on *ICPR* 24.

IACM has expressed the view that *AMR* 17 (5) is violated where the domestic law of a State discriminates between the rights of legitimate and illegitimate children, dividing the latter into 'natural' children (where their fathers have recognized them) and children of an 'illicit' union (where they are the issue of an adulterous or incestuous relationship).[27]

The Privy Council has held that, where a national constitution guarantees fundamental rights and freedoms, the term 'child' in that instrument cannot be restricted to legitimate children.[28]

Under the supervision procedure for *ESC* (see §32), EUCE has provided the following interpretations of the relevant provisions in that Charter:

Article 7 applies only to children and young people once they have reached school age; pre-school children are covered by Article 17.[29]

Article 7, paragraph (1) applies to all categories of work, including agricultural and domestic work, which cannot automatically be considered as 'light'.[30] Nor is work in the tertiary sector necessarily 'light' for this purpose.[31] In order for a State Party to comply with this provision, the types of work to which children under 15 may be admitted must be laid down in a limitative list, be genuinely light, and in no way prejudice their moral welfare, health, or education.[32]

Article 7, paragraph (2). The 'minimum age' here means an age higher than 15 years;[33] a State in which the minimum age for admission to notoriously dangerous or unhealthy work is 18 for girls and between 16 and 18 for boys fulfils the obligation under this paragraph.[34]

Article 7, paragraph (3). In order to comply with this obligation, it is not enough to ensure school attendance without taking additional measures to avoid any interference, through occupational activities, with the education provided.[35] Specific measures must be taken to set a maximum limit on the duration of work done by children before or after school hours, and to restrict the permissible types of work to prescribed light occupations.[36] Where it is

---

[27] El Salvador 160. But the decision of a court reversing the conviction of a medical practitioner for terminating a pregnancy does not violate *ADRD* VII: Case 2141 (USA) 6 March 1981.

[28] *Minister of Home Affairs* v. *Fisher* [1979] 3 All ER 21 (on appeal from Bermuda).

[29] I, 41.

[30] I, 42.

[31] IV, 53.

[32] V, 55.

[33] I, 186.

[34] III, 39.

[35] V, 57.

[36] III, 40.

possible for children still subject to compulsory education to be employed for periods of up to 25 hours in a week, the obligation is not satisfied;[37] nor is it where the limit is 3 hours on school days, and 6 to 8 hours on weekdays when there is no school.[38] A general recognition of the possibility of employing children related to the employer on household jobs and in agriculture outside school hours is also not compatible with the obligation under this paragraph, particularly in the absence of other limitations on hours of work.[39]

Article 7, paragraph (4). A limitation to 8 hours per day and 40 hours per week does not adequately meet the requirements of this paragraph, since it does not allow young persons to enjoy the benefit of appropriate vocational training.[40] (Note that *ESC* 33 applies to this paragraph.)

Article 7, paragraph (5). Although the value of an apprentice's training ought obviously to be taken into account, after two or three years' vocational training he is fitted to render services such that one could hardly go on considering him as an apprentice.[41] Where the duration of the apprenticeship is excessive (sometimes as long as five years), the differences between apprentices and young workers tends to disappear and in those circumstances young workers do not enjoy fair rates of pay, since they do not normally reach the adult rate until the age of 21.[42] There is really no basic reason for not paying the same wage to young workers for the same output. Though certain reductions may be justified because their needs are less, these must not be too substantial and ought to be for a limited time.[43] Where young workers are paid 30 per cent less than adult workers, that is not 'fair' within the meaning of the paragraph.[44] But apprentices may be paid less than this: if their wages range generally between one and two thirds of the average for adults, the obligation under this paragraph is fulfilled.[45]

Article 7, paragraph (6). The employer's consent mentioned in this paragraph may have some bearing in defining the way in which the young persons' rights under this provision are to be exercised, but it is not a condition *sine qua non* for the grant of the right.[46] The provision that time spent in vocational training during normal working hours 'shall be treated as forming part of the working day' implies that such time must be remunerated (either by the employer or by public funds), and that it must not give rise to any form of recuperation which would result in the total number of working hours of the person concerned being extended accordingly.[47] (Note that *ESC* 33 applies to this paragraph.)

Article 7, paragraph (7). The obligation here is to guarantee children and young people three weeks' leave, the number of working days granted depending on the length of the working week.[48] Where young people working at home constitute the only category not entitled to three weeks' holiday with pay, the State obligation under this paragraph may be fulfilled if the conditions of *ESC* 33 (which applies to it) are satisfied.[49]

Article 7, paragraph (8). Where legislation forbids the employment of persons under 16 between 7 p.m. and 6 a.m., and the employment of persons under 18 between 10 p.m. and 5 a.m., the obligation under this paragraph is fulfilled.[50]

[37] II, 32.　[38] IV, 54.
[39] I, 187.　[40] I, 44.
[41] II, 33.　[42] I, 188.
[43] II, 33.　[44] IV, 58.
[45] III, 44.　[46] V, 67.
[47] V, 67.　[48] I, 45.
[49] IV. 60.　[50] II, 36.

Article 7, paragraph (9). The requirement here is for regular (i.e. periodic) medical supervision,[51] which must be compulsory.[52] Where the national laws or regulations only provide for medical examination, but not specifically at regular intervals, the obligation is not fulfilled.[53] Nor is it if the interval between the prescribed medical examinations is as long as three years.[54]

Article 7, paragraph (10). This paragraph is far broader in scope than the nine which precede it: it obliges the State Parties to protect young people against any dangers which threaten them, even if they are not connected with their work,[55] from the age at which they are required to attend school until the age at which they become adults.[56]

Article 8 applies solely to women in paid employment, and not to self-employed women.[57]

Article 8, paragraph (1). It is not enough that the right to maternity leave is established by custom, however firmly: a right of such capital importance must be guaranteed by law.[58] The choice is not between providing leave of at least 12 weeks, and providing allowances over that period; the leave must be provided in any event, and the choice is only whether the consequent loss of earnings should be compensated by the employer, by social security benefits, or by benefits from public funds.[59] However, it is in order for women to elect not to avail themselves of this right over a part of the 12 weeks' period in question.[60] Certain maternity allowances have been held to be adequate, and others not.[61]

Article 8, paragraph (2). This paragraph does not prevent the employment being terminated during absence on maternity leave if the period prescribed in the employment contract has expired, or if the employed woman has been guilty of misconduct which justifies breaking off the employment relationship.[62] Where this protection is not extended to household workers and domestic employees, the obligation under the paragraph is not satisfied;[63] likewise, where female domestic servants may be dismissed between the end of the fifth month of pregnancy and childbirth, thus depriving them of the right to paid maternity leave.[64]

Article 8, paragraph (3). Where female domestic workers, female family workers, and women working at home are not guaranteed adequate time off for nursing, this obligation is not satisfied.[65] 'Sufficient' time off for nursing is constituted by two daily rest periods for a year for the purpose of feeding, deemed to be hours of work and remunerated as such, of an hour each where the employer has not provided a crèche or nursing room, and otherwise of half an hour each.[66]

Article 8, paragraph (4). 'Industrial employment' in paragraph (4) (*a*) does not include non-industrial employment in industrial premises.[67]

Article 17. A State Party may fulfil its obligations under this Article where assistance to mothers and children comes very largely from private sources, since in those circumstances State intervention might not be 'necessary'.[68]

---

[51] I, 190.
[52] IV, 61.
[53] II, 37.
[54] II, 37.
[55] I, 41.
[56] V, 73-4.
[57] I, 49.
[58] III, 48, 49.
[59] V, 76.
[60] I, 50.
[61] I, 50; II, 39.
[62] I, 51.
[63] IV, 66-7.
[64] V, 77.
[65] III, 50; VI, 64.
[66] I, 51.
[67] I, 192.
[68] I, 177.

Although the Article does not in terms mention legal protection for those concerned, it is not possible to disregard the legal position of the mother and her child in establishing the extent of the social and economic protection on which they may call, and so determining whether a State Party fulfils its obligation.[69] The basic principle is that mothers should be in a position of medical and financial security both before and after confinement.[70]

The Article applies to children of pre-school age.[71] A State whose legislation manifestly discriminates against children born out of wedlock cannot be held to satisfy its obligations.[72] Likewise, where illegitimate children have no legal status unless and until it has been conferred upon them as a result of action taken under legitimation laws,[73] where they are deprived of any claim to inherit from their father's estate,[74] where they cannot claim a reasonable share of a parent's inheritance if the will contains no clause in their favour, and where, if their mother dies intestate, they are only entitled to a share of her inheritance if she leaves no direct legitimate descendant.[75] The mere absence of unjust discrimination against unmarried mothers is not enough: special measures are necessary, such as the institution of services of guidance and assistance, including financial assistance.[76]

Homeless children should be provided with the nearest possible approximation to a normal home environment.[77]

---

[69] IV, 103.   [70] III, 80.   [71] I, 41.
[72] III, 80; cf., under *EHR* 8, *Marckx* v. *Belgium* (6833/74) Report: 10 December 1977; Judgment: 2 EHRR 330.
[73] III, 81.   [74] IV, 104; see also *Marckx* v. *Belgium, supra.*
[75] I, 77.   [76] III, 80.   [77] III, 80.

§18. WORK

§18.1 The right to work

§18.1.1 TEXTS

UDHR

23 (1) Everyone has the right to work, to free choice of employment, . . . and to protection against unemployment.

ADRD

XIV. Every person has the right to work, under proper conditions, and to follow his vocation freely, in so far as existing conditions of employment permit.

XXXVII. It is the duty of every person to work, as far as his capacity and possibilities permit, in order to obtain the means of livelihood or to benefit his community.

ICES

6 (1) The States Parties to the present Covenant recognize the right to work, which includes the right of everyone to the opportunity to gain his living by work which he freely chooses or accepts, and will take appropriate steps to safeguard this right.

(2) The steps to be taken by a State Party to the present Covenant to achieve the full realization of this right shall include technical and vocational guidance and training programmes, policies and techniques to achieve steady economic, social and cultural development and full and productive employment under conditions safeguarding fundamental political and economic freedoms to the individual.

ESC

I, (1) Everyone shall have the opportunity to earn his living in an occupation freely entered upon.

II, 1. With a view to ensuring the effective exercise of the right to work, the Contracting Parties undertake:
(1) to accept as one of their primary aims and responsibilities the achievement and maintenance of as high and stable a level of employment as possible, with a view to the attainment of full employment;

(2) to protect effectively the right of the worker to earn his living in an occupation freely entered upon;

(*App.*: This provision shall not be interpreted as prohibiting or authorizing any union security clause or practice.)

(3) to establish or maintain free employment services for all workers;
(4) to provide or promote appropriate vocational guidance, training and rehabilitation.

[*AFR*]

15. Every individual shall have the right to work.

29. The individual shall also have the duty: . . .
    (6) To work to the best of his abilities and competence . . .

§18.1.2 CROSS-REFERENCES

State obligation: Absolute and immediate under [*AFR*]: see §6.3. Qualified and progressive under *ICES* and *ESC*: see §6.4. For the juridical status of obligations under *UDHR* and *ADRD*, see §6.2.

Signatures, ratifications, accessions, reservations, and interpretations: See Table A for the State Parties bound by these provisions on 1 January 1982, and any reservations and interpretations notified by them.

Derogation: Non-derogable in any circumstances under *ICES* and [*AFR*]; derogable in exceptional circumstances under *ESC*: see §11.

Non-discrimination: No discrimination of any kind (except against non-nationals, for developing countries only, under *ICES*) is allowed in respect of this right: see §7 for the relevant provisions in the instruments.

Abuse: See §9 for the relevant provisions in these instruments.

Savings: See §10 for the relevant provisions in these instruments.

Restrictions and limitations: See §8 for the general provisions in these instruments.

International supervision, interpretation, application and enforcement: By [*AFCM*] under [*AFR*] (see §30); supervision only by ECOSOC under *ICES* (see §31), and by EUCE under *ESC* (see §32). See also §6.6 for the obligation to provide domestic remedies under *UDHR*, *ADRD*, and [*AFR*].

Subsidiary instruments: ILO 122 (see §18.1.5); *ILO 111* (see §7.0.5); also *ILO 2*.

See also: §18.4 as to forced or compulsory labour; §19.1 for other references to unemployment in *UDHR* and *ADRD*; §20 as to vocational training.

§18.1.3 COMMENT

UDHR 23 (1) here enumerates three rights: the right to work; the right to free choice of employment; and the right to protection against unemployment.

ICES 6 (1) 'includes' the second of these rights in the first, but enlarges it to a right to the opportunity to gain a living; *ESC* I, (1) gives that right only, without in addition specifying a 'right to work'. *ADRD* makes no mention of protection against unemployment: indeed, the phrase 'in so far as existing conditions of employment permit' appears to exclude this. Neither do *ICES* or *ESC*, but each of them specifies 'full employment' as a State policy objective — limited, however, in the case of *ICES* by the requirement of 'conditions safeguarding fundamental political and economic freedoms to the individual'. Both *ICES* 6 (2) and *ESC* II, 1 list several means for the achievements of their respective ends, which overlap in large part. [*AFR* 15] simply declares a 'right to work'. Only *ADRD* XXXVII and [*AFR* 29 (6)] treat work also as a duty.[1]

Note that *ESC* here refers to 'everyone'.

§18.1.4 JURISPRUDENCE

In its reports to ECOSOC (see §31), the ILO's Committee of Experts on the Application of Conventions and Recommendations has given some indications of matters which may be relevant in considering how far a State Party has made progress in achieving the observance of the provisions of *ICES* 6.

These include the existence of discrimination in employment, on the grounds of political activity which neither constitutes an activity against the security of the State nor is incompatible with the requirements of the forms of the employment concerned;[2] the existence of a penal offence of 'leading a parasitic form of life', without any express limit to the scope of that offence;[3] the existence of model collective farm rules under which a member may terminate his membership only with the consent of the management committee;[4] and the existence of special labour services in construction or agriculture in lieu of military service.[5]

Under the supervision procedure for *ESC* (see §32), EUCE has provided the following interpretations of the four paragraphs of Article 1 in Part II of the Charter:

Paragraph (1). This provision imposes an obligation as to means rather than as to results. If a State at any time abandoned the objective of full employment in favour of an economic system providing for a permanent pool of unemployment, it would be infringing this obligation.[6] The provision requires the existence of a planned policy of employment,[7] and special measures to help those who are at a disadvantage in seeking work, either because of regional imbalance, or of disparities based on sex or age.[8]

---

[1] This is how it in fact appears to many millions of subsistence farmers and their families, who claim no 'right' to tend their crops, but would rapidly starve if they did not.

[2] 1979, 54.

[3] 1979, 99.

[4] 1979, 99; 1980, 5.

[5] 1980, 5.

[6] I, 13–14.

[7] II, 3.

[8] IV, General Introduction.

Paragraph (2). This provision is closely bound up with the prohibition of forced labour and the eradication of all forms of discrimination in employment.[9] The coercion of any worker to carry out work against his wishes, and without his freely expressed consent, is contrary to this provision. The same applies to coercion of any worker to carry out work he had previously freely agreed to do, but which he subsequently no longer wants to carry out. However, the peculiar status of the military may justify penal sanctions for breach of a voluntary engagement without infringing this prohibition.[10]

The provision is infringed where penal sanctions may be imposed on a public servant or other person responsible for a public service (so defined as not to be restricted to essential services, that is to say services whose interruption would jeopardize the safety or well-being of the whole or part of the population) in the event of his unwarranted refusal or failure to perform, or unwarranted delay in performing, the duties of his office or service, or in the event of any interruption or abandonment of the service with intent to disturb its regularity, or having the effect of so doing.[11] Mere disobedience to orders, or the interruption or abandonment of service by certain categories of staff, must not be subjected to penal measures unless the act giving rise to the charge endangered, or was capable of endangering, the safety of property or the life or health of individuals. So long as such penal legislation exists, the provision is infringed, even if the legislation is not applied in practice.[12]

A requirement that female civil servants should resign on marriage, and that married women cannot enter the civil service, is incompatible with this provision.[13]

Paragraph (3). This provision places an obligation on each contracting State not only to create or maintain free employment services for all workers, without exception,[14] but also to ensure that they are properly operated and, where necessary, supervized in collaboration with both sides of industry.[15] 'Free' means that no charge may be made either to employers or to workers for any placement.[16]

Paragraph (4). The obligations under this paragraph are identical to those imposed by *ESC* II, 9, 10 and 15:[17] see §§ 19.4 and 20.4.

§18.1.5 SUBSIDIARY INSTRUMENTS

The ILO Convention concerning Employment Policy (*ILO 122*) provides that its State Parties shall 'declare and pursue, as a major goal, an active policy designed to promote full, productive and freely chosen employment'.[18] This policy shall aim at ensuring that

(*a*) there is work for all who are available for and seeking work;
(*b*) such work is as productive as possible;
(*c*) there is freedom of choice of employment and the fullest possible opportunity for each worker to qualify for, and to use his skills and endowments in, a job for which he is well suited, irrespective of race, colour, sex, religion, political opinion, national extraction or social origin.[19]

[9] I, 15
[10] III, 5.
[11] IV, 7–8.
[12] V, 6.
[13] I, 166.
[14] II, 5.
[15] I, 16.
[16] IV, 10; V, 11; VI, 10.
[17] I, 16.
[18] *ILO 122* 1(1).
[19] *ILO 122* 1(2).

The policy 'shall be pursued by methods that are appropriate to national conditions and practices.'[20]

§18.2 Pay and conditions of work

§18.2.1 TEXTS

UDHR

23 (1) Everyone has the right . . . to just and favourable conditions of work . . .

(2) Everyone, without any discrimination, has the right to equal pay for equal work.

(3) Everyone who works has the right to just and favourable remuneration ensuring for himself and his family an existence worthy of human dignity, and supplemented, if necessary, by other means of social protection.

ADRD

XIV. Every person who works has the right to receive such remuneration as will, in proportion to his capacity and skill, assure him a standard of living suitable for himself and for his family.

ICES

7. The States Parties to the present Covenant recognize the right of everyone to the enjoyment of just and favourable conditions of work, which ensure, in particular:
   (*a*) Remuneration which provides all workers, as a minimum, with:
      (i) Fair wages and equal remuneration for work of equal value without distinction of any kind, in particular women being guaranteed conditions of work not inferior to those enjoyed by men, with equal pay for equal work;
      (ii) A decent living for themselves and their families in accordance with the provisions of the present Covenant;
   (*b*) Safe and healthy working conditions;
   (*c*) Equal opportunity for everyone to be promoted in his employment to an appropriate higher level, subject to no considerations other than those of seniority and competence;

ESC

I, (3) All workers have the right to safe and healthy working conditions.

---

[20] *ILO 122* 1 (3).

(4) All workers have the right to a fair remuneration sufficient for a decent standard of living for themselves and their families.

II, 3. With a view to ensuring the effective exercise of the right to safe and healthy working conditions, the Contracting Parties undertake:
(1) to issue safety and health regulations;
(2) to provide for the enforcement of such regulations by measures of supervision;
(3) to consult, as appropriate, employers' and workers' organizations on measures intended to improve industrial safety and health.

II, 4. With a view to ensuring the effective exercise of the right to a fair remuneration, the Contracting Parties undertake:
(1) to recognize the right of workers to a remuneration such as will give them and their families a decent standard of living;
(2) to recognize the right of workers to an increased rate of remuneration for overtime work, subject to exceptions in particular cases;
(3) to recognize the right of men and women workers to equal pay for work of equal value;
(4) to recognize the right of all workers to a reasonable period of notice for termination of employment;

(*App.*: This provision shall be so understood as not to prohibit immediate dismissal for any serious offence.)

(5) to permit deductions from wages only under conditions and to the extent prescribed by national laws or regulations or fixed by collective agreements or arbitration awards.

(*App.*: It is understood that a Contracting Party may give the undertaking required in this paragraph if the great majority of workers are not permitted to suffer deductions from wages either by law or through collective agreements or arbitration awards, the exceptions being those persons not so covered.)

The exercise of these rights shall be achieved by freely concluded collective agreements, by statutory wage-fixing machinery, or by other means appropriate to national conditions.

[*AFR*]

15. Every individual shall have the right to work under equitable and satisfactory conditions and shall receive equal pay for equal work.

§18.2.2 CROSS-REFERENCES

State obligation: Absolute and immediate under [*AFR*]: see §6.3. Qualified and progressive under *ICES* and *ESC*: see §6.4. For the juridical status of obligations under *UDHR* and *ADRD*, see §6.2.

Signatures, ratifications, accessions, reservations, and interpretations: See Table A for the State Parties bound by these provisions on 1 January 1982, and any reservations and interpretations notified by them.

Derogation: Non-derogable in any circumstances under *ICES* and [*AFR*]; derogable in exceptional circumstances under *ESC*: see §11.

Non-discrimination: No discrimination of any kind (except against non-nationals, for developing countries only, under *ICES*) is allowed in respect of these rights: see §7 for the relevant provisions in the instruments. Note also the specific references in *UDHR* 23 (2) and *ICES* 7.

Abuse: See §9 for the relevant provisions in these instruments.

Savings: See §10 for the relevant provisions in these instruments.

Restrictions and limitations: see §8 for the general provisions in these instruments.

International supervision, interpretation, application, and enforcement: By [*AFCM*] under [*AFR*] (see §30); supervision only by ECOSOC under *ICES* (see §31), and by EUCE under *ESC* (see §32). See also §6.6 for the obligation to provide domestic remedies under *UDHR* and *ADRD*.

Subsidiary instruments: *ILO 100*, EEC Directives 75/117 and 76/207 (see §18.2.5). Many other ILO Conventions are also in force relating to pay and conditions of work, and to occupational safety and health.

See also: §18.3 for a reference to 'just conditions of work' in *ESC* I, (2).

§18.2.3 COMMENT

Four distinct rights are protected by these provisions.

The right to fair pay

UDHR 23 (3) calls this 'just and favourable remuneration', *ICES* 7(*a*) (i) 'fair wages', and *ESC* I, (4) 'fair remuneration'. In each case, the test is the standard of living which the pay must provide for the worker and his family, defined as 'an existence worthy of human dignity' in *UDHR*, 'suitable' and 'in proportion to his capacity and skill' in *ADRD*, 'a decent living' in *ICES*, and 'a decent standard of living' in *ESC*. Only *UDHR* 23 (3) envisages 'topping-up' of the standard of living by social benefits. [*AFR*] is silent as to this right.

The right to equal pay for equal work

UDHR and [*AFR*] declare this generally as between all workers, and not only as between men and women. So does *ICES* for 'work of equal value', adding a specific requirement for 'equal pay for equal work' as between men and women. *ESC* requires 'equal pay for work of equal value' for men and women workers, but mentions this only in II, (4) as one of several requirements, and not in the corresponding Article in Part I. *ADRD* does not mention this right.

The right to proper working conditions

UDHR 23 (1) and *ICES* 7 call these 'just and favourable', [*AFR*] 'equitable and satisfactory', and both *ICES* 7(b) and *ESC* I, (3) require them to be 'safe and healthy'. Only *ESC* II, 3 prescribes any means for achieving that end. It is *ESC* I, (2) which requires 'just conditions of work', but the corresponding Article in *ESC* II relates entirely to rest and leisure (see §18.3).

The right to promotion

Only *ICES* 7(c) prescribes this, as a right of equal opportunity on the basis of seniority and competence only.

§18.2.4 HISTORY

The development of international standards in this field goes back to the establishment of the ILO in 1919.

§18.2.5 JURISPRUDENCE

In its reports to ECOSOC (see §31), the ILO's Committee of Experts on the Application of Conventions and Recommendations has given some indications of matters which may be relevant in considering how far a State Party has made progress in achieving the observance of the provisions of *ICES* 7. These include differences in minimum wage rates between men and women in the same types of work;[21] the lack of a general power to make orders with immediate executory force in the event of imminent danger to workers;[22] the absence of provisions requiring the notification of occupational diseases in the case of employment in mines;[23] the absence of provisions to prohibit the sale, hire, other transfer or exhibition of unguarded machinery;[24] lack of frequency of inspection visits to agricultural undertakings.[25] the sufficiency of the number of labour inspectors and their transport facilities;[26] the participation of labour inspectors in inquiries into occupational accidents and diseases;[27] and the strictness of regulation of the amount of overtime authorized.[28]

Under the supervision procedure for *ESC* (see §32), EUCE has provided the following interpretations of the relevant Articles of this Charter:

Article 3 requires the issue of safety and health regulations for all economic sectors, adequate enforcement of such regulations through inspection and civil and criminal sanctions, and the arrangement and actual carrying out of all necessary consultations on safety and health matters between governments and both sides of industry.[29] The Article applies to self-employed workers as well as to wage and salary earners.[30] Where regulations relating to safe and healthy working conditions are applied neither to self-employed workers in the agricultural sector or in industry and commerce, nor to members of their families, the State obligation is not satisfied.[31] It is not enough to make provisions for consultation at national, regional, local, or possibly enterprise level: consultations must actually be held whenever the need arises.[32]

21 1979, 108.   22 1980, 13.
23 Ibid.   24 1980, 20.
25 Ibid.   26 1980, 26.
27 1980, 27.   28 Ibid.
29 I, 22.   30 III, 17.
31 II, 12.   32 I, 24.

Article 4, paragraph (1) applies to the private sector and not only to public service employees.[33] The term 'a decent standard of living' means different things in different countries.[34] Account must be taken of the fact that the socio-economic status of the worker and his family changes, and that his basic needs, which at first are centred on the provision of purely material basic necessities such as food and housing, subsequently move towards concerns of a more advanced and complex nature, such as educational facilities and cultural and social benefits.[35] The concept of 'a decent standard of living' must take account of the fundamental social, economic, and cultural needs of workers and their families in relation to the stage of development reached by the society in which they live; it must also for the present be judged in the light of the economic and social situation in the country which is being considered.[36] In a given country and at a given time the wage paid to the largest number of workers can be taken as representative of the wage level in that country: any lower wage which deviates from this to an excessive extent cannot be considered as sufficient to permit 'a decent standard of living' in the society under consideration.[37] The State obligation under this paragraph can only be said to be fulfilled if an end is put in practice to remuneration which does not make it possible, bearing in mind national economic and social conditions as well as social benefits and benefits in kind, to guarantee those receiving them and their families a decent standard of living.[38]

Article 4, paragraph (2). 'Overtime' includes work performed in special circumstances outside or in addition to normal working hours.[39] Not only must the worker receive payment for this, but the rate of such payment must also be higher than the normal wage rate.[40]

Article 4, paragraph (3). The ultimate objective of this paragraph is the real establishment of equal pay between male and female workers.[41] This provision obliges the State Parties to recognize the principle of equal pay for work of equal value, not only in law but also in fact.[42] If that right cannot be ensured for all workers simply through the operation of collective agreements, the State is required to intervene by way of statutory wage-fixing machinery, or any other appropriate method.[43] The obligation is met where the 'equal pay for equal work' rule is established *de iure* and *de facto*, and the State concerned has taken all steps in its power to achieve equality of remuneration for work of comparable value.[44] Since *ESC* 33 does not apply to this paragraph, its provisions must be put into effect for the entire workforce of both sexes: even if only a very few working women are excluded, the obligation is not satisfied.[45]

Article 4, paragraph (4). No absolute definition of a 'reasonable' period of notice can be given.[46] The criteria are those of fairness, such as a worker's period of service with a firm.[47] The obligation is not satisfied where the period of notice is in the first place governed by the contract of employment which leaves the parties free to agree that there should be no period of notice at all,

---

[33] II, 17.   [34] II, 16.
[35] I, 26.   [36] V, 25–6.
[37] V, 25–6.   [38] III, 23.
[39] I, 28.   [40] I, 28.
[41] I, 28.   [42] I, 28.
[43] II, 18–19.   [44] II, 18–19.
[45] IV, 33.   [46] I, 29.
[47] IV, 35.

or where in the absence of an agreement the period of notice of a weekly-paid worker is generally fixed at one week, irrespective of the length of his service, and under existing legislation workers are not entitled to more than one week's notice after up to two years' employment,[48] or two weeks' notice after four years' service.[49]

Article 4, paragraph (5). A State Party will conform with this provision when deductions from wages are permitted for the large majority of workers only where they are expressly authorized by laws, regulations, collective agreements, or arbitration awards.[50]

§18.2.6 SUBSIDIARY INSTRUMENTS

The ILO Convention concerning Equal Remuneration for Men and Women Workers for Work of Equal Value (*ILO 100*) obliges its State Parties, 'by means appropriate to the methods in operation for determining rates of remuneration', to 'promote and, insofar as is consistent with such methods, ensure the application to all workers of the principle of equal remuneration for men and women workers for work of equal value'.[51] 'Remuneration' is defined to include not only wages and salaries, but also 'any additional emoluments whatsoever payable directly or indirectly, whether in cash or in kind, by the employer to the worker and arising out of the worker's employment'.[52] The phrase 'equal remuneration' in the principle refers to rates of remuneration established without discrimination based on sex.[53] However, differential rates between workers are not contrary to the principle if they correspond, without regard to sex, to differences determined by objective appraisal of jobs on the basis of the work to be performed.[54]

Similar provisions are contained in Directive 75/117 of the Council of the European Communities, addressed to the Member States of the Treaty of Rome; Directive 76/207 of that Council extends this to equal treatment as regards access to employment, vocational training and promotion, and working conditions.

§18.3 Rest and leisure

§18.3.1 TEXTS

UDHR

24. Everyone has the right to rest and leisure, including reasonable limitation of working hours and periodic holidays with pay.

ADRD

XV. Every person has the right to leisure time, to wholesome recreation, and to the opportunity for advantageous use of his free time to his spiritual, cultural and physical benefit.

[48] VI, 27.
[49] I, 177.
[50] V. 34–5.
[51] *ILO 100* 2(1).
[52] *ILO 100* 1(e).
[53] *ILO 100* 1(b).
[54] *ILO 100* 3(3).

ICES

7. The States Parties to the present Covenant recognize the right of everyone to the enjoyment of just and favourable conditions of work, which ensure, in particular: . . .

(*d*) Rest, leisure and reasonable limitation of working hours and periodic holidays with pay, as well as remuneration for public holidays.

ESC

I, (2) All workers have the right to just conditions of work.

II, 2. With a view to ensuring the effective exercise of the right to just conditions of work, the Contracting Parties undertake:

(1) to provide for reasonable daily and weekly working hours, the working week to be progressively reduced to the extent that the increase of productivity and other relevant factors permit;

(2) to provide for public holidays with pay;

(3) to provide for a minimum of two weeks' annual holiday with pay;

(4) to provide for additional paid holidays or reduced working hours for workers engaged in dangerous or unhealthy occupations as prescribed;

(5) to ensure a weekly rest period which shall, as far as possible, coincide with the day recognized by tradition or custom in the country or region concerned as a day of rest.

§18.3.2 CROSS-REFERENCES

State obligation: Qualified and progressive under *ICES* and *ESC*: see §6.4. (Note that *ESC* 33 applies to all five paragraphs of *ESC* II, 2.) For the juridical status of obligations under *UDHR* and *ADRD*, see §6.2.

Signatures, ratifications, accessions, reservations, and interpretations: See Table A for the State Parties bound by these provisions on 1 January 1982, and any reservations and interpretations notified by them.

Derogation: Non-derogable in any circumstances under *ICES*; derogable in exceptional circumstances under *ESC*: see §11.

Non-discrimination: No discrimination of any kind (except against non-nationals, for developing countries only, under *ICES*) is allowed in respect of these rights: see §7 for the relevant provisions in the instruments.

Abuse: See §9 for the relevant provisions in these instruments.

Savings: See §10 for the relevant provisions in these instruments.

Restrictions and limitations: See §8 for the general provisions in these instruments.

International supervision, interpretation, application, and enforcement: Supervision only by ECOSOC under *ICES* (see §31), and by EUCE under *ESC* (see §32). See also §6.6 for the obligation to provide domestic remedies under *UDHR* and *ADRD*.

Subsidiary instruments: A number of ILO Conventions in force relate to hours of work, weekly rest, and paid leave.

§18.3.3 COMMENT

UDHR 24 here lists only a single right to 'rest and leisure', but includes within it 'reasonable limitation of working hours', and 'holidays with pay'. *ICES* 7 (*d*) appears to treat these as four distinct rights, and adds a right to remuneration for public holidays. *ESC* II, 2 repeats and expands these in much greater detail, but attaches them to the corresponding Article in Part I which does not appear to relate to rest and leisure, but to 'just conditions of work'. *ADRD* makes no reference to either work or holidays, and instead recites some objectives of the use of leisure. [*AFR*] has no comparable provision.

§18.3.4 HISTORY

The development of international standards in this field goes back to the establishment of the ILO in 1919.

§18.3.5 JURISPRUDENCE

The provisions of *ICES* 7 have not yet been authoritatively interpreted or applied in the course of the international supervision procedure laid down in that Covenant (see §31).

Under the supervision procedure for *ESC* (see §32), EUCE has provided the following interpretations of the five paragraphs of *ESC* II, 2, bearing in mind the fact that *ESC* 33 applies to all these paragraphs:

Paragraph (1). A State Party cannot be considered as complying with this obligation unless reasonable daily and weekly working hours are established either by law or regulations or by collective agreement, or by some other process imposing an obligation whose performance is subject to the supervision of an appropriate authority.[55] What are 'reasonable' working hours cannot be laid down in absolute terms: it will vary from place to place and from time to time, depending on productivity and other factors.[56] Hours of work for family workers in agriculture are included in this provision.[57]

Paragraph (2). Within the CE countries, a range of 9 to 17 public holidays with pay per annum is reasonable.[58]

Paragraph (3). An arrangement whereby the annual holiday may not be taken until the 12 working months for which it is due have fully elapsed is not incompatible with this provision.[59] It is not clear whether the annual holiday must be taken in one uninterrupted period, or may be split up.[60] Workers must not be able to waive their right to annual holidays, even in consideration of an extra payment by the employer. But this does not prevent the payment

---

[55] I, 169.   [56] I, 18.
[57] III, 12.   [58] I, 19.
[59] I, 20.   [60] I, 170.

of a lump sum to an employee at the end of his employment in compensation for a paid holiday to which he has become entitled, but which he has not yet taken.[61]

Paragraph (4). This obligation cannot be compounded by awarding increased pay for dangerous or unhealthy work, instead of increasing the holidays or reducing the working hours.[62] Nor must employment in other occupations be allowed during days worked in dangerous or unhealthy operations for which a limitation of working hours is prescribed.[63] A State Party which has already reduced the general working week to 40 hours and fixed the annual paid holiday at four weeks is not exempt from the obligation to take further action under this paragraph: those who do dangerous or unhealthy work are entitled to receive additional benefits over others.[64]

Paragraph (5). Here too, the worker must not be allowed to forego his weekly rest period.[65]

§18.4 Slavery, servitude, and forced labour

§18.4.1 TEXTS

UDHR

4. No one shall be held in slavery or servitude; slavery and the slave trade shall be prohibited in all their forms.

ADRD

XXXIV. It is the duty of every able-bodied person to render whatever civil and military service his country may require for its defense and preservation, and, in case of public disaster, to render such services as may be in his power.

ICPR

8 (1) No one shall be held in slavery; slavery and the slave-trade in all their forms shall be prohibited.

(2) No one shall be held in servitude.

(3)

(*a*) No one shall be required to perform forced or compulsory labour;

(*b*) Paragraph 3 (*a*) shall not be held to preclude, in countries where imprisonment with hard labour may be imposed as a punishment for a crime, the performance of hard labour in pursuance of a sentence to such punishment by a competent court;

(*c*) For the purpose of this paragraph the term 'forced or compulsory labour' shall not include:

(i) Any work or service, not referred to in sub-paragraph (*b*), normally required of a person who is under detention in consequence of a lawful order of a court, or of a person during conditional release from such detention;

---

[61] I, 170: V, 14.　　[62] III, 4.　　[63] IV, 18.　　[64] V, 17; VI, 14.　　[65] I, 172.

(ii) Any service of a military character and, in countries where conscientious objection is recognized, any national service required by law of conscientious objectors;

(iii) Any service exacted in cases of emergency or calamity threatening the life or well-being of the community;

(iv) Any work or service which forms part of normal civil obligations.

EHR

4 (1) No one shall be held in slavery or servitude.

(2) No one shall be required to perform forced or compulsory labour;

(3) For the purpose of this Article the term 'forced or compulsory labour' shall not include:

(*a*) any work required to be done in the ordinary course of detention imposed according to the provisions of Article 5 of this Convention or during conditional release from such detention;

(*b*) any service of a military character or, in case of conscientious objectors in countries where they are recognized, service exacted instead of compulsory military service;

(*c*) any service exacted in case of an emergency or calamity threatening the life or well-being of the community;

(*d*) any work or service which forms part of normal civic obligations.

AMR

6 (1) No one shall be subject to slavery or to involuntary servitude, which are prohibited in all their forms, as are the slave trade and traffic in women.

(2) No one shall be required to perform forced or compulsory labor. This provision shall not be interpreted to mean that, in those countries in which the penalty established for certain crimes is deprivation of liberty at forced labor, the carrying out of such a sentence imposed by a competent court is prohibited. Forced labor shall not adversely affect the dignity or the physical or intellectual capacity of the prisoner.

(3) For the purposes of this article the following do not constitute forced or compulsory labor:

(*a*) work or service normally required of a person imprisoned in execution of a sentence or formal decision passed by the competent judicial authority. Such work or service shall be carried out under the supervision and control of public authorities, and any persons performing such work or service shall not be placed at the disposal of any private party, company, or juridical person;

(*b*) military service and, in countries in which conscientious objectors are recognized, national service that the law may provide for in lieu of military service;

(*c*) service exacted in time of danger or calamity that threatens the existence or the well-being of the community; or

(*d*) work or service that forms part of normal civic obligations.

[*AFR*]

5. . . . All forms of exploitation and degradation of man, particularly slavery, slave trade, . . . shall be prohibited.

§18.4.2 CROSS-REFERENCES

State obligation: Absolute and immediate under *ICPR, EHR, AMR,* and [*AFR*]: see §6.3. For the juridical status of obligations under *UDHR* and *ADRD*, see §6.2.

Signatures, ratifications, accessions, reservations, and interpretations: See Table A for the State Parties bound by these provisions on 1 January 1982, and any reservations and interpretations notified by them.

Derogation: Non-derogable in any circumstances for *ICPR* 8(1) and (2), *EHR* 4(1), *AMR*, and [*AFR*]; derogable in exceptional circumstances for the remaining provisions: see §11.

Non-discrimination: No discrimination of any kind is allowed in respect of these rights or freedoms: see §7 for the relevant provisions in the instruments.

Abuse: See §9 for the relevant provisions in these instruments.

Savings: See §10 for the relevant provisions in these instruments.

Restrictions and limitations: None, other than the specific provisions in *ICPR* 8(3) (*c*), *EHR* 4(3), *AMR* 6(3), and [*AFR* 29(2) and (5)]. As to these, see §8 for the principles governing all restriction and limitation clauses.

International supervision, interpretation, application, and enforcement: By HRC under *ICPR* (see §27); by EUCM and EUCT under *EHR* (see §28); by IACM and IACT under *AMR* (see §29); by [AFCM] under [*AFR*] (see §30). See also §6.6 for the obligation to provide domestic remedies under *UDHR, ADRD, ICPR, EHR, AMR,* and [*AFR*].

Subsidiary instruments: SC_1, SC_2, *CP, ILO 29,* and *ILO 105* (see §18.4.6); CW_1 6 (see §7.0.5); *CM* (see §17.1.5).

See also: §18.1 as to forced or compulsory labour.

§18.4.3 COMMENT

These provisions between them cover four different practices: slavery, the slave trade, servitude, and forced (or compulsory) labour. Only *ICPR* 8 and *AMR* 6 probibit them all: *UDHR* 4 omits forced labour, *EHR* 4 the slave trade, and [*AFR* 5] both servitude and forced labour. *AMR* 6(1) alone adds 'traffic in women'. *ICPR, EHR,* and *AMR* exclude from the definition of 'forced or compulsory labour' prison work, military service or national service in lieu, emergency or calamity work, and work which 'forms part of normal civic obligations'. *ADRD* XXXIV imposes the last three of these as a duty; so, by implication, do *AMR* 29(2) and (5).

§18.4.4 HISTORY

Freedom from slavery was the first human right, properly so called, to become a subject matter of *international* law. As early as 1885, the General Act of the Berlin Conference on Central Africa was able to affirm that 'trading in slaves is forbidden in conformity with the principles of international law', and SC_1 (which entered into force in 1927) is the first true multilateral human rights treaty. And ever since its establishment in 1919, the ILO has contributed to the development of international standards in this field.

§18.4.5 JURISPRUDENCE

Slavery and the slave trade

None of the major instruments defines these terms; relevant definitions are found only in the subsidiary instruments.

SC_1 (see §18.4.6) defines [66] slavery as

the status or condition of a person over whom any or all of the powers attaching to the right of ownership are exercised.

SC_2 (see §18.4.6), replacing an earlier and very similar definition in SC_1, defines [67] the 'slave trade' to mean and include

all acts involved in the capture, acquisition or disposal of a person with intent to reduce him to slavery; all acts involved in the acquisition of a slave with a view to selling or exchanging him; all acts of disposal by sale or exchange of a person acquired with a view to being sold or exchanged; and, in general, every act of trade or transport in slaves by whatever means of conveyance.

Servitude

None of the major instruments defines this term. However, SC_2 defines [68] the following 'institutions and practices similar to slavery':

(1) debt bondage, that is the status or condition arising from a pledge by a debtor of his personal services or of those of a person under his control as security for a debt, if the value of those services as reasonably assessed is not applied towards the liquidation of the debt or the length and nature of those services are not respectively limited and defined;

(2) serfdom, that is the condition or status of a tenant who is by law, custom, or agreement bound to live and labour on land belonging to another person and to render some determinate service to such other person, whether for reward or not, and is not free to change his status;

(3) any institution or practice whereby:

(a) a woman, without the right to refuse, is promised or given in marriage on

---

[66] SC_1 1.
[67] SC_2 1.
[68] SC_2 7.

payment of a consideration in money or in kind to her parents, guardian, family, or any other person or group; or

(b) the husband of a woman, his family, or his clan, has the right to transfer her to another person for value received or otherwise; or

(c) a woman on the death of her husband is liable to be inherited by another person;

(4) any institution or practice whereby a child or young person under the age of 18 years is delivered by either or both of his natural·parents or by his guardian to another person, whether for reward or not, with a view to the exploitation of the child or young person or of his labour.

The major instruments formally distinguish 'servitude' from 'forced or compulsory labour'. Although the two categories must in fact often overlap, they cannot be treated as equivalent; for example, the exceptions from the scope of the term 'forced or compulsory labour' listed in *EHR* 4(3) are not relevant to an examination of the prohibition directed against 'slavery or servitude'.[69]

In *W, X, Y and Z* v. *United Kingdom*,[70] EUCM examined the question whether military service required of the applicants, who had joined the services as minors but who now wished to be discharged, constituted 'servitude'. While recalling that there were historical examples of uncontestable slavery or servitude being used for the purposes of military service, the Commission observed that the young age at which a person entered into the service cannot in itself attribute the character of 'servitude' to the normal condition of a soldier. Moreover, since in the present instance the applicants had been recruited with parental consent, the Commission saw no difference between them and adult servicemen in respect of whom, admittedly, the terms of service did not amount to a state of servitude.

Nor is it 'servitude' to be 'placed at the government's disposal', for a limited time and subject to revision, by a court following a criminal trial, even if that involves compulsory work in a penal colony: it does not affect the legal status of the person concerned, nor does it entail an obligation to live on another's property, or the impossibility of changing his condition.[71]

On the other hand, the High Court of Kenya has held that, where conditions are such that a husband can enforce compliance by his wife with his physical demands without exposing himself to a criminal charge, a court order for restitution of conjugal rights would subject the wife to the effective dominion of the husband to an extent which constitutes 'servitude' within the meaning of the constitution of Kenya.[72]

Forced or compulsory labour

The expression 'forced or compulsory labour' is not defined in any of the major instruments. *ILO 29* in fact defines[73] it to mean

all work or service which is exacted from any person under the menace of any penalty and for which the said person has not offered himself voluntarily

with exceptions similar to those in *EHR* 4(3).[74]

[69] *W, X, Y and Z* v. *United Kingdom* (3435-8/67) CD 28, 109.
[70] *Supra.*
[71] *Van Droogenbroek* v. *Belgium* (7906/77) Report: 9 July 1980 (referred to EUCT).
[72] *Republic* v. *Khadi, Kisumu, ex p. Nasreen* [1973] EA 153.
[73] *ILO 29* 2(1).
[74] *ILO 29* 2(2).

Fawcett, discussing the technical difficulty of any definition, comments that 'the margin between the planned use of labour and the direction of labour, between free and compulsory employment, can become almost indiscernibly narrow.'[75] However, EUCM has observed that historically the term 'forced or compulsory labour' was associated with labour conditions in non-self-governing territories, and the purpose of the prohibition of forced and compulsory labour in a number of studies, recommendations, and conventions was to end slavery, colonial oppression, and the exploitation of manpower.[76] EUCM has further observed[77] that it was not considered necessary to insert a definition of forced labour in *EHR* 4 because of the existing definition in *ILO 29*, and the provisions of *ILO 105* (see §18.4.6).

The concept of 'forced or compulsory labour' cannot therefore be understood solely in terms of the literal meaning of the words. In interpreting it, it is reasonable to have regard to the relevant ILO Conventions from which EUCM has extracted two elements: firstly, that the work or service is performed by the worker against his will; and secondly, that the requirement that the work or service be performed is unjust or oppressive, or that the work or service itself involves unavoidable hardship.[78]

IACM has stated that *ILO 29* and *ILO 105* are violated where a government uses forced labour as a means of coercion against individuals who have certain political views, for political prisoners after their realease, and for would-be emigrants before they are granted permission to leave.[79]

In *Cyprus* v. *Turkey*,[80] EUCM observed that allegations of Greek-Cypriot women being made to clean out Turkish-occupied houses, including pulling out dead bodies, and of Greek-Cypriot men being compelled to do construction work or to clean up water courses could, if established, constitute 'forced or compulsory labour'.

In *Iversen* v. *Norway*,[81] EUCM examined the complaint of a dentist who had been required by law to perform obligatory public dental service in a remote part of the country for up to two years. Four members of the Commission (with whom two others agreed on different grounds[82]) held that such service was neither unjust nor oppressive, since the service was for a short period, provided favourable remuneration, did not involve any diversion from chosen professional work, was only applied in the case of posts not filled after being duly advertised, and did not involve any discriminatory, arbitrary or punitive application. Four other members, however, were of the view that the conditions under which the applicant was required to perform his work — as regards, for instance, salary, time limit, and professional facilities — did not as such exclude the applicability of *EHR* 4(2), since the work in question was imposed upon the applicant subject to penal sanctions.

In *X* v. *Federal Republic of Germany*,[83] EUCM examined the complaint of a

---

[75] *The Application of the European Convention on Human Rights*, 48.
[76] *X and Y* v. *Federal Republic of Germany* (7641/76) DR 10, 224.
[77] *Ibid.*
[78] *Iversen* v. *Norway* (1468/62) CD 12, 80; *X* v. *Federal Republic of Germany* (4653/70) CD 46, 22.
[79] 6 Cuba 13.
[80] (6780/74; 6950/75) Report: 10 July 1976.
[81] *Supra.*
[82] That the service was reasonably required of him in an emergency threatening the well-being of the community, and was therefore not forced or compulsory labour.
[83] (4653/70) CD 46, 22. See also *X and Y* v. *Federal Republic of Germany*, *supra.*

lawyer who had been appointed by a court to represent a defendant who had been granted legal aid in a divorce case. The Commission observed that the applicant had not been required to work against his will since he had freely chosen his profession as an advocate, knowing that advocates have, according to German law, the obligation to represent poor clients if a court appoints the, as legal aid counsel. Moreover, the work required of the applicant was not unjust, since the right to receive legal aid is provided for under *EHR*, and is thus recognized as an obligation of the State. There was also no hardship involved since the work required was an advocate's normal professional work. Nor could the alleged financial loss be regarded as causing the applicant any real hardship. The same reasoning has been applied to notaries, where their services are required at reduced fees.[84] But where a court appoints defence counsel in criminal proceedings to act for no fee at all, will not even reimburse his clerical expenses, and will release him only for sickness or a conflict of interests, complex issues are raised under *EHR* 4.[85]

The obligation imposed by law on a person to accept, in order to qualify for unemployment benefits, a job offer not in conformity with his qualifications, does not contravene *EHR* 4(2).[86] Nor does the legal obligation imposed on corporate bodies, in their capacity as employers, to calculate and withhold certain taxes, social security contributions, etc., from the salaries of their employees.[87]

Work required to be done in the ordinary course of detention
imposed according to the provisions of EHR 5, or during conditional
release from such detention

In *De Wilde, Ooms and Versyp* v. *Belgium*,[88] EUCT, disagreeing with EUCM, held that the duty to work which had been imposed on persons detained for vagrancy had not exceeded the 'ordinary' limits, within the meaning of *EHR* 4(3)(*a*), because it aimed at their rehabilitation and was based on a general standard. Nor does compulsory work exceed the 'ordinary' limits if it is designed to enable prisoners to earn enough to cover the cost of their board and lodging for the first month after their release.[89]

EHR 4 does not contain any provision concerning the remuneration of prisoners for their work, nor enabling them to be covered by social security systems.[90] Dealing with a complaint from certain prisoners that part of the work required of them during their detention was performed on behalf of private firms under contracts concluded with the prison administration, EUCM observed that *EHR* 4(3)(*a*) does not prevent a State from concluding such contracts: nor does it indicate that a prisoner's obligation to work must be limited to work to be performed within the prison and for the State itself. The underlying reason for the term '*normalement réquis*' was the intention

---

[84] *X* v. *Federal Republic of Germany* (8410/78) DR 18, 216.

[85] *Gussenbauer* v. *Austria* (4897/71) CD 42, 41; *Van der Mussele* v. *Belgium* (8919/80) Decision: 17 March 1981.

[86] *X* v. *Netherlands* (7602/76) DR 7, 161.

[87] *Four Companies* v. *Austria* (7427/76) DR 7, 148; Decision of 10 May 1971, VfGH, Austria (ÖJZ 1972, 305).

[88] (2832/66; 2835/66; 2899/66) Judgment: 1 EHRR 373. See also Report: 19 July 1969; *X* v. *Austria* (2742/66) CD 19, 95.

[89] *Van Droogenbroek* v. *Belgium* (7906/77) Report: 9 July 1980 (referred to EUCT).

[90] *21 Detained Persons* v. *Federal Republic of Germany* (3134/67; 3188–206/67) CD 27, 97; cf. *X* v. *Switzerland* (8500/79) DR 18, 238.

to provide a safeguard against arbitrary decision by authorities with regard to the work that might be required.[91]

Service of a military character or, in the case of conscientious
objectors in countries where they are recognized, service
exacted instead of compulsory military service

In *W, X, Y and Z* v. *United Kingdom*,[92] EUCM examined the question whether this exception also covered military service into which a person had entered as a volunteer. Having regard to the fact that both *EHR* and *ICPR* had replaced the term 'any work or service exacted in virtue of compulsory military service laws', which appears in the exception clause in *ILO 29*, by the term 'any service of a military character', the Commission felt that it was safe to assume that in omitting the word 'compulsory' it was intended to cover also the obligation to continue a service entered into on a voluntary basis.

By including the words 'in countries where they are recognised', a choice is left to the State Parties whether or not to recognize conscientious objectors and, if they do, whether or not to require some substitute service from them.[93]

§18.4.6 SUBSIDIARY INSTRUMENTS

The Slavery Convention (SC_1) was adopted in 1926 under the auspices of the League of Nations, entered into force in the following year, and may be regarded as the first true international human rights law treaty. It has since been amended by a Protocol adopted in 1953, which substitutes references to the UN for those to the League of Nations.

The Convention defines 'slavery' and 'the slave trade':[94] for those definitions, see §18.4.5. The State Parties undertake to 'bring about, progressively and as soon as possible, the complete abolition of slavery in all its forms', and 'to prevent and suppress the slave trade'.[95] For the latter end, they will adopt all appropriate measures within their territorial waters and on vessels flying their flags,[96] and will give each other every assistance.[97] They will impose severe penalties for infractions of laws and regulations enacted to give effect to the Convention's purposes.[98] They will also 'take all necessary measures to prevent compulsory or forced labour from developing into conditions analagous to slavery', and exact such labour only for 'public services'; where it still survives for other purposes, that practice will be discontinued as soon as possible, and will meanwhile invariably be of an exceptional character, adequately remunerated, and not involve the removal of the labourers from their usual place of residence.[99]

The Supplementary Convention on the Abolition of Slavery, the Slave

---

[91] *Ibid.* Neither *ICPR* 8 nor *EHR* 4 has adopted in its entirety Article 2(2)(*c*) of *ILO 29*, which provides that 'forced or compulsory labour' shall not include 'any work or service exacted from any person as a consequence of a conviction in a court of law, provided that the said work or service is carried out under the supervision and control of a public authority and that the said person is not hired to or placed at the disposal of private individuals, companies or associations'. That proviso is, however, included in *AMR* 6(3)(*a*).

[92] (3435–8/67) CD 28, 109.

[93] *X* v. *Austria* (5591/72) CD 43, 61.

[94] SC_1 1; a slightly revised definition appears in SC_2 7.

[95] SC_1 2

[96] SC_1 3.

[97] SC_1 4.

[97] SC_1 6.

[99] SC_1 5.

Trade, and Institutions and Practices similar to Slavery (SC_2) defines certain 'institutions and practices similar to slavery'[100] see (§18.4.5 for those definitions), and requires its State Parties to 'take all practicable and necessary legislative and other measures to bring about progressively and as soon as possible' their 'complete abolition or abandonment where they still exist'.[101] The State Parties will take 'all effective measures' to prevent their ships, aircraft, ports, airfields, and coasts from being used to convey slaves,[102] and will also adopt certain measures which have since been more fully elaborated in *CM* (see §17.1.5).[103]

SC_2 also requires its State Parties to create a number of criminal offences, namely

(1) conveying, or attempting to convey, slaves from one country to another, or being accessory thereto;[104]
(2) conveying slaves in ships or aircraft, or using national flags for that purpose;[105]
(3) mutilating, branding, or otherwise marking a slave or a person of servile status in order to indicate his status, or as a punishment, or for any other reason, or of being accessory thereto;[106]
(4) enslaving another person or inducing another person to give himself or a person dependent upon him into slavery, or attempting these acts, or being accessory thereto, or being a party to a conspiracy to accomplish them;[107]
(5) inducing another person to place himself or a person dependent upon him into a servile status, or any attempt to perform such acts, being accessory thereto, or being a party to a conspiracy to accomplish them.[108]

For this purpose, 'servile status' means the condition or status resulting from any of the 'institutions and practices similar to slavery' defined in the Convention.[109]

Finally, 'any slave who takes refuge on board any vessel of a State Party . . . shall *ipso facto* be free'.[110]

Under the ILO Convention concerning Forced Labour (*ILO 29*), the State Parties undertake to 'suppress the use of forced or compulsory labour in all its forms within the shortest possible period'.[111] Until then, it may be used only for public purposes, as an exceptional measure, and subject to a series of elaborate conditions and guarantees.[112] The illegal exaction of forced and compulsory labour shall be a penal offence, punished with 'really adequate' penalties.[113]

The later ILO Convention concerning the Abolition of Forced Labour (*ILO 105*) goes further, requiring its State Parties

---

[100] SC_2 1,
[101] *Ibid.*
[102] SC_2 3(2).
[103] SC_2 2.
[104] SC_2 3(1); this offence is to be subject to 'very severe penalties'.
[105] SC_2 3(2) (*a*).
[106] SC_2 5.
[107] SC_2 6(1).
[108] SC_2 6(2).
[109] SC_2 7(*b*).
[110] SC_2 4.
[111] *ILO 29* 1(1).
[112] *ILO 29* 1(2).
[113] *ILO 29* 25.

to suppress and not to make use of any form of forced or compulsory labour:

(a) as a means of political coercion or education or as a punishment for holding or expressing political views or views ideologically opposed to the established political, social or economic system;
(b) as a method of mobilising and using labour for purposes of economic development;
(c) as a means of labour discipline;
(d) as a punishment for having participated in strikes;
(e) as a means of racial, social, national or religious discrimination.[114]

Under the Convention for the Suppression of the Traffic in Persons and of the Exploitation of the Prostitution of Others (*CP*), the State Parties agree

to punish any person who, to gratify the passions of another:

(1) procures, entices or leads away, for purposes of prostitution, another person, even with the consent of that person;
(2) exploits the prostitution of another person, even with the consent of that person.[115]

They likewise agree to punish any person who:

(1) keeps or manages, or knowingly finances or takes part in the financing of, a brothel;
(2) knowingly lets or rents a building or other place or any part thereof for the purpose of the prostitution of others.[116]

Attempts to commit any of these offences,[117] and intentional participation in them,[118] shall also be punishable. All these offences are to be extraditeable.[119]

The State Parties will not subject prostitutes to special registration, or to the possession of a special document, or to exceptional supervision or notification requirements.[120] They will take or encourage measures for the prevention of prostitution and the rehabilitation and social adjustment of its victims,[121] as well as measures to check the international traffic of persons of either sex for the purpose of prostitution,[132] to care for the victims of that traffic,[123] and to supervise employment agencies in order to prevent persons seeking employment from being exposed to the danger of prostitution.[124]

[114] *ILO 105* 1.   [115] *CP* 2.
[116] *Ibid.*   [117] *CP* 3.
[118] *CP* 4.   [119] *CP* 8–10.
[120] *CP* 6.   [121] *CP* 16.
[122] *CP* 17.   [123] *CP* 19.
[124] *CP* 20.

§19. SOCIAL SECURITY,
ASSISTANCE, AND WELFARE

§19.0.1 TEXTS

UDHR

22. Everyone, as a member of society, has the right to social security and is entitled to realization, through national effort and international co-operation and in accordance with the organization and resources of each State, of the economic, social and cultural rights indispensable for his dignity and the free development of his personality.

25 (1) Everyone has the right to a standard of living adequate for the health and well-being of himself and of his family, including food, clothing, housing and medical care and necessary social services, and the right to security in the event of unemployment, sickness, disability, widowhood, old age or other lack of livelihood in circumstances beyond his control.

ADRD

XVI. Every person has the right to social security which will protect him from the consequences of unemployment, old age, and any disabilities arising from causes beyond his control that make it physically or mentally impossible for him to earn a living.

XXXV. It is the duty of every person to cooperate with the state and the community with respect to social security and welfare, in accordance with his ability and with existing circumstances.

XXXVI. It is the duty of every person to pay the taxes established by law for the support of public services.

ICES

9. The States Parties to the present Covenant recognize the right of everyone to social security, including social insurance.

ESC

I, (12) All workers and their dependents have the right to social security.

(13) Anyone without adequate resources has the right to social and medical assistance.

(14) Everyone has the right to benefit from social welfare services.

(15) Disabled persons have the right to vocational training, rehabilitation and resettlement, whatever the origin and nature of their disability.

II, 12. With a view to ensuring the effective exercise of the right to social security, the Contracting Parties undertake:
(1) to establish or maintain a system of social security;
(2) to maintain the social security system at a satisfactory level at least equal to that required for ratification of International Labour Convention (No. 102) Concerning Minimum Standards of Social Security;
(3) to endeavour to raise progressively the system of social security to a higher level;
(4) to take steps, by the conclusion of appropriate bilateral and multilateral agreements, or by other means, and subject to the conditions laid down in such agreements, in order to ensure:
   (*a*) equal treatment with their own nationals of the nationals of other Contracting Parties in respect of social security rights, including the retention of benefits arising out of social security legislation, whatever movements the persons protected may undertake between the territories of the Contracting Parties;
   (*b*) the granting, maintenance and resumption of social security rights by such means as the accumulation of insurance or employment periods completed under the legislation of each of the Contracting Parties.

(*App.*: The words 'and subject to the conditions laid down in such agreements' in the introduction to this paragraph are taken to imply *inter alia* that with regard to benefits which are available independently of any insurance contribution a Contracting Party may require the completion of a prescribed period of residence before granting such benefits to nationals of other Contracting Parties.)

II, 13. With a view to ensuring the effective exercise of the right to social and medical assistance, the Contracting Parties undertake:
(1) to ensure that any person who is without adequate resources and who is unable to secure such resources either by his own efforts or from other sources, in particular by benefits under a social security scheme, be granted adequate assistance, and, in case of sickness, the care necessitated by his condition;

(2) to ensure that persons receiving such assistance shall not, for that reason, suffer from a diminution of their political or social rights;

(3) to provide that everyone may receive by appropriate public or private services such advice and personal help as may be required to prevent, to remove, or to alleviate personal or family want;

(4) to apply the provisions referred to in paragraphs 1, 2 and 3 of this Article on an equal footing with their nationals to nationals of other Contracting Parties lawfully within their territories, in accordance with their obligations under the European Convention on Social and Medical Assistance, signed at Paris on 11 December 1953.

(*App.*: Governments not Parties to the European Convention on Social and Medical Assistance may ratify the Social Charter in respect of this paragraph provided that they grant to nationals of other Contracting Parties a treatment which is in conformity with the provisions of the said Convention.)

II, 14. With a view to ensuring the effective exercise of the right to benefit from social welfare services, the Contracting Parties undertake:

(1) to promote or provide services which, by using methods of social work, would contribute to the welfare and development of both individuals and groups in the community, and to their adjustment to the social environment;

(2) to encourage the participation of individuals and voluntary or other organizations in the establishment and maintenance of such services.

II, 15. With a view to ensuring the effective exercise of the right of the physically or mentally disabled to vocational training, rehabilitation and resettlement, the Contracting Parties undertake:

(1) to take adequate measures for the provision of training facilities, including, where necessary, specialized institutions, public or private;

(2) to take adequate measures for the placing of disabled persons in employment, such as specialized placing services, facilities for sheltered employment and measures to encourage employers to admit disabled persons to employment.

[*AFR*]

13 (1) Every individual shall have the right of access to public property and services in strict equality of all persons before the law.

18 (4) The aged and the disabled shall also have the right to special measures of protection in keeping with their physical or moral needs.

29. The individual shall also have the duty: . . .
   (6) to pay taxes imposed by law in the interest of society;

§19.0.2 CROSS-REFERENCES

State obligation: Absolute and immediate under [*AFR*]: see §6.3. Qualified and progressive under *ICES* and *ESC*: see §6.4. For the juridical status of obligations under *UDHR* and *ADRD*, see §6.2.

Signatures, ratifications, accessions, reservations, and interpretations: See Table A for the State Parties bound by these provisions on 1 January 1982, and any reservations and interpretations notified by them.

Derogation: Non-derogable in any circumstances under *ICES* and [*AFR*]; derogable in exceptional circumstances under *ESC*: see §11.

Non-discrimination: No discrimination of any kind (except against non-nationals, for developing countries only, under *ICES*) is allowed in respect of these rights: see §7 for the relevant provisions in the instruments.

Abuse: See §9 for the relevant provisions in these instruments.

Savings: See §10 for the relevant provisions in these instruments.

Restrictions and limitations: See §8 for the general provisions in these instruments.

International supervision, interpretation, application, and enforcement: By [AFCM] under [*AFR*] (see §30); supervision only by ECOSOC under *ICES* (see §31), and by EUCE under *ESC* (see §32). See also §6.6 for the obligation to provide domestic remedies under *UDHR* and *ADRD*.

Subsidiary instruments: ILO 102. There is also a large number of other ILO Conventions in force relating to various social security standards.

See also: §18.2 for a further reference to social protection in *UDHR* 23(3); §18.1 for a further reference to protection against unemployment in *UDHR* 23(1).

§19.0.3 COMMENT

The simple 'right to social security' stated in *UDHR* 22 is expanded in *UDHR* 25(1) into a right to security in six specified eventualities: unemployment, sickness, disability, widowhood, old age, and 'other lack of livelihood in circumstances beyond his control'. *ADRD* does not specifically mention sickness or widowhood, but the category of 'causes beyond his control that make it physically or mentally impossible for him to earn a living' would probably include at least the first of these. *ICES* 9 repeats the simple 'right to social security, including social insurance', but does not specify any eventualities in which the security is to be provided.

ESC is much more specific than any of the other instruments, devoting four separate Articles to this right in Part I, and prescribing (in the corresponding Articles in Part II) no fewer than thirteen different groups of measures to be taken by the State Parties in support of it. Note that *ESC* I, (13) and (14) extend to 'everyone', but *ESC* I, (12) extends only to 'workers and their dependents'.

ADRD XXXV and XXXVI call for contributions from the individual towards services provided by the State, in the form both of co-operation and the payment of taxes 'established by law'; [*AFR* 29(6)] also declares a duty to pay taxes 'imposed by law', though that Charter declares no right to social security.

§19.0.4 JURISPRUDENCE

The provisions of *ICES* 9 have not yet been authoritatively interpreted or applied in the course of the international supervision procedure laid down in that Covenant (see §31).

Under the supervision procedure for *ESC* (see §32), EUCE has provided the following interpretations of the relevant Articles of that Charter:

Article 12, paragraph (1). Where there is social insurance legislation providing benefits covering certain risks, but there are substantial gaps in it and many benefits are very low, there may be serious doubt as to whether the measures in force could be termed a 'social security' system.[1] But a system may be a genuine system of social security even though some risks (benefit in kind for sickness and maternity, and family benefits) are not covered.[2]

Article 12, paragraph (2). Whenever a social security system is at least equal in level to that required for the ratification of *ILO 102*, the obligation under this paragraph is satisfied.[3] *ILO 102* has four parts, and the conditions for ratifying it are the fulfilment of at least three of these. Where a State only fulfils two of them, it cannot fulfil the obligations of this paragraph of *ESC*.[4] Where legislation requires the wife of the insured to contribute to hospital confinement costs for her maternity care, and the dependants of an insured person who is in prison might, in certain circumstances, be denied benefits, *ILO 102* would not be satisfied, nor would the obligation under this paragraph of *ESC*.[5]

Article 12, paragraph (3) requires a higher level of social security than that of *ILO 102*. Accordingly, where a State's social security system fails to attain the level required for the ratification of that Convention, the obligation under this paragraph cannot be satisfied.[6]

Article 12, paragraph (4) cannot be regarded as having been honoured unless equality between a country's own nationals and those of other State Parties is effectively safeguarded under national legislation, and adequate efforts are made to conclude and implement international agreements whereby migrants' rights are maintained or restored.[7] In the absence of bilateral or multilateral agreements, unilateral measures must be taken.[8] A provision under which a social security benefit or pension is restricted to citizens of a certain State alone is incompatible with this paragraph.[9] Likewise, where benefits for disablement and for survivors are not granted to persons living abroad unless they are nationals of the State concerned, even if in practice the transfer of these

[1] III, 62. [2] IV, 81.
[3] I, 62. [4] IV, 81.
[5] III, 62. [6] II, 192; III, 63.
[7] III, 64. [8] VI, 84.
[9] IV, 84–5; VI, 85.

benefits would not be refused.[10] However, where payment abroad of family allowances is prohibited alike to nationals and to aliens, there is at least formal equality of treatment and therefore no incompability with the requirements of this paragraph.[11]

Article, 13, paragraph (1) makes it compulsory to accord assistance to necessitous persons as of right. The State Parties are no longer merely empowered to grant assistance as they think fit; they are under an obligation, which they may be called on in court to honour.[12] Where, with a few exceptions, social assistance is only guaranteed by a State Party for persons born there or resident there for at least five years, it is not clear whether and to what extent seasonal workers benefit from social assistance in general, and there does not seem to be sufficient foundation on economic grounds to justify excluding those workers from unemployment benefits, the State concerned does not wholly fulfil its obligation under this paragraph.[13] Unemployment benefits for workers who lose their jobs relate to Article 12 of the Charter on social security, and not to social assistance.[14]

Article 13, paragraph (2) makes it compulsory for State Parties to eradicate from their legislation any remnants of social and political discrimination against persons receiving assistance, who are not to be regarded as second-class citizens merely because they are unable to support themselves.[15] Legislation which provides that a person who has received assistance benefits may not become a member of an assistance authority until after the expiration of a period of 12 months amounts to a 'diminution' of the rights of the person concerned within the meaning of this paragraph.[16] But the paragraph will only be infringed if discrimination against persons receiving public assistance results from an express statutory provision, such as an electoral provision or a provision governing admittance to the public service.[17]

Article 13, paragraph (3). This obligation is much more precise and more restricted than that in Article 14, and concerns only advisory services for persons without, or liable to be without, adequate resources; whereas Article 14 is concerned with social welfare services in general. Accordingly, a State Party could comply with either of these provisions while failing to comply with the other.[18]

Article 13, paragraph (4) is not an autonomous provision, insofar as it merely indicates which persons are to receive protection under the previous three paragraphs.[19] Where, in the absence of a bilateral agreement, nationals of one State Party can be repatriated from another simply because they are in need, the requirements of this paragraph are not satisfied.[20] Likewise where, in part of the territory of a State Party, only persons born there or having lived there for at least five years are entitled to social and medical assistance.[21]

---

[10] III, 65.
[11] I, 201.
[12] I, 64.
[13] III, 67; IV, 88. Cf. *Shapiro v. Thompson* 394 US 618.
[14] IV, 88.
[15] I, 64.
[16] I, 203.
[17] I, 67.
[18] I, 64.
[19] I, 67.
[20] IV, 91.
[21] IV, 92.

Article 14 applies to a much larger number of beneficiaries than Article 13(3), which covers only persons who do not have adequate resources of their own. Where Article 13(3) is limited to assistance, Article 14 includes any action taken to facilitate the development of individuals and their adjustment to society. Accordingly, beyond a certain level of social development, a State wishing to comply with the provisions of Article 14 must promote the establishment of services providing advice and individual help, rather than merely encourage the granting of material assistance.[22]

Article 14, paragraph (2). A State Party which rejects the idea of direct administration of social services by private persons or bodies, but which nevertheless encourages their participation in the upkeep of these services, satisfies the obligations under this paragraph.[23]

Article 15. In order to comply with the obligations under this Article, the criteria used to certify a person as physically or mentally disabled must be clearly specified.[24]

Article 15, paragraph (2) covers both physically and mentally handicapped persons,[25] and requires a continuous effort to ensure its application.[26]

---

[22] I, 69.
[23] IV, 95.
[24] III, 74.
[25] I, 208.
[26] IV, 99.

§20. EDUCATION AND TRAINING

UDHR

26 (1) Everyone has the right to education. Education shall be free, at least in the elementary and fundamental stages. Elementary education shall be compulsory. Technical and professional education shall be made generally available and higher education shall be equally accessible to all on the basis of merit.

(2) Education shall be directed to the full development of the human personality and to the strengthening of respect for human rights and fundamental freedoms. It shall promote understanding, tolerance and friendship among all nations, racial or religious groups, and shall further the activities of the United Nations for the maintenance of peace.

(3) Parents have a prior right to choose the kind of education that shall be given to their children.

ADRD

XII. Every person has the right to an education, which should be based on the principles of liberty, morality and human solidarity.

Likewise every person has the right to an education that will prepare him to attain a decent life, to raise his standard of living, and to be a useful member of society.

The right to an education includes the right to equality of opportunity in every case, in accordance with natural talents, merit and the desire to utilize the resources that the state or the community is in a position to provide.

Every person has the right to receive, free, at least a primary education.

XXXI. It is the duty of every person to acquire at least an elementary education.

ICES

13 (1) The States Parties to the present Covenant recognize the right of everyone to education. They agree that education shall be directed to the full development of the human personality and the sense of its dignity, and shall strengthen the respect for human rights

and fundamental freedoms. They further agree that education shall enable all persons to participate effectively in a free society, promote understanding, tolerance and friendship among all nations and all racial, ethnic or religious groups, and further the activities of the United Nations for the maintenance of peace.

(2) The States Parties to the present Covenant recognize that, with a view to achieving the full realization of this right:

(*a*) Primary education shall be compulsory and available free to all;

(*b*) Secondary education in its different forms, including technical and vocational secondary education, shall be made generally available and accessible to all by every appropriate means, and in particular by the progressive introduction of free education;

(*c*) Higher education shall be made equally accessible to all, on the basis of capacity, by every appropriate means, and in particular by the progressive introduction of free education;

(*d*) Fundamental education shall be encouraged or intensified as far as possible for those persons who have not received or completed the whole period of their primary education;

(*e*) The development of a system of schools at all levels shall be actively pursued, an adequate fellowship system shall be established, and the material conditions of teaching staff shall be continuously improved.

(3) The States Parties to the present Covenant undertake to have respect for the liberty of parents and, when applicable, legal guardians, to choose for their children schools, other than those established by the public authorities, which conform to such minimum educational standards as may be laid down or approved by the State and to ensure the religious and moral education of their children in conformity with their own convictions.

(4) No part of this article shall be construed so as to interfere with the liberty of individuals and bodies to establish and direct educational institutions, subject always to the observance of the principles set forth in paragraph 1 of this Article and to the requirement that the education given in such institutions shall conform to such minimum standards as may be laid down by the State.

14. Each State Party to the present Covenant which, at the time of becoming a Party, has not been able to secure in its metropolitan territory or other territories under its jurisdiction compulsory primary education, free of charge, undertakes, within two years, to work out and adopt a detailed plan of action for the progressive implementation, within a reasonable number of years to be fixed in the plan, of the principle of compulsory education free of charge for all.

ICPR

18 (4) The States Parties to the present Covenant undertake to have respect for the liberty of parents and, when applicable, legal guardians to ensure the religious and moral education of their children in conformity with their own convictions.

EHR P1

2. No person shall be denied the right to education. In the exercise of any functions which it assumes in relation to education and to teaching, the State shall respect the right of parents to ensure such education and teaching in conformity with their own religious and philosophical convictions.

ESC

I, (9) Everyone has the right to appropriate facilities for vocational guidance with a view to helping him choose an occupation suited to his personal aptitude and interests.

(10) Everyone has the right to appropriate facilities for vocational training.

II, 9. With a view to ensuring the effective exercise of the right to vocational guidance, the Contracting Parties undertake to provide or promote, as necessary, a service which will assist all persons, including the handicapped, to solve problems related to occupational choice and progress, with due regard to the individual's characteristics and their relation to occupational opportunity: this assistance should be available free of charge, both to young persons, including school children, and to adults.

II, 10. With a view to ensuring the effective exercise of the right to vocational training, the Contracting Parties undertake:
(1) to provide or promote, as necessary, the technical and vocational training of all persons, including the handicapped, in consultation with employers' and workers' organizations, and to grant facilities for access to higher technical and university education, based solely on individual aptitude;
(2) to provide or promote a system of apprenticeship and other systematic arrangements for training young boys and girls in their various employments;
(3) to provide or promote, as necessary:
    (a) adequate and readily available training facilities for adult workers;
    (b) special facilities for the re-training of adult workers needed

as a result of technological development or new trends in employment;

(4) to encourage the full utilization of the facilities provided by appropriate measures such as:

  (*a*) reducing or abolishing any fees or charges;

  (*b*) granting financial assistance in appropriate cases;

  (*c*) including in the normal working hours time spent on supplementary training taken by the worker, at the request of his employer, during employment;

  (*d*) ensuring, through adequate supervision, in consultation with the employers' and workers' organizations, the efficiency of apprenticeship and other training arrangements for young workers, and the adequate protection of young workers generally.

AMR

12 (4) Parents or guardians, as the case may be, have the right to provide for the religious and moral education of their children or wards that is in accord with their own convictions.

[*AFR*]

17 (1) Every individual shall have the right to education.

(3) The promotion and protection of morals and traditional values recognized by the community shall be the duty of the State.

§20.0.2 CROSS-REFERENCES

State obligation: Absolute and immediate under *ICPR, EHR, AMR*, and [*AFR*]: see §6.3. Qualified and progressive under *ICES* and *ESC*: see §6.4. (Note that *ESC* 33 applies to all four paragraphs of *ESC* II, 10.) For the juridical status of obligations under *UDHR* and *ADRD*, see §6.2.

Signatures, ratifications, accessions, reservations, and interpretations: See Table A for the State Parties bound by these provisions on 1 January 1982, and any reservations and interpretations notified by them.

Derogation: Non-derogable in any circumstances under *ICES, ICPR, AMR*, and [*AFR*]. Derogable in exceptional circumstances under *EHR* and *ESC*: see §11.

Non-discrimination: No discrimination of any kind (except against non-nationals, for developing countries only, under *ICES*) is allowed in respect of these rights or freedoms: see §7 for the relevant provisions in the instruments.

Abuse: See §9 for the relevant provisions in these instruments.

Savings: See §10 for the relevant provisions in these instruments.

Restrictions and limitations: Note the specific provisions in *ICES* 13(4); see §8 for the general provisions in these instruments, and the principles governing all restriction and limitation clauses.

International supervision, interpretation, application, and enforcement: By HRC under *ICPR* (see §27); by EUCM and EUCT under *EHR* (see §28); by IACM and IACT under *AMR* (see §29); by [AFCM] under [*AFR*] (see §30); supervision only by ECOSOC under *ICES* (see §31); by EUCE under *ESC* (see §32). See also §6.6 for the obligation to provide domestic remedies under *UDHR, ADRD, ICPR, EHR, AMR*, and [*AFR*].

Subsidiary instruments: CE (see §7.0.5); *ILO 142.*

See also: §19.1 for another reference to vocational training in *ESC* 15; §18.1 for another reference to technical and vocational guidance and training programmes in *ICES* 6(2); §23.3 for freedom of conscience and religion.

§20.0.3 COMMENT

These Articles cover several related matters.

The right to education

This is declared or recognized in UDHR 26(1), *ADRD* XII, *ICES* 13(1), *EHR P1* 2, and [*AFR* 17(1)]. Only *ADRD* XII explicitly mentions 'equality of opportunity' at all levels of education, 'in accordance with natural talents, merit and the desire' to take advantage of it. *EHR P1* 2 alone states it in negative form.

Free education

UDHR 26(1) requires this 'at least in the elementary and fundamental stages', *ADRD* XII for 'at least a primary education', and *ICES* 13(2) for 'primary education' absolutely, and for secondary and higher education progressively. Note the specific (and unique) time limit for the obligation in *ICES* 14.

Compulsory education

UDHR 26(1) requires this for 'elementary' education, *ICES* 13(2)(*a*) for 'primary' education. *ADRD* XXXI instead imposes on individuals the duty 'to acquire at least an elementary education'.

Secondary education

UDHR 26(1) calls for 'technical and professional' education to be made 'generally available'. *ICES* 13(2)(*b*) contains a similar call for secondary education in all its forms, including the 'technical and vocational' ones, and says that this should be 'accessible to all by every appropriate means'.

Higher education

UDHR 26(1) and *ICES* 13(2)(*c*) both call for this to be 'equally accessible to all', in *UDHR* 'on the basis of merit', and in *ICES* 'on the basis of capacity'. *ESC* II, 10(1) requires the grant of 'facilities for access', based 'solely on individual aptitude'.

Purposes of education

UDHR 26(2) lists four objectives for education:

(1) the full development of the human personality;
(2) strengthening of respect for human rights and fundamental freedoms;

(3) the promotion of understanding, tolerance and friendship among all nations, racial or religious groups;
(4) the furtherance of the activities of the UN for the maintenance of peace.

To these, *ICPR* 13(1) adds three more:

(5) the development of the sense of human dignity;
(6) enabling all persons to participate effectively in a free society;
(7) the promotion of understanding, tolerance and friendship among *ethnic* groups.

ADRD XII instead says that education 'should be based on the principles of liberty, morality and human solidarity', and should prepare people to attain a decent life, raise their standards of living, and be useful members of society.

Parents' rights in education

UDHR 26(3) declares a 'prior right' for parents to choose 'the kind of education' their children should be given. *ICES* 13(3), *ICPR* 18(4), and *AMR* 12(4) confine this to the children's 'religious and moral' education in accordance with the convictions of their parents or legal guardians; *EHR P1* 2 to education and teaching in conformity with the parents' 'religious and philosophical' convictions. *ICES* 13(3) adds a parental right to choose private rather than public schools, provided these conform to the minimum educational standards laid down or approved by the State.

Vocational guidance and training

ESC II, 9 and 10 contain detailed provisions about these, which apply to 'everyone', and not only to workers.

Morals and traditional values

Only [*AFR* 17(3)] places upon the State the express duty to promote and protect these.

§20.0.4 JURISPRUDENCE

The provisions of *ICES* 13 and 14 have not yet been authoritatively interpreted or applied in the course of the international supervision procedure laid down in that Covenant (see §31).

In the *Belgian Linguistic Case*,[1] EUCT examined the scope of the 'right to education' within the meaning of the first sentence of *EHR P1* 2. Having regard to the fact that, at the time of the opening of the Protocol for signature, all the Member States of the CE possessed general and official educational systems, the Court concluded that what was here guaranteed to persons subject to the jurisdiction of those States was the right, in principle, to avail themselves of the means of instruction existing at a given time. The negative formulation indicated that the State Parties did not recognize such a right to education as would have required them to establish at their own expense, or to subsidize, education of any particular type or at any particular level. EUCM had been

---

[1] 6 *Groups of Belgian Citizens* v. *Belgium* (1474/62, etc.) Judgment: 1 EHRR 252. See also *X* v. *United Kingdom* (7782/77) DR 14, 179; *X* v. *Austria* (5492/72) CD 44, 63; *Inhabitants of Les Fourons* v. *Belgium* (2209/64) Report: 30 March 1971.

of the view that the first sentence prohibited States from taking any action that might prevent persons under their jurisdiction from educating themselves.[2]

The right of access to educational institutions existing at a given time constitutes only a part of the right to education. Although the first sentence of *EHR P1 2* does not specify the language in which education must be conducted in order that the right to education should be respected, EUCT has observed that this right would be meaningless if it did not imply, in favour of its beneficiaries, the right to be educated in the national language, or in one of the national languages, as the case may be. Moreover, for the right to education to be effective, it is also necessary that the individual who is the beneficiary should have the possibility of drawing profit from the education received; that is to say, the right to obtain, in conformity with the rules in force in each State, and in one form or another, official recognition of the studies which he has completed.[3]

The right to education, by its very nature, calls for regulation by the State: regulation which may vary in time and place according to the needs and resources of the community and of individuals. Such regulation must not injure the substance of the right to education, nor conflict with other rights enshrined in *EHR*,[4] but it imposes no obligation on a State to recognize, or continue to recognize, any particular institution as an educational establishment:[5]

The right to education envisaged in *EHR P1 2* is concerned primarily with elementary education, and not necessarily with advanced studies such as technology,[6] or retraining programmes.[7] However, instruction in sex, pregnancy, birth, and venereal disease, whether in physical or biological terms, or in terms of human love and responsibilities, is 'education' in the sense of this provision.[8]

For the purposes of *EHR P1 2*, an adoption order confers on the adopters the same rights and obligations with regard to a child as had existed up to that moment between the natural parents and the child.[9] But a corporate body, being a legal and not a natural person, is incapable of having or exercising any such rights.[10]

Parental convictions

In *Kjeldsen et al.* v. *Denmark*,[11] EUCT examined the scope of the second sentence of *EHR P1 2*. It noted that the right set out in that sentence was an adjunct of the fundamental right to education: the two sentences must be read not only in the light of each other, but also of the other provisions of *EHR*, and in particular Articles 8, 9, and 10. *EHR P1 2* requires the State to respect the rights of parents *while* exercising its functions in education. The State's functions in that sentence include matters such as the allocation of places in secondary schools and the organization of the system of secondary education in

---

[2] Report: 24 June 1965. This Article not only prohibits the State from preventing parents from arranging the education of their children outside the public schools, but also requires the State actively to respect parental convictions within the public schools.
[3] *6 Groups of Belgian Citizens v. Belgium, supra.*
[4] *Ibid.*
[5] *Church of X v. United Kingdom* (3798/68) CD 29, 74.
[6] *X v. United Kingdom* (5962/72) DR 2, 50.
[7] *X v. Belgium* (7010/75) DR 3, 162.
[8] *Kjeldsen et al. v. Denmark* (5095/71; 5920/72; 5926/72) Report: 21 March 1975.
[9] *X v. United Kingdom* (7627/76) DR 11, 160.
[10] *X v. Sweden* (4733/71) CD 39, 75.
[11] Judgment: 1 EHRR 711.

general;[12] the setting and planning of the curriculum;[13] and, where the State chooses to assume that responsibility, the grant of financial assistance to private schools.[14]

EHR P1 2 does not prevent States from imparting, through teaching or education, information or knowledge of a directly or indirectly religious or philosophical kind. It does not even permit parents to object to the integration of such teaching or education in the school curriculum. But it does imply that the State in fulfilling the functions it assumes in regard to education and teaching must take care that information or knowledge included in the curriculum is conveyed in an objective, critical and pluralistic manner. The State is forbidden to pursue an aim of indoctrination that might be considered as not respecting parents' religious and philosophical convictions. That is the limit that must not be exceeded.[15]

HRC also has expressed the view that, where parents or guardians object to religious instruction for their children at school, it is not incompatible with *ICPR* 18(4) for domestic legislation to require that instruction should instead be given in the study of the history of religion and ethics, provided that this is done in a neutral and objective way and respects the convictions of parents and guardians who do not believe in any religion.[16]

According to EUCM, the words 'any function' in *EHR P1 2* are not confined to the contents of the school curriculum: they include the development and moulding of children's characters and mental powers, of which discipline is an inseparable part. However, fundamental objections to the use or threatened use of physical violence are 'philosophical convictions' in the sense of forming part of an outlook on life — including, in particular, a concept of human behaviour in society. Accordingly, where some parents object, as a matter of such conviction, to the use of corporal punishment as a disciplinary measure in a State's schools, the State is bound to respect those convictions, notwithstanding the availability of alternative private schools, and regardless of the fact that these convictions are not shared by the generality of the parents concerned.[17]

Vocational guidance and training

Under the supervision procedure for *ESC* (see §32), EUCE has provided the following interpretations of the relevant Articles of that Charter:

Article 9. The vocational guidance facilities here referred to must be placed at the disposal not only of unemployed persons, but of all categories of students, and particularly young people leaving school.[18] Nor should vocational guidance be approached only from a medico-psychological angle.[19]

Article 10. This is subject, in respects of all its four paragraphs, to the provisions of *ESC* 33.

[12] *X and Y v. United Kingdom* (7527/76) DR 11, 147; *Church of X v. United Kingdom, supra.*

[13] *Kjeldsen et al. v. Denmark, supra.*

[14] *Ibid.*

[15] *Ibid*: Danish legislation which provided for integrated sex education did not violate *EHR P1 2*. See also *6 Groups of Belgian Citizens v. Belgium, supra*: this provision does not require of States that they should, in the sphere of education or teaching, respect parents' linguistic preferences, but only their religious and philosophical convictions.

[16] *Hartikainen et al. v. Finland* (R. 9/40) HRC 36, 147.

[17] *Campbell and Cosans v. United Kingdom* (7511/76; 7743/76) Report: 16 May 1980 (referred to EUCT).

[18] I, 53.

[19] IV, 70.

Article 10, paragraph (1). Where severe restrictions are imposed on the access of young foreigners to vocational training assistance, this obligation is not satisfied.[20]

Article 10, paragraph (2). The apprenticeship facilities referred to here should be conceived in broad terms and comprise full, co-ordinated, and systematic training.[21] They must not be conditioned on a date of entry into the country, or on residence or employment qualifications for the apprentice's parents.[22] A State Party bound by this provision is not prevented from making arrangements aimed at gradually replacing apprenticeship by a more institutionalized vocational training.[23] The compulsory periods of practical experience forming part of the training of, for example, students in medicine, dentistry, law, and education, whether in the course of their university studies or afterwards, are within the scope of this paragraph.[24]

Article 10, paragraph (3) lays a particular obligation on any State Party that still has a considerable number of unemployed.[25] Where measures under which the only workers who may receive State aid for vocational training are nationals of the State concerned who have at least six years of employment, and persons who pay contributions, this might, in certain circumstances and under certain conditions, be considered as compatible with this provision. But it could create difficulties in respect of foreign workers.[26]

Article 10, paragraph (4). It is doubtful whether measures comply with the obligation under this paragraph if they are applicable only to trainees (young and adult) in certain designated industrial activities which constitute only part of the total economic activity in the State concerned.[27]

[20] VI, 70.
[21] I, 57.
[22] VI, 71.
[23] I, 57.
[24] III, 55.
[25] I, 58.
[26] V, 84–5.
[27] V, 86.

§21. PROPERTY

UDHR

17 (1) Everyone has the right to own property alone as well as in association with others.

(2) No one shall be arbitrarily deprived of his property.

ADRD

XXIII. Every person has a right to own such private property as meets the essential needs of decent living and helps to maintain the dignity of the individual and his home.

XXXVI. It is the duty of every person to pay the taxes established by law for the support of public services.

EHR P1

1. Every natural or legal person is entitled to the peaceful enjoyment of his possessions. No one shall be deprived of his possessions except in the public interest and subject to the conditions provided for by law and by the general principles of international law.

The preceding provisions shall not, however, in any way impair the right of a State to enforce such laws as it deems necessary to control the use of property in accordance with the general interest or to secure the payment of taxes or other contributions or penalties.

AMR

21 (1) Everyone has the right to the use and enjoyment of his property. The law may subordinate such use and enjoyment to the interest of society.

(2) No one shall be deprived of his property except upon payment of just compensation, for reasons of public utility or social interest, and in the cases and according to the forms established by law.

(3) Usury and any other form of exploitation of man by man shall be prohibited by law.

[*AFR*]

14. The right to property shall be guaranteed. It may only be encroached upon in the interest of public need or in the general interest of the community and in accordance with the provisions of appropriate laws.

29. The individual shall also have the duty:

(6) .. to pay taxes imposed by law in the interest of the society;

§21.0.2 CROSS-REFERENCES

State obligation: Absolute and immediate under *EHR, AMR*, and [*AFR*]: see §6.3. For the juridical status of obligations under *UDHR* and *ADRD*, see §6.2.

Signatures, ratifications, accessions, reservations, and interpretations: See Table A for the State Parties bound by these provisions on 1 January 1982, and any reservations and interpretations notified by them.

Derogation: Non-derogable in any circumstances under [*AFR*]; derogable in exceptional circumstances under *EHR* and *AMR*: see §11.

Non-discrimination: No discrimination of any kind is allowed in respect of these rights: see §7 for the relevant provisions in the instruments.

Abuse: See §9 for the relevant provisions in these instruments.

Savings: See §10 for the relevant provisions in these instruments.

Restrictions and limitations: Note the specific provisions in *EHR P1* 1, *AMR* 21(1) and (2), and [*AFR* 14]. See §8 for the general provisions in these instruments, and the principles governing all restriction and limitation clauses.

International supervision, interpretation, application, and enforcement: By EUCM and EUCT under *EHR* (see §28); by IACM and IACT under *AMR* (see §29); by [*AFCM*] under [*AFR*] (see §30). See also §6.6 for the obligation to provide domestic remedies under *UDHR, ADRD, EHR, AMR*, and [*AFR*].

Subsidiary Instruments: 'Charter of Economic Rights and Duties of States' (UNGA Resolution 3281/XXIX).

§21.0.3 COMMENT

The right to own property

Although *UDHR* 17(1) declares a right to own property,[1] neither of the Covenants mentions any such right. Only *UDHR* has the phrase 'alone or in association with others'. *ADRD* XXIII limits the right to 'the essential needs of decent living' and helping 'to maintain the dignity of the individual and the home'.[2]

---

[1] This provision was cited by Judge Levi Carneiro in the *Anglo-Iranian Oil Company Case (Jurisdiction)*; ICJ Reports 1952, 168.

[2] IACM has expressed the view that this Article supports measures for agrarian reform: AR 1969/70, 17.

Neither *EHR P1* nor *AMR* speaks of ownership. *EHR P1* 1 instead declares a right to 'the peaceful enjoyment of his possessions', and *AMR* 21(1) to 'the use and enjoyment of his property'. [*AFR* 14] simply guarantees 'the right to property'.

EHR P1, *AMR*, and [*AFR*] all allow for legal restrictions: *EHR P1* on 'use' in accordance with 'the general interest'; *AMR* on 'use and enjoyment' in the 'interest of society'; [*AFR*] allows 'encroachments', 'in the interest of public need or in the general interest of the community'. *EHR P1* also allows laws 'to secure the payment of taxes or other contributions or penalties'; [*AFR* 29(6)] declares a duty to pay taxes 'imposed by law in the interests of society'; so does *ADRD* XXXVI where they are 'established by law for the support of public services'.

Deprivation of property

UDHR, *EHR P1* and *AMR* all contemplate circumstances in which persons may be lawfully deprived of their property. *UDHR* 17(2) only says that this shall not be done 'arbitrarily'. *EHR P1* 1 requires it to be 'in the public interest'; *AMR* 21(2) 'for reasons of public utility or social interest'. *AMR* restricts it to 'the cases and according to the forms established by law'; *EHR P1* to 'the conditions provided for by law and by the general principles of international law'.

AMR alone requires the 'payment of just compensation'.

Only *AMR* 21(3) requires 'usury and any other form of exploitation of man by man' to be prohibited by law.

§ 21.0.4 JURISPRUDENCE

'Possessions'

EUCM has said that this clearly means both moveable and immoveable property.[3] In certain circumstances, the duty to contribute to a State's social security scheme may give rise to a property right over certain assets: that may depend on how the assets are used for the payment of a pension.[4] 'Possessions' does not include a child's right to acquire its parent's property on intestacy or by gifts or bequests,[5] nor the income from the letting of property,[6] but it may include so-called 'perpetual' burial rights.[7] A notary's claim for fees only becomes a 'possession' when he has rendered services for which he is entitled to charge under the existing regulations: the mere expectation that these will not be changed in the future is not a property right.[8]

The Privy Council has held[9] that the right of a public officer not to be transferred against his will is not a right of property; the High Court of Uganda has held[10] that the word 'property' in that State's Constitution includes a contract.

---

[3] *Wiggins* v. *United Kingdom* (7456/76) DR 13, 40.
[4] *Müller* v. *Austria* (5849/72) DR 1, 46.
[5] *Marckx* v. *Belgium* (6833/74) Report: 10 December 1977.
[6] *X* v. *Austria* (8003/77) Report: 3 EHRR 285.
[7] *X* v. *Federal Republic of Germany* (8363/78) DR 20, 163.
[8] *X* v. *Federal Republic of Germany* (8410/78) DR 18, 216.
[9] *Harrikisson* v. *Attorney-General* [1979] 3 WLR 62 (on appeal from Trinidad and Tobago).
[10] *Shah* v. *Attorney-General* [1970] EA 523.

'Peaceful enjoyment'; 'deprived'

EHR P1 1 can only be violated if there is a direct and sufficient causative relationship between the act complained of and the right claimed.[11]

Even where there is a right to benefit from a State pension fund, that does not constitute an entitlement to a pension of any particular amount. Downward fluctuations during a deflationary trend do not constitute a deprivation, but a substantial reduction which affects the very substance of the right to benefit could do so.[12] There is no interference with the right where pensions are reduced in accordance with legal provisions which were already in force when the contributions were paid.[13]

The compulsory acquisition by the State of privately held debenture stock is a deprivation of possessions, not a control of their use.[14] So is the refusal of a licence which deprives the owner of a house of his right to live in it,[15] or the removal of the licence number and the licence and tax card of a motor car.[16] But a law which restricts a landlord's right to terminate lettings to tenants, or to increase their rents, or the use he makes of the rents received, is not a deprivation of his property, since income is not a property right within the meaning of *EHR P1* 1.[17]

If a local authority has a right to expropriate urban land for development, but does not exercise it for many years during which no construction can take place on it and its value therefore remains depressed, that can constitute an interference with the peaceful enjoyment of the land even though the legal title to it remains unaffected and it could still be let or sold.[18]

Legislation which restricts a mother's right to give or bequeath a share of her property to her illegitimate child interferes with her right to dispose of her property, and so violates *EHR P1* 1.[19] But a lawyer is not deprived of any property right if the State pays him less for an appearance for a legally aided client than he could obtain for the same work in private practice: no property right accrues to him until the legal aid is granted.[20] Nor does the refusal of an advance on his legal aid fees deprive him of any possessions.[21] Nor is *EHR P1* 1 violated where prison authorities retain a proportion of a prisoner's earnings from his prison work in order to pay it over to him on release, even if they pay him no interest on it.[22]

One cannot derive from *EHR P1* 1 a general obligation for States to maintian the purchasing power of sums deposited with banking or financial institutions by systematically indexing savings.[23]

---

[11] *X, Y and Z* v. *Federal Republic of Germany* (7655-7/76) DR 12, 111.

[12] *Müller* v. *Austria, supra.*

[13] *X* v. *Austria* (7624/76) DR 19, 100.

[14] *A, B, C and D* v. *United Kingdom* (3039/67) CD 23, 66.

[15] *Wiggins* v. *United Kingdom, supra.*

[16] Decision of 8 March 1971, VfGH Austria (JB 1972, 311).

[17] *X* v. *Austria* (8033/77) Report: 3 EHRR 285.

[18] *Sporrong and Lönnroth* v. *Sweden* (7151-52/75) Report: 8 October 1980 (referred to EUCT).

[19] *Marckx* v. *Belgium, supra.*

[20] *X* v. *Federal Republic of Germany* (4653/70) CD 46, 22; seel also *Van der Mussele* v. *Belgium* (8919/80) Decision: 17 March 1981.

[21] *X and Y* v. *Federal Republic of Germany* (7641/76) DR 10, 224.

[22] *X* v. *Federal Republic of Germany* (4984/71) DR 43, 28; *X* v. *Austria* (8346/78) DR 19, 230.

[23] *X* v. *Federal Republic of Germany* (8724/79) DR 20, 226.

The Supreme Court of Iceland has held[24] that the seizure of a boat caught fishing illegally in territorial waters, and its sale to recover the fine imposed on the person responsible, does not contravene *EHR P1* 1.

Deprivation 'in the public interest'

The qualification 'except in the public interest' is an exception clause to the application of which the usual rules apply, including the doctrine of governmental margin of appreciation (see § 8). However, unlike the formulation for the 'general interest' which qualifies the *control of use* of property by the State (see below), *EHR P1* 1 does not say that *deprivation* of property must be 'necessary' in the public interest.[25]

A measure forming part of financial and monetary reforms after a war, considered necessary by the competent authorities for establishing a sound economic basis for a new democratic society, and designed to ensure that the economic burdens arising out of the war, and out of changes in the value of the currency, should be distributed proportionately amongst the citizens, is in the public interest[26] and no compensation need be paid for any resulting deprivation of property.[27] And where a State's legislature enacts a measure entitling the State to acquire compulsorily the debenture stock outstanding from an entire industry, for the purpose of establishing a sound economic base for that industry, and regards that measure as essential for that purpose, the State has not exceeded the margin of appreciation as to what measures are in the public interest.[28]

'The general principles of international law'; compensation

These are the principles established in general international law relating to the confiscation of the property of *foreign* nationals, and the compensation that must be paid for this (see § 1.5). It follows that, in the absence of a specific treaty clause to the contrary, measures taken by a State with respect to the property of its *own* nationals are not subject to these 'general principles of international law'. *EHR* contains no such clause, and its *travaux préparatoires* confirm that the High Contracting Parties did not intend it to extend the application of those principles to the taking of the property of a State's own nationals.[29] Accordingly, a State which deprives its nationals of their possessions in the public interest, and subject to the conditions provided for by its laws, is not bound to compensate them under *EHR P1* 1.[30]

Even if *EHR P1* 1 in principle presupposed a right to compensation in the case of an expropriation, that would not give a right to any particular amount. Though a substantial reduction might affect the very substance of a right to compensation, a payment based exclusively on the agricultural value of land, and excluding mineral wealth which was not intended to be realized in the foreseeable future as well as loss of profit not directly caused by the expropriation, would not interfere with the substance of the right.[31]

---

[24] Decision of 25 June 1963 (No. 66/1063).
[25] *A, B, C and D* v. *United Kingdom, supra.*
[26] *X* v. *Federal Republic of Germany* (551/59) CD 3.
[27] *X* v. *Federal Republic of Germany* (1870/63) CD 18, 54.
[28] *A, B, C and D* v. *United Kingdom, supra.*
[29] *Gudmundsson* v. *Iceland* (511/59) CD 4.
[30] *X* v. *Federal Republic of Germany* (1870/63) CD 18, 54.
[31] *X* v. *Austria* (7987/77) DR 18, 31.

The Supreme Court of Cyprus has held[32] that *EHR P1* 1 does not limit the discretion of the legislature in establishing general principles for the assessment of compensation by a civil court.

Control of use 'in accordance with the general interest'

EUCM has found the following justified under this head, in support of some particular 'legitimate aim of social policy':

(1) The refusal to allow the owner of a house to live in it, under a law designed to counter the danger of over-population;[33]
(2) Restrictions on a landlord's right to terminate domestic tenancies, increase rents, and use the rents collected, during a shortage of (cheap) housing;[34]
(3) A measure regulating the closing hours for shops;[35]
(4) The suspension of payment of a social security pension to a foreigner established abroad;[36]
(5) A restriction to 40 years of 'perpetual' burial rights, in order to prevent an excessive extension of cemeteries.[37]

The Supreme Court of Cyprus has held that the restrictions and limitations on the use of property entailed by a street-widening scheme are justified by the interests of town and country planning.[38] But EUCM has said that a threat of expropriation of urban land for many years, during which construction on it was prohibited, was disproportionate to the legitimate purpose ·of planning control, even in the complex circumstances of the centre of a capital city.[39]

'Taxes' and 'penalties'

It is within the sovereign power of any State to enact laws imposing taxes or other contributions, the proceeds of which are to be appropriated to public purposes. A tax levied in order to achieve monetary and economic stability within a State is for a public purpose, and in the public interest, even if it takes the form of a levy of up to 25 per cent of the real value of capital assets, which may be paid by instalments over ten years.[40]

The Supreme Court of British Guyana held in 1964 that a compulsory levy on the emoluments of every individual employed within the Colony, to be used for works of development there and for the issue of bonds repayable with interest after six years was not a tax, but a forced loan.[41] But the Supreme Court of Mauritius has held[42] that a compulsory deposit of 50 per cent of the c.i.f. value of goods imported, repayable to the importer within three months without interest, was not a forced loan.

[32] *Papadopoulou et al.* v. *Republic of Cyprus* [1971] 3 CLR 317.
[33] *Wiggins* v. *United Kingdom, supra.*
[34] *X* v. *Austria* (8003/77) Report: 3 EHRR 285.
[35] *X* v. *Federal Republic of Germany* (1307/61) CD 9, 53.
[36] *X* v. *Federal Republic of Germany* (6572/74) DR 8, 70.
[37] *X* v. *Federal Republic of Germany* (8363/78) DR 20, 163.
[38] *Sofroniou et al.* v. *Municipality of Nicosia* (1976) 6 JSC 874.
[39] *Sporrong and Lönnroth* v. *Sweden, supra.*
[40] *Gudmundsson* v. *Iceland, supra*; for loss of property or income suffered in order to secure the payment of taxes, see *X and Y* v. *United Kingdom* (5302/71) CD 44, 29; *Four Companies* v. *Austria* (7427/76) DR 7, 148.
[41] *Lilleyman et al.* v. *Inland Revenue Commissioners et al.* (1964) 13 WIR 244.
[42] *Hawoldar* v. *Government of Mauritius* SCR 19985, No. 54 of 1978.

EUCM has said that *EHR P1* 1 does not prescribe any limitation, either of form or of size, on laws which impose penalties, or regulate their enforcement. These are left to what each State Party 'deems necessary'.[43]

---

[43] *Denmark, Norway, Sweden and Netherlands* v. *Greece* (3321–3/67; 3344/67) Report : YB 12 *bis.*

§22. LEGAL INTEGRITY

§22.1 Nationality

§22.1.1 TEXTS

UDHR

15 (1) Everyone has the right to a nationality.

(2) No one shall be arbitrarily deprived of his nationality nor denied the right to change his nationality.

ADRD

XIX. Every person has the right to the nationality to which he is entitled by law and to change it, if he so wishes, for the nationality of any other country that is willing to grant it to him.

ICPR

24 (3) Every child has the right to acquire a nationality.

AMR

20 (1) Every person has the right to a nationality.

(2) Every person has the right to the nationality of the state in whose territory he was born if he does not have the right to any other nationality.

(3) No one shall be arbitrarily deprived of his nationality or of the right to change it.

§22.1.2 CROSS-REFERENCES

State obligation: Absolute and immediate under *ICPR* and *AMR*: see §6.3. For the juridical status of obligations under *UDHR* and *ADRD*, see §6.2.

Signatures, ratifications, accessions, reservations, and interpretations: See Table A for the State Parties bound by these provisions on 1 January 1982, and any reservations and interpretations notified by them.

Derogation: Non-derogable in any circumstances under *AMR*; derogable in exceptional circumstances under *ICPR*: see §11.

Non-discrimination: No discrimination of any kind is allowed in respect of these rights or freedoms: see §7 for the relevant provisions in the instruments.

Abuse: See §9 for the relevant provisions in these instruments.

Savings: See § 10 for the relevant provisions in these instruments.

Restrictions and limitations: See § 8 for the general provisions in these instruments.

International supervision, interpretation, application, and enforcement: By HRC under *ICPR* (see § 27); by IACM and IACT under *AMR* (see § 29). See also § 6.6 for the obligation to provide domestic remedies under *UDHR*, *ADRD*, *ICPR*, and *AMR*.

Subsidiary instruments: CS_2 and CW_3 (see § 22.1.5).

See also: § 14.5 for the rights of stateless persons under CS_1.

§ 22.1.3 COMMENT

The right to a nationality

The definition of this right varies considerably between the instruments. Only *UDHR* 15(1) and *AMR* 20(1) declare it without qualification. In *ICPR* 24(3), it is expressed as the right to 'acquire' a nationality, and confined to children; *ADRD* XIX seems tautologous in declaring no more than whatever right (if any) a person already has to a nationality under some national law. Only *AMR* 20(2) requires its State Parties to confer their nationality by the *ius soli* if the person concerned would otherwise be stateless (cf., in that connexion, CS_2 1: § 22.1.5).

Change of nationality

ADRD declares an absolute right to change one's nationality, provided only that another country is willing to grant it. *AMR* 20(3) only requires that no one should be 'arbitrarily' deprived of that right. In *UDHR* 15(2) it is not entirely clear whether the prohibition of denial of the right to change one's nationality is absolute, or confined only to arbitrary denials: the former seems the better interpretation. *ICPR* has no comparable provision.

Deprivation of nationality

UDHR 15(2) and *AMR* 20(3) both prohibit, in identical terms, 'arbitrary' deprivation of nationality. *ADRD* and *ICPR* contain no comparable prohibition.
  None of these rights is expressly declared in *EHR* or [*AFR*].

§ 22.1.4 JURISPRUDENCE

IACM has stated that deprivation of citizenship, by decree of the Ministry of the Interior, is a legally unjustifiable penalty that violates *ADRD* XIX.[1] *UDHR* 15(1) has been referred to in a dissenting opinion in the International Court of Justice.[2]

§ 22.1.5 SUBSIDIARY INSTRUMENTS

There are two subsidiary instruments in this field.
  The Convention on the Reduction of Statelessness (CS_2) requires its State

---

[1] 3 Chile (AR 1977) 93–4.
[2] *Nottebohm Case (Second phase), per* Judge *ad hoc* Guggenheim; ICJ Reports 1955, 63.

Parties to grant their nationalities, subject to a few exceptions, to persons born within their territories,[3] and to the children of one of their citizens,[4] who would otherwise be stateless. The State Parties are also required not to allow their nationalities to be lost, if that would result in statelessness, by various voluntary or involuntary acts such as change in personal status,[5] loss of nationality by a parent or spouse,[6] operation of law,[7] or indeed deprivation of nationality[8] — again subject to some exceptions. A further Article[9] specifically provides that 'a Contracting State may not deprive any person or group of persons of their nationality on racial, ethnic, religious or political grounds'.

The Convention on the Nationality of Married Women (CW_3) provides that neither marriage nor its dissolution shall automatically affect the nationality of a wife,[10] that a wife shall be able to retain her nationality even if her husband voluntarily acquires or renounces a nationality,[11] and that, where a wife cannot acquire her husband's nationality on request as a matter of right, she should be able to acquire it through specially privileged naturalization procedures, 'subject to such limitations as may be imposed in the interests of national security or public policy'.[12]

§22.2 Recognition before the law

§22.2.1 TEXTS

UDHR

6. Everyone has the right to recognition everywhere as a person before the law.

ADRD

XVII. Every person has the right to be recognized everywhere as a person having rights and obligations, and to enjoy the basic civil rights.

ICPR

16. Everyone shall have the right to recognition everywhere as a person before the law.

AMR

3. Every person has the right to recognition as a person before the law.

[AFR]

5. Every individual shall have the right . . . to the recognition of his legal status.

---

[3] CS_2 1.   [4] CS_2 4.   [5] CS_2 5.   [6] CS_2 6.   [7] CS_2 7.
[8] CS_2 8.   [9] CS_2 9.   [10] CW_3 1.   [11] CW_3 2.   [12] CW_2 3.

§ 22.2.2 CROSS-REFERENCES

State obligation: Absolute and immediate under *ICPR, AMR*, and [*AFR*]: see §6.3. For the juridical status of obligations under *UDHR* and *ADRD*, see §6.2.

Signatures, ratifications, accessions, reservations, and interpretations: See Table A for the State Parties bound by these provisions on 1 January 1982, and any reservations and interpretations notified by them.

Derogation: Non-derogable in any circumstances: see §11.

Non-discrimination: No discrimination of any kind is allowed in respect of this right: see §7 for the relevant provisions in the instruments.

Abuse: See §9 for the relevant provisions in these instruments.

Savings: See §10 for the relevant provisions in these instruments.

Restrictions and limitations: None.

International supervision, interpretation, application, and enforcement: By HRC under *ICPR* (see §27); by IACM and IACT under *AMR* (see §29); by [AFCM] under [*AFR*] (see §30). See also §6.6 for the obligation to provide domestic remedies under *UDHR, ADRD, ICPR, AMR*, and [*AFR*].

See also: § 22.3.1 for equality before the law.

§ 22.2.3 COMMENT

The language of *UDHR* 6, *ICPR* 16, and *AMR* 3 is identical, except that *AMR* omits 'everywhere'. *ADRD* XVII differs in substituting 'having rights and obligations, and to enjoy the basic civil rights' for 'before the law'; [*AFR* 5] instead speaks of recognition of 'legal status'.

§ 22.2.4 JURISPRUDENCE

None of these provisions has yet been interpreted or applied by any of the competent independent international institutions.

§ 22.3 Equality before the law

§ 22.3.1 TEXTS

UDHR

7. All are equal before the law and are entitled without any discrimination to equal protection of the law. All are entitled to equal protection against any discrimination in violation of this Declaration and against any incitement to such discrimination.

ADRD

II. All persons are equal before the law and have the rights and duties established in this Declaration, without distinction as to race, sex, language, creed or any other factor.

XXXIII. It is the duty of every person to obey the law and other legitimate commands of the authorities of his country and those of the country in which he may be.

ICPR

14 (1) All persons shall be equal before the courts and tribunals.

26. All persons are equal before the law and are entitled without any discrimination to the equal protection of the law. In this respect, the law shall prohibit any discrimination and guarantee to all persons equal and effective protection against discrimination on any ground such as race, colour, sex, language, religion, political or other opinion, national or social origin, property, birth or other status.

AMR

24. All persons are equal before the law. Consequently, they are entitled, without discrimination, to equal protection of the law.

[AFR]

3 (1) Every individual shall be equal before the law.
   (2) Every individual shall be entitled to equal protection of the law.

§22.3.2 CROSS-REFERENCES

State obligation: Absolute and immediate under *ICPR, AMR*, and *[AFR]*: see §6.3. For the juridical status of obligations under *UDHR* and *ADRD*, see §6.2.

Signatures, ratifications, accessions, reservations, and interpretations: See Table A for the State Parties bound by these provisions on 1 January 1982, and any reservations and interpretations notified by them.

Derogation: Non-derogable in any circumstances under *[AFR]*; derogable in exceptional circumstances under *ICPR* and *AMR*: see §11.

Non-discrimination: See §7 for the general provisions in these instruments.

Abuse: See §9 for the relevant provisions in these instruments.

Savings: See §10 for the relevant provisions in these instruments.

Restrictions and limitations: See §8 for the general provisions in these instruments.

International supervision, interpretation, application, and enforcement: By HRC under *ICPR* (see §27); by IACM and IACT under *AMR* (see §29); by [AFCM] under *[AFR]* (see §30). See also §6.6 for the obligation to provide domestic remedies under *UDHR, ADRD, ICPR, AMR*, and *[AFR]*.

See also: §22.2 for recognition before the law; §26.2 for another prohibition of incitement to discrimination.

§22.3.3 COMMENT

Three related concepts are enshrined in these texts: equality before the law, equal protection of the law, and protection from discrimination.

Equality before the law

All the instruments say that 'all [persons] are equal before the law'. *ICPR* 14(1) adds that they shall also be equal before the courts and tribunals. *ADRD* II adds that they have the rights and duties 'established' in that instrument.

Equal protection of the law

All the instruments except *ADRD* say that all persons 'are entitled to [the] equal protection of the law'.

Protection from discrimination

The 'equal protection' provision includes, in all cases except [*AFR*], the phrase 'without [any] discrimination'. But in addition, *UDHR* 7 calls for equal protection *against* discrimination, and against any incitement to such discrimination. *ICPR* 26 refines this to a requirement that the law should prohibit any discrimination, and should guarantee equal and effective protection against it on any of the grounds listed in the standard *UDHR* catalogue (see §7). This Article may be said to declare an independent 'right not to be discriminated against', and is supported by *ICPR* 20(2) which requires 'incitement to discrimination' to be prohibited by law (see §26.2).

ADRD XXXIII alone adds duties to obey the law, and the other legitimate commands of relevant state authorities.

§22.3.4 HISTORY

The concept of equality before the law goes back at least as far as the French *déclaration des droits de l'homme et du citoyen* of 1789, which asserted (in Article 7) that the law 'should be the same for all, whether it protects or punishes', and that all were 'equal in its sight'. (The US Bill of Rights in 1791 contains no parallel provision.)

The *locus classicus* of the concept of 'equal protection of the law' is the Fourteenth Amendment to the US Constitution, passed in 1868 in connection with the abolition of slavery in the aftermath of the American Civil War, which forbids each of the States to 'deny to any person within its jurisdiction the equal protection of the laws'.

Since then, both these concepts have been incorporated in numerous national constitutions.

§22.3.5 JURISPRUDENCE

So far, only two of these provisions have been considered by competent independent international institutions.

HRC has expressed the view that there is a violation of *ICPR* 26 (as well as of *ICPR* 2(1) and (3) in conjunction with *ICPR* 23(1)) where the laws of a State enable it to restrict access to, and remove from, its territory the alien husbands of female nationals, but not the alien wives of male nationals, so failing to give the 'equal protection of the law' to families 'without any discrimination'.[1]

---

[1] *Aumeeruddy-Cziffra et al.* v. *Mauritius* (R. 9/35) HRC, 36, 134.

HRC has also expressed the view that, while *ICPR* 25 allows the imposition of reasonable restrictions on the political rights there protected, *ICPR* 26 (as well as *ICPR* 2(1)) requires that in no case may a person be subjected to such sanctions solely because of his or her political opinion.[2]

IACM has considered that *ADRD* II is violated where, under domestic law, adultery alone is a sufficient ground for divorcing a wife, but must be accompanied by 'public scandal' or 'abandonment of the woman' before it can be a ground for divorcing a husband; and where the law distinguishes between legitimate and illegitimate children, the latter being divided into those that are 'natural' (i.e. recognized by the father) and those that issue from an 'illicit' (i.e. adulterous or incestuous) union.[3]

There is however a rich national jurisprudence on the 'equal protection' provision of the Fourteenth Amendment in the US Supreme Court; and the Supreme Court of India has on many occasions considered the provisions for equality before the law, and for equal protection of the laws, contained in Article 14 of the Indian Constitution. Canadian courts have also contributed some jurisprudence on the equivalent provision in that country's Bill of Rights.

The meaning and effect of the Fourteenth Amendment to the US Constitution is summarized as follows by Willis:[4]

The guaranty of the equal protection of the laws means the protection of equal laws.[5] It forbids class legislation, but does not forbid classification which rests upon reasonable grounds of distinction. It does not prohibit legislation, which is limited either in the objects to which it is directed or by the territory within which it is to operate. It merely requires that all persons subjected to such legislation shall be treated alike under like circumstances and conditions both in the privileges conferred and in the liabilities imposed. The inhibition of the amendment . . . was designed to prevent any person or class from being singled out as a special subject for discriminating and hostile legislation.[6] It does not take from the states the power to classify either in the adoption of police laws, or tax laws, or eminent domain laws, but permits to them the exercise of a wide scope of discretion, and nullifies what they do only when it is without any reasonable basis. Mathematical nicety and perfect equality are not required. Similarity, not identity of treatment, is enough. If any state of facts can reasonably be conceived to sustain a classification, the existence of that state of facts must be assumed. One who assails a classification must carry the burden of showing that it does not rest upon any reasonable basis.

The jurisprudence of the Supreme Court of India has been concerned with the meaning, scope, and effect of Article 14 of the Indian Constitution which provides that 'The State shall not deny to any person equality before the law or the equal protection of the laws within the territory of India.' It is now well settled that while Article 14 forbids class legislation, it does not forbid reasonable classification for the purposes of legislation. In order, however, to pass the test of permissible classification, two conditions must both be fulfilled:

---

[2] *Pietraroia* v. *Uruguay* (R. 10/44) HRC 36, 153.

[3] El Salvador 160. But the decision of a court reversing the conviction of a medical practitioner for terminating a pregnancy does not violate *ADRD* II: Case 2141 (USA) 6 March 1981.

[4] Constitutional Law (1st ed.), 579.

[5] *Yick Wo* v. *Hopkins* 118 US 356 at 369; *Southern Railway Co.* v. *Greene* 216 US 400.

[6] *Gulf C. & S.F.R. Co.* v. *Ellis* 163 US 150.

(1) The classification must be founded on an intelligible *differentia* which distinguishes persons or things that are grouped together from others left out of the group;

(2) That *differentia* must have a rational relation to the object sought to be achieved by the statute in question. The classification may be founded on different bases, namely geographical,[7] or according to objects,[8] occupations or the like.[9] What is necessary is that there must be a nexus between the basis of classification and the object of the Act under consideration. Further, Article 14 condemns discrimination not only by a substantive law but also by a law of procedure.[10]

In applying these principles, the Supreme Court has held that

(*a*) a law may be constitutional even though it relates to a single individual if, on account of some special circumstances or reasons applicable to him and not applicable to others, that single individual may be treated as a class by himself;[11]

(*b*) there is always a presumption in favour of the constitutionality of an enactment, and the burden is upon him who attacks it to show that there has been a clear transgression of the constitutional principles;[12]

(*c*) it must be presumed that the legislature understands and correctly appreciates the needs of its own people, that its laws are directed to problems made manifest by experience, and that its discriminations are based on adequate grounds;[13]

(*d*) the legislation is free to recognize degrees of harm and may confine its restrictions to those cases where the need is deemed to be the clearest;[14]

(*e*) in order to sustain the presumption of constitutionality, the court may

---

[7] *Punjab* v. *Ajaib Singh* [1953] SCR 254; *Nagaland* v. *Ratan Singh* [1966] 3 SCR 830; *Shri Krishan Singh* v. *Rajasthan* [1955] SCR 531; *Joshi D. P.* v. *M. B. State* [1955] SCR 1215; *Purushottam Govindji Halai* v. *Desai* [1955] SCR 887; *Madhya Pradesh* v. *Mandawar* [1955] SCR 599; *Rajasthan* v. *Rao Manohar Singh Ji* [1954] SCR 996.

[8] *Prabhakar Rao N. Mawle* v. *Andra Pradesh* [1965] 3 SCR 743; *Mahant Moti Das* v. *Sahi* [1959] Supp 2 SCR 563; *Roshan Lal Mehra* v. *Ishwar Das* [1962] 2 SCR 947; *Harman Singh* v. *R. T. A.* [1954] SCR 371; *Rashid & Sons* v. *I. T. Officer* [1964] 6 SCR 826.

[9] Such as historical considerations: *Lachman Das* v. *Punjab* [1963] SCR 925; *Ram Parshad* v. *Punjab* [1966] 3 SCR 486; *Madyn Pradesh* v. *Bhopal Sugar Industries* [1964] 6 SCR 846; *Mohanlal Jain* v. *Man Singhji* [1962] 1 SCR 702; *Narottam Kishore* v. *Union of India* [1964] 7 SCR 55; or according to the nature of persons: *Matajog Dobey* v. *Bhari* [1955] SCR 925; *Bombay* v. *Balsara* [1951] SCR 682; *Rehman Shagoo* v. *State of J. K.* [1960] 1 SCR 680; *Makhan Lal Malhotra* v. *Union of India* [1961] 2 SCR 120; *Pratap Singh* v. *State of V. P.* [1961] 2 SCR 509; *Balaji* v. *I. T. Officer* [1962] 2 SCR 983; *Uttar Pradesh* v. *Kaushliya* [1964] 4 SCR 1002; or according to the nature of business: *B. I. C.* v. *Collector, Control Excise* [1963] 3 SCR 642; *Western India Theatres* v. *Cantonment Board* [1959] Supp 2 SCR 63; *Abbas* v. *Union of India* [1970] 2 SCR 780; *A. P. Grain & Steel Merchants Association* v. *Union of India* [1971] 1 SCR 166; *Harakchand Ratanchand Banthia* v. *Union of India* [1970] 1 SCR 479; or treating the State differently from private persons: *Lachman Das* v. *Punjab, supra*; *Nav Rattanmal* v. *Rajasthan* [1962] 2 SCR 324; *Katra Education Society* v. *Uttar Pradesh* [1966] 3 SCR 328; or with reference to time: *Mohd. Sahed Mahboob Medico* v. *Dy. Custodian-General* [1962] 2 SCR 371; *Roshan Lal Mehra* v. *Ishwar Das, supra*.

[10] *Budhan Choudry et al.* v. *Bihar* [1955] 1 SCR 1045.

[11] See *Shri Ram Krishna Dalmia* v. *Shri Justice S. R. Tendolkar et al.* [1959] SCR 279, at 297.

[12] *State of J & K* v. *Khosa* [1974] 1 SCR 19.

[13] See also *Middleton* v. *Texas Power and Light Co.* 249 US 152 at 157.

[14] See also *Radice* v. *New York* 264 US 294.

take into consideration matters of common knowledge, matters of common report, and the history of the times, and may assume every state of facts which can be conceived of existing at the time of the legislation;

(f) while good faith and knowledge of the existing conditions on the part of a legislature are to be presumed, if there is nothing on the face of the law or the surrounding circumstances brought to the notice of the court on which the classification may reasonably be regarded as based, the presumption of constitutionality cannot be carried to the extent of always holding that there must be some undisclosed and unknown reasons for subjecting certain individuals or corporations to hostile or discriminating legislation.

An impugned statute may fall into one or other of the following five categories:

(i) It may itself indicate the persons or things to whom its provisions are intended to apply. The basis of the classification of such persons or things may appear on its face, or may be gathered from the surrounding circumstances known to or brought to the notice of the court. In determining the validity of such a statute, the court will apply the test of permissible classification, where conditions (1) and (2) above must both be satisfied. Where the court finds that they are, it will uphold the validity of the law.[15]

(ii) It may direct its provisions against one individual person or thing or to several individual persons or things, but no reasonable basis of classification may appear on the face of it or be deducible from the surrounding circumstances, or be a matter of common knowledge. In such a case, the court will strike down the statute as an instance of naked discrimination.[16]

(iii) It may not itself make any classification of the persons or things for the purpose of applying its provisions, but may leave this to the discretion of the government. In determining the validity of such a statute, the court will not strike down the law out of hand only because no classification appears on its face, or because a discretion is given to the government to make the selection or classification, but will go on to ascertain whether the statute has laid down any principle or policy for the guidance of the exercise of the government's discretion. If there is none, the court will strike down the statute on the ground that it provides for the delegation of arbitrary and uncontrolled power to the government to discriminate between persons or things similarly situated, and that the discrimination is therefore inherent in the statute itself. In such a case, the court will strike down both the statute and the executive action taken under it.[17]

(iv) If such a statute lays down a policy or principle for the guidance of the exercise of the government's discretion in the matter of the selection or classification, the court will uphold the law as constitutional.[18]

(v) However, if the government, in making the selection or classification, does not proceed on, or follow, the policy or principle laid down, the court

---

[15] *Chiranjitlal Chowdhri* v. *Union of India* [1950] SCR 869; *Bombay* v. *Balsara* [1951] SCR 682; *Kedar Nath Bajoria* v. *West Bengal* [1954] SCR 30; *V. M. Syed Mohammad & Co.* v. *State of Andhra* [1954] SCR 1117; *Budhan Choudry* v. *Bihar, supra*.

[16] *Ameerunnissa Begum* v. *Mahboob Begum* [1953] SCR 404; *Ramprasad Narain Sahi* v. *Bihar* [1953] SCR 1129.

[17] *West Bengal* v. *Anwar Ali Sarkar* [1952] SCR 284; *Dwarka Prasad Laxmi Narain* v. *Uttar Pradesh* [1954] SCR 803; *Dhirendra Krishna Mandal* v. *The Superintendent and Remembrancer of Legal Affairs* [1955] SCR 224.

[18] *Kathi Raning Rawat* v. *Saurashtra* [1952] SCR 435.

will hold that the executive action, but not the statute, should be condemned as unconstitutional.[19]

In the context of the guarantee of equality before the law contained in section 1(6) of the Canadian Bill of Rights, Canadian courts have held that

(*a*) a provision of the Indian Act denying the widow of an Indian the right to administer the estate of her late husband infringes this guarantee and is accordingly inoperative;[20]

(*b*) however, the guarantee is not infringed by laws which punish rape only when committed by males;[21] allow an interference of living on the avails of protitution to be drawn more readily against males than against females;[22] or allow heavier sentences to be imposed in some Provinces upon persons in a particular age group.

§22.4 Fair trial

§22.4.1 Texts

UDHR

10. Everyone is entitled in full equality to a fair and public hearing by an independent and impartial tribunal, in the determination of his rights and obligations and of any criminal charge against him.

ADRD

XXVI. Every person accused of an offense has the right to be given an impartial and public hearing, and to be tried by courts previously established in accordance with pre-existing laws. . .

ICPR

14 (1) . . . In the determination of any criminal charge against him, or of his rights and obligations in a suit at law, everyone shall be entitled to a fair and public hearing by a competent, independent and impartial tribunal established by law. The Press and the public may be excluded from all or part of a trial for reasons of morals, public order (*ordre public*) or national security in a democratic society, or when the interest of the private lives of the parties so requires, or to the extent strictly necessary in the opinion of the court in special circumstances where publicity would prejudice the interests of justice; but any judgment rendered in a criminal case

---

[19] *Ibid.*

[20] *Canard* v. *Attorney-General of Canada* [1972] 5 WWR 678 (Court of Appeal, Manitoba).

[21] *R* v. *Krenn et al.* (1976) 27 CCC (2nd) 168 (Supreme Court, British Columbia).

[22] *R* v. *Odgers* (1978) 37 CCC (2nd) 554 (Supreme Court, Alberta).

[23] *R* v. *Burnshine* [1974] 4 WWR 49 (Supreme Court of Canada).

or in a suit at law shall be made public except where the interest of juvenile persons otherwise requires or the proceedings concern matrimonial disputes or the guardianship of children.

EHR

6 (1) In the determination of his civil rights and obligations or of any criminal charge against him, everyone is entitled to a fair and public hearing within a reasonable time by an independent and impartial tribunal established by law. Judgment shall be pronounced publicly but the press and public may be excluded from all or part of the trial in the interest of morals, public order or national security in a democratic society, where the interests of juveniles or the protection of the private life of the parties so require, or to the extent strictly necessary in the opinion of the court in special circumstances where publicity would prejudice the interests of justice.

AMR

8 (1) Every person has the right to a hearing, with due guarantees and within a reasonable time, by a competent, independent, and impartial tribunal, previously established by law, in the substantiation of any accusation of a criminal nature made against him or for the determination of his rights and obligations of a civil, labor, fiscal, or any other nature.

(5) Criminal proceedings shall be public, except insofar as may be necessary to protect the interests of justice.

[*AFR*]

7 (1) Every individual shall have the right to have his cause heard. This comprises:

(*d*) the right to be tried within a reasonable time by an impartial court or tribunal.

26. States parties to the present Charter shall have the duty to guarantee the independence of the Courts.

§22.4.2 CROSS-REFERENCES

State obligation: Absolute and immediate under *ICPR, EHR, AMR*, and [*AFR*]: see §6.3. For the juridical status of obligations under *UDHR* and *ADRD*, see §6.1.

Signatures, ratifications, accessions, reservations, and interpretations: See Table A for the State Parties bound by these provisions on 1 January 1982, and any reservations and interpretations notified by them.

Derogation: Non-derogable in any circumstances under [*AFR*]; derogable in exceptional circumstances under *ICPR*, *EHR*, and *AMR*: see §11.

Non-discrimination: No discrimination of any kind is allowed in respect of these rights: see §7 for the relevant provisions in the instruments.

Abuse: See §9 for the relevant provisions in these instruments.

Savings: See §10 for the relevant provisions in these instruments.

Restrictions and limitations: Note the specific provisions in *ICPR* 14(1), *EHR* 6(1), and *AMR* 8(5). See §8 for the general provisions in these instruments, and the principles governing all restriction and limitation clauses.

International supervision, interpretation, application, and enforcement: By HRC under *ICPR* (see §27); by EUCM and EUCT under *EHR* (see §28); by IACM and IACT under *AMR* (see §29); by [AFCM] under [*AFR*] (see §30). See also §6.6 for the obligation to provide domestic remedies under *UDHR*, *ADRD*, *ICPR*, *EHR*, *AMR*, and [*AFR*].

See also: §14.2 for arrest and detention; §22.3 for equality before the law; §22.6 for the rights of accused persons; §22.7 for remedies for miscarriages of justice.

§22.4.3 COMMENT

Only *ADRD* XXVI confines this provision to criminal proceedings: the other instruments extend it to other proceedings also. *UDHR* 10 specifies 'the determination of . . . rights and obligations'; *ICPR* 14(1) adds 'in a suit at law'; *AMR* 8(1) adds 'of a civil, labor, fiscal, or any other nature'; *EHR* 6(1) confines itself to 'civil rights and obligations';[1] [*AFR* 7(1)] simply refers to 'his cause'.

The obligation common to all the instruments is that there must be a 'hearing'. *UDHR*, *ICPR*, and *EHR* require the hearing to be both 'fair' and 'public'; *ADRD* substitutes, for the requirement of fairness, 'impartial', and *AMR* 'with due guarantees'. *ADRD* also requires the proceedings to be 'public', but *AMR* 8(5) confines this to criminal ones.

All the instruments other than *ADRD* and [*AFR*] require that the tribunal before which the hearing takes place must be both 'independent' and 'impartial'. [*AFR* 7(1)(d)] here omits the requirement of independence: but see [*AFR* 26]. Both *ICPR* and *AMR* require the tribunal, in addition, to be 'competent'. All the treaties except [*AFR*] also require it to be 'established by law' — 'previously' in the case of *AMR*. *ADRD* requires not only the 'previous' establishment of the court, but also that the laws in accordance with which it is established should be 'pre-existing' (see §22.5).

ICPR, *EHR*, and *AMR* all contemplate exceptions to the principle of publicity. *AMR* 8(5) confines this to cases where it 'may be necessary to protect the interests of justice'. *EHR* requires the judgment to be pronounced publicly in all cases, but lists six specific reasons why the press and the public may be excluded from the trial. *ICPR* lists five of these reasons for doing likewise (the

---

[1] Until the day before *EHR* was signed in Rome in November 1950, both it and the then concurrent draft of *ICPR* had used the term 'rights and obligations in a suit at law'. But at the last moment the English text of *EHR* was altered to its present wording in order to make it conform more closely to the French expression '*droits et obligations de caractère civil*', while *ICPR* retained the original version.

exception being 'the interests of juveniles'), and also requires judgments to be made public — except where 'the interest of juvenile persons' otherwise requires, or the proceedings concern family matters.

All the treaties except *ICPR* require the hearing to be 'within a reasonable time'. (*ICPR* 9(3), like *EHR* 5(3) and *AMR* 7(5), requires *detained* persons to be tried 'within a reasonable time' if they are not released: see §14.2. *ICPR* 14(3)(c) also requires *accused* persons to be tried 'without undue delay': see §22.6. But unlike the other three treaties, *ICPR* appears to have no express provisions about delays in proceedings other than criminal ones.)

Only [*AFR* 26] imposes a specific State obligation 'to guarantee the independence of the Courts'.

§22.4.4 HISTORY

As early as 1215, the English Magna Carta declared: 'We will sell to no man, we will not deny or defer to any man either justice or right',[2] and: 'No sheriff, constable, coroners, or others of our bailiffs, [that is, Royal officers] shall hold pleas of our Crown [that is, criminal trials]'.[3]

In reaffirming Magna Carta in 1354, King Edward III undertook that no man, of whatever estate or condition, should be harmed except *per due process de ley*. From that beginning, through Coke, Madison, and many others, there grew the great modern edifice of 'due process of law', now enshrined in many national constitutions.

§22.4.5 JURISPRUDENCE

Right of access to courts

In *Golder* v. *United Kingdom*,[4] the question arose whether *EHR* 6(1) was limited to guaranteeing the right to a fair trial in legal proceedings which were already pending, or whether in addition it secured a right of access to the courts for every person who *wished* to commence an action in order to have his civil rights and obligations determined. In the latter eventuality, a further question arose whether there were any 'inherent' limitations on the right of access, or on the exercise of that right. The applicant, a prisoner, had petitioned the Home Secretary for permission to consult a solicitor with a view to bringing a civil action for libel against a prison officer. His petition had been refused.[5] Both EUCM[6] and EUCT[7] held that the right of access to a court or tribunal, though not stated in express terms, constituted an element which is inherent in the right protected by *EHR* 6(1). The Court added that

Article 6(1) secures to everyone the right to have any claim relating to his civil rights and obligations brought before a court or tribunal. In this way, the Article

---

[2] Ch. 29 in the version confirmed by King Edward I in 1297; 6 Halsbury's Statutes (3rd ed.) 401.
[3] Ch. 24 in the original version; see McKechnie, *Magna Carta*.
[4] (4451/70) Judgment: 1 EHRR 524. See also *Reed* v. *United Kingdom* (7630/76) DR 19, 113; Report: 17 December 1981.
[5] Rejecting the government's argument that the applicant, on obtaining his release from prison, would have been in a position to have recourse to the courts at will, the Court observed that 'hindering the effective exercise of a right may amount to a breach of that right, even if the hindrance is of a temporary character'.
[6] Report: 1 June 1973.   [7] *Supra*.

embodies the 'right to a court', of which the right of access, that is the right to institute proceedings before courts in civil matters, constitutes one aspect only. To this are added the guarantees laid down by Article 6(1) as regards both the organisation and composition of the court, and the conduct of the proceedings. In sum, the whole makes up the right to a fair hearing.[8]

But the right of access to the courts is not absolute. *EHR* 6(1) itself contains an important limitation in the term 'civil rights and obligations'. The interpretation of this term excludes large areas of administrative proceedings from the right to judicial review (see below). Besides, before there can be a dispute, there must be a claim, but not every claim can give rise to a right of access to a court. What is critical is the nature of the claim: and the test is whether, when an individual objects to an action which affects his private rights, he is claiming in substance that the adverse party has acted in a way in which he was not entitled to act under the applicable domestic law.[9] Nor does the right entail that a court must always pronounce on the merits of a claim: immunity,[10] prescription, etc. may be grounds for not doing so. Nor does it mean that a court cannot deny jurisdiction (e.g. *ratione materiae* or *ratione loci*), or that the exercise of the right must be unconditional, or that the bringing of actions by infants, persons of unsound mind, bankrupts, and vexatious litigants may not be restricted. Moreover, the exercise of the right will always be subject to procedural and administrative conditions such as time limits, security for costs, office hours, the use of prescribed forms, etc.[11]

But both the Commission and the Court agreed that there are no 'inherent' limitations on the right of a convicted prisoner to institute proceedings, and for that purpose to have unrestricted access to a lawyer.[12] Indeed, any limitations must not injure the substance of the right, nor conflict with any other protected rights.[13]

The right of access to a court cannot be understood as a mere general right which can be made ineffective by economic and other obstacles. In *Airey* v. *Ireland*,[14] the applicant complained that the prohibitive cost of litigation prevented her from bringing proceedings before the Irish High Court for the purpose of petitioning for judicial separation. The respondent government argued that the applicant did enjoy access to the High Court, since she was free to go before that court without the assistance of a lawyer. But EUCT held that *EHR* was intended to guarantee not rights that are theoretical or illusory, but rights that are practical and effective. Accordingly, it had to be ascertained whether the applicant's appearance before the High Court without the assistance of a lawyer would be effective, in the sense of whether she would be able to present her case properly and satisfactorily. If her husband were represented by a lawyer and she were not, it seemed certain to the Court that she would be at a disadvantage. Quite apart from that eventuality, the Court observed that it was not realistic

---

[8] The right may imply that facilities should be made available to a prisoner for the preparation of a civil claim — including, in a personal injury case, facilities for medical examination: *Campbell* v. *United Kingdom* (7819/77) DR 14, 186.

[9] *Kaplan* v. *United Kingdom* (7598/76) Report: 17 July 1980.

[10] For Parliamentary immunity, see *X* v. *Austria* (3374/67) CD 29, 29; *Agee* v. *United Kingdom* (7729/76) DR 7, 164.

[11] *Golder* v. *United Kingdom*, Report, *supra*.

[12] *Supra*.

[13] *Belgian Linguistic Case* (1474/62, etc.) Judgment: 1 EHRR 252, which was applied in *Golder* v. *United Kingdom*, *supra*.

[14] *Airey* v. *Ireland* (6289/73) Report: 9 March 1978; Judgment: 2 EHRR 305.

to suppose that, in litigation of that nature, the applicant could effectively conduct her own case, despite the assistance which judges afford to parties acting in person. Having regard to the Commission's finding that the applicant was not in a financial position to meet the high costs required in proceedings for judicial separation, the Court held that she did not enjoy an effective right of access to the High Court and that, accordingly, there had been a breach of *EHR* 6(1).[15]

The right of access to a court, which is a constituent element of the right to a fair trial, is equally applicable in criminal matters. In *Deweer* v. *Belgium*,[16] the applicant, whose shop was closed after an inspection by an official, and who then availed himself of an offer from the *procureur du Roi* to avoid prosecution by payment of a sum of BFr. 10,000, complained of a violation of *EHR* 6(1). EUCT held that, although the applicant had waived his right to have his case dealt with by a tribunal, his waiver of a fair trial attended by all the guarantees which *EHR* requires was tainted. The Court observed that, in a democratic society, too great an importance attaches to the 'right to a court' for its benefit to be forfeited solely because an individual is a party to a settlement reached in the course of a procedure ancillary to court proceedings.

The right of access to the courts, however, does not include the right to bring criminal proceedings against a third person, by means either of a public or of a private prosecution.[17] Nor does it compel a State to establish courts of appeal or of *cassation*.[18] But it covers questions of fact just as much as questions of law: the court must therefore have jurisdiction to rectify factual errors, and to examine whether the sanction is proportionate to the fault.[19]

IACM has stated that, where a warrant has been issued for someone's arrest, and that person then receives a message from the Minister of the Interior to the effect that the National Guard 'were not guaranteeing his life' if he surrendered to the warrant, there is a violation of the right to due process under *ADRD* XXVI.[20] And a law which retrospectively deems a person's detention during a state of emergency to have been legal and constitutional, and prohibits him from bringing any action before any court to determine its legality, attempts to take away the fundamental right of access to the court.[21]

---

[15] The Court warned, however, that it would be erroneous to generalize from this conclusion. In certain eventualities, the possibility of appearing before a court in person, even without a lawyer's assistance, will meet the requirements of *EHR* 6(1); there may be occasions when such a possibility secures adequate access even to the High Court. The Court also emphasized that this conclusion did not imply that the State must provide free legal aid for every dispute relating to a 'civil right'. But *EHR* 6(1) may sometimes compel the State to provide for the assistance of a lawyer when such assistance proves indispensable for effective access to a court, either because legal representation is rendered compulsory (as it is by the domestic law of certain States for various types of litigation) or by reason of the complexity of the procedure or of the case.

[16] (6903/75) 2 EHRR 439. Here too, it is not an absolute right, and is subject to implied limitations, e.g. a decision not to prosecute or an order for discontinuance of the proceedings.

[17] *Kiss* v. *United Kingdom* (6224/73) DR 7, 55; *X* v. *Federal Republic of Germany* (7116/75) DR 7, 91.

[18] *Delcourt* v. *Belgium* (2689/65) Judgment: 1 EHRR 355; *Müller* v. *Austria* (5849/72) DR 1, 46.

[19] *Le Compte, Van Leuven and de Meyere* v. *Belgium* (6878/75; 7238/75) Judgment: 23 June 1981.

[20] Case 2509 (Panama) AR 1979/80, 63.

[21] *Attorney-General* v. *Reynolds* (1977) 24 WIR 552 (Court of Appeal of Grenada and West Indian Associated States).

'Criminal charge'

In criminal matters, the aim of *EHR* 6(1) is to ensure that accused persons do
not remain for too long in a state of uncertainty about their fate. An accused
person cannot insist that the charge against him is heard at a time of his choice:
the prosecution may formally discontinue the proceedings, or simply drop the
charge. But so long as the prosecution intends to proceed, it must proceed within
a reasonable time.[22]

The 'determination' of a criminal charge means a decision on the merits. So
long as the proceedings pursue that purpose, the guarantees of *EHR* 6(1) continue to apply. They will normally cease to apply if the proceedings are terminated before any decision on the merits is reached, but they may remain applicable if, for example, an issue arises as to the length of time the proceedings have
taken before they were terminated.[23]

EUCT has defined the 'charge' as the official notification given to an individual by the competent authority of an allegation that he has committed a
criminal offence.[24] In *Engel et al.* v. *Netherlands*,[25] EUCM stated that the terms
'criminal' and 'charge' ('*matière penale*' and '*accusation*') are autonomous: they
are not to be construed solely by reference to the domestic law of the State
concerned, but must be interpreted independently. Nevertheless, there is generally
a distinction between acts that are punishable offences, subject to a criminal
charge and appropriate proceedings in the ordinary courts of law, and acts which
constitute offences against the discipline, internal order or proper conduct of
the armed services or the civil administration. But a problem arises where an act
or omission is both a disciplinary offence and a criminal offence. Are the public
authorities concerned entitled to deal with it solely as a disciplinary offence by
way of disciplinary proceedings, or are they bound — and can the individual
offender require them — to deal with it by a criminal charge to which *EHR* 6
would apply in full? The Commission concluded that the State cannot substitute disciplinary proceedings for the purpose of depriving the individual
offender of the protection of *EHR* 6. Nevertheless, where disciplinary proceedings are taken to deal with an offence which is both disciplinary and criminal,
there are factors which should be taken into account as indicating that there
was not such a purpose. Such factors would include that

(1) the proceedings are already prescribed by law;
(2) any penalty imposed as a result of the proceedings is directly connected with,
    and contributes to, the proper functioning of the service or administration
    concerned, and is not disproportionate in nature or severity;
(3) the proceedings are conducted fairly, the minimum standards described in
    EHR 6(3) being observed;
(4) appeal from their findings lies to an independent tribunal.

EUCT, however, did not entirely subscribe to this approach.[26] While observing that the word 'charge' must be understood 'within the meaning of' *EHR*, the

---

[22] *X* v. *United Kingdom* (8233/78) Report: 3 EHRR 271; see also *Fletcher* v. *United
Kingdom* (3034/67) CD 25, 76.
[23] *Adolf* v. *Austria* (8269/78) Report: 8 October 1980 (referred to EUCT).
[24] *Deweer* v. *Belgium*, Judgment, *supra*, n. 16.
[25] (5100–2/71; 5354/72; 5370/72) Report: 19 July 1974.
[26] Judgment: 1 EHRR 647.

Court considered that the question of the autonomy of the concept of 'criminal' did not call for exactly the same reply. It explained that —

The Convention without any doubt allows the States, in the performance of their function as guardians of the public interest, to maintain or establish a distinction between criminal law and disciplinary law, and to draw the dividing line, but only subject to certain conditions. The Convention leaves the States free to designate as a criminal offence an act or omission not constituting the normal exercise of one of the rights that it protects . . . Such a choice, which has the effect of rendering applicable Articles 6 and 7, in principle escapes supervision by the Court. The converse choice, for its part, is subject to stricter rules. If the Contracting States were able at their discretion to classify an offence as disciplinary instead of criminal, or to prosecute the author of a 'mixed' offence on the disciplinary rather than on the criminal plane, the operation of the fundamental clauses of Articles 6 and 7 would be subordinated to their sovereign will. A latitude extending thus far might lead to results incompatible with the purpose and object of the Convention. The Court therefore has jurisdiction, under Article 6 . . . to satisfy itself that the disciplinary does not improperly encroach upon the criminal.

In short, the autonomy of the concept of 'criminal' operates, as it were, one way only.

Limiting itself to the sphere of military service[27] which was the subject matter of the applications, the Court laid down the following criteria for the purpose of ascertaining whether a 'charge' treated by the State as disciplinary had nonetheless the character of a criminal charge within the meaning of *EHR* 6:

(1) Whether the provisions defining the offence charged belong, according to the legal system of the respondent State, to criminal law, disciplinary law, or both concurrently;
(2) Consideration of the nature of the offence;
(3) Consideration of the degree of severity of the penalty that the person concerned risks incurring.

The following matters have been held to involve the determination of a 'criminal charge' within the meaning of *EHR* 6(1):

(1) The determination of sentence following conviction;[28]
(2) The enforcement of a legislative decree designed to 'repress offences against rules relating to the country's supplies' by imprisonment, fine, forfeiture, court-ordered closure of premises and publicizing of the judgment;[29]
(3) Charges against servicemen of having published articles tending to undermine military discipline;[30]
(4) Proceedings in *cassation*.[31]

---

[27] EUCM later applied these criteria to a case of a prison disciplinary offence: *Kiss* v. *United Kingdom, supra*, n. 17.
[28] *X* v. *United Kingdom* (4623/70) CD 39, 66.
[29] *Deweer* v. *Belgium, supra*, n. 16.
[30] *Engel et al.* v. *Netherlands, supra*, n. 25.
[31] *Delcourt* v. *Belgium, supra*, n. 18.

Several other matters have been held not to involve the determination of a criminal charge.[32]

'Civil rights and obligations'

Both EUCM and EUCT have been influenced by French jurisprudence in interpreting the term 'civil rights and obligations'. In *Ringeisen* v. *Austria*,[33] the Commission observed that the French text reflected the intentions of the authors more faithfully than the English one. According to French legal terminology, *'droits civils'* refers to rights and obligations under civil law, as distinct from public law and penal law. This is a classical distinction in the legal systems derived from Roman law; the term 'civil' in that context refers to the legal relations between individuals and other private subjects of law, as distinct from legal relations between private subjects and public authorities. Accordingly, the Commission considered that the term 'civil rights and obligations' must be interpreted restrictively so as to comprise only such legal relationships as are typical of relations between private individuals,[34] to the exclusion of the legal relations in which the private subject is confronted with those who exercise public authority. However, in its judgment in the same case,[35] the Court gave the term a decidedly wider meaning. It held that —

For Article 6(1) to be applicable to a case (*'contestation'*), it is not necessary that both parties to the proceedings should be private persons . . . The wording of Article 6(1) is far wider; the French expression *'contestations sur [des] droits et obligations de caractère civil'* covers all proceedings the result of which is decisive for private rights and obligations. The English text, 'determination of . . . civil rights and obligations', confirms this interpretation. The character of the legislation which governs how the matter is to be determined (civil, commercial, administrative law, etc.) and that of the authority which is invested with jurisdiction in the matter (ordinary court, administrative body, etc.) are therefore of little consequence.

In *König* v. *Federal Republic of Germany*[36] EUCT confirmed its previous

---

[32] These include the regulation of citizenship: *X* v. *Austria* (5212/71) CD 43, 69; the exercise, after the conclusion of criminal proceedings, of the prerogative of mercy: *X* v. *Austria* (1127/61) CD 8, 9; the examination of a petition for a retrial submitted after the conclusion of criminal proceedings: *X* v. *Austria* (913/60) CD 8, 43; proceedings before a Disciplinary Court on charges laid against civil servants: *X* v. *Federal Republic of Germany* (734/60) CD 6, 29; the decision, after the conclusion of criminal proceedings, whether a convicted person should be released on probation: *X* v. *Austria* (606/59) CD 7, 111; vagrancy: *De Wilde, Ooms and Versyp* v. *Belgium* (2832/66; 2835/66; 2899/66) Report: 19 July 1969; the deportation of an alien: *Agee* v. *United Kingdom, supra*, n. 10; the authorization of surveillance: *Klass* v. *Federal Republic of Germany* (5029/71) Judgment: 2 EHRR 214; the procedure for release pending trial: *Matznetter* v. *Austria* (2178/64) Report: 4 April 1967; a charge against a serviceman of failure to obey an order about the performance of fatigues in peacetime: *Eggs* v. *Switzerland* (7341/76) Report: DR 15, 35; a charge against a prisoner of making a false and malicious allegation against a prison officer: *Kiss* v. *United Kingdom, supra*, n. 17; proceedings before a Social Defence Board on an application for the release of a detained person: Decision of 20 April 1970, Cour de Cassation, Belgium (Pas. belge 1970, 724); proceedings before the Constitutional Court against an amendment to the Census Act: *X* v. *Austria* (8142/78) DR 18, 88.
[33] (2614/65) Report: 19 March 1970.
[34] But including legal as well as natural persons: *Church of X* v. *United Kingdom* (3798/68) CD 29, 74.
[35] 1 EHRR 455.
[36] (6232/73) Judgment: 2 EHRR 170.

decision and stated that the concept of 'civil rights and obligations' is auto-nomous.[37] If the case concerns a dispute between an individual and a public authority, the question whether the latter has acted as a private person or in its sovereign capacity is not conclusive. Accordingly, in ascertaining whether a case ('*contestation*') concerns the determination of a civil right, only the character of the right at issue is relevant. But a tenuous connection with such a right, or remote consequences, are not enough: the result of the proceedings must be directly decisive for the right concerned.[38]

The following matters have been held to involve the determination of a 'civil right' within the meaning of *EHR* 6(1):

(1) A judicial separation;[39]
(2) The withdrawal of authorization to practice medicine;[40]
(3) The authorization of a contract for the sale of land;[41]
(4) Land redistribution proceedings;[42]
(5) The payment of compensation for loss of holidays and pay during illness;[43]
(6) The ownership of a patent;[44]
(7) The right to enjoy a good reputation, and the right to have determined before a tribunal the justification of attacks upon such a reputation;[45]
(8) The payment of compensation for damage caused by game;[46]
(9) The right to conduct insurance business;[47]
(10) Loss of capacity to deal personally with one's property;[48]
(11) The fixing of compensation following an expropriation.[49]

Many matters have also been held not to involve the determination of a 'civil right' in that sense.[50]

---

[37] i.e. it must not be construed as a mere reference to the domestic law of a State but, on the contrary, must be interpreted independently of the rights existing in the law of the State concerned.

[38] *Le Compte, Van Leuven and de Meyere* v. *Belgium* (6878/75; 7238/75) Judgment: 23 June 1981.

[39] *Airey* v. *Ireland*, Judgment, *supra*, n. 14.

[40] *König* v. *Federal Republic of Germany*, Judgment, *supra*, n. 36; *Le Compte, Van Leuven and de Meyere* v. *Belgium* (6878/75; 7238/75) Report: 14 December 1979; Judgment: 23 June 1981.

[41] *Ringeisen* v. *Austria*, Judgment, *supra*, n. 33.

[42] *X* v. *Austria* (7620/76) DR 11, 156.

[43] *X and Y* v. *Federal Republic of Germany* (1013/61) CD 8, 106.

[44] *X* v. *Switzerland* (8000/77) DR 13, 81; but not the registration of a patent: *X* v. *Austria* (7830/77) DR 14, 200.

[45] *X* v. *Federal Republic of Germany* (7116/75) DR 7, 91; *Isop* v. *Austria* (808/60) CD 8, 80.

[46] Decision of 14 October 1965, VfGH Austria (ÖJZ 1966, 248).

[47] *Kaplan* v. *United Kingdom* (7598/76) Report: 17 July 1980.

[48] *Winterwerp* v. *Netherlands* (6301/73) Judgment: 2 EHRR 387.

[49] *X* v. *Austria* (7987/77) DR 18, 31; *Sporrong and Lönnroth* v. *Sweden* (7151-2/75) Report: 8 October 1980 (referred to EUCT).

[50] These include proceedings concerned with conduct as servicemen and with their military obligations: *Engel et al.* v. *Netherlands*, Report, *supra*, n. 25; proceedings for release pending trial: *Matznetter* v. *Austria*, Report, *supra*, n. 32; *Neumeister* v. *Austria* (1936/63) Report: 27 May 1966; the authorization of surveillance: *Klass* v. *Federal Republic of Germany*, Judgment, *supra*, n. 32; the conditional release of a convicted person: *X* v. *Austria* (1760/63) CD 20, 1; a claim to obtain legal aid: *X* v. *Federal Republic of Germany* (3011/67) CD 25, 70; an application to set aside the decision of planning authorities to widen a street: *X* v. *Federal Republic of Germany* (5428/72) CD 44, 49; a claim for research funds and salary: *X* v. *Sweden* (6776/74) DR 2, 123; a dispute on an issue of faith or

But even if the right concerned *is* a civil one, it does not follow that the State Parties must submit the *'contestation'* to procedures which meet the requirements of *EHR* 6(1) at each of their stages. Flexibility and efficiency, which can be fully compatible with the protection of human rights, may favour the prior intervention of administrative or professional bodies — or, *a fortiori,* of judicial bodies which do not satisfy all the requirements of *EHR* 6(1).[51] Decisions affecting civil rights may be taken in the first instance by administrative authorities exercising legal powers: even though these affect civil rights or obligations, they do not 'determine' them, and *EHR* 6(1) does not therefore apply to them. But if they then give rise to a claim, dispute or *'contestation'* about a civil right, *EHR* 6(1) comes into play in the 'determination' of that claim.[52]

'Fair' hearing

When interpreting the concept of a 'fair' hearing, allowance must be made for the existence of different legal systems. For instance, in certain systems the court is required to invite the parties to make submissions on those points of law which appear to the court to be significant. In other systems, such a requirement does not exist. It does not necessarily follow that the absence of such a requirement constitutes an infringement of the principle of 'fair hearing'.[53]

religious practice: *X* v. *Denmark* (7374/76) DR 5, 157; a decision to grant or refuse entry into a country: *X, Y, Z, V and W* v. *United Kingdom* (3325/67) YB 10, 528; the deportation of an alien: *Agee* v. *United Kingdom, supra,* n. 10; the termination of a residence permit granted to an alien: *X* v. *United Kingdom* (7902/77) DR 9, 224; *Uppal et al.* v. *United Kingdom* (8244/78) DR 17, 149; the right to participate in the work of the House of Lords: *X* v. *United Kingdom* (8208/78) DR 16, 162; the right to be admitted and to exercise the function of an advocate: *X* v. *Belgium* (2568/65) CD 26, 10; disciplinary proceedings concerning a person's conduct as a member of the legal profession: *X* v. *Austria* (2793/66) CD 23, 125; Decision of 29 September 1970, VfGH Austria (ÖJZ 1971, 413); proceedings of a hospital committee resulting in termination of employment: *X* v. *United Kingdom* (5934/72) CD 45, 116; proceedings concerning the imposition and recovery of tax: *A, B, C and D* v. *Netherlands* (1904/63; 2029/63; 2094/63; 2217/64) CD 19, 105; *Kantara Shipping Ltd.* v. *Republic of Cyprus* [1971] 3 CLR 176 (Supreme Court of Cyprus); Decision of 29 October 1971, Cour de Cassation, Belgium (Cassation, 1st Chamber, No. F 361 N); Decision of 29 October 1971, Cour de Cassation, Belgium (Pas. belge 1972, 213); Decision of 8 September 1972, Cour de Cassation, Belgium (Cassation, 1st Chamber, No. 7.D.7783); litigation concerning the granting of a non-contributory pension: *X* v. *Austria* (8149/78), DR 14, 252; *X* v. *Austria* (3959/69) CD 35, 109; a claim to be discharged from the armed forces: *W, X, Y and Z* v. *United Kingdom* (3435-38/67) CD 25, 117; a claim for compensation for injuries and losses resulting from expulsion or damage taking place during or after the Second World War: *X* v. *Federal Republic of Germany* (4505/70) CD 39, 51; *X* v. *Federal Republic of Germany* (2942/66) CD 23, 51; *X* v. *Federal Republic of Germany* (4523/70) CD 38, 115; proceedings before a Disciplinary Court: *X* v. *Federal Republic of Germany* (734/60) *supra,* n. 32; the recognition of an educational establishment for the purpose of admission of foreign students: *Church of X* v. *United Kingdom* (3798/68) CD 29, 74; a decision to expropriate, but not the fixing of the compensation: *X* v. *Austria* (7987/77) DR 18, 31; *Sporrong and Lönnroth* v. *Sweden* (7151-2/75) Report: 8 October 1980 (referred to EUCT); proceedings before a Constitutional Court against an amendment to the Census Act: *X* v. *Austria* (8142/78) DR 18, 88; a dispute about the rights of a police officer to continue to carry out his duties: *X* v. *United Kingdom* (8496/79) DR 21, 168.

[51] *Le Compte, Van Leuven and de Meyere* v. *Belgium,* Judgment, *supra,* n. 38.
[52] *Kaplan* v. *United Kingdom,* Report, *supra,* n. 47.
[53] *X & Co. (England) Ltd.* v. *Federal Republic of Germany* (3147/67) CD 27, 119.

In *Ofner and Hopfinger* v. *Austria*,[54] EUCM examined the question whether the notion of a 'fair trial' embodied any right relating to the defence beyond and above the minimum rights laid down in *EHR* 6(3) (see §22.6). The Commission stated that what is generally called the 'equality of arms' — that is, the procedural equality of the accused with the prosecutor — is an inherent element of a 'fair trial'.[55] This principle was applied in *Pataki and Dunshirn* v. *Austria*,[56] where the Commission observed that the presence of the public prosecutor, without the presence of the accused or his counsel, at a session of the Court of Appeal when the case was heard and decided, constituted an inequality in the representation of the parties which was incompatible with the notion of a fair trial.[57]

Applying the same principle — namely, that anyone who is a party to either civil or criminal proceedings should have a reasonable opportunity of presenting his case to the court under conditions which do not place him at a substantial disadvantage *vis-à-vis* his opponent — EUCM has said that the right to a fair hearing implies a right to be present in person at the hearing of the case, particularly where the personal character and manner of life of the party concerned is directly relevant to the formation of the court's opinion.[58] Similarly, while the right to free legal aid in civil cases is not expressly included among the rights guaranteed by *EHR*, the denial of free legal aid can in some circumstances constitute a violation of the right to a fair hearing.[59]

In each of the following situations the question could arise whether or not there has been a violation of the right to a fair hearing:

(1) where the trial judge expresses very strong views as to the merits and the conduct of the defence and thereby raises doubts as to his impartiality;[60]
(2) Where a virulent press campaign precedes the trial, particularly when laymen participate as jurors in the proceedings;[61]
(3) Where the court obtains, and bases its judgment on, evidence which may be described as 'hearsay', and which the party affected is unable to challenge as to its substance;[62]

---

[54] (524/69; 617/59) Report: 23 November 1962; see also *Nielsen* v. *Denmark* (343/57) Report: 15 March 1961; *X* v. *Denmark* (4764/71) CD 39, 87; *X* v. *Norway* (7945/77) DR 14; 228; *Artico* v. *Italy* (6694/74) Judgment: 3 EHRR 1.

[55] See also *X* v. *Federal Republic of Germany* (3139/67) CD 26, 77; *Neumeister* v. *Austria* (1936/63) Judgment: 1 EHRR 91; *Delcourt* v. *Belgium* (2689/65) Judgment: 1 EHRR 355.

[56] (596/59; 789/60) Report: 28 March 1963.

[57] See also Decision of 20 March 1972, Cour de Cassation, Belgium (Cassation, 2nd Chamber, No. 6401): any decision relating to an accused person based on elements not contained in the file communicated to the latter's counsel, or taken from other files to which neither the accused nor his counsel have had access, violates the principle of equality of arms.

[58] *X* v. *Sweden* (434/58) CD 1; *X* v. *Federal Republic of Germany* (1169/61) CD 13, 1; *X* v. *Switzerland* (7370/76) DR 9, 95. See also *X* v. *Austria* (8289/78) DR 18, 166.

[59] *X* v. *Federal Republic of Germany* (2857/66) CD 29, 15; *X* v. *Switzerland* (6958/75) DR 3, 155; cf. *Airey* v. *Ireland* (6289/73) Judgment: 2 EHRR 305.

[60] *Mr and Mrs X* v. *United Kingdom* (4991/71) CD 45, 1.

[61] *X* v. *Austria* (1476/62) CD 11, 31; *X* v. *Norway* (3444/67) CD 35, 37; *Ensslin, Baader and Raspe* v. *Federal Republic of Germany* (7572/76; 7586-7/76) DR 14, 64; *Krause* v. *Switzerland* (7986/77) DR 13, 73; cf. 2 Nicaragua 81-2.

[62] *X* v. *Austria* (4428/70) CD 40, 1. But see *X* v. *Federal Republic of Germany* (8414/78) DR 17, 231: hearsay evidence may sometimes be relied on, provided that its use is not unfair in the circumstances.

(4) Where evidence is obtained from an accomplice by granting him immunity from prosecution, and such evidence is used at the trial;[63]

(5) Where the court refuses to consider documents properly submitted to it by a party in support of its claim, merely because they are in a language other than that used in the proceedings;[64]

(6) Where police officers threaten to use coercion to take a blood sample in order to establish the level of alcohol in the blood, while being aware that the person who takes the blood sample is not a physician;[65]

(7) Where, in the preparatory stage of a court decision, fundamental principles of law have been neglected;[66]

(8) Where costs of interpretation are eventually charged to an accused person, thus inducing a defendant to defend himself in a language with which he is not very familiar, rather than incur additional expense;[67]

(9) Where the court declines to authorise the payment out of public funds of the expenses of calling expert witnesses for the defence;[68]

(10) Where a magistrate, after hearing defence counsel, reads out a judgment he has written, signed and dated more than two weeks before.[69]

HRC has stated that it is not the Committee's function to examine whether the court of trial has made errors of fact, or to review its application of its own domestic law, but only to determine whether the provisions of *ICPR* have been observed.[70] But there can be no fair hearing where the proceedings are conducted in writing, and neither the accused nor his counsel have the right to be present at the trial.[71]

'Public' hearing

In *Le Compte, Van Leuven and de Meyere* v. *Belgium*, EUCM said that there is not a 'public hearing' unless the court dealing with the matter holds its proceedings in public both when considering the facts and when deciding on the law.[72] In that case, EUCT held that there were no grounds for holding the proceedings *in camera*.[73] However, public proceedings may not always be necessary, and can sometimes be replaced by some other form of procedure, provided that it is 'fair' to the interests of the parties.[74]

The fact that the public may be excluded in certain cases, e.g. where the protection of the private lives of the parties so require, does not confer on the parties a right to be tried *in camera*, not even for the protection of their private lives.[75]

---

[63] *X* v. *United Kingdom* (7306/75) DR 7, 115.

[64] Decision of 7 January 1971, Cour de Cassation, Belgium (Pas. belge 1971, 419).

[65] Decision of 17 March 1971, BG, Federal Republic of Germany (NJW 1971, 1097).

[66] Decision of 3 December 1971, Hoge Raad, Netherlands (NJ 1972, 137).

[67] *Luedicke, Belkacem and Koç* v. *Federal Republic of Germany* (6210/73; 6877/75; 7132/75) Report: 18 May 1977.

[68] *Kouphs* v. *The Republic* (1977) 11 JSC 1860.

[69] *Satharasinghe* v. *Jurianz* 66 NLR 490 (Supreme Court of Ceylon).

[70] *Pinkney* v. *Canada* (R. 7/27) published 14 December 1981.

[71] *Weinberger* v. *Uruguay* (R. 7/28) HRC 36, 114; *Pietraroia* v. *Uruguay* (R. 10/44) HRC 36, 153; *Antonaccio* v. *Uruguay* (R. 14/63) published 14 December 1981.

[72] Report: 14 December 1979. See also *Engel et al.* v. *Netherlands*, Judgment, *supra*, n. 25.

[73] *Supra*, n. 38.

[74] Decision of 27 June 1957, BG, Federal Republic of Germany (NJW 1957, 1480).

[75] Decision of 2 July 1969, BG, Federal Republic of Germany (NJW 1969, 2107).

Where only some members of the public are prevented, from time to time, from entering the court but there has been no general exclusion of the public, the hearing is still in open court.[76] But where it takes place in a library which can only be reached through a door marked 'Private', the public has been denied the right to be present, notwithstanding that the judge has announced that he was 'sitting in open court'.[77]

HRC has expressed the view that there is no public hearing where the proceedings are conducted in writing, and the judgment is not made public.[78]

'Within a reasonable time'

In *Buchholz* v. *Federal Republic of Germany*,[79] EUCT said that *EHR* imposes a duty on its State Parties so to organize their legal systems as to allow their courts to comply with the requirements of *EHR* 6(1), including that of trial within a 'reasonable time'. A temporary backlog of business may not put them under a liability, but they must take prompt remedial action to deal with it. EUCM has pointed out in this connection that court vacations and rules of procedure fall within the State Parties' own jurisdiction,[80] and the Supreme Court of India has said forcefully that the State cannot avoid its constitutional obligation to provide speedy trials by pleading financial or administrative inability.[81]

In respect of criminal charges, EUCT and EUCM have both said that the period to be taken into consideration begins with the date on which a person is charged.[82] The term 'charge' cannot be construed only in terms of the domestic law of the State concerned, but must be interpreted autonomously. However, it may be necessary to have regard to the whole system and practice of criminal procedure of the relevant State in order to interpret (and thus delimit) the notion of 'charge' for the purpose of applying that notion to the facts of the particular case under consideration.[83] Three possible starting dates emerge from the Strasbourg jurisprudence: the date of the applicant's arrest,[84] the date of the opening of the preliminary investigation against him,[85] or the date of the filing of the indictment.[86] In order to identify with certainty the particular moment when a person can be said to have been charged, EUCM observed in *Neumeister* v. *Austria*[87] that the relevant stage is that at which the situation of the person concerned has been substantially affected as a result of the suspicion against him.

---

[76] *Re Weekes* (1972) 21 WIR 526 (High Court of Trinidad and Tobago).

[77] *McPherson* v. *McPherson* [1935] All ER 105 (Privy Council).

[78] *Weinberger* v. *Uruguay* (R. 7/28) HRC 36, 114; *Tourón* v. *Uruguay* (R. 7/32) HRC 36, 120; *Pietraroia* v. *Uruguay* (R. 10/44) HRC 36, 153.

[79] (7759/77) Judgment: 3 EHRR 547.

[80] *Corigliano* v. *Italy* (8304/78) Report: 16 March 1981 (referred to EUCT).

[81] *Hussainara Khatoon* v. *Home Secretary, State of Bihar* AIR [1979] SC 1369.

[82] *Neumeister* v. *Austria* (1936/63) Judgment: 1 EHRR 91; *Wemhoff* v. *Federal Republic of Germany* (2122/64) Judgment: 1 EHRR 55; *Ringeisen* v. *Austria* (2614/65) Report: 19 March 1970; Judgment: 1 EHRR 455.

[83] *Soltikow* v. *Federal Republic of Germany* (2257/64) Report: 3 February 1970.

[84] *Dr X* v. *Austria* (2278/64) CD 24, 8; *Haase* v. *Federal Republic of Germany* (7412/76) DR 11, 78; *Ringeisen* v. *Austria*, Report, *supra*; *Hätti* v. *Federal Republic of Germany* (6181/73) Report: DR 6, 22.

[85] *X* v. *Italy and Federal Republic of Germany* (5078/71) CD 46, 42; *X* v. *Federal Republic of Germany* (4649/70) CD 46, 1.

[86] *Soltikow* v. *Federal Republic of Germany*, Report: *supra*. See also *X* v. *United Kingdom* (6728/74) DR 14, 26 where the Commission preferred the date on which 'the suspicion against the applicant was seriously investigated and the prosecution case compiled' to the date on which the indictment was actually issued.

[87] Report: *supra*; see also *X* v. *Federal Republic of Germany* (6946/75) DR 6, 114.

When a person has been provisionally released from detention, the obligation to bring him to trial within a reasonable time ceases under *EHR* 5(3) (see § 14.2), but continues under *EHR* 6(1).[88] The relevant period may be said to end when criminal charges are finally determined by an acquittal or a conviction, even if this determination is made on appeal by a court which pronounces upon the merits of the charge. The same result can be achieved when the criminal proceedings terminate otherwise, for example by their discontinuance.[89]

The question whether the length of criminal proceedings exceeded the limits of a reasonable time has to be decided in relation to the particular circumstances of the proceedings concerned, and in particular with regard to —

(1) the complexity of the case as a whole;
(2) the manner in which the case has been handled by the national judicial authorities and courts; and
(3) the accused's own conduct.[90]

None of these elements is conclusive in itself, but they are factors in the case which might explain the length of the particular proceedings concerned. Each of them should be examined separately, and evaluated with a view to determining its contribution towards the length of the proceedings. Finally, in the light of all these factors taken together, the total period under consideration must be evaluated in order to determine whether or not it was 'reasonable'.[91]

In *Huber* v. *Austria*,[92] EUCM examined the extent to which an accused person's conduct could be relevant. The Commission observed that a distinction must be made between three forms of conduct in this context: the accused person's reliance on procedural rights which are available to him under the law, his failure to co-operate in the investigation and trial, and any deliberate obstruction on his part. While an accused person is under no obligation to renounce his procedural rights or to co-operate in the criminal proceedings against him, the Commission concluded that any unco-operative or even obstructive attitude on his part during the proceedings against him, although it cannot defeat his claim under *EHR* 6(1), must nevertheless be taken into consideration in any examination of the question whether or not there has been a violation of his right to a hearing within a reasonable time.

In civil matters, the reasonable time may begin to run, in certain circumstances, even before the issue of the writ commencing proceedings in the court to which the plaintiff submits his dispute.[93] A prospective plaintiff might, for instance, be unable to seize the competent court before having the lawfulness and the expediency of the impugned acts examined in preliminary proceedings.[94]

[88] *X* v. *United Kingdom* (8233/78) Report: 3 EHRR 271.
[89] *Neumeister* v. *Austria*, Judgment; *Wemhoff* v. *Federal Republic of Germany*, Judgment; *Ringeisen* v. *Austria*, Report, Judgment; all *supra*, n. 82. But see also *X* v. *Federal Republic of Germany* (3911/69) CD 30, 76.
[90] *Ibid.* See also *Soltikow* v. *Federal Republic of Germany*, Report, *supra*, n. 84; *Hätti* v. *Federal Republic of Germany*, Report, *supra*, n. 84; *X* v. *Italy and Federal Republic of Germany*, *supra*, n. 85.
[91] *Huber* v. *Austria* (4517/70) Report: DR 2, 11; *Kofler* v. *Italy* (8261/78) Decision: 8 July 1981; *Eckle* v. *Federal Republic of Germany* (8130/78) Report: 19 February 1981 (referred to EUCT); *Foti et al.* v. *Italy* (7604/76, etc.) Report: 9 March 1981 (referred to EUCT).
[92] *Ibid.*
[93] *Golder* v. *United Kingdom* (4471/70) Judgment: 1 EHRR 524.
[94] *König* v. *Federal Republic of Germany* (6232/73) Judgment: 2 EHRR 170.

The period to which *EHR* 6(1) applies is no different in the case of disputes (*'contestations'*) over civil rights and obligations, and the same criteria as in criminal proceedings apply to the question whether the duration of the proceedings exceeded a 'reasonable time',[95] with the addition of the defendant's behaviour, and what is at stake for the plaintiff.[96] EUCM has also said that in civil matters the exercise of the right to a hearing 'within a reasonable time' is often dependent on the diligence of the interested party.[97] It is of course only a delay attributable to the State that can justify a finding of a violation of the 'reasonable time' requirement of *EHR* 6(1).[98]

In certain national jurisdictions, when the right to a hearing 'within a reasonable time' is violated in an intolerable way, so that the prolongation of the proceedings can be regarded as a denial of justice, the violation may be regarded as a bar to proceedings.[99]

The Supreme Court of Guyana has observed that an accused cannot be said to have been 'afforded a fair hearing within a reasonable time' if he is called upon to defend himself against the written depositions of prosecution witnesses read in evidence against him more than three years after he was committed for trial.[100]

HRC has expressed the view that there is a violation of *ICPR* 14(3)(c) (see §22.6.1) where an appeal against conviction cannot be heard for 34 months because the transcript of the trial is not made available.[101]

'Independent and impartial tribunal established by law'

The term 'a tribunal established by law' envisages the whole organizational structure of the courts, including not only the matters coming within the jurisdiction of certain categories of courts, but also the establishment of the individual courts and the determination of their local jurisdiction. EUCM has stated more than once that the object and purpose of requiring that the courts shall be 'established by law' is that the organization of justice in a democratic society must not depend on the discretion of the Executive, but must be regulated by laws emanating from Parliament. However, this does not mean that delegated legislation is as such unacceptable in matters concerning the judicial organization. *EHR* 6(1) does not require the legislature to regulate each and every detail in this field by formal Act of Parliament, provided that it establishes at least the organizational framework for the judicial organization.[102]

It is not necessary that the tribunal should be comprised exclusively of persons learned in the law. A tribunal of lay judges may equally be provided for, and properly established, by law.[103] But, in the view of IACM, the requirements

---

[95] *Ibid.*

[96] *Buchholz* v. *Federal Republic of Germany* (7759/77) Judgment: 3 EHRR 597.

[97] *X* v. *Federal Republic of Germany* (2472/65) CD 23, 42; *X* v. *Switzerland* (7370/76) DR 9, 95.

[98] *Buchholz* v. *Federal Republic of Germany*, Judgment, *supra.*

[99] Decision of 13 October 1971, OLG Koblenz (NJW 1972, 404); but see, *per contra*, Decision of 10 November 1971, BG, Federal Republic of Germany (NJW 1972, 402); Decision of 10 January 1972, OLG Karlsruhe (1 Ss 220/71; Justiz 1972, 120).

[100] *R* v. *Edwin Ogle* (1966) 11 WIR 439.

[101] *Pinkney* v. *Canada* (R. 7/27) published 14 December 1981.

[102] *Zand* v. *Austria* (7360/76) Report: DR 15, 70; *Piersack* v. *Belgium* (8692/79) Report: 15 May 1981 (referred to EUCT). See also *Ringeisen* v. *Austria*, Judgment, *supra*, n. 82; *Le Compte, Van Leuven and de Meyere* v. *Belgium*, Report, *supra*, n. 38; Decision of 3 July 1965, VfGH, Austria (G 26/64; G 10/65, 11).

[103] *X* v. *Austria* (1476/62) CD 11, 31; *X* v. *Austria* (5481/72) CD 44, 127.

of independence and impartiality in *AMR* 8(1) are not satisfied by Special Tribunals established after a revolution, where the accused are submitted to the legal judgment of people, some of whom at least were not lawyers; to the judicial decision of people who were not judges; to the verdict of political enemies; and to the judgment of people, influenced by the psychology of their victory, who were more inclined to be severe rather than fair.[104]

The term 'independent' comprises two elements, namely the tribunals' independence from the Executive, and their independence from the parties.[105] In *Sutter* v. *Switzerland*,[106] EUCM observed that a judge's independence does not necessarily entail that he should be appointed for life or that he should be irremovable in law; that is, that he cannot be given other duties without his consent. But it is essential that he should enjoy a certain stability, if only for a specific period, and that he should not be subject to any authority in the performance of his duties as a judge. In *Zand* v. *Austria*,[107] however, the Commission emphasized that the irremovability of judges during their term of office, whether it be for a limited period of time or for life, is a necessary corollary of their independence and is thus included in the guarantees of *EHR* 6(1).

The Supreme Court of Ceylon has said that the independence of judges under the Constitution requires that they should be appointed by the Head of State on the advice of an independent Judicial Service Commission, that they should hold office 'during good behaviour' (i.e. that they should not be removeable except upon proof of gross misconduct), that their salaries should be provided and paid by Parliament, and that their transfer and disciplinary control should be exercised exclusively by the Judicial Service Commission.[108] Accordingly, any measure empowering the Minister of Justice to nominate particular judges to try particular cases is *ultra vires*.[109] There is, incidentally, no distinction between a slight interference by the Executive with the judiciary, and a major interference: in either case the independence of the judiciary would be compromised, and this must be condemned.[110]

The English legal maxim: 'justice must not only be done; it must also manifestly and undoubtedly be seen to be done' is also reflected in *EHR* 6(1).[111] So, where the president of the court of trial had been involved three times in the investigation of the case as senior deputy public prosecutor, the court could not offer all the requisite guarantees of impartiality.[112]

The Sub-Commission of CHR is currently conducting a study on the independence and impartiality of the judiciary, jurors and assessors, and the independence of lawyers.

Rendering of judgment

EUCM has stated that *EHR* 6 requires a court to give reasons for its decision. This applies to civil as well as criminal proceedings. However, if a court gives

---

[104] 2 Nicaragua 75. 90.
[105] *Zand* v. *Austria*, Report, *supra*; See also *Huber* v. *Austria* (5523/72) CD 46, 99; *Engel et al.* v. *Netherlands*, Judgment, *supra*, n. 25.
[106] (8209/78) DR 16, 166.
[107] *Supra*, n. 102.
[108] *Senadhira* v. *Bribery Commission* 63 NLR 313.
[109] *The Queen* v. *Liyanage et al.* 64 NLR 313.
[110] *In re Agnes Nona* 53 NLR 106, *per* Dias, J at 116.
[111] *Delcourt* v. *Belgium*, Judgment, *supra*, n. 18. See also *Le Compte, Van Leuven and de Meyere* v. *Belgium*, Report, *supra*, n. 38; *Piersack* v. *Belgium*, Report, *supra*, n. 102.
[112] *Piersack* v. *Belgium*, Report, *supra*.

reasons, then *prima facie* the requirements of *EHR* 6 in this respect are satisfied, and this presumption is not upset simply because the judgment does not deal specifically with one point considered by a party to be material. It does not follow from *EHR* 6 that the reasons given by a court should deal specifically with all the points which one party may consider to be essential to his case; a party does not have an absolute right to require reasons to be given for rejecting each of his arguments. On the other hand, if an applicant were to show that the court had ignored a fundamental defence which had been clearly put before it and which, if successful, would have discharged him in whole or in part from liability, then this would be enough to rebut the presumption of a fair hearing, and it would be open to the Commission to find that *EHR* 6 had been violated.[113]

§ 22.5 Retroactive penal laws

§ 22.5.1 TEXTS

UDHR

11 (2) No one shall be held guilty of any penal offence on account of any act or omission which did not constitute a penal offence, under national or international law, at the time when it was committed. Nor shall a heavier penalty be imposed than the one that was applicable at the time the penal offence was committed.

ICPR

15 (1) No one shall be held guilty of any criminal offence on account of any act or omission which did not constitute a criminal offence, under national or international law, at the time when it was committed. Nor shall a heavier penalty be imposed than the one that was applicable at the time when the criminal offence was committed. If, subsequent to the commission of the offence, provision is made by law for the imposition of a lighter penalty, the offender shall benefit thereby.

(2) Nothing in this article shall prejudice the trial and punishment of any person for any act or omission which, at the time when it was committed, was criminal according to the general principles of law recognised by the community of nations.

EHR

7 (1) No one shall be held guilty of any criminal offence on account of any act or omission which did not constitute a criminal offence

---

[113] *Firestone Tyre and Rubber Co. Ltd. and International Synthetic Rubber Co. Ltd.* v. *United Kingdom* (5460/72) CD 43, 99.

under national or international law at the time when it was committed. Nor shall a heavier penalty be imposed than the one that was applicable at the time the criminal offence was committed.

(2) This Article shall not prejudice the trial and punishment of any person for any act or omission which, at the time when it was committed, was criminal according to the general principles of law recognized by civilized nations.

AMR

9. No one shall be convicted of any act or omission that did not constitute a criminal offense, under the applicable law, at the time it was committed. A heavier penalty shall not be imposed than the one that was applicable at the time the criminal offense was committed. If subsequent to the commission of the offense the law provides for the imposition of a lighter punishment, the guilty person shall benefit therefrom.

[AFR]

7 (2) No one may be condemned for an act or omission which did not constitute a legally punishable offence at the time it was committed. No penalty may be inflicted for an offence for which no provision was made at the time it was committed.

§22.5.2 CROSS-REFERENCES

State obligation: Absolute and immediate under *ICPR, EHR, AMR*, and [*AFR*]: see §6.3. For the juridical status of obligations under *UDHR* and *ADRD*, see §6.2.

Signatures, ratifications, accessions, reservations, and interpretations: See Table A for the State Parties bound by these provisions on 1 January 1982, and any reservations and interpretations notified by them.

Derogation: Non-derogable in any circumstances: see §11.

Non-discrimination: No discrimination of any kind is allowed in respect of these rights or freedoms: see §7 for the relevant provisions in the instruments.

Abuse: See §9 for the relevant provisions in these instruments.

Savings: See §10 for the relevant provisions in these instruments.

Restrictions and limitations: Note the specific provisions in *ICPR* 15(2) and *EHR* 7(2). See §8 for the general provisions in these instruments, and the principles governing all restriction and limitation clauses.

International supervision, interpretation, application, and enforcement: By HRC under *ICPR* (see §27); by EUCM and EUCT under *EHR* (see §28); by IACM and IACT under *AMR* (see §29); by [*AFCM*] under [*AFR*] (see §30). See also §6.6 for the obligation to provide domestic remedies under *UDHR, ADRD, ICPR, EHR, AMR*, and [*AFR*].

§22.5.3 COMMENT

The purpose of these provisions is that no one should be prejudiced for any conduct by changes in the domestic laws of a State after that conduct has occurred. Two such changes are contemplated: laws which create new criminal offences (or repeal old ones), and laws which impose heavier (or lighter) penalties for existing criminal offences.

There are only minor differences in the texts of the five instruments concerned. *UDHR* 11(2) speaks of 'penal' offences; [*AFR* 7(2)] of 'legally punishable' ones; the others of 'criminal' ones. *AMR* 9 uses the phrase 'under the applicable law'; [*AFR* 7(2)] omits this altogether; the others say 'under national or international law.' [*AFR* 7(2)] appears to make no provision about increases in penalties after the commission of the offence. *ICPR* 15(1) and *AMR* 9 contain an additional provision, in very similar language, to the effect that the offender should benefit from any lightening of the penalty (*ICPR*) or punishment (*AMR*) after the commission of the offence. There is no such provision in *EHR* or [*AFR*].

ICPR 15(2) and *EHR* 7(2) alone have a saving for crimes recognized by customary international law — that is, conduct which, at the time of its commission, was criminal according to 'the general principles of law' recognized by 'the community of nations' (*ICPR*) or 'civilised nations' (*EHR*) (see §5.3). In recent years, there have been added to these some new 'international crimes' created by specific treaties, such as genocide under *CG* (see §14.1.6) and *apartheid* under *CA* (see §7.0.5).

§22.5.4 HISTORY

Article 8 of the French *déclaration des droits de l'homme et du citoyen* of 1789 provided that 'no one ought to be punished but by virtue of a law promulgated before the offence', and even before the passage in 1791 of the ten Amendments constituting the US Bill of Rights, the US Constitution already contained a provision saying that 'no Bill of Attainder or ex post facto law shall be passed'.

§22.5.5 JURISPRUDENCE

New criminal offences, or the repeal of old ones

HRC has expressed the view that *ICPR* 15(1) is violated where a person is convicted of 'subversive association' or 'conspiracy to violate the constitution' on the ground of trade union activities which were lawful at the time they were engaged in,[1] or of membership of a political party which was not banned until after the period concerned.[2]

EHR 7(1) does not merely prohibit — except as provided in paragraph (2) — retroactive application of the criminal law to the detriment of the accused. It confirms, more generally, the principle of the statutory nature of offences and their punishment (*'nullum crimen, nulla poena sine lege'*).[3] This principle requires that a person cannot be held guilty under an obsolete law if the acts of which he is accused were performed after the abrogation of that law, because a conviction in those circumstances would relate to 'an act or omission which did not

---

[1] *Pietraroia* v. *Uruguay* (R. 10/44) HRC 36, 153.

[2] *Weinberger* v. *Uruguay* (R. 7/28) HRC 36, 114.

[3] *X* v. *Federal Republic of Germany* (1169/61) CD 13, 1; *X* v. *Netherlands* (7721/76) DR 11, 209.

constitute a criminal offence under national . . . law at the time when it was committed', no distinction being made in *EHR* 7(1) between an act or omission which 'no longer constituted' a criminal offence, and an act or omission which 'did not yet' constitute one. For this purpose, it is immaterial whether the abrogation of a criminal law be express or implicit, provided that the latter form of abrogation exists in the domestic legal system of the State concerned.[4]

EHR 7(1) prohibits, in particular, extension of the application of the criminal law *'in malam partem'* by analogy.[5] In *Handyside* v. *United Kingdom*,[6] EUCM said that this principle includes the requirement that the offence should be clearly described by law. However, the requirement of certainty in the law cannot mean that the concrete facts giving rise to criminal liability should be set out in detail in the statute concerned: it is satisfied where it is possible to determine from the relevant statutory provision what act or omission is subject to criminal liability, even if such a determination derives from a court's interpretation of the provision concerned.[7]

Although it is not normally for EUCM to ascertain the proper interpretation of national law by national courts, the case is different where *EHR* expressly refers to national law, as it does in *EHR* 7. Under that Article, the application of a provision of national penal law to an act which that provision does not cover results in a direct conflict with *EHR*, so that the Commission can and must take cognizance of allegations of false national interpretations of national laws. Its supervisory function therefore consists of making sure that, at the moment when the accused person performed the act which led to his being prosecuted, there was in force a legal provision which made that act punishable, and that the punishment imposed does not exceed the limits fixed by that provision. This supervisory function includes consideration of the question whether the national court, in reaching its decision, has not unreasonably interpreted, and applied to the applicant, the national law concerned.[8]

EHR 7 embodies the principle of the legality of crimes and punishments. The concept of 'guilty' in *EHR* 7 is autonomous, but it does not cover a decision to grant the extradition of an individual.[9] 'Criminal offence' in *EHR* 7 does not envisage a disciplinary offence.[10] In *Lawless* v. *Ireland*,[11] where the applicant had been detained for the sole purpose of restraining him from engaging in activities prejudicial to the preservation of public peace and order or the security of the State, EUCT held that his detention, being a preventive measure, could not be deemed to be due to his having been held guilty of a criminal offence, and that accordingly *EHR* 7 had no bearing on the case.

EHR 7 is concerned with the sentencing of an accused person and not with the enforcement of a sentence already pronounced.[12] *EHR* 7(1) refers to 'penalties'. The conditions of probation do not constitute a 'penalty', but are a measure touching upon the effects of the penalty imposed.[13]

---

[4] *Ibid.*   [5] *Ibid.*
[6] (5493/72) CD 45, 23. See also *X* v. *Federal Republic of Germany* (7900/77) DR 13, 70.
[7] Cf. *X* v. *United Kingdom* (6683/74) DR 3, 95.
[8] *Murphy* v. *United Kingdom* (4681/70) CD 43. 1.
[9] *X* v. *Netherlands* (7512/76) DR 6, 184.
[10] *X* v. *Federal Republic of Germany* (4274/69) CD 35, 158; see also *X* v. *Federal Republic of Germany* (7705/76) DR 9, 196.
[11] (332/57) Judgment: 1 EHRR 15.
[12] *X* v. *Austria* (1760/63) CD 20, 1.
[13] *X* v. *Federal Republic of Germany* (3347/67) CD 27, 136.

In *X* v. *Belgium*,[14] EUCM noted that, according to the *travaux préparatoires*, *EHR* 7 does not affect laws which, under the very exceptional circumstances at the end of the Second World War, were passed in order to suppress war crimes, treason, and collaboration with the enemy, and does not aim at any legal or moral condemnation of these laws.

In India, where the Constitution provides that 'No person shall be convicted of any offence except for violation of a law in force at the time of the commission of the act charged as an offence',[15] the Supreme Court has held that the phrase 'law in force' must be understood in its natural sense as being the law in fact in existence and in operation at the time of the commission of the offence, as distinct from the law 'deemed' to have become operative by virtue of the power of the legislature to pass retrospective laws.[16]

Interpreting the provision in the US Constitution which provides that 'No Bill of Attainder or ex post facto law shall be passed',[17] the US Supreme Court has observed that while the ban on *ex post facto* laws applies strictly to legislative acts, 'it reaches every form in which the legislative power of a State can be exerted, whether it is a constitution, a constitutional amendment, an enactment of the legislature, a by-law or ordnance of a municipal corporation, or a regulation or order of some other instrumentality of the State exercising delegated legislative authority.'[18] In *Bouie* v. *Columbia*, the Court noted that an unforeseeable judicial enlargement of a criminal statute, applied retrospectively, operated precisely like an *ex post facto* law.[19]

The *ex post facto* effect of a law cannot be evaded by giving a civil form to that which is essentially criminal.[20] However, a defendant does not have a vested right in the remedies and methods of procedure employed in criminal trials, provided that a statutory procedural change does not deprive him of a substantial right or immunity possessed at the time of the commission of the offence charged.[21]

Legislation which aggravates the degree of the crime resulting from an act committed before its passage would violate the prohibition of *ex post facto* laws.[22] So would legislation which eliminates, after the date of a criminal act, a defence which was available to the accused at the time the act was committed,[23] or which alters the legal rules of evidence so as to require less proof, in order to convict the accused, than the law required at the time of the commission

---

[14] (1038/61) YB 4, 324.

[15] Art. 20(1).

[16] *Rao Shiv Bahadur Singh* v. *Vindhya Pradesh* [1953] SCR 394; see also *Chief Inspector of Mines* v. *Thapar* [1962] 1 SCR 9.

[17] Art. I(9)3.

[18] *Ross* v. *Oregon* 227 US 150.

[19] 378 US 347: 'If a state legislature is barred by the ex post facto clause from passing such a law, it must follow that a State Supreme Court is barred ... from achieving precisely the same result by judicial construction.'

[20] *Burgess* v. *Salmon* 97 US 381. But deportation of an alien, however severe its consequences, involves a civil rather than a criminal proceeding: *Bugajewitz* v. *Adama* 228 US 585; *Harisiades* v. *Shaughnessy* 342 US 580; *Galvan* v. *Press* 347 US 522; *Flemming* v. *Nestor* 363 US 603; *Mahler* v. *Eby* 264 US 32.

[21] *Mallet* v. *North Carolina* 181 US 589; *Beazell* v. *Ohio* 269 US 167; *Hopt* v. *Utah* 110 US 574; *Thompson* v. *Missouri* 171 US 380; *Gut* v. *State* 76 US 35; *Duncan* v. *Missouri* 152 US 377; *Cook* v. *United States* 138 US 157; *Rao Shiv Bahadur Singh* v. *Vindhaya Pradesh*, supra, n. 16.

[22] *Calder* v. *Bull* 3 US 386; *Malloy* v. *South Carolina* 237 US 180.

[23] *Kring* v. *Missouri* 107 US 221; *Dobbert* v. *Florida* 432 US 282.

of the offence.[24] A statute which operates to disqualify a person from holding public office or engaging in a profession or other calling because of his refusal to take an oath denying the commission of past acts not previously punishable as crimes also constitutes an *ex post facto* law in violation of the Constitution.[25] Equally repugnant would be a statute which takes away a person's right to vote because of some prior, non-criminal conduct,[26] or a statute which authorizes the seizure of a person's property for previously non-criminal conduct.[27]

Although *EHR* forms no part of the domestic laws of the United Kingdom, the House of Lords has said that, in view of the provisions of *EHR* 7 (as well as of *UDHR* 11) 'it is hardly credible that any government department would promote or that Parliament would pass retrospective criminal legislation.'[28]

In *Liyanage et al.* v. *The Queen*,[29] the Privy Council condemned as 'wholly bad' a law which it found, in effect, to be a special direction to the judiciary as to the trial of particular prisoners (who were identifiable from a previously published White Paper) charged with particular offences on a particular occasion, and which purported to legalize their imprisonment while they were awaiting trial, made admissible their statements inadmissibly obtained during that period, altered the law of evidence so as to facilitate their conviction, and altered *ex post facto* the punishment to be imposed on them.

Changes in penalties

Where there has been a reduction in the criminal penalties after the commission of an offence *EHR* 7, unlike *ICPR* 15(7), does not guarantee the right to have the most favourable criminal law applied.[30]

The US Supreme Court has held that a law which imposes additional punishment to that prescribed when a criminal act was committed is an *ex post facto* law prohibited by the Constitution.[31] In determining whether legislation increases the punishment for a prior offence, the key question is whether the new law makes it *possible* for the accused to receive a greater punishment, even though it remains possible for him to receive the same punishment under the new law as could have been imposed under the prior law.[32]

In the USA, laws have been construed as imposing additional punishment —

(1) where the original statute allowed the court to impose a sentence less than the 15-year maximum term of imprisonment, while the amended law required the court to impose that maximum sentence upon conviction;[33]
(2) where a statute took away parole eligibility for offences which had been subject to parole according to the law at the time they were committed;[34]
(3) where a statute required that persons sentenced to death be placed in solitary

---

[24] *Ibid.*
[25] *Cummings* v. *Missouri* 71 US 277; *Ex parte Garland* 71 US 333; cf. *Garner* v. *Board of Public Works* 341 US 716.
[26] *Johannessen* v. *United States* 225 US 227.
[27] *Fletcher* v. *Peek* 10 US 87.
[28] *Waddington* v. *Miah* [1974] 2 All ER 377.
[29] [1966] 1 All ER 650 (on appeal from Ceylon).
[30] *X* v. *Federal Republic of Germany* (7900/77) DR 13, 70.
[31] *Calder* v. *Bull, supra,* n. 22; *Re Medley* 134 US 160; see also *Kedar Nath Bajoria* v. *State of W. B.* [1954] SCR 30.
[32] *Lindsey* v. *Washington* 301 US 397.
[33] *Ibid.*
[34] *Warden, Lewisburg Penitentiary* v. *Marrero* 417 US 653.

confinement awaiting execution, and was applied to persons who had committed their capital offences before the effective date of the statute;[35]

(4) where a statute altered the manner in which the death penalty may be carried out by authorizing a prison official to set the time of execution.[36]

The US Supreme Court has held that several other laws did not impose additional punishment.[37]

The Supreme Court of Sierra Leone has held that, where an enactment creating an offence has been repealed and re-enacted with heavier penalties, an offence committed before the repeal should be punished only in accordance with the earlier enactment.[38]

§22.6 Rights of accused persons

§22.6.1 TEXTS

UDHR

11 (1) Everyone charged with a penal offence has the right to be presumed innocent until proved guilty according to law in a public trial at which he has had all the guarantees necessary for his defence.

ADRD

XXVI. Every accused person is presumed to be innocent until proved guilty.

ICPR

14 (2) Everyone charged with a criminal offence shall have the right to be presumed innocent until proved guilty according to law.

(3) In the determination of any criminal charge against him, everyone shall be entitled to the following minimum guarantees, in full equality:

---

[35] *Re Medley, supra*, n. 31; *Holden* v. *Minnesota* 137 US 483; *McElvaine* v. *Brush* 142 US 155; cf. *Rooney* v. *North Dakota* 196 US 319.

[36] *Re Medley, supra*; *Re Savage* 134 US 176.

[37] These include an habitual offender statute which increased the punishment for a current offence if the accused had been convicted of one or more previous offences, as applied in the prosecution of an offence committed after its enactment: *Donald* v. *Massachusetts* 180 US 311; *Gryger* v. *Burke* 334 US 728; a statute re-establishing the death penalty in cases of murder, as applied to a murder committed under a prior death penalty statute which was declared unconstitutional: *Dobbert* v. *Florida, supra*, n. 23; a statute prescribing a series of new regulations as to the way in which death sentences should be carried out: *Rooney* v. *North Dakota* 196 US 319; a change in the method of inflicting the death penalty from hanging to electrocution: *Malloy* v. *South Carolina* 237 US 180; a statute disenfranchizing certain criminal offenders: *Murphy* v. *Ramsay* 114 US 15; a statute providing that one who had been convicted of crime should no longer be permitted to engage in the practice of medicine: *Hawker* v. *New York* 170 US 189.

[38] *Buckle* v. *Commissioner of Police* [1964-6] ALR S. L. 265.

(*a*) To be informed promptly and in detail in a language which he understands of the nature and cause of the charge against him;

(*b*) To have adequate time and facilities for the preparation of his defence and to communicate with counsel of his own choosing;

(*c*) To be tried without undue delay;

(*d*) To be tried in his presence, and to defend himself in person or through legal assistance of his own choosing; to be informed, if he does not have legal assistance, of this right; and to have legal assistance assigned to him, in any case where the interests of justice so require, and without payment by him in any such case if he does not have sufficient means to pay for it;

(*e*) To examine, or have examined, the witnesses against him and to obtain the attendance and examination of witnesses on his behalf under the same conditions as witnesses against him;

(*f*) To have the free assistance of an interpreter if he cannot understand or speak the language used in court;

(*g*) Not to be compelled to testify against himself or to confess guilt.

(4) In the case of juvenile persons, the procedure shall be such as will take account of their age and the desirability of promoting their rehabilitation.

(5) Everyone convicted of a crime shall have the right to his conviction and sentence being reviewed by a higher tribunal according to law.

(7) No one shall be liable to be tried or punished again for an offence for which he has already been finally convicted or acquitted in accordance with the law and penal procedure of each country.

EHR

6 (2) Everyone charged with a criminal offence shall be presumed innocent until proved guilty according to law.

(3) Everyone charged with a criminal offence has the following minimum rights:

(*a*) to be informed promptly, in a language which he understands and in detail, of the nature and cause of the accusation against him;

(*b*) To have adequate time and facilities for the preparation of his defence;

(*c*) to defend himself in person or through legal assistance of his own choosing or, if he has not sufficient means to pay for legal assistance, to be given it free when the interests of justice so require;

(*d*) to examine or have examined witnesses against him and to obtain the attendance and examination of witnesses on his behalf under the same conditions as witnesses against him;

(*e*) to have the free asistance of an interpreter if he cannot under-stand or speak the language used in court.

AMR

8 (2) Every person accused of a criminal offense has the right to be presumed innocent so long as his guilt has not been proven according to law. During the proceedings, every person is entitled, with full equality, to the following minimum guarantees:

(*a*) the right of the accused to be assisted without charge by a translator or interpreter, if he does not understand or does not speak the language of the tribunal or court;

(*b*) prior notification in detail to the accused of the charges against him;

(*c*) adequate time and means for the preparation of his defense;

(*d*) the right of the accused to defend himself personally or to be assisted by legal counsel of his own choosing, and to communicate freely and privately with his counsel;

(*e*) the inalienable right to be assisted by counsel provided by the state, paid or not as the domestic law provides, if the accused does not defend himself personally or engage his own counsel within the time period established by law;

(*f*) the right of the defense to examine witnesses present in the court and to obtain the appearance, as witnesses, of experts or other persons who may throw light on the facts;

(*g*) the right not to be compelled to be a witness against himself or to plead guilty; and

(*h*) the right to appeal the judgment to a higher court.

(3) A confession of guilt by the accused shall be valid only if it is made without coercion of any kind.

(4) An accused person acquitted by a nonappealable judgment shall not be subjected to a new trial for the same cause.

[*AFR*]

7 (1) Every individual shall have the right to have his cause heard. This comprises: . . .

(*b*) the right to be presumed innocent until proved guilty by a competent court or tribunal;

(*c*) the right to defence, including the right to be defended by counsel of his choice;

§22.6.2 CROSS-REFERENCES

State obligation: Absolute and immediate under *ICPR, EHR, AMR*, and [*AFR*]: see §.6.3. For the juridical status of obligations under *UDHR* and *ADRD*, see §6.2.

Signatures, ratifications, accessions, reservations, and interpretations: See Table A for the State Parties bound by these provisions on 1 January 1982, and any reservations and interpretations notified by them.

Derogation: Non-derogable in any circumstances under [*AFR*]; derogable in exceptional circumstances under *ICPR, EHR*, and *AMR*: see §11.

Non-discrimination: No discrimination of any kind is allowed in respect of these rights or freedoms: see §7 for the relevant provisions in the instruments.

Abuse: See §9 for the relevant provisions in these instruments.

Savings: See §10 for the relevant provisions in these instruments.

Restrictions and limitations: See §8 for the general provisions in these instruments.

International supervision, interpretation, application, and enforcement: By HRC under *ICPR* (see §27); by EUCM and EUCT under *EHR* (see §28); by IACM and IACT under *AMR* (see §29); by [*AFCM*] under [*AFR*] (see §30). See also §6.6 for the obligation to provide domestic remedies under *UDHR, ADRD, ICPR, EHR, AMR*, and [*AFR*].

See also: §14.2 for arrest and detention; §22.3 for equality before the law; §22.4 for the right to a fair trial (including delays before trial); §22.7 for remedies for miscarriages of justice.

§22.6.3 COMMENT

Unlike the right to a fair trial considered in §22.4, these provisions apply only to criminal proceedings. They fall into several distinct categories.

The presumption of innocence

This is declared in all the six instruments. In *ADRD* XXVI, the beneficiary is the 'accused person'; in [*AFR* 7(1)(*b*)] 'every individual'; in all the other instruments, it is the person 'charged with a criminal' (or, in the case of *UDHR* 11(1) only, a 'penal') 'offence'. Except in the case of *ADRD* and [*AFR*], all the instruments require the guilt to be proved 'according to law'; [*AFR*] instead requires 'a competent court or tribunal'.

Guarantees for the defence

UDHR simply stipulates 'all the guarantees necessary for his defence'. *ADRD* has no comparable provision. [*AFR* 7(1)(*c*)] simply declares 'the right to defence', and includes in this the 'right to be defended by counsel of his choice'. The other three treaties all set out lists of 'minimum' guarantees to which the person charged is entitled — in the case of *ICPR* 14(3) and *AMR* 8(2) 'in [or 'with'] full equality'. The following express guarantees are common to all the treaties other than [*AFR*]:

(1) Notification in detail of the charges — 'prior' in the case of *AMR*, 'promptly' and 'in a language which he understands' in the case of *ICPR* and *EHR*;

(2) Adequate time and facilities (or, in the case of *AMR*, means) for the preparation of the defence;

(3) The right of the accused to defend himself either in person or through a lawyer of his own choosing (this being the only specific right included in the 'right to defence' in [*AFR* 7(1)(c)]);

(4) The attendance and examination of witnesses both against him and in his favour — in the case of *ICPR* and *EHR* 'under the same conditions', and in the case of *AMR* in the shape of 'experts or other persons who may throw light on the facts';

(5) The free services of a court interpreter where he cannot understand or speak the language used in court.

In respect of the following further minimum guarantees, these three treaties diverge:

(6) All of them make provision for free legal aid, but with important differences: *EHR* limits it to cases 'when the interests of justice so require' and the accused 'has not sufficient means to pay' for it; so does *ICPR*, but in such cases it requires legal assistance to be 'assigned' to the accused; *AMR* instead declares an 'inalienable' right to assistance by counsel provided by the State — paid or not as the domestic law provides — whenever the accused fails to defend himself or to engage his own lawyer;

(7) Only *ICPR* and *AMR* expressly provide a right to communicate with counsel — in the case of *AMR* alone, 'freely and privately';

(8) *ICPR* 14(5) and *AMR* (but not *EHR*) declare a right of appeal to a higher court;

(9) *ICPR* and *AMR* (but not *EHR*) prohibit compulsory self-incrimination;

(10) *AMR* 7(3) alone provides that confessions shall only be valid if they are made without any kind of coercion;

(11) *ICPR* alone requires that the accused must be tried 'in his presence';

(12) *ICPR* alone requires that he should be informed of his right to be tried in his presence, and to defend himself in person or through a lawyer of his choosing;

(13) *ICPR* 14(4) alone requires special procedures for juveniles.

Delays before trial

ICPR 14(3)(c) requires only criminal trials to take place 'without undue delay'. By contrast, *EHR* 6(1), *AMR* 8(1) and [*AFR* 7(1)(d)] require *all* trials — not only criminal ones — to take place 'within a reasonable time': see §22.4. As a separate matter, *ICPR* 9(3), *EHR* 5(3), and *AMR* 7(5) all require *detained* persons to be tried 'within a reasonable time if they are not released' (see §14.2).

Ne bis in idem

Only *ICPR* 14(7) and *AMR* 8(4) provide protection against double jeopardy — *ICPR* in the case of both final convictions and acquittals; *AMR* only in the case of final acquittals.

§ 22.6.4 HISTORY

As long ago as 1789, Article 9 of the French *déclaration des droits de l'homme et du citoyen* began 'Every man being counted innocent until convicted . . .'. From at least that time onwards, the presumption of innocence has been accepted as a central safeguard against the exercise of arbitrary power by public authorities.

But the French *déclaration* had nothing to say about the rights of an accused person after his arrest. By contrast, the Fifth and Sixth Amendments to the US Bill of Rights of 1791 already contain many of the safeguards now elaborated in the modern international instruments:

V. [No person shall be] subject for the same offence to be twice put in jeopardy of life or limb; nor shall be compelled in any criminal case to be a witness against himself . . .
VI. In all criminal prosecutions, the accused shall enjoy the right to a speedy and public trial, by an impartial jury . . ., and to be informed of the nature and cause of the accusations; to be confronted with the witnesses against him; to have compulsory process for obtaining witnesses in his favor; and to have the assistance of counsel for his defence.

§ 22.6.5 JURISPRUDENCE

'Presumed innocent until proved guilty according to law'

In *Austria* v. *Italy*,[1] EUCM stated that *EHR* 6(2) requires, firstly, that judges in fulfilling their duties should not start with the conviction or assumption that the accused committed the act with which he is charged. The burden to prove guilt falls upon the prosecution, and any doubt is for the benefit of the accused. Secondly, judges must permit the accused to produce evidence in rebuttal. They can find a person guilty only on the basis of direct or indirect evidence sufficiently strong in the eyes of the law to establish his guilt.

EHR 6(2) is thus primarily concerned with the spirit in which judges must carry out their task. The attitude of other persons taking part in the proceedings, such as counsel for the prosecution and witnesses, who express themselves towards the accused in flights of language such as might disturb the calm of the court by their violence or insulting nature, would not affect the presumption of innocence except inasmuch as the presiding judge, by failing to react against such behaviour, might give the impression that the court shared the obvious animosity to the accused and regarded him from the outset as guilty.[2] The same considerations apply if the accused, during the preliminary investigation, has been subjected to any maltreatment with the aim of extracting a confession from him, and any admissions extracted in this manner are subsequently accepted as evidence by the court.[3]

In *Krause* v. *Switzerland*,[4] EUCM said that while the principle of the presumption of innocence is in the first instance a procedural guarantee applying in any kind of criminal procedure, its application is in fact wider. It constitutes

---

[1] (788/60) Report: 30 March 1963. See also *X* v. *Federal Republic of Gemany* (4124/69) CD 35, 132.

[2] *Ibid.* See also *Nielsen* v. *Denmark* (343/57) YB 2, 412.

[3] *Ibid.*

[4] (7986/77) DR 13, 73. See also *Ensslin, Baader and Raspe* v. *Federal Republic of Germany* (7572/76; 7586–7/76) DR 14, 64; *X* v. *Austria* (2343/64) CD 22, 38; *Liebig* v. *Federal Republic of Germany* (6659/74) DR 17, 5.

a fundamental principle which protects everybody against being treated by public officials as if they were guilty of an offence before that is established according to law by a competent court. *EHR* 6(2) may therefore be violated by public officials if they declare that someone is responsible for criminal acts without a court having so found. This does not mean, of course, that the authorities may not inform the public about criminal investigations. They do not violate *EHR* 6(2) if they state that a suspicion exists, that people have been arrested, that they have confessed, etc. What is excluded, however, is a formal declaration that somebody is guilty.

EHR 6(2) is therefore violated where a court, in deciding to terminate criminal proceedings before trial, states that the accused has committed an act which fulfils the description of a criminal offence;[5] or where a court terminates such proceedings because the period of limitation has expired, but orders the applicant to pay part of the costs on the ground of an appraisal of his guilt.[6]

In common-law jurisdictions, it has frequently been held that the presumption of innocence is imperilled if the prosecutor expressly invites the jury to draw an adverse influence against the accused from the fact that he has chosen to exercise his right to silence during police interrogation, or his right not to give evidence at the trial.

The presumption of innocence extends only to the proof of guilt, and not to the kind or level of punishment. It does not therefore prevent a judge, when deciding upon the penalty to be imposed on an accused lawfully convicted of an offence submitted to his adjudication, from having regard to factors relating to the accused's personality.[7]

A rebuttable presumption of fact which the defence may, in turn, disprove (e.g. a statutory provision which states that, when certain facts have been proved by the prosecution, certain other facts shall be presumed) is not a presumption of guilt. However, if widely or unreasonably worded, it could have the same effect. EUCM has therefore said that it is not enough to examine only the form in which the presumption is drafted; it is necessary to examine its substance and effect.[8] The Austrian Supreme Court has held that the principle of reversing the burden of proof, in respect of an offence under the Vagrancy Act, was not unknown to the Austrian legal system and that there could be no question of its being in conflict with *EHR* 6(2).[9]

The following conduct has been held not to infringe the rule in *EHR* 6(2):

(1) Handcuffing the accused in front of the jury while the trial was pending;[10]
(2) The medical examination of an accused person;[11]
(3) Obliging the driver of a motor vehicle suspected of being under the influence of alcohol to submit to a blood test;[12]
(4) Taking photographs and fingerprints and keeping these, or other documents, for identification purposes;[13]

---

[5] *Adolf* v. *Austria* (8269/78) Report: 8 October 1980 (referred to EUCT).
[6] *Minelli* v. *Switzerland* (8660/79) Report: 6 May 1981 (referred to EUCT).
[7] *Engel et al.* v. *Netherlands* (5100-2/71; 5354/72; 5370/72) Judgment: 1 EHRR 647; *X* v. *Federal Republic of Germany* (5620/72) CD 46, 110. See also *X* v. *Denmark* (2518/65) CD 18, 44, where the jury was informed of the accused's previous convictions before they had determined the issue of his guilt in respect of two charges of rape.
[8] *X* v. *United Kingdom* (5124/71) CD 42, 135.
[9] Decision of 14 January 1971, OGH Austria (ÖJZ 1971, 469).
[10] *X* v. *Austria* (2291/64) CD 24, 20.
[11] *X* v. *Federal Republic of Germany* (986/61) CD 9, 23.
[12] *X* v. *Netherlands* (8239/78) DR 16, 184.
[13] Decision of 25 October 1960, BVwG, Federal Republic of Germany (NJW 1961, 571).

(5) A court making use of facts determined at another trial;[14]

(6) Recovering the expenses of a deceased accused from his estate.[15]

HRC appears to take the view that violations of *ICPR* 14(1) and (3) which deprive the accused person of the safeguards of a fair trial also constitute a violation of the presumption of innocence in *ICPR* 14(2).[16]

IACM has expressed the view that the use of circumstantial evidence alone to establish the accused's guilt is not, in and of itself, violative of the presumption of innocence in *AMR* 8(2).[17]

'To be informed promptly, in a language which he understands and in detail, of the nature and cause of the accusation against him'

This provision relates to the information which must be given to the accused in connection with the criminal *proceedings* against him: for the information to which he is entitled on arrest and detention, see § 14.2.

In *Ofner* v. *Austria*,[18] EUCM held that an accused person has the right to be informed not only of the *grounds* for the accusation — that is, the acts with which he is charged and on which his indictment is based — but also of the *nature* of the accusation, namely the legal classification of those acts. This is all the more necessary as, under *EHR* 6(3)(*b*), the accused has the right 'to have adequate time and facilities for the preparation of his defence': there is a logical connexion between *EHR* 6(3)(*a*) and 6(3)(*b*). Consequently, the information about the nature and grounds for the accusation should contain such particulars as will enable the accused to prepare an adequate defence.

The Supreme Court of Ceylon has held[19] that, in a criminal case on indictment tried before it on the prosecution of the Attorney-General, the accused are entitled, before the trial begins, to lists of all prosecution witnesses and documents; copies of all statements made by those witnesses, and by the accused, to the investigating officers which will be produced in evidence; and copies of the documents on which the prosecution relies.

The Supreme Court of Sierra Leone has said that an accused should be supplied, not less than fourteen days before his trial, with copies (certified as true by a law officer) of the evidence which the prosecution witnesses will give, if he has not had an earlier opportunity to hear their evidence.[20]

EHR 6(3)(*a*) requires that any summons served on an accused person should be accompanied by a translation in a language which he understands.[21] It does not, however, give a general right for the accused to have the court files translated,[22] but only those procedural documents which are necessary for his defence.[23]

---

[14] Decision of 10 March 1971, OLG Celle, CDNC 3, 25.

[15] Decision of 18 June 1971, OLG Celle (NJW 1971, 2180).

[16] *Perdomo and de Lanza* v. *Uruguay* (R. 2/8) HRC 35, 111.

[17] 2 Nicaragua, 91.

[18] (524/59) YB 3, 322.

[19] *The Queen* v. *Liyanage* 65 NLR 337.

[20] *Macauley* v. *Attorney-General* [1968-9] ALR S. L. 58.

[21] Decision of 26 April 1971, Rechtbank Breda, Netherlands, CDNC 3, 35; Decision of 1 December 1971, LG München (NJW 1972, 405). Cf. Decision of 19 May 1971, Rechtbank Amsterdam, Netherlands, CDNC 3, 36; Decision of 17 December 1972, Cour de Cassation, Belgium (Cassation, 2nd Chamber, No. 7.D.8081); Decision of 2 February 1972, Hof Den Bosch, Netherlands, CDNC 4, 30.

[22] *X* v. *Austria* (6185/73) DR 2, 68.

[23] Decision of 27 July 1972, OGH Austria (ÖJZ 1973, 127).

'To have adequate time and facilities for the preparation of his defence'

The time necessary for the preparation of the defence must be assessed on a different basis at the various stages of the proceedings,[24] having regard also to the question whether the accused defends himself in person, or through a lawyer.[25] IACM has expressed the view that 24 or 48 hours are not 'adequate' times for the preparation of the defence.[26]

The facilities guaranteed to an accused person do not include an absolute right of access to the court file, although it may be implied that in certain circumstances he or his lawyer must have reasonable access to it.[27]

Trial 'without undue delay'

HCR has not so far had occasion to distinguish between the right of a *detained* person, under *ICPR* 9(3), to be tried 'within a reasonable time' if he is not released, and the right of an *accused* person to be tried 'without undue delay' under *ICPR* 14(3): in all but one case,[28] whenever it has found the former to be violated, it has found the latter to be violated also.[29]

The provisions in *EHR* 6(1) and *AMR* 8(1) for trials to be held 'within a reasonable time' apply to all trials, and not only criminal ones: the relevant jurisprudence is therefore noted in § 22.4, in which the general provisions for all 'fair trials' are considered.

'To defend himself in person or through legal assistance of his own choosing,
or, if he has not sufficient means to pay for legal assistance, to be given it
free when the interests of justice so require'

In *Artico* v. *Italy*, EUCM said that *EHR* 6(3)(c) guarantees a right recognized as an essential feature of the concept of a fair trial.[30] That provision guarantees to an accused person that the proceedings against him will not take place without an adequate representation of the case for the defence. It guarantees the right to an effectual defence, either in person or through a lawyer. That right is reinforced by the obligation to provide free legal assistance if two conditions are complied with: if the accused has not the means to pay for legal representation, and if the interests of justice so require.[31]

In that case, the officially appointed lawyer withdrew and was not replaced, despite repeated action taken by the accused. Rejecting the respondent government's submission that *EHR* 6(3)(c) would be violated 'only if an accused person had suffered an actual disadvantage from the fact that he did not receive effectual legal assistance' as an interpretation for which there was no foundation either in the wording or in the spirit of that provision, EUCM stated that it

---

[24] *X* v. *Belgium* (7628/76) DR 9, 169.

[25] *X* v. *Federal Republic of Germany* (6501/74) DR 1, 80.

[26] 2 Nicaragua, 80; 94.

[27] *X* v. *Austria* (7138/75) DR 9, 50. See also *X* v. *United Kingdom* (5282/71) CD 42, 99.

[28] *de Casariego* v. *Uruguay* (R. 13/56) HRC 36, 185.

[29] *Sequeira* v. *Uruguay* (R. 1/6) HRC 35, 127; *Burgos* v. *Uruguay* (R. 12/52) HRC 36, 176; *Perdomo and de Lanza* v. *Uruguay* (R. 2/8) HRC 35, 111; *Ambrosini* v. *Uruguay* (R. 1/5) HRC 34, 124; *Massera* v. *Uruguay* (R. 1/5) HRC 34, 124; *de Massera* v. *Uruguay* (R. 1/5) HRC 34, 124; *Weinberger* v. *Uruguay* (R. 7/28) HRC 36, 114. See also *Antonaccio* v. *Uruguay* (R. 14/63) published 14 December 1981.

[30] (6694/74) Report: 8 March 1979. See also *Airey* v. *Ireland* (6289/73) Judgment: 2 EHRR 305; *X* v. *Austria* (4338/69) CD 36, 79.

[31] (6694/74) Report: 8 March 1979.

contains an absolute guarantee of the right to defence.[32] Affirming this decision, EUCT pointed out that *EHR* 9(3)(*c*) speaks of 'assistance' and not of 'nomination': mere nomination does not ensure effective assistance, since the lawyer appointed for legal aid purposes may die, fall seriously ill, be prevented for a protracted period from acting, or shirk his duties. If they are notified of the situation, the authorities must then either replace him or cause him to fulfil his obligations,[33] unless it is plain that no lawyer complying with his professional duties to the court could conduct the accused's defence in accordance with his instructions.[34]

By stipulating that an accused may have legal assistance of his own choosing, *EHR* 6(3)(*c*) does not secure the right to an unlimited number of defence lawyers. The purpose of the provision is to ensure that both sides of the case are actually heard by giving the accused, as necessary, the assistance of an independent professional. In *Ensslin, Baader and Raspe* v. *Federal Republic of Germany*,[35] EUCM found that a domestic law which limited the number of lawyers freely chosen by the accused to three, without prejudice to the *ex officio* addition of other defence counsel appointed by the court, did not violate the right secured by this provision.

In the same case, the Commission also examined the situation created by the refusal to accept, or the exclusion of, defence counsel by a court. While observing that such a measure may intimidate other potential defence counsel or cast discredit on the defence in general, and that a succession of defence lawyers may be damaging to the presentation of the case and introduce greater uncertainty into the lawyer's role as 'the watchdog of procedural regularity', the Commission concluded that the right to defend one's case with the assistance of counsel of one's choice is limited by the State's right to make the appearance of lawyers before the courts subject to regulations, and the obligation of defence counsel not to transgress certain principles of professional ethics.[36]

EHR does not expressly secure the right of an accused person to *communicate* with the counsel of his choice. However, in *Bonzi* v. *Switzerland*,[37] EUCM affirmed that this right can be inferred from the provisions of *EHR* 6(3)(*b*) and (*c*), since the opportunity for the accused to confer with his counsel is a necessary condition for the preparation of his defence.

HRC has expressed the view that *ICPR* 14(3) is violated where persons detained pending trial are given no access of any kind to legal counsel,[38] or where defence lawyers are assigned to them whom they do not want,[39] or with whom they are given no opportunity to communicate,[40] or if the procedure is in

[32] But see earlier decisions of the Commission which express different views: *X* v. *Federal Republic of Germany* (722/60) CD 9, 1; *X* v. *Austria* (2676/65) CD 23, 31; *X* v. *Norway* (5923/72) DR 3, 43.
[33] (6694/74) Judgment: 3 EHRR 1.
[34] *X* v. *United Kingdom* (8386/78) DR 21, 126.
[35] (7572/76. 7586-7/76) DR 14, 64.
[36] *Ibid.*; see also *X and Y* v. *Federal Republic of Germany* (5217/71; 5376/72) CD 42, 139; *X* v. *Norway* (5923/72) DR 3, 43.
[37] (7854/77) DR 12, 185; *Fell* v. *United Kingdom* (7878/77) Decision: 14 March 1981. But see also *Schertenleib* v. *Switzerland* (8329/78) DR 17, 180, where EUCM added that the right to communicate with counsel might be subject to some restrictions.
[38] *Ramirez* v. *Uruguay* (R. 1/4) HRC 35, 121; *Sequeira* v. *Uruguay* (R. 1/6) HRC 35, 127; *Weinberger* v. *Uruguay* (R. 7/28) HRC 36, 114; *Carballal* v. *Uruguay* (R. 8/33) HRC 36, 125; *Touròn* v. *Uruguay* (R. 7/32) HRC 36, 120.
[39] *Burgos* v. *Uruguay* (R. 12/52) HRC 36, 176; *de Casariego* v. *Uruguay* (R. 13/56) HRC 36, 185.
[40] *Perdomo and de Lanza* v. *Uruguay* (R. 2/8) HRC 35, 111; *Antonaccio* v. *Uruguay* (R. 14/63) published 14 December 1981.

writing, and neither the accused nor his counsel has the right to be present at the trial.[41]

IACM has expressed the view that fundamental human rights are violated in a State where lawyers who assume responsibility for defending individuals detained for political reasons are subjected to threats and acts of intimidation, including such measures as withholding their licences to practise;[42] *a fortiori* where they are killed, detained, maltreated, or 'disappear'.[43]

Canadian Courts have held that the 'right to retain and instruct counsel without delay' under that country's Bill of Rights was violated where a person arrested was refused permission to speak to his lawyer before taking a breathalyser test,[44] or to telephone his wife,[45] where there was any interference with the privacy of the communication with counsel,[46] even by the mere presence of a police officer who heard nothing of the conversation,[47] and where the court refused to adjourn the trial when the counsel of the accused's choice was not available.[48]

The Supreme Court of India has held that the constitutional protection given to an *arrested* person of the 'right to consult, and to be defended by, a legal practitioner of his choice' cannot be denied to someone who is not under arrest or in custody.[49]

The Supreme Court of Ceylon has held that the right to representation by counsel was infringed where cross-examination by counsel of a prosecution witness was refused when the accused had already questioned that witness himself;[50] and where an adjournment of the trial, in order to enable the accused to prepare his case, was refused on the mistaken assumption that he had been on bail when he had in fact been in custody.[51]

The Nigerian Constitution also protects the right of an accused to defend himself 'by legal representatives of his choice', but the Supreme Court of Nigeria has held that this does not prevent the Minister from refusing entry to the country of a foreign lawyer enrolled as a legal practitioner in Nigeria whom the accused had engaged to represent him.[52]

A Belgian Court has held that the right to legal assistance of the accused's own choosing under *EHR* 6(3)(c) is not violated by a requirement that the lawyer chosen must be able to use the official language in which the proceedings are conducted.[53]

---

[41] *Burgos* v. *Uruguay, supra*; *Antonaccio* v. *Uruguay, supra*.

[42] 3 Paraguay, 86–7.

[43] Argentina, 233.

[44] *Brownridge* v. *The Queen* [1972] SCR 926 (Supreme Court of Canada).

[45] *R* v. *Martel* (1968) 64 WWR 152 (District Court, Alberta).

[46] *R* v. *Makismchuk* [1974] 2 WWR 668; *R* v. *Irwin* [1974] 5 WWR 744; *R* v. *Penner* [1973] 6 WWR 94 (all Court of Appeal, Manitoba); *R* v. *McGuirk* (1976) 24 CCC (2nd) 386 (Supreme Court, Prince Edward Island); *R* v. *Balkan* (1973) 6 WWR 617 (Supreme Court, Alberta); *R* v. *Paterson* (1978) 39 CCC (2nd) 355 (High Court, Ontario). Cf. *Thornhill* v. *Attorney-General* (1974) 27 WIR 281 (High Court of Trinidad and Tobago).

[47] *R* v. *Straightnose* [1974] 2 WWR 662 (District Court, Saskatchewan).

[48] *Gilberg* v. *Attorney-General for Alberta* [1974] 2 WWR 474 (Supreme Court, Alberta).

[49] *Nandini Satpathy* v. *Dani* AIR [1978] SC 1025.

[50] *Subramaniam* v. *Inspector of Police, Kankesanturai* 71 NLR 204.

[51] *Premaratne* v. *Gunaratne* 71 NLR 113.

[52] *Awolowo* v. *Sarki* [1966] 1 All NLR 178.

[53] Decision of 26 January 1967, Tribunal de Première Instance, Bruxelles (Parquet No. 4506/SOC/65).

'To examine or have examined witnesses against him and to obtain the attendance and examination of witnesses on his behalf under the same conditions as witnesses against him'

In *Austria* v. *Italy*,[54] EUCM, examining the scope of *EHR* 6(3)(*d*), observed that this provision aims at ensuring for the defence, in this respect, complete equality of treatment with the prosecution and the civil plaintiff. On the other hand, it does not imply the right to have witnesses called without restriction. The provision does not therefore mean that municipal law cannot lay down conditions for the admission and examination of witnesses, provided that such conditions are identical for witnesses on both sides. Similarly, the competent judicial authorities in States are free, subject to respect for the terms of *EHR* and in particular the principle of equality established by this provision, to decide whether the hearing of a witness for the defence is likely to assist in ascertaining the truth and, if not, to refuse to hear that witness.

The same principles apply to the actual examination of witnesses. Under *EHR* 6(3)(*d*), an accused person does not have an unrestricted right to put questions to witnesses testifying against him in court. The exercise of this right must be governed by the court's appreciation of whether such questions are likely to assist in, and are thus necessary for, ascertaining the truth.[55] *EHR* 6(3)(*d*) does not require the presence of the accused when witnesses are examined before the trial, provided they are heard again at the trial and the accused can then examine them.[56]

The words 'under the same conditions' do not refer to legal conditions only. It is not enough to verify that the legal conditions were identical for witnesses for the defence, for the prosecution, and for the civil plaintiff: it must also be ascertained whether the court created any inequality of treatment in its application of the law.[57]

IACM has expressed doubts about systems of 'free evidence' and 'free evaluation of evidence'. In its view, these are 'procedures more conducive to judicial error than the system of legal evidence'.[58]

The Court of Appeal of Guyana has held that the trial judge is bound, *ex debito iustitiae*, to inform an unrepresented accused of his right to call defence witnesses,[59] and that it is a denial of the right to representation for the trial judge to refuse to allow vital prosecution witnesses, who had testified when the accused was unrepresented, to be recalled in order that his counsel could cross-examine them.[60]

The Supreme Court of Nigeria has held that an accused is entitled to an adjournment because of the absence of a witness if he satisfies the court that the witness is material to his defence, that he has not neglected to procure the witness' attendance, and that there is a reasonable expectation that the witness will attend on the proposed date.[61]

---

[54] (788/60) Report: 30 March 1963. See also *X* v. *Austria* (2281/64) CD 24, 20; *X* v. *Austria* (1476/62) CD 11, 31; *Hopfinger* v. *Austria* (617/59) CD 5; *M* v. *Austria* (1290/61) (unpublished.)

[55] *X* v. *Austria* (4428/70) CD 40, 1; Decision of 11 February 1970, OGH, Austria (ÖJZ 1970, 411).

[56] *X* v. *Federal Republic of Germany* (8414/78) DR 17, 231. See also *In the matter of an application by Ioannis Ktimatias* (1977) 6 JSC 1043 (Supreme Court of Cyprus).

[57] *Austria* v. *Italy*, Report, *supra*, n. 54.

[58] 2 Nicaragua, 81.

[59] *The State* v. *Cleveland Clarke* (1976) 22 WIR 249.

[60] *The State* v. *Fitzpatrick Darrell* (1976) 24 WIR 211.

[61] *Yanov* v. *The State* [1965] 1 All NLR 193.

'To have the free assistance of an interpreter if he cannot understand or speak the language used in court'

In *Luedicke, Belkacem and Koç* v. *Federal Republic of Germany*,[62] EUCM observed that *EHR* 6(3)(e) is not only concerned with the conduct of a fair trial, but tries to minimize the disadvantages of a person who does not know the language of the court and may not have the resources to pay an interpreter. Whereas, in *EHR* 6(3)(c), two conditions are attached to the word 'free' in relation to legal assistance — namely, that the accused 'has not sufficient means to pay' and that 'the interests of justice so require' — the word 'free' in *EHR* 6(3)(e) is without any qualification. An interpreter must therefore be provided free without regard to the financial situation of the accused. The Commission interpreted the word 'free' to mean 'completely and definitely free', and EUCT in the same case held that the words 'free' and *'gratuitement'* (in the French text) have in themselves an ordinary meaning that is clear and determinate: they denote a once-and-for-all exemption or exoneration from liability to pay interpretation expenses, and not a conditional remission, temporary exemption, or suspension.[63]

In that case, the respondent government argued that the rights enumerated in *EHR* 6(3) were intended to ensure a fair trial for persons 'accused' of a criminal offence and that, once they had been finally convicted, there was no longer any trial whose fairness had to be ensured; accordingly, there was no objection to reclaiming interpretation expenses from someone after his conviction. EUCM rejected this argument, pointing out that the government's interpretation would in practice deny the benefit of *EHR* 6(3)(e) to any accused who was eventually convicted, and would leave in existence the disadvantages suffered by an accused who does not understand or speak the language used in court, as compared with an accused who is familiar with that language; consequently, the right to a fair trial which *EHR* 6 seeks to safeguard would itself be adversely affected. The Court held that *EHR* 6(3)(e) accordingly entailed, for anyone who could not speak or understand the language used in court, the right to receive the free assistance of an interpreter, without subsequently having claimed back from him payment of the costs thereby incurred.[64]

The guarantee in *EHR* 6(3)(e) is not limited to interpretation at the oral hearing only, but extends to the translation or interpretation of all those documents or statements in the proceedings which it is necessary for the accused to understand in order to have the benefit of a fair trial.[65]

EUCM has said that the term 'language used in court' could not be given such a wide significance as to cover the relations between the accused and his counsel. It only applies to the relations between the accused and the judge.[66] Nor does it require that speeches made by defence counsel be interpreted.[67] However, in some national jurisdictions, the right of defence enshrined in *EHR*

---

[62] (6210/73; 6877/75; 7132/75) Report: 18 May 1977.

[63] Judgment: 2 EHRR 433.

[64] *Ibid.*; see also *Geerk* v. *Switzerland* (7640/76) Report: DR 16, 56; Decision of 14 March 1972, Cour de Cassation, Belgium (Cassation, 2nd Chamber, No. 1248); Decision of 21 June 1971, AG Geilenkirchen, Federal Republic of Germany (NJW 1971, 2320); Decision of 18 October 1962, AG Bremerhaven, Federal Republic of Germany (NJW 1963, 827); *Öztürk* v. *Federal Republic of Germany* (8544/79) Decision: 15 December 1981.

[65] *Luedicke, Belcacem and Koç* v. *Federal Republic of Germany*, Judgment, *supra.*

[66] *X* v. *Austria* (6185/73) DR 2, 68.

[67] Decision of 27 January 1970, Cour de Cassation, Belgium, (No. 5280).

6 has been construed to imply that an interpreter should be provided to enable a foreign prisoner to communicate with his counsel.[68]

The Supreme Court of Nigeria has held[69] that the right to an interpreter must be claimed at the trial, and only a refusal at that stage will provide grounds for an appeal.

'Not to be compelled to testify against himself or to confess guilt'

The Constitution of the United States provides that no person 'shall be compelled in any criminal case',[70] and the Constitution of India that 'no person accused of any offence shall be compelled',[71] 'to be a witness against himself'. Both constitutions embody the principle of protection against compulsory self-incrimination which has been one of the fundamental canons of the British system of criminal jurisprudence since the abolition of the notorious Court of Star Chamber in the seventeenth century.

The Indian Supreme Court has explained that this provision consists of two components:

(1) A protection against 'compulsion to be a witness';
(2) A protection against such compulsion resulting in the accused giving evidence 'against himself'.[72]

In the United States, it has been held that unreasonable searches and seizures of documents fall within the meaning of this provision, and that documents or other evidence so obtained are inadmissible in evidence.[73] This view also prevailed in India[74] until 1961, when a bench of the Supreme Court consisting of eleven judges disagreed with that interpretation and defined the scope of the protection thus:

Self-incrimination must mean conveying information based upon the personal knowledge of the person giving the information and cannot include merely the mechanical process of producing documents in court which may throw a light on any of the points in the controversy, but which do not contain any statement of the accused based on his personal knowledge. For example, the accused person may be in possession of a document which is in his writing or which contains his signature or his thumb-impression. The production of such a document, with a view to comparison of the writing or the signature or the impression, is not the statement of an accused person, which can be said to be of the nature of a personal testimony.[75]

Accordingly, the Indian Supreme Court held in that case that giving thumb impressions, or impressions of foot or palm or fingers, or specimen writings,

---

[68] Decision of 10 August 1968, Bureau d'assistance judiciaire du Tribunal de Bruxelles (Journal de Droit International no. 4, 1971, 856).
[69] *The Queen* v. *Eguabor* [1962] 1 All NLR 287.
[70] Fifth Amendment.
[71] Art. 20(3).
[72] *Sharma et al.* v. *Satish Chandra et al* [1954] SCR 1077: A person can 'be a witness' not merely by giving oral evidence, but also by producing documents or making intelligible gestures as in the case of a dumb witness. To 'be a witness' is nothing more than 'to furnish evidence', and such evidence can be furnished through the lips, or by production of a thing, or a document, or in other modes.
[73] *Boyd* v. *United States* 116 US 616; *Weeks* v. *United States* 232 US 383.
[74] *Sharma et al.* v. *Satish Chandra et al., supra.*
[75] *Bombay* v. *Kathi Kalu Oghad* [1962] 3 SCR 10.

or showing parts of the body, by way of identification were not included in the expression 'to be a witness'.

Likewise, the Supreme Court of Canada has held[76] that the compulsory provision of a sample of breath or blood to prove its alcohol content is not precluded by the 'protection against self-incrimination' in the Canadian Bill of Rights.

The Indian Supreme Court has also held that it must be shown that the accused was compelled to make a statement which is of such a character that by itself it should have the tendency to incriminate the maker. The prohibition would not, therefore, apply to a confession made by an accused without any inducement, threat or promise, or to a retracted confession.[77]

HRC has expressed the view that ICPR 14(3)(g) is violated where an accused person is compelled to sign a statement which incriminates him.[78]

'To have the conviction and sentence reviewed by a higher tribunal according to law'

IACM has stated that 'the existence of a higher tribunal necessarily implies a re-examination of the facts presented in the lower court', and that the omission of the opportunity for such an appeal deprives defendants of due process.[79]

HRC has expressed the view that *ICPR* 14(5) is violated where an appeal against a criminal conviction cannot be heard for 34 months because the transcript of the original trial is not made available.[80]

'Not to be tried or punished again for an offence for which he has already been finally convicted or acquitted in accordance with law and penal procedure'

None of the competent independent international institutions has yet had occasion to consider this provision. However, the Supreme Court of India has held that, in order to attract the protection against double jeopardy in the Indian Constitution, it must be shown that there was a previous conviction, and a previous punishment, for the same offence.[81]

§22.7 Miscarriage of justice

§22.7.1 TEXTS

ICPR

14 (6) When a person has by a final decision been convicted of a criminal offence and when subsequently his conviction has been reversed or he has been pardoned on the ground that a new or newly discovered fact shows conclusively that there has been a miscarriage of justice, the person who has suffered punishment as a result of such

---

[76] *Curr* v. *The Queen* [1972] SCR 889.
[77] *Kalawati* v. *H. P. State* [1953] SCR 546.
[78] *Burgos* v. *Uruguay* (R. 12/52) HRC 36, 176.
[79] 2 Nicaragua, 86.
[80] *Pinkney* v. *Canada* (R. 7/27) published 14 December 1981.
[81] *Dana* v. *Punjab* [1959] Supp 1 SCR 274.

conviction shall be compensated according to law, unless it is proved that the non-disclosure of the unknown fact in time is wholly or partly attributable to him.

AMR

10. Every person has the right to be compensated in accordance with the law in the event he has been sentenced by a final judgment through a miscarriage of justice.

§ 22.7.2 CROSS-REFERENCES

State obligation: Absolute and immediate under *ICPR* and *AMR*: see §6.3.

Signatures, ratifications, accessions, reservations, and interpretations: See Table A for the State Parties bound by these provisions on 1 January 1982, and any reservations and interpretations notified by them.

Derogation: Derogable in exceptional circumstances under *ICPR* and *AMR*: see §11.

Non-discrimination: No discrimination of any kind is allowed in respect of this right: see §7 for the relevant provisions in the instruments.

Abuse: See §9 for the relevant provisions in these instruments.

Savings: See §10 for the relevant provisions in these instruments.

Restrictions and limitations: See §8 for the general provisions in these instruments.

International supervision, interpretation, application, and enforcement: By HRC under *ICPR* (see §27); by IACM and IACT under *AMR* (see §29). See also §6.6 for the obligation to provide domestic remedies under *ICPR* and *AMR*.

See also: §14.2 for compensation for unlawful arrest or detention.

§ 22.7.3 COMMENT

Both *ICPR* 14(6) and *AMR* 10 require compensation in accordance with the law — that is, they require the State Parties to have in force domestic laws which provide for such compensation.

But before the right to compensation can arise, several conditions must be satisfied, which are not quite the same in the two treaties. First, there must have been a 'final' decision (*ICPR*) or judgment (*AMR*) — that is, one which is no longer subject to appeal. Secondly, the victim must have 'suffered punishment' (*ICPR*) or 'been sentenced' (*AMR*). Lastly, there must have been a 'miscarriage of justice'. Neither of the treaties attempts to define this. But *ICPR* limits compensation to cases where the miscarriage has been 'conclusively' established by a 'new or newly discovered fact', and requires the conviction to have been reversed, or the victim of the miscarriage to have been pardoned. *ICPR* also deprives the victim of the right to compensation if he is himself responsible for the non-disclosure, in sufficient time, of the 'unknown' fact, the burden of establishing this being on the State concerned.

§22.7.4 JURISPRUDENCE

None of these provisions has yet been interpreted or applied by any of the competent independent international institutions.

§23. MENTAL AND MORAL INTEGRITY

§23.1 Dignity, personality, and name

§23.1.1 TEXTS

UDHR

1. All human beings are born free and equal in dignity and rights. They are endowed with reason and conscience and should act towards one another in a spirit of brotherhood.

29 (1) Everyone has duties to the community in which alone the free and full development of his personality is possible.

ADRD

XXIX. It is the duty of the individual so to conduct himself in relation to others that each and every one may fully form and develop his personality.

ICPR

24 (2) Every child shall be registered immediately after birth and shall have a name.

AMR

6 (1) Every person has the right to have his physical, mental, and moral integrity respected.

11 (1) Everyone has the right to have his honor respected and his dignity recognised.

18. Every person has the right to a given name and to the surnames of his parents or that of one of them. The law shall regulate the manner in which this right shall be ensured for all, by the use of assumed names if necessary.

[AFR]

5. Every individual shall have the right to the respect of the dignity inherent in a human being.

§23.1.2 CROSS-REFERENCES

State obligation: Absolute and immediate under *ICPR*, *AMR*, and [*AFR*]: see §6.3. For the juridical status of obligations under *UDHR* and *ADRD*, see §6.2.

Signatures, ratifications, accessions, reservations, and interpretations: See Table A for the State Parties bound by these provisions on 1 January 1982, and any reservations and interpretations notified by them.

Derogation: Non-derogable in any circumstances under *AMR* and [*AFR*]; derogable in exceptional circumstances under *ICPR*: see §11.

Non-discrimination: No discrimination of any kind is allowed in respect of these rights or freedoms: see §7 for the relevant provisions in the instruments.

Abuse: See §9 for the relevant provisions in these instruments.

Savings: See §10 for the relevant provisions in these instruments.

Restrictions and limitations: See §8 for the general provisions in these instruments.

International supervision, interpretation, application, and enforcement: By HRC under *ICPR* (see §27); by IACM and IACT under *AMR* (see §29); by [*AFCM*] under [*AFR*] (see §30). See also §6.6 for the obligation to provide domestic remedies under *UDHR*, *ADRD*, *ICPR*, *AMR*, and [*AFR*].

§23.1.3 COMMENT

UDHR 1, *AMR* 11(1), and [*AFC* 5] contain general declarations about the inherent dignity of human beings. None of the other instruments does. *AMR* 5(1) establishes an additional right of respect for 'mental and moral', as well as physical, 'integrity'. 'Personality' is seen in both *UDHR* 29(1) and *ADRD* XXIX as a characteristic whose growth requires the fulfilment of duties to others. The right to a name is considered only in *ICPR* 24(2) and *AMR* 18. The former confines it to children, the latter requires both a given name and a surname.

§23.1.4 JURISPRUDENCE

None of these provisions has yet been authoritatively interpreted or applied by any of the competent independent international institutions.

However, although *EHR* contains no express provisions about the registration of children at birth, both EUCM and EUCT have said that the right to respect for family life under *EHR* 8(1) requires the registration of a child's birth without further formalities, regardless of whether its mother was married, in order to transform the biological bond, automatically and immediately, into a legal one.[1]

---

[1] *Marckx* v. *Belgium* (6833/74) Report: 10 December 1977; Judgment: 2 EHRR 330. See also *48 Kalderas' Gypsies* v. *Federal Republic of Germany and Netherlands* (7823-4/77) DR 11, 221: the failure to issue a birth certificate may constitute an interference with the right to respect for family life.

§23.2 Privacy, honour, and reputation

§23.2.1 TEXTS

UDHR

12. No one shall be subjected to arbitrary interference with his privacy, family, home or correspondence, nor to attacks upon his honour and reputation. Everyone has the right to the protection of the law against such interference or attacks.

ADRD

V. Every person has the right to the protection of the law against abusive attacks upon his honor, his reputation, and his private and family life.

IX. Every person has the right to the inviolability of his home.

X. Every person has the right to the inviolability and transmission of his correspondence.

ICPR

17 (1) No one shall be subjected to arbitrary or unlawful interference with his privacy, family, home or correspondence, nor to unlawful attacks on his honour and reputation.

(2) Everyone has the right to the protection of the law against such interference or attacks.

EHR

8 (1) Everyone has the right to respect for his private and family life, his home and his correspondence.

(2) There shall be no interference by a public authority with the exercise of this right except such as is in accordance with the law and is necessary in a democratic society in the interests of national security, public safety or the economic well-being of the country, for the prevention of disorder or crime, for the protection of health or morals, or for the protection of the rights and freedoms of others.

AMR

11 (1) Everyone has the right to have his honor respected and his dignity recognized.

(2) No one may be the object of arbitrary or abusive interference with his private life, his family, his home, or his correspondence, or of unlawful attacks on his honor or reputation.

(3) Everyone has the right to the protection of the law against such interference or attacks

14 (1) Anyone injured by inaccurate or offensive statements or ideas disseminated to the public in general by a legally regulated medium of communication has the right to reply or make a correction using the same communications outlet, under such conditions as the law may establish.

(2) The correction or reply shall not in any case remit other legal liabilities that may have been incurred.

(3) For the effective protection of honor and reputation, every publisher, and every newspaper, motion picture, radio, and television company, shall have a person responsible, who is not protected by immunities or special privileges.

§23.2.2 CROSS-REFERENCES

State obligation: Absolute and immediate under *ICPR*, *EHR*, and *AMR*; see §6.3. For the juridical status of obligations under *UDHR* and *ADRD*, see §6.2.

Signatures, ratifications, accessions, reservations, and interpretations: See Table A for the State Parties bound by these provisions on 1 January 1982, and any reservations and interpretations notified by them.

Derogation: Derogable in exceptional circumstances under *ICPR*, *EHR*, and *AMR*: see §11.

Non-discrimination: No discrimination of any kind is allowed in respect of these rights or freedoms: see §7 for the relevant provisions in the instruments.

Abuse: See §9 for the relevant provisions in these instruments.

Savings: See §10 for the relevant provisions in these instruments.

Restrictions and limitations: Note the specific provisions in *EHR* 8(2). See §8 for the general provisions in these instruments, and the principles governing all restriction and limitation clauses.

International supervision, interpretation, application, and enforcement: By HRC under *ICPR* (see §27); by EUCM and EUCT under *EHR* (see §28); by IACM and IACT under *AMR* (see §29). See also §6.6 for the obligation to provide domestic remedies under *UDHR*, *ADRD*, *ICPR*, *EHR*, and *AMR*.

See also: §17.1 for other provisions relating to the family.

§23.2.3 COMMENT

UDHR 12 and *ICPR* 17(1) use the word 'privacy'; *ADRD* V, *EHR* 8(1) and *AMR* 11(2) the expression 'private life'.[1] *ADRD* and *EHR* protect 'family life'; the other three instruments the 'family'. All these instruments protect,

---

[1] Robertson states that, in the case of *EHR*, this does not reflect any difference of substance, but rather an attempt to secure concordance between the English and French texts, since the French texts of *UDHR*, *ICPR* and *EHR* all use the expression *'vie privée'*: *Human Rights in Europe* 86. Likewise, the Spanish texts of *ADRD* and *AMR* use the expression *'vida privada'*.

in addition, 'home' and 'correspondence'. 'Honour' and 'reputation' are protected by all of them other than *EHR*.

EHR 8(1) alone confers its protection in absolute terms, listing in Article 8(2) eight specific grounds on which public authorities may, under domestic law which is 'necessary in a democratic society' (see §8), interfere with the exercise of the protected right. The other instruments protect only against interference with privacy or family which is 'arbitrary' (*UDHR*, *ICPR*, and *AMR*), 'abusive' (*ADRD* and *AMR*), or 'unlawful' (*ICPR*). The same qualifications apply to interference with home or correspondence in *UDHR*, *ICPR*, and *AMR*, but both these are declared to be absolutely 'inviolable' in *ADRD*. The protection against attacks on honour and reputation is absolute in *UDHR*, but confined to 'unlawful' ones in *ICPR* and *AMR*.

Al the instruments other than *EHR* stipulate that everyone 'has the right to the protection of the law against' such interference or attacks. As the exceptions in *EHR* 8(2) explicitly apply only to public authorities, it could be argued that the obligation to provide domestic remedies under *EHR* 13 requires the State Parties to that Convention to protect the right declared in *EHR* 8(1) against all interference from other quarters.

Only *AMR* 14 establishes a specific 'right of reply' against personal attacks in the communications media.

[*AFR*] contains no corresponding provisions.

§23.2.4 JURISPRUDENCE

The 'right to respect'

Although the primary object of *EHR* 8 is that of protecting the individual from arbitrary interference by public authorities,[2] it does not merely compel the State to abstain from such interference. In addition to this primarily negative requirement, it also imposes some positive obligations to respect the right referred to in this Article. For instance, in *Airey* v. *Ireland*,[3] EUCT observed that respect for family life obliges a government to make the courts effectively accessible to anyone who may wish to have recourse to them to obtain a decree of judicial separation. In *Van Oosterwijck* v. *Belgium*,[4] an application by a female-born transsexual who had achieved the appearance of the male sex, EUCM considered that the failure of the respondent government to contemplate measures which would make it possible to take account in the applicant's civil status of the change in sex which had lawfully occurred amounted not only to an interference with the applicant's exercise of his right to respect for private life, but to a veritable failure to recognize the respect due to his private life within the meaning of *EHR* 8(1). (EUCT later refused to consider this case on its merits, on the ground that the applicant's domestic remedies had not been exhausted before the application was made.[5])

---

[2] *Belgian Linguistic Case* (1474/62, etc.) Judgment: 1 EHRR 252.

[3] (6289/73) Judgment: 2 EHRR 305.

[4] (7654/76) Report: 1 March 1979. See also *X* v. *Federal Republic of Germany* (6699/74) DR 11, 16.

[5] Judgment: 3 EHRR 557.

'Private life'

A number of Anglo-Saxon and French authors understand the right to respect for 'private life' only as the right to live, as far as one wishes, protected from publicity.[6] However, EUCM has observed that the right to respect for private life does not end there. It comprises also, for instance, the right to establish and develop relationships with other human beings, especially in the emotional field, for the development and fulfilment of one's own personality.[7] In principle, therefore, whenever the State formulates rules for the behaviour of the individual within this sphere, it interferes with the respect for private life and such interference can then only be justified by reference to *EHR* 8(2).[8]

In *X* v. *United Kingdom*,[9] EUCM said that the prosecution and punishment of a person for having had homosexual relationships with adolescents under the age of consent was necessary for the protection of the rights and freedoms of others; as would be the fixing by legislation of the age of consent. However, in *Dudgeon* v. *United Kingdom*,[10] EUCT has held that a law which makes *all* homosexual conduct between males — including such conduct in private between consenting persons over 21 — a criminal offence, even though in practice no one is ever prosecuted under it, constitutes an interference with the right to respect for the private lives (which includes the sexual lives) of persons of homosexual orientation if it causes them fear, suffering, and psychological distress; moreover, such a wide law is not necessary in a democratic society either for the protection of morals, or for the protection of the rights and freedoms of others.

While a large proportion of the laws existing in every State has some immediate or remote effect on the individual's possibility of developing his personality by doing what he wants to do, not all these can be considered to constitute an interference with private life. In fact, the claim to respect for private life is automatically reduced to the extent that the individual brings his private life into contact with public life, or into close connection with other protected interests. In *Brüggemann and Scheuten* v. *Federal Republic of Germany*,[11] EUCM said that while a person's sexual life is undoubtedly an important aspect of his private life, *EHR* 8(1) cannot be interpreted to mean that pregnancy and its termination are, as a principle, solely a matter of the private life of the mother. Noting that whenever a woman is pregnant, her private life becomes closely connected with the developing foetus, the Commission upheld a German law which did not permit an abortion to be carried out merely because the pregnancy was unwanted.

In *X* v. *Iceland*,[12] EUCM observed that the protection afforded by *EHR* 8(1)

---

[6] Cf. numerous references quoted by Velu in 'Privacy and Human Rights', *Third International Colloquy about the European Convention on Human Rights* (Manchester) 27–8. See also Black's *Law Dictionary* (4th ed., 1951) under 'Privacy'. For a wider view, see Sieghart, *Privacy and Computers* (London, 1976), Ch. 1.

[7] *X* v. *Iceland* (6825/74) DR 5, 86. See also *X* v. *Switzerland* (8257/78) DR 13, 248, which concerned a court order restoring custody of a foster child to its natural parents.

[8] *Brüggemann and Scheuten* v. *Federal Republic of Germany* (6959/75) Report: DR 10, 100. For Decision, see DR 5, 103.

[9] (7215/75) Report: DR 19, 66. See also *X* v. *Federal Republic of Germany* (530/59) CD 2; *X* v. *Federal Republic of Germany* (5935/72) DR 3, 46; *X* v. *United Kingdom* (7525/76) DR 11, 117.

[10] (7525/76) Judgment: 22 October 1981.

[11] *Supra*, n. 8.

[12] *Supra*, n. 7.

cannot be extended to relationships of the individual with his entire immediate surroundings, insofar as they do not involve human relationships and notwithstanding the desire of the individual to keep such relationships within the private sphere. Accordingly, it considered that since the keeping of dogs is by the very nature of that animal necessarily associated with certain interferences with the lives of others and even with public life, *EHR* 8(1) cannot be interpreted so as to secure to everybody the right to keep a dog. Nor is the compulsory wearing of safety belts by the drivers and passengers of motor vehicles in any sense an interference with a person's 'private life', however broadly that expression may be be interpreted.[13]

In a number of earlier cases, EUCM expressed the view that it was an 'inherent feature' of lawful imprisonment that a prisoner should be restricted in his private life.[14] More recently, the Commission has looked for justification of such restrictions among the specific grounds listed in *EHR* 8(2). Accordingly, the denial to married prisoners of an opportunity to continue their conjugal life in prison,[15] as well as the close surveillance of visits made to a prisoner by his wife and children,[16] while interfering with the exercise of the right to respect for their private lives, have been found to be justified as necessary in a democratic society in the interests of public safety, for the prevention of disorder or crime, and for the protection of the rights and freedoms of others.[17] So have the wearing of prison uniform, surveillance and searches by prison warders, and restrictions on association with other prisoners.[18]

The seizure of a private document required for a criminal investigation interferes with the right to respect for private life, but may be necessary for the prevention of disorder or crime.[19] Similarly, the disclosure to, or improper discovery by, third persons of facts relating to an individual's physical condition, health or personality, or of material contained in a person's criminal record, could constitute an interference with his private life.[20] However, EUCM has observed that the taking and retention of photographs by the police of persons taking part in a public demonstration would not constitute an invasion of privacy,[21] and that the production in evidence of intimate photographs,[22] and the keeping of records, including documents, photographs, and fingerprints relating to previous criminal cases,[23] could be necessary in a democratic society for the prevention of crime and in the interests of public safety respectively. So may the placing of a juvenile under observation as part of a judicial investigation concerning him, in accordance with the law in force.[24]

---

[13] *X v. Belgium* (8707/79) DR 18, 255.
[14] *X v. Federal Republic of Germany* (3819/68) CD 32, 23. See also *X v. Federal Republic of Germany* (530/59) *supra*, n. 9; *X v. Netherlands* (1983/63) CD 18, 19.
[15] *X and Y v. Switzerland* (8166/78) DR 13, 241. See also *X v. Federal Republic of Germany* (3603/68) CD 31, 48; *X v. United Kingdom* (6564/74) DR 2, 105.
[16] *X v. United Kingdom* (8065/77) DR 14, 246.
[17] See also *Wemhoff v. Federal Republic of Germany* (3448/67) CD 30, 56: the interests of security require that a remand prisoner should not have knowledge of the manner by which his personal effects and the security installations of his cell are checked.
[18] *McFeeley et al. v. United Kingdom* (8317/78) Report: 3 EHRR 161.
[19] *X v. Federal Republic of Germany* (530/59) *supra*, n. 9; *X v. Federal Republic of Germany* (6794/74) DR 3, 104.
[20] *Van Oosterwijck v. Belgium* (7654/76) Report: 1 March 1979. See also *X v. Norway* (7945/77) DR 14, 228.
[21] *X v. United Kingdom* (5877/72) CD 45, 90.
[22] *X v. Federal Republic of Germany* (5339/72) CD 43, 156.
[23] *X v. Federal Republic of Germany* (1307/61) CD 9, 53; cf. Decision of 12 October 1965, VfGH Austria (ÖJZ 1966, 400).
[24] *X v. Switzerland* (8500/79) DR 18, 238.

The protection of the right to private life from interferences made possible by modern scientific and technical devices was considered by EUCT in *Klass v. Federal Republic of Germany*.[25] The Court noted that judicial notice must be taken of two important facts; first, the technical advances made in the means of espionage and, correspondingly, of surveillance; and secondly, the development of terrorism in Europe in recent years. The Court observed that democratic societies now find themselves threatened by highly sophisticated forms of espionage and by terrorism, with the result that the State must be able, in order to counter such threats effectively, to undertake the secret surveillance of subversive elements operating within its jurisdiction. The Court therefore accepted that the existence of some legislation granting powers of secret surveillance over the mail, post and telecommunications is, under exceptional conditions, necessary in a democratic society in the interests of national security and/or for the protection of disorder or crime. However, this does not mean that States enjoy an unlimited discretion to subject persons within their jurisdictions to secret surveillance. Since such a law poses the danger of undermining or even destroying democracy on the ground of defending it, States may not, in the name of the struggle against espionage and terrorism, adopt whatever measures they deem appropriate. The Court stressed that whenever a system of surveillance is adopted, there must exist adequate and effective guarantees against abuse.

In *Association X v. United Kingdom*.[26] EUCM found that a voluntary vaccination scheme designed to protect the health of society, and made subject to a proper system of control in order to minimize the risks involved, does not interfere with the right to respect for private life. Nor does *EHR* 8 impose an obligation on the State to provide specific detailed information to parents on either contra-indications or the risks associated with particular vaccines.

The compulsory taking of samples for a paternity test, though only a minor medical intervention, is an interference within the meaning of *EHR* 8. However, being harmless, scientifically validated, and intended to assist in the determination by the courts of paternity rights, the interference is proportionate to the purpose sought for it and may therefore be justified as being necessary in a democratic society for the protection of the rights of others.[27]

The Austrian Supreme Court has held that the letting of a room by a hotel proprietor to an unmarried couple of different sexes did not in itself constitute an act encouraging the possibility of prostitution. A contrary interpretation would mean that the provision of the penal code involved would, by laying down penal sanctions, impose obligations on every hotel proprietor to watch over the intimate relations of his guests. Such an interpretation, the Court observed, would be contrary to the right to respect for private life guaranteed in *EHR* 8.[28]

'Family life'

HRC has expressed the view that the common residence of husband and wife has to be considered as the normal behaviour of a family. Accordingly, where domestic law protects the right of residence within the State of the alien wives of male nationals, but requires 'residence permits' for the foreign husbands of

---

[25] (5029/71) Judgment: 2 EHRR 214. See also *Malone v. United Kingdom* (8691/79) Decision: 13 July 1981.

[26] (7154/75) DR 14, 31.

[27] *X v. Austria* (8278/78) DR 18, 154.

[28] Decision of 8 June 1970, OGH, Austria (ÖJZ 1971, 158).

female nationals which may be refused or withdrawn at any time by the Minister of the Interior, whereupon the husbands concerned may be deported under a ministerial order which is not subject to judicial review, the wives of such husbands (being discriminated against on the grounds of sex) are victims of a violation of *ICPR* 2(1) and 3, in conjunction with *ICPR* 17(1). It is therefore unnecessary to determine whether in such circumstances *ICPR* 17(1) is infringed on its own, in that the interference with the family might be 'arbitrary' even if it is not 'unlawful'.[29]

In order to ascertain whether in a particular case it is appropriate to speak of 'family life', it is necessary to consider whether, apart from the legal ties of relationship by blood or marriage, there is some factual bond or link establishing family life.[30] For instance, the fact that persons live together and that they are financially dependent on one another may constitute such a link.[31] EUCM has pointed out that *EHR* 8 concerns not *de jure*, but *de facto* family life.[32]

The fact of birth, that is, the existence of a biological bond between mother and child, creates 'family life' within the meaning of *EHR* 8. Accordingly, the automatic and immediate transformation of the biological bond into a bond of legal relationship is essential for the recognition of the existence of family life. In *Marckx* v. *Belgium*,[33] both EUCM and EUCT found that the right to respect for family life therefore required that, irrespective of whether the mother was married, the registration of the child's birth should without further formalities have the effect of the recognition of a legal bond of relationship with the mother.

The right to respect for family life is not confined to 'legitimate' families. Relations between a child born out of wedlock and his natural parents, that is both his father and his mother, are in principle covered by the term 'family life'.[34] Indeed, EUCT has held that the concept of family life in *EHR* 8 must be understood in the broad sense and that it includes at least the ties between near relatives — for instance, those between grandparents and grandchildren. The State is therefore obliged to act in a manner calculated to allow those ties to develop normally.[35] At the same time, a prospective father does not have a right to be consulted on, or to seize the authorities of, the question of a proposed termination of his wife's pregnancy. In so far as this may constitute an interference with his right to respect for his family life, it is justified as necessary for the protection of the rights of others.[36]

---

[29] *Aumeeruddy-Cziffra* v. *Mauritius* (R. 9/35) HRC 36, 134.

[30] *X* v. *Switzerland* (8257/78) DR 13, 248; *Marckx* v. *Belgium* (6833/74) DR 3, 112.

[31] *X and Y* v. *United Kingdom* (7229/75) DR 12, 32. See also *X* v. *Federal Republic of Germany* (3110/67) CD 27, 77 (uncle and nephew/niece); *X and Y* v. *United Kingdom* (5269/71) CD 39, 104 (adult daughter and her parents); *X* v. *United Kingdom* (5532/72) CD 43, 119 (son and mother, brother and sister); *X* v. *Belgium and Netherlands* (6482/74) DR 7, 75 (adoptive single parent and adoptive child).

[32] *X and Y* v. *United Kingdom* (5302/71) CD 44, 29. But where the relationship between two persons falls short of 'family life' because there is no common household or they do not permanently live together, it may still amount to 'private life' within the meaning of *EHR* 8: *X and Y* v. *Switzerland* (7289/75; 7349/76) DR 9, 57.

[33] (6833/74) Report: 10 December 1977; Judgment: 2 EHRR 330. See also *48 Kalderas' Gypsies* v. *Federal Republic of Germany and Netherlands* (7823-4/77) DR 11, 221: the failure to issue a birth certificate may constitute an interference with the right to respect for family life.

[34] *Marckx* v. *Belgium, supra.*

[35] *Ibid.*

[36] *X* v. *United Kingdom* (8416/78) DR 19, 244. See also Decision of 31 October 1980, Conseil d'Etat, France, 6 *Human Rights Review*, 75.

It is not a requirement of *EHR* 8 that a child should be entitled to some share in the estates of his parents or other near relatives. But it is essential that children, whether legitimate or illegitimate, should have the same capacity to inherit on intestacy. Family life does not include only social, moral, or cultural relations; it also comprises interests of a material kind. Therefore, matters of intestate succession, and of disposition, between near relatives are intimately connected with family life. In *Marckx* v. *Belgium*,[37] EUCT agreed with the minority view of EUCM that the right of succession between children and parents, and between grandchildren and grandparents, is so closely related to family life that it comes within the sphere of *EHR* 8.

The family of a person who has been married twice includes the children of both marriages, but *EHR* 8 assigns no priority as between the children in respect of their financial maintenance.[38]

In the *Belgian Linguistic Case*[39] EUCM, while considering that *EHR* 8 did not guarantee the right to education (considered as a corollary of the freedom of private life), or the rights of parents with regard to their children's education (considered as a consequence of the right to respect for family life), observed that it is not impossible for educational measures to affect the respect for private and family life. Any school system might violate *EHR* 8 if, though not disregarding parents' rights to educate and bring up their children in accordance with their religious and philosophical convictions, it was so organized as to separate parents and children. This might be the case, for instance, if, where education was compulsory, the children were obliged to live in boarding schools, or if school hours were deliberately arranged in such a way as to prevent contact between children and their parents, or to reduce such contact to a minimum. Similarly, provisions relating to the language of instruction may entail grave disturbances in private or family life. Under certain conditions such provisions might be considered incompatible with *EHR* 8. But this incompatibility would be due not to the State's failure to respect parents' wishes with regard to the language of education, but to the grave and unjustified disturbances caused in private or family life. In that case, the Commission found that the respondent government, in spite of the compulsory schooling it had introduced, was not bound by *EHR* 8 to provide French education for French-speaking persons living in the Flemish region of Belgium; nor was it bound to open existing French schools to them or to subsidize French schools attended by the applicants' children under conditions other than those laid down in the national linguistic legislation.

EUCT, while affirming this decision, pointed out that *EHR* 8 in no way guaranteed the right to be educated in the language of one's parents by the public authorities or with their aid; to require a child to study in depth a national language which was not his own could not be characterized as an act of 'depersonalisation'. Accordingly, the Court stressed that if the legislation in question leads certain parents to send their children to schools outside their region and thus separate themselves from their children, such a separation is not imposed by the legislation: it is the result of their own choice.[40]

In *Kjeldsen et al.* v. *Denmark*,[41] where the issue raised was whether or not

[37] *Supra.*
[38] *X* v. *Federal Republic of Germany* (8604/79) DR 20, 206.
[39] (1474/62, etc.) Report: 24 June 1965.
[40] Judgment: 1 EHRR 252. See also *Inhabitants of Les Fourons* v. *Belgium* (2209/64) Report: 30 March 1971.
[41] (5095/71; 5920/72; 5926/72) Report: 21 March 1975.

compulsory integrated sex education in the Danish public schools contravened *EHR* 8, EUCM observed that if sex education is handled with all due respect for the different convictions of parents, the danger of a disturbance of private or family life will be greatly diminished. If, in specific cases, that disturbance would still result — and it cannot be completely avoided — sex education would not be unjustifiable or arbitrary. It would be the unavoidable result of the difficult balancing between the interests of the community and the individual in the sphere of education which is implied in *EHR P1 2*.

EHR 8 guarantees the right to respect for *existing* family life. It does not oblige a State to grant a foreign citizen entry to its territory for the purpose of establishing a new family relationship there.[42] A measure of prohibition of entry can therefore only be considered as interfering with a person's private or family life where that life is already firmly established in the territory concerned,[43] but not if there are no legal obstacles for that person and his spouse to establish their family life effectively in another country connected with either of them.[44] The same principle applies to the expulsion of a person from a country in which close members of his family are living.[45] Entry and immigration clearance procedures designed to establish the truth of alleged family links do not violate *EHR* 8 if they allow those concerned to vindicate their rights to respect for family life.[46]

The separation of a prisoner from his family, and the hardship resulting from it, have been said in some of the older cases to be 'inherent consequences' of the execution of a sentence and not therefore to violate *EHR* 8.[47] More recently, they have been found to be justified under *EHR* 8(2) as necessary for the prevention of disorder.[48] The consequences of a long-term service engagement freely entered into have also been said not to violate *EHR* 8.[49]

The right to respect for family life may be violated in a case where the authorities impose intolerable living conditions on a person or his family,[50] or where the State attempts to separate two persons united by an adoption contract, or forbids them to meet.[51]

The family life of parents with their children is not absolutely linked with marriage; indeed, it does not cease because of the divorce of a married couple. However, it is legitimate, or even necessary, for the national law to provide rules governing the relationship between parents and children where the communal life of the parents is practically non-existent or interrupted, which differ from the rules which normally apply when the family unit is still

---

[42] *X and Y v. United Kingdom* (7229/75) DR 12, 32; *X v. United Kingdom* (7048/75) DR 9, 42.

[43] *X and Y v. Switzerland* (7289/75; 7349/76) DR 9, 57. See also *X v. Denmark* (1855/63) CD 16, 50; *Alan and Khan v. United Kingdom* (2991/66) Report: 17 December 1968; *X v. United Kingdom* (5301/71) CD 43, 82.

[44] *X and Y v. United Kingdom* (5269/71) CD 39, 104; *X v. United Kingdom* (5301/71), *supra*; *X and Y v. United Kingdom* (5445-6/72) CD 42, 146; *Agee v. United Kingdom* (7729/76) DR 7, 164.

[45] *X v. United Kingdom* (3898/68) CD 35, 102; *X v. Federal Republic of Germany* (6357/73) DR 1, 77; *X and Y v. Federal Republic of Germany* (7816/77) DR 9, 219; *X v. Federal Republic of Germany* (8041/77) DR 12, 197; *Agee v. United Kingdom*, *supra*.

[46] *Kamel v. United Kingdom* (8378/78) DR 20, 168.

[47] *X v. Austria* (2676/65) CD 23, 31; *X v. Federal Republic of Germany* (3603/68) CD 31, 48; *X v. Federal Republic of Germany* (4185/60) CD 35, 140; *X v. United Kingdom* (5229/71) CD 42, 140; *X v. United Kingdom* (5712/72) CD 46, 112.

[48] *McFeeley et al. v. United Kingdom* (8317/78) Report: 3 EHRR 161.

[49] *W, X, Y and Z v. United Kingdom* (3435-8/67) CD 28, 109.

[50] *Guzzardi v. Italy* (7367/76) Report: 7 December 1978.

[51] *X v. Belgium and Netherlands* (6482/74) DR 7, 75.

maintained.[52] In the event of a divorce, the question of custody must necessarily be decided in favour of one of the parties, an act which necessarily interferes with the family life of the other parent.[53] The parent who is deprived of the custody may not be precluded, under *EHR* 8(1), from access to that child unless special circumstances as defined in *EHR* 8(2) so demand. In deciding this question, domestic courts, exercising a considerable measure of discretion in the matter, may properly take into account a child's mental stability and physical well-being. But whenever a domestic court refuses a parent a right of access to his or her children, EUCM may ultimately have the task of judging whether such a refusal is justifiable under *EHR* 8(2).[54]

'Home'

In *Wiggins* v. *United Kingdom*,[55] EUCM considered that a house which the applicant had lawfully bought and renovated, and in which he lived together with his wife during their marriage, must be regarded as having been their 'home' within the meaning of *EHR* 8(1). It remained the applicant's home also *after* his separation from his wife. Her leaving their common household gave rise to no change in that respect. Accordingly, the refusal of the housing authority to grant the applicant a licence for his continued occupancy of the house, and their order that he should vacate the premises, *prima facie* interfered with his right to respect for his home as guaranteed by *EHR* 8(1).

An unlawful search of a person's home may constitute an interference with this right.[56] So too may legislation providing for the secret surveillance of telephone conversations.[57] In *Denmark, Norway, Sweden and Netherlands* v. *Greece*,[58] the evidence was that the Greek law on the state of siege of 1967 authorized the military authorities to search a house by day or night, that

[52] *X* v. *Federal Republic of Germany* (2699/65) CD 26, 33; *X* v. *Federal Republic of Germany* (7770/77) DR 14, 175.
[53] *X* v. *Netherlands* (1449/62) CD 10, 1; *X* v. *Federal Republic of Germany* (4284/69) CD 37, 74. See also *X* v. *Netherlands* (6061/73) CD 45, 120 on the question whether the consequent order for maintenance violates *EHR* 8(1).
[54] *X* v. *Sweden* (172/56) YB 1, 211; *X* v. *Sweden* (911/60) CD 7, 7; *X* v. *Austria* (514/59) CD 2; *X* v. *Denmark* (1329/62) CD 9, 28; *X* v. *Netherlands* (1449/62) CD 10, 1; *X* v. *Federal Republic of Germany* (2699/65) CD 26, 33; *X* v. *Austria* (3053/67) CD 25, 88; *W.X and H.X* v. *United Kingdom* (4004/69) CD 33, 18; *X* v. *Federal Republic of Germany* (4185/69) CD 35, 140; *X* v. *Federal Republic of Germany* (4284/69) CD 37, 74; *X* v. *United Kingdom* (5608/72) CD 44, 66; *X and Y* v. *Netherlands* (6753/74) DR 2, 118; *X* v. *United Kingdom* (7434/76) DR 9, 103; *X* v. *United Kingdom* (7626/76) DR 11, 160; *X* v. *Federal Republic of Germany* (7770/77) DR 14, 175; *X* v. *Sweden* (7911/77) DR 12, 192; *X* v. *Switzerland* (8257/78) DR 13, 248.
[55] (7456/76) DR 13, 40. The Housing Control (Guernsey) Law of 1969, which was one in a series of laws that had been introduced after the Second World War in order to prevent over-population harmful to Guernsey's economy, reserved all dwellings below a certain rateable value for people either born on the island or having otherwise close connections with it. It also took into account the size of a dwelling in relation to the number of persons occupying it. The Commission found that this law was pursuing a legitimate aim which was necessary for the economic well-being of Guernsey and for the protection of the rights and freedoms of others, and accordingly rejected the application as inadmissible on that ground.
[56] *X* v. *United Kingdom* (6148/73) DR 6, 19. But not the search of a motor vehicle on the highway by the police: Decision of 27 September 1971, Cour de Cassation, Belgium (Pas. belge 1972, 87); or the fluoridation of drinking water: Decision of 14 August 1970, Koninklijk Besluit, Netherlands, CDNC 3, 40.
[57] *Klass* v. *Federal Republic of Germany* (5029/71) EUCT, Judgment; 2 EHRR 214.
[58] (3321-3/67; 3344/67) Report: YB 12 *bis*.

such searches in fact took place frequently without a warrant, and that arrests of suspects normally occurred in their houses at night. The Commission found that *EHR* 8 had thereby been violated.

'Correspondence'

The opening and examination, or 'stopping', of a person's correspondence clearly constitutes an interference by a public authority with his right to respect for his correspondence within the meaning of *EHR* 8(1).[59] In *Golder* v. *United Kingdom*,[60] EUCM observed that while there is obviously a failure to respect correspondence if the authorities read, 'stop', and destroy a person's letters, it is equally a failure to respect correspondence if the authorities destroy letters without reading them. In that case, a prisoner requested permission to 'consult' a solicitor. As he had no opportunity of meeting a solicitor in the ordinary course of his confinement, this meant that he was in fact requesting permission to write to a solicitor. When permission was refused, he was in exactly the position in which he would have been had he written a letter which was later 'stopped'. For all practical purposes, there was an implied refusal of his right to correspond, and the Commission found that this amounted to an interference with his right to respect for his correspondence. Upholding this finding, EUCT observed that impeding someone from initiating correspondence constitutes the most far-reaching form of 'interference' with the exercise of the right to respect for his correspondence.[61]

EUCM has now come to the view that a prisoner's right to respect for his correspondence is the same as that of a person at liberty, and envisages a free flow of such communications, even if they are intended for publication. Any interference with these must be specifically justified under *EHR* 8(2).[62]

Discouraging a person from sending a letter may not amount to an interference;[63] nor would a public authority to which a letter has been submitted be prevented by *EHR* 8 from communicating this letter, or disclosing its contents, to another authority.[64] And *EHR* 8(1) does not confer a right to a postal service that functions perfectly, and in which no letter ever miscarries.[65]

---

[59] *X* v. *Federal Republic of Germany* (2279/64) CD 23, 114; *X* v. *Austria* (2291/64) CD 24, 20; *De Wilde, Ooms, Versyp* v. *Belgium* (2832/66; 2835/66; 2899/66) Report: 19 July 1969; Judgment: 1 EHRR 373; *X* v. *Federal Republic of Germany* (4445/70) CD 37, 119; *X and Y* v. *United Kingdom* (5459/72) CD 40, 75; *McMahon* v. *United Kingdom* (7113/75) DR 10, 205; *Carne* v. *United Kingdom* (7052/75) DR 10, 154; *Silver et al* v. *United Kingdom* (5947/72, etc.) Report: 11 October 1980 (referred to EUCT). See also Decision of 26 June 1972, Cour Superieure de Justice, Luxembourg (Pas. Lux. 1973, 216) on the question whether the opening of a letter addressed to a third party which has not yet been posted constitutes a violation of *EHR* 8(1). For restrictions which may be imposed on prisoners in regard to their correspondence, see *X* v. *Netherlands* (1983/63) CD 18, 19; *X* v. *Switzerland* (7736/76) DR 9, 206; *X* v. *Ireland* 3717/68) CD 31, 96; *X* v. *Federal Republic of Germany* (1628/62) CD 12, 61. See also *X* v. *United Kingdom* (6084/73) DR 3, 62 where a letter was suppressed in the interests of public safety.
[60] (4451/70) Report: 1 June 1973.
[61] *Ibid.*, Judgment: 1 EHRR 524.
[62] *Silver et al.* v. *United Kingdom* (5947/72, etc.) Report: 11 October 1980 (referred to EUCT). HRC has also expressed the view that legislation which authorizes, in very general terms, the censorship or 'stopping' of prisoners' correspondence does not provide satisfactory legal safeguards against 'arbitrary' interference in the context of *ICPR* 17(1): *Pinkney* v. *Canada* (R. 7/27) published 14 December 1981.
[63] *Wemhoff* v. *Federal Republic of Germany* (2122/64) CD 15, 1.
[64] *X* v. *Sweden* (3788/68) CD 35, 56.
[65] *X* v. *Federal Republic of Germany* (8383/78) DR 17, 227.

In *Klass* v. *Federal Republic of Germany*,[66] both EUCM and EUCT said that although telephone conversations are not expressly mentioned in *EHR* 8(1), such conversations are covered by the notions of 'private life' and 'correspondence' referred to in that provision. Accordingly, the secret surveillance of such conversations would be an interference with the individual's right to respect for his private life and his correspondence. Indeed, the Court went further and observed that in the mere existence of legislation providing for secret surveillance there is involved, for all those to whom the legislation could be applied, a menace of surveillance; this menace necessarily strikes at freedom of communication between users of the postal and telecommunication services and thereby constitutes an 'interference by a public authority' with the exercise of the applicant's right to respect for private and family life and for correspondence.[67] EUCM has since said that the recording of any telephone conversation without the authority of the parties constitutes an interference with their 'correspondence' within the meaning of *EHR* 8, though it may in certain circumstances be justified as being necessary in a democratic society for the prevention of disorder or crime under *EHR* 8(2).[68]

§23.3 Thought, conscience, and religion

§23.3.1 TEXTS

UDHR

18. Everyone has the right to freedom of thought, conscience and religion; this right includes freedom to change his religion or belief, and freedom, either alone or in community with others and in public or private, to manifest his religion or belief in teaching, practice, worship and observance.

ADRD

III. Every person has the right freely to profess a religious faith, and to manifest and practice it both in public and in private.

ICPR

18 (1) Everyone shall have the right to freedom of thought, conscience and religion. This right shall include freedom to have or to adopt a religion or belief of his choice, and freedom, either individually or in community with others and in public or private, to manifest his religion or belief in worship, observance, practice and teaching.

(2) No one shall be subject to coercion which would impair his freedom to have or to adopt a religion or belief of his choice.

[66] (5029/71) Report: 9 March 1977; Judgment: 2 EHRR 214; see also *Malone* v. *United Kingdom* (8691/79) Decision: 13 July 1981.
[67] *Ibid.*
[68] *A, B, C and D* v. *Federal Republic of Germany* (8290/78) DR 18, 176; see also Decision of 20 May 1958, BG, Federal Republic of Germany (E/BG/Z 27, 284).

(3) Freedom to manifest one's religion or beliefs may be subject only to such limitations as are prescribed by law and are necessary to protect public safety, order, health, or morals or the fundamental rights and freedoms of others.

(4) The States Parties to the present Covenant undertake to have respect for the liberty of parents and, when applicable, legal guardians to ensure the religious and moral education of their children in conformity with their own convictions.

EHR

9 (1) Everyone has the right to freedom of thought, conscience and religion; this right includes freedom to change his religion or belief, and freedom, either alone or in community with others and in public or private, to manifest his religion or belief, in worship, teaching, practice and observance.

(2) Freedom to manifest one's religion or beliefs shall be subject only to such limitations as are prescribed by law and are necessary in a democratic society in the interests of public safety, for the protection of public order, health or morals, or for the protection of the rights and freedoms of others.

EHR P1

2. No person shall be denied the right to education. In the exercise of any functions which it assumes in relation to education and to teaching, the State shall respect the right of parents to ensure such education and teaching in conformity with their own religious and philosophical convictions.

AMR

12 (1) Everyone has the right to freedom of conscience and of religion. This includes freedom to maintain or to change one's religion or beliefs, and freedom to profess or disseminate one's religion or beliefs either individually or together with others, in public or in private.

(2) No one shall be subject to restrictions that might impair his freedom to maintain or to change his religion or beliefs.

(3) Freedom to manifest one's religion and beliefs may be subject only to the limitations prescribed by law that are necessary to protect public safety, order, health, or morals, or the rights or freedoms of others.

(4) Parents or guardians, as the case may be, have the right to provide for the religious and moral education of their children or wards that is in accord with their own convictions.

[*AFR*]

8. Freedom of conscience, the profession and free practice of religion shall be guaranteed. No one may, subject to law and order, be submitted to measures restricting the exercise of these freedoms.

§23.3.2 CROSS-REFERENCES

State obligation: Absolute and immediate under *ICPR, EHR, AMR*, and [*AFR*]: see §6.3. For the juridical status of obligations under *UDHR* and *ADRD*, see §6.2.

Signatures, ratifications, accessions, reservations, and interpretations: See Table A for the State Parties bound by these provisions on 1 January 1982, and any reservations and interpretations notified by them.

Derogation: Non-derogable in any circumstances under *ICPR, AMR*, and [*AFR*]; derogable in exceptional circumstances under *EHR*: see §11.

Non-discrimination: No discrimination of any kind is allowed in respect of these rights or freedoms: see §7 for the relevant provisions in the instruments.

Abuse: See §9 for the relevant provisions in these instruments.

Savings: See §10 for the relevant provisions in these instruments.

Restrictions and limitations: Note the specific provisions in *ICPR* 18(3), *EHR* 9(2), and *AMR* 12(3). See §8 for the general provisions in these instruments, and the principles governing all restriction and limitation clauses.

International supervision, interpretation, application, and enforcement: By HRC under *ICPR* (see §27); by EUCM and EUCT under *EHR* (see §28); by IACM and IACT under *AMR* (see §29); by [AFCM] under [*AFR*] (see §30). See also §6.6 for the obligation to provide domestic remedies under *UDHR, ADRD, ICPR, EHR, AMR*, and [*AFR*].

Subsidiary instruments: See §23.3.6.

See also: §20 in relation to the education of children; §26.2 for prohibitions of advocacy of religious hatred; §26.6 for the rights of religious minorities.

§23.3.3 COMMENT

UDHR 18, *ICPR* 18(1), and *EHR* 9(1) all declare 'the right to freedom of thought, conscience and religion'. *AMR* 12(1) follows the same formulation, but omits 'thought' (which appears instead in *AMR* 13(1): see §23.4); [*AFR* 8] confines itself here to 'conscience'.

All the instruments other than *AMR* and [*AFR*] add a right to 'manifest' one's religion or belief in practice, worship, observance, and teaching; *ADRD AMR*, and [*AFR*] a right to 'profess' it; *ADRD* and [*AFR*] to 'practise' it; and *AMR* to 'disseminate' it. All the instruments other than [*AFR*] say that these things may be done 'in public or in private', and all except *ADRD* and [*AFR*] that they may be done either alone or in community (or together) with others.[1] The principal right includes, in *UDHR* and *AMR*, a freedom to 'change' one's religion or belief, in *AMR* an additional freedom to 'maintain' it, and in *ICPR* a freedom 'to have or to adopt a religion or belief' of one's choice.

ICPR 18(2) prohibits coercion, and *AMR* 9(2) and [*AFR*] restrictions, on these freedoms.

[*AFR*] provides a general exception in the form 'subject to law and order'; the exceptions allowed by *ICPR* 18(3), *EHR* 9(2), and *AMR* 12(3) are confined to the freedom to 'manifest'; they must be 'prescribed by law'; and they must be 'necessary' (here, only *EHR* adds 'in a democratic society') for the purposes of public safety, public order, public health, public morals, or the protection of the rights and freedoms of others — which, in the case of *ICPR* only, must be 'fundamental' rights and freedoms.

ICPR 8(4), *EHR P1* 2, and *AMR* 12(4) contain additional provisions relating to the education of children: see §20.

§ 23.3.4 HISTORY

It is not unusual in the animal kingdom for members of a species to be ill-treated or persecuted because of differences from the norm in their appearance or behaviour. But *homo sapiens* appears to be unique in displaying a consistent pattern of persecuting its members for their heterodox opinions or beliefs, especially when these are systematically manifested in the form of a religion or philosophy. Few of the major human religions have not at one time or another suffered persecution, or themselves persecuted — through the authority of a State in which they have become established — the members of other religions, or heretics within their own fold. For a substantial proportion of the worst atrocities perpetrated in recorded history, the ostensible justification has been the alleged need for the dominance or maintenance of one belief system rather than another.

This is not the place to recite a catalogue of religious persecutions over the ages, let alone to describe the iniquities perpetrated either by, or against, any particular religious group. Suffice it to recall that the movement for 'freedom of belief' precedes every other in the history of the struggle for human rights and fundamental freedoms: in Europe, for example, it goes back to at least the sixteenth century, if not the Roman Empire. Traces of the religious struggles and wars accompanying the Christian Reformation still persist in the modern human rights instruments, especially in their concern with freedom of 'thought'.

§ 23.3.5 JURISPRUDENCE

Pacifism[2] as a philosophy falls within the ambit of the right to freedom of thought and conscience: it may therefore be seen as a 'belief' protected by *EHR* 9(1). But the term 'practice' as employed in *EHR* 9(1) does not cover every act which is motivated or influenced by a religion or belief. In *Arrowsmith* v. *United Kingdom*,[3] EUCM observed that while public declarations generally

---

[1] EUCM has said that these are not mutually exclusive alternatives, leaving the authorities with a choice as to which of them to grant: they only recognize that religion may be practised in either form: *Ahmad* v. *United Kingdom* (8160/78) Decision: 12 March 1981.

[2] That is, the commitment, in both theory and practice, to the philosophy of securing one's political or other objectives without resort to the threat or use of force against another human being in any circumstances, even in response to the threat or use of force.

[3] (7050/75) DR 19, 5.

proclaiming the idea of pacifism and urging the acceptance of a commitment to non-violence may be considered as a normal and recognized manifestation of pacifist belief, a pacifist does not, by distributing leaflets which do not expresss such pacifist views, manifest his belief in the sense of *EHR* 9(1).

In view of *EHR* 4(3)(*b*), *EHR* 9(1) does not impose on a State the obligations to recognize conscientious objectors. Accordingly, a State which has not recognized them is not prevented from punishing those who refuse to perform military service.[4] Alternatively, conscientious objectors may be required to perform civilian service in substitution for compulsory military service, and the State may impose sanctions on those who refuse such service.[5]

A church is an organized religious community based on identical, or at least substantially similar, views. Through the right guaranteed to its members under *EHR* 9, the church itself is protected in its right to manifest its religion, to organize and carry out worship, teaching, practice, and observance, and it is free to act out and enforce uniformity in these matters. Further, in a State church system its servants are employed for the purpose of applying and teaching a specific religion. Their individual freedom of thought, conscience, and religion is exercised at the moment they accept or refuse employment as clergymen, and their right to leave the church guarantees their freedom of religion in the event that they come to oppose its teachings. The church is therefore not obliged to provide religious freedom to its servants and members, as is the State as such for everyone within its jurisdiction. Accordingly, in *X* v. *Denmark*,[6] EUCM found that *EHR* 9(1) does not include the right of a clergyman, in his capacity of a civil servant in a State church system, to set up conditions for baptism which are contrary to the direction of the highest administrative authority within that church, that is, the church Minister. Nor is there an interference with *EHR* 9(1) where a Muslim schoolteacher is compelled to transfer from a full-time to a part-time contract if he wishes to worship at a mosque during normal school hours on Fridays.[7]

If a church is organized as a legal (as opposed to a natural) person, it is capable neither of having nor of exercising the rights mentioned in *EHR* 9(1). And the denial to its members, or the withdrawal, of student status, work permits, employment vouchers, or extensions of stay within the territory of a State does not prevent them from manifesting their religion or belief.[8]

The Supreme Court of India has held that religious practices, or performances of acts in pursuance of religious belief, are as much a part of religion as faith or belief in particular doctrines.[9] But it has been held in the Netherlands that a requirement to give prior notice to the administrative authorities before slaughtering a goat by way of worship is not a limitation on the freedom to manifest one's religion, and therefore requires no justification under *EHR* 9(2).[10]

EHR 9 does not protect the taxpayer from the use of public funds for the subvention of parties which he does not support. This freedom is therefore not infringed by an election campaign subsidy.[11]

---

[4] *X* v. *Austria* (5591/72) CD 43, 61.
[5] *X* v. *Federal Republic of Germany* (7705/76) DR 9, 196.
[6] (7374/76) DR 5, 157.
[7] *Ahmad* v. *United Kingdom, supra,* n. 1.
[8] *Church of X* v. *United Kingdom* (3798/68) CD 29, 74; nor is any particular creed or confession entitled to be protected from all forms of criticism: *Church of Scientology* v. *Sweden* (8282/78) DR 21, 109.
[9] *Ratilal Panchand Gandhi* v. *State of Bombay* AIR [1954] SC 388.
[10] Decision of 4 November 1969, Hoge Raad, Netherlands, CDNC 1, 52.
[11] *Association X, Y and Z* v. *Federal Republic of Germany* (6850/74) DR 5, 90.

The requirement for a motor-cyclist to wear a crash helmet, which obliges a Sikh to remove his turban (the continuous wearing of which is a religious requirement for him) when riding his motor-cycle, interferes with his freedom of religion, but is justified for the protection of public health.[12] So is compulsory membership of a health service, where this is required of farmers for the prevention of tuberculosis among cattle.[13] Compulsory motor insurance, to which a person may have objections of conscience, has as its purpose the safeguarding of the rights of third parties who may become victims of motor accidents, and is therefore necessary for the protection of the rights and freedoms of others.[14]

EHR 9 does not oblige a State to put at the disposal of prisoners books which they consider necessary for the exercise of their religion or for the development of their philosophy of life.[15] The retention by the prison authorities of a book which, although religious or philosophical in character, contains a chapter dedicated to the martial arts is a measure which, while limiting the prisoner's freedom of religion, may be considered necessary for the protection of the rights and freedoms of others.[16] The refusal of permission to a prisoner to grow a beard or to obtain a prayer chain, while infringing *EHR* 9(1), could be justified as being necessary for the protection of public order.[17] Nor does *EHR* 9 confer any right to a preferential status on any category of prisoners, such as a right to wear their own clothes, or to be relieved from prison work.[18]

IACM has expressed the view that the withdrawal of the juridical personality of a religious congregation constitutes a restriction on the right to religious freedom of worship,[19] as does a provision in a State's constitution saying that

political propaganda cannot be made in any way by clergy, secular persons, or ministers of any faith, invoking religious motives and basing their endorsement on the religious beliefs of the people. In the temples, furthermore, upon the celebration of acts of the faith or religious propaganda, criticism cannot be made of the laws of the State, of the government, or of public officials in particular.[20]

HRC has expressed the view that, where parents or guardians object to religious instruction for their children at school, it is not incompatible with *ICPR* 18(4) for domestic legislation to require that instruction should instead be given in the study of the history of religions and ethics, provided that this is done in a neutral and objective way and respects the convictions of parents and guardians who do not believe in any religion.[21]

§23.3.6 SUBSIDIARY INSTRUMENTS

As long ago as 1967, ECOSOC transmitted to the UNGA a draft Convention, prepared by CHR, on the Elimination of all Forms of Intolerance and Discrimination based on Religion and Belief. However, no draft has yet been adopted.

[12] *X v. United Kingdom* (7992/77) DR 14, 234.
[13] *X v. Netherlands* (1068/61) YB 5, 278.
[14] *X v. Netherlands* (2988/66) CD 23, 137. See also Decision of 22 June 1971, Hoge Raad, Netherlands, CDNC 3, 41.
[15] *X v. Austria* (1753/63) CD 16, 20.
[16] *X v. United Kingdom* (6886/75) DR 5, 100.
[17] *X v. Austria, supra.*
[18] *McFeeley et al. v. United Kingdom* (8317/78) Report: 3 EHRR 161.
[19] AR 1979/80, 118.
[20] 1 Nicaragua, 69.
[21] *Hartikainen et al. v. Finland* (R. 9/40) HRC 36, 147.

§23.4 Opinion and expression

§23.4.1 TEXTS

UDHR

19. Everyone has the right to freedom of opinion and expression; this right includes freedom to hold opinions without interference and to seek, receive and impart information and ideas through any media and regardless of frontiers.

ADRD

IV. Every person has the right to freedom of investigation, of opinion, and of the expression and dissemination of ideas, by any medium whatsoever.

ICPR

19 (1) Everyone shall have the right to hold opinions without interference.

(2) Everyone shall have the right to freedom of expression; this right shall receive freedom to seek, receive and impart information and ideas of all kinds, regardless of frontiers, either orally, in writing or in print, in the form of art, or through any other media of his choice.

(3) The exercise of the right provided for in paragraph 2 of this Article carries with it special duties and responsibilities. It may therefore be subject to certain restrictions, but these shall only be such as are provided by law and are necessary:

(*a*) For respect of the rights or reputations of others;

(*b*) For the protection of national security or of public order (*ordre public*), or of public health or morals.

EHR

10 (1) Everyone has the right to freedom of expression. This right shall include freedom to hold opinions and to receive and impart information and ideas without interference by public authority and regardless of frontiers. This Article shall not prevent States from requiring the licensing of broadcasting, television or cinema enterprises.

(2) The exercise of these freedoms, since it carries with it duties and responsibilities, may be subject to such formalities, conditions, restrictions or penalties as are prescribed by law and are necessary in a democratic society, in the interests of national security, territorial integrity or public safety, for the prevention of disorder or crime, for the protection of health or morals, for the protection of the

reputation or rights of others, for preventing the disclosure of information received in confidence, or for maintaining the authority and impartiality of the judiciary.

AMR

13 (1) Everyone shall have the right to freedom of thought and expression. This right shall include freedom to seek, receive, and impart information and ideas of all kinds, regardless of frontiers, either orally, in writing, in print, in the form of art, or through any other medium of one's choice.

(2) The exercise of the right provided for in the foregoing paragraph shall not be subject to prior censorship but shall be subject to subsequent imposition of liability, which shall be expressly established by law to the extent necessary in order to ensure:

(*a*) respect for the rights or reputations of others; or

(*b*) the protection of national security, public order, or public health or morals.

(3) The right of expression may not be restricted by indirect methods or means, such as the abuse of government or private controls over newsprint, radio broadcasting frequencies, or equipment used in the dissemination of information, or by any other means tending to impede the communication and circulation of ideas and opinions.

(4) Notwithstanding the provisions of paragraph 2 above, public entertainments may be subject by law to prior censorship for the sole purpose of regulating access to them for the moral protection of childhood and adolescence.

[*AFR*]

9 (1) Every individual shall have the right to receive information.

(2) Every individual shall have the right to express and disseminate his opinions within the law.

§ 23.4.2 CROSS-REFERENCES

State obligation: Absolute and immediate under *ICPR, EHR, AMR*, and [*AFR*]: see § 6.3. For the juridical status of obligations under *UDHR* and *ADRD*, see § 6.2.

Signatures, ratifications, accessions, reservations, and interpretations: See Table A for the State Parties bound by these provisions on 1 January 1982, and any reservations and interpretations notified by them.

Derogation: Non-derogable in any circumstances under [AFR]; derogable in exceptional circumstances under *ICPR, EHR*, and *AMR*: see § 11.

Non-discrimination: No discrimination of any kind is allowed in respect of these rights or freedoms: see §7 for the relevant provisions in the instruments.

Abuse: See §9 for the relevant provisions in these instruments.

Savings: See §10 for the relevant provisions in these instruments.

Restrictions and limitations: Note the specific provisions in *ICPR* 19(3), *EHR* 10(2), and *AMR* 13(2) and (4). See §8 for the general provisions in these instruments, and the principles governing all restriction and limitation clauses.

International supervision, interpretation, application, and enforcement: By HRC under *ICPR* (see §27); by EUCM and EUCT under *EHR* (see §28); by IACM and IACT under *AMR* (see §29); by [AFCM] under [*AFR*] (see §30). See also §6.6 for the obligation to provide domestic remedies under *UDHR*, *ADRD*, *ICPR*, *EHR*, *AMR*, and [*AFR*].

Subsidiary instruments: CC (see §23.4.6).

See also: §23.2 for the 'right of reply' provided by *AMR* 14; §26.2 for the prohibitions of propaganda for war, and of advocacy of national, racial, or religious hatred, in *ICPR* 20 and *AMR* 13(5).

§23.4.3 COMMENT

The relationship between 'opinion' and 'expression' varies somewhat between the six instruments which deal with these rights. The two Declarations speak of 'the right to freedom' of both opinion and expression, to which *ADRD* IV adds 'investigation'. *AMR* 13(1) here follows *UDHR* 19, but substitutes 'thought' for 'opinion'. *ICPR* 19(1) declares an independent right 'to hold opinions without interference'; *EHR* 10(1) too declares a right 'to hold opinions', but says that it is included in the right to freedom of expression. [*AFR* 9(2)] conflates the two, by declaring the right 'to express and disseminate his opinions'.

Beyond opinions, all the instruments other than *ADRD* and [*AFR*] protect a two-way flow of 'information and ideas' (to which *ICPR* 19(2) and *AMR* 13(1) add 'of all kinds') by declaring the right to 'seek, receive and impart' these, in all cases, 'regardless of frontiers', and in the case of *EHR* alone 'without interference by public authority'. All the instruments other than *EHR* and [*AFR*] say that this may be done through any media, *ICPR* and *AMR* adding 'of his (or one's) choice' and exemplifying the matter by the phrase 'either orally, in writing or in print [or] in the form of art'. By contrast, *ADRD* and [*AFR*] appear to contemplate only one-way flows of such material: outbound ideas in the case of the first, and inbound information in the case of the second.

All four treaties subject these rights to restrictions and limitations. In [*AFR* 9(2)], the phrase is simply 'within the law'. *ICPR* 19(3), *EHR* 10(2), and *AMR* 13(2) also require that the restrictions should be provided (or prescribed, or expressly established) by law, but only to the extent 'necessary' (*EHR* alone here adds 'in a democratic society') in support of one or more of a list of objectives. For *ICPR* and *AMR*, that list includes five items; for *EHR*, it includes no fewer than ten — the longest such list in any of the instruments (see §8.0.3). The rights and reputations of others, national security, health and morals are common to all three of these treaties. *ICPR* and *AMR* add public order, for which *EHR* substitutes the prevention of disorder or crime. *EHR* then adds territorial integrity, preventing the disclosure of information received in confidence, and maintaining the authority and impartiality of the judiciary.

ICPR and *EHR* — but not *AMR* — base the need for these restrictions and limitations on the 'duties and responsibilities' which the right to freedom of expression carries with it. *AMR* 13(2) confines the effect of such restrictions to the subsequent imposition of liability on the publisher, and expressly forbids prior censorship except (by Article 13(4)) in the case of public entertainments for the moral protection of children and adolescents.

EHR 10(1) allows States to license broadcasting, television, or cinema enterprises; *AMR* 10(3) says instead that governments or private interests may not abuse such controls to restrict the right of expression.

§ 23.4.4 HISTORY

The major battles in the Anglo-Saxon world over 'freedom of speech' began during the seventeenth century. The English Bill of Rights in 1688 provided

that the freedom of speech and debate or proceedings in Parliament ought not to be impeached or questioned in any court or place out of Parliament,

but made no similar provision for the benefit of ordinary citizens. However, the scope of the freedom was gradually expanded in a series of English judicial decisions over the next century:[1] by 1791, the first Article of the US Bill of Rights, far from protecting the freedom of speech of legislators, was more concerned to ensure that the legislators would not attempt to stifle that of the citizens:

Congress shall make no law . . . abridging the freedom of speech, or of the press.

Article 11 of the French *déclaration des droits de l'homme et du citoyen* resembles rather more closely the formulation adopted in the modern human rights treaties:

The unrestrained communication of thoughts or opinions being one of the most precious rights of man, every citizen may speak, write and publish freely, provided he be responsible for the abuse of this liberty, in the cases determined by law.

Since then, conflicts over freedom of speech between public authorities and individuals, and indeed between different private interests, have continued in many parts of the world, and indeed still continue today. Most modern constitutions contain provisions on this subject, though always with some restrictions.

§ 23.4.5 JURISPRUDENCE

Freedom of expression

Freedom of expression constitutes one of the essential foundations of a democratic society; one of the basic conditions for its progress and for the development of

[1] See, for example, *Wilkes* v. *Wood* (1763) 19 ST 1153; *Leach* v. *Money* (1765) 19 ST 1002; *Entick* v. *Carrington* (1765) 19 ST 1030; *Stockdale* v. *Hansard* (1839) 8 LJQB 294.

every one of its members. In *Handyside* v. *United Kingdom*,[2] EUCT observed that, subject to paragraph 2, *EHR* 10 applies not only to 'information' or 'ideas' that are favourably received or regarded as inoffensive or as a matter of indifference, but also to those that offend, shock, or disturb the State or any sector of the population.[3]

In *Sunday Times* v. *United Kingdom*,[4] EUCT noted that these principles applied even to the field of the administration of justice. The courts cannot operate in a vacuum. Whilst they are the forum for the settlement of disputes, this does not mean that there can be no prior discussion of disputes elsewhere, be it in specialized journals, in the general press or amongst the public at large. Indeed, the Court observed that, while the mass media must not overstep the bounds imposed in the interests of the proper administration of justice, it is incumbent on them to impart information and ideas concerning matters that come before the courts, just as in other areas of public interest. Not only do the media have the task of imparting such information and ideas: the public also has a right to receive them.

EHR 10 covers the right of expression of legal or artificial as well as of natural persons.[5] It applies to servicemen just as it does to other persons within the jurisdiction of a State.[6] But it does not accord to public officials a special right of information which is wider than that of other persons.[7]

The concept of 'expression' in *EHR* 10 concerns the expression of opinion and the receiving and imparting of information and ideas, but it does not encompass any notion of the physical expression of feelings, such as the sexual act.[8] Freedom of expression includes freedom to circulate the ideas expressed,[9] in paper-back books,[10] leaflets and circulars,[11] but not necessarily by personal business advertisements.[12] Joining a procession may be considered as an expression of opinion;[13] but not the sale or display of merchandise.[14]

EHR 10 does not guarantee that a motion tabled by a member of Parliament

---

[2] (5493/72) Report: 30 September 1975; Judgment: 1 EHRR 737. See also Decision of 30 January 1970, Tribunal de Première Instance de Bruxelles, Belgium, CDNC 1, 55; *Terminiello* v. *Chicago* 337 US 1.

[3] See also *Street* v. *New York* 394 US 576; *New York Times* v. *Sullivan* 376 US 254; *Roth* v. *United States* 354 US 476; *Bachellar* v. *Maryland* 397 US 564.

[4] (6538/74) Judgment: 2 EHRR 245.

[5] *Attorney-General of Antigua and another* v. *Antigua Times Ltd.* [1975] 3 All ER 81 (Privy Council).

[6] *Engel et al.* v. *Netherlands* (5100–2/71; 5354/72; 5370/72) Report: 19 July 1974; Judgment: 1 EHRR 647.

[7] *17 Austrian Communes and some of their Councillors* v. *Austria* (5767/72, etc.) CD 46, 118.

[8] *X* v. *United Kingdom* (7215/75) Report: DR 19, 66.

[9] *Romesh Thappar* v. *State of Madras* 37 AIR (1950) SC 124.

[10] Decision of 22 March 1960, Hoge Raad, Netherlands (NJ 1960, 707).

[11] *Mills* v. *Alabama* 384 US 214; *Talley* v. *California* 362 US 60.

[12] *Hamdad Dawakhana (Wakf) Lal Kuan, Delhi* v. *Union of India* [1960] 2 SCR 671 (Supreme Court of India).

[13] Decision of 7 November, Hoge Raad, Netherlands (NJ 1968, 266); see also the earlier Decision of 24 January 1967 of the same court (NJ 1967, 747) which held a Decree which forbade owners or tenants to write, leave, or permit advertisements on buildings to be inconsistent with Article 7 of the Constitution which guaranteed freedom of expression; and the Decision of 30 May 1967 (NJ 1968, 14) which held a regulation which made driving, walking, or standing on the public highway with advertising or publicity media subject to prior authorization from the Mayor to be contrary to the same Article; cf. *Kameshwar Prasad* v. *State of Bihar* AIR [1962] SC 1166 (Supreme Court of India).

[14] Decision of 15 April 1975, Hoge Raad, Netherlands (NJ No. 3, 1976). The plaintiff had offered oranges for sale, to be thrown at a map of South Africa.

shall be included in the agenda of Parliament against its will as expressed by a vote;[15] nor the right to vote;[16] nor a right to use a particular language;[17] nor a right to receive particular information by post within a specified time.[18] The freedom to 'impart information and ideas' cannot be taken to include a general and unfettered right for all private citizens and organizations to have access to broadcasting time on radio and television in order to forward their opinions.[19] Indeed, this freedom does not mean that anyone has the right to compel another to listen to him.[20] The guarantee of freedom of expression in *EHR* 10 does not preclude a court, confronted with the duty of arriving at an appreciation of an individual's character and personality, from taking into consideration statements made by him out of court, whether orally or in writing, which may throw light, favourable or unfavourable, on his character or personality.[21]

An alien's rights under *EHR* 10 are independent of his right to stay in the country, and do not protect the latter right.[22]

In some of its earlier decisions, EUCM expressed the view that it was an 'inherent feature' of lawful imprisonment that certain restrictions should be imposed on a prisoner's freedom to exercise his rights under *EHR* 10; for example, restrictions on correspondence,[23] purchase of books and other reading material,[24] visits from newspaper reporters,[25] receipt of radio programmes,[26] and publication.[27] In accordance with the Commission's more recent jurisprudence, these restrictions would need to be justified on one or more of the specific grounds set out in *EHR* 10(2).

Restrictions and limitations

As regards the relationship of paragraph (2) of *EHR* 10 to paragraph (1), it is clearly that of an exception to the general rule. The general rule is the protection of the freedom: the exception is its restriction. The restriction — interpreted in the light of the general rule — may not be applied in a sense such that the expression or dissemination of an opinion in a particular matter is completely suppressed: it may be restricted only in so far as this is necessary for preserving the values protected in paragraph (2) of *EHR* 10. The grounds permitting such restrictions are exhaustively enumerated in that paragraph.[28]

When an interference is alleged, the question that arises is whether or not the interference complained of was prescribed by law and was, in the circumstances, necessary in a democratic society for any of the criteria enumerated

---

[15] *X* v. *Switzerland* (7758/77) DR 9, 214.

[16] *X* v. *Netherlands* (6573/74) DR 1 87.

[17] *X* v. *Ireland* (4137/69) CD 35, 137. But see the Decision of 8 November 1966 of the Tribunal de Première Instance de Bruxelles, Belgium (see YB 9, 746): the *imposition* of the use of a specific language on industrial, commercial and financial undertakings for the drafting of their official documents is contrary to *EHR* 10(1) and 14.

[18] *X* v. *Federal Republic of Germany* (8383/78) DR 17, 227.

[19] *X* v. *United Kingdom* (4515/70) CD 38, 86.

[20] Decision of 9 July 1974, Hof Arnhem, Netherlands (see YB 18, 427).

[21] *X* v. *Sweden* (911/60) CD 7, 7.

[22] *Agee* v. *United Kingdom* (7729/76) DR 7, 164.

[23] *X* v. *Austria* (4517/70) YB 14, 548; *X* v. *Austria* (1760/63) CD 20, 1; *X* v. *Austria* (1753/63) CD 16, 20; *X* v. *United Kingdom* (5270/71) CD 46, 54.

[24] *X* v. *Federal Republic of Germany* (1860/63) CD 18, 47.

[25] *X* v. *Belgium* (3914/69) CD 34, 20.

[26] Decision of 17 July 1971, VfGH, Austria (ÖJZ 1972, 306).

[27] *X* v. *United Kingdom* (5442/72) DR 1, 41.

[28] *Handyside* v. *United Kingdom* (5493/72) Report: 30 September 1975; Judgment: 1 EHRR 737.

in *EHR* 10(2), having regard to the duties and responsibilities which the exercise of the freedom of expression under *EHR* 10 carries with it.[29] But *EHR* never puts the various organs of the State Parties under an *obligation* to limit the rights and freedoms it guarantees. In particular, in no case does *EHR* 10(2) compel a State to impose 'restrictions' or 'penalties' in the field of freedom of expression; it never prevents a State from *not* availing itself of the expedients it provides for the State (cf. the words *'may* be subject'). Indeed, *EHR* 10 certainly does not oblige a State to introduce prior censorship.[30]

EHR 10(2) contemplates primarily the conditions, restrictions and penalties to which freedom of expression is commonly subject in a democratic society as being necessary to prevent seditious, libellous, blasphemous, and obscene publications, to ensure the proper administration of justice, to protect the secrecy of confidential information, etc. It does not permit the infliction of incapacities in regard to freedom of expression, whether this is done by way of penal sanctions or preventive measures, except where the nature of the offence itself obviously necessitates such incapacities. Accordingly, a law which inflexibly takes away for life, without reference to the evolution of public morals or public order, all freedom of publication for the non-political, as well as the political, writings of a person convicted of having collaborated with the enemy during a war, goes beyond what is justifiable under *EHR* 10(2).[31]

IACM has expressed the view that a limitation on freedom of the press is justified only when order and the security of the State are truly compromised. Such a limitation may then be in effect only for a limited period of time and under certain specific circumstances, and any restrictions must be clearly established so that everyone may know precisely what is prohibited, and what is subject to censorship. There is a serious risk of infringement of *AMR* 13 where the legislation prohibits publications which 'in any way damage or compromise the economic stability of the nation', or 'harm the national defence', adding the phrase 'or other similar cases'[32]

Examples

HRC has expressed the view that *ICPR* 19 is violated where, under a country's military penal code, persons may be detained, charged, and convicted for 'subversive association' or 'assistance to subversive associations', apparently on no basis other than their political views and connections, and the government concerned has submitted no evidence to show that this was 'necessary' for any of the purposes specified in *ICPR* 19(3).[33] ICPR 19(2) is also violated where the real grounds for such persecution are that the person concerned has taken part in trade union activities,[34] or disseminated information about such activities.[35]

Between them, EUCT, EUCM, and a variety of national courts have decided that a person's freedom of expression would be interfered with by a public authority, and that the interference would therefore require justification on grounds such as those set out in *EHR* 10(2), if

[29] *Ibid.*
[30] *Ibid.*
[31] *De Becker* v. *Belgium* (214/56) Report: 21 August 1961; Judgment: 1 EHRR 43.
[32] 2 Nicaragua, 118.
[33] *Perdomo and de Lanza* v. *Uruguay* (R. 2/8) HRC 35, 111; followed in *Carballal* v. *Uruguay* (R. 8/33) HRC 36, 125 and *Petraroia* v. *Uruguay* (R. 10/44) HRC 36, 153.
[34] *Burgos* v. *Uruguay* (R. 12/52) HRC 36, 176.
[35] *Weinberger* v. *Uruguay* (R. 7/28) HRC 36, 114.

(1) he is arrested, prosecuted, or punished for having published a book, article, pamphlet, or advertisement;[36]
(2) copies of a book written by him are seized, forfeited, or destroyed;[37]
(3) an injunction is issued by a court restraining him from publishing an article,[38] or pre-censorship is imposed on a journal;[39]
(4) he is ordered to pay costs despite an acquittal on a charge arising out of the publication of a book;[40]
(5) he is restricted by law for life from editing, printing, or distributing a newspaper or other publication; and from organizing or managing any cultural, philanthropic, or sporting acitivity, or public entertainment, theatrical publication, film, or broadcast;[41]
(6) the publication of any text directly or indirectly criticizing the Government in the discharge of its duties is prohibited;[42]
(7) notices of 'left-wing organizations' are prohibited;[43]
(8) an absolute duty of secrecy is imposed on the medical profession;[44]
(9) the employees of a government department are prohibited from taking 'newspapers which are condemned by the church authorities' into the various departmental premises;[45]
(10) a law makes the right to publish newspapers subject to the deposit of $10,000 to satisfy any judgment for libel;[46]
(11) a law seeks to regulate the prices of newspapers in relation to the numbers of their pages and their sizes, and to regulate the allocation of space for advertising matter,[47] or their circulation;[48]

---

[36] *Handyside* v. *United Kingdom, supra,* n. 28. See also *Arrowsmith* v. *United Kingdom* (7050/75) Report: DR 19, 5 (necessary for the protection of national security and the prevention of disorder in the army); *X, Y and Z* v. *Belgium* (6782-4/74) DR 9, 13 (necessary for the protection of morals); *Engel et al.* v. *Netherlands* (5100/71, etc.) Judgment: 1 EHRR 647 (necessary both for the prevention of disorder and for the protection of the reputation or rights of others); *X* v. *Austria* (753/60) CD 4 (necessary for the protection of the reputation or rights of others); *X* v. *Federal Republic of Germany* (1167/61) CD 12, 70 (necessary for the protection of the morals of young persons); Decision of 12 April 1972, Hoog Militair Gerechtshof, Netherlands (MRT 1972, 338); Decision of 19 June 1970, OGH, Austria (JB 1970, 629) (necessary for the protection of morals); Decision of 18 January 1972, Hoge Raad, Netherlands (NJ 1972, 545) (necessary to prevent disorder); Decision of 30 January 1968, Hoge Raad, Netherlands (NJ 1968, 199) (necessary for the protection of public morals).
[37] *Handyside* v. *United Kingdom, supra,* n. 28.
[38] *Sunday Times* v. *United Kingdom* (6538/74) Judgment: 2 EHRR 245.
[39] *Brij Bushan* v. *State of Delhi* [1950] SCR 605 (Supreme Court of India).
[40] *Geerk* v. *Switzerland* (7640/76) DR 12, 103.
[41] *De Becker* v. *Belgium* (214/56) Report: 21 August 1961; Judgment: 1 EHRR 43.
[42] *Denmark, Norway, Sweden and Netherlands* v. *Greece* (3321-3/67; 3344/67) Report: YB 12 *bis.* But see Decision of 24 March 1961, Conseil d'Etat, Belgium, CDNC (necessary in the interests of *ordre public*).
[43] *Ibid.*
[44] Decision of 16 October 1972, VfGH Austria (JB 1972 196).
[45] *Olivier et al.* v. *Buttigieg* [1966] 2 All ER 459 (Privy Council, on appeal from the Supreme Court of Malta).
[46] *Attorney-General of Antigua and another* v. *Antigua Times Ltd.* [1975] 3 All ER 81 (Privy Council) (justified under the Constitution as being reasonably required . . . for the purpose of protecting the reputations and rights . . . of other persons. A mere right of action did not give true protection to an injured person's reputation: unless there was a reasonable prospect of his obtaining damages and costs for libel, he might be deterred from initiating proceedings.)
[47] *Sakal Papers (P) Ltd.* v. *Union of India* [1962] 3 SCR 842 (Supreme Court of India).
[48] *Bennett Coleman & Co.* v. *Union of India* [1973] 1 SCR 177 (Supreme Court of India).

(12) a law stipulates that no speech may be made in public and in the open air without police authorization;[49]
(13) disciplinary proceedings are taken by a professional body for the use of aggressive or insulting language;[50]
(14) the publication of offers of employment from abroad is prohibited without the prior authorization of the Federal Employment Office;[51]
(15) processions on public highways are prohibited without prior authorization.[52]

On the other hand, various national courts (and in one case EUCM) have said that the following do not constitute interference by a public authority with freedom of expression:

(1) the prohibition of criticism of the government 'in a malignant manner', rather than 'by means of fair argument';[53]
(2) the award of damages for defamation by a court;[54]
(3) the payment of an annual licence fee of $600 as a condition for the lawful publication of a newspaper;[55]
(4) the prohibition of the import of newsprint and printing equipment except under licence;[56]
(5) the denial to a performer of a State subsidy, or of permission to perform in schools;[57]
(6) the regulation of the use of loudspeakers at public meetings;[58]
(7) restrictions voluntarily accepted by entering on an office or into a contract of employment.[59]

An Italian court has held that the acquisition by a group of persons of entry tickets, each of which entitles the holder to vote for a song in a public poll, amounts to a fraudulent method of choosing the best song insofar as the number of tickets exceeds the number of spectators, and therefore constitutes a violation of the freedom of expression of the spectators who are no longer in a position to express their true choice.[60]

It has been decided in the Federal Republic of Germany that a person who is attacked in a newspaper article is entitled under *EHR* 10 to have his reply published in the newspaper.[61]

---

[49] Decision of 6 February 1968, Hof van Justitie, Netherlands Antilles (NJ 1969, 128).

[50] *X v. Federal Republic of Germany* (4561/70) CD 39, 58 (necessary for the protection of the reputation or rights of others).

[51] Decision of 14 February 1964, BSG, Federal Republic of Germany (NJW 1964, 1691) (necessary in the interests of public safety and the preservation of order).

[52] Decision of 30 May 1967, Hoge Raad, Netherlands (NJ 1968, 18) (necessary for the prevention of disorder).

[53] *DPP v. Obi* [1961] All NLR 186 (Supreme Court of Nigeria).

[54] *Jagan v. Burnham* (1973) 20 WIR 96 (Court of Appeal, Guyana).

[55] *Attorney-General of Antigua and another v. Antigua Times Ltd. supra*, n. 46 (Privy Council).

[56] *Hope v. New Guyana Co. Ltd. and Teekah* (Civil Appeal No. 33 of 1976, Court of Appeal, Guyana).

[57] *X v. Federal Republic of Germany* (2834/66; 4038/69) YB 13, 250.

[58] *Francis v. Chief of Police* [1973] 2 All ER 251 (Privy Council, on appeal from St. Christopher, Nevis & Anguilla).

[59] *Stewart v. Public Service Staff Relations Board* [1978] 1 FC 133 (Federal Court of Canada).

[60] Decison of 29 May 1970, Court of Appeal, Milano, Italy, CDNC 1, 56.

[61] Decision of 12 August 1955, LG Mannheim, Federal Republic of Germany (NJW 1956, 384).

'Duties and responsibilities'

In assessing the grounds specified in *EHR* 10(2) for the justification of restrictions or limitations, regard must be had to the particular situation of the person seeking to exercise the freedom of expression, and to the duties and responsibilities which are incumbent on him by reason of that situation. Thus, different standards may apply to different categories of persons, such as civil servants, soldiers, policemen, journalists, politicians, etc., whose duties and responsibilities must be seen in relation to their functions in society. In *Engel et al.* v. *Netherlands*,[62] EUCM was concerned with members of the armed forces. One of their duties and responsibilities is to maintain discipline and order within the armed forces, and it was against that background that the interference with their exercise of the right to freedom of expression therefore fell to be examined.

In *Handyside* v. *United Kingdom*, the case concerned the publisher of a book intended to be read by schoolchildren. EUCM applied the same principle,[63] and EUCT stressed that the scope of the 'duties and responsibilities' depends on the situation of the person who exercises his freedom of expression, and the technical means he uses.[64]

The 'duties and responsibilities' referred to in *EHR* 10(2) find an even stronger expression in *EHR* 17[65] (see § 9).

Licensing of broadcasting, television, or cinema enterprises

EHR 10(1) does not state whether these enterprises shall be organized as private or public corporations, or whether they may be granted a monopoly in the field of this particular activity, or whether competing enterprises must exist at the same time. In *X* v. *Sweden*,[66] the applicant argued that the fact that a licensing system was provided for in *EHR* 10 did not mean that States had a right to establish a monopoly system by licensing only one enterprise in the country concerned. EUCM observed that the use of the plural term 'enterprises' was grammatically consistent with the previous references in the text to 'States' in the plural, as opposed to a 'State' in the singular. Having regard to the practice in the different Member States of the CE, the Commission concluded that the term 'licensing' cannot be understood to exclude a public television monopoly.

The notion of licensing implies that, in granting a licence, the State may subject radio and television broadcasting to certain regulations. In *X* v. *United Kingdom*,[67] EUCM considered that, having regard to the practice in different Member States of the CE, *EHR* 10(1) should be interpreted as permitting the State, in granting a licence, to exclude certain specified categories of advertising, for example political advertising. However, the system of licensing must be prescribed by law, and the criteria set out in *EHR* 10(2) must be observed in the granting of licences.[68]

---

[62] (5100-2/71; 5354/72; 5370/72) Report: 19 July 1974.
[63] (5493/72) Report: 30 September 1975.
[64] Judgment: 1 EHRR 737.
[65] *Glimmerveen and Hagenbeek* v. *Netherlands* (8349/78; 8406/78) DR 18, 187.
[66] (3071/67) CD 26, 71. See also *X* v. *United Kingdom* (4750/71) CD 40, 29; Royal Decree No. 39 of 14 November 1975, Netherlands (YB 20, 771); Royal Decree No. 18 of 27 December 1976, Netherlands (YB 20, 787).
[67] (4515/70) CD 38, 86.
[68] Decision of 25 May 1964, Gerecht in eerste aanlag, Netherlands (NJ 1965, 412).

Data about television or radio programmes constitute 'information', as opposed to 'opinions' or 'ideas', within the meaning of *EHR* 10. The freedom to impart such information is only granted to the person or body who produces, provides, or organizes the data, as the author, originator or otherwise the intellectual owner of the information concerned.[69]

In the area of 'information' — that is to say, in the area of facts and news as opposed to 'ideas' and 'opinions' — the protection which *EHR* 10 seeks to secure concerns the free flow of such information to the public in general.[70]

§23.4.6 SUBSIDIARY INSTRUMENTS

The Convention on the International Right of Correction (*CC*) provides that, where a State Party contends that a news dispatch (as there defined) 'capable of injuring its relations with other States or its national prestige or dignity', transmitted from one country to another and published or disseminated abroad, is 'false or distorted', it may submit its version of the facts in the form of a communiqué to the State Parties within whose territories the dispatch has been published or disseminated.[71] The communiqué must be no longer than is necessary, and must be without comment or expression of opinion.[72]

The State Parties receiving such a communiqué must then, within not more than five clear days, release it through their own customary press channels.[73] If they do not, the originating State Party may send it to the Secretary-General of the UN, who must release it through his own information channels within ten clear days, together with any comments he has received from any State Party that has failed to release it.[74]

§23.5 Culture, arts, and science

§23.5.1 TEXTS

UDHR

27 (1) Everyone has the right freely to participate in the cultural life of the community, to enjoy the arts and to share in scientific advancement and its benefits.

(2) Everyone has the right to the protection of the moral and material interests resulting from any scientific, literary or artistic production of which he is the author.

---

[69] *De Geillustreerde Pers N.V.* v. *Netherlands* (5178/71) Report: DR 8, 5. Such programme data are not simple facts, or news in the proper sense of the word. They are a compilation of facts and they are news in the sense that they provide an orientation guide for television viewers or radio listeners before or during a particular week with a view to assisting them in the selection of forthcoming programmes. The characteristic feature of such information is that it can only be produced and provided by the broadcasting organizations charged with the production of the programmes themselves. See also Decision of 25 June 1965, Hoge Raad, Netherlands (NJ 1966, 115).
[70] *Ibid.*
[71] *CC* II(1).
[72] *CC* II(2).
[73] *CC* III(1).
[74] *CC* IV(2).

ADRD

XIII. Every person has the right to take part in the cultural life of the community, to enjoy the arts, and to participate in the benefits that result from intellectual progress, especially discoveries.

He likewise has the right to the protection of his moral and material interests as regards his inventions or any literary, scientific or artistic works of which he is the author.

ICES

15 (1) The States Parties to the present Covenant recognize the right of everyone:
(*a*) To take part in cultural life;
(*b*) To enjoy the benefits of scientific progress and its applications;
(*c*) To benefit from the protection of the moral and material interests resulting from any scientific, literary or artistic production of which he is the author.

(2) The steps to be taken by the States Parties to the present Covenant to achieve the full realization of this right shall include those necessary for the conservation, the development and the diffusion of science and culture.

(3) The States Parties to the present Covenant undertake to respect the freedom indispensable for scientific research and creative activity.

(4) The States Parties to the present Covenant recognize the benefits to be derived from the encouragement and development of international contacts and co-operation in the scientific and cultural fields.

[*AFR*]

17 (2) Every individual may freely take part in the cultural life of his community.

§23.5.2 CROSS-REFERENCES

State obligation: Absolute and immediate under [*AFR*]: see §6.3. Qualified and progressive under *ICES*: see §6.4. For the juridical status of obligations under *UDHR* and *ADRD*, see § 6.2.

Signatures, ratifications, accessions, reservations, and interpretations: See Table A for the State Parties bound by these provisions on 1 January 1982, and any reservations and interpretations notified by them.

Derogation: Non-derogable in any circumstances: see §11.

Non-discrimination: No discrimination of any kind is allowed in respect of these rights or freedoms: see §7 for the relevant provisions in the instruments.

Abuse: See §9 for the relevant provisions in these instruments.

Savings: See §10 for the relevant provisions in these instruments.

Restrictions and limitations: See §8 for the general provisions in these instruments.

International supervision, interpretation, application, and enforcement: By [AFCM] under [AFR] (see §30); supervision only by ECOSOC under *ICES* (see §31). See also §6.6 for the obligation to provide domestic remedies under *UDHR* and *ADRD*.

Subsidiary instruments: See the UNESCO Recommendations on the Status of Scientific Researchers of 1974, and the World Federation of Scientific Workers' Declaration of the Rights of Scientific Workers of 1969.

See also: §26.6 for the rights of minorities to enjoy their own culture.

§23.5.3 COMMENT

UDHR 27(1), the first paragraph of *ADRD* XIII, paragraphs (*a*) and (*b*) of *ICES* 15(1), and [*AFR* 17(2)] are concerned with the rights of the consumers of cultural, artistic, and scientific creativity; *UDHR* 27(2), the second paragraph of *ADRD* XIII, and paragraph (*c*) of *ICES* 15(1) with the rights of its producers — that is, in the latter case, with the 'moral and material' benefits of the production for its authors.

Only *ICES* 15(3) specifically mentions 'the freedom indispensable for scientific research and creative activity'.

§23.5.4 JURISPRUDENCE

None of these provisions has yet been interpreted or applied by any of the competent independent international institutions.

§24. JOINT ACTIVITIES

§24.1 Assembly

§24.1.1 Texts

UDHR

20 (1) Everyone has the right to freedom of peaceful assembly . . .

ADRD

XXI. Every person has the right to assemble peaceably with others in a formal public meeting or an informal gathering, in connection with matters of common interest of any nature.

ICPR

21. The right of peaceful assembly shall be recognized. No restrictions may be placed on the exercise of this right other than those imposed in conformity with the law and which are necessary in a democratic society in the interests of national security or public safety, public order (*ordre public*), the protection of public health or morals or the protection of the rights and freedoms of others.

EHR

11 (1) Everyone has the right to freedom of peaceful assembly . . .

(2) No restrictions shall be placed on the exercise of these rights other than such as are prescribed by law and are necessary in a democratic society in the interests of national security or public safety, for the prevention of disorder or crime, for the protection of health or morals or for the protection of the rights and freedoms of others. This Article shall not prevent the imposition of lawful restrictions on the exercise of these rights by members of the armed forces, of the police or of the administration of the State.

AMR

15. The right of peaceful assembly, without arms, is recognized. No restrictions may be placed on the exercise of this right other than those imposed in conformity with the law and necessary in a democratic society in the interest of national security, public safety or public order, or to protect public health or morals or the rights or freedoms of others.

[*AFR*]

11. Every individual shall have the right to assemble freely with others. The exercise of this right shall be subject only to necessary restrictions provided for by law, in particular those enacted in the interest of national security, the safety, health, ethics and rights and freedoms of others.

§24.1.2 CROSS-REFERENCES

State obligation: Absolute and immediate under *ICPR, EHR, AMR*, and [*AFR*]: see §6.3. For the juridical status of obligations under *UDHR* and *ADRD*, see §6.2.

Signatures, ratifications, accessions, reservations, and interpretations: See Table A for the State Parties bound by these provisions on 1 January 1982, and any reservations and interpretations notified by them.

Derogation: Non-derogable in any circumstances under [*AFR*]; derogable in exceptional circumstances under *ICPR, EHR*, ar.d *AMR*: see §11.

Non-discrimination: No discrimination of any kind is allowed in respect of these rights or freedoms: see §7 for the relevant provisions in the instruments.

Abuse: See §9 for the relevant provisions in these instruments.

Savings: See §10 for the relevant provisions in these instruments.

Restrictions and limitations: Note the specific provisions in *ICPR* 21, *EHR* 11(2), *AMR* 15, and [*AFR* 11]. See §8 for the general provisions in these instruments, and the principles governing all restriction and limitation clauses.

International supervision, interpretation, application and enforcement: By HRC under *ICPR* (see §27); by EUCM and EUCT under *EHR* (see §28); by IACM and IACT under *AMR* (see §29); by [AFCM] under [*AFR*] (see §30). See also §6.6 for the obligation to provide domestic remedies under *UDHR, ADRD, ICPR, EHR*, AMR, and [*AFR*].

§24.1.3 COMMENT

Only [*AFR* 11] omits the otherwise universal qualification of 'peaceful' from the right of assembly. *AMR* 15 adds the additional qualification 'without arms'; only *ADRD* says that the assembly may be a formal public meeting or an informal gathering, and refers to 'matters of common interest of any nature'.

All the four treaties allow restrictions, which must be 'imposed in conformity with', 'prescribed by' or 'provided for by' law. In all cases, these must be 'necessary', and (except for [*AFR*]) they must be necessary 'in a democratic society'. The catalogue of grounds justifying such a restriction has in common, for all the four treaties, the four items of national security, public safety, health, and the rights and freedoms of others. To this, [*AFR*] adds 'ethics' and the others add 'morals'; *ICPR* and *AMR* add 'public order', and *EHR* instead adds 'the prevention of disorder or crime'. However, the introduction of the catalogue in [*AFR*] by the words 'in particular' suggests that in the case of that instrument the list may not be intended to be exhaustive.

EHR alone contains an additional exception for members of the armed forces, the police, and public administrators.

§24.1.4 JURISPRUDENCE

EUCM has said that, like the right to freedom of expression, the right to peaceful assembly is a fundamental right, and one of the foundations of a democratic society. It covers both private and public meetings. The latter may require authorizations, in order to ensure that they remain peaceful. That accords with *EHR* 11(1), but complete bans on all demonstrations do not, unless they can be specifically justified under *EHR* 11(2).[1]

The Supreme Court of India has held that the State can only make regulations *in aid of* the right of assembly of all citizens, and can therefore impose reasonable restrictions to safeguard their rights, and to preserve public order. But that does not entitle the State to prohibit *all* meetings and processions.[2]

In *Denmark, Norway, Sweden and Netherlands* v. *Greece,*[3] EUCM observed that freedom of assembly is a major part of the political and social life of any country. It is an essential part of the activities of political parties and of the conduct of elections. In that case, the Commission found that in Greece:

(1) meetings for political purposes were prohibited if they were to be held in public, and could take place in private only with the permission of the competent police authority;
(2) indoor meetings for the purpose of a lecture required the authorization of the competent military authority.

EUCM considered that none of these restrictions was consistent with *EHR* 11. The Commission observed that to subject indoor meetings to the discretion of the police, and lectures to that of the military authorities, without any clear prescription in law as to how that discretion was to be exercised and without further control, was to create a police state which was the antithesis of a 'democratic society'.

IACM has expressed the view that the right of assembly was violated where, following a birthday banquet at which the guest of honour allegedly improvised a speech 'tinged with political implications', over a hundred of the guests were arrested and interrogated, seven were dismissed from their official posts, and four had their State pensions reduced by a third for one year by Presidential decree.[4]

EHR 11 has also been cited in a judgment of the English Court of Appeal in the context of the use of the highway for public meetings.[5]

---

[1] *Rassemblement Jurassien and Unité Jurassienne* v. *Switzerland* (8191/78) DR 17, 93. But a general ban on all public processions in a capital city for two months may be justified if there is a real danger of their resulting in disorder which cannot be prevented by less stringent measures: *Christians against Racism and Fascism* v. *United Kingdom* (8440/78) DR 21, 138.

[2] *Himat Lal K. Shah* v. *Commissioner of Police* [1973] 1 SCR 227.

[3] (3321–3/67; 3344/67) Report: YB 12 *bis*.

[4] AR 1979/80, 129–30.

[5] *Hubbard* v. *Pitt* [1945] 1 All ER 1056.

§24.2 Association

§24.2.1 TEXTS

UDHR

20 (1) Everyone has the right to freedom of . . . association.

(2) No one may be compelled to belong to an association.

ADRD

XXII. Every person has the right to associate with others to promote, exercise and protect his legitimate interests of a political, economic, religious, social, cultural, professional, labor union or other nature.

ICPR

22 (1) Everyone shall have the right to freedom of association with others, . . .

(2) No restrictions may be placed on the exercise of this right other than those which are prescribed by law and which are necessary in a democratic society in the interests of national security or public safety, public order (*ordre public*), the protection of public health or morals or the protection of the rights and freedoms of others. This Article shall not prevent the imposition of lawful restrictions on members of the armed forces and of the police in their exercise of this right.

EHR

11 (1) Everyone has the right . . . to freedom of association with others, . . .

(2) No restrictions shall be placed on the exercise of these rights other than such as are prescribed by law and are necessary in a democratic society in the interests of national security or public safety, for the prevention of disorder or crime, for the protection of health or morals or for the protection of the rights and freedoms of others. This Article shall not prevent the imposition of lawful restrictions on the exercise of these rights by members of the armed forces, of the police or of the administration of the State.

AMR

16 (1) Everyone has the right to associate freely for ideological, religious, political, economic, labor, social, cultural, sports, or other purposes.

(2) The exercise of this right shall be subject only to such restrictions established by law as may be necessary in a democratic society, in the interest of national security, public safety or public order, or

to protect public health or morals or the rights and freedoms of others.

(3) The provisions of this article do not bar the imposition of legal restrictions, including even deprivation of the exercise of the right of association, on members of the armed forces and the police.

[*AFR*]

10 (1) Every individual shall have the right to free association provided that he abides by the law.

(2) Subject to the obligation of solidarity provided for in Article 29 no one may be compelled to join an association.

§24.2.2 CROSS-REFERENCES

State obligation: Absolute and immediate under *ICPR, EHR, AMR*, and [*AFR*]: see §6.3. For the juridical status of obligations under *UDHR* and *ADRD*, see §6.2.

Signatures, ratifications, accessions, reservations, and interpretations: See Table A for the State Parties bound by these provisions on 1 January 1982, and any reservations and interpretations notified by them.

Derogation: Non-derogable in any circumstances under [*AFR*]; derogable in exceptional circumstances under *ICPR, EHR*, and *AMR*: see §11.

Non-discrimination: No discrimination of any kind is allowed in respect of these rights or freedoms: see §7 for the relevant provisions in the instruments.

Abuse: See §9 for the relevant provisions in these instruments.

Savings: See §10 for the relevant provisions in these instruments.

Restrictions and limitations: Note the specific provisions in *ICPR* 22(2), *EHR* 11(2), *AMR* 16(2), and [*AFR* 10(1)]. See §8 for the general provisions in these instruments, and the principles governing all restriction and limitation clauses.

International supervision, interpretation, application, and enforcement: By HRC under *ICPR* (see §27); by EUCM and EUCT under *EHR* (see §28); by IACM and IACT under *AMR* (see §29); by [AFCM] under [*AFR*] (see §30). See also §6.6 for the obligation to provide domestic remedies under *UDHR, ADRD, ICPR, EHR, AMR*, and [*AFR*].

See also: §24.3 for the right to form and join trade unions.

§24.2. 3 COMMENT

The right to 'freedom of association' (or, in the case of [*AFR*], to 'associate freely') is recognized by all these instruments. Only *ADRD* XXII and *AMR* 16(1) specify the purposes of the association: common to both instruments are political, economic, religious, social, cultural, labour, and 'other' purposes; to these, *ADRD* adds 'professional', and *AMR* 'ideological' and 'sports'. Only

UDHR 20(2) and [*AFR* 10(2)] explicitly add a correlative right not to be 'compelled to belong to (or join) an association' — subject, in the case of [*AFR*], to the 'obligation of solidarity' in [*AFR* 29]: see §25.

[*AFR* 10(1)] allows a general exception in the form 'provided that he abides by the law'. The exceptions in *ICPR* 22(2), *EHR* 11(2), and *AMR* 16(2), by contrast, are specific. They must be 'prescribed' or 'established' by law, and must be 'necessary in a democratic society' in the interests of national security or public safety, or the protection of public health, public morals, or the rights and freedoms of others. *ICPR* and *AMR* also include public order, *EHR* instead the prevention of disorder or crime.

The three treaties other than [*AFR*] also allow the imposition of lawful restrictions on members of the armed forces or of the police, to which *EHR* alone adds public administrators.

Trade unions are a special case of freedom of association, and are considered separately in §24.3.

§24.2.4 JURISPRUDENCE

The term 'association' presupposes a voluntary grouping for a common goal. The relationship between workers employed by the same employer cannot be understood as an association, because it depends only on the contractual relationship between employee and employer.[6] Nor can the establishment of a *'studentkår'* as part of a university, as a formal way of organizing student participation in its administration, since *EHR* 11(1) offers its protection only in respect of private associations, not in respect of public institutions.[7]

In *Le Compte, Van Leuven and de Meyere* v. *Belgium*,[8] EUCM said that a medical organization created by the State, whose object was to ensure the observance of medical ethics and maintain the honour, discretion, probity, and dignity of its members, was not an 'association' within the meaning of *EHR* 11(1) because of its legal nature and its specifically public functions. Freedom of association does not prevent a citizen from being obliged to belong to public law institutions, such as a province or a district. Nor does it prevent persons practising a profession, the exericse of which affects the general interest, from being for that reason incorporated, by or under the law, in a strictly regulated professional organization, in order both to manage some of their common interests and, in the general interest, to protect the health of the community. This is so even if, in order to organize this body, use has been made of some of the technical forms of an association. Confirming this, EUCT held in the same case[9] that it was not a violation of *EHR* 11 for the State to require all its medical practitioners to be registered with, and subject to the authority, of such an organization, provided they remained free to form and join other associations of their choice to protect their professional interests.

Freedom of association is a general capacity for citizens to join, without interference by the State, in associations in order to attain various ends. However, *EHR* 11 does not guarantee a right to the successful attainment of such ends.[10]

---

[6] *James, Young and Webster* v. *United Kingdom* (7601/76; 7806/77) Report: 14 December 1979.

[7] *Association X* v. *Sweden* (6094/73) DR 9, 5.

[8] (6878/75; 7238/75) Report: 14 December 1979.

[9] Judgment: 23 June 1981.

[10] *Association X* v. *Sweden* (6094/73) *supra*; cf. *AIBE Association* v. *NI Tribunal* AIR [1962] SC 171 (Supreme Court of India).

Freedom of association does not by itself entail a freedom to bargain collectively or a freedom to strike,[11] nor does it include the right of a prisoner to 'associate' with other prisoners.[12]

EHR 11 cannot be interpreted as prohibiting a State from deporting an alien on the ground that he has been in contact with foreign intelligence officers even if, under *EHR* 11, he were entitled to have contact with such persons whilst in the jurisdiction of the State concerned.[13] Nor can it be contended that disciplinary punishment for writing articles found to undermine military discipline could hamper the activities of a servicemen's association so as to amount to an interference with its freedom of association.[14]

IACM has expressed the view that restrictions on the formation of political parties that have a 'tie or connection' with institutions abroad, such tie or connection being inferred from the mere existence in other countries of organizations with a similar 'ideology, principles or name', are irreconcilable with *ADRD* XXII.[15] IACM has also expressed the view that the freedom of association was violated where, following a birthday banquet at which the guest of honour allegedly improvised a speech 'tinged with political implications', over a hundred of the guests were arrested and interrogated, seven were dismissed from their official posts, and four had their State pensions reduced by a third for one year by Presidential decree.[16]

§24.3 Trade unions

§24.3.1 TEXTS

UDHR

23 (4) Everyone has the right to form and to join trade unions for the protection of his interests.

ICPR

22 (1) Everyone shall have the right to freedom of association with others, including the right to form and join trade unions for the protection of his interests.

(2) No restrictions may be placed on the exercise of this right other than those which are prescribed by law and which are necessary in a democratic society in the interests of national security or public safety, public order (*ordre public*), the protection of public health or morals or the protection of the rights and freedoms of others. This Article shall not prevent the imposition of lawful restrictions on members of the armed forces and of the police in their exercise of this right.

---

[11] *Collymore* v. *Attorney-General* [1969] 2 All ER 1207 (Privy Council, on appeal from Trinidad and Tobago).
[12] *McFeeley et al.* v. *United Kingdom* (8317/78) Report: 3 EHRR 161.
[13] *Agee* v. *United Kingdom* (7729/76) DR 7, 164.
[14] *Engel et al.* v. *Netherlands* (5100–2/71; 5354/72; 5370/72) Judgment: 1 EHRR 647.
[15] AR 1979/80, 123.
[16] AR 1979/80, 129–30.

(3) Nothing in this article shall authorize States Parties to the International Labour Organization Convention of 1948 concerning Freedom of Association and Protection of the Right to Organize to take legislative measures which would prejudice, or to apply the law in such a manner as to prejudice, the guarantees provided for in that Convention.

ICES

8 (1) The States Parties to the present Covenant undertake to ensure:

(*a*) The right of everyone to form trade unions and join the trade union of his choice, subject only to the rules of the organization concerned, for the promotion and protection of his economic and social interests. No restrictions may be placed on the exercise of this right other than those prescribed by law and which are necessary in a democratic society in the interests of national security or public order or for the protection of the rights and freedoms of others;

(*b*) The right of trade unions to establish national federations or confederations and the right of the latter to form or join international trade union organizations;

(*c*) The right of trade unions to function freely subject to no limitations other than those prescribed by law and which are necessary to a democratic society in the interests of national security or public order or for the protection of the rights and freedoms of others;

(*d*) The right to strike, provided that it is exercised in conformity with the laws of the particular country.

(2) This article shall not prevent the imposition of lawful restrictions on the exercise of these rights by members of the armed forces or of the police or of the administration of the State.

(3) Nothing in this article shall authorize States Parties to the International Labour Organization Convention of 1948 concerning Freedom of Association and Protection of the Right to Organize to take legislative measures which would prejudice, or apply the law in such a manner as would prejudice, the guarantees provided for in that Convention.

EHR

11 (1) Everyone has the right . . . to freedom of association with others, including the right to form and to join trade unions for the protection of his interests.

(2) No restrictions shall be placed on the exercise of these rights other than such as are prescribed by law and are necessary in a

democratic society in the interests of national security or public safety, for the prevention of disorder or crime, for the protection of health or morals or for the protection of the rights and freedoms of others. This Article shall not prevent the imposition of lawful restrictions on the exercise of these rights by members of the armed forces, of the police or of the administration of the State.

ESC

I, (5) All workers and employers have the right to freedom of association in national or international organizations for the protection of their economic and social interests.

(6) All workers and employers have the right to bargain collectively.

II, 5. With a view to ensuring or promoting the freedom of workers and employers to form local, national or international organizations for the protection of their economic and social interests and to join those organizations, the Contracting Parties undertake that national law shall not be such as to impair, nor shall it be so applied as to impair, this freedom. The extent to which the guarantees provided for in this Article shall apply to the police shall be determined by national laws or regulations. The principle governing the application to the members of the armed forces of these guarantees and the extent to which they shall apply to persons in this category shall equally be determined by national laws or regulations.

II, 6. With a view to ensuring the effective exercise of the right to bargain collectively, the Contracting Parties undertake:
(1) to promote joint consultation between workers and employers;
(2) to promote, where necessary and appropriate, machinery for voluntary negotiations between employers or employers' organizations and workers' organizations, with a view to the regulation of terms and conditions of employment by means of collective agreements;
(3) to promote the establishment and use of appropriate machinery for conciliation and voluntary arbitration for the settlement of labour disputes;
and recognize:
(4) the right of workers and employers to collective action in cases of conflicts of interest, including the right to strike, subject to obligations that might arise out of collective agreements previously entered into.

(*App.*: It is understood that each Contracting Party may, insofar as it is concerned, regulate the exercise of the right to strike by law, provided that any further restriction that this might place on the right can be justified under the terms of Article 31.)

§24.3.2 CROSS-REFERENCES

State obligation: Absolute and immediate under *ICPR* and *EHR*: see §6.3. Qualified and progressive under *ICES* and *ESC*: see §6.4. For the juridical status of obligations under *UDHR*, see §6.2.

Signatures, ratifications, accessions, reservations, and interpretations: See Table A for the State Parties bound by these provisions on 1 January 1982, and any reservations and interpretations notified by them.

Derogation: Non-derogable in any circumstances under *ICES*; derogable in exceptional circumstances under *ICPR, EHR,* and *ESC*: see §11.

Non-discrimination: No discrimination of any kind is allowed in respect of these rights or freedoms: see §7 for the relevant provisions in the instruments.

Abuse: See §9 for the relevant provisions in these instruments.

Savings: Note the specific provisions in *ICPR* 22(3) and *ICES* 8(3) saving *ILO 87*, and see §10 for the general provisions in these instruments.

Restrictions and limitations: Note the specific provisions in *ICPR* 22(2), *ICES* 8(1)(*a*) and (*c*) and 8(2), and *EHR* 11(2). See §8 for the general provisions in these instruments (including *ESC* 31), and the principles governing all restriction and limitation clauses.

International supervision, interpretation, application and enforcement: By HRC under *ICPR* (see §27); by EUCM and EUCT under *EHR* (see §28); supervision only by ECOSOC under *ICES* (see §31); by EUCE under *ESC* (see §32). See also §6.6 for the obligation to provide domestic remedies under *UDHR, ICPR,* and *EHR*.

Subsidiary instruments: ILO 87, ILO 98, and *ILO 135* (see §24.3.5).

See also: §24.2 for freedom of association generally.

§24.3.3 COMMENT

Four separate rights are protected by these provisions.

The right to form and to join trade unions

This right is specifically declared in *UDHR* 23(4), *ICPR* 22(1), *ICES* 8(1)(*a*), *EHR* 11(1), and *ESC* 5. *ADRD, AMR,* and [*AFR*] do not mention it in terms, but they do protect a general right of association (see §24.2), and this presumably includes the right to form and join trade unions as a special case — the more so as *ICPR* 22(1) and *EHR* 11(1) expressly treat the latter right as included in the former. *UDHR* 20(2) and [*AFR* 10(2)] both state that 'no one may be compelled to belong to (or join) an association' — subject, in the case of [*AFR*], to the 'obligation of solidarity' in [*AFR* 29]: see §25. None of the other treaties expressly repeats this provision, though *ICES* alone qualifies the trade unions concerned as those 'of his choice'. Since the right to form and join trade unions is expressed in favour of 'everyone', it presumably extends to employers as well as workers, to the self-employed, and to workers in co-operatives and collectives as well as to those working under a contract of employment.

The four treaties that expressly recognize the right to form and join trade unions all contain specific exceptions to this right. All these must be 'prescribed by law', and be 'necessary in a democratic society' for one of a defined list of purposes. Common to that list in all the four treaties are the interests of national security, and the protection of the rights and freedoms of others. To that common core, *ICPR* 20(2), *EHR* 11(2), and *ESC* 31 add the protection of health or morals, *ICPR* and *EHR* the interest of public safety, *ICPR* and *ICES* the interest of public order, *EHR* instead the prevention of disorder or crime, and *ESC* the public interest.

Both the Covenants expressly save *ILO 87*: see § 24.3.5.

The rights of trade unions

Only *ICES* 8(1)(*b*) and (*c*) deal with these, establishing a right for trade unions to associate with each other, and to 'function freely' — again subject to the same limitations as *ICES* allows for the right to form and join trade unions.

The right to bargain collectively

Only *ESC* 6 expressly protects this right.

The right to strike

This is specifically protected in *ICES* 8(1)(*d*), 'provided that it is exercised in conformity with the laws of the particular country'. It is also included in *ESC* II, 6(4) as part of the right to bargain collectively and is there made subject to the exceptions in *ESC* 31.

The position of public servants

ESC 5 envisages that national laws and regulations may deal differently with the right to form and join trade unions for members of the police and the armed forces. The other three treaties all permit 'the imposition of lawful restrictions' on these two categories of persons in the exercise of their trade unions rights (including, in the case of *ICES*, the right to strike); *ICES* 8(2) and *EHR* 11(2) add a further category of 'members of the administration of the State'.

§ 24.3.4 JURISPRUDENCE

The right to form and to join trade unions

In a case where a trade union leader was abducted, detained, tortured, charged, and convicted by a military court of unspecified 'subversive activities', HRC has expressed the view that *ICPR* 22(1) was violated in conjunction with *ICPR* 19(1) and (2).[17]

EHR 11(1) presents trade union freedom as one form, or a special aspect, of freedom of association. In interpreting its meaning and scope, EUCT has

---

[17] *Burgos* v. *Uruguay* (R. 12/52) HRC 36, 176.

stated that regard should be had to the contents and interpretation of the two principal ILO Conventions in this field: *ILO 87* and *ILO 98* (see §24.3.5). Both these Conventions reflect widely accepted labour law standards which have been elaborated and clarified by the competent organs of the ILO, and therefore enable *EHR* to keep pace with the rules of international labour law and ensure that its concepts remain in harmony with the concepts used in international labour law and practice.[18]

EHR 11(1) uses the terms 'freedom' ('*liberté*') and 'right' ('*droit*') in both authentic texts. Since the 'right' to form and join trade unions is expressly guaranteed as included in the 'right . . . to freedom of association', EUCM has observed that no legal distinction can be made between a freedom and a right in this context. Therefore, the right to freedom of association is the over-all concept, with the right to form and to join trade unions as an element in that concept, rather than as a separate and distinct right.[19]

EHR 11 does not secure any particular treatment of trade unions or their members by the State, such as a right to be consulted by it,[20] or a right that the State should conclude any given collective agreement with it.[21] EUCT has held that such rights are not indispensable for the effective enjoyment of trade union freedom, and do not constitute an element necessarily inherent in the right which is guaranteed by *EHR* 11(1).[22]

However, the words 'for the protection of his interests', clearly denoting purpose, show that *EHR* 11 safeguards the freedom to protect the occupational interests of trade union members by trade union action, the conduct and development of which the State must both permit and make possible. It follows that the members of a trade union have a right, in order to protect their interests, that the trade union should be heard, but not that the State authorities should actively support an individual member in a particular case.[23] *EHR* 11 leaves each State a free choice of the means to be used towards this end. While consultations, collective bargaining, the conclusion of collective agreements or the grant of a right to strike are some of those means, there are others. What *EHR* 11 requires is that under national law trade unions should be enabled, in conditions not at variance with *EHR* 11, to strive for the protection of their members' interests. In *Svenska Lokmannaforbundet* v. *Sweden*,[24] EUCT held that the fact that the National Collective Bargaining Office had in principle refused to enter into collective agreements with a particular union, because of a general policy of limiting the number of organizations with which collective agreements were to be concluded, was not on its own incompatible with trade union freedom; nor, as EUCT held in *National Union of Belgian*

---

[18] *National Union of Belgian Police* v. *Belgium* (4464/70) Judgment: 1 EHRR 578: *Svenska Lokmannaforbundet* v. *Sweden* (5614/72) Judgment: 1 EHRR 67. For the ILO procedures, see § 35.

[19] *James, Young and Webster* v. *United Kingdom* (7601/76; 7806/77) Report: 14 December 1979.

[20] *National Union of Belgian Police* v. *Belgium, supra.*

[21] *Svenska Lokmannaforbundet* v. *Sweden, supra*; *Schmidt and Dahlström* v. *Sweden* (5589/72) Judgment: 6 February 1976. In *National Union of Belgian Police* v. *Belgium* (Report: 27 May 1974) EUCM explained that the right to bargain collectively is a freedom and a capacity, rather than a right against employers, or the State as an employer. Cf. *Banton et al.* v. *Alcoa Minerals of Jamaica et al.* (1971) 17 WIR 275 (Supreme Court of Jamaica).

[22] *Ibid.* See also *Trade Union X* v. *Belgium* (7361/76) DR 14, 40.

[23] *Gallogly* v. *United Kingdom* (7990/77), DR.

[24] *Supra*, n. 18.

Police v. *Belgium*,[25] was the fact that the Minister of the Interior did not consult a particular union on such matters as staff structures, or conditions, or recruitment and promotion, again because of a general policy of limiting the number of organizations to be consulted.

EHR 11 is binding upon the State as an employer, whether its relations with its employees are governed by public or by private law.[26] It also obliges the State to protect individuals through appropriate measures taken against some forms of interference by other individuals, groups or organizations. While these themselves may not, under *EHR*, be held responsible for any such acts which are in breach of the Convention, the State may, in certain circumstances, be responsible for them.[27] In *X* v. *Ireland*,[28] EUCM expressed the view that threats of dismissal or other actions intended to bring about the relinquishment by an employee of his office as a shop steward could in principle raise an issue under *EHR* 11, as such interference could, in certain circumstances, seriously restrict or impede the lawful exercise of the freedom of association in relation to trade unions; in particular, the right of workers' and employers' organizations to elect their representatives in full freedom and to organize their administration.

The standards which *EHR* 11 might provide for the conduct of the State as an employer seem to be identical in substance with those which the State might be obliged under *EHR* 11 to impose upon private employers. In *Schmidt and Dahlström* v. *Sweden*,[29] EUCM observed that if some action taken by the State as an employer violates *EHR* 11, then the same action taken by a private employer should also be considered a breach for which the State may be held responsible under *EHR* if it fails to secure, by legislation or otherwise, conformity of private employers' actions with the standards concerned.

EHR 11 envisages associations which may be created by private initiative. A system of unions set up by the State itself, without allowing private activity in that field, would not be compatible with *EHR* 11.[30]

EHR 11 uses the plural 'unions', indicating that a trade union monopoly is excluded. There must be room for more than one union. A person must therefore be free to choose which of the existing unions he wants to join if he does not intend to form a new one. The words 'for the protection of his interests' also imply that a worker must be able to choose the union which in his opinion best protects his interests — and, if he considers that none of the existing trade unions does so effectively, to associate with other workers in order to form a new one. In *James, Young and Webster* v. *United Kingdom*,[32] where the applicants were dismissed because they refused to join specific unions following a 'closed shop' agreement between those unions and the employer concluded after the applicants had taken up their work, EUCM found (without

---

[25] *Supra*, n. 18.

[26] *Schmidt and Dahlström* v. *Sweden, supra*, n. 21; *Svenska Lokmannaforbundet* v. *Sweden, supra*, n. 18.

[27] *National Union of Belgian Police* v. *Belgium, supra*, n. 18. Throughout the drafting of *EHR* 11, reference was made to the discussions in the UN on the preparation of *ICPR* and *ICES*. During the UN debates a proposal was made that the right of association, including trade union rights, should be protected only against 'governmental interference'. But this proposal was rejected, since it was generally considered that the individual should be protected against all kinds of interference in the exercise of this right: *Collected Edition of the travaux préparatoires* 2, 230–5; *Annotation on draft Covenants, prepared by the Secretary-General*, Doc. A/2929, 155–9 and 160–5.

[28] (4125/69) CD 37, 42.

[29] (5589/72) Report: 17 July 1974.

[30] *James, Young and Webster* v. *United Kingdom, supra*, n. 19.

[31] *Ibid.*

expressing any opinion on the system of 'closed shops' in general) that there was an interference in respect of each applicant's right to form or join a trade union for the protection of his interests in accordance with his personal convictions or wishes.

In the same case,[32] EUCT upheld that view, holding that although not every compulsion to join a particular trade union necessarily violated *EHR* 11, compulsion amounting to a threat of dismissal involving loss of livelihood, especially for those who had been engaged before the agreement came into force, strikes at the very substance of the freedom guaranteed by *EHR* 11. Such a freedom cannot be enjoyed if in reality it is either non-existent, or so reduced as to be of no practical value. Moreover, *EHR* 11 serves also to protect the freedoms of personal opinion guaranteed by *EHR* 9 and 10, and cannot therefore be used to compel someone to join an association contrary to his convictions.

In its reports to ECOSOC (see §31), the ILO's Committee of Experts on the Application of Conventions and Recommendations has given some indication of the matters which may be relevant in considering how far a State Party has made progress in achieving the observance of the provisions of *ICES* 8 in this respect.

These include questions whether an administrative authority may refuse, without appeal to the courts, to register an occupational association on any ground (including the allegation that its rules contain provisions contrary to the national constitution, or to national laws), or can deprive union leaders of their office, or can dissolve the association, or can require the association to deal with its assets in some particular manner;[33] whether a constitutional provision which assigns a leading or guiding role to a particular political party can be compatible with the right of workers to organize their activities and formulate their programmes as they choose;[34] whether a prohibition imposed on workers' associations from participating in party politics or political activities could be used to prohibit trade unions from taking a public stand on questions of economic and social policy affecting their members;[35] whether trade union activity is confined to a single group of organizations recognized by law, or whether members have the right to establish organizations of their choosing, both at the basic as well as the federation and confederation levels;[36] whether members of collective farms are able, if they so wish, to establish trade unions which can operate effectively to represent, further, and defend their interests;[37] whether a minimum number of workers is required in a bargaining unit before a union can be formed, or a minimum number of affiliated local unions before a federation can be formed;[38] whether the managing committee or the membership of the union must consist exclusively of employees of the undertaking concerned;[39] whether trade union rights discriminate between members of different races, or different nationalities;[40] whether a federation can cover more than one industry;[41] whether domestic law allows public servants to form trade

[32] *Ibid.*, Judgment: 13 August 1981.
[33] 1978, 47; 1979, 36; 1979, 37; 1979, 44; 1979, 112; 1980, 29.
[34] 1979, 93; 1979, 103; 1980, 9.
[35] 1978, 19; 1979, 44.
[36] 1978, 25; 1979, 57; 1979, 87; 1979, 93; 1979, 103.
[37] 1978, 30; 1979, 57; 1979, 93; 1980, 9.
[38] 1978, 47; 1979, 44; 1980, 29.
[39] 1978, 19; 1978 25; 1978, 41; 1979, 44.
[40] 1980, 29.
[41] 1978, 47.

unions;[42] whether there are restrictions on the freedom of election and the
holding of trade union office, and in particular whether former trade union
officers may be re-elected;[43] whether federations and confederations may
carry out trade union functions, and whether they may group more than one
industry;[44] and whether the managers of enterprises have the right to establish
separate trade unions from those of the workers.[45]

Freedom to organize

Under the supervision procedure for *ESC* (see §32), EUCE has provided the
following interpretations of Article 5 of that Charter:

The Article imposes two obligations, one negative and the other positive.
The first requires the absence, in the municipal law of each State Party, of
any legislation or regulation, or any administrative practice, which impairs
the freedom of employers or workers to form or join their respective organizations. The second obliges each State Party to take adequate legislative or
other measures to guarantee the exercise of the right to organize, and in particular to protect workers' organizations from any interference on the part
of employers.[46] Apart from restrictions in respect of members of the police
and the armed forces, the Article guarantees the freedom to organize to all
classes of employers and workers, including public servants.[47] A State Party may
be permitted to limit the freedom of organization of the members of the police,
but it is not justified in depriving them of all the guarantees which the Article
provides. But a State Party may limit in any way — and even suppress entirely
— the freedom to organize of members of the armed forces.[48] Although the
Article does not rule on the admissibility of union security clauses or practices,
any form of compulsory unionism imposed by law must be considered as incompatible with it.[49] Any restriction prohibiting civil servants from membership
of trade unions other than those composed exclusively of civil servants could
not be regarded as compatible with this obligation; this also applies to similar
restrictions on the freedom of civil servants' trade union organizations to be
members of federations or confederations of their choice. However, all workers
and all trade union organizations should be free to decide to which trade union,
or professional or technical association, they wish to belong.[50]

Restrictions under which foreign workers cannot become eligible for administrative or managerial functions in a trade union until they have worked in the
country for five years, and even then cannot make up more than one third of
such managers and administrators, are not compatible with this provision.[51]

The principle of the compulsory registration of trade unions is not by itself
incompatible with this Article, so long as the applicants have adequate administrative and jurisdictional protection against abuse of the power to refuse to
register a trade union.[52] By itself, an obligation on trade unions to obtain a
negotiating licence need not be incompatible with the Article;[53] but if, in order
to obtain such a licence, a trade union has to have at least 500 members and has
to deposit a sum ranging between £5,000 and £15,000, this is not compatible
with the Article.[54] Authorization to create a trade union empowered to exercise
the right of collective bargaining must not require a minimum number of

---

[42] 1979, 36; 1979, 51; 1979, 112   [43] 1979, 37.   [44] 1979, 37; 1979, 112.
[45] 1979, 87.   [46] I, 31.   [47] *Ibid.*
[48] *Ibid.*   [49] *Ibid.*   [50] II, 184.
[51] VI, 30.   [52] II, 184.   [53] II, 22.
[54] III, 31.

members, nor the deposit of an excessively large sum of money;[55] at most, any payment demanded should cover only minimal administrative costs.[56] The right to organize is not satisfied if a trade union needs to be recognized by a Minister, or if its members can only include the members of the staff of a single firm, and the freedom to organize at an inter-professional level is completely excluded.[57]

The requirements of the Article are not satisfied if members of the police can only take part in joint bodies: there must be proper workers' associations.[58] It is not a compliance if such personnel are forbidden to form their organizations or to join organizations of their own choosing, but are compelled to become members of an organization established by or under the statute or regulation itself.[59] Where the bodies in question are not even 'staff associations', since they consist only of certain representatives elected by the police, who otherwise have no right to form a union nor to affiliate to existing unions, the requirements of the Article are not satisfied.[60]

The right to function freely

In its reports to ECOSOC (see §31), the ILO's Committee of Experts on the Application of Conventions and Recommendations has indicated that one of the matters which may be relevant in considering how far a State Party has made progress in achieving the observance of the provisions of *ICES* 8(1)(c) is whether a provision of domestic law which prohibits trade unions in general terms from engaging in 'political activities' may in practice restrict the right of trade unions to function without interference.[61]

The right to bargain collectively

Under the supervision procedure for *ESC* (see §32), EUCE has provided the following interpretations of the first three paragraphs of Article 6 of that Charter:

Paragraph 1 refers to consultation on the basis of equal representation within joint committees established at national, regional, and local levels, within firms and various sectors of the economy, as well as the civil service, in order to enable employers and workers to consult one another on questions of common interest.[62] Joint consultations at national level are not enough: they must be provided for also at regional and local level, and not be confined to certain undertakings, certain sectors of the economy, or a limited number of questions.[63] They must not be confined to employees in the private sector, but must extend also to public officials subject to regulations, though with the modifications obviously necessary in respect of persons bound not by contractual conditions, but by regulations laid down by the public authorities. Here, the consultation machinery should extend to the drafting and implementation of the regulations concerned.[64] Both sides of industry should have an equal say in the consultations, but there is no objection to government representatives taking part, or acting as chairmen.[65]

Paragraph 2. The obligation to 'promote' machinery for voluntary negotiations presupposes the guarantee of a complete freedom to organize.[66] The obligation is not only one to recognize, in legislation, that employers and

---

[55] III, 30.   [56] IV, 39.   [57] IV, 40–41.   [58] I, 180.
[59] II, 22.   [60] *Ibid.*   [61] 1979, 13; 1979, 37. [62] V, 41.
[63] II, 25.   [64] III, 33.   [65] V, 41.   [66] IV, 46.

workers may settle their mutual relations by means of collective agreements; the State Party must also actively promote the conclusion of such agreements if their spontaneous development is not satisfactory, and to ensure that each side is prepared to bargain collectively with the other.[67]

Paragraph 3. The machinery envisaged in this provision may be established by legislation, collective agreements, or industrial practice, and its object may be the settlement of any kind of labour dispute. However, where conciliation machinery established on the basis of collective agreements is sufficiently efficacious, the government concerned need not in addition establish arbitration procedures, or promote their use.[68]

The right to strike

In its reports to ECOSOC (see § 31), the ILO's Committee of Experts on the Application of Conventions and Recommendations has given some indication of matters which may be relevant in considering how far a State Party has made progress in achieving the observance of the provisions of *ICES* 8 in this respect.

These include questions whether the right to strike can be generally suspended or otherwise prohibited;[69] whether compulsory arbitration procedures directly or indirectly prohibit strikes after an award has been given;[70] whether the right to strike in 'vital' industries is limited to essential services in the strict sense of the term;[71] and whether works councils have the exclusive right to represent workers in proceedings with regard to the settlement of disputes and strikes, or whether trade unions, federations, and confederations also have rights in these areas.[72]

Under the supervision procedure for *ESC* (see § 32), EUCE has provided the following interpretations of *ESC* II, 6(4):

This provision relates to both strikes and lock-outs, even though the latter are not explicitly mentioned in the paragraph: the lock-out is the principal, if not the only, form of collective action which employers can take in defence of their interests.[71] The right to collective action under this provision arises only in cases of conficts of *interest*, not in cases of conflicts of *right*, such as disputes concerning the existence, validity, or interpretation of a collective agreement, or its violation.[74] If restrictions are imposed by a collective agreement on recourse to collective action, even in cases of conflicts of interest, these are compatible with the provision.[75] The same applies to a 'cooling-off' period prescribed by legislation, for periods of negotiation or conciliation, or arbitration proceedings, between employers and workers: such a provision does not impose a real restriction on the right to collective action, since it merely regulates its exercise.[76] But a law which forbids any strike not called or recognized by a trade union is not compatible with this provision, which recognizes the right of 'workers' — and not merely of their trade unions — to collective action.[77]

Whether legislation denying the right to strike to persons employed in essential public services is, by virtue of Article 31, compatible with the Charter

---

[67] I, 35.   [68] I, 37.   [69] 1979, 37; 1980, 29.
[70] 1978, 19; 1978, 47; 1979, 112; 1980, 15.
[71] 1978, 47; 1979, 44; 1980, 15; 1980, 22.   [72] 1978, 19.
[73] I, 38, followed by BAG, Federal Republic of Germany, in two Decisions of 10 June 1980 (1 AZR 168/79 and 1 AZR 822/79); VI, 39; 40.
[74] I, 38.   [75] *Ibid.*   [76] *Ibid.*   [77] VI, 39–40.

depends on the extent to which the life of the community is dependent on the services involved. The same consideration applies to legislation for the compulsory settlement of conflicts of interest which are likely to expose the national economy to serious danger.[78] Article 31 permits restrictions on the right to strike of certain categories of public servants, including members of the police and armed forces, judges, and senior civil servants. But it does not extend to a denial of the right to strike to public servants as a whole.[79]

The provision is not violated by the application of legal provisions or principles making individual members of trade unions or employers' associations criminally or civilly liable in the event of their organization resorting to illegal collective action.[80] A rule according to which a strike terminates contracts of employment is, in principle, not compatible with the provisions of this paragraph. But matters may be different if, in practice, those participating in a strike are, after its termination, fully reinstated and if their previously acquired rights — for example, as regards pensions, holidays and seniority — are not impaired.[81]

A rule of municipal law under which workers only have the right to strike if the union to which they belong has first acquired a 'negotiating licence' from a public authority, and the grant of that licence is in the discretion of the authority and not subject to judicial review, is incompatible with the provisions of this paragraph.[82] So is the refusal to recognize the right to strike for paid employees in non-profit-making activities.[83] The provision is likewise violated if all strikes whose aim is not the conclusion of new collective agreements are illegal.[84]

On the other hand, the paragraph does not extend to political strikes: it is designed only to protect the right to bargain collectively, and such strikes are quite outside the purview of collective bargaining. Likewise, a ban on strikes that are contrary to the public interest or morals is permissible, provided it falls within the terms of Article 31.[85] Nor is the submission of a strike declaration to a secret ballot of the workers concerned incompatible with this provision, since the vote does not prevent the expression of the free collective will of the interested parties.[86]

§24.3.5 SUBSIDIARY INSTRUMENTS

The State Parties to the ILO Convention concerning Freedom of Association and Protection of the Right to Organise (*ILO 87*) undertake to give effect to a number of provisions.

Workers and employers, without distinction whatsoever, shall have the right to establish and, subject only to the rules of the organization concerned, to join organizations of their own choosing without previous authorization.[87] (Such organizations mean organizations 'for furthering and defending the interests of workers or of employers'.[88])

Those organizations shall have the right to draw up their constitutions and rules, to elect their representatives in full freedom, to organize their administration and activities and to formulate their programmes,[89] and public authorities

---

[78] I, 38.
[79] VI, 38; 39.
[80] I, 38.
[81] *Ibid.*
[82] I, 183.
[83] *Ibid.*
[84] I, 184.
[85] II, 27.
[86] II, 187.
[87] *ILO 87* 2.
[88] *ILO 87* 10.
[89] *ILO 87* 3(1).

shall not restrict this right or impede its lawful exercise.[90] Nor shall administrative authorities have the power to dissolve or suspend such organizations.[91] The organizations shall have the right to federate and confederate, and affiliate with international organizations.[92] The workers and employers, and their organizations, shall respect the law of the land,[93] but that law shall not impair the guarantees of the Convention.[94] However, the extent to which those guarantees shall apply to the armed forces and the police 'shall be determined by national laws or regulations'.[95] The State Parties will also 'take all necessary and appropriate measures to ensure that workers and employers may exercise freely the right to organize.'[96]

The ILO Convention concerning the Application of the Principles of the Right to Organise and to Bargain Collectively (*ILO 98*) provides that workers shall enjoy adequate protection against acts of anti-union discrimination in respect of their employment.[97] Employment should not be conditional on the worker not joining, or leaving, a trade union, nor should workers be dismissed or prejudiced for union membership or activities.[98]

Workers' and employers' organizations shall enjoy adequate protection against any acts of interference by each other, or each others' agents or members, in their establishment, functioning, or administration:[99] domination or financial or other support by employers of workers' organizations is such an act of interference.[100] There should be 'measures appropriate to national conditions' to encourage and promote negotiating machinery, and the regulation of terms and conditions of employment by means of collective agreements, between employers' and workers' organizations.[101] Again, the extent to which these guarantees shall apply to the armed forces and the police 'shall be determined by national laws or regulations',[102] and the Convention does not apply to 'public servants engaged in the administration of the State'.[103]

The ILO Convention concerning Protection and Facilities to be Afforded to Workers' Representatives in the Undertaking (*ILO 135*) provides that workers' representatives (that is, representatives designated by trade unions or elected by the workers themselves[104]) in an undertaking shall be protected against dismissal or other prejudicial acts based on their status or activities, 'insofar as they act in conformity with existing laws or collective agreements or other jointly agreed arrangements'.[105] The representatives should be given appropriate facilities in the undertaking in order that they can carry out their functions promptly and efficiently,[106] provided that the granting of such facilities does not impair the efficient operation of the undertaking.[107]

---

[90] *ILO 87* 3(2).
[91] *ILO 87* 4.
[92] *ILO 87* 5.
[93] *ILO 87* 8(1).
[94] *ILO 87* 8(2).
[95] *ILO 87* 9.
[96] *ILO 87* 11.
[97] *ILO 98* 1(1).
[98] *ILO 98* 1(2).
[99] *ILO 98* 2(1).
[100] *ILO 98* 2(2).
[101] *ILO 98* 4.
[102] *ILO 98* 5(1).
[103] *ILO 98* 6.
[104] *ILO 135* 3.
[105] *ILO 135* 1.
[106] *ILO 135* 2(1).
[107] *ILO 135* 2(3).

§25. POLITICS AND DEMOCRACY

§25.0.1 Texts

UDHR

21 (1) Everyone has the right to take part in the government of his country, directly or through freely chosen representatives.

(2) Everyone has the right of equal access to public service in his country.

(3) The will of the people shall be the basis of the authority of government; this will shall be expressed in periodic and genuine elections which shall be by universal and equal suffrage and shall be held by secret vote or by equivalent free voting procedures.

ADRD

XX. Every person having legal capacity is entitled to participate in the government of his country, directly or through his representatives, and to take part in popular elections, which shall be by secret ballot, and shall be honest, periodic and free.

XXIV. Every person has the right to submit respectful petitions to any competent authority, for reasons of either general or private interest, and the right to obtain a prompt decision thereon.

XXXII. It is the duty of every person to vote in the popular elections of the country of which he is a national, when he is legally capable of doing so.

XXXIV. It is likewise his duty to hold any public office to which he may be elected by popular vote in the state of which he is a national.

XXXVIII. It is the duty of every person to refrain from taking part in political activities that, according to law, are reserved exclusively to the citizens of the state in which he is an alien.

ICPR

25. Every citizen shall have the right and the opportunity, without any of the distinctions mentioned in Article 2 and without unreasonable restrictions:

(a) To take part in the conduct of public affairs, directly or through freely chosen representatives;

(*b*) To vote and to be elected at genuine periodic elections which shall be by universal and equal suffrage and shall be held by secret ballot, guaranteeing the free expression of the will of the electors;

(*c*) To have access, on general terms of equality, to public service in his country.

EHR P1

3. The High Contracting Parties undertake to hold free elections at reasonable intervals by secret ballot, under conditions which will ensure the free expression of the opinion of the people in the choice of the legislature.

EHR

16. Nothing in Articles 10, 11, and 14 shall be regarded as preventing the High Contracting Parties from imposing restrictions on the political activity of aliens.

AMR

23 (1) Every citizen shall enjoy the following rights and opportunities:

(*a*) to take part in the conduct of public affairs, directly or through freely chosen representatives;

(*b*) to vote and to be elected in genuine periodic elections, which shall be by universal and equal suffrage and by secret ballot that guarantees the free expression of the will of the voters; and

(*c*) to have access, under general conditions of equality, to the public service of his country.

(2) The law may regulate the exercise of the rights and opportunities referred to in the preceding paragraph only on the basis of age, nationality, residence, language, education, civil and mental capacity, or sentencing by a competent court in criminal proceedings.

[*AFR*]

13 (1) Every citizen shall have the right to freely participate in the government of his country, either directly or through freely chosen representatives in accordance with the provisions of the law.

(2) Every citizen shall have the right of equal access to the public service of his country.

27 (1) Every individual shall have duties towards . . . society, the State and other legally recognized communities and the international community.

29. The individual shall also have the duty:

(2) To serve his national community by placing his physical and intellectual abilities at its service;
(3) Not to compromise the security of the State whose national or resident he is;
(4) To preserve and strengthen social and national solidarity, particularly when the latter is threatened;
(5) To preserve and strengthen the national independence and the territorial integrity of his country and to contribute to its defence in accordance with the law;

(7) To preserve and strengthen positive African cultural values in his relations with other members of the society, in the spirit of tolerance, dialogue and consultation and, in general, to contribute to the promotion of the moral well being of society;
(8) To contribute to the best of his abilities, at all times and at all levels, to the promotion and achievement of African unity.

§25.0.2 CROSS-REFERENCES

State obligation: Absolute and immediate under *ICPR, EHR, AMR*, and [*AFR*]: see §6.3. For the juridical status of obligations under *UDHR* and *ADRD*, see §6.2.

Signatures, ratifications, accessions, reservations, and interpretations: See Table A for the State Parties bound by these provisions on 1 January 1982, and any reservations and interpretations notified by them.

Derogation: Non-derogable in any circumstances under *AMR* and [*AFR*]; derogable in exceptional circumstances under *ICPR* and *EHR*: see §11.

Non-discrimination: No discrimination of any kind is allowed in respect of these rights: see §7 for the relevant provisions in the instruments.

Abuse: See §9 for the relevant provisions in these instruments.

Savings: See §10 for the relevant provisions in these instruments.

Restrictions and limitations: Note the specific provisions in *EHR* 16 and *AMR* 23(2). See §8 for the general provisions in these instruments, and the principles governing all restriction and limitation clauses.

International supervision, interpretation, application, and enforcement: By HRC under *ICPR* (see §27); by EUCM and EUCT under *EHR* (see §28); by IACM and IACT under *AMR* (see §29); by [*AFCM*] under [*AFR*] (see §30). See also §6.6 for the obligation to provide domestic remedies under *UDHR, ADRD, ICPR, EHR, AMR*, and [*AFR*].

Subsidiary instruments; CW_2 (see §25.0.5).

§ 25.0.3 COMMENT

Several distinct but connected rights are protected by these provisions.

The right to take part in government

This is protected by *UDHR* 21(1), *ADRD* XX (for those of 'legal capacity'), and [*AFR* 13(1)]; *ICPR* 25(*a*) and *AMR* 23(1) (*a*) refer instead to a right to take part in 'the conduct of public affairs'. The right is confined to citizens, explicitly in *ICPR* and *AMR*, and implicitly in the other instruments by their references to the government of 'his country'. *EHR* contains no equivalent provision.

The right to democratic government

All the instruments refer to 'representatives', 'freely chosen' except for *ADRD* XX. The 'will' (or, in the case of *EHR P1* 3, the 'opinion') of the people is to be expressed — in all cases except [*AFR*] — in elections. Of the remaining instruments, *UDHR* 21(3), *ADRD* XX, *ICPR* 25(*b*), and *AMR* 23(1)(*b*) require the elections to be 'periodic' and *EHR P1* to be held 'at reasonable intervals'; under *EHR P1* they must be 'free'; under *ICPR* and *AMR* 'genuine'; and under *ADRD* 'popular' and 'honest' as well as 'free'. All the instruments — again apart from [*AFR*] — require secret ballots (or, in the case of *UDHR*, 'equivalent free voting procedures'), and — except for *ADRD* and *EHR P1* — 'universal and equal suffrage'.

The right to vote, and to stand for election

Only *ICPR* 25(*b*) and *AMR* 23(1)(*b*) expressly declare this right. Where it exists, it is again confined to citizens — expressly in the case of *ICPR* and *AMR*, and by the operation of the specific exclusions in the case of *ADRD* XXXVIII and *EHR* 16.

The right to equal access to public service

This is protected in all the instruments except *ADRD* and *EHR*.

The right of petition

This is unique to *ADRD* XXIV,[1] which requires petitions to be 'respectful', declares the right to extend to either general or private interests, and includes a right to 'obtain a prompt decision' on such petitions.

Political duties

ADRD XXXII and XXXIV respectively declare duties to exercise the right to vote in popular elections, and to hold elected offices. [*AFR* 29] adds a whole catalogue of political duties, which it describes in [*AFR* 10(2)] (see § 24.2.1) as 'the obligation of solidarity' (see also § 26).

Restrictions

Apart from the restriction, already mentioned, of some of the relevant rights to citizens of the countries concerned, only *AMR* 23(2) expressly allows restrictions

---

[1] Early drafts of *UDHR* also contained a right of petition, but this was deleted before the Declaration was adopted.

for political rights on the additional grounds of age, residence, language, education, civil and mental capacity, or criminal convictions.[2]

§25.0.4 JURISPRUDENCE

'Free expression of the opinion of the people'

Although the wording of *EHR Pl* 3 seems to provide only for an institutional guarantee of free elections, EUCM has said that it implies a representative legislature,[3] as well as a recognition of the principle of universal suffrage and, in that context, individual rights — namely the right to vote and the right to stand for election to the legislature. However, this right is neither absolute nor without limitations, but subject to such restrictions imposed by each State as are not arbitrary and do not interfere with the free expression of the people's opinion. Among the conditions commonly imposed on the possession or exercise of a right to vote in parliamentary elections are citizenship, residence, and age.[4]

In *X* v. *Netherlands*,[5] EUCM upheld a law which deprived persons convicted of 'uncitizenlike conduct' during the Second World War of their right to vote for life, since the purpose of that law was to prevent persons who had grossly misused their right to participate in public life in wartime from misusing their political rights in the future. Similarly, the prevention from voting of convicted prisoners serving their sentence does not affect the free expression of the opinion of the people.[6] Nor is *EHR Pl* 3 available for those who wish to participate in elections for a purpose incompatible with *EHR* 17 — that is, to destroy the rights and freedoms set forth in *EHR*.[7]

In *X* v. *United Kingdom*,[8] EUCM considered that the requirement whereby a citizen must be resident in a constituency before he can be registered as an elector did not amount to an infringement of the principles laid down in *EHR Pl* 3. The Commission observed that the reason justifying the residence requirements are: first, the assumption that a non-resident citizen is less directly or continuously interested in, and has less day-to-day knowledge of, its problems; secondly, the impracticability for parliamentary candidates to present the different electoral issues to citizens abroad so as to secure a free expression of opinion; thirdly, the need to prevent electoral fraud, the danger of which is increased in uncontrolled postal votes; and finally, the link between the right of representation in the parliamentary vote and the obligation to pay taxes, not always imposed on those in voluntary and continuous residence abroad.

In *W, X, Y and Z* v. *Belgium*,[9] EUCM observed that the minimum age (25)

---

[2] Although there is no mention of restrictions on the grounds of residence, age or criminal convictions in *EHR Pl* 3, EUCM has upheld such restrictions as being consistent with that provision: see nn. 4, 5, 6, and 8, *infra*.

[3] *Denmark, Norway, Sweden and Netherlands* v. *Greece* (3321–3/67; 3344/67) Report: 5 November 1969.

[4] *X* v. *United Kingdom* (7566/76) DR 9, 121. See also *W, X, Y and Z* v. *Belgium* (6745–6/74) DR 2, 110; *X* v. *Belgium* (8701/79), DR 18, 250.

[5] (6573/74) DR 1, 87; cf. *X* v. *Belgium, supra*.

[6] *X* v. *Federal Republic of Germany* (2728/66) CD 25, 38; *X* v. *Federal Republic of Germany* (4984/71) CD 43, 28.

[7] *Glimmerveen and Hagenbeek* v. *Netherlands* (8348/78; 8406/78) DR 18, 187.

[8] (7566/76) DR 9, 121. See also *X and Y* v. *United Kingdom* (5302/71) CD 44, 29.

[9] *Supra*, n. 4.

required for those wishing to stand for election to the House of Representatives cannot be regarded as an unreasonable or arbitrary condition, or one likely to interfere with the free expression of the opinion of the people in the choice of the legislature. As for the minimum age required for candidates to the Senate (40), the Commission noted that under a bicameral system the condition affects only one part of the legislature; those aged under 40 are not prevented from entering the legislature since they may be elected to the House of Representatives which has the same powers as the Senate, and exercises them jointly with the latter. Moreover, in a bicameral system it is not arbitrary to arrange things so that one House is composed of those who by virtue of their age have acquired greater political experience.

A law which requires an electoral list to be signed by at least three members of the regional legislature or to be supported by at least 200 signatures of other persons, and which must be officially certified, does not infringe *EHR P1* 3.[10] In *Association X, Y and Z* v. *Federal Republic of Germany*,[11] EUCM examined the validity of an election campaign subsidy, paid to political parties which had taken part in the election and obtained a certain minimum percentage of votes, as compensation for the costs of the election campaign at the rate of DM 3.50 per vote obtained. The Commission noted that the purpose of the subsidy was to make the parties more independent of sources of money which might unduly influence their political actions. Whether the subsidy is paid at all, and what amount is paid to any particular party, depends on its success in the election, and therefore reflects the real importance of the party concerned. The Commission concluded that neither the subsidy as such, nor the way in which it is allotted to the various parties, can be said to be a condition which fails to ensure the free expression of the opinion of the people.

The Italian Supreme Court has held that a regulation governing election campaigns which imposes penalties for putting up posters otherwise than on the hoardings provided for the purpose by the competent authorities accords with *EHR P1* 3, since it guarantees equality of treatment in the campaign to the different candidates and political groups.[12]

In *X* v. *United Kingdom*,[13] the applicant, a member of the Liberal Party, complained that he was deprived of his right to a just and fair representation of his opinion in the House of Commons by virtue of the 'first past the post' electoral system which existed in the United Kingdom, and contended that only an electoral system which contained at least an element of proportional representation could ensure conformity with *EHR P1* 3. EUCM explained that the words 'free expression of the opinion of the people' primarily signify that the elections cannot be held under any form of pressure in the choice of one or more candidates, and that in this choice the elector must not be unduly induced to vote for one party or another. Furthermore, the word 'choice' signifies that the different political parties must be assured a reasonable opportunity to present their candidates at elections. But *EHR P1* 3 may not be interpreted as imposing a particular kind of electoral system which would guarantee that

---

[10] *X* v. *Austria* (7008/75) DR 6, 120.

[11] (6850/74) DR 5, 90.

[12] Decision of 12 October 1972, Corte Suprema di Cassazione, Italy, CDNC 4, 41.

[13] (7140/75) DR 7, 95. EUCM also noted that, at the time of the signature of *EHR*, some States possessed a simple majority system of elections, while others utilized systems of proportional representation. Both these systems of election may therefore be considered as part of the common heritage of political traditions to which reference is made in the Preamble to *EHR*. See also *Liberal Party et al.* v. *United Kingdom* (8765/79) DR 21, 211.

the total number of votes cast for each candidate or group of candidates must necessarily always be reflected in the composition of the legislative assembly.

'Legislature' in *EHR P1* 3 must be interpreted in the light of the institutions established by the constitutions of the Member States of the CE: for instance, Article 26 of the Belgian Constitution provides that 'legislative power shall be exercised jointly by the King, the House of Representatives and the Senate'. Neither regional councils in Belgium,[14] nor local authorities in Northern Ireland[15], are 'legislatures' within the meaning of this term. A referendum on EEC membership held in the United Kingdom was not an election for the choice of a legislature: it was purely consultative, and there was no legal obligation to organize it.[16] Nor does *EHR P1* 3 impose on States an obligation to consult the population before the conclusion of an international treaty. This question is governed exclusively by the internal law of the State in question.[17]

The right 'to take part in the conduct of public affairs'

HRC has expressed the view that *ICPR* 25 is violated by a national decree which prohibits, for a term of 15 years, the engagement 'in any of the activities of a political nature authorised by the Constitution of the Republic' by persons who were

(1) candidates for elective office at certain elections on the list of Marxist or pro-Marxist political parties or groups which were declared illegal by decrees made some time after those elections;
(2) candidates for elective office at those elections on the lists of political organizations which were 'electorally associated' with those parties or groups, 'under the same coincidental or joint slogan or subslogan';
(3) 'tried for crimes against the nation';
(4) 'tried for offences against the public administration committed during the exercise of their political functions'.[18]

Even in a situation of emergency, the Committee could not see why, to restore peace and order, it should be necessary to deprive all the candidates of some political groups at some past elections of all future political rights for a period as long as 15 years, regardless of whether they had sought to promote their political opinions by peaceful means or by using or advocating violence.[19] *ICPR* 25 only prohibits 'unreasonable restrictions', but *ICPR* 2(1) and 26 require that no one may be subjected to such sanctions merely because of his or her political opinion.[20] Furthermore, the principle of proportionality requires that a measure as harsh as the deprivation of all political rights for a period of 15 years be specifically justified.[21]

IACM has expressed the view that the 'right to participate in government' under *ADRD* XX is seriously limited where the participation of the armed

[14] *W, X, Y and Z v. Belgium* (6745–6/74) DR 2, 110.
[15] *X v. United Kingdom* (5155/71) DR 6, 13.
[16] *X v. United Kingdom* (7096/75) DR 3, 165.
[17] *X v. Federal Republic of Germany* (6742/74) DR 3, 103.
[18] *Massera v. Uruguay* (R. 1/5) HRC 34, 124.
[19] *Silva et al. v. Uruguay* (R. 8/34) HRC 36, 130.
[20] *Weinberger v, Uruguay* (R 7/28) HRC 36, 114.
[21] *Pietraroia v. Uruguay* (R. 10/44) HRC 36, 153.

forces in wide areas of government is mandatory, and where organs of the executive power may remove elected officials,[22] and that this freedom is incompatible with the institution of a Presidency-for-life.[23]

'Honest, periodic and free' elections

IACM has stated that the postponement of all elections for 10 years contradicts *ADRD* XX.[24]

§25.0.5 SUBSIDIARY INSTRUMENTS

The Convention on the Political Rights of Women (CW_2) provides that women, on equal terms with men, without any discrimination, shall be entitled to vote in all elections,[25] to hold public office and exercise all public functions established by national law,[26] and to be eligible for election to all publicly elected bodies established by national law.[27]

[22] AR 1979/80, 123–4.
[23] 4 Haiti, 69.
[24] AR 1977, 93.
[25] CW_2 I.
[26] CW_2 III.
[27] CW_2 II.

§26. COLLECTIVE RIGHTS

Throughout the centuries over which the concepts of 'human rights' and 'fundamental freedoms' have developed and been refined, it has been an axiom of all the underlying theory that the beneficiaries of those rights and freedoms are individual human beings, in whom they 'inhere', 'inalienably', by virtue of their humanity, and the dignity and integrity to which that characteristic entitles them. When some such rights have been ascribed to sub-classes of the universal class of human beings — such as workers, women, mothers, children, or prisoners — those rights have still been seen as attaching to individual members of the sub-class concerned, rather than to the sub-class as an abstract entity. That has hitherto formed the basis for the definition, interpretation and application of all 'human' rights.

The rights considered in the present section — with the partial exception of the rights of minorities considered in § 26.6 — are expressed in a form that is difficult to reconcile with any classical theory of human rights. They are, very largely, expressed to attach to 'peoples', rather than to 'persons' or 'individuals'. Without seeking to question either the validity or the legitimacy of such rights, some difficulties must be mentioned here to which this formulation gives rise when it is sought to incorporate them into a catalogue of *human* rights.

First, there is no generally accepted definition of what constitutes a 'people': yet, clearly, not every group within a State can be entitled to call itself a 'people', and thereupon (for instance) claim the 'right of self-determination' as a legitimate ground for seceding from the State. Nor is there any unambiguous test of whether any given individual does or does not form part of any particular 'people',[1] and so shares that people's rights.

Secondly, it is easy to identify the State, or its government and its other public authorities, as the entities that have the obligation to respect and secure the rights of individuals; but it is less easy to identify the entities that are obliged to respect and secure the rights of peoples. To be of practical utility, obligations should be imposed only on those who have it in their power to perform them: it is not immediately clear in whose identifiable power it lies, for example, to ensure for a people 'the right to dispose of its natural wealth and resources'.

---

[1] A classical example of this difficulty was reflected in the notorious 'Nürnberg laws' of National Socialist Germany, which provided the legal foundation for discrimination against Jews. Under those laws, any German who could produce the baptismal certificates of all four grandparents was 'Aryan' (that is, non-Jewish), and therefore not subject to adverse discrimination — and indeed bound, during the Second World War, to serve in the German armed forces. If those grandparents had in fact all been born into the Jewish faith and later converted to Christianity, such a person's parents would have been classified under those laws as 'full Jews'; thus, while they perished in a concentration camp, their sons might perish in battle, wearing German uniforms and bound to defend the National Socialist cause with their lives. Ironically, the Supreme Court of Israel has had to face the same difficulty in deciding who is a Jew for the purposes of the Israeli 'Law of the Return', under which Jews are entitled to automatic Israeli citizenship: see, for example, *Rufeisen* v. *Minister of the Interior* (1962) 16 PD 2428; *Shalit* v. *Minister of the Interior* (1969) 23 PD 477.

That power may be spread so widely and thinly over other States, public and private national and international bodies, and many individuals, that it may prove impossible to demonstrate that any one or more of them has failed to perform the obligation.

Thirdly, abstract concepts have in the past only too often presented grave dangers to the enjoyment by individuals of their human rights and fundamental freedoms. Some of the worst violations of those rights have been perpetrated in the service of some inspiring abstraction, such as 'the one true faith', 'the nation', 'the State' (including, as a recent example, *'das Reich'*) 'the economy' (including 'a strong dollar (or pound)'), and indeed 'the masses'. A 'people' is no less an abstraction than any of these: it cannot in reality consist of anything more than the individuals who compose it. If any of the individual rights and freedoms protected by modern international human rights law ever came to be regarded as subservient to the rights of a 'people' — without, that is, the most stringent qualifications such as 'prescribed by law, and necessary in a democratic society' for the protection of specifically defined collective interests (see § 8) — there would be a very real risk that legitimacy might yet again be claimed on such a ground for grave violations of the human rights of individuals.[2]

That said, there are now several rights ascribed to 'peoples' which are declared in international human rights instruments (though the instrument that declares the largest number of them is not yet in force). Those rights must therefore be considered here. Sometimes called 'solidarity rights'[3] or 'third-generation rights', they reflect the most recent developments in international human rights law — and are, for that reason, still in an early stage of legal evolution.

§ 26.1 Self-determination, liberation, and equality

§ 26.1.1 TEXTS

ICPR

1 (1) All peoples have the right of self-determination. By virtue of that right they freely determine their political status and freely pursue their economic, social and cultural development.

(3) The States Parties to the present Covenant, including those having responsibility for the administration of Non-Self-Governing and Trust Territories, shall promote the realization of the right of self-determination, and shall respect that right, in conformity with the provisions of the Charter of the United Nations.

---

[2] In the words of Heribert Golsung, then Director of Human Rights at the CE, 'In the final analysis, it is an attempt to make the safeguard of human rights dependent upon *"raison d'état"*, that elusive concept which has been and still is used so frequently to disguise the most cruel violations of human dignity.' *Forum Europe* 1979, No. 1.

[3] [*AFR* 23 and 29] (see § 26.2.1 and (§ 25.0.1) contain the first mention of the word 'solidarity' in a human rights *treaty*; it had previously only appeared in the context of education in *ADRD* XII.

ICES

1 (1) All peoples have the right of self-determination. By virtue of that right they freely determine their political status and freely pursue their economic, social and cultural development.

(3) The States Parties to the present Covenant, including those having responsibility for the administration of Non-Self-Governing and Trust Territories, shall promote the realization of the right of self-determination, and shall respect that right, in conformity with the provisions of the Charter of the United Nations.

[AFR]

19. All peoples shall be equal: they shall enjoy the same respect and shall have the same rights. Nothing shall justify the domination of a people by another.

20 (1) All peoples shall have the right to existence. They shall have the unquestionable and inalienable right to self-determination. They shall freely determine their political status and shall pursue their economic and social development according to the policy they have freely chosen.

(2) Colonized or oppressed peoples shall have the right to free themselves from the bonds of domination by resorting to any means recognized by the international community.

(3) All peoples shall have the right to the assistance of the States Parties to the present Charter in their liberation struggle against foreign domination, be it political, economic or cultural.

§26.1.2 CROSS-REFERENCES

State obligation: Absolute and immediate under *ICPR* and *[AFR]*: see §6.3. Qualified and progressive under *ICES*: see §6.4.

Signatures, ratifications, accessions, reservations, and interpretations: See Table A for the State Parties bound by these provisions on 1 January 1982, and any reservations and interpretations notified by them.

Derogation: Non-derogable in any circumstances under *ICES* and *[AFR]*; derogable in exceptional circumstances under *ICPR*: see §11.

Non-discrimination: No discrimination of any kind is allowed in respect of these rights: see §7 for the relevant provisions in the instruments.

Abuse: See §9 for the relevant provisions in these instruments.

Savings: See § 10 for the relevant provisions in these instruments.

Restrictions and limitations: See §8 for the general provisions in these instruments.

International supervision, interpretation, application, and enforcement: By HRC under *ICPR* (see §27); by [AFCM] under [*AFR*] (see §30); supervision only by ECOSOC under *ICES* (see §31). See also §6.6 for the obligation to provide domestic remedies under *ICPR* and [*AFR*].

§26.1.3 COMMENT

The 'principle of equal rights and self-determination of peoples' is cited in *UNCH* 1(2) as a basis for friendly relations among nations, itself there declared to be one of the four purposes of the UN. Throughout its existence, the UN has undertaken and supported many measures to promote and protect the 'right of self-determination', especially in encouraging and accelerating the grant of independence to colonial countries, trust territories and other non-self-governing territories, 75 of which became independent between the entry into force of *UNCH* in 1945 and the end of 1977.[4] One of those measures was the incorporation of the right of self-determination as a human right in the UN Covenants.

In both the Covenants, the right of self-determination is declared in identical form; [*AFR* 20(1)] qualifies it with the additional adjectives 'unquestionable' and 'inalienable', omits the word 'cultural', and substitutes for the word 'freely' the phrase 'according to the policy they have freely chosen'.

[*AFR* 20(1)] adds a 'right to existence'; [*AFR* 20(2)] declares a further right to liberation from the bonds of domination, the means for doing so being restricted only by the limitation that they must be 'recognised by the international community'; and [*AFR* 20(3)] declares a further right to assistance from the other State Parties in any such 'liberation struggle'.

§26.1.4 JURISPRUDENCE

None of these provisions has yet been interpreted or applied by any of the competent independent international institutions.

§26.2 International peace and security

§26.2.1 TEXTS

UDHR

28. Everyone is entitled to a social and international order in which the rights and freedoms set forth in this Declaration can be fully realised.

ICPR

20 (1) Any propaganda for war shall be prohibited by law.

(2) Any advocacy of national, racial or religious hatred that constitutes incitement to discrimination, hostility or violence shall be prohibited by law.

---

[4] For a full list of these, see *UN Action in the Field of Human Rights*, 44.

AMR

13 (5) Any propaganda for war and any advocacy of national, racial, or religious hatred that constitute incitements to lawless violence or to any other similar illegal action against any person or group of persons on any grounds including those of race, color, religion, language, or national origin shall be considered as offenses punishable by law.

[*AFR*]

23 (1) All peoples shall have the right to national and international peace and security. The principles of solidarity and friendly relations implicitly affirmed by the Charter of the United Nations and re-affirmed by that of the Organization of African Unity shall govern relations between States.

(2) For the purpose of strengthening peace, solidarity and friendly relations, States parties to the present Charter shall ensure that:

(a) any individual enjoying the right of asylum under Article 12 of the present Charter shall not engage in subversive activities against his country of origin or any other State party to the present Charter;

(b) their territories shall not be used as bases for subversive or terrorist activities against the people of any other State party to the present Charter.

§26.2.2 CROSS-REFERENCES

State obligation: Absolute and immediate under *ICPR*, *AMR*, and [*AFR*]: see §6.3. For the juridical status of obligations under *UDHR*, see §6.2.

Signatures, ratifications, accessions, reservations, and interpretations: See Table A for the State Parties bound by these provisions on 1 January 1982, and the reservations and interpretations (some of them specifically concerned with these provisions) notified by them.

Derogation: Non-derogable in any circumstances under [*AFR*]; derogable in exceptional circumstances under *ICPR* and *AMR*: see §11.

Non-discrimination: see §7 for the other relevant provisions in these instruments.

Abuse: See §9 for the relevant provisions in these instruments.

Savings: See §10 for the relevant provisions in these instruments.

Restrictions and limitations: See §8 for the general provisions in these instruments.

International supervision, interpretation, application, and enforcement: By HRC under *ICPR* (see §27); by IACM and IACT under *AMR* (see §29); by [*AFCM*] under [*AFR*] (see §30). See also §6.6 for the obligation to provide domestic remedies under *UDHR*, *AMR*, and [*AFR*].

§ 26.2.3 COMMENT

It almost goes without saying that the objective of international peace and security is fundamental to the UN, and to all other regional and national organizations concerned with human rights, whether inter-governmental or non-governmental. That objective is reflected affirmatively in *UDHR* 28 and [*AFR* 25(1)], and negatively in *ICPR* 20(1) and *AMR* 13(5) which require the State Parties to prohibit by law 'any propaganda for war' — without however specifying the relationship between this requirement and the protection for the right to freedom of expression contained elsewhere in these instruments (see § 23.4).

ICPR 20(2) and *AMR* 13(5) require the State Parties also to prohibit by law 'any advocacy of national, racial or religious hatred'; in the case of *ICPR* if it constitutes 'incitement to discrimination, hostility or violence', and in the case of *AMR* if it constitutes, more narrowly, incitement to 'lawless' violence or 'any other similar illegal action' against persons or groups on grounds of a limited discrimination catalogue.

None of the other instruments contains any provisions comparable to [*AFR* 25(2) (*a*) or (*b*)].

§ 26.2.4 JURISPRUDENCE

None of these provisions has yet been interpreted or applied by any of the competent independent international institutions.

§ 26.3 Use of wealth and resources

§ 26.3.1 TEXTS

ICPR

1 (2) All peoples may, for their own ends, freely dispose of their natural wealth and resources without prejudice to any obligations arising out of international economic co-operation, based upon the principle of mutual benefit, and international law. In no case may a people be deprived of its own means of subsistence.

47. Nothing in the present Covenant shall be interpreted as impairing the inherent right of all peoples to enjoy and utilize fully and freely their natural wealth and resources.

ICES

1 (2) All peoples may, for their own ends, freely dispose of their natural wealth and resources without prejudice to any obligations arising out of international economic co-operation, based upon the principle of mutual benefit, and international law. In no case may a people be deprived of its own means of subsistence.

25. Nothing in the present Covenant shall be interpreted as impairing the inherent right of all peoples to enjoy and utilize fully and freely their natural wealth and resources.

[*AFR*]

21 (1) All peoples shall freely dispose of their wealth and natural resources. This right shall be exercised in the exclusive interest of the people. In no case shall a people be deprived of it.

(2) In case of spoliation the dispossessed people shall have the right to lawful recovery of its property as well as to an adequate compensation.

(3) The free disposal of wealth and natural resources shall be exercised without prejudice to the obligation of promoting international economic cooperation based on mutual respect, equitable exchange and the principles of international law.

(4) States Parties to the present Charter shall individually and collectively exercise the right to free disposal of their wealth and natural resources with a view to strengthening African unity and solidarity.

(5) States Parties to the present Charter shall undertake to eliminate all forms of foreign economic exploitation particularly that practised by international monopolies so as to enable their peoples to fully benefit from the advantages derived from their national resources.

§26.3.2 CROSS-REFERENCES

State obligation: Absolute and immediate under *ICPR* and [*AFR*]; see §6.3. Qualified and progressive under *ICES*: see §6.4.

Signatures, ratifications, accessions, reservations, and interpretations: See Table A for the State Parties bound by these provisions on 1 January 1982, and any reservations and interpretations notified by them.

Derogation: Non-derogable in any circumstances under *ICES* and [*AFR*]; derogable in exceptional circumstnaces under *ICPR*: see §11.

Non-discrimination: No discrimination of any kind is allowed in respect of these rights: see §7 for the relevant provisions in the instruments.

Abuse: See §9 for the relevant provisions in these instruments.

Savings: See §10 for the relevant provisions in these instruments.

Restrictions and limitations: Note the specific provisions in [*AFR* 21(3)]. See §8 for the general provisions in these instruments, and the principles governing all restriction and limitation clauses.

International supervision, interpretation, application, and enforcement: By HRC under *ICPR* (see §27); by [AFCM] under [*AFR*] (see §30); supervision only by ECOSOC under *ICES* (see §31). See also §6.6 for the obligation to provide domestic remedies under *ICPR* and [*AFR*].

Subsidiary Instruments: 'Charter of Economic Rights and Duties of States' (UNGA Resolution 3281/XXIX).

§26.3.3 COMMENT

These provisions reflect the modern version of the traditional doctrine of 'territorial' sovereignty (see §1.5).

The question of the permanent sovereignty of peoples and nations over their natural resources forms part of the 'principle of equal rights and self-determination of peoples' cited in *UNCH* 1, where the purposes of the UN are declared. The word 'natural' qualifies both 'wealth' and 'resources' in all these Articles in *ICPR* and *ICES*, but only 'resources' in [*AFR* 21]. The right is limited in all three treaties by 'obligations arising out of international economic co-operation', and by international law; *ICPR* 1(2) and *ICES* 1(2) found the co-operation on 'the principle of mutual benefit'; [*AFR* 21(3)] instead on 'mutual respect' and 'equitable exchange'. The deprivation prohibited in all three of the treaties refers, in the Covenants, to a people's 'own means of subsistence', and in [*AFR*] to the principal right itself. *ICPR* 47 and *ICES* 25 restate the same right in the form of a general limitation on their other provisions (see §8).

None of the other instruments contains any provisions comparable to [*AFR* 21(2), (4), or (5)].

§26.3.4 JURISPRUDENCE

None of these provisions has yet been interpreted or applied by any of the competent independent international institutions.

§26.4 Development

§26.4.1 TEXT

[*AFR*]

22 (1) All peoples shall have the right to their economic, social and cultural development with due regard to their freedom and identity and in the equal enjoyment of the common heritage of mankind.

(2) States shall have the duty, individually or collectively, to ensure the exercise of the right to development.

§26.4.2 CROSS-REFERENCES

State obligation: Absolute and immediate: see §6.3.

Derogation: Non-derogable in any circumstances: see §11.

Non-discrimination: No discrimination of any kind is allowed in respect of this right: see §7 for the relevant provisions in this instrument.

Restrictions and limitations: None.

International supervision, interpretation, application, and enforcement: By [AFCM] (see §30). See also §6.6 for the obligation to provide domestic remedies.

§26.4.3 COMMENT

The 'right to development' has been the subject of much debate in recent years, partly because the economic circumstances of many of the world's countries are such as to deprive their inhabitants of many of their human rights of all kinds, but partly also because some programmes for the *economic* development of such countries may themselves result in major violations of human rights and fundamental freedoms for those inhabitants. Economic development has therefore often come to be seen as antithetical to the maintenance of many human rights, especially those in the 'civil and political' group — though there is in fact no empirical evidence to support the proposition that there must necessarily be any such conflict. The limitation 'with due regard to their freedom' in [*AFR* 22(1)] is therefore of particular importance.

There is as yet no generally agreed definition of the nature or scope of a 'right to development' in the context of human rights.[5] An international conference[6] convened by the International Commission of Jurists in 1981 has proposed the following formulation:

Development should . . . be seen as a global concept including, with equal emphasis, civil and political rights and economic, social and cultural rights . . .

True development requires a recognition that the different human rights are inseparable from each other,[7] and development is inseparable from human rights and the Rule of Law. Likewise, justice and equity at the international level are inseparable from justice and equity at the national level . . .

Development should be understood as a process designed progressively to create conditions in which every person can enjoy, exercise and utilise under the Rule of Law all his human rights, whether economic, social, cultural, civil or political.

Every person has the right to participate in, and benefit from, development in the sense of a progressive improvement in the standard and quality of life.

The concept of the right to development . . . serves to express the right of all people all over the world, and of every citizen, to enjoy all human rights

The primary obligation to promote development, in such a way as to satisfy this right, rests upon each State for its own territory and for the persons under its jurisdiction.

---

[5] See, for example, *The International Dimensions of the Right to Development as a Human Right in relation with other Human Rights*, Report of the UN Secretary-General to CHR, E/CN.4/1334) (1979); *Some Preliminary Views on the Relationship between Civil and Political Rights and Economic, Social and Cultural Rights in the Context of Development and on the Right to Development*, International Commission of Jurists (1978); *Human Rights and Development*, International Commission of Jurists (1977).

[6] Reported in *Development, Human Rights and the Rule of Law* (Pergamon, 1981).

[7] See also, to this effect, UNGA Resolution 32/130 of 16 December 1977.

§26.4.4 JURISPRUDENCE

These provisions have not yet been interpreted or applied by the only competent independent international institution, since [AFCM] has not yet been established.

§26.5 Environment

§26.5.1 TEXT

[*AFR*]

24. All peoples shall have the right to a general satisfactory environment favourable to their development.

§26.5.2 CROSS-REFERENCES

State obligation: Absolute and immediate: see §6.3.

Derogation: Non-derogable in any circumstances: see §11.

Non-discrimination: No discrimination of any kind is allowed in respect of this right; see §7 for the relevant provisions in this instrument.

Restrictions and limitations: None.

International supervision, interpretation, application, and enforcement: By [AFCM] (see §30). See also §6.6 for the obligation to provide domestic remedies.

§26.5.3 COMMENT

The 'right to the environment' is another 'third-generation' human right which has been proposed in recent years. [*AFR* 24] is the first international instrument of human rights law to adopt that proposal, qualifying the environment concerned as 'general', 'satisfactory', and 'favourable to . . . development'.

§26.5.4 JURISPRUDENCE

This provision has not yet been interpreted or applied by the only competent independent international institution, since [AFCM] has not yet been established.

§26.6 Minorities

§26.6.1 TEXT

ICPR

27. In those States in which ethnic, religious or linguistic minorities exist, persons belonging to such minorities shall not be denied the right, in community with the other members of their group, to enjoy their own culture, to profess and practise their own religion, or to use their own language.

§26.6.2 Cross-references

State obligation: Absolute and immediate: see § 6.3.

Signatures, ratifications, accessions, reservations, and interpretations: See Table A for the State Parties bound by these provisions on 1 January 1982, and any reservations and interpretations notified by them.

Derogation: Derogable in exceptional circumstances: see §11.

Non-discrimination: No discrimination of any kind is allowed in respect of these rights: see §7 for the relevant provisions in this instrument.

Abuse: See §9 for the relevant provisions in this instrument.

Savings: See §10 for the relevant provisions in this instrument.

Restrictions and limitations: See §8 for the general provisions in this instrument.

International supervision, interpretation, application, and enforcement: By HRC (see § 27). See also §6.6 for the obligation to provide domestic remedies.

See also: §23.3 for the freedom to profess and practise religion; §23.5 for the right to take part in cultural life; §26.2 for prohibitions of advocacy of national or religious hatred.

§26.6.3 Comment

Although this right is declared in terms to attach to 'persons', it may be said to be a collective right in so far as its exercise is protected 'in community with the other members of' the 'minorities' referred to. The individual's right to take part in cultural life is separately protected in *ICES* 15(1)(*a*) (see §23.5), and his right to profess and practise a religion in *ICPR* 18(1) (see §23.3), but the right to use a language is not.[8]

§26.6.4 History

This is one of the few rights which was already the subject of international treaties before 1945. Articles 86 and 93 of the Treaty of Versailles of 1919 contained protections for minorities, and the Polish-German Upper Silesia Treaty of 1922 not only guaranteed certain rights — including life, liberty, and the free exercise of religion — for all inhabitants, and equal treatment before the law and the same civil and political rights for all nationals, but also

(1) the same treatment and security in law and in fact to all linguistic, religious, or ethnic minority groups of nationals; and
(2) the right of minority groups to establish schools and religious institutions, and to use their own language for publications, at public meetings, and before the courts.

---

[8] But EUCT, in the context of *EHR P1* 2, has held that the right to education would be meaningless if it did not imply, in favour of its beneficiaries, the right to be educated in their national language: *6 Groups of Belgian Citizens* v. *Belgium* (1474/62, etc.) Judgment: 1 EHRR 252.

§26.6.5 JURISPRUDENCE

HRC has expressed the view that a person who is born and brought up on an Indian tribal reserve, and has kept ties with that community which he wishes to maintain, must normally be considered as 'belonging' to that minority within the meaning of *ICPR* 27. Although the right to live on a tribal reserve is not as such guaranteed by this Article, if domestic law precludes a person who belongs to the tribe from living there, that can be an interference with his right of access to his native culture and language 'in community with the other members' of his group, if no such community exists outside the reserve. Not every such interference is a denial of rights under *ICPR* 27, but where an Indian is prevented by law from returning to her native reserve after her marriage to a non-Indian has been dissolved, such a denial is neither reasonable nor objectively justifiable (for example, as being necessary to preserve the identity of the tribe), and so constitutes an infringement of the Article, when read together with *ICPR* 2, 3, 12, 17, 23, and 26.[9]

[9] *Lovelace* v. *Canada* (R. 6/24) HRC 36, 166.

Part IV

International Interpretation, Application, Enforcement, and Supervision

Note: Since this book is concerned with substantive rather than procedural law, only the minimum of essential comment follows the texts reproduced in this Part.

§27. THE UN HUMAN RIGHTS COMMITTEE (HRC)

§27.1 Composition and organization

ICPR

28 (1) There shall be established a Human Rights Committee (hereafter referred to in the present Covenant as the Committee). It shall consist of eighteen members and shall carry out the functions hereinafter provided.

(2) The Committee shall be composed of nationals of the States Parties to the present Covenant who shall be persons of high moral character and recognized competence in the field of human rights, consideration being given to the usefulness of the participation of some persons having legal experience.

(3) The members of the Committee shall be elected and shall serve in their personal capacity.

29 (1) The members of the Committee shall be elected by secret ballot from a list of persons possessing the qualifications prescribed in Article 28 and nominated for the purpose by the States Parties to the present Covenant.

(2) Each State Party to the present Covenant may nominate not more than two persons. These persons shall be nationals of the nominating State.

(3) A person shall be eligible for renomination.

30 (1) The initial election shall be held no later than six months after the date of the entry into force of the present Covenant.

(2) At least four months before the date of each election to the Committee, other than an election to fill a vacancy declared in accordance with Article 34, the Secretary-General of the United Nations shall address a written invitation to the States Parties to the present Covenant to submit their nominations for membership of the Committee within three months.

(3) The Secretary-General of the United Nations shall prepare a list in alphabetical order of all the persons thus nominated, with an indication of the States Parties which have nominated them, and shall submit it to the States Parties to the present Covenant no later than one month before the date of each election.

(4) Elections of the members of the Committee shall be held at a meeting of the States Parties to the present Covenant convened by the Secretary-General of the United Nations at the Headquarters of the United Nations. At that meeting, for which two thirds of the States Parties to the present Covenant shall constitute a quorum, the persons elected to the Committee shall be those nominees who obtain the largest number of votes and an absolute majority of the votes of the representatives of States Parties present and voting.

31 (1) The Committee may not include more than one national of the same State.

(2) In the election of the Committee, consideration shall be given to equitable geographical distribution of membership and to the representation of the different forms of civilization and of the principal legal systems.

32 (1) The members of the Committee shall be elected for a term of four years. They shall be eligible for re-election if renominated. However, the terms of nine of the members elected at the first election shall expire at the end of two years; immediately after the first election, the names of these nine members shall be chosen by lot by the Chairman of the meeting referred to in Article 30, paragraph 4.

(2) Elections at the expiry of office shall be held in accordance with the preceding articles of this part of the present Covenant.

33 (1) If, in the unanimous opinion of the other members, a member of the Committee has ceased to carry out his functions for any cause other than absence of a temporary character, the Chairman of the Committee shall notify the Secretary-General of the United Nations, who shall then declare the seat of that member to be vacant.

(2) In the event of the death or the resignation of a member of the Committee, the Chairman shall immediately notify the Secretary-General of the United Nations, who shall declare the seat vacant from the date of death or the date on which the resignation takes effect.

34 (1) When a vacancy is declared in accordance with Article 33 and if the term of office of the member to be replaced does not expire within six months of the declaration of the vacancy, the Secretary-General of the United Nations shall notify each of the States Parties to the present Covenant, which may within two months submit nominations in accordance with Article 29 for the purpose of filling the vacancy.

(2) The Secretary-General of the United Nations shall prepare a list in alphabetical order of the persons thus nominated and shall

submit it to the States Parties to the present Covenant. The election to fill the vacancy shall then take place in accordance with the relevant provisions of this part of the present Covenant.

(3) A member of the Committee elected to fill a vacancy declared in accordance with Article 33 shall hold office for the remainder of the term of the member who vacated the seat on the Committee under the provisions of that Article.

35. The members of the Committee shall, with the approval of the General Assembly of the United Nations, receive emoluments from United Nations resources on such terms and conditions as the General Assembly may decide, having regard to the importance of the Committee's responsibilities.

36. The Secretary-General of the United Nations shall provide the necessary staff and facilities for the effective performance of the functions of the Committee under the present Covenant.

37 (1) The Secretary-General of the United Nations shall convene the initial meeting of the Committee at the Headquarters of the United Nations.

(2) After its initial meeting, the Committee shall meet at such times as shall be provided in its rules of procedure.

(3) The Committee shall normally meet at the Headquarters of the United Nations or at the United Nations Office at Geneva.

38. Every member of the Committee shall, before taking up his duties, make a solemn declaration in open committee that he will perform his functions impartially and conscientiously.

39 (1) The Committee shall elect its officers for a term of two years. They may be re-elected.

(2) The Committee shall establish its own rules of procedure, but these rules shall provide, *inter alia*, that:

(*a*) Twelve members shall constitute a quorum;

(*b*) Decisions of the Committee shall be made by a majority vote of the members present.

43. The members of the Committee, and of the *ad hoc* conciliation commissions which may be appointed under Article 42, shall be entitled to the facilities, privileges and immunities of experts on mission for the United Nations as laid down in the relevant sections of the Convention on the Privileges and Immunities of the United Nations.

44. The provisions for the implementation of the present Covenant shall apply without prejudice to the procedures prescribed in the

field of human rights by or under the constituent instruments and the conventions of the United Nations and of the specialized agencies and shall not prevent the States Parties to the present Covenant from having recourse to other procedures for settling a dispute in accordance with general or special international agreements in force between them.

45. The Committee shall submit to the General Assembly of the United Nations through the Economic and Social Council, an annual report on its activities.

§27.2 State communications

ICPR

41 (1) A State Party to the present Covenant may at any time declare under this article that it recognizes the competence of the Committee to receive and consider communications to the effect that a State Party claims that another State Party is not fulfilling its obligations under the present Covenant. Communications under this Article may be received and considered only if submitted by a State Party which has made a declaration recognizing in regard to itself the competence of the Committee. No communication shall be received by the Committee if it concerns a State Party which has not made such a declaration. Communications received under this article shall be dealt with in accordance with the following procedure:

(*a*) If a State Party to the present Covenant considers that another State Party is not giving effect to the provisions of the present Covenant, it may, by written communication, bring the matter to the attention of that State Party. Within three months after the receipt of the communication, the receiving State shall afford the State which sent the communication an explanation or any other statement in writing clarifying the matter, which should include, to the extent possible and pertinent, reference to domestic procedures and remedies taken, pending, or available in the matter.

(*b*) If the matter is not adjusted to the satisfaction of both States Parties concerned within six months after the receipt by the receiving State of the initial communication, either State shall have the right to refer the matter to the Committee, by notice given to the Committee and to the other State.

(*c*) The Committee shall deal with a matter referred to it only after it has been ascertained that all available domestic remedies have been invoked and exhausted in the matter, in conformity with the generally recognized principles of international law. This shall not be the rule where the application of the remedies is unreasonably prolonged.

(*d*) The Committee shall hold closed meetings when examining communications under this article.

(*e*) Subject to the provisions of sub-paragraph (*c*), the Committee shall make available its good offices to the States Parties concerned with a view to a friendly solution of the matter on the basis of respect for human rights and fundamental freedoms as recognized in the present Covenant.

(*f*) In any matter referred to it, the Committee may call upon the States Parties concerned, referred to in sub-paragraph (*b*), to supply any relevant information.

(*g*) The States Parties concerned, referred to in sub-paragraph (*b*), shall have the right to be represented when the matter is being considered in the Committee and to make submissions orally and/or in writing.

(*h*) The Committee shall, within twelve months after the date of receipt of notice under sub-paragraph (*b*), submit a report:

(i) If a solution within the terms of sub-paragraph (*e*) is reached, the Committee shall confine its report to a brief statement of the facts and of the solution reached;

(ii) If a solution within the terms of sub-paragraph (*e*) is not reached, the Committee shall confine its report to a brief statement of the facts; the written submissions and record of the oral submissions made by the States Parties concerned shall be attached to the report.

In every matter, the report shall be communicated to the States Parties concerned.

(2) The provisions of this article shall come into force when ten States Parties to the present Covenant have made declarations under paragraph 1 of this article. Such declarations shall be deposited by the States Parties with the Secretary-General of the United Nations, who shall transmit copies thereof to the other States Parties. A declaration may be withdrawn at any time by notification to the Secretary-General. Such a withdrawal shall not prejudice the consideration of any matter which is the subject of a communication already transmitted under this Article; no further communication by any State Party shall be received after the notification of withdrawal of the declaration has been received by the Secretary-General, unless the State Party concerned has made a new declaration.

42 (1)

(*a*) If a matter referred to the Committee in accordance with Article
41 is not resolved to the satisfaction of the States Parties concerned, the Committee may, with the prior consent of the States
Parties concerned, appoint an *ad hoc* Conciliation Commission
(hereinafter referred to as the Commission). The good offices
of the Commission shall be made available to the States Parties
concerned with a view to an amicable solution of the matter on
the basis of respect for the present Covenant.

(*b*) The Commission shall consist of five persons acceptable to the
States Parties concerned. If the States Parties concerned fail to
reach agreement within three months on all or part of the composition of the Commission the members of the Commission
concerning whom no agreement has been reached shall be elected
by secret ballot by a two-thirds majority vote of the Committee
from among its members.

(2) The members of the Commission shall serve in their personal
capacity. They shall not be nationals of the States Parties concerned,
or of a State not party to the present Covenant, or of a State Party
which has not made a declaration under Article 41.

(3) The Commission shall elect its own Chairman and adopt its
own rules of procedure.

(4) The meetings of the Commission shall normally be held at
the Headquarters of the United Nations or at the United Nations
Office in Geneva. However, they may be held at such other convenient places as the Commission may determine in consultation
with the Secretary-General of the United Nations and the States
Parties concerned.

(5) The secretariat provided in accordance with Article 36 shall
also service the commissions appointed under this Article.

(6) The information received and collated by the Committee
shall be made available to the Commission and the Commission
may call upon the States concerned to supply any other relevant
information.

(7) When the Commission has fully considered the matter, but in
any event not later than twelve months after having been seized of
the matter, it shall submit to the Chairman of the Committee a
report for communication to the States Parties concerned.

(*a*) If the Commission is unable to complete its consideration of the
matter within twelve months, it shall confine its report to a brief
statement of the status of its consideration of the matter.

(*b*) If an amicable solution to the matter on the basis of respect for
human rights as recognized in the present Covenant is reached,

the Commission shall confine its report to a brief statement of the facts and of the solution reached.

(c) If a solution within the terms of sub-paragraph (b) is not reached, the Commission's report shall embody its findings on all questions of fact relevant to the issues between the States Parties concerned, and its views on the possibilities of an amicable solution of the matter. This report shall also contain the written submissions and a record of the oral submissions made by the States Parties concerned.

(d) If the Commission's report is submitted under sub-paragraph (c), the States Parties concerned shall, within three months of the receipt of the report, notify the Chairman of the Committee whether or not they accept the contents of the report of the Commission.

(8) The provisions of this Article are without prejudice to the responsibilities of the Committee under Article 41.

(9) The States Parties concerned shall share equally all the expenses of the members of the Commission in accordance with estimates to be provided by the Secretary-General of the United Nations.

(10) The Secretary-General of the United Nations shall be empowered to pay the expenses of the members of the Commission, if necessary, before reimbursement by the States Parties concerned, in accordance with paragraph 9 of this Article.

COMMENT

ICPR 41 entered into force on 22 August 1979. HRC has adopted detailed Rules of Procedure,[1] but by 1 January 1982 it had not yet received any State communications under this Article.

§27.3 Individual communications

ICPR OP

1. A State Party to the Covenant that becomes a party to the present Protocol recognizes the competence of the Committee to receive and consider communications from individuals subject to its jurisdiction who claim to be victims of a violation by that State Party of any of the rights set forth in the Covenant. No communication shall be received by the Committee if it concerns a State Party to the Covenant which is not a party to the present Protocol.

---

[1] These are published by the UN (Doc. CCPR/C/3/ Rev. 1).

2. Subject to the provisions of Article 1, individuals who claim that any of their rights enumerated in the Covenant have been violated and who have exhausted all available domestic remedies may submit a written communication to the Committee for consideration.

3. The Committee shall consider inadmissible any communication under the present Protocol which is anonymous, or which it considers to be an abuse of the right of submission of such communications or to be incompatible with the provisions of the Covenant.

4 (1) Subject to the provisions of Article 3, the Committee shall bring any communications submitted to it under the present Protocol to the attention of the State Party to the present Protocol alleged to be violating any provision of the Covenant.

(2) Within six months, the receiving State shall submit to the Committee written explanations or statements clarifying the matter and the remedy, if any, that may have been taken by that State.

5 (1) The Committee shall consider communications received under the present Protocol in the light of all written information made available to it by the individual and by the State Party concerned.

(2) The Committee shall not consider any communication from an individual unless it has ascertained that:

(*a*) The same matter is not being examined under another procedure of international investigation or settlement:

(*b*) The individual has exhausted all available domestic remedies. This shall not be the rule where the application of the remedies is unreasonably prolonged.

(3) The Committee shall hold closed meetings when examining communications under the present Protocol.

(4) The Committee shall forward its views to the State Party concerned and to the individual.

6. The Committee shall include in its annual report under Article 45 of the Covenant a summary of its activities under the present Protocol.

7. Pending the achievement of the objectives of resolution 1514 (XV) adopted by the General Assembly of the United Nations on 14 December 1960 concerning the Declaration on the Granting of Independence to Colonial Countries and Peoples, the provisions of the present Protocol shall in no way limit the right of petition granted to these peoples by the Charter of the United Nations and other international conventions and instruments under the United Nations and its specialized agencies.

COMMENT

In common with the procedure before EUCM (see §28.3), the communication under this procedure[2] must come from a victim of the alleged violation. However, unlike the procedures before EUCM, IACM under *AMR* (see §29.2.3), [AFCM] (see §30.5), CHR (see §31.1), and the UNESCO Committee (see §34), there is no time limit after domestic remedies have been exhausted, nor is there a requirement not to admit communications which are 'manifestly ill-founded' (as for EUCM) or 'manifestly groundless or obviously out of order' (as for IACM).

HRC has decided that it is competent to consider violations alleged to have been committed by a State Party's agents outside its own territory: the reference in *ICPR OP* 1 to 'individuals subject to its jurisdiction' is not to the place where the violation occurs, but to the relationship between the State and the victim, wherever it occurs.[3]

HRC has decided that 'another procedure of international investigation or settlement' within the meaning of *ICPR OP* 5(2)(*a*) includes the procedure before IACM,[4] but not the procedure before CHR.[5] It has not yet determined whether the UNESCO procedure (see §34) falls within this category. As for the exhaustion of domestic remedies, it is for the respondent government to specify what effective remedies are still available to the alleged victim in the particular case: general descriptions of remedies are not enough.[6] Where, four and a half years after a person's arrest, no final judgment has been rendered in his case, the application of the remedies is 'unreasonably prolonged'.[7] HRC has also decided that it is able to form its views on 'facts which have not been contradicted by the State Party'.[8]

The views of HRC expressed on communications under this procedure and published before 1 January 1982 are noted in the relevant sections in Parts II and III above.[9]

§27.4 Supervision

ICPR

40 (1) The States Parties to the present Covenant undertake to submit reports on the measures they have adopted which give effect to

---

[2] HRC's Rules of Procedure (*supra*) cover individual as well as State communications.

[3] *Burgos* v. *Uruguay* (R. 12/52) HRC 36, 176; *de Casariego* v. *Uruguay* (R. 13/56) HRC 36, 185.

[4] But not where an unrelated third party submits a communication to IACM about the same case after the victim's legal representative has already submitted one to HRC: *de Casariego* v. *Uruguay, supra*; or where such a communication to IACM is withdrawn after one has been submitted to HRC: *Antonaccio* v. *Uruguay* (R. 14/63) published 14 December 1981.

[5] HRC 33, 99–100.

[6] HRC 35, 91.

[7] *Weinberger* v. *Uruguay* (R. 7/28) HRC 36, 114.

[8] *Ambrosini et al.* v. *Uruguay* (R. 1/5) HRC 34, 124; *Sequeira* v. *Uruguay* (R. 1/6) HRC 35, 127.

[9] For an authoritative account of the performance of HRC's functions under *ICPR OP*, see Möse and Opsahl, 'The Optional Protocol to the International Covenant on Civil and Political Rights', 20 *Santa Clara L. R.* 271.

the rights recognized herein and on the progress made in the enjoyment of those rights:

(*a*) Within one year of the entry into force of the present Covenant for the States Parties concerned;

(*b*) Thereafter whenever the Committee so requests.

(2) All reports shall be submitted to the Secretary-General of the United Nations, who shall transmit them to the Committee for consideration. Reports shall indicate the factors and difficulties, if any, affecting the implementation of the present Covenant.

(3) The Secretary-General of the United Nations may, after consultation with the Committee, transmit to the specialized agencies concerned copies of such parts of the reports as may fall within their field of competence.

(4) The Committee shall study the reports submitted by the States Parties to the present Covenant. It shall transmit its reports, and such general comments as it may consider appropriate, to the States Parties. The Committee may also transmit to the Economic and Social Council these comments along with the copies of the reports it has received from States Parties to the present Covenant.

(5) The States Parties to the present Covenant may submit to the Committee observations on any comments that may be made in accordance with paragraph 4 of this Article.

COMMENT

HRC published its first 'general comments' under *ICPR* 40(4) in its Annual Report to the thirty-sixth session of UNGA.[10] These are noted in the relevant sections in Part III above.

[10] HRC 36, 107–110.

§28. THE EUROPEAN COMMISSION AND COURT OF HUMAN RIGHTS (EUCM and EUCT)

§28.1 Institutions

EHR

19. To ensure the observance of the engagements undertaken by the High Contracting Parties in the present Convention, there shall be set up:
1. A European Commission of Human Rights, hereinafter referred to as 'the Commission';
2. A European Court of Human Rights, hereinafter referred to as 'the Court'.

§28.2 EUCM: Composition and organization

EHR

20. The Commission shall consist of a number of members equal to that of the High Contracting Parties. No two members of the Commission may be nationals of the same State.

21 (1) The members of the Commission shall be elected by the Committee of Ministers by an absolute majority of votes, from a list of names drawn up by the Bureau of the Consultative Assembly; each group of the Representatives of the High Contracting Parties in the Consultative Assembly shall put forward three candidates, of whom two at least shall be its nationals.

(2) As far as applicable, the same procedure shall be followed to complete the Commission in the event of other States subsequently becoming Parties to this Convention, and in filling casual vacancies.

22[1] (1) The members of the Commission shall be elected for a period of six years. They may re-elected. However, of the members elected at the first election, the terms of seven members shall expire at the end of three years.

---

[1] As amended by *EHR P5* 1 and 2.

391

(2) The members whose terms are to expire at the end of the initial period of three years shall be chosen by lot by the Secretary-General of the Council of Europe immediately after the first election has been completed.

(3) In order to ensure that, as far as possible, one half of the membership of the Commission shall be renewed every three years, the Committee of Ministers may decide, before proceeding to any subsequent election, that the term or terms of office of one or more members to be elected shall be for a period other than six years but not more than nine and not less than three years.

(4) In cases where more than one term of office is involved and the Committee of Ministers applies the preceding paragraph, the allocation of the terms of office shall be effected by the drawing of lots by the Secretary-General, immediately after the election.

(5) A member of the Commission elected to replace a member whose term of office has not expired shall hold office for the remainder of his predecessor's term.

(6) The members of the Commission shall hold office until replaced. After having been replaced, they shall continue to deal with such cases as they already have under consideration.

23. The members of the Commission shall sit on the Commission in their individual capacity.

37. The secretariat of the Commission shall be provided by the Secretary-General of the Council of Europe.

58. The expenses of the Commission . . . shall be borne by the Council of Europe.

59. The members of the Commission . . . shall be entitled, during the discharge of their functions, to the privileges and immunities provided for in Article 40 of the Statute of the Council of Europe and in the agreements made thereunder.

§28.3 EUCM: Competence

EHR

24. Any High Contracting Party may refer to the Commission, through the Secretary-General of the Council of Europe, any alleged breach of the provisions of the Convention by another High Contracting Party.

25 (1) The Commission may receive petitions addressed to the Secretary-General of the Council of Europe from any person, non-

governmental organization or group of individuals claiming to be the victim of a violation by one of the High Contracting Parties of the rights set forth in this Convention, provided that the High Contracting Party against which the complaint has been lodged has declared that it recognizes the competence of the Commission to receive such petitions. Those of the High Contracting Parties who have made such a declaration undertake not to hinder in any way the effective exercise of this right.

(2) Such declarations may be made for a specific period.

(3) The declarations shall be deposited with the Secretary-General of the Council of Europe who shall transmit copies thereof to the High Contracting Parties and publish them.

(4) The Commission shall only exercise the powers provided for in this Article when at least six High Contracting Parties are bound by declarations made in accordance with the preceding paragraphs.

26. The Commission may only deal with the matter after all domestic remedies have been exhausted, according to the generally recognized rules of international law, and within a period of six months from the date on which the final decision was taken.

27 (1) The Commission shall not deal with any petition submitted under Article 25 which:

(*a*) is anonymous, or

(*b*) is substantially the same as a matter which has already been examined by the Commission or has already been submitted to another procedure of international investigation or settlement and if it contains no relevant new information.

(2) The Commission shall consider inadmissible any petition submitted under Article 25 which it considers incompatible with the provisions of the present Convention, manifestly ill-founded, or an abuse of the right of petition.

(3) The Commission shall reject any petition referred to it which it considers inadmissible under Article 26.

COMMENT

Note that EUCM may consider any State communication at any time, but may consider individual petitions only where the respondent State has made the appropriate declaration of competence. (As to these, see Table A.) For IACM under *AMR*, the position is the converse: see §29.2.3; [AFCM] will need no prior declarations of competence for either source of communication: see §§30.4 and 30.5.

In common with the procedure before HRC (see §27.3), the communication under this procedure must come from a victim of the alleged violation. The time limit of six months after the exhaustion of domestic remedies is also required for the procedure before IACM under *AMR*, as is the requirement that the petition must not be manifestly ill-founded.

§28.4 EUCM: Procedure

EHR

28. In the event of the Commission accepting a petition referred to it:

(*a*) it shall, with a view to ascertaining the facts, undertake together with the representatives of the parties an examination of the petition and, if need be, an investigation, for the effective conduct of which the States concerned shall furnish all necessary facilities, after an exchange of views with the Commission:

(*b*) it shall place itself at the disposal of the parties concerned with a view to securing a friendly settlement of the matter on the basis of respect for human rights as defined in this Convention.

29.[2] After it has accepted a petition submitted under Article 25, the Commission may nevertheless decide unanimously to reject the petition if, in the course of its examination, it finds that the existence of one of the grounds for non-acceptance provided for in Article 27 has been established.

In such a case, the decision shall be communicated to the parties.

30.[3] If the Commission succeeds in effecting a friendly settlement in accordance with Article 28, it shall draw up a Report which shall be sent to the States concerned, to the Committee of Ministers and to the Secretary-General of the Council of Europe for publication. This Report shall be confined to a brief statement of the facts and of the solution reached.

31 (1) If a solution is not reached, the Commission shall draw up a Report on the facts and state its opinion as to whether the facts found disclose a breach by the State concerned of its obligations under the Convention. The opinions of all the members of the Commission on this point may be stated in the Report.

(2) The Report shall be transmitted to the Committee of Ministers. It shall also be transmitted to the States concerned, who shall not be at liberty to publish it.

---

[2] As amended by *EHR P3* 1.
[3] As amended by *EHR P3* 2.

(3) In transmitting the Report to the Committee of Ministers the Commission may make such proposals as it thinks fit.

32 (1) If the question is not referred to the Court in accordance with Article 48 of this Convention within a period of three months from the date of the transmission of the Report to the Committee of Ministers, the Committee of Ministers shall decide by a majority of two-thirds of the members entitled to sit on the Committee whether there has been a violation of the Convention.

(2) In the affirmative case the Committee of Ministers shall prescribe a period during which the Contracting Party concerned must take the measures required by the decision of the Committee of Ministers.

(3) If the High Contracting Party concerned has not taken satisfactory measures within the prescribed period, the Committee of Ministers shall decide by the majority provided for in paragraph 1 above what effect shall be given to its original decision and shall publish the Report.

(4) The High Contracting Parties undertake to regard as binding on them any decision which the Committee of Ministers may take in application of the preceding paragraphs.

33. The Commission shall meet *in camera*.

34.[4] Subject to the provisions of Article 29, the Commission shall take its decisions by a majority of the Members present and voting.

35. The Commission shall meet as the circumstances require. The meetings shall be convened by the Secretary-General of the Council of Europe.

36. The Commission shall draw up its own rules of procedure.[5]

COMMENT

EUCM's published Reports interpreting and applying the provisions of *EHR* are noted in the relevant sections in Parts II and III above; so are published Decisions on admissibility where they contain important interpretations of the provisions of the Convention.

As the Committee of Ministers is essentially a political rather than an independent body, its functions in this area fall outside the scope of the present work.

---

[4] As amended by *EHR P3* **3**.
[5] The current edition of these is reproduced in *European Convention on Human Rights: Collected Texts* (CE).

§ 28.5 EUCT: Composition and organization

EHR

38. The European Court of Human Rights shall consist of a number of judges equal to that of the Members of the Council of Europe. No two judges may be nationals of the same State.

39 (1) The members of the Court shall be elected by the Consultative Assembly by a majority of the votes cast from a list of persons nominated by the Members of the Council of Europe; each Member shall nominate three candidates, of whom two at least shall be its nationals.

(2) As far as applicable, the same procedure shall be followed to complete the Court in the event of the admission of new members of the Council of Europe, and in filling casual vacancies.

(3) The candidates shall be of high moral character and must either possess the qualifications required for appointment to high judicial office or be jurisconsults of recognized competence.

40[6] (1) The members of the Court shall be elected for a period of nine years. They may be re-elected. However, of the members elected at the first election the terms of four members shall expire at the end of six years.

(2) The members whose terms are to expire at the end of the initial periods of three and six years shall be chosen by lot by the Secretary-General immediately after the first election has been completed.

(3) In order to ensure that, as far as possible, one third of the membership of the Court shall be renewed every three years, the Consultative Assembly may decide, before proceeding to any subsequent election, that the term or terms of office of one or more members to be elected shall be for a period other than nine years but not more than twelve and not less than six years.

(4) In cases where more than one term of office is involved and the Consultative Assembly applies the preceding paragraph, the allocation of the terms of office shall be effected by the drawing of lots by the Secretary-General immediately after the election.

(5) A member of the Court elected to replace a member whose term of office has not expired shall hold office for the remainder of his predecessor's term.

(6) The members of the Court shall hold office until replaced. After having been replaced, they shall continue to deal with such cases as they already have under consideration.

---

[6] As amended by *EHR P5* 3 and 4.

41. The Court shall elect its President and Vice-President for a period of three years. They may be re-elected.

42. The members of the Court shall receive for each day of duty a compensation to be determined by the Committee of Ministers.

43. For the consideration of each case brought before it the Court shall consist of a Chamber composed of seven judges. There shall sit as an *ex officio* member of the Chamber the judge who is a national of any State party concerned, or, if there is none, a person of its choice who shall sit in the capacity of judge; the names of the other judges shall be chosen by lot by the President before the opening of the case.

58. The expenses of . . . the Court shall be borne by the Council of Europe.

59. The members of . . . the Court shall be entitled, during the discharge of their functions, to the privileges and immunities provided for in Article 40 of the Statute of the Council of Europe and in the agreements made thereunder.

§28.6 EUCT: Jurisdiction

EHR

44. Only the High Contracting Parties and the Commission shall have the right to bring a case before the Court.

45. The jurisdiction of the Court shall extend to all cases concerning the interpretation and application of the present Convention which the High Contracting Parties or the Commission shall refer to it in accordance with Article 48.

62. The High Contracting Parties agree that, except by special agreement, they will not avail themselves of treaties, conventions or declarations in force between them for the purpose of submitting, by way of petition, a dispute arising out of the interpretation or application of this Convention to a means of settlement other than those provided for in this Convention.

46 (1) Any of the High Contracting Parties may at any time declare that it recognizes as compulsory *ipso facto* and without special agreement the jurisdiction of the Court in all matters concerning the interpretation and application of the present Convention.

(2) The declarations referred to above may be made uncondi-

tionally or on condition of reciprocity on the part of several or certain other High Contracting Parties or for a specified period.

(3) These declarations shall be deposited with the Secretary-General of the Council of Europe who shall transmit copies thereof to the High Contracting Parties.

47. The Court may only deal with a case after the Commission has acknowledged the failure of efforts for a friendly settlement and within the period of three months provided for in Article 32.

48. The following may bring a case before the Court, provided that the High Contracting Party concerned, if there is only one, or the High Contracting Parties concerned, if there is more than one, are subject to the compulsory jurisdiction of the Court or, failing that, with the consent of the High Contracting Party concerned, if there is only one, or of the High Contracting Parties concerned if there is more than one:

(*a*) the Commission;

(*b*) a High Contracting Party whose national is alleged to be a victim;

(*c*) a High Contracting Party which referred the case to the Commission;

(*d*) a High Contracting Party against which the complaint has been lodged.

49. In the event of dispute as to whether the Court has jurisdiction, the matter shall be settled by the decision of the Court.

EHR P2

1 (1) The Court may, at the request of the Committee of Ministers, give advisory opinions on legal questions concerning the interpretation of the Convention and the Protocols thereto.

(2) Such opinions shall not deal with any question relating to the content or scope of the rights or freedoms defined in Section I of the Convention and in the Protocols thereto, or with any other question which the Commission, the Court, or the Committee of Ministers might have to consider in consequence of any such proceedings as could be instituted in accordance with the Convention.

(3) Decisions of the Committee of Ministers to request an advisory opinion of the Court shall require a two-thirds majority vote of the representatives entitled to sit on the Committee.

2. The Court shall decide whether a request for an advisory opinion submitted by the Committee of Ministers is within its consultative competence as defined in Article 1 of this Protocol.

COMMENT

Note that an individual petitioner cannot be a party, and has no *locus standi*, before EUCT, though the Court generally allows his representative either to assist the Commission, or to be heard as *amicus curiae*.

EUCT's reported judgments are noted in the relevant sections in Parts II and III above.

§ 28.7 EUCT: Procedure

EHR

50. If the Court finds that a decision or a measure taken by a legal authority or any other authority of a High Contracting Party is completely or partially in conflict with the obligations arising from the present Convention, and if the internal law of the said Party allows only partial reparation to be made for the consequences of this decision or measure, the decision of the Court shall, if necessary, afford just satisfaction to the injured party.

51 (1) Reasons shall be given for the judgment of the Court.

(2) If the judgment does not represent in whole or in part the unanimous opinion of the judges, any judge shall be entitled to deliver a separate opinion.

52. The judgment of the Court shall be final.

53. The High Contracting Parties undertake to abide by the decision of the Court in any case to which they are parties.

54. The judgment of the Court shall be transmitted to the Committee of Ministers which shall supervise its execution.

55. The Court shall draw up its own rules and shall determine its own procedure.[7]

EHR P2

3 (1) For the consideration of requests for an advisory opinion, the Court shall sit in plenary session.

(2) Reasons shall be given for advisory opinions of the Court.

(3) If the advisory opinion does not represent in whole or in part the unanimous opinion of the judges, any judge shall be entitled to deliver a separate opinion.

---

[7] These are reproduced in the current edition of *European Convention on Human Rights: Collected Texts* (CE).

(4) Advisory opinions of the Court shall be communicated to the Committee of Ministers.

4. The powers of the Court under Article 55 of the Convention shall extend to the drawing up of such rules and the determination of such procedure[8] as the Court may think necessary for the purposes of this Protocol.

§28.8 Supervision

EHR

57. On receipt of a request from the Secretary-General of the Council of Europe any High Contracting Party shall furnish an explanation of the manner in which its internal law ensures the effective implementation of any of the provisions of this Convention.

COMMENT

Unlike the supervision procedures for *ICPR* (see §27.4), *ICES* (see §31.2), and *ESC* (see §32), this procedure makes no provision for the expression of any comments or conclusions by the Secretary-General on the material submitted to him.

---

[8] These are reproduced in the current edition of *European Convention on Human Rights: Collected Texts* (CE).

§29. THE INTER-AMERICAN COMMISSION AND COURT OF HUMAN RIGHTS (IACM and IACT)

§29.1 IACM's functions and powers in respect of OAS Member States which are not parties to *AMR*

IACM, which has its seat at the General Secretariat of the OAS in Washington, DC, USA, was first established in 1959.[1] In the following year, the OAS Council promulgated the Commission's Statute, Article 1 of which declared that its function was 'to promote respect for human rights'. Article 2 went on to declare that, 'for the purpose of this Statute, human rights are understood to be those set forth in [*ADRD*].' IACM's original powers were set out as follows in Article 9:

In carrying out its assignment of promoting respect for human rights, the Commission shall have the following functions and powers:
(a) To develop an awareness of human rights among the peoples of America;
(b) To make recommendations to the governments of the member states in general, if it considers such action advisable, for the adoption of progressive measures in favor of human rights within the framework of their domestic legislation and, in accordance with their constitutional precepts, appropriate measures to further the faithful observance of those rights;
(c) To prepare such studies or reports as it considers advisable in the performance of its duties;
(d) To urge the governments of the member states to supply it with information on the measures adopted by them in matters of human rights;
(e) To serve the Organization of American States as an advisory body in respect of human rights.

From the beginning, the Commission interpreted paragraph (b) of this Article as a power to make general recommendations to individual Member States of the OAS, as well as to all of them,[2] and in pursuance of this power it has carried out a number of detailed 'country studies' on the situation of human rights in various American republics, some of which have included investigations *in loco*.

Following the Second Special Inter-American Conference in Rio de Janeiro, Brazil, in 1965, IACM's powers were enlarged to include the consideration of 'communications' by the addition to its then Statute of a new Article 9 *bis* in the following terms:

The Commission shall have the following additional functions and powers:
(a) To give particular attention to observance of the human rights referred to in Articles I, II, III, IV, XVIII, XXV, and XXVI of the American Declaration of the Rights and Duties of Man;

[1] By Resolution VIII of the Fifth Meeting of Consultation of the OAS Ministers of Foreign Affairs.
[2] IACM, *Report on the Work Accomplished During its First Session* (OEA/Ser. L/V/II.1, doc. 32).

401

(*b*) To examine communications submitted to it and any other available information; to address the government of any American state for information deemed pertinent by the Commission; and to make recommendations, when it deems this appropriate, with the objective of bringing about more effective observance of fundamental human rights;

(*c*) To submit a report annually to the Inter-American Conference or to the Meeting of Consultation of Ministers of Foreign Affairs, which should include: (i) a statement of progress achieved in realization of the goals set forth in the American Declaration; (ii) a statement of areas in which further steps are needed to give effect to the human rights set forth in the American Declaration; and (iii) such observations as the Commission may deem appropriate on matters covered in the communications submitted to it and in other information available to the Commission;

(*d*) To verify, as a condition precedent to the exercise of the powers set forth in paragraphs (*b*) and (*c*) of the present article, whether the internal legal procedures and remedies of each member state have been duly applied and exhausted.

The OAS Charter was revised, with effect from 27 February 1970, by the Protocol of Buenos Aires which had been signed three years earlier. Article 51 of the Revised Charter designates the IACM as a 'principal organ' of the OAS; Article 112 declares that its 'principal function shall be to promote the observance and protection of human rights and to serve as a consultative organ of the Organisation in these matters'; and Article 150 provides that, until *AMR* enters into force, the 'present' IACM 'shall keep vigilance over the observance of human rights'.

AMR in fact entered into force in 1978, and its provisions for IACM are set out in §29.2 below. However, the Commission's functions and powers under the revised OAS Charter of 1970 remain in effect for those OAS Member States which have not yet become parties to *AMR*, and the IACM's new Statute[3] now contains the following consolidated powers in respect of those States:

18. The Commission shall have the following powers with respect to the member states of the Organization of American States:

(*a*) to develop an awareness of human rights among the people of the Americas;

(*b*) to make recommendations to the governments of the states on the adoption of progressive measures in favor of human rights in the framework of their legislation, constitutional provisions and international commitments, as well as appropriate measures to further observance of those rights;

(*c*) to prepare such studies or reports as it considers advisable for the performance of its duties;

(*d*) to request that the governments of the states provide it with reports on measures they adopt in matters of human rights;

(*e*) to respond to inquiries made by any member state through the General Secretariat of the Organization on matters related to human rights in that state and, within its possibilities, to provide those states with the advisory services they request;

(*f*) to submit an annual report to the General Assembly of the Organization, in which due account shall be taken of the legal regime applicable to those States Parties to the American Convention on Human Rights and of that system applicable to those that are not Parties;

---

[3] Adopted by the OAS General Assembly at its Ninth Regular Session in La Paz, Bolivia, in October 1979. For the full text of the Statute, see IACM, *Handbook of Existing Rules Pertaining to Human Rights* (OEA/Ser. L/V/II.50, doc. 6).

(*g*) to conduct on-site observations in a state, with the consent or at the invitation of the government in question, and

(*h*) to submit the program-budget of the Commission to the Secretary General, so that he may present it to the General Assembly.

20. In relation to those member states of the Organization that are not Parties to the American Convention on Human Rights, the Commission shall have the following powers, in addition to those designated in Article 18:

(*a*) to pay particular attention to the observance of the human rights referred to in Articles I, II, III, IV, XVIII, XXV, and XXVI of the American Declaration of the Rights and Duties of Man;

(*b*) to examine communications submitted to it and any other available information, to address the government of any member state not a Party to the Convention for information deemed pertinent by this Commission, and to make recommendations to it, when it finds this appropriate, in order to bring about more effective observance of fundamental human rights, and

(*c*) to verify, as a prior condition to the exercise of the powers granted under subparagraph (*b*) above, whether the domestic legal procedures and remedies of each member state not a Party to the Convention have been duly applied and exhausted.

IACM's jurisprudence under *ADRD*, as published in its annual reports to the OAS and in its 'country studies', is noted in the relevant sections in Parts II and III above.

§29.2 The provisions of *AMR* for IACM and IACT

§29.2.1 INSTITUTIONS AND MANDATE

AMR

33. The following organs shall have competence with respect to matters relating to the fulfillment of the commitments made by the States Parties to this Convention:

(*a*) the Inter-American Commission on Human Rights, referred to as 'The Commission'; and

(*b*) the Inter-American Court of Human Rights, referred to as 'The Court'.

41. The main functions of the Commission shall be to promote respect for and defense of human rights. In the exercise of its mandate, it shall have the following functions and powers:

(*a*) to develop an awareness of human rights among the peoples of America;

(*b*) to make recommendations to the governments of the member states, when it considers such action advisable, for the adoption of progressive measures in favor of human rights within the framework of their domestic law and constitutional provisions as well as appropriate measures to further the observance of those rights;

(c) to prepare such studies or reports as it considers advisable in the performance of its duties;

(d) to request the governments of the member states to supply it with information on the measures adopted by them in matters of human rights;

(e) to respond, through the General Secretariat of the Organization of American States, to inquiries made by the member states on matters related to human rights and, within the limits of its possibilities, to provide those states with the advisory services they request;

(f) to take action on petitions and other communications pursuant to its authority, under the provisions of Articles 44 through 51 of this Convention; and

(g) to submit an annual report to the General Assembly of the Organization of American States.

§ 29.2.2 IACM: COMPOSITION AND ORGANIZATION

AMR

34. The Inter-American Commission on Human Rights shall be composed of seven members, who shall be persons of high moral character and recognized competence in the field of human rights.

35. The Commission shall represent all the member countries of the Organization of American States.

36 (1) The members of the Commission shall be elected in a personal capacity by the General Assembly of the Organization from a list of candidates proposed by the governments of the member states.

(2) Each of those governments may propose up to three candidates, who may be nationals of the states proposing them or of any other member state of the Organization of American States. When a slate of three is proposed, at least one of the candidates shall be a national of a state other than the one proposing the slate.

37 (1) The members of the Commission shall be elected for a term of four years and may be reelected only once, but the terms of three of the members chosen in the first election shall expire at the end of two years. Immediately following that election the General Assembly shall determine the names of those three members of the Commission by lot.

38. Vacancies that may occur on the Commission for reasons other than the normal expiration of a term shall be filled by the Permanent Council of the Organization in accordance with the provisions of the Statute of the Commission.

39. The Commission shall prepare its Statute,[4] which it shall submit to the General Assembly for approval. It shall establish its own Regulations.[4]

40. Secretariat services for the Commission shall be furnished by the appropriate specialized unit of the General Secretariat of the Organization. This unit shall be provided with the resources required to accomplish the tasks assigned to it by the Commission.

70 (1) The . . . members of the Commission shall enjoy, from the moment of their election and throughout their term of office, the immunities extended to diplomatic agents in accordance with international law. During the exercise of their official function they shall, in addition, enjoy the diplomatic privileges necessary for the performance of their duties.

(2) At no time shall . . . the members of the Commission be held liable for any decisions or opinions issued in the exercise of their functions.

71. The position of . . . member of the Commission is incompatible with any other activity that might affect the independence or impartiality of such . . . member, as determined in the respective statutes.

72. The . . . members of the Commission shall receive emoluments and travel allowances in the form and under the conditions set forth in their statutes, with due regard for the importance and independence of their office. Such emoluments and travel allowances shall be determined in the budget of the Organization of American States.

73. The General Assembly may, only at the request of the Commission, . . . determine sanctions to be applied against members of the Commission . . . when there are justifiable grounds for such action as set forth in the respective statutes. A vote of a two-thirds majority of the member states of the Organization shall be required for a decision in the case of members of the Commission.

§ 29.2.3 IACM: COMPETENCE

AMR

44. Any person or group of persons, or any nongovernmental entity legally recognized in one or more member states of the Organization, may lodge petitions with the Commission containing denunciations or complaints of violation of this Convention by a State Party.

---

[4] Both these are reproduced in the Commission's *Handbook of Existing Rules Pertaining to Human Rights* (OAS/Ser. L/V/II.50, doc. 6).

45 (1) Any State Party may, when it deposits its instrument of ratification of or adherence to this Convention, or at any later time, declare that it recognizes the competence of the Commission to receive and examine communications in which a State Party alleges that another State Party has committed a violation of a human right set forth in this Convention.

(2) Communications presented by virtue of this article may be admitted and examined only if they are presented by a State Party that has made a declaration recognizing the aforementioned competence of the Commission. The Commission shall not admit any communication against a State Party that has not made such a declaration.

(3) A declaration concerning recognition of competence may be made to be valid for an indefinite time, for a specified period, or for a specific case.

(4) Declarations shall be deposited with the General Secretariat of the Organization of American States, which shall transmit copies thereof to the member states of that Organization.

46 (1) Admission by the Commission of a petition or communication lodged in accordance with Articles 44 or 45 shall be subject to the following requirements:

(a) that the remedies under domestic law have been pursued and exhausted in accordance with generally recognized principles of international law;

(b) that the petition or communication is lodged within a period of six months from the date on which the party alleging violation of his rights was notified of the final judgment;

(c) that the subject of the petition or communication is not pending before another international procedure for settlement; and

(d) that, in the case of Article 44, the petition contains the name, nationality, profession, domicile, and signature of the person or persons or of the legal representative of the entity lodging the petition.

(2) The provisions of paragraphs 1(a) and 1(b) of this article shall not be applicable when:

(a) the domestic legislation of the state concerned does not afford due process of law for the protection of the right or rights that have allegedly been violated;

(b) the party alleging violation of his rights has been denied access to the remedies under domestic law or has been prevented from exhausting them; or (*c*) there has been unwarranted delay in rendering a final judgment under the aforementioned remedies.

47. The Commission shall consider inadmissible any petition or communication submitted under Articles 44 or 45 if:

(*a*) any of the requirements indicated in Article 46 has not been met;

(*b*) the petition or communication does not state facts that tend to establish a violation of the rights guaranteed by this Convention;

(*c*) the statements of the petitioner or of the state indicate that the petition or communication is manifestly groundless or obviously out of order; or

(*d*) the petition or communication is substantially the same as one previously studied by the Commission or by another international organization.

COMMENT

Note that the preconditions for the competence of IACM under *AMR* are the converse of those for EUCM (see § 28.3): the Commission may consider individual petitions at any time, but may consider State communications only where the respondent State has made the appropriate declaration of competence. (As to these, see Table A.) No such prior declarations will be required for the consideration by [AFCM] of communications from either source: see §§ 30.4 and 30.5.

Unlike the procedure before HRC (see § 27.3) and EUCM, the petition need not come from the victim of the alleged violation. The time limit of six months after the exhaustion of domestic remedies is also required for the procedure before EUCM, as is the requirement that the petition must not be manifestly groundless. But, unlike all the other procedures, there is no requirement that the petition must be 'compatible' with the Convention.

The jurisprudence of IACM under *AMR* is noted in the relevant sections in Parts II and III above.

§ 29.2.4 IACM: PROCEDURE

AMR

48 (1) When the Commission receives a petition or communication alleging violation of any of the rights protected by this Convention, it shall proceed as follows:

(*a*) If it considers the petition or communication admissible, it shall request information from the government of the state indicated as being responsible for the alleged violations and shall furnish that government a transcript of the pertinent portions of the petition or communication. This information shall be submitted within a reasonable period to be determined by the Commission in accordance with the circumstances of each case.

(*b*) After the information has been received, or after the period established has elapsed and the information has not been received, the Commission shall ascertain whether the grounds for the petition or communication still exist. If they do not, the Commission shall order the record to be closed.

(*c*) The Commission may also declare the petition or communication inadmissible or out of order on the basis of information or evidence subsequently received.

(*d*) If the record has not been closed, the Commission shall, with the knowledge of the parties, examine the matter set forth in the petition or communication in order to verify the facts. If necessary and advisable, the Commission shall carry out an investigation, for the effective conduct of which it shall request, and the states concerned shall furnish to it, all necessary facilities.

(*e*) The Commission may request the states concerned to furnish any pertinent information and, if so requested, shall hear oral statements or receive written statements from the parties concerned.

(*f*) The Commission shall place itself at the disposal of the parties concerned with a view to reaching a friendly settlement of the matter on the basis of respect for the human rights recognized in this Convention.

(2) However, in serious and urgent cases, only the presentation of a petition or communication that fulfills all the formal requirements of admissibility shall be necessary in order for the Commission to conduct an investigation with the prior consent of the state in whose territory a violation has allegedly been committed.

49. If a friendly settlement has been reached in accordance with paragraph 1 (*f*) of Article 48, the Commission shall draw up a report, which shall be transmitted to the petitioner and to the States Parties to this Convention, and shall then be communicated to the Secretary General of the Organization of American States for publication. This report shall contain a brief statement of the facts and of the solution reached. If any party in the case so requests, the fullest possible information shall be provided to it.

50 (1) If a settlement is not reached, the Commission shall, within the time limit established by its Statute, draw up a report setting forth the facts and stating its conclusions. If the report, in whole or in part, does not represent the unanimous agreement of the members of the Commission, any member may attach to it a separate opinion.

The written and oral statements made by the parties in accordance with paragraph 1 (*e*) of Article 48 shall also be attached to the report.

(2) The report shall be transmitted to the states concerned, which shall not be at liberty to publish it.

(3) In transmitting the report, the Committee may make such proposals and recommendations as it sees fit.

51 (1) If, within a period of three months from the date of the transmittal of the report of the Commission to the states concerned, the matter has not either been settled or submitted by the Commission or by the state concerned to the Court and its jurisdiction accepted, the Commission may, by the vote of an absolute majority of its members, set forth its opinion and conclusions concerning the question submitted for its consideration.

(2) Where appropriate, the Commission shall make pertinent recommendations and shall prescribe a period within which the state is to take the measures that are incumbent upon it to remedy the situation examined.

(3) When the prescribed period has expired, the Commission shall decide by the vote of an absolute majority of its members whether the state has taken adequate measures and whether to publish its report.

§ 29.2.5 IACT: COMPOSITION AND ORGANIZATION

AMR

52 (1) The Court shall consist of seven judges, nationals of the member states of the Organization, elected in an individual capacity from among jurists of the highest moral authority and of recognized competence in the field of human rights, who possess the qualifications required for the exercise of the highest judicial functions in conformity with the law of the state of which they are nationals or of the state that proposes them as candidates.

(2) No two judges may be nationals of the same state.

53 (1) The judges of the Court shall be elected by secret ballot by an absolute majority vote of the States Parties to the Convention in the General Assembly of the Organization, from a panel of candidates proposed by those states.

(2) Each of the States Parties may propose up to three candidates, nationals of the state that proposes them or of any other member state of the Organization of American States. When a slate of three

is proposed, at least one of the candidates shall be a national of a state other than the one proposing the slate.

54 (1) The judges of the Court shall be elected for a term of six years and may be reelected only once. The term of three of the judges chosen in the first election shall expire at the end of three years. Immediately after the election, the names of the three judges shall be determined by lot in the General Assembly.

(2) A judge elected to replace a judge whose term has not expired shall complete the term of the latter.

(3) The judges shall continue in office until the expiration of their term. However, they shall continue to serve with regard to cases that they have begun to hear and that are still pending, for which purposes they shall not be replaced by the newly elected judges.

55 (1) If a judge is a national of any of the States Parties to a case submitted to the Court, he shall retain his right to hear that case.

(2) If one of the judges called upon to hear a case should be a national of one the States Parties to the case, any other State Party in the case may appoint a person of its choice to serve on the Court as an *ad hoc* judge.

(3) If among the judges called upon to hear a case none is a national of any of the States Parties to the case, each of the latter may appoint an *ad hoc* judge.

(4) An *ad hoc* judge shall possess the qualifications indicated in Article 52.

(5) If several States Parties to the Convention should have the same interest in a case, they shall be considered as a single party for purposes of the above provisions. In case of doubt, the Court shall decide.

56. Five judges shall constitute a quorum for the transaction of business by the Court.

57. The Commission shall appear in all cases before the Court.

58 (1) The Court shall have its seat at the place determined by the States Parties to the Convention in the General Assembly of the Organization; however, it may convene in the territory of any member state of the Organization of American States when a majority of the Court consider it desirable, and with the prior consent of the state concerned.

The seat of the Court may be changed by the States Parties to the Convention in the General Assembly by a two thirds vote.

(2) The Court shall appoint its own Secretary.

(3) The Secretary shall have his office at the place where the Court has its seat and shall attend the meetings that the Court may hold away from its seat.

59. The Court shall establish its Secretariat, which shall function under the direction of the Secretary of the Court, in accordance with administrative standards of the General Secretariat of the Organization in all respects not incompatible with the independence of the Court. The staff of the Court's Secretariat shall be appointed by the Secretary General of the Organization, in consultation with the Secretary of the Court.

70 (1) The judges of the Court . . . shall enjoy, from the moment of their election and throughout their term of office, the immunities extended to diplomatic agents in accordance with international law. During the exercise of their official function they shall, in addition, enjoy the diplomatic privileges necessary for the performance of their duties.

(2) At no time shall the judges of the Court . . . be held liable for any decisions or opinions issued in the exercise of their functions.

71. The position of judge of the Court . . . is incompatible with any other activity that might affect the independence or impartiality of such judge . . ., as determined in the respective statutes.

72. The judges of the Court . . . shall receive emoluments and travel allowances in the form and under the conditions set forth in their statutes, with due regard for the importance and independence of their office. Such emoluments and travel allowances shall be determined in the budget of the Organization of American States, which shall also include the expenses of the Court and its Secretariat. To this end, the Court shall draw up its own budget and submit it for approval to the General Assembly through the General Secretariat. The latter may not introduce any changes in it.

73. The General Assembly may, only at the request of . . . the Court, . . . determine sanctions to be applied against . . . judges of the Court when there are justifiable grounds for such action as set forth in the respective statutes. A vote of a two-thirds majority of the member states of the Organization shall be required for a decision . . . and . . . a two-thirds majority vote of the States Parties to the Convention shall also be required.

§ 29.2.6 IACT: JURISDICTION

AMR

61 (1) Only the States Parties and the Commission shall have the right to submit a case to the Court.

(2) In order for the Court to hear a case, it is necessary that the procedures set forth in Articles 48 to 50 shall have been completed.

62 (1) A State Party may, upon depositing its instrument of ratification or adherence to this Convention, or at any subsequent time, declare that it recognizes as binding, *ipso facto*, and not requiring special agreement, the jurisdiction of the Court on all matters relating to the interpretation or application of this Convention.

(2) Such declaration may be made unconditionally, on the condition of reciprocity, for a specified period, or for specific cases. It shall be presented to the Secretary General of the Organization, who shall submit copies thereof to the other member states of the Organization and to the Secretary of the Court.

(3) The jurisdiction of the Court shall comprise all cases concerning the interpretation and application of the provisions of this Convention that are submitted to it, provided that the States Parties to the case recognize or have recognized such jurisdiction, whether by special declaration pursuant to the preceding paragraphs, or by a special agreement.

64 (1) The member states of the Organization may consult the Court regarding the interpretation of this Convention or of other treaties concerning the protection of human rights in the American states. Within their spheres of competence, the organs listed in Chapter X of the Charter of the Organization of American States, as amended by the Protocol of Buenos Aires, may in like manner consult the Court.

(2) The Court, at the request of a member state of the Organization, may provide that state with opinions regarding the compatibility of any of its domestic laws with the aforesaid international instruments.

65. To each regular session of the General Assembly of the Organization of American States the Court shall submit, for the Assembly's consideration, a report on its work during the previous year. It shall specify, in particular, the cases in which a state has not complied with its judgments, making any pertinent recommendations.

COMMENT

Note that, as in the case of EUCT, an individual petitioner cannot be a party, and has no *locus standi* as such, before IACT.

By 1 January 1982, IACT had not yet delivered or published any final judgments, nor had it decided whether it had jurisdiction to entertain a case directly referred to it by a State Party at first instance — that is, without the prior consideration of any communication by IACM — the State Party having expressly waived both the need for the exhaustion of domestic remedies and the provisions of *AMR* 61(2).[5]

§ 29.2.7 IACT: PROCEDURE

AMR

60. The Court shall draw up its Statute,[6] which it shall submit to the General Assembly for approval. It shall adopt its own Rules of Procedure.[6]

63 (1) If the Court finds that there has been a violation of a right or freedom protected by this Convention, the Court shall rule that the injured party be ensured the enjoyment of his right or freedom that was violated. It shall also rule, if appropriate, that the consequences of the measure or situation that constituted the breach of such right or freedom be remedied and that fair compensation be paid to the injured party.

(2) In cases of extreme gravity and urgency, and when necessary to avoid irreparable damage to persons, the Court shall adopt such provisional measures as it deems pertinent in matters it has under consideration. With respect to a case not yet submitted to the Court, it may act at the request of the Commission.

66 (1) Reasons shall be given for the judgment of the Court.

(2) If the judgment does not represent in whole or in part the unanimous opinion of the judges, any judge shall be entitled to have his dissenting or separate opinion attached to the judgment.

67. The judgment of the Court shall be final and not subject to appeal. In case of disagreement as to the meaning or scope of the judgment, the Court shall interpret it at the request of any of the parties, provided the request is made within ninety days from the date of notification of the judgment.

---

[5] See its interlocutory judgment of 22 July 1981, No. G.101/81, in *Government of Costa Rica, in the matter of Viviana Gallardo et al.*

[6] Both are reproduced in IACT's Annual Report for 1980 to the General Assembly of the OAS (OEA/Ser. L/V/III.3/doc. 13).

68 (1) The States Parties to the Convention undertake to comply with the judgment of the Court in any case to which they are parties.

(2) That part of a judgment that stipulates compensatory damages may be executed in the country concerned in accordance with domestic procedure governing the execution of judgments against the state.

69. The parties to the case shall be notified of the judgment of the Court and it shall be transmitted to the States Parties to the Convention.

§ 29.2.8 SUPERVISION

AMR

42. The States Parties shall transmit to the Commission a copy of each of the reports and studies that they submit annually to the Executive Committees of the Inter-American Economic and Social Council and the Inter-American Council for Education, Science, and Culture, in their respective fields, so that the Commission may watch over the promotion of the rights implicit in the economic, social, educational, scientific, and cultural standards set forth in the Charter of the Organization of American States as amended by the Protocol of Buenos Aires.

43. The States Parties undertake to provide the Commission with such information as it may request of them as to the manner in which their domestic law ensures the effective application of any provisions of this Convention.

COMMENT

Note that, unlike the supervision procedures for *ICPR* (see §27.4), *ICES* (see §31.2), and *ESC* (see §32), this procedure confers no explicit powers on IACM to express its own comments or conclusions on the reports and information transmitted to it by the State Parties.

§30. THE AFRICAN COMMISSION ON HUMAN AND PEOPLES' RIGHTS ([AFCM])

§30.1 Institution and mandate

[*AFR*]

30. An African Commission on Human and Peoples' Rights, hereinafter called "the Commission", shall be established within the Organization of African Unity to promote human and peoples' rights and ensure their protection in Africa.

45. The functions of the Commission shall be:

1. To promote human and peoples' rights and in particular:

(*a*) To collect documents, undertake studies and researches on African problems in the field of human and peoples' rights, organize seminars, symposia and conferences, disseminate information, encourage national and local institutions concerned with human and peoples' rights, and should the case arise, give its views or make recommendations to Governments.

(*b*) To formulate and lay down principles and rules aimed at solving legal problems relating to human and peoples' rights and fundamental freedoms upon which African Governments may base their legislations.

(*c*) To co-operate with other African and international institutions concerned with the promotion and protection of human and peoples' rights.

2. Ensure the protection of human and peoples' rights under conditions laid down by the present Charter.

3. Interpret all the provisions of the present Charter at the request of a State Party, an institution of the OAU or an African organization recognized by the OAU.

4. Perform any other tasks which may be entrusted to it by the Assembly of Heads of State and Government.

COMMENT

As [*AFR*] has not yet entered into force, [AFCM] has not yet been established.

§ 30.2 Composition and organization

[*AFR*]

31 (1) The Commission shall consist of eleven members chosen from amongst African personalities of the highest reputation, known for their high morality, integrity, impartiality and competence in matters of human and peoples' rights; particular consideration being given to persons having legal experience.

(2) The members of the Commission shall serve in their personal capacity.

32. The Commission shall not include more than one national of the same State.

33. The members of the Commission shall be elected by secret ballot by the Assembly of Heads of State and Government, from a list of persons nominated by the States parties to the present Charter.

34. Each State party to the present Charter may nominate not more than two candidates. The candidates must have the nationality of one of the State parties to the present Charter. When two candidates are nominated by a State, one of them may not be a national of that State.

35 (1) The Secretary General of the Organization of African Unity shall invite State parties to the present Charter at least four months before the elections to nominate candidates.

(2) The Secretary General of the Organization of African Unity shall make an alphabetical list of the persons thus nominated and communicate it to the Heads of State and Government at least one month before the elections.

36. The members of the Commission shall be elected for a six year period and shall be eligible for re-election. However, the term of office of four of the members elected at the first election shall terminate after two years, and the term of office of three others at the end of four years.

37. Immediately after the first election, the Chairman of the Assembly of Heads of State and Government of the Organization of African Unity shall draw lots to decide the names of those members referred to in Article 36.

38. After their election, the members of the Commission shall make a solemn declaration to discharge their duties impartially and faithfully.

39 (1) In case of death or resignation of a member of the Commission, the Chairman of the Commission shall immediately inform the Secretary General of the Organization of African Unity, who shall declare the seat vacant from the date of death or from the date on which the resignation takes effect.

(2) If, in the unanimous opinion of other members of the Commission, a member has stopped discharging his duties for any reason other than a temporary absence, the Chairman of the Commission shall inform the Secretary General of the Organization of African Unity, who shall then declare the seat vacant.

(3) In each of the cases anticipated above, the Assembly of Heads of State and Government shall replace the member whose seat became vacant for the remaining period of his term unless the period is less than six months.

40. Every member of the Commission shall be in office until the date his successor assumes office.

41. The Secretary General of the Organization of African Unity shall appoint the Secretary of the Commission. He shall also provide the staff and services necessary for the effective discharge of the duties of the Commission. The Organization of African Unity shall bear the cost of the staff and services.

42 (1) The Commission shall elect its Chairman and Vice Chairman for a two-year period. They shall be eligible for re-election.

(2) The Commission shall lay down its rules of procedure,

(3) Seven members shall form the quorum.

(4) In case of an equality of votes, the Chairman shall have a casting vote.

(5) The Secretary General may attend the meetings of the Commission. He shall neither participate in deliberations nor shall he be entitled to vote. The Chairman of the Commission may, however, invite him to speak.

43. In discharging their duties, members of the Commission shall enjoy diplomatic privileges and immunities provided for in the General Convention on the Privileges and Immunities of the Organization of African Unity.

44. Provision small be made for the emoluments and allowances of the members of the Commission in the Regular Budget of the Organization of African Unity.

COMMENT

As [*AFR*] has not yet entered into force, the members of [AFCM] have not yet been appointed.

§30.3 Procedure

[*AFR*]

46. The Commission may resort to any appropriate method of investigation; it may hear from the Secretary General of the Organization of African Unity or any other person capable of enlightening it.

60. The Commission shall draw inspiration from international law on human and peoples' rights, particularly from the provisions of various African instruments on human and peoples' rights, the Charter of the United Nations, the Charter of the Organization of African Unity, the Universal Declaration of Human Rights, other instruments adopted by the United Nations and by African countries in the field of human and peoples' rights as well as from the provisions of various instruments adopted within the Specialised Agencies of the United Nations of which the parties to the present Charter are members.

61. The Commission shall also take into consideration, as subsidiary measures to determine the principles of law, other general or special international conventions, laying down rules expressly recognized by member States of the Organization of African Unity, African practices consistent with international norms on human and peoples' rights, customs generally accepted as law, general principles of law recognized by African states as well as legal precedents and doctrine.

COMMENT

Although [AFCM]'s powers of investigation, and competent sources of information, will be very wide, the general tenor of [*AFR* 60 and 61] might on one construction be read as precluding the Commission from considering any of the jurisprudence of the competent institutions under any of the other *regional* human rights treaties. However, it may be that these are admitted by the references to 'international law on human . . . rights' at the beginning of [*AFR* 60], and to 'legal precedents' at the end of [*AFR* 61].

§30.4 State communications

[AFR]

47. If a State party to the present Charter has good reasons to believe that another State party to this Charter has violated the provisions of the Charter, it may draw, by written communication, the attention of that State to the matter. This communication shall also be addressed to the Secretary General of the OAU and to the Chairman of the Commission. Within three months of the receipt of the communication, the State to which the communication is addressed shall give the enquiring State a written explanation or statement elucidating the matter. This should include as much as possible relevant information relating to the laws and rules of procedure applied and applicable and the redress already given or course of action available.

48. If within three months from the date on which the original communication is received by the State to which it is addressed, the issue is not settled to the satisfaction of the two States involved through bilateral negotiation or by any other peaceful procedure, either State shall have the right to submit the matter to the Commission through the Chairman and shall notify the other State involved.

49. Notwithstanding the provisions of Article 47, if a State party to the present Charter considers that another State party has violated the provisions of the Charter, it may refer the matter directly to the Commission by addressing a communication to the Chairman, to the Secretary General of the Organization of African Unity and the State concerned.

50. The Commission can only deal with a matter submitted to it after making sure that all local remedies, if they exist, have been exhausted, unless it is obvious to the Commission that the procedure of achieving these remedies would be unduly prolonged.

51 (1) The Commission may ask the States concerned to provide it with all relevant information.

(2) When the Commission is considering the matter, States concerned may be represented before it and submit written or oral representations.

52. After having obtained from the States concerned and from other sources all the information it deems necessary and after having tried all appropriate means to reach an amicable solution based on the respect of human and peoples' rights, the Commission shall prepare, within a reasonable period of time from the notification referred to

in Article 48, a report stating the facts and its findings. This report shall be sent to the State concerned and communicated to the Assembly of Heads of State and Government.

53. While transmitting its report, the Commission may make to the Assembly of Heads of State and Government such recommendations as it deems useful.

54. The Commission shall submit to each Ordinary Session of the Assembly of Heads of State and Government a report on its activities.

COMMENT

Note that, unlike IACM under *AMR* (see §29.2.3), [AFCM] will require no prior declarations of competence to consider State communications.

§30.5 Other communications

[*AFR*]

55 (1) Before each Session, the Secretary of the Commission shall make a list of the communications other than those of State parties to the present Charter and transmit them to the Members of the Commission, who shall indicate which communications should be considered by the Commission.

(2) A communication shall be considered by the Commission if a simple majority of its members so decide.

56. Communications relating to human and peoples' rights referred to in Article 55 received by the Commission shall be considered if they:

(1) indicate their authors even if the latter request anonymity,
(2) are compatible with the Charter of the Organization of African Unity or with the present Charter,
(3) are not written in disparaging or insulting language directed against the State concerned and its institutions or to the Organization of African Unity,
(4) are not based exclusively on news disseminated through the mass media,
(5) are sent after exhausting local remedies, if any, unless it is obvious that this procedure is unduly prolonged,
(6) are submitted within a reasonable period from the time local remedies are exhausted or from the date the Commission is seized of the matter, and
(7) do not deal with cases which have been settled by these States

involved in accordance with the principles of the Charter of the United Nations, or the Charter of the Organization of African Unity, or the provisions of the present Charter.

57. Prior to any substantive consideration, all communications shall be brought to the knowledge of the State concerned by the Chairman of the Commission.

58 (1) When it appears after deliberations of the Commission that one or more communications apparently reveal the existence of a series of serious or massive violations of human and peoples' rights, the Commission shall draw the attention of the Assembly of Heads of State and Government to them.

(2) The Assembly of Heads of State and Government may then request the Commission to undertake an in-depth study of these situations and make a factual report, accompanied by its findings and recommendations.

(3) A case of emergency duly noticed by the Commission shall be submitted by the latter to the Chairman of the Assembly of Heads of State and Government who may request an in-depth study.

59 (1) All measures taken within the provisions of the present Charter shall remain confidential until such a time as the Assembly of Heads of State and Government shall otherwise decide.

(2) However, the report shall be published by the Chairman of the Commission upon the decision of the Assembly of Heads of State and Government.

(3) The report on the activities of the Commission shall be published by its Chairman after it has been considered by the Assembly of Heads of State and Government.

COMMENT

Note that, unlike EUCM (see § 28.3), [AFCM] will require no prior declarations of competence to consider these communications.

Unlike the procedure before HRC (see § 27.3) and EUCM, these communications need not come from the victim of the alleged violations. As in the case of the procedures before CHR (see § 31.1) and the UNESCO Committee (see § 34), the requirement under this procedure is that the case must not 'have been settled' by the State concerned, rather than — as in the case of the other procedures — that it must not be 'pending' under another procedure. The time limit is 'a reasonable period' after the exhaustion of domestic remedies, as in the case of the procedures before CHR and UNESCO, and unlike the six months' limit in the procedures before EUCM (see § 28.3) and IACM under *AMR* (see § 29.2.3). The requirements that the communication must not be 'insulting' to the State concerned, or based exclusively on reports in the mass media, are also to be found in the procedures before CHR and UNESCO, but not in any of the others.

§30.6 Supervision

[*AFR*]

62. Each State party shall undertake to submit every two years, from the date the present Charter comes into force, a report on the legislative or other measures taken with a view to giving effect to the rights and freedoms recognized and guaranteed by the present Charter.

COMMENT

Unlike the supervision procedures for *ICPR* (see §27.4), *ICES* (see §31.2) and *ESC* (see §32), this procedure makes no provision for the expression of any comments or conclusions by [AFCM] on the material submitted to it.

§31. THE UN ECONOMIC AND SOCIAL COUNCIL (ECOSOC)

ECOSOC derives its existence from Chapter X of *UNCH*. It is an intergovernmental organ, consisting of 27 of the UN's Member States, elected by the UNGA.[1] One of its functions is that it 'may make recommendations for the purpose of promoting respect for, and observance of, human rights and fundamental freedoms for all'.[2] It is under an obligation to set up Commissions, among other things 'for the promotion of human rights'.[3]

By its constitution, ECOSOC is essentially a political rather than a judicial organ. However, for the purposes of the present work, it has two potentially important functions: parentage of CHR, and supervision of *ICES*.

§ 31.1 The UN Commission on Human Rights (CHR)

The initial terms of reference under which ECOSOC established CHR in 1946 were as follows:

To submit proposals, recommendations, and reports to [ECOSOC] regarding
(a) an international bill of rights;
(b) international declarations or conventions on civil liberties, the status of women, freedom of information, and similar matters;
(c) the protection of minorities;
(d) the prevention of discrimination on grounds of race, sex, language or religion; and
(e) any other matter concerning human rights not covered by items (a), (b), (c) and (d).[4]

The members of CHR sit as representatives of their governments. A Sub-Commission on Prevention of Discrimination and Protection of Minorities has also been established, whose members sit in their capacities as individual experts.

For the first twenty years of its existence, CHR took the view that it had no power 'to take any action in regard to any complaints concerning human rights',[5] although the UN Secretary-General regularly transmitted to the Commission lists of complaints (formally called 'communications') received by the UN, with indications of their substance, under a succession of ECOSOC resolutions eventually consolidated into Resolution 728F (XXVIII).[6] However, in 1967 CHR sought — and by ECOSOC Resolution 1235 (XLII)[7] obtained — powers to receive information, through the Sub-Commission, on violations of human rights and fundamental freedoms from 'all available sources', including information relevant to 'gross violations of human rights' contained in the com-

---

[1] *UNCH* 61(1).
[2] *UNCH* 62(2).
[3] *UNCH* 68.
[4] ECOSOC Resolutions 6(I) of 16 February 1946 and 9(II) of 21 June 1946.
[5] ECOSOC Resolution 75(V) of 5 August 1947.
[6] 30 July 1959.
[7] 6 June 1967.

munications listed under Resolution 728F, and 'to make a thorough study of situations which reveal a consistent pattern of violations of human rights, and to report with recommendations thereon' to ECOSOC.

Under Resolution 1235, therefore, CHR has power to consider complaints from any source containing information about 'gross' violations of human rights, and to initiate a 'thorough study' of the situation if that information reveals a 'consistent pattern' of violations of human rights. CHR has in fact carried out several such studies.

Three years later,[8] ECOSOC adopted a further resolution — Resolution 1503 (XLVIII) — of which the following is the full text:

Procedure for dealing with communications relating to violations of human rights and fundamental freedoms

The Economic and Social Council,

Noting resolutions 7 (XXVI) and 17 (XXV) of the Commission on Human Rights and resolution 2 (XXI) of the Sub-Commission on Prevention of Discrimination and Protection of Minorities,

1. *Authorizes* the Sub-Commission on Prevention of Discrimination and Protection of Minorities to appoint a working group consisting of not more than five of its members, with due regard to geographical distribution, to meet once a year in private meetings for a period not exceeding ten days immediately before the sessions of the Sub-Commission to consider all communications, including replies of Governments thereon, received by the Secretary-General under Council resolution 728 F (XXVIII) of 30 July 1959 with a view to bringing to the attention of the Sub-Commission those communications, together with replies of Governments, if any, which appear to reveal a consistent pattern of gross and reliably attested violations of human rights and fundamental freedoms within the terms of reference of the Sub-Commission;

2. *Decides* that the Sub-Commission on Prevention of Discrimination and Protection of Minorities should, as the first stage in the implementation of the present resolution, devise at its twenty-third session appropriate procedures for dealing with the question of admissibility of communications received by the Secretary-General under Council resolution 728 F (XXVIII) and in accordance with Council resolution 1235 (XLII) of 6 June 1967;

3. *Requests* the Secretary-General to prepare a document on the question of admissibility of communications for the Sub-Commission's consideration at its twenty-third session;

4. *Further requests* the Secretary-General:

(*a*) To furnish to the members of the Sub-Commission every month a list of communications prepared by him in accordance with Council resolution 728 F (XXVIII) and a brief description of them, together with the text of any replies received from Governments,

(*b*) To make available to the members of the working group at their meetings the originals of such communications listed as they may request, having due regard to the provisions of paragraph 2(*b*) of Council resolution 728F (XXVIII) concerning the divulging of the identity of the authors of communications;

(*c*) To circulate to the members of the Sub-Commission, in the working languages, the originals of such communications as are referred to the Sub-Commission by the working group;

5. *Requests* the Sub-Commission on Prevention of Discrimination and Protection of Minorities to consider in private meetings, in accordance with paragraph 1 above, the communications brought before it in accordance with the decision of a majority of the members of the working group and any replies of

[8] 27 May 1970.

Governments relating thereto and other relevant information, with a view to determining whether to refer to the Commission on Human Rights particular situations which appear to reveal a consistent pattern of gross and reliably attested violations of human rights requiring consideration by the Commission;

6. *Requests* the Commission on Human Rights after it has examined any situation referred to it by the Sub-Commission to determine:

(a) Whether it requires a thorough study by the Commission and a report and recommendations thereon to the Council in accordance with paragraph 3 of Council resolution 1235 (XLII);

(b) Whether it may be a subject of an investigation by an *ad hoc* committee to be appointed by the Commission which shall be undertaken only with the express consent of the State concerned and shall be conducted in constant co-operation with that State and under conditions determined by agreement with it. In any event, the investigation may be undertaken only if:

   (i) All available means at the national level have been resorted to and exhausted;

   (ii) The situation does not relate to a matter which is being dealt with under other procedures prescribed in the constituent instruments of, or conventions adopted by, the United Nations and the specialized agencies, or in regional conventions, or which the State concerned wishes to submit to other procedures in accordance with general or special international agreements to which it is a party.

7. *Decides* that if the Commission on Human Rights appoints an *ad hoc* committee to carry on an investigation with the consent of the State concerned:

(a) The composition of the committee shall be determined by the Commission. The members of the committee shall be independent persons whose competence and impartiality is beyond question. Their appointment shall be subject to the consent of the Government concerned;

(b) The committee shall establish its own rules of procedure. It shall be subject to the quorum rule. It shall have authority to receive communications and hear witnesses, as necessary. The investigation shall be conducted in co-operation with the Government concerned;

(c) The committee's procedure shall be confidential, its proceedings shall be conducted in private meetings and its communications shall not be publicized in any way;

(d) The committee shall strive for friendly solutions before, during and even after the investigation;

(e) The committee shall report to the Commission on Human Rights with such observations and suggestions as it may deem appropriate;

8. *Decides* that all actions envisaged in the implementation of the present resolution by the Sub-Commission on Prevention of Discrimination and Protection of Minorities or the Commission on Human Rights shall remain confidential until such time as the Commission may decide to make recommendations to the Economic and Social Council;

9. *Decides* to authorize the Secretary-General to provide all facilities which may be required to carry out the present resolution, making use of the existing staff of the Division of Human Rights of the United Nations Secretariat;

10. *Decides* that the procedure set out in the present resolution for dealing with communications relating to violations of human rights and fundamental freedoms should be reviewed if any new organ entitled to deal with such communications should be established within the United Nations or by international agreement.

As to admissibility, the Sub-Commission[9] has adopted the following procedure:

[9] By its Resolution 1(XXIV) of 13 August 1971.

(1) *Standards and criteria*

(a) The object of the communication must not be inconsistent with the relevant principles of the Charter, of the Universal Declaration of Human Rights and of the other applicable instruments in the field of human rights.

(b) Communications shall be admissible only if, after consideration thereof, together with the replies of any of the Governments concerned, there are reasonable grounds to believe that they may reveal a consistent pattern of gross and reliably attested violations of human rights and fundamental freedoms, including policies of racial discrimination and segregation and of *apartheid* in any country, including colonial and other dependent countries and peoples.

(2) *Source of communications*

(a) Admissible communications may originate from a person or group of persons who, it can be reasonably presumed, are victims of the violations referred to in subparagraph (1)(b) above, any person or group of persons who have direct and reliable knowledge of those violations, or non-governmental organizations acting in good faith in accordance with recognized principles of human rights, not resorting to politically motivated stands contrary to the provisions of the Charter of the United Nations and having direct and reliable knowledge of such violations.

(b) Anonymous communications shall be inadmissible; subject to the requirements of subparagraph 2(b) of resolution 728F (XXVIII) of the Economic and Social Council, the author of a communication, whether an individual, a group of individuals or an organization, must be clearly identified.

(c) Communications shall not be inadmissible solely because the knowledge of the individual authors is second-hand, provided that they are accompanied by clear evidence.

(3) *Contents of communications and nature of allegations*

(a) The communication must contain a description of the facts and must indicate the purpose of the petition and the rights that have been violated.

(b) Communications shall be inadmissible if their language is essentially abusive and in particular if they contain insulting references to the State against which the complaint is directed. Such communications may be considered if they meet the other criteria for admissibility after deletion of the abusive language.

(c) A communication shall be inadmissible if it has manifestly political motivations and its subject is contrary to the provisions of the Charter of the United Nations.

(d) A communication shall be inadmissible if it appears that it is based exclusively on reports disseminated by mass media.

(4) *Existence of other remedies*

(a) Communications shall be inadmissible if their admission would prejudice the functions of the specialized agencies of the United Nations system.

(b) Communications shall be inadmissible if domestic remedies have not been exhausted, unless it appears that such remedies would be ineffective or unreasonably prolonged. Any failure to exhaust remedies should be satisfactorily established.

(c) Communications relating to cases which have been settled by the State concerned in accordance with the principles set forth in the Universal Declaration of Human Rights and other applicable documents in the field of human rights will not be considered.

(5) *Timeliness*

A communication shall be inadmissible if it is not submitted to the United Nations within a reasonable time after the exhaustion of the domestic remedies as provided above.

It will be seen that, unlike the procedures before HRC (see §27.3) and EUCM (see §28.3), the communication need not come from any victim of the alleged violations. As in the case of the procedures before [AFCM] (see §30.5) and the UNESCO Committee (see §34), the requirement under this procedure is that the case must not 'have been settled' by the State concerned, rather than — as in the case of the other procedures — that it must not be 'pending' under another procedure. The time limit is 'a reasonable period' after the exhaustion of domestic remedies, as in the case of the procedure before [AFCM], and unlike the six months' limit in the procedures before EUCM (see §28.3) and IACM under *AMR* (see §29.2.3). The requirements that the communication must not be 'insulting' to the State concerned, or based exclusively on reports in the mass media, are also to be found in the procedures before [AFCM] and UNESCO, but not in any of the others.

Note that there is no provision to ensure that complainants have an opportunity of seeing, and commenting on, any replies received from the governments concerned.

The '1503 procedure' in fact comprises three stages:

(1) The Working Group on Communications screens the incoming material, and refers to the Sub-Commission any of it which appears to 'reveal a consistent pattern of gross and reliably attested violations of human rights and fundamental freedoms';
(2) The Sub-Commission then decides which of such 'particular situations' it should refer to CHR;
(3) CHR then decides whether to undertake a 'thorough study' under Resolution 1235, or an 'investigation' under paragraph 6(*b*) of Resolution 1503.

As CHR's competence does not derive directly from the assent of a limited number of State Parties to some specific treaty, it is competent to receive and consider complaints about violations of human rights from any source, and directed against any State. But there must be enough of them to indicate that there is a 'particular situation' in that State revealing a 'consistent pattern' of 'gross' violations of human rights and fundamental freedoms. Accordingly, CHR has no competence to consider, let alone furnish a remedy for, any single complaint by or on behalf of an invididual victim of a violation of his or her human rights.

CHR is composed of governmental representatives, rather than independent individuals. This may account for the fact that, although it has had many 'particular situations' referred to it over the past twelve years, it has not yet made any 'reports and recommendations' on any of them to ECOSOC in pursuance of Resolution 1503.[10]

§31.2 Supervision of *ICES*

ICES

16 (1) The States Parties to the present Covenant undertake to submit in conformity with this part of the Covenant reports on the

---

[10] For an authoritative account of the history and workings of these procedures, see Jakob Th. Möller, 'Petitioning the United Nations'; 1 *Universal Human Rights* 57.

measures which they have adopted and the progress made in achieving the observance of the rights recognized herein.

(2) (*a*) All reports shall be submitted to the Secretary-General of the United Nations, who shall transmit copies to the Economic and Social Council for consideration in accordance with the provisions of the present Covenant.

(*b*) The Secretary-General of the United Nations shall also transmit to the specialized agencies copies of the reports, or any relevant parts therefrom, from States Parties to the present Covenant which are also members of these specialized agencies in so far as these reports, or parts therefrom, relate to any matters which fall within the responsibilities of the said agencies in accordance with their constitutional instruments.

17 (1) The States Parties to the present Covenant shall furnish their reports in stages, in accordance with a programme to be established by the Economic and Social Council within one year of the entry into force of the present Covenant after consultation with the States Parties and the specialized agencies concerned.

(2) Reports may indicate factors and difficulties affecting the degree of fulfilment of obligations under the present Covenant.

(3) Where relevant information has previously been furnished to the United Nations or to any specialized agency by any State Party to the present Covenant, it will not be necessary to reproduce that information, but a precise reference to the information so furnished will suffice.

18. Pursuant to its responsibilities under the Charter of the United Nations in the field of human rights and fundamental freedoms, the Economic and Social Council may make arrangements with the specialized agencies in respect of their reporting to it on the progress made in achieving the observance of the provisions of the present Covenant falling within the scope of their activities. These reports may include particulars of decisions and recommendations on such implementation adopted by their competent organs.

19. The Economic and Social Council may transmit to the Commission on Human Rights for study and general recommendation or as appropriate for information the reports concerning human rights submitted by States in accordance with Articles 16 and 17, and those concerning human rights submitted by the specialized agencies in accordance with Article 18.

20. The States Parties to the present Covenant and the specialized agencies concerned may submit comments to the Economic and

Social Council on any general recommendation under Article 19 or reference to such general recommendation in any report of the Commission on Human Rights or any documentation referred to therein.

21. The Economic and Social Council may submit from time to time to the General Assembly reports with recommendations of a general nature and a summary of the information received from the States Parties to the present Covenant and the specialized agencies on the measures taken and the progress made in achieving general observance of the rights recognized in the present Covenant.

22. The Economic and Social Council may bring to the attention of other organs of the United Nations, their subsidiary organs and specialized agencies concerned with furnishing technical assistance any matters arising out of the reports referred to in this part of the present Covenant which may assist such bodies in deciding, each within its field of competence, on the advisability of international measures likely to contribute to the effective progressive implementation of the present Covenant.

COMMENT

Unlike the procedure for the supervision of *ESC* (see §32), this procedure does not require any consideration of the 'country reports' by any group of independent experts (such as EUCE), as opposed to governmental representatives. However, the ILO's Committee of Experts on the Application of Conventions and Recommendations has in fact studied[11] these reports; where this Committee has expressed views in that connection on the interpretation and application of provisions of *ICES*, they are noted in the relevant section of Part III above.

Although *ICES* has been in force since January 1976 and ECOSOC has received many of these country reports, the formal study of which it has remitted[12] to a Sessional Working Group of Governmental Experts, by 1 January 1982 it had not yet transmitted any of them to CHR, nor had it made any recommendations, even 'of a general nature', to UNGA under *ICES* 21.[13]

---

[11] These studies have been conducted pursuant to *ICES* 18, and their outcome takes the form of Reports to ECOSOC by the ILO Committee, subsequently reissued as UN documents.

[12] By ECOSOC Resolution 1988 (LX) of 11 May 1976, supplemented by Decision 1978/10 of 3 May 1978 and Decision 1981/102 of 6 February 1981.

[13] See the successive Annual Reports of ECOSOC to UNGA, down to the latter's thirty-sixth Session in 1981 (A/36/3/Rev. 1, Ch. XXV); see also *The Review* of the International Commission of Jurists, No. 27, 26.

§32. THE EUROPEAN COMMITTEE OF EXPERTS (EUCE)

ESC

PART IV

21. The Contracting Parties shall send to the Secretary-General of the Council of Europe a report at two-yearly intervals, in a form to be determined by the Committee of Ministers, concerning the application of such provisions of Part II of the Charter as they have accepted.

22. The Contracting Parties shall send to the Secretary-General, at appropriate intervals as requested by the Committee of Ministers, reports relating to the provisions of Part II of the Charter which they did not accept at the time of their ratification or approval or in a subsequent notification. The Committee of Ministers shall determine from time to time in respect of which provisions such reports shall be requested and the form of the reports to be provided.

23 (1) Each Contracting Party shall communicate copies of its reports referred to in Articles 21 and 22 to such of its national organizations as are members of the international organizations of employers and trade unions to be invited under Article 27, paragraph 2, to be represented at meetings of the Sub-committee of the Governmental Social Committee.

(2) The Contracting Parties shall forward to the Secretary-General any comments on the said reports received from these national organizations, if so requested by them.

24. The reports sent to the Secretary-General in accordance with Articles 21 and 22 shall be examined by a Committee of Experts, who shall have also before them any comments forwarded to the Secretary-General in accordance with paragraph 2 of Article 23.

25 (1) The Committee of Experts shall consist of not more than seven members appointed by the Committee of Ministers from a list of independent experts of the highest integrity and of recognized competence in international social questions, nominated by the Contracting Parties.

(2) The members of the Committee shall be appointed for a period of six years. They may be reappointed. However, of the

members first appointed, the terms of office of two members shall expire at the end of four years.

(3) The members whose terms of office are to expire at the end of the initial period of four years shall be chosen by lot by the Committee of Ministers immediately after the first appointment has been made.

(4) A member of the Committee of Experts appointed to replace a member whose term of office has not expired shall hold office for the remainder of his predecessor's term.

26. The International Labour Organization shall be invited to nominate a representative to participate in a consultative capacity in the deliberations of the Committee of Experts.

27 (1) The reports of the Contracting Parties and the conclusions of the Committee of Experts shall be submitted for examination to a Sub-committee of the Governmental Social Committee of the Council of Europe.

(2) The Sub-committee shall be composed of one representative of each of the Contracting parties. It shall invite no more than two international organizations of employers and no more than two international trade union organizations as it may designate to be represented as observers in a consultative capacity at its meetings. Moreover, it may consult no more than two representatives of international non-governmental organizations having consultative status with the Council of Europe, in respect of questions with which the organizations are particularly qualified to deal, such as social welfare, and the economic and social protection of the family.

(3) The Sub-committee shall present to the Committee of Ministers a report containing its conclusions and append the report of the Committee of Experts.

28. The Secretary-General of the Council of Europe shall transmit to the Consultative Assembly the conclusions of the Committee of Experts. The Consultative Assembly shall communicate its views on these Conclusions to the Committee of Ministers.

29. By a majority of two-thirds of the members entitled to sit on the Committee, the Committee of Ministers may, on the basis of the report of the Sub-committee, and after consultation with the Consultative Assembly, make to each Contracting Party any necessary recommendations.

COMMENT

Of all the institutions mentioned in this Part of *ESC*, only EUCE is composed of independent experts, rather than governmental or elected representatives. Its Conclusions are therefore the only part of this supervision procedure which is noted in Part III above.

EUCE has completed a succession of the 'supervision cycles' provided for in *ESC* Part IV. In its Conclusions on the first two of these, it proposed that the Committee of Ministers of the CE should make various 'recommendations' under *ESC* 29 to a number of the State Parties concerned. However, the Committee of Ministers on both occasions declined to do so, and has in fact so far contented itself with drawing the attention of the State Parties to EUCE's Conclusions, the Reports of the Governmental Committee, and the Opinions of the Assembly.[1]

Nonetheless, several of the State Parties have modified their domestic laws, regulations, and practices in order to comply with their obligations under *ESC*, both before and after ratification.[2]

---

[1] See *The European Social Charter*, CE, SOC (80) 3, App. II (1980).

[2] *Ibid.*, 14-15. See also Wiebringhaus, '*Les effets de la charte sociale européenne en droit interne*', in *In Memoriam Sir Otto Kahn-Freund*, Beck (1980).

§33. THE UN SECRETARIAT'S DIVISION OF HUMAN RIGHTS (DHR)

Under *UNCH*, the UN Secretariat is a 'principal organ' of the UN, comprising the Secretary-General, who is the UN's chief administrative officer, and his staff. Their responsibilities are exclusively international, and they may neither seek nor receive instructions from any government, or any other authority outside the UN Organization.

DHR, which has its seat in Geneva, Switzerland, is the Division of the UN Secretariat responsible for assisting in the carrying out of the mandates of *UNCH* in the field of human rights, as established by the competent UN organs. It now reports to the Secretary-General through the Under-Secretary-General for Political and General Assembly Affairs. It is headed by a Director, assisted by a Deputy Director and an Assistant Director, and is organized into three sections — one for international instruments and procedures; one for research, studies, and the prevention of discrimination; and one for advisory services and publications. These sections are in their turn are divided into specialized units.

DHR's functions are to provide secretariat services to all the UN organs concerned with human rights, including HRC, ECOSOC, and CHR and its Sub-Commission; to carry out research on human rights; to handle material and prepare reports; to collect and disseminate information and publications; and to provide appropriate advisory services.

As a secretariat, DHR of course has no direct responsibility either for creating international human rights law, or for making it effective. However, in practice its influence in both these fields has been, and remains, substantial. For example, the first drafts of all the UN's major and subsidiary human rights instruments — including *UDHR*, *ICPR*, and *ICES* — were prepared by DHR, as were HRC's Rules of Procedure. DHR continues to be active in the field of defining and codifying new human rights, such as the 'third-generation' or 'solidarity' rights considered in §26, as well as elaborating subsidiary instruments for existing human rights, such as [*CT*].

DHR also lends its help to the interpretation and application of the instruments in force by their respective competent organs; its International Instruments Unit, for example, has particular responsibilities in connection with the procedures under *ICPR*, *ICES*, *CD*, and *CA*.

§34. THE UN EDUCATIONAL, SCIENTIFIC AND CULTURAL ORGANISATION (UNESCO)

UNESCO is one of the UN's 'specialized agencies', with its headquarters in Paris, France. Article 1 of its Constitution, adopted in 1945, defines its purpose as being

To contribute to peace and security by promoting collaboration among the nations through education, science and culture in order to further universal respect for justice, for the Rule of Law and for the human rights and fundamental freedoms which are affirmed for the peoples of the world . . . by the Charter of the United Nations.

Its principal concerns in the field of human rights are the right to education (see §20), in connection with which its General Conference adopted *CE* (see §20.0.5); freedom of opinion and expression (see §23.4), the rights relating to culture, arts, and science (see §§23.5 and 26.6); as well as the teaching of human rights.

Like CHR (see §31.1), UNESCO began by taking the view that it had no power to take any action on complaints directed to it about violations of human rights.[1] However, after experimenting with a number of procedures over the years,[2] it adopted in 1978 an entirely new procedure for considering such 'communications', by a Decision of the Executive Board[3] of which the following are the relevant parts:

The Executive Board . . .
13. *Decides* that the Committee will henceforth be designated 'the Committee on Conventions and Recommendations';
14. *Decides* that the Committee will continue to carry out its functions with respect to conventions and recommendations and will consider communications received by the Organization concerning cases and questions or violations of human rights within Unesco's fields of competence in accordance with the following conditions and procedures:

Conditions
(*a*) Communications shall be deemed admissible if they meet the following conditions:
  (i) The communication must not be anonymous;
  (ii) the communication must originate from a person or a group of persons who, it can be reasonably presumed, are victims of an alleged violation of any of the human rights referred to in paragraph (iii) below. It may also originate from any person, group of persons or non-governmental organization having reliable knowledge of those violations;

---

[1] Decision 11.3 (1952) of the Executive Board.

[2] For a summary of these, see P. Alston, 'UNESCO's procedures for dealing with human rights violations', 20 *Santa Clara L. R.* 665.

[3] 3.3 (1978).

(iii) the communication must concern violations of human rights falling within Unesco's competence in the fields of education, science, culture and information and must not be motivated exclusively by other considerations;

(iv) the communication must be compatible with the principles of the Organization, the Charter of the United Nations, the Universal Declaration of Human Rights, the international covenants on human rights and other international instruments in the field of human rights;

(v) the communication must not be manifestly ill-founded and must appear to contain relevant evidence;

(vi) the communication must be neither offensive nor an abuse of the right to submit communications. However, such a communication may be considered if it meets all other criteria of admissibility after the exclusion of the offensive or abusive parts;

(vii) the communication must not be based exclusively on information disseminated through the mass media;

(viii) the communication must be submitted within a reasonable time-limit following the facts which constitute its subject-matter or within a reasonable time-limit after the facts have become known;

(ix) the communication must indicate whether an attempt has been made to exhaust available domestic remedies with regard to the facts which constitute the subject-matter of the communication and the results of such an attempt, if any;

(x) communications relating to matters already settled by the States concerned in accordance with the human rights principles set forth in the Universal Declaration of Human Rights and the international covenants on human rights shall not be considered;

Procedures
(b) The Director-General shall:
   (i) acknowledge receipt of communications and inform the authors thereof of the above-mentioned conditions governing admissibility;
   (ii) ascertain that the author of the communication has no objection to his communication, after having been communicated to the government concerned, being brought to the notice of the Committee and to his name being divulged;
   (iii) upon receipt of an affirmative answer from the author of the communication, transmit the communication to the government concerned, informing it that the communication will be brought to the notice of the Committee, together with any reply the government may wish to make;
   (iv) transmit the communication to the Committee, together with the reply, if any, of the government concerned and additional relevant information from the author, taking into account the need to proceed without delay;

(c) The Committee shall examine in private session the communications transmitted to it by the Director-General;

(d) The Committee shall decide on the admissibility of communications in accordance with the above-mentioned conditions;

(e) Representatives of the governments concerned may attend meetings of the Committee in order to provide additional information or to answer questions from members of the Committee on either admissibility or the merits of the communication;

(f) The Committee may avail itself of the relevant information at the disposal of the Director-General;

(g) In consideration of a communication, the Committee may, in exceptional circumstances, request the Executive Board to authorize it under Rule 29 of the Rules of Procedure to take appropriate action;

(*h*) The Committee may keep a communication submitted to it on its agenda while seeking additional information it may consider necessary for the disposition of the matter;

(*i*) The Director-General shall notify the author of the communication and the government concerned of the Committee's decision on the admissibility of the communication;

(*j*) The Committee shall dismiss any communication which, having been found admissible, does not, upon examination of the merits, appear to warrant further action. The author of the communication and the government concerned shall be notified accordingly;

(*k*) Communications which warrant further consideration shall be acted upon by the Committee with a view to helping to bring about a friendly solution designed to advance the promotion of the human rights falling within Unesco's fields of competence;

15. *Decides further* that the Committee shall submit confidential reports to the Executive Board at each session on the carrying out of its mandate under the present decision. These reports shall contain appropriate information arising from its examination of the communications which the Committee considers it useful to bring to the notice of the Executive Board. The reports shall also contain recommendations which the Committee may wish to make either generally or regarding the disposition of a communication under consideration;

16. *Decides* to consider confidential reports of the Committee in private session and to take further action as necessary in accordance with Rule 28 of the Rules of Procedure;

17. *Decides also* that communications transmitted to it by the Committee which testify to the existence of a question shall be dealt with in accordance with paragraph 18 below;

18. *Considers* that questions of massive, systematic or flagrant violations of human rights and fundamental freedoms — including, for example, those perpetrated as a result of policies of aggression, interference in the internal affairs of States, occupation of foreign territory and implementation of a policy of colonialism, genocide, apartheid, racialism, or national and social oppression — falling within Unesco's fields of competence should be considered by the Executive Board and the General Conference in public meetings.

It will be seen that, as in the case of CHR (see §31.1), the UNESCO Committee is competent to consider communications emanating from any source, and directed against any State. The violations must be of a human right 'falling within UNESCO's competence in the fields of education, science, culture and information',[4] but they need not 'reveal a consistent pattern' of 'gross' violations, as in the case of CHR's '1503 procedure'. The Committee's powers to seek information are very wide.

However, as in the case of CHR's '1503 procedure', the complainant does not appear to have any opportunity of seeing, or commenting on, the respondent government's reply, and only the respondent government, and not the complainant, can appear before the Committee when it considers the communication either as to admissibility or on the merits.

The procedure is confidential, and by 1 January 1982 UNESCO had not published any recommendations that may have been made, or indicated whether any action had been taken on them.

---

[4] For a discussion of what these are, see Alston, *op. cit.*, 674-6.

The independent Conciliation and Good Offices Commission, established under the Protocol to *CE* (see §7.0.5) to seek the amicable settlement of disputes between State Parties to that Convention, also operates under the auspices of UNESCO. However, by 1 January 1982 no dispute had yet been referred to it.

§35. THE INTERNATIONAL LABOUR ORGANISATION (ILO)

The ILO, which has its Office in Geneva, Switzerland, was founded in 1919 by the Treaty of Versailles. It was the first 'specialized agency' to be given that status by the UN, under an agreement with ECOSOC (see §31). Its paramount concern is social justice, and the promotion and protection of the human rights and fundamental freedoms most closely linked to that objective. Uniquely, the ILO functions in a tripartite fashion: that is, most of its organs are composed not only of representatives of governments, but also of an equal number of representatives of workers and employers.

Throughout its existence, the ILO has sponsored international conventions in its field of concern, of which more than 150 are now in force which between them have attracted close to 5,000 ratifications, some of them from over 100 States. Several of these are noted in Part III of the present work. The application of these Conventions is controlled by four different procedures.[1]

§35.1 The supervision procedure

Under Article 22 of the ILO's Constitution, each of its Member States is bound to report 'on the measures it has taken to give effect to the provisions of Conventions to which it is a party'. For the most important Conventions, these reports are now required at two-year intervals; for the rest, at four-year ones. They are then examined by a Committee of Experts on the Application of Conventions and Recommendations, consisting of 18 independent persons appointed for terms of three years. That Committee may address direct 'requests' to a State Party in confidence, or include 'observations' in its published reports, which it submits to the annual sessions of the International Labour Conference, where they are examined by a specially appointed tripartite Conference Committee on the Application of Conventions and Recommendations.

§35.2 The representations procedure

This derives from the following Articles in the ILO's Constitution:

24. In the event of any representation being made to the International Labour Office by an industrial association of employers or of workers that any of the Members has failed to secure in any respect the effective observance within its jurisdiction of any Convention to which it is a party, the Governing Body may communicate this representation to the government against which it is made, and may invite that government to make such statement on the subject as it may think fit.

---

[1] For a comprehensive description of this system, see Valticos, *International Labour Law* (Kluwer, 1979).

25. If no statement is received within a reasonable time from the government in question, or if the statement when received is not deemed to be satisfactory by the Governing Body, the latter shall have the right to publish the representation and the statement, if any, made in reply to it.

Standing Orders, originally adopted by the Governing Body in 1932 and most recently revised in 1980,[2] regulate the procedure to be adopted. Under these, the Governing Body first determines, on a report of its Officers, whether the representation is receivable, If it is, it is examined in private by a tripartite Committee of members of the Governing Body, which hears both sides and reports back. The Governing Body then determines, in private, whether to adopt the Committee's recommendations.

§ 35.2 The complaints procedure

This is laid down by the following Articles of the ILO's Constitution:

26 (1) Any of the Members shall have the right to file a complaint with the International Labour Office if it is not satisfied that any other Member is securing the effective observance of any Convention which both have ratified in accordance with the foregoing articles.

(2) The Governing Body may, if it thinks fit, before referring such a complaint to a Commission of Inquiry, as hereinafter provided for, communicate with the government in question in the manner described in article 24.

(3) If the Governing Body does not think it necessary to communicate the complaint to the government in question, or if, when it has made such communication, no statement in reply has been received within a reasonable time which the Governing Body considers to be satisfactory, the Governing Body may appoint a Commission of Inquiry to consider the complaint and to report thereon.

(4) The Governing Body may adopt the same procedure either of its own motion or on receipt of a complaint from a delegate to the Conference.

(5) When any matter arising out of article 25 or 26 is being considered by the Governing Body, the government in question shall, if not already represented thereon, be entitled to send a representative to take part in the proceedings of the Governing Body while the matter is under consideration. Adequate notice of the date on which the matter will be considered shall be given to the government in question.

27. The Members agree that, in the event of the reference of a complaint to a Commission of Inquiry under article 26, they will each, whether directly concerned in the complaint or not, place at the disposal of the Commission all the information in their possession which bears upon the subject-matter of the complaint.

28. When the Commission of Inquiry has fully considered the complaint, it shall prepare a report embodying its findings on all questions of fact relevant to determining the issue between the parties and containing such recommendations as it may think proper as to the steps which should be taken to meet the complaint and the time within which they should be taken.

29 (1) The Director-General of the International Labour Office shall communicate the report of the Commission of Inquiry to the Governing Body and

[2] ILO document GB. 212/14/21.

to each of the governments concerned in the complaint, and shall cause it to be published.

(2) Each of these governments shall within three months inform the Director-General of the International Labour Office whether or not it accepts the recommendations contained in the report of the Commission; and if not, whether it proposes to refer the complaint to the International Court of Justice.

31. The decision of the International Court of Justice in regard to a complaint or matter which has been referred to it in pursuance of article 29 shall be final.

32. The International Court of Justice may affirm, vary or reverse any of the findings or recommendations of the Commission of Inquiry, if any.

33. In the event of any Member failing to carry out within the time specified the recommendations, if any, contained in the report of the Commission of Inquiry, or in the decision of the International Court of Justice, as the case may be, the Governing Body may recommend to the Conference such action as it may deem wise and expedient to secure compliance therewith.

34. The defaulting government may at any time inform the Governing Body that it has taken the steps necessary to comply with the recommendations of the Commission of Inquiry or with those in the decision of the International Court of Justice, as the case may be, and may request it to constitute a Commission of Inquiry to verify its contention. In this case the provisions of articles 27, 28, 29, 31 and 32 shall apply, and if the report of the Commission of Inquiry or the decision of the International Court of Justice is in favour of the defaulting government, the Governing Body shall forthwith recommend the discontinuance of any action taken in pursuance of article 33.

Commissions of Inquiry determine their own procedures: these are not regulated by Standing Orders.

§35.4 The special procedure for complaints about infringements of trade union rights

This procedure does not derive from the ILO's Constitution, but was established in 1950 by the common consent of the ILO's Governing Body and ECOSOC, since which time it has undergone considerable development. Complaints may be made by national organizations directly interested in the matter, or by certain international organizations of employers or workers. They may be made to the UN or the ILO, against Member States of either organization. The ILO Governing Body's Committee on Freedom of Association — a tripartite committee of 9 regular and 9 substitute members of the Governing Body, sitting in their personal capacities — determines whether the complaint is receivable, and (after preliminary examination) makes recommendations to the Governing Body about the action to be taken. This may, at the request or with the consent of the government concerned, include referral of the complaint to the ILO's Fact-finding and Conciliation Commission on Freedom of Association, which is composed of 3 to 5 independent persons appointed by the Governing Body. After examination, that Commission reports back to the Governing Body. The reports of the Committee under this procedure are published in the ILO's *Official Bulletin*; those of the Commission are published separately.[3]

[3] For a more detailed description of this procedure, see ILO document GB/LS/March 1977.

§35.5 Supervision of *ICES* and *ESC*

Apart from operating its own procedures in connection with its own Conventions, the ILO may also take part in the supervision procedures for two of the major human rights treaties.

Under *ICES* 18, the UN specialized agencies (including the ILO) may report to ECOSOC 'on the progress made in achieving the observance of the provisions' of *ICES*, and under *ICES* 20 the specialized agencies may comment to ECOSOC on 'general recommendations' relating to the State reports submitted under *ICES* 16. ECOSOC may pass on summaries of the specialized agencies' reports in its own reports to the UNGA under *ICES* 21 (see §31.2). Comments on provisions of *ICES* under this procedure by the ILO's Committee of Experts on the Application of Conventions and Recommendations are noted in the relevant sections in Part III above.

In the case of *ESC*, the ILO is entitled to 'participate in a consultative capacity' in the deliberations of EUCE under *ESC* 26 (see §32), but its views on the interpretation of the provisions of *ESC* are not separately published.

§36. NON-GOVERNMENTAL ORGANIZATIONS

By themselves, laws are no more than abstractions composed of empty words. What brings them to life is the people who make them, and those who apply them.

Left to themselves, the individual victims of human rights violations would have few opportunities either to make laws, or to apply them. That burden has traditionally fallen on others, individually more fortunate than the victims, who have banded together to give of their time and effort, often unpaid, and sometimes at the risk of their own liberties, livelihoods, and even their lives, in order to improve the lot of those who have suffered deprivation, oppression, and persecution.

In the nature of things, such organizations cannot be composed of governmental officials (though they do not always lack private sympathy in those circles), nor could they operate with any degree of success if they had formal governmental endorsement. They must necessarily be 'non-governmental organizations' (NGOs).

It would scarcely be possible to exaggerate the influence that NGOs have had on the development of international human rights law. There is not a single resolution, declaration, or treaty in this field which does not ultimately owe its very existence — and frequently its formulation, its adoption, and its later entry into force — to the untiring efforts of NGOs. Moreover, NGOs are better placed than anyone else to monitor the continuing performance — or lack of it — by national governments of the obligations by which they become bound in international law, and to pass their information on to the institutions called upon to supervise, interpret, apply, and enforce them.[1]

There are today hundreds, if not thousands, of NGOs throughout the world concerned with various aspects of human rights, but it is not the function of the present work to list them, or to describe their particular interests or activities.[2] Only very few of them have as their principal and direct concern the development and elaboration of substantive international human rights *law*; among the most active of these are the International Commission of Jurists, the International Law Association, the International Association of Penal Law, the International Association of Democratic Lawyers, and the *Mouvement International des Juristes Catholiques (Pax Romana)*. But the development of international human rights law also forms a subsidiary part of the concerns and activities of many other international NGOs, such as for example the International Committee of the Red Cross, Amnesty International, the World Council of Churches, the Anti-Slavery Society for the Protection of Human Rights, and the Minority Rights Group.

Some NGOs enjoy a limited degree of recognition by inter-governmental organizations. So, for example, *UNCH* 71 allows ECOSOC 'to make suitable

---

[1] See, for example, Opsahl, 'The Protection of Human Rights in the Council of Europe and in the United Nations', YB 26, 109, n. 26.

[2] For the most comprehensive lists and descriptions available, see the *Human Rights Directories* published by Human Rights Internet of Washington, DC, USA.

arrangements for consultation with non-governmental organisations which are concerned with matters within its competence', and in pursuance of that provision ECOSOC has conferred various degrees of 'consultative status' on a number of NGOs, as have UN specialized agencies and other intergovernmental organizations. Again, under ECOSOC Resolutions 1235 and 1503 (see §31.1), CHR and the Sub-Commission are able to receive information — and sometimes even oral representations — direct from NGOs. Likewise, the Sub-Committee of the Governmental Social Committee of the CE established under *ESC* 27(1) is entitled, under paragraph 2 of that Article, to consult certain international NGOs on certain specific questions: see §32. In practice, of course, NGOs also play a vital role in the preparation and submission of complaints, petitions, applications, and other forms of 'communication' to HRC, EUCM, IACM, and the other institutions that are competent to consider these.

TABLE A
Signatures, ratifications, accessions, adherences, reservations, and interpretations

This Table describes the full status of the five major human rights treaties in force — *ICPR, ICES, EHR, ESC,* and *AMR* — on 1 January 1982, and summarizes the status of the Subsidiary Instruments and the relevant ILO Conventions on that date. Further details, and information about subsequent changes, are available from:

ICPR, ICES, Subsidiary Instruments	Department of Public Information, United Nations, New York City, NY 10017, USA
	Office of Public Information, United Nations, Palais des Nations, CH-1211 Geneva 10, Switzerland
	National and local UN Information Centres or Offices
EHR and *ESC*	Council of Europe, B.P. 431 R6, 67006 Strasbourg Cedex, France
AMR	Information Office, Organisation of American States, 17th and Constitution Avenue, NW, Washington, DC 20006, USA
ILO Conventions	International Labour Office, CH-1211 Geneva 22, Switzerland

In this Table, no distinctions are drawn between ratifications, accessions, and adherences; nor between declarations of express reservation and of restrictive interpretation. Most of the declarations and reservations are translations from the original languages.

To save space, the following are omitted:

Notices of derogation;
Declarations relating only to the territorial application of a treaty to dependent territories;
Objections to reservations;
Statements relating only to disputes about the status of China or West Berlin.

ICPR

(Entry into force 23 March 1976)

State	Signature	Ratification, accession	Declaration under Art. 41
Algeria	10 December 1968		
Argentina	19 February 1968		
Australia*	18 December 1972	13 August 1980	
Austria*	10 December 1973	10 September 1978	10 September 1978
Barbados*		5 January 1973	
Belgium	10 December 1968		
Bulgaria*	8 October 1968	21 September 1970	
Byelorussian SSR*	19 March 1968	12 November 1973	
Canada		19 May 1976	29 October 1979
Central African Republic		8 May 1981	
Chile	16 September 1969	10 February 1972	
Colombia	21 December 1966	29 October 1969	
Costa Rica	19 December 1966	29 November 1968	
Cyprus	19 December 1966	2 April 1969	
Czechoslovakia*	7 October 1968	23 December 1975	
Democratic Kampuchea	17 October 1980		
Denmark*	20 March 1968	6 January 1972	6 April 1978
Dominican Republic		4 January 1978	
Ecuador	4 April 1968	6 March 1969	
Egypt	4 August 1967		
El Salvador	21 September 1967	30 November 1979	
Finland*	11 October 1967	19 August 1975	19 August 1975
France*		4 November 1980	
Gambia*		22 March 1979	
German Democratic Republic*	27 March 1973	8 November 1973	
Germany, Federal Republic of*	9 October 1968	17 December 1973	28 March 1981
Guinea*	28 February 1967	24 January 1978	
Guyana*	22 August 1968	15 February 1977	
Honduras	19 December 1966		

447

State	Signature	Ratification, accession	Declaration under Art. 41
Hungary*	25 March 1969	17 January 1974	
Iceland*	30 December 1968	22 August 1979	22 August 1979
India*		10 April 1979	
Iran	4 April 1968	24 June 1975	
Iraq*	18 February 1969	25 January 1971	
Ireland	1 October 1973		
Israel	19 December 1966		
Italy*	18 January 1967	15 September 1978	15 September 1978
Jamaica	19 December 1966	3 October 1975	
Japan*	30 May 1978	21 June 1979	
Jordan	30 June 1972	28 May 1975	
Kenya		1 May 1972	
Korea, Democratic People's Republic of		14 September 1981	
Lebanon		3 November 1972	
Liberia	18 April 1967		
Libyan Arab Jamahiriya*		15 May 1970	
Luxembourg	26 November 1974		
Madagascar	17 September 1969	21 June 1971	
Mali		16 July 1974	
Mauritius		12 December 1973	
Mexico*		23 March 1981	
Mongolia*	5 June 1968	18 November 1974	
Morocco	19 January 1977	3 May 1979	
Netherlands*	25 June 1969	11 December 1978	11 December 1978
New Zealand*	12 November 1968	28 December 1978	28 December 1978
Nicaragua		12 March 1980	
Norway*	20 March 1968	13 September 1972	31 August 1972
Panama	27 July 1976	8 March 1977	
Peru	11 August 1977	28 April 1978	
Philippines	19 December 1966		
Poland	2 March 1967	18 March 1977	
Portugal	7 October 1976	15 June 1978	
Romania*	27 June 1968	9 December 1974	

Rwanda		16 April 1975	
St. Vincent and the Grenadines		9 November 1981	
Senegal	6 July 1970	13 February 1978	5 January 1981
Spain	28 September 1976	27 April 1977	
Sri Lanka		11 June 1980	11 June 1980
Suriname		28 December 1976	
Sweden*	29 September 1967	6 December 1971	26 November 1971
Syrian Arab Republic*		21 April 1969	
Trinidad and Tobago*		21 December 1978	
Tunisia	30 April 1968	18 March 1969	
Ukrainian SSR*	20 March 1968	12 November 1973	
Union of Soviet Socialist Republics*	18 March 1968	16 October 1973	
United Kingdom*	16 September 1968	20 May 1976	20 May 1976
United Republic of Tanzania		11 June 1976	
United States of America	5 October 1977		
Uruguay	21 February 1967	1 April 1970	
Venezuela*	24 June 1969	10 May 1978	
Yugoslavia	8 August 1967	2 June 1971	
Zaire		1 November 1976	

*Reservations and Interpretations

AUSTRALIA

Upon ratification:

Articles 2 and 50. Australia advises that, the people having united as one people in a Federal Commonwealth under the Crown, it has a federal constitutional system. It accepts that the provisions of the Covenant extend to all parts of Australia as a federal State without any limitations or exceptions. It enters a general reservation that Article 2, paragraphs 2 and 3, and Article 50 shall be given effect consistently with and subject to the provisions in Article 2, paragraph 2.

Under Article 2, paragraph 2, steps to adopt measures necessary to give effect to the rights recognized in the Covenant are to be taken in accordance with each State Party's Constitutional processes which, in the case of Australia, are the processes of a federation in which legislative, executive, and judicial powers to give effect to the rights recognized in the Covenant are distributed among the federal (Commonwealth) authorities and the authorities of the constituent States.

In particular, in relation to the Australian States the implementation of those provisions of the Covenant over whose subject-matter the federal authorities exercise legislative, executive, and judicial jurisdiction will be a matter for those authorities; and the implementation of those provisions of the Covenant over whose subject-matter the authorities of the constituent States exercise legislative, executive and judicial jurisdiction will be a matter for those authorities; and where a provision has both federal and State aspects, its implementation will accordingly be a matter for the respective constitutionally appropriate authorities (for the purpose of implementation, the Northern Territory will be regarded as a constituent State).

To this end, the Australian Government has been in consultation with the responsible State and Territory Ministers with the object of developing cooperative arrangements to co-ordinate and facilitate the implementation of the Covenant.

Article 10. Australia accepts the principle stated in paragraph 1 of Article 10 and the general principles of the other paragraphs of that Article, but makes the reservation that these and other provisions of the Covenant are without prejudice to laws and lawful arrangements of custodial discipline in penal establishments. In relation to paragraph 2(*a*), the principle of segregation is accepted as an objective to be achieved progressively. In relation to paragraphs 2(*b*) and 3 (second sentence) the obligation to segregate is accepted only to the extent that such segregation is considered by the responsible authorities to be beneficial to the juveniles or adults concerned.

Article 14. Australia accepts paragraph 3(*b*) on the understanding that the reference to adequate facilities does not recognize provision to prisoners of all the facilities available to a prisoner's legal representative.

Australia accepts the requirement in paragraph 3(*d*) that everyone is entitled to be tried in his presence, but reserves the right to exclude an accused person where his conduct makes it impossible for the trial to proceed.

Australia interprets paragraph 3(*d*) of Article 14 as consistent with the operation of schemes of legal assistance in which the person assisted is required to make a contribution towards the cost of the defence related to his capacity to pay and determined according to law, or in which assistance is granted in respect of other than indictable offences only after having regard to all relevant matters.

Australia makes the reservation that the provision of compensation for miscarriages of justice in the circumstances contemplated in paragraph 6 of Article 14 may be by administrative procedures rather than pursuant to specific legal provision.

Article 17. Australia accepts the principles stated in Article 17 without prejudice to the right to enact and administer laws which, insofar as they authorize action which impinges on a person's privacy, family, home, or correspondence, are necessary in a democratic society in the interests of national security, public safety, the economic well-being of the country, the protection of public health or morals, or the protection of the rights and freedoms of others.

Article 19. Australia interprets paragraph 2 of Article 19 as being compatible with the regulation of radio and television broadcasting in the public interest with the object of providing the best possible broadcasting services to the Australian people.

Article 20. Australia interprets the rights provided for by Articles 19, 21, and 22 as consistent with Article 20; accordingly, the Commonwealth and constituent States, having legislated with respect to the subject-matter of the Article in matters of practical concern in the interests of public order (*ordre public*), the right is reserved not to introduce any further legislative provision on these matters.

Article 25. The reference in paragraph (*b*) of Article 25 to 'universal and equal suffrage' is accepted without prejudice to laws which provide that factors such as regional interests may be taken into account in defining electoral divisions, or which establish franchises for municipal and other local government elections related to the sources of revenue and the functions of such government.

Convicted persons. Australia declares that laws now in force in Australia relating to the rights of persons who have been convicted of serious criminal offences are generally consistent with the requirements of Articles 14, 18, 19, 25, and 26 and reserves the right not to seek amendment of such laws.

Discrimination and distinction. The provisions of Articles 2(1) and 24(1), 25, and 26 relating to discrimination and distinction between persons shall be without prejudice to laws designed to achieve for the members of some class or classes of persons equal enjoyment of the rights defined in the Covenant. Australia accepts Article 26 on the basis that the object of the provision is to confirm the right of each person to equal treatment in the application of the law.

AUSTRIA

Upon ratification:

1. Article 12, paragraph 4, of the Covenant will be applied provided that it will not affect the Act of April 3, 1919, State Law Gazette No. 209, concerning the Expulsion and the Transfer of Property of the House of Hapsburg-Lorraine as amended by the Act of October 30, 1919, State Law Gazette No. 501, the Federal Constitutional Act of July 30, 1925, Federal Law Gazette No. 292, and the Federal Constitutional Act of January 26, 1928, Federal Law Gazette No. 30, read in conjunction with the Federal Constitutional Act of July 4, 1963, Federal Law Gazette No. 172.

2. Article 9 and article 14 of the Covenant will be applied provided that legal regulations governing the proceedings and measures of deprivation of liberty as provided for in the Administrative Procedure Acts and in the Financial Penal Act remain permissible within the framework of the judicial review by the Federal Administrative Court or the Federal Constitutional Court as provided by the Austrian Federal Constitution.

3. Article 10, paragraph 3, of the Covenant will be applied provided that legal regulations allowing for juvenile prisoners to be detained together with adults under 25 years of age who give no reason for concern as to their possible detrimental influence on the juvenile prisoner remain permissible.

4. Article 14 of the Covenant will be applied provided that the principles governing the publicity of trials as set forth in article 90 of the Federal Constitutional Law as amended in 1929 are in no way prejudiced and that
(a) paragraph 3, sub-paragraph (d) is not in conflict with legal regulations which stipulate that an accused person who disturbs the orderly conduct of the trial or whose presence would impede the questioning of another accused person, of a witness or of an expert can be excluded from participation in the trial;
(b) paragraph 5 is not in conflict with legal regulations which stipulate that after an acquittal or a lighter sentence passed by a court of the first instance, a higher tribunal may pronounce conviction or a heavier sentence for the same offense, while they exclude the convicted person's right to have such conviction or heavier sentence reviewed by a still higher tribunal;
(c) paragraph 7 is not in conflict with legal regulations which allow proceedings that led up to a person's final conviction or acquittal to be reopened.

5. Articles 19, 21 and 22 in connection with article 2(1) of the Covenant will be applied provided that they are not in conflict with legal restrictions as provided for in article 16 of the European Convention for the Protection of Human Rights and Fundamental Freedoms.

6. Article 26 is understood to mean that it does not exclude different treatment of Austrian nationals and aliens, as is also permissible under article 1, paragraph 2, of the International Convention on the Elimination of All Forms of Racial Discrimination.

BARBADOS

The Government of Barbados states that it reserves the right not to apply in full, the guarantee of free legal assistance in accordance with paragraph 3(d) of Article 14 of the Covenant, since, while accepting the principles contained in the same paragraph, the problems of implementation are such that full application cannot be guaranteed at present.

BULGARIA

The People's Republic of Bulgaria deems it necessary to underline that the provisions of article 48, paragraphs 1 and 3, of the International Covenant on Civil and Political Rights, and article 26, paragraphs 1 and 3, of the International Covenant on Economic, Social and Cultural Rights, under which a number of States are deprived of the opportunity to become parties to the Covenants, are of a discriminatory nature. These provisions are inconsistent with the very nature of the Covenants, which are universal in character and should be open for accession by all States. In accordance with the principle of sovereign equality, no State has the right to bar other States from becoming parties to a covenant of this kind.

BYELORUSSIAN SOVIET SOCIALIST REPUBLIC

Declaration made upon signature and confirmed upon ratification:

The Byelorussian Soviet Socialist Republic declares that the provisions of paragraph 1 of article 26 of the International Covenant on Economic, Social and Cultural Rights and of paragraph 1 of article 48 of the International Covenant on Civil and Political Rights, under which a number of States cannot become parties to these Covenants, are of a discriminatory nature and considers that the Covenants, in accordance with the principle of sovereign equality of States, should be open for participation by all States concerned without any discrimination or limitation.

CZECHOSLOVAKIA

Upon signature:

The Czechoslovak Socialist Republic declares that the provisions of article 48, paragraph 1, of the International Covenant on Civil and Political Rights are in contradiction with the principle that all States have the right to become parties to multilateral treaties governing matters of general interest.

Upon ratification:

The provision of article 48, paragraph 1, is in contradiction with the principle that all States have the right to become parties to multilateral treaties regulating matters of general interest.

DENMARK

1. The Government of Denmark makes a reservation in respect of Article 10, paragraph 3, second sentence. In Danish practice, considerable efforts are made to ensure appropriate age distribution of convicts serving sentences of imprisonment, but it is considered valuable to maintain possibilities of flexible arrangements.

2. (*a*) Article 14, paragraph 1, shall not be binding on Denmark in respect of public hearings.
In Danish law, the right to exclude the press and the public from trials may go beyond what is permissible under this Covenant and the Government of Denmark finds that this right should not be restricted.
(*b*) Article 14, paragraphs 5 and 7, shall not be binding on Denmark.
The Danish Administration of Justice Act contains detailed provisions regulating the matters dealt with in these two paragraphs. In some cases, Danish legislation is less restrictive than the Covenant (e.g. a verdict returned by a jury on the question of guilt cannot be reviewed by a higher tribunal, cf. paragraph 5); in other cases, Danish legislation is more restrictive than the Covenant (e.g. with respect to resumption of a criminal case in which the accused party was acquitted, cf. paragraph 7).

3. Reservation is further made to Article 20, paragraph 1. This reservation is in accordance with the vote cast by Denmark in the XVI General Assembly of the United Nations in 1961 when the Danish Delegation, referring to the preceding article concerning freedom of expression, voted against the prohibition against propaganda for war.

FINLAND

Upon ratification:

Reservations

1. With respect to article 9, paragraph 3, of the Covenant Finland declares that according to the present Finnish legislation the administrative authorities may take decisions concerning arrest or imprisonment, in which event the case is taken up for decision in court only after a certain time lapse;

2. With respect to article 10, paragraph 2 (*b*) and 3, of the Covenant, Finland declares that although juvenile offenders are, as a rule, segregated from adults, it does not deem appropriate to adopt an absolute prohibition not allowing for more flexible arrangements;

3. With respect to article 13 of the Covenant, Finland declares that the article does not correspond to the present Finnish legislation regarding an alien's right to be heard or lodge a complaint in respect of a decision concerning his expulsion;

4. With respect to article 14, paragraph 1, of the Covenant, Finland declares that under Finnish law a sentence can be declared secret if its publication could be an affront to morals or endanger national security;

5. With respect to article 14, paragraph 3 (*d*), of the Covenant, Finland declares that the contents of this paragraph do not correspond to the present legislation in Finland inasmuch as it is a question of the defendant's absolute right to have legal assistance already at the stage of preliminary investigations;

6. With respect to article 14, paragraph 7, of the Covenant, Finland declares that it is going to pursue its present practice, according to which a sentence can be changed to the detriment of the convicted person, if it is established that a member or an official of the court, the prosecutor or the legal counsel have through criminal or fraudulous activities obtained the acquittal of the defendant or a substantially more lenient penalty, or if false evidence has been presented with the same effect, and according to which an aggravated criminal case may be taken up for reconsideration if within a year until then unknown evidence is presented, which would have led to conviction or a substantially more severe penalty;

7. With respect to article 20, paragraph 1, of the Covenant, Finland declares that it will not apply the provisions of this paragraph, this being compatible with the standpoint Finland already expressed at the 16th United Nations General Assembly by voting against the prohibition of propaganda for war, on the grounds that this might endanger the freedom of expression referred in article 19 of the Covenant.

FRANCE

1. The Government of the Republic considers that, in accordance with Article 103 of the Charter of the United Nations, in case of conflict between its obligations under the Covenant and its obligations under the Charter (especially Articles 1 and 2 thereof), its obligations under the Charter will prevail.

2. The Government of the Republic enters the following reservation concerning Article 4(1): firstly, the circumstances enumerated in Article 16 of the Constitution in respect of its implementation, in Article 1 of the Act of 3 April 1978 and in the Act of 9 August 1849 in respect of the declaration of a state

of siege, in Article 1 of the Act No. 55–385 of 3 April 1955 in respect of the declaration of a state of emergency and which enable these instruments to be implemented, are to be understood as meeting the purpose of Article 4 of the Covenant; and secondly, for the purpose of interpreting and implementing Article 16 of the Constitution of the French Republic, the terms 'to the extent strictly required by the exigencies of the situation' cannot limit the power of the President of the Republic to take 'the measures required by circumstances'.

3. The Government of the Republic enters a reservation concerning Articles 9 and 14 to the effect that these Articles cannot impede enforcement of the rules pertaining to the disciplinary regime in the armies.

4. The Government of the Republic declares that Article 13 cannot derogate from Chapter IV of Order No. 45–2658 of 2 November 1945 concerning the entry into, and sojourn in, France of aliens, nor from the other instruments concerning the expulsion of aliens in force in those parts of the territory of the Republic in which the Order of 2 November 1945 does not apply.

5. The Government of the Republic interprets Article 14, paragraph 5, as stating a general principle to which the law may make limited exceptions; for example, in the case of certain offences subject to the initial and final adjudication of a police court and of criminal offences. However, an appeal against a final decision may be made to the Court of Cassation which rules on the legality of the decision concerned.

6. The Government of the Republic declares that Articles 19, 21, and 22 of the Covenant will be implemented in accordance with Articles 10, 11 and 16 of the European Convention on Human Rights of 4 November 1950. However, the Government of the Republic enters a reservation concerning Article 19 which cannot derogate from the monopoly of the French radio and television broadcasting system.

7. The Government of the Republic declares that the term 'war' appearing in Article 20, paragraph 1, is to be understood to mean war in contravention of international law and considers, in any case, that French legislation in this matter is adequate.

8. In the light of Article 2 of the Constitution of the French Republic, the French Government declares that Article 27 is not applicable so far as the Republic is concerned.

GAMBIA

For financial reasons free legal assistance for accused persons is limited in our constitution to persons charged with capital offences only. The Government of the Gambia therefore wishes to enter a reservation in respect of article 14(3) (*d*) of the Covenant in question.

GERMAN DEMOCRATIC REPUBLIC

The German Democratic Republic considers that article 48, paragraph 1, of the Covenant runs counter to the principle that all States which are guided in their policies by the purposes and principles of the United Nations Charter have the right to become parties to conventions which affect the interest of all States.

GERMANY, FEDERAL REPUBLIC OF

1. Articles 19, 21 and 22 in conjunction with Article 2 (1) of the Covenant shall be applied within the scope of Article 16 of the Convention of 4 November 1950 for the Protection of Human Rights and Fundamental Freedoms.

2. Article 14 (3) (*d*) of the Covenant shall be applied in such manner that it is for the court to decide whether an accused person held in custody has to appear in person at the hearing before the court of review (*Revisionsgericht*).

3. Article 14 (5) of the Covenant shall be applied in such manner that:
(*a*) A further appeal does not have to be instituted in all cases solely on the grounds the accused person — having been acquitted by the lower court — was convicted for the first time in the proceedings concerned by the appellate court.
(*b*) In the case of criminal offences of minor gravity the review by a higher tribunal of a decision not imposing imprisonment does not have to be admitted in all cases.

4. Article 15 (1) of the Covenant shall be applied in such manner that when provision is made by law for the imposition of a lighter penalty the hitherto applicable law may for certain exceptional categories of cases remain applicable to criminal offences committed before the law was amended.

GUINEA

Upon ratification:

In accordance with the principle whereby all States whose policies are guided by the purposes and principles of the Charter of the United Nations are entitled to become parties to covenants affecting the interests of the international community, the Government of the Republic of Guinea considers that the provisions of article 48, paragraph 1, of the International Covenant on Civil and Political Rights are contrary to the principle of the universality of international treaties and the democratization of international relations.

GUYANA

Upon ratification:

*In respect of sub-paragraph (*d*) of paragraph 3 of article 14*

While the Government of the Republic of Guyana accept the principle of Legal Aid in all appropriate criminal proceedings, is working towards that end and at present apply it in certain defined cases, the problems of implementation of a comprehensive Legal Aid Scheme are such that full application cannot be guaranteed at this time.

In respect of paragraph 6 of article 14

While the Government of the Republic of Guyana accept the principle of compensation for wrongful imprisonment, it is not possible at this time to implement such a principle.

HUNGARY

Upon signature:

The Government of the Hungarian People's Republic declares that paragraph 1 of article 26 of the International Covenant on Economic, Social and Cultural Rights and paragraph 1 of article 48 of the International Covenant on Civil and Political Rights according to which certain States may not become signatories to the said Covenants are of a discriminatory nature and are contrary to the basic principle of international law that all States are entitled to become signatories to general multilateral treaties. These discriminatory provisions are incompatible with the objectives and purposes of the Covenants.

Upon ratification:

The Presidential Council of the Hungarian People's Republic declares that the provisions of article 48, paragraphs 1 and 3, of . . . the International Covenant on Civil and Political Rights, and article 26, paragraphs 1 and 3, of the International Covenant on Economic, Social and Cultural Rights are inconsistent with the universal character of the Covenants. It follows from the principle of sovereign equality of States that the Covenants should be open for participation by all States without any discrimination or limitation.

ICELAND

1. Article 8, paragraph 3(*a*), in so far as it affects the provisions of Icelandic law which provide that a person who is not the main provider of his family may be sentenced to a term at a labour facility in satisfaction of arrears in support payments for his child or children.

2. Article 10, paragraph 2(*b*), and paragraph 3, second sentence, with respect to the separation of juvenile prisoners from adults. Icelandic law in principle provides for such separation but it is not considered appropriate to accept an obligation in the absolute form called for in the provisions of the Covenant.

3. Article 13, to the extent that it is inconsistent with the Icelandic legal provisions in force relating to the right of aliens to object to a decision on their expulsion.

4. Article 14, paragraph 7, with respect to the resumption of cases which have already been tried. The Icelandic law of procedure has detailed provisions on this matter which it is not considered appropriate to revise.

5. Article 20, paragraph 1, with reference to the fact that a prohibition against propaganda for war could limit the freedom of expression. This reservation is consistent with the position of Iceland at the General Assembly at its 16th session.

Other provisions of the Covenant shall be inviolably observed.

INDIA

Declarations

I. With reference to . . . article 1 of the International Covenant on Civil and Political Rights, the Government of the Republic of India declares that the words 'the right of self-determination' appearing in [this article] apply only to the peoples under foreign domination and that these words do not apply to sovereign independent States or to a section of a people or nation — which is the essence of national integrity.

II. With reference to article 9 of the International Covenant on Civil and Political Rights, the Government of the Republic of India takes the position that the provisions of the article shall be so applied as to be in consonance with the provisions of clauses (3) to (7) of article 22 of the Constitution of India. Further under the Indian Legal System, there is no enforceable right to compensation for persons claiming to be victims of unlawful arrest or detention against the State.

Reservation

III. With respect to article 13 of the International Covenant on Civil and Political Rights, the Government of the Republic of India reserves its right to apply its law relating to foreigners.

Declaration

IV. With reference to . . . articles 12, 19 (3), 21 and 22 of the International Covenant on Civil and Political Rights, the Government of the Republic of India declares that the provisions of the said articles shall be so applied as to be in conformity with the provisions of article 19 of the Constitution of India.

IRAQ

Upon signature and confirmed upon ratification:

The entry of the Republic of Iraq as a party to the International Covenant on Economic, Social and Cultural Rights and the International Covenant on Civil and Political Rights shall in no way signify recognition of Israel nor shall it entail any obligations towards Israel under the said two Covenants.

The entry of the Republic of Iraq as a party to the above two Covenants shall not constitute entry by it as a party to the Optional Protocol to the International Covenant on Civil and Political Rights.

Upon ratification:

Ratification by Iraq . . . shall in no way signify recognition of Israel nor shall it be conducive to entry with her into such dealings as are regulated by the said [Covenant].

ITALY

Upon ratification:

Article 9, paragraph 5. The Italian Republic, considering that the expression 'unlawful arrest or detention' contained in article 9, paragraph 5, could give rise to differences of interpretation, declares that it interprets the aforementioned expression as referring exclusively to cases of arrest or detention contrary to the provisions of article 9, paragraph 1.

Article 12, paragraph 4. Article 12, paragraph 4, shall be without prejudice to the application of transitional provision XIII of the Italian Constitution, respecting prohibition of the entry into and sojourn in the national territory of certain members of the House of Savoy.

Article 14, paragraph 3. The provisions of article 14, paragraph 3 (*d*) are deemed to be compatible with existing Italian provisions governing trial of the accused in his presence and determining the cases in which the accused may present his own defence and those in which legal assistance is required.

Article 14, paragraph 5. Article 14, paragraph 5, shall be without prejudice to the application of existing Italian provisions which, in accordance with the Constitution of the Italian Republic, govern the conduct, at one level only, of proceedings instituted before the Constitutional Court in respect of charges brought against the President of the Republic and its Ministers.

Article 15, paragraph 1. With reference to article 15, paragraph 1, last sentence: 'If subsequent to the commission of the offence, provision is made by law for the imposition of a lighter penalty, the offender shall benefit thereby', the Italian Republic deems this provision to apply exclusively to cases in progress.

Consequently, a person who has already been convicted by a final decision shall not benefit from any provision made by law, subsequent to that decision, for the imposition of a lighter penalty.

Article 19, paragraph 3. The provisions of article 19, paragraph 3, are interpreted as being compatible with the existing licensing system for national radio and television and with the restrictions laid down by law for local radio and television companies and for stations relaying foreign programmes.

JAPAN

Upon signature and confirmed upon ratification:

Recalling the position taken by the Government of Japan, when ratifying the Convention (No. 87) concerning Freedom of Association and Protection of the Right to Organise, that 'the police' referred to in article 9 of the said Convention be interpreted to include the fire service of Japan, the Government of Japan declares that 'members — of the police' referred to in paragraph 2 of article 8 of the International Covenant on Economic, Social and Cultural Rights as well as in paragraph 2 of article 22 of the International Covenant on Civil and Political Rights be interpreted to include fire service personnel of Japan.

LIBYAN ARAB JAMAHIRIYA

The acceptance and the accession to this Covenant by the Libyan Arab Republic shall in no way signify a recognition of Israel or be conducive to entry by the Libyan Arab Republic into such dealings with Israel as are regulated by the Covenant.

MEXICO

Article 9, paragraph 5. Under the Political Constitution of the United Mexican States and the relevant implementing legislation, every individual enjoys the guarantees relating to penal matters embodied therein, and consequently no person may be unlawfully arrested or detained. However, if by reason of false accusation or complaint any individual suffers an infringement of this basic right, he has, *inter alia*, under the provisions of the appropriate laws, an enforceable right to just compensation.

Article 18. Under the Political Constitution of the United Mexican States, every person is free to profess his preferred religious belief and to practise its ceremonies, rites, and religious acts, with the limitation, with regard to public religious acts, that they must be performed in places of worship and, with regard

459

to education, that studies carried out in establishments designed for the professional education of ministers of religion are not officially recognized. The Government of Mexico believes that these limitations are included among those established in paragraph 3 of this Article.

Article 13. The Government of Mexico makes a reservation to this Article, in view of the present text of Article 33 of the Political Constitution of the United Mexican State.

Article 25, subparagraph (b). The Government of Mexico also makes a reservation to this provision, since Article 130 of the Political Constitution of the United Mexican States provides that ministers of religion shall have neither an active nor a passive vote, nor the right to form associations for political purposes.

MONGOLIA

Declaration made upon signature and renewed upon ratification:

Mongolia declares that the provisions of paragraph 1 of article 26 of the International Covenant on Economic, Social and Cultural Rights and of paragraph 1 of article 48 of the International Covenant on Civil and Political Rights, under which a number of States cannot become parties to these Covenants, are of a discriminatory nature and considers that the Covenants, in accordance with the principle of sovereign equality of States, should be open for participation by all States concerned without any discrimination or limitation.

NETHERLANDS

Upon ratification:

Reservations

Article 10. The Kingdom of the Netherlands subscribes to the principle set out in paragraph 1 of this article, but it takes the view that ideas about the treatment of prisoners are so liable to change that it does not wish to be bound by the obligations set out in paragraph 2 and paragraph 3 (second sentence) of this article.

Article 12, paragraph 1. The Kingdom of the Netherlands regards the Netherlands and the Netherlands Antilles as separate territories of a State for the purpose of this provision.

Article 12, paragraphs 2 and 4. The Kingdom of the Netherlands regards the Netherlands and the Netherlands Antilles as separate countries for the purpose of these provisions.

Article 14, paragraph 3(d). The Kingdom of the Netherlands reserves the statutory option of removing a person charged with a criminal offence from the courtroom in the interests of the proper conduct of the proceedings.

Article 14, paragraph 5. The Kingdom of the Netherlands reserves the statutory power of the Supreme Court of the Netherlands to have sole jurisdiction to try certain categories of persons charged with serious offences committed in the discharge of a public office.

Article 14, paragraph 7. The Kingdom of the Netherlands accepts this provision only insofar as no obligations arise from it further to those set out in article 68 of the Criminal Code of the Netherlands and article 70 of the Criminal Code of the Netherlands Antilles as they now apply. They read:

1. Except in cases where court decisions are eligible for review, no person may be prosecuted again for an offence in respect of which a court in the Netherlands or the Netherlands Antilles has delivered an irrevocable judgment.
2. If the judgment has been delivered by some other court, the same person may not be prosecuted for the same offence in the case of (I) acquittal or withdrawal of proceedings or (II) conviction followed by complete execution, remission or lapse of the sentence.

Article 19, paragraph 2. The Kingdom of the Netherlands accepts the provision with the proviso that it shall not prevent the Kingdom from requiring the licensing of broadcasting, television or cinema enterprises.

Article 20, paragraph 1. The Kingdom of the Netherlands does not accept the obligation set out in this provision in the case of the Netherlands.

Article 25 (c). The Kingdom of the Netherlands does not accept this provision in the case of the Netherlands Antilles.

Explanation

[The Kingdom of the Netherlands] clarify that although the reservations [. . .] are partly of an interpretational nature, [it] has preferred reservations to interpretational declarations in all cases, since if the latter form were used doubt might arise concerning whether the text of the Covenant allows for the interpretation put upon it. By using the reservation-form the Kingdom of the Netherlands wishes to ensure in all cases that the relevant obligations arising out of the Covenant will not apply to the Kingdom, or will apply only in the way indicated.

NEW ZEALAND

Upon ratification:

Reservations

The Government of New Zealand reserves the right not to apply article 10(2)(*b*) or article 10(3) in circumstances where the shortage of suitable facilties makes the mixing of juveniles and adults unavoidable; and further reserves the right not to apply article 10(3) where the interests of other juveniles in an establishment require the removal of a particular juvenile offender or where mixing is considered to be of benefit to the persons concerned.

  The Government of New Zealand reserves the right not to apply article 14(6) to the extent that it is not satisfied by the existing system for ex gratia payments to persons who suffer as a result of a miscarriage of justice.

  The Government of New Zealand having legislated in the areas of the advocacy of national and racial hatred and the exciting of hostility or illwill against any group of persons, and having regard to the right of freedom of speech, reserves the right not to introduce further legislation with regard to article 20.

  The Government of New Zealand reserves the right not to apply article 22 as it relates to trade unions to the extent that existing legislative measures, enacted to ensure effective trade union representation and encourage orderly industrial relations, may not be fully compatible with that article.

NORWAY

Subject to reservations to . . . article 10, paragraph 2 (*b*) and paragraph 3 'with regard to the obligation to keep accused juvenile persons and juvenile offenders segregated from adults' and to article 14, paragraphs 5 and 7 and to article 20, paragraph 1.

ROMANIA

Upon signature:

The Government of the Socialist Republic of Romania declares that the provisions of article 48, paragraph 1, of the International Covenant on Civil and Political Rights are at variance with the principle that all States have the right to become parties to multilateral treaties governing matters of general interest.

Upon ratification:

(*a*) The State Council of the Socialist Republic of Romania considers that the provisions of article 48 (1) of the International Covenant on Civil and Political Rights are inconsistent with the principle that multilateral international treaties whose purposes concern the international community as a whole must be open to universal participation.

(*b*) The State Council of the Socialist Republic of Romania considers that the maintenance in a state of dependence of certain territories referred to in article 1 (3) of the International Covenant on Civil and Political Rights is inconsistent with the Charter of the United Nations and the instruments adopted by the Organization on the granting of independence to colonial countries and peoples, including the Declaration of Principles of International Law concerning Friendly Relations and Co-operation among States in accordance with the Charter of the United Nations, adopted unanimously by the United Nations General Assembly in its resolution 2625 (XXV) of 1970, which solemnly proclaims the duty of States to promote the realization of the principle of equal rights and self-determination of peoples in order to bring a speedy end to colonialism.

SWEDEN

Sweden reserves the right not to apply the provisions of article 10, paragraph 3, with regard to the obligation to segregate juvenile offenders from adults, the provisions of article 14, paragraph 7, and the provisions of article 20, paragraph 1, of the Covenant.

SYRIAN ARAB REPUBLIC

1. The accession of the Syrian Arab Republic to these two Covenants shall in no way signify recognition of Israel or entry into a relationship with it regarding any matter regulated by the said two Covenants.

2. The Syrian Arab Republic considers that paragraph 1 of article 26 of the Covenant on Economic, Social and Cultural Rights and paragraph 1 of article 48 of the Covenant on Civil and Political Rights are incompatible with the purposes and objectives of the said Covenants, inasmuch as they do not allow all States, without distinction or discrimination, the opportunity to become parties to the said Covenants.

TRINIDAD AND TOBAGO

(i) The Government of the Republic of Trinidad and Tobago reserves the right not to apply in full the provision of paragraph 2 of article 4 of the Covenant since section 7(3) of its Constitution enables Parliament to enact legislation even though it is inconsistent with sections (4) and (5) of the said Constitution;

(ii) Where at any time there is a lack of suitable prison facilities, the Government of the Republic of Trinidad and Tobago reserves the right not to apply article 10(2)(*b*) and 10(3) so far as those provisions require juveniles who are detained to be accommodated separately from adults;

(iii) The Government of the Republic of Trinidad and Tobago reserves the right not to apply paragraph 2 of article 12 in view of the statutory provisions requiring persons intending to travel abroad to furnish tax clearance certificates;

(iv) The Government of the Republic of Trinidad and Tobago reserves the right not to apply paragraph 5 of article 14 in view of the fact that section 43 of its Supreme Court of Judicature Act No. 12 of 1962 does not confer on a person convicted on indictment an unqualified right of appeal and that in particular cases, appeal to the Court of Appeal can only be done with the leave of the Court of Appeal itself or of the Privy Council;

(v) While the Government of the Republic of Trinidad and Tobago accepts the principle of compensation for wrongful imprisonment, it is not possible at this time to implement such a principle in accordance with paragraph 6 of article 14 of the Covenant;

(vi) With reference to the last sentence of paragraph 1 of article 15 — 'If, subsequent to the commission of the offence, provision is made by law for the imposition of a lighter penalty, the offender shall benefit thereby', the Government of the Republic of Trinidad and Tobago deems this provision to apply exclusively to cases in progress. Consequently, a person who has already been convicted by a final decision shall not benefit from any provision made by law, subsequent to that decision, for the imposition of a lighter penalty;[1]

(vii) The Government of the Republic of Trinidad and Tobago reserves the right to impose lawful and or reasonable restrictions with respect to the right of assembly under article 21 of the Covenant;

(viii) The Government of the Republic of Trinidad and Tobago reserves the right not to apply the provision of article 26 of the Covenant in so far as it applies to the holding of property in Trinidad and Tobago, in view of the fact that licences may be granted to or withheld from aliens under the Aliens Landholding Act of Trinidad and Tobago.

UKRAINIAN SOVIET SOCIALIST REPUBLIC

Declaration made upon signature and confirmed upon ratification:

The Ukrainian Soviet Socialist Republic declares that the provisions of paragraph 1 of article 26 of the International Covenant on Economic, Social and Cultural Rights and of paragraph 1 of article 48 of the International Covenant on Civil and Political Rights, under which a number of States cannot become parties to these Covenants, are of a discriminatory nature and considers that the Covenants, in accordance with the principle of sovereign equality of States, should be open for participation by all States concerned without any discrimination or limitation.

UNION OF SOVIET SOCIALIST REPUBLICS

Declaration made upon signature and confirmed upon ratification:

The Union of Soviet Socialist Republics declares that the provisions of paragraph 1 of article 26 of the International Covenant on Economic, Social and

---

[1] In a communication received by the Secretary-General on 31 January 1979, the Government of Trinidad and Tobago confirmed that paragraph (vi) above constituted an interpretative declaration which did not aim to exclude nor modify the legal effect of the provisions of the Covenant.

Cultural Rights and of paragraph 1 of article 48 of the International Covenant on Civil and Political Rights, under which a number of States cannot become parties to these Covenants, are of a discriminatory nature and considers that the Covenants, in accordance with the principle of sovereign equality of States, should be open for participation by all States concerned without any discrimination or limitation.

UNITED KINGDOM OF GREAT BRITAIN AND NORTHERN IRELAND

Upon signature:

First, the Government of the United Kingdom declare their understanding that, by virtue of Article 103 of the Charter of the United Nations, in the event of any conflict between their obligations under Article 1 of the Covenant and their obligations under the Charter (in particular, under Articles 1, 2 and 73 thereof) their obligations under the Charter shall prevail.

Secondly, the Government of the United Kingdom declare that:

(a) In relation to Article 14 of the Covenant, they must reserve the right not to apply, or not to apply in full, the guarantee of free legal assistance contained in sub-paragraph (d) of paragraph 3 in so far as the shortage of legal practitioners and other considerations render the application of this guarantee in British Honduras, Fiji and St. Helena impossible;

(b) In relation to Article 23 of the Covenant, they must reserve the right not to apply the first sentence of paragraph 4 in so far as it concerns any inequality which may arise from the operation of the law of domicile;

(c) In relation to Article 25 of the Covenant, they must reserve the right not to apply:

(i) Sub-paragraph (b) in so far as it may require the establishment of an elected legislature in Hong Kong and the introduction of equal suffrage, as between different electoral rolls, for elections in Fiji; and

(ii) Sub-paragraph (c) in so far as it applies to jury service in the Isle of Man and to the employment of married women in the Civil Service of Northern Ireland, Fiji, and Hong Kong.

Lastly the Government of the United Kingdom declare that the provisions of the Covenant shall not apply to Southern Rhodesia unless and until they inform the Secretary-General of the United Nations that they are in a position to ensure that the obligations imposed by the Covenant in respect of that territory can be fully implemented.

Upon ratification:

Firstly the Government of the United Kingdom maintain their declaration in respect of article 1 made at the time of signature of the Covenant.

The Government of the United Kingdom reserve the right to apply to members of and persons serving with the armed forces of the Crown and to persons lawfully detained in penal establishments of whatever character such laws and procedures as they may from time to time deem to be necessary for the preservation of service and custodial discipline and their acceptance of the provisions of the Covenant is subject to such restrictions as may for these purposes from time to time be authorised by law.

Where at any time there is a lack of suitable prison facilities or where the mixing of adults and juveniles is deemed to be mutually beneficial, the Government of the United Kingdom reserve the right not to apply article 10(2) (b) and 10(3), so far as those provisions require juveniles who are detained to be accommodated separately from adults, and not to apply article 10(2) (a) in

Gibraltar, Montserrat and the Turks and Caicos Islands in so far as it requires segregation of accused and convicted persons.

The Government of the United Kingdom reserve the right not to apply article 11 in Jersey.

The Government of the United Kingdom reserve the right to interpret the provisions of article 12(1) relating to the territory of a State as applying separately to each of the territories comprising the United Kingdom and its dependencies.

The Government of the United Kingdom reserve the right to continue to apply such immigration legislation governing entry into, stay in and departure from the United Kingdom as they may deem necessary from time to time and, accordingly, their acceptance of article 12(4) and of the other provisions of the Covenant is subject to the provisions of any such legislation as regards persons not at the time having the right under the law of the United Kingdom to enter and remain in the United Kingdom. The United Kingdom also reserves a similar right in regard to each of its dependent territories.

The Government of the United Kingdom reserve the right not to apply article 13 in Hong Kong in so far as it confers a right of review of a decision to deport an alien and a right to be represented for this purpose before the competent authority.

The Government of the United Kingdom reserve the right not to apply or not to apply in full the guarantee of free legal assistance in sub-paragraph (d) of paragraph 3 of article 14 in so far as the shortage of legal practitioners renders the application of this guarantee impossible in the British Virgin Islands, the Cayman Islands, the Falkland Islands, the Gilbert Islands, the Pitcairn Islands Group, St. Helena and Dependencies and Tuvalu.

The Government of the United Kingdom interpret article 20 consistently with the rights conferred by articles 19 and 21 of the Covenant and having legislated in matters of practical concern in the interests of public order (*ordre public*) reserve the right not to introduce any further legislation. The United Kingdom also reserve a similar right in regard to each of its dependent territories.

The Government of the United Kingdom reserve the right to postpone the application of paragraph 3 of article 23 in regard to a small number of customary marriages in the Solomon Islands.

The Government of the United Kingdom reserve the right to enact such nationality legislation as they may deem necessary from time to time to reserve the acquisition and possession of citizenship under such legislation to those having sufficient connection with the United Kingdom or any of its dependent territories and accordingly their acceptance of article 24(3) and of the other provisions of the Covenant is subject to the provisions of any such legislation.

The Government of the United Kingdom reserve the right not to apply sub-paragraph (b) of article 25 in so far as it may require the establishment of an elected Executive or Legislative Council in Hong Kong and sub-paragraph (c) of article 25 in so far as it relates to jury service in the Isle of Man.

Lastly the Government of the United Kingdom declare that the provisions of the Covenant shall not apply to Southern Rhodesia unless and until they inform the Secretary-General of the United Nations that they are in a position to ensure that the obligations imposed by the Covenant in respect of that territory can be fully implemented.

VENEZUELA

Upon ratification:

Article 60, paragraph 5, of the Constitution of the Republic of Venezuela establishes that: 'No person shall be convicted in a criminal trial unless he has first been personally notified of the charges and heard in the manner prescribed by law. Persons accused of an offence against the *res publica* may be tried *in absentia*, with the guarantees and in the manner prescribed by law'. Venezuela is making this reservation because article 14, paragraph 3 (*d*), of the Covenant makes no provision for persons accused of an offence against the *res publica* to be tried *in absentia*.

ICPR OP

(Entry into force 23 March 1976)

State	Signature	Ratification, accession
Austria	10 December 1973	
Barbados		5 January 1973
Canada		19 May 1976
Central African Republic		8 May 1981
Colombia	21 December 1966	29 October 1969
Costa Rica	19 December 1966	29 November 1968
Cyprus	19 December 1966	
Denmark*	20 March 1968	6 January 1972
Dominican Republic		4 January 1978
Ecuador	4 April 1968	6 March 1969
El Salvador	21 September 1967	
Finland	11 December 1967	19 August 1975
Guinea	19 March 1975	
Honduras	19 December 1966	
Iceland*		22 August 1979
Italy*	30 April 1976	15 September 1978
Jamaica	19 December 1966	3 October 1975
Madagascar	17 September 1969	21 June 1971
Mauritius		12 December 1973
Nicaragua		12 March 1980
Netherlands	25 June 1969	11 December 1978
Norway*	20 March 1968	13 September 1972
Panama	27 July 1976	8 March 1977
Peru	11 August 1977	3 October 1980
Philippines	19 December 1966	
Portugal	1 August 1978	
St. Vincent & the Grenadines		9 November 1981
Senegal	6 July 1970	13 February 1978
Suriname		28 December 1976
Sweden*	29 September 1967	6 December 1971
Trinidad & Tobago		14 November 1980
Uruguay	21 February 1967	1 April 1970
Venezuela*	15 November 1976	10 May 1978
Zaire		1 November 1976

*Reservations and Interpretations

DENMARK

Upon ratification:

With reference to Article 5, paragraph 2 (*a*), the Government of Denmark makes a reservation with respect to the competence of the Committee to consider a communication from an individual if the matter has already been considered under other procedures of international investigation.

ICELAND

Iceland . . . accedes to the said Protocol subject to a reservation, with reference to article 5, paragraph 2, with respect to the competence of the Human Rights Committee to consider a communication from an individual if the matter is being examined or has been examined under another procedure of international investigation or settlement. Other provisions of the Covenant shall be inviolably observed.

ITALY

Upon ratification:

The Italian Republic ratifies the Optional Protocol to the International Covenant on Civil and Political Rights, it being understood that the provisions of article 5, paragraph 2, of the Protocol mean that the Committee provided for in article 28 of the Covenant shall not consider any communication from an individual unless it has ascertained that the same matter is not being and has not been examined under another procedure of international investigation or settlement.

NORWAY

Upon ratification:

Subject to the following reservation to article 5, paragraph 2:
. . . The Committee shall not have competence to consider a communication from an individual if the same matter has already been examined under other procedures of international investigation or settlement.

SWEDEN

Upon ratification:

On the understanding that the provisions of article 5, paragraph 2, of the Protocol signify that the Human Rights Committee provided for in article 28 of the said Covenant shall not consider any communication from an individual unless it has ascertained that the same matter is not being examined or has not been examined under another procedure of international investigation or settlement.

VENEZUELA

Upon ratification:

Article 60, paragraph 5, of the Constitution of the Republic of Venezuela establishes that: 'No person shall be convicted in a criminal trial unless he has first been personally notified of the charges and heard in the manner prescribed by law. Persons accused of an offence against the *res publica* may be tried *in absentia*, with the guarantees and in the manner prescribed by law'. Venezuela is making this reservation because article 14, paragraph 3 (*d*), of the Covenant makes no provision for persons accused of an offence against the *res publica* to be tried *in absentia*.

Signatures, Ratifications, Accessions, etc.

ICES
(Entry into force 3 January 1976)

State	Signature		Ratification,	accession
Algeria	10 December	1968		
Argentina	19 February	1968		
Australia	18 December	1972	10 December	1975
Austria	10 December	1973	10 September	1978
Barbados*			5 January	1973
Belgium	10 December	1968		
Bulgaria*	8 October	1968	21 September	1970
Byelorussian SSR*	19 March	1968	12 November	1973
Canada			19 May	1976
Central African Republic			8 May	1981
Chile	16 September	1969	10 February	1972
Colombia	21 December	1966	29 October	1969
Costa Rica	19 December	1966	29 November	1968
Cyprus	9 January	1967	2 April	1969
Czechoslovakia*	7 October	1968	23 December	1975
Democratic Kampuchea	17 October	1980		
Denmark*	20 March	1968	6 January	1972
Dominican Republic			4 January	1978
Ecuador	29 September	1967	6 March	1969
Egypt	4 August	1967		
El Salvador	21 September	1967	30 November	1979
Finland	11 October	1967	19 August	1975
France*			4 November	1980
Gambia			29 December	1978
German Democratic Republic*	27 March	1973	8 November	1973
Germany, Federal Republic of	9 October	1968	17 December	1973
Guinea*	28 February	1967	24 January	1978
Guyana	22 August	1968	15 February	1977
Honduras	19 December	1966	17 February	1981
Hungary*	25 March	1969	17 January	1974
Iceland	30 December	1968	22 August	1979
India*			10 April	1979
Iran	4 April	1968	24 June	1975
Iraq*	18 February	1969	25 January	1971
Ireland	1 October	1973		
Israel	19 December	1966		
Italy	18 January	1967	15 September	1978
Jamaica	19 December	1966	3 October	1975
Japan*	30 May	1978	21 June	1979
Jordan	30 June	1972	28 May	1975
Kenya*			1 May	1972
Korea, Democratic People's Republic of			14 September	1981
Lebanon			3 November	1972
Liberia	18 April	1967		
Libyan Arab Jamahiriya*			15 May	1970
Luxembourg	26 November	1974		
Madagascar*	14 April	1970	22 September	1971
Mali			16 July	1974

State	Signature		Ratification, accession	
Malta*	22 October	1968		
Mauritius			12 December	1973
Mexico*			23 March	1981
Mongolia*	5 June	1968	18 November	1974
Morocco	19 January	1977	3 May	1979
Netherlands*	25 June	1969	11 December	1978
New Zealand*	12 November	1968	28 December	1978
Nicaragua			12 March	1980
Norway*	20 March	1968	13 September	1972
Panama	27 July	1976	8 March	1977
Peru	11 August	1977	28 April	1978
Philippines	19 December	1966	7 June	1974
Poland	2 March	1967	18 March	1977
Portugal	7 October	1976	31 July	1978
Romania*	27 June	1968	9 December	1974
Rwanda*			16 April	1975
St. Vincent & the Grenadines			9 November	1981
Senegal	6 July	1970	13 February	1978
Spain	28 September	1976	27 April	1977
Sri Lanka			11 June	1980
Suriname			28 December	1976
Sweden*	29 September	1967	6 December	1971
Syrian Arab Republic*			21 April	1969
Trinidad and Tobago*			8 December	1978
Tunisia	30 April	1968	18 March	1969
Ukrainian SSR*	20 March	1968	12 November	1973
Union of Soviet Socialist Republics*	18 March	1968	16 October	1973
United Kingdom*	16 September	1968	20 May	1976
United Republic of Tanzania			11 June	1976
United States of America	5 October	1977		
Uruguay	21 February	1967	1 April	1970
Venezuela	24 June	1969	10 May	1978
Yugoslavia	8 August	1967	2 June	1971
Zaire			1 November	1976

*Reservations and Interpretations

BARBADOS

The Government of Barbados states that it reserves the right to postpone —
(a) The application of sub-paragraph (a) (1) of article 7 of the Covenant in so far as it concerns the provision of equal pay to men and women for equal work;
(b) The application of article 10(2) in so far as it relates to the special protection to be accorded mothers during a reasonable period during and after childbirth; and
(c) The application of article 13(2) (a) of the Covenant, in so far as it relates to primary education;
since, while the Barbados Government fully accepts the principles embodied in the same articles and undertakes to take the necessary steps to apply them in their entirety, the problems of implementation are such that full application of the principles in question cannot be guaranteed at this stage.

BULGARIA

The People's Republic of Bulgaria deems it necessary to underline that the provisions of article 48, paragraphs 1 and 3, of the International Covenant on Civil and Political Rights, and article 26, paragraphs 1 and 3, of the International Covenant on Economic, Social and Cultural Rights, under which a number of States are deprived of the opportunity to become parties to the Covenants, are of a discriminatory nature. These provisions are inconsistent with the very nature of the Covenants, which are universal in character and should be open for accession by all States. In accordance with the principle of sovereign equality, no State has the right to bar other States from becoming parties to a covenant of this kind.

BYELORUSSIAN SOVIET SOCIALIST REPUBLIC

Declaration made upon signature and confirmed upon ratification:

The Byelorussian Soviet Socialist Republic declares that the provisions of paragraph 1 of article 26 of the International Covenant on Economic, Social and Cultural Rights and of paragraph 1 of article 48 of the International Covenant on Civil and Political Rights, under which a number of States cannot become parties to these Covenants, are of a discriminatory nature and considers that the Covenants, in accordance with the principle of sovereign equality of States, should be open for participation by all States concerned without any discrimination or limitation.

CZECHOSLOVAKIA

Upon signature:

The Czechoslovak Socialist Republic declares that the provisions of article 26, paragraph 1, of the International Covenant on Economic, Social and Cultural Rights are in contradiction with the principle that all States have the right to become parties to multilateral treaties governing matters of general interest.

Upon ratification:

The provision of article 26, paragraph 1, of the Covenant is in contradiction with the principle that all States have the right to become parties to multilateral treaties regulating matters of general interest.

DENMARK

The Government of Denmark cannot, for the time being, undertake to comply entirely with the provisions of Article 7 (*d*) on remuneration for public holidays.

FRANCE

(1) The Government of the Republic considers that, in accordance with Article 103 of the Charter of the United Nations, in case of conflict between its obligations under the Covenant and its obligations under the Charter (especially Articles 1 and 2 thereof), its obligations under the Charter will prevail.

(2) The Government of the Republic declares that Articles 6, 9, 11 and 13 are not to be interpreted as derogating from provisions governing the access of aliens to employment or as establishing residence requirements for the allocation of certain social benefits.

(3) The Government of the Republic declares that it will implement the provisions of Article 8 in respect of the right to strike in conformity with Article 6, paragraph 4, of the European Social Charter according to the interpretation thereof given in the annex to that Charter.

GERMAN DEMOCRATIC REPUBLIC

The German Democratic Republic considers that article 26, paragraph 1, of the Covenant runs counter to the principle that all States which are guided in their policies by the purposes and principles of the United Nations Charter have the right to become parties to conventions which affect the interests of all States.

GUINEA

Upon ratification:

In accordance with the principle whereby all States whose policies are guided by the purposes and principles of the Charter of the United Nations are entitled to become parties to covenants affecting the interests of the international community, the Government of the Republic of Guinea considers that the provisions of article 26, paragraph 1, of the International Covenant on Economic, Social and Cultural Rights are contrary to the principle of the universality of international treaties and the democratization of international relations.

The Government of the Republic of Guinea likewise considers that article 1, paragraph 3, and the provisions of article 14 of that instrument are contrary to the provisions of the Charter of the United Nations, in general, and United Nations resolutions on the granting of independence to colonial countries and peoples, in particular.

The above provisions are contrary to the Declaration on Principles of International Law Concerning Friendly Relations and Co-operation among States contained in General Assembly resolution 2625 (XXV), pursuant to which every State has the duty to promote realization of the principle of equal rights and self-determination of peoples in order to put an end to colonialism.

HUNGARY

Upon signature:

The Government of the Hungarian People's Republic declares that paragraph 1 of article 26 of the International Covenant on Economic, Social and Cultural Rights and paragraph 1 of article 48 of the International Covenant on Civil and Political Rights according to which certain States may not become signatories to the said Covenants are of a discriminatory nature and are contrary to the basic principle of international law that all States are entitled to become signatories to general multilateral treaties. These discriminatory provisions are incompatible with the objectives and purposes of the Covenants.

Upon ratification:

The Presidential Council of the Hungarian People's Republic declares that the provisions of article 48, paragraphs 1 and 3, of . . . the International Covenant on Civil and Political Rights, and article 26, paragraphs 1 and 3, of the International Covenant on Economic, Social and Cultural Rights are inconsistent with the universal character of the Covenants. It follows from the principle of sovereign equality of States that the Covenants should be open for participation by all States without any discrimination or limitation.

INDIA

Declarations

I. With reference to article 1 of the International Covenant on Economic, Social and Cultural Rights, . . . the Government of the Republic of India declares that the words 'the right of self-determination' appearing in [this article] apply only to the peoples under foreign domination and that these words do not apply to sovereign independent States or to a section of a people or nation — which is the essence of national integrity.

IV. With reference to articles 4 and 8 of the International Covenant on Economic, Social and Cultural Rights, . . . the Government of the Republic of India declares that the provisions of the said [article] shall be so applied as to be in conformity with the provisions of article 19 of the Constitution of India.

V. With reference to article 7 (c) of the International Covenant on Economic, Social and Cultural Rights, the Government of the Republic of India declares that the provisions of the said article shall be so applied as to be in conformity with the provisions of article 16 (4) of the Constitution of India.

IRAQ

Upon signature and confirmed upon ratification:

The entry of the Republic of Iraq as a party to the International Covenant on Economic, Social and Cultural Rights and the International Covenant on Civil and Political Rights shall in no way signify recognition of Israel nor shall it entail any obligations towards Israel under the said two Covenants.

The entry of the Republic of Iraq as a party to the above two Covenants shall not constitute entry by it as a party to the Optional Protocol to the International Covenant on Civil and Political Rights.

Upon ratification:

Ratification by Iraq . . . shall in no way signify recognition of Israel nor shall it be conducive to entry with her into such dealings as are regulated by the said [Covenant].

JAPAN

Upon signature and confirmed upon ratification:

1. In applying the provisions of paragraph (*d*) of article 7 of the International Covenant on Economic, Social and Cultural Rights, Japan reserves the right not to be bound by 'remuneration for public holidays' referred to in the said provisions.

2. Japan reserves the right not to be bound by the provisions of sub-paragraph (*d*) of paragraph 1 of article 8 of the International Covenant on Economic Social and Cultural Rights, except in relation to the sectors in which the right referred to in the said provisions is accorded in accordance with the laws and regulations of Japan at the time of ratification of the Covenant by the Government of Japan.

3. In applying the provisions of sub-paragraphs (*b*) and (*c*) of paragraph 2 of article 13 of the International Covenant on Economic, Social and Cultural Rights, Japan reserves the right not to be bound by 'in particular by the progressive introduction of free education' referred to in the said provisions.

4. Recalling the position taken by the Government of Japan, when ratifying the Convention (No. 87) concerning Freedom of Association and Protection of the Right to Organise, that 'the police' referred to in article 9 of the said Convention be interpreted to include the fire service of Japan, the Government of Japan declares that 'members — of the police' referred to in paragraph 2 of article 8 of the International Covenant on Economic, Social and Cultural Rights as well as in paragraph 2 of article 22 of the International Covenant on Civil and Political Rights be interpreted to include fire service personnel of Japan.

KENYA

While the Kenya Government recognizes and endorses the principles laid down in paragraph 2 of article 10 of the Covenant, the present circumstances obtaining in Kenya do not render necessary or expedient the imposition of those principles by legislation.

LIBYAN ARAB JAMAHIRIYA

The acceptance and the accession to this Covenant by the Libyan Arab Republic shall in no way signify a recognition of Israel or be conducive to entry by the Libyan Arab Republic into such dealings with Israel as are regulated by the Covenant.

MADAGASCAR

The Government of Madagascar states that it reserves the right to postpone the application of article 13, paragraph 2, of the Covenant, more particularly in so far as relates to primary education, since, while the Malagasy Government fully accepts the principles embodied in the said paragraph and undertakes to take the necessary steps to apply them in their entirety at the earliest possible date, the problems of implementation, and particularly the financial implications, are such that full application of the principles in question cannot be guaranteed at this stage.

MALTA

The Government of Malta recognises and endorses the principles laid down in paragraph 2 of article 10 of the Covenant. However, the present circumstances obtaining in Malta do not render necessary and do not render expedient the imposition of those principles by legislation.

MEXICO

The Government of Mexico accedes to [the Covenant] with the understanding that Article 8 of the Covenant shall be applied in the Mexican Republic under the conditions and in conformity with the procedures established in the applicable provisions of the Political Constitution of the United Mexican States and the relevant implementing legislation.

MONGOLIA

Declaration made upon signature and renewed upon ratification:

Mongolia declares that the provisions of paragraph 1 of article 26 of the International Covenant on Economic, Social and Cultural Rights and of paragraph 1 of article 48 of the International Covenant on Civil and Political Rights, under which a number of States cannot become parties to these Covenants, are of a discriminatory nature and considers that the Covenants, in accordance with the principle of sovereign equality of States, should be open for participation by all States concerned without any discrimination or limitation.

NETHERLANDS

Upon ratification:

Reservation

Article 8, paragraph 1 (d). The Kingdom of the Netherlands does not accept this provision in the case of the Netherlands Antilles with regard to the latter's central and local government bodies.

Explanation

[The Kingdom of the Netherlands] clarify that although it is not certain whether the reservation [. . .] is necessary, [it] has preferred the form of a reservation to that of a declaration. In this way the Kingdom of the Netherlands wishes to ensure that the relevant obligation under the Covenant does not apply to the Kingdom as far as the Netherlands Antilles is concerned.

NEW ZEALAND

Upon ratification:

The Government of New Zealand reserves the right not to apply article 8 to the extent that existing legislative measures, enacted to ensure effective trade union representation and encourage orderly industrial relations, may not be fully compatible with that article.

The Government of New Zealand reserves the right to postpone, in the economic circumstances foreseeable at the present time, the implementation of article 10(2) as it relates to paid maternity leave or leave with adequate social security benefits.

NORWAY

Subject to reservations to article 8, paragraph 1 (d) to the effect that the current Norwegian practice of referring labour conflicts to the State Wages Board (a permanent tripartite arbitral commission in matters of wages) by Act of Parliament for the particular conflict, shall not be considered incompatible with the right to strike, this right being fully recognised in Norway.

ROMANIA

Upon signature:

The Government of the Socialist Republic of Romania declares that the provisions of article 26, paragraph 1, of the International Covenant on Economic, Social and Cultural Rights are at variance with the principle that all States have the right to become parties to multilateral treaties governing matters of general interest.

Upon ratification:

(a) The State Council of the Socialist Republic of Romania considers that the provisions of article 26 (1) of the International Covenant on Economic, Social and Cultural Rights are inconsistent with the principle that multilateral international treaties whose purposes concern the international community as a whole must be open to universal participation.

477

(*b*) The State Council of the Socialist Republic of Romania considers that the maintenance in a state of dependence of certain territories referred to in articles 1 (3) and 14 of the International Covenant on Economic, Social and Cultural Rights is inconsistent with the Charter of the United Nations and the instruments adopted by the Organization on the granting of independence to colonial countries and peoples, including the Declaration on Principles of International Law concerning Friendly Relations and Co-operation among States in accordance with the Charter of the United Nations, adopted unanimously by the United Nations General Assembly in its resolution 2625 (XXV) of 1970, which solemnly proclaims the duty of States to promote the realization of the principle of equal rights and self-determination of peoples in order to bring a speedy end to colonialism.

RWANDA

The Rwandese Republic [is] bound, however, in respect of education, only by the provisions of its Constitution.

SWEDEN

Sweden enters a reservation in connexion with article 7 (*d*) of the Covenant in the matter of the right to remuneration for public holidays.

SYRIAN ARAB REPUBLIC

1. The accession of the Syrian Arab Republic to these two Covenants shall in no way signify recognition of Israel or entry into a relationship with it regarding any matter regulated by the said two Covenants.

2. The Syrian Arab Republic considers that paragraph 1 of article 26 of the Covenant on Economic, Social and Cultural Rights and paragraph 1 of article 48 of the Covenant on Civil and Political Rights are incompatible with the purposes and objectives of the said Covenants, inasmuch as they do not allow all States, without distinction or discrimination, the opportunity to become parties to the said Covenant.

TRINIDAD AND TOBAGO

In respect to article 8(1)(d) and 8(2): The Government of Trinidad and Tobago reserves the right to impose lawful and or reasonable restrictions on the exercise of the aforementioned rights by personnel engaged in essential services under the Industrial Relations Act or under any Statute replacing same which has been passed in accordance with the provisions of the Trinidad and Tobago Constitution.

UKRAINIAN SOVIET SOCIALIST REPUBLIC

Declaration made upon signature and confirmed upon ratification:

The Ukrainian Soviet Socialist Republic declares that the provisions of paragraph 1 of article 26 of the International Covenant on Economic, Social and

and Cultural Rights and of paragraph 1 of article 48 of the International Covenant on Civil and Political Rights, under which a number of States cannot become parties to these Covenants, are of a discriminatory nature and considers that the Covenants, in accordance with the principle of sovereign equality of States, should be open for participation by all States concerned without any discrimination or limitation.

UNION OF SOVIET SOCIALIST REPUBLICS

Declaration made upon signature and confirmed upon ratification:

The Union of Soviet Socialist Republics declares that the provisions of paragraph 1 of article 26 of the International Covenant on Economic, Social and Cultural Rights and of paragraph 1 of article 48 of the International Covenant on Civil and Political Rights, under which a number of States cannot become parties to these Covenants, are of a discriminatory nature and considers that the Covenants, in accordance with the principle of sovereign equality of States, should be open for participation by all States concerned without any discrimination or limitation.

UNITED KINGDOM OF GREAT BRITAIN AND NORTHERN IRELAND

Upon signature:

First, the Government of the United Kingdom declare their understanding that, by virtue of Article 103 of the Charter of the United Nations, in the event of any conflict between their obligations under Article 1 of the Covenant and their obligations under the Charter (in particular, under Articles 1, 2 and 73 thereof) their obligations under the Charter shall prevail.

Secondly, the Government of the United Kingdom declare that they must reserve the right to postpone the application of sub-paragraph (*a*) (i) of Article 7 of the Covenant in so far as it concerns the provision of equal pay to men and women for equal work, since, while they fully accept this principle and are pledged to work towards its complete application at the earliest possible time, the problems of implementation are such that complete application cannot be guaranteed at present.

Thirdly, the Government of the United Kingdom declare that, in relation to Article 8 of the Covenant, they must reserve the right not to apply sub-paragraph (*b*) of paragraph 1 in Hong Kong, in so far as it may involve the right of trade unions not engaged in the same trade or industry to establish federations or confederations.

Lastly, the Government of the United Kingdom declare the the provisions of the Covenant shall not apply to Southern Rhodesia unless and until they inform the Secretary-General of the United Nations that they are in a position to ensure that the obligations imposed by the Covenant in respect of that territory can be fully implemented.

Upon ratification:

Firstly, the Government of the United Kingdom maintain their declaration in respect of article 1 made at the time of signature of the Covenant.

The Government of the U. ited Kingdom declare that for the purposes of article 2(3) the British Virgin Islands, the Cayman Islands, the Gilbert Islands, the Pitcairn Islands Group, St. Helena and Dependencies, the Turks and Caicos Islands and Tuvalu are developing countries.

The Government of the United Kingdom reserve the right to interpret article 6 as not precluding the imposition of restrictions, based on place of birth or residence qualifications, on the taking of employment in any particular region or territory for the purpose of safeguarding the employment opportunities of workers in that region or territory.

The Government of the United Kingdom reserve the right to postpone the application of sub-paragraph (i) of paragraph (*a*) of Article 7, in so far as it concerns the provision of equal pay to men and women for equal work in the private sector in Jersey, Guernsey, the Isle of Man, Bermuda, Hong Kong and the Solomon Islands.

The Government of the United Kingdom reserve the right not to apply sub-paragraph 1 (*b*) of article 8 in Hong Kong.

The Government of the United Kingdom while recognising the right of everyone to social security in accordance with article 9 reserve the right to postpone implementation of the right in the Cayman Islands and the Falkland Islands because of shortage of resources in these territories.

The Government of the United Kingdom reserve the right to postpone the application of paragraph 1 of article 10 in regard to a small number of customary marriages in the Solomon Islands and the application of paragraph 2 of article 10 in so far as it concerns paid maternity leave in Bermuda and the Falkland Islands.

The Government of the United Kingdom maintain the right to postpone the application of sub-paragraph (*a*) of paragraph 2 of article 13, and article 14, in so far as they require compulsory primary education, in the Gilbert Islands, the Solomon Islands and Tuvalu.

Lastly the Government of the United Kingdom declare that the provisions of the Covenant shall not apply to Southern Rhodesia unless and until they inform the Secretary-General of the United Nations that they are in a position to ensure that the obligations imposed by the Covenant in respect of that territory can be fully implemented.

EHR (Entry into force 3 September 1943)
EHR P1 (Entry into force 18 May 1954)
EHR P4 (Entry into force 2 May 1968)

State	Signature EHR	Ratification EHR	Ratification EHR P1	Ratification EHR P4	Current declaration under	
					Art. 25	Art. 26
Austria*	13 December 1957	3 September 1958	3 September 1958	18 September 1969	3 September 1979[2]	3 September 1979[2]
Belgium	4 November 1950	14 June 1955	14 June 1955	21 September 1970	30 June 1977[3]	29 June 1977[3]
Cyprus	16 December 1961	6 October 1962	6 October 1962		24 January 1980[2]	24 January 1980[2]
Denmark	4 November 1950	13 April 1953	13 April 1953	30 September 1964	7 April 1977[3]	7 April 1977[3]
France*	4 November 1950	3 May 1974	3 May 1974	3 May 1974	2 October 1981[3]	16 July 1980[2]
Federal Republic of Germany*	4 November 1950	5 December 1952	13 February 1957	1 June 1968	1 July 1981[3]	1 July 1981[3]
Greece*	28 November 1950	28 November 1974	28 November 1974		3 September 1979[3]	30 January 1979[2]
Iceland	4 November 1950	29 June 1953	29 June 1953	16 November 1967	25 March 1960	3 September 1979[3]
Ireland*	4 November 1950	25 February 1953	25 February 1953	29 October 1968	25 February 1953	25 February 1953
Italy	4 November 1950	26 October 1955	26 October 1955		1 August 1981[2]	1 August 1981[2]
Liechtenstein	23 November 1978					
Luxembourg*	4 November 1950	3 September 1953	3 September 1953	2 May 1968	28 April 1981[3]	28 April 1981[3]
Malta*	12 December 1966	23 January 1967	23 January 1967			
Netherlands*	4 November 1950	31 August 1954	31 August 1954	15 November 1963	1 September 1979	1 September 1979
Norway	4 November 1950	15 January 1952	18 December 1952	12 June 1964	29 June 1977[3]	29 June 1977[3]
Portugal*	22 September 1976	9 November 1978	9 November 1978	9 November 1978	9 November 1980[1]	9 November 1981[1]
Spain*	24 November 1977	4 October 1979	23 February 1978	23 February 1978	1 July 1981[1]	15 October 1979
Sweden*	28 November 1950	4 February 1952	22 June 1953	13 June 1964	4 March 1952	13 May 1981[3]
Switzerland*	21 December 1972	28 November 1974	19 May 1976		28 November 1980[2]	28 November 1974
Turkey*	4 November 1950	18 May 1954	18 May 1954			
United Kingdom*	4 November 1950	8 March 1951	3 November 1952		14 January 1981[3]	14 January 1981[3]

[1] For two years
[2] For three years
[3] For five years

481

*Reservations and Interpretations

AUSTRIA

The Federal President declares the Covention to be ratified with the reservation:
1. The provisions of Article 5 of the Convention shall be so applied that there shall be no interference with the measures for the deprivation of liberty prescribed in the laws on administrative procedure, BGB1 No. 172/1950, subject to review by the Administrative Court or the Constitutional Court as provided for in the Austrian Federal Constitution;
2. The provisions of Article 6 of the Convention shall be so applied that there shall be no prejudice to the principles governing public court hearings laid down in Article 90 of the 1929 version of the Federal Constitution Law;

and being desirous of avoiding any uncertainty concerning the application of Article 1 of the Protocol in connection with the State Treaty of 15 May 1955 for the Restoration of an Independent and Democratic Austria, declares the Protocol ratified with the reservations that there shall be no intereference with the provisions of Part IV 'Claims arising out of the War' and Part V 'Property, Rights and Interests' of the above-mentioned State Treaty.

Protocol No. 4 is signed with the reservation that Article 3 shall not apply to the provisions on the Law of 3 April 1919, StGB1. No. 209 concerning the banishment of the House of Habsburg-Lorraine and the confiscation of their property, as set out in the Act of 30 October 1919, StGB1. No. 501, in the Constitutional Law of 30 July 1925, BGB1. No. 292, in the Federal Constitutional Law of 26 January 1928, BGB1. No. 30, and taking account of the Federal Constitutional Law of 4 July 1963, BGB1. No. 172.

FRANCE

In depositing this instrument of ratification, the Government of the Republic in accordance with Article 64 of the Convention, makes a reservation in respect of:
1. Articles 5 and 6 thereof, to the effect that those articles shall not hinder the application of the provisions governing the system of discipline in the armed forces contained in Section 27 of Act No. 72–662 of 13 July 1972, determining the general legal status of military servicemen, nor of the provisions of Article 375 of the Code of Military Justice;
2. paragraph 1 of Article 15, to the effect, firstly, that the circumstances specified in Article 16 of the Constitution regarding the implementation of that Article, in Section 1 of the Act of 3 April 1878 and in the Act of 9 August 1849 regarding proclamation of a state of siege, and in Section 1 of Act No. 55–385 of 3 April 1955 regarding proclamation of a state of emergency, and in which it is permissible to apply the provisions of those texts, must be understood as complying with the purpose of Article 15 of the Convention and that, secondly, for the interpretation and application of Article 16 of the Constitution of the Republic, the terms 'to the extent strictly required by the exigencies of the situation' shall not restrict the power of the President of the Republic to take 'the measures required by the circumstances'.

The Government of the Republic declares that it interprets the provisions of Article 10 as being compatible with the system established in France under Act No. 72-553 of 10 July 1972, determining the legal status of the French Radio and Television.

FEDERAL REPUBLIC OF GERMANY

In conformity with Article 64 of the Convention the German Federal Republic makes the reservation that it will only apply the provisions of Article 7 paragraph 2 of the Convention within the limits of Article 103 clause 2 of the Basic Law of the German Federal Repulic. This provides that 'any act is only punishable if it was so by law before the offence was committed'.

The Federal Republic of Germany adopts the opinion according to which the second sentence of Article 2 of the (First) Protocol entails no obligation on the part of the State to finance schools of a religious or philosophical nature, or to assist in financing such schools, since this question, as confirmed by the concurring declaration of the Legal Committee of the Consultative Assembly and the Secretary General of the Council of Europe, lies outside the scope of the Convention for the Protection of Human Rights and Fundamental Freedoms and of its Protocol.

GREECE

The application of the word 'philosophical' which is the penultimate word of the second sentence of Article 2, will, in Greece, conform with the relevant provisions of internal legislation.

IRELAND

. . . the Government of Ireland do hereby confirm and ratify the aforesaid Convention and undertake faithfully to perform and carry out all the stipulations therein contained, subject to the reservation that they do not interpret Article 6 (3)(c) of the Convention as requiring the provision of free legal assistance to any wider extent than is now provided in Ireland.

At the time of signing the (First) Protocol the Irish Delegate puts on record that, in the view of the Irish Government, Article 2 of the Protocol is not sufficiently explicit in ensuring to parents the right to provide education for their children in their homes or in schools of the parents' own choice, whether or not such schools are private schools or are schools recognised or established by the State.

Upon signature of EHR P4:

The reference to extradition contained in paragraph 21 of the Report of the Committee of Experts on this Protocol and concerning paragraph 1 of Article 3 of the Protocol includes also laws providing for the execution in the territory of one Contracting Party of warrants of arrest issued by the authorities of another Contracting Party.

LUXEMBOURG

The Government of the Grand Duchy of Luxembourg, having regard to Article 64 of the Convention and desiring to avoid any uncertainty as regards the application of Article 1 of the Protocol in relation to the Luxembourg Law of 26 April 1951 concerning the liquidation of certain ex-enemy property, rights and interests subject to measures of sequestration, makes a reservation relating to the provisions of the above-mentioned Law of 26 April 1951.

MALTA

I. The Government of Malta, having regard to Article 64 of the Convention, and desiring to avoid any uncertainty as regards the application of Article 10 of the Convention declares that the Constitution of Malta allows such restrictions to be imposed upon public officers in regard to their freedom of expression as are reasonably justifiable in a democratic society. The Code of conduct of public officers in Malta precludes them from taking an active part in political discussions or other political activity during working hours or on official premises.

II. The Government of Malta, having regard to Article 64 of the Convention declares that the principle of lawful defence admitted under sub-paragraph (*a*) of paragraph 2 of Article 2 of the Convention shall apply in Malta also to the defence of property to the extent required by the provisions of paragraphs (*a*) and (*b*) of section 238 of the Criminal Code of Malta, the text whereof, along with the text of the preceding section 237, is as follows:

'237. No offence is committed when a homicide or a bodily harm is ordered or permitted by a law or by a lawful authority, or is imposed by actual necessity either in lawful self-defence or in the lawful defence of another person.

238. Cases of actual necessity of lawful defence shall include the following:

(*a*) where the homicide or bodily harm is committed in the act of repelling, during the night-time, the scaling or breaking of enclosures, walls, or the entrance doors of any house or inhabited apartment, or of the appurtenances thereof having a direct or an indirect communication with such house or apartment;

(*b*) where the homicide or bodily harm is committed in the act of defence against any person committing theft or plunder, with violence, or attempting to commit such theft or plunder, with violence, or attempting to commit such theft or plunder;

(*c*) where the homicide or bodily harm is imposed by the actual necessity of the defence of one's own chastity or of the chastity of another person.'

III. The Government of Malta, having regard to Article 64 of the Convention, declares that the principle affirmed in the second sentence of Article 2 of the Protocol is accepted by Malta only in so far as it is compatible with the provision of efficient instruction and training, and the avoidance of unreasonable public expenditure, having regard to the fact that the population of Malta is overwhelmingly Roman Catholic.

The Government of Malta declares that it interprets paragraph 2 of Article 6 of the Convention in the sense that it does not preclude any particular law from imposing upon any person charged under such law the burden of proving particular facts.

NETHERLANDS

As to the Convention:

. . . the Convention apply to Surinam and the Dutch West Indies except as regards the provisions of free legal assistance under Article 6(3)(*c*).

As to the Protocol:

In the opinion of the Netherlands Government the State should not only respect the rights of parents in the matter of education but, if need be, ensure the possibility of exercising those rights by appropriate financial measures.

PORTUGAL

I. Article 5 of the Convention will be applied subject to Articles 27 and 28 of the Military Discipline Regulations, which provide for the placing under arrest of members of the armed forces.

Articles 27 and 28 of the Military Discipline Regulations read as follows:
Article 27:
1. *Arrests consist of the detention of the offender in a building intended for the purpose, in an appropriate place, barracks or military establishment, in suitable quarters on board ship or, failing these, in a place determined by the competent authority.*
2. *Between the reveille and sundown, during the period of detention, the members of the armed forces can perform the duties assigned to them.*

Article 28:
Close arrest consists of the detention of the offender in a building intended for the purpose.

II. Article 7 of the Convention will be applied subject to Article 309 of the Constitution of the Portuguese Republic, which provides for the indictment and trial of officers and personnel of the State Police Force (PIDE-DGS).

Article 309 of the Constitution reads as follows:
Article 309:
1. *Law No. 8/75 of 25 July 1975 shall remain in force with the amendments made by Law No. 16/75 of 23 December 1975 and Law No. 18/75 of 26 December 1975.*
2. *The offences referred to in Articles 2(2), 3, 4(b) and 5 of the Law referred to in the foregoing paragraph may be further defined by Law.*
3. *The exceptional extenuating circumstances as provided for in Article 7 of the said Law may be specifically regulated by law.*

(Act No. 8/75 lays down the penalties applicable to officers, officials and associates of the former General Directorate of Security (beforehand the International and State Defence Police), disbanded after 24 April 1974, and stipulates that the military courts have jurisdiction in such cases).

III. Article 10 of the Convention will be applied subject to Article 38 (6) of the Constitution of the Portuguese Republic, which provides that the television may not be privately owned.

Article 38 (6) of the Constitution reads as follows:
Article 38:
6. *The television shall not be privately owned.*

IV. Article 11 of the Convention will be applied subject to Article 60 of the Constitution of the Portuguese Republic, which prohibits lock-outs.

Article 60 of the Constitution reads as follows:
Article 60:
Lock-outs shall be prohibited.

V. Article 4 (3) (*b*) of the Convention will be applied subject to Article 276 of the Constitution of the Portuguese Republic, which provides for compulsory civic service.

Article 276 of the Constitution reads as follows:
Article 276:
1. *The defence of the country is a fundamental duty of every Portuguese.*
2. *Military service shall be compulsory, for a period and on conditions to be laid down by law.*
3. *Persons considered unfit for armed military service and conscientious objectors shall perform unarmed military service or civic service suited to their situations.*

4. *Civic service may be established as a substitute for or as a complement to military service and may be made compulsory by law for citizens not subject to military service.*
5. *No citizen shall keep or obtain any office in the state or in any other public body if he fails to perform his military service or civic service, if compulsory.*
6. *Performance by a citizen of military service or compulsory civic service shall be without prejudice to his post, social security benefits or permanent career.*

VI. Article 11 of the Convention will be applied subject to Article 46 (4) of the Constitution of the Portuguese Republic, which prohibits organisations with allegiance to a fascist ideology.

Article 46 (4) of the Constitution reads as follows:

Article 46:
4. *Armed, military-type, militarised or para-military associations outside the state and the Armed Forces and organisations which adopt Fascist ideology shall not be permitted.*

VII. Article 1 of the Protocol will be applied subject to Article 82 of the Constitution of the Portuguese Republic, which provides that expropriations of large landowners, big property owners and entrepreneurs or shareholders may be subject to no compensation under the conditions to be laid down by the law.

Article 82 of the Constitution reads as follows:

Article 82:
1. *The law shall determine the methods and forms of intervention, nationalisation and socialisation of the means of production and criteria for fixing compensation.*
2. *The law may stipulate that expropriations of large landowners, big property owners and entrepreneurs or shareholders shall not be subject to any compensation whatsoever.*

VIII. Article 2 of the Protocol will be applied subject to Articles 43 and 75 of the Constitution of the Portuguese Republic, which provide for the non-denominationality of public education, the supervision of private education by the State and the validity of legal provisons concerning the setting-up of private educational establishments.

Articles 43 and 75 of the Constitution read as follows:

Article 43:
1. *The freedom to learn and teach shall be safeguarded.*
2. *The state shall not arrogate to itself the right to plan education and culture in accordance with any philosophical, aesthetic, political, ideological or religious guidelines.*
3. *Public education shall not be denominational.*

Article 75:
1. *The state shall establish a network of official education institutions to meet the needs of the whole population.*
2. *The state shall supervise private education which is complementary to public education.*

SPAIN

I. Articles 5 and 6, insofar as they may be incompatible with the disciplinary provisions concerning the armed forces, as they appear in Book 2, Part XV and Book 3, Part XXIV of the Code of Military Justice.

Brief statement of the relevant provisions:
The Code of Military Justice provides that the punishment of minor

offences may be ordered directly by an offender's official superior, after having elucidated the facts. The punishment of serious offences is subject to an investigation of a judicial character, in the course of which the accused must be given a hearing. The penalties and the power to impose them are defined by law. In any case, the accused can appeal against the punishment to his immediate superior and so on, up to the Head of State.

II. Article 11, insofar as it may be incompatible with Articles 28 and 127 of the Spanish Constitution.

Brief statement of the relevant provisions:

Article 28 of the Constitution recognises the right to organise, but provides that legislation may restrict the exercise of this right or make it subject to exception in the case of the armed forces or other corps subject to military discipline and shall regulate the manner of its exercise in the case of civil servants.

Article 127, paragraph 1, specifies that serving judges, law officers and prosecutors may not belong to either political parties or trade unions and provides that legislation shall lay down the system and modalities as to the professional association of these groups.

Spain declares that it interprets:

I. the provisions of the last sentence in Article 10, paragraph 1, as being compatible with the present system governing the organisation of radio and television broadcasting in Spain.

II. the provisions of Articles 15 and 17 to the effect that they permit the adoption of the measures contemplated in Articles 55 and 116 of the Spanish Constitution.

SWEDEN

. . . We do ratify, approve and accept the (First) Protocol with all its Articles and clauses with the reservation in respect of Article 2 of the Protocol, to the effect that Sweden could not grant to parents the right to obtain, by reason of their philosophical convictions, dispensation for their children from the obligation of taking part in certain parts of the education in the public schools, and also to the effect that the dispensation from the obligation of taking part in the teaching of Christianity in these schools could only be granted for children of another faith than the Swedish Church in respect of whom a satisfactory religious instruction had been arranged. This reservation is based on the provisions of the new rule of 17 March 1933 for the establishment of secondary education within the Kingdom and also on the analogous provisions concerning other educational establishments.

SWITZERLAND

I. The provisions of Article 5 of the Convention shall not affect the operation of the cantonal legislation authorising the detention of certain categories of persons by decision of an administrative authority or cantonal provisions governing the procedure for placing a child or ward in an institution in accordance with federal legislation on paternal authority or guardianship (Articles 284, 386, 406 and 421.13 of the Swiss Civil Code).

II. The rule contained in Article 6, paragraph 1, of the Convention that hearings shall be in public shall not apply to proceedings relating to the determination of civil rights and obligations or of any criminal charge which, in accordance with cantonal legislation, are heard before an administrative authority.

III. The rule that judgment must be pronounced publicly shall not affect the operation of cantonal legislation on civil or criminal procedure providing that judgment shall not be delivered in public but notified to the parties in writing.

The Swiss Federal Council considers that the guarantee of fair trial in Article 6 paragraph 1 of the Convention, in the determination of civil rights and obligations or any criminal charge against the person in question, is intended solely to ensure ultimate control by the judiciary over the acts or decisions of the public authorities relating to such rights or obligations or the determination of such a charge.

The Swiss Federal Council declares that it interprets the guarantee of free legal assistance and the free assistance of an interpreter, in Article 6, paragraph 3, (c) and (e) of the Convention, as not permanently absolving the beneficiary from payment of the resulting costs.

TURKEY

Having seen and examined the Convention and the (First) Protocol, we have approved the same with the reservation set out in respect of Article 2 of the Protocol by reason of the provisions of Law No. 6366 voted by the National Grand Assembly of Turkey dated 10 March 1954.

Article 3 of the said Law No. 6366 reads: 'Article 2 of the Protocol shall not affect the provisions of Law No. 430 of 3 March 1924 relating to the unification of education.'

UNITED KINGDOM

At the time of signing the present (First) Protocol, I declare that, in view of certain provisions of the Education Acts in force in the United Kingdom, the principle affirmed in the second sentence of Article 2 is accepted by the United Kingdom only so far as it is compatible with the provision of efficient instruction and training, and the avoidance of unreasonable public expenditure.

ESC
(Entry into force 26 February 1965)

State	Signature	Ratification	Articles NOT accepted
Austria	22 July 1963	29 October 1969	2(1); (4); 6(4); 7(1); 7(6); 18(3); 19(4), (7), (8), (10)
Belgium	18 October 1961		
Cyprus	22 May 1967	7 March 1968	2; 4. 7; 8; 10; 13; 16; 17; 18
Denmark	18 October 1961	3 March 1965	2(1), (4); 4(4), (5); 7; 8(2), (3), (4); 19
France	18 October 1961	9 March 1973	2(4); 13(2)
Federal Republic of Germany	18 October 1961	27 January 1965	4(4); 7(1); 8(2), (4); 10(4)
Greece	18 October 1961		
Iceland	15 January 1976	15 January 1976	2(2), (4); 7; 8; 9; 10; 19
Ireland	18 October 1961	7 October 1964	4(3); 7(1), (7), (9); 8(2), (3); 11(1), (2); 12(2)
Italy	18 October 1961	22 October 1965	
Luxembourg	18 October 1961		
Netherlands	18 October 1961	22 April 1980	6(4) for civil servants; 19(10)
Norway*	18 October 1961	26 October 1962	7(1), (4), (9); 8; 18; 19(8)
Spain*	27 April 1978	6 May 1980	
Sweden	18 October 1961	17 December 1962	2(1), (2), (4); 4(2), (5); 7(5), (6); 8(2), (4); 12(4)
Switzerland	6 May 1976		
Turkey	18 October 1961		
United Kingdom	18 October 1961	11 July 1962	2(1); 4(3); 7(1), (4), (7); 8(2), (3); 12(2), (3), (4)

*Reservations and Interpetations

NORWAY

Upon ratification:

As regards Article 12, the undertaking is subject to the reservation that Norway under paragraph 4 of this Article will be permitted in the bilateral and multilateral agreements therein mentioned to stipulate as a condition for granting equal treatment that foreign seamen should be domiciled in the country to which the vessel belongs.

SPAIN

Upon ratification:

Spain declares that it will interpret and apply Articles 5 and 6 of the European Social Charter, read with Article 31 and the Appendix to the Charter, in such a way that their provisions will be compatible with those of Articles 28, 37, 103.3 and 127 of the Spanish Constitution.

AMR

(Entry into force 18 July 1978)

State	Signature	Ratification, accession or adherence	Declarations under Art. 45	Art. 62
Barbados	20 June 1978	5 November 1981		
Bolivia		19 July 1979		
Chile	22 November 1969			
Colombia	22 November 1969	31 July 1973		
Costa Rica	22 November 1969	8 April 1970	2 July 1980	2 July 1980
Dominican Republic*	7 September 1977	19 April 1978		
Ecuador	22 November 1969	28 December 1977		
El Salvador*	22 November 1969	23 June 1978		
Grenada	14 July 1978	18 July 1978		
Guatemala*	22 November 1969	25 May 1978		
Haiti		27 September 1977		
Honduras	22 November 1969	8 September 1977		
Jamaica	16 September 1977	7 August 1978	7 August 1978	
Mexico*		24 March 1981		
Nicaragua	22 November 1969	25 September 1979		
Panama	22 November 1969	22 June 1978		
Paraguay	22 November 1969			
Peru	27 July 1977	28 July 1978	21 January 1981	21 January 1981
USA	1 June 1977			
Uruguay*	22 November 1969			
Venezuela*	22 November 1969	9 August 1977	9 August 1977	

*Reservations and Interpretations

DOMINICAN REPUBLIC

Upon signature:

The Dominican Republic aspires that the principle pertaining to abolition of the death penalty shall become purely and simply that, with general application throughout the states of the American region, and likewise maintains the observations and comments made on the aforementioned Draft Convention which it distributed to the delegations to the Council of the Organization of American States on June 20, 1969.

EL SALVADOR

Upon ratification:

. . . with the reservation that such ratification is understood without prejudice to those provisions of the Convention that might be in conflict with express precepts of the Political Constitution of the Republic.

GUATEMALA

Upon ratification:

. . . with a reservation as to Article 4, paragraph 4 thereof, since the Constitution of the Republic of Guatemala, in its Article 54, only excludes the application of the death penalty to political crimes, but not to common crimes related to political crimes.

MEXICO

Interpretative Declarations

With respect to paragraph 1 of Article 4, considers that the expression 'in general' used in this paragraph does not constitute an obligation to adopt or maintain in force legislation which protects life 'from the moment of conception' since this matter belongs to the domain reserved to States.

Furthermore, in the view of the Government of Mexico, the limitation established by the Political Constitution of the United Mexican States, in the sense that all public religious acts must be performed strictly within places of worship, is within the scope of paragraph 3 of Article 12.

Reservation

The Government of Mexico makes an express reservation as to paragraph 2 of Article 23 since the Political Constitution of the United Mexican States, in its Article 130, provides that ministers of religion shall have neither an active nor a passive vote, nor the right to form associations for political purposes.

URUGUAY

Upon signature:

Article 80.2 of the Constitution of Uruguay provides that citizenship is suspended for a person indicted according to law in a criminal prosecution that may result in a sentence of imprisonment in a penitentiary. This restriction on the exercise of the rights recognized in Article 23 of the Convention is not envisaged among the circumstances provided for in this respect by paragraph 2 of Article 23, for which reason the Delegation of Uruguay expresses a reservation on this matter.

VENEZUELA

Upon ratification:

Article 60, paragraph 5 of the Constitution of the Republic of Venezuela establishes that: No one may be convicted in a criminal trial without first having been personally notified of the charges and heard in the manner prescribed by law. Persons accused of an offense against the *res publica* may be tried *in absentia*, with the guarantees and in the manner prescribed by law.

Signatures, Ratifications, Accessions, etc.

Subsidiary Instruments

See §	Instrument	Number of State Parties on 1 January 1982
14.1.6	CG	86
7.0.5	CA	62
7.0.5	CD	110
14.5.5	CR	87
14.5.5	CS_1	32
22.1.5	CS_2	10
7.0.5	CW_1	31
25.0.5	CW_2	87
22.1.5	CW_3	54
17.1.5	CM	31
7.0.5	CE	69
18.4.6	SC_1	90
18.4.6	SC_2	96
18.4.6	CP	52
23.4.6	CC	11

ILO Conventions

See §	Convention	Number of State Parties on 1 January 1982
18.4.6	*ILO 29*	124
24.3.5	*ILO 87*	93
24.3.5	*ILO 98*	110
18.2.6	*ILO 100*	100
18.4.6	*ILO 105*	107
7.0.5	*ILO 111*	101
18.1.5	*ILO 122*	68
24.3.5	*ILO 135*	37

TABLE B
Judgments, Decisions, and Reports cited

This Table lists all the jurisprudence noted in the present work, and shows (under the heading '§; n.') the sections and footnotes where it is cited. The Table is divided by reference to the global, regional, and national institutions from which the jurisprudence emanates, in the following order:

Global	*Regional*	*National*
Permanent Court of	EUCM	British Commonwealth
International Justice	EUCT	USA
International Court	EUCE	Europe
of Justice	European Court	
International Arbitral	of Justice	
Tribunals	IACM	
HRC	IACT	
ECOSOC		

Explanations of citations, publications, and abbreviations may be found at the beginnings of the relevant lists.

Judgments, Decisions, and Reports cited

Permanent Court of International Justice

Case	Reference	§; *n.*
Jurisdiction of the Courts of Danzig (Advisory Opinion)	Annual Digest 1927–8, No. 187	1; 21
Treatment of Polish Nationals and Other Persons of Polish Origin or Speech in the Danzig Territory (Advisory Opinion)	Series A/B, No. 44	4; 3 6; 22
Free Zones of Upper Savoy and District of Gex Case	Series A/B, No. 46	4; 3
Exchange of Greek and Turkish Populations (Advisory Opinion)	Series B, No. 10	4; 3 6; 21

International Court of Justice

Case	ICJ Reports	§; *n.*
Colombian-Peruvian Asylum Case	1950, 339	14.5; 4
Reservations to the Genocide Convention (Advisory Opinion)	1951, 15	1; 29 3; 19 14.1; 26
Anglo-Iranian Oil Company Case (Jurisdiction)	1952, 168	21; 1
Nottebohm Case (Second Phase)	1955, 63	22.1; 2
South-West African Cases (Second Phase)	1966, 289	1; 23 6; 13
Legal Consequences of the Continued Presence of South Africa in Namibia (Advisory Opinion)	1971, 16	6; 4

International Arbitral Tribunals

Case	Reference	§; *n.*
Alabama Claims Arbitration (Mixed Tribunal of Arbitration under Treaty of Washington 1871)	Moore 1 Int. Arb. 445	4; 3
Steiner and Goss v. *The Polish State* (Upper Silesian Arbitral Tribunal)	Annual Digest 1927–8, Nos. 188 and 287	1; 16

HRC

HRC's jurisprudence comes from its case reports under *ICPR OP* (see §27.3), and from its 'general comments' under *ICPR* 40(4) (see §27.4). Except for two case reports published individually at the end of 1981, all references are to HRC's Annual Reports, under *ICPR* 45, to the UNGA through ECOSOC. They are here numbered by reference to the session of the UNGA to which they were submitted, and as part of whose official records they are published.[1]

---

[1] The official UN document numbers are:

HRC 32 (1977)	A/32/44
HRC 33 (1978)	A/33/40
HRC 34 (1979)	A/34/40
HRC 35 (1980)	A/35/40
HRC 36 (1981)	A/36/40

CASES

Applicant and State	Case No.	Annual Report, p.	§; n.
Ambrosini v. *Uruguay*	R.1/5	HRC 34, 124	14.2; 86, 126 14.3; 75, 76, 79, 83 22.6; 29 27; 8
Antonaccio v. *Uruguay*	R. 14/63	**published 14 December 1981**	1; 27 14.2; 128 14.3; 78 22.4; 71 22.6; 29, 40, 41 27; 4
Aumeeruddy-Cziffra et al. v. *Mauritius*	R. 9/35	HRC 36, 134	7; 2 14.2; 149 17; 1, 16, 20 22.3; 1 23.2; 29
Burgos v. *Uruguay*	R. 12/52	HRC 36, 176	6; 24 9; 7 14.2; 44, 124, 149 14.3; 84 22.6; 29, 39, 41, 78 23.4; 34 24; 17 27; 3
Carballal v. *Uruguay*	R. 8/33	HRC 36, 125	8; 20 14.2; 85, 106, 111, 149 14.3; 77, 84 22.6; 38 23.4; 33
de Bouton v. *Uruguay*	R. 9/37	HRC 36, 143	14.2; 83, 111, 149 14.3; 82
de Casariego v. *Uruguay*	R. 13/56	HRC 36, 185	6; 24 9; 7 14.2; 44, 149 14.3; 79 22.6; 28, 39 27; 3, 4
de Massera v. *Uruguay*	R. 1/5	HRC 34, 124	22.6; 29
Hartikainen v. *Finland*	R. 9/40	HRC 36, 147	20; 16 23.3; 21
Lovelace v. *Canada*	R. 6/24	HRC 36, 166	14.6; 6 26; 9

Judgments, Decisions, and Reports Cited   TABLE B: HRC

Applicant and State	Case No.	Annual Report, p.	§; n.
Maroufidou v. Sweden	R. 13/58	HRC 36, 160	8; 19, 96 14.4; 37
Massera v. Uruguay	R. 1/5	HRC 34, 124	14.2; 106, 126, 127 22.6; 29 25; 18
Motta v. Uruguay	R. 2/11	HRC 35, 132	14.2; 111, 149 14.3; 84, 85
Perdomo and de Lanza v. Uruguay	R. 2/8	HRC 35, 111	14.2; 87, 125, 149 14.3; 82 22.6; 16, 29, 40 23.4; 33
Pietraroia v. Uruguay	R. 10/44	HRC 36, 153	8; 32 14.2; 106 14.3; 79 22.3; 2 22.4; 71, 78 22.5; 1 23.4; 33 25; 21
Pinkney v. Canada	R. 7/27	published 14 December 1981	8; 96 14.3; 79, 84 22.4; 70, 101 22.6; 80 23.2; 62
Ramirez v. Uruguay	R. 1/4	HRC 35, 121	14.2; 84, 149 14.3; 84 22.6; 38
Sequeira v. Uruguay	R. 1/6	HRC 35, 127	14.2; 123, 149 14.3; 83 22.6; 29, 38 27; 8
Silva et al. v. Uruguay	R. 8/34	HRC 36, 130	11; 23 14.2; 149 25; 19
Touròn v. Uruguay	R. 7/32	HRC 36, 120	14.2; 111, 149 22.4; 78 22.6; 38
Valcada v. Uruguay	R. 2/9	HRC 35, 107	14.2; 149
Weinberger v. Uruguay	R. 7/28	HRC 36, 114	14.2; 111, 128, 149 14.3; 78 22.4; 71, 78 22.5; 2 22.6; 29, 38 23.4; 33 25; 20 27; 7

GENERAL COMMENTS

No.	Annual Report, p.	§; n
3/13	HRC 36, 109	6; 23
		27; 10
4/13	HRC 36, 109	7; 1
		27; 10
5/13	HRC 36, 110	11; 1
		27; 10

ECOSOC

Neither ECOSOC itself under *ICES* 21, nor CHR under *ICES* 19 or ECOSOC Resolutions 1235 (XLII) or 1503 (XLVIII) (see § 31) have so far published any jurisprudence on matters within their respective competences under these provisions.

However, in a series of annual reports[2] to ECOSOC pursuant to *ICES* 18, the ILO's Committee of Experts on the Application of Conventions has given certain indications of matters which may be relevant in considering how far State Parties have made progress in achieving the observance of the provisions of *ICES* 6, 7, 8, and 9, and these are noted in the relevant sections of Part III of the present work.

---

[2] The years of the reports, and the document numbers under which they have been reissued by the UN, are:

Year	UN Document No.
1978	E/1978/27
1979	E/1979/33
1980	E/1980/35

EUCM

EUCM's jurisprudence arises from its exercise of two successive functions: the making of Decisions on the admissibility of applications under *EHR* 27(2), and the rendering of Reports under *EHR* 30 and 31 on applications which it has decided to be admissible (see §§28.3 and 28.4). Some (but not all) of these are published individually, and many of them may also be found in the following collections published from Strasbourg:

	Abbreviation
Yearbook of the European Convention on Human Rights, published since 1955, and annually since 1960, in successively numbered volumes.	YB
Collection of Decisions, published in 46 successively numbered volumes (containing no Reports) from 1960 to 1974. (The first five of these were not paginated.)	CD
Decisions and Reports, published in successively numbered volumes (containing Reports as well as Decisions) since July 1975.	DR

Where a Decision is reported in both CD (or DR) and YB, only the CD or DR reference is given in the relevant footnotes, but both references may be included in this Table. Where a Decision or Report is not included in a volume of DR published before 1 January 1982, it is referred to in the present work only by its date. Some Reports are now also being republished in the European Human Rights Reports (abbreviated here as 'EHRR'): those references are also given in this Table. (Where a case has subsequently been referred to and adjudicated by EUCT, EUCM's Report will also be included in the papers in 'Series B' published by the Court in relation to that case.) Where a case has been referred to EUCT, but not adjudicated, before 1 January 1982, references to EUCM's Report are marked 'referred to EUCT' in the relevant footnote, and with an asterisk in this Table.

Since many applicants to EUCM wish to remain anonymous and their cases are therefore entitled '*X* v. [*the respondent State*]', all the Decisions and Reports of EUCM cited in this book are listed here in the order of the application numbers which the Commission assigns to them (or, where there is more than one, the first of these), rather than in the more usual alphabetical order of the applicants' names. '*Federal Republic of Germany*' and '*United Kingdom*' are abbreviated in this Table to '*FRG*' and '*UK*' respectively.

Application	Applicant and State	Decision	Report	§; n.
86/55	X v. FRG	YB 1, 198		7; 4
95/55	X v. Belgium	YB 1, 201		7; 4
165/56	X v. FRG	YB 1, 203		7; 4
167/56	X v. FRG	YB 1, 235		7; 15
172/56	X v. Sweden	YB 1, 211		23.2; 54
176/56	Greece v. UK	YB 2, 182	unpublished	8; 76
				11; 5
214/56	De Becker v. Belgium	YB 2, 214	21 August 1961	8; 28, 58
				23.4; 31, 41
235/56	X v. FRG	YB 2, 256		6; 29
238/56	X v. Denmark	YB 1, 205		7; 10, 19
250/57	German Communist Party v. FRG	YB 1, 222		9; 1
332/57	Lawless v. Ireland	YB 2, 308	19 December 1959	8; 77, 78
				9; 3
343/57	Nielsen v. Denmark	YB 2, 412		14.2; 60
				14.2; 99
				22.6; 2
434/58	X v. Sweden	CD 1		22.4; 58
		YB 2, 354		
436/58	X v. FRG	CD 1		7; 4
		YB 2, 386		
448/59	X v. FRG	CD 3		6; 43
		YB 3, 254		
462/59	X v. Austria	CD 1		14.3; 51
		YB 2, 382		
493/59	X v. Ireland	CD 7, 85		11; 8
		YB 4, 302		
511/59	Gudmundsson v. Iceland	CD 4		7; 20
		YB 3, 394		21; 29, 40

514/59	X v. Austria	CD 2 / YB 3, 196		23.2; 54
524/59	Ofner v. Austria	YB 3, 322	23 November 1962	22.4; 54 / 22.6; 18
530/59	X v. FRG	CD 2 / YB 3, 184		23.2; 9, 14, 19
551/59	X v. FRG	CD 3		21; 26
596/59 789/60	Pataki and Dunshirn v. Austria	YB 3, 244 / YB 3, 356	28 March 1963	22.4; 56
606/59	X v. Austria	YB 4, 186 / CD 7, 111		22.4; 32
617/59	Hopfinger v. Austria	YB 4, 340 / CD 5 / YB 3, 370	23 November 1962	22.6; 54
712/60	Retimag S.A. v. FRG	CD 8, 29 / YB 4, 384		9; 1
722/60	X v. FRG	CD 9, 1 / YB 5, 104		22.6; 32
734/60 753/60	X v. FRG X v. Austria	CD 6, 29 / CD 4		22.4; 32, 50 / 8; 88
788/60	Austria v. Italy	YB 3, 310 / YB 4, 138	30 March 1963	23.4; 36 / 1; 29
808/60	Isop v. Austria	CD 8, 80 / YB 5, 108		22.6; 1, 54, 57 / 7; 13
858/60	X v. Belgium	CD 6, 5 / YB 4, 224		22.4; 45 / 14.2; 137
867/60	X v. Norway	CD 6, 34 / YB 4, 270		14.1; 5

Application	Applicant and State	Decision	Report	§; n.
911/60	X v. Sweden	CD 7, 7 YB 4, 198		7; 15 8; 50, 82 23.2; 54 23.4; 21
913/60	X v. Austria	CD 8, 43		22.4; 32
984/61	X v. Belgium	CD 6, 39		14.3; 46
986/61	X v. FRG	CD 9, 23 YB 5, 192		22.6; 11
1013/61	X and Y v. FRG	CD 8, 106 YB 5, 158		22.4; 43
1038/61	X v. Belgium	YB 4, 324		22.5; 14
1068/61	X v. Netherlands	YB 5, 278		8; 56, 84 23.3; 13
1092/61	X v. Austria	CD 9, 37 YB 5, 210		6; 35
1103/61	X v. Belgium	CD 8, 113 YB 5, 168		14.2; 97
1127/61	X v. Austria	CD 8, 9		22.4; 32
1167/61	X v. FRG	CD 12, 70 YB 6, 204		7; 12, 14 8; 88 23.4; 36
1169/61	X v. FRG	CD 13, 1 YB 6, 520		22.4; 58
1197/61	X v. FRG	CD 8, 68 YB 5, 88		22.5; 3 6; 25
1211/61	X v. Netherlands	CD 9, 46 YB 5, 224		14.2; 95
1216/61	X v. FRG	CD 11, 1		14.2; 100
1287/61	X v. FRG	unpublished		14.1; 10

504

1290/61	M v. Austria	unpublished		22.6; 54
1307/61	X v. FRG	CD 9, 53		21; 35
		YB 5, 230		23.2; 23
1329/62	X v. Denmark	CD 9, 28		8; 83
		YB 5, 200		23.2; 54
1404/62	Wiechert v. FRG	CD 15, 15		14.3; 41
		YB 7, 104		
1449/62	X v. Netherlands	CD 10, 1		8; 83
		YB 6, 262		23.2; 53, 54
1465/62	X v. FRG	CD 9, 63		14.3; 46
		YB 5, 256		
1468/62	Iversen v. Norway	CD 12, 80	24 June 1965	8; 85, 86
		YB 6, 278		18; 78, 81
1474/62	6 Groups of Belgian Citizens	YB 6, 332		20; 2
1677/62	v. Belgium ('Belgian Linguistic	YB 7, 140		23.2; 39
1691/62	Case')			
1769/63				
1994/63				
2126/64				
1476/62	X v. Austria	CD 11, 31		22.4; 61, 103
				22.6; 54
1602/62	Stögmüller v. Austria	YB 7, 168	9 February 1967	14.2; 115
1611/62	X v. FRG	CD 17, 42		6; 25
		YB 8, 158		
1628/62	X v. FRG	CD 12, 61		23.2; 59
1747/62	X v. Austria	CD 13, 42		8; 35, 59, 88
		YB 6, 424		
1753/63	X v. Austria	CD 16, 20		8; 38
		YB 8, 174		23.3; 15, 17
				23.4; 23
1760/63	X v. Austria	CD 20, 1		22.4; 50
		YB 9, 166		22.5; 12
				23.4; 23

Application	Applicant and State	Decision	Report	§; n.
1802/63	X v. FRG	CD 10, 26 YB 6, 462		14.3; 46
1850/63	Köplinger v. Austria	CD 19, 71 YB 9, 240		14.2; 139
1855/63	X v. Denmark	CD 16, 50 YB 8, 200		23.2; 43
1860/63	X v. FRG	CD 18, 47		8; 97
1870/63	X v. FRG	YB 8, 204 CD 18, 54 YB 8, 218		23.4; 24 21; 27, 30
1904/63 2029/63 2217/64	A, B, C and D v. Netherlands	CD 19, 105 YB 9, 268		22.4; 50
1936/63	Neumeister v. Austria	YB 7, 224	27 May 1966	14.2; 101, 115 22.4; 50, 87
1983/63	X v. Netherlands	CD 18, 19 YB 8, 228		14.3; 48
2065/63	X v. Netherlands	CD 18, 40 YB 8, 266		23.2; 14, 59 7; 16
2122/64	Wemhoff v. FRG	CD 15, 1 YB 7, 280	1 April 1966	14.2; 115 23.2; 63
2143/64	X v. Austria and Yugoslavia	CD 14, 15 YB 7, 314		14.3; 46
2178/64	Matznetter v. Austria	YB 7, 330	4 April 1967	14.2; 115 22.4; 32, 50 7; 15, 21
2209/64	Inhabitants of Les Fourons v. Belgium		30 March 1971	20; 1
2257/64	Soltikow v. FRG	YB 11, 180	3 February 1970	23.2; 40 22.4; 83, 86, 90

App. No.	Case	Date	Citation	References
2278/64	Dr X v. Austria		CD 24, 8	22.4; 84
2279/64	X v. FRG		YB 10, 188	23.2; 59
2291/64	X v. Austria		CD 23, 114	14.3; 65
			CD 24, 20	22.6; 10, 54, 59
2299/64	Grandrath v. FRG	12 December 1966	YB 8, 324	7; 11, 16
2333/64	Inhabitants of Leeuw-St Pierre v. Belgium		CD 16, 58	7; 16
			YB 8, 338	
			YB 11, 228	
2343/64	X v. Austria		CD 22, 38	22.6; 4
			YB 10, 176	
2413/65	X v. FRG		CD 23, 1	14.3; 51
2472/65	X v. FRG		CD 23, 42	22.4; 97
2518/65	X v. Denmark		CD 18, 44	22.6; 7
			YB 8, 370	
2568/65	X v. Belgium		CD 26, 10	22.4; 50
2604/65	Jentzsch v. FRG	6 October 1970	YB 10, 218	14.2; 117
2614/65	Ringeisen v. Austria	19 March 1970	YB 15, 678	14.2; 115
			YB 11, 268	22.4; 33, 82, 84, 89
2621/65	X v. Netherlands		CD 19, 100	14.2; 96
			YB 9, 474	
2676/65	X v. Austria		CD 23, 31	22.6; 32
				23.2; 47
2689/65	Delcourt v. Belgium		CD 22, 48	7; 14
			YB 10, 238, 282	14.2; 104
2699/65	X v. FRG		CD 26, 33	8; 50, 66
			YB 11, 366	23.2; 52, 54
2717/66	X v. FRG		CD 29, 1	6; 43
			CD 35, 1	7; 20
			YB 13, 200	
2728/66	X v. FRG		CD 25, 38	25; 6
			YB 10, 336	

Application	Applicant and State	Decision	Report	§; n.
2742/66	X v. Austria	CD 19, 95 / YB 9, 550 / YB 10, 342		14.2; 54 / 18; 88
2749/66	De Courcy v. UK	CD 24, 93 / YB 10, 388		8; 97 / 14.3; 49
2758/66	X v. Belgium	CD 30, 11 / YB 12, 174		14.1; 18
2792/66	X v. Norway	CD 21, 64 / YB 9, 556		7; 15
2793/66	X v. Austria	CD 23, 125		22.4; 50
2795/66	X v. FRG	CD 30, 23 / YB 12, 192		8; 97
2804/66	Struppat v. FRG	CD 27, 61 / YB 11, 380		7; 13
2832/66, 2835/66, 2899/66	De Wilde, Oooms and Versyp v. Belgium	YB 10, 420	19 July 1969	18; 88 / 22.4; 32 / 23.2; 59
2834/66, 4038/69	X v. FRG	CD 35, 29 / YB 13, 250		7; 17 / 23.4; 57
2857/66	X v. FRG	CD 29, 15		22.4; 59
2914/66	Van den Berghe v. Belgium	CD 28, 62		7; 15, 21
2942/66	X v. FRG	CD 23, 51		22.4; 50
2988/66	X v. Netherlands	CD 23, 137 / YB 10, 472		8; 68
2991/66	Alan and Khan v. UK	YB 10, 478	17 December 1968	23.3; 14 / 23.2; 43
3011/67	X v. FRG	CD 25, 70		22.4; 50
3034/67	Fletcher v. UK	CD 25, 76		22.4; 22
3039/67	A, B, C and D v. UK	CD 23, 66 / YB 10, 506		8; 74, 87 / 21; 14, 25, 28

Application	Case	Report	Reference
3040/67	X v. FRG	CD 22, 133	14.3; 46
3053/67	X v. Austria	YB 10, 518	23.2; 54
3071/67	X v. Sweden	CD 25, 88	23.4; 66
3110/67	X v. FRG	CD 26, 71; YB 11, 456	23.2; 31
3134/67, 3172/67, 3188–3206/67	21 Detained Persons v. FRG	CD 27, 77; YB 11, 494; CD 27, 97; YB 11, 528	18; 90, 91
3139/67	X v. FRG	CD 26, 77	22.4; 55
3147/67	X and Co. (England) Ltd. v. FRG	CD 27, 119	22.4; 53
3266/67	X v. FRG	CD 30, 53; YB 12, 242	7; 12
3321/67, 3322/67, 3323/67, 3344/67	Denmark, Norway, Sweden and Netherlands v. Greece	YB 11, 690, 730; YB 12 bis	8; 81; 11; 3, 18; 14.3; 7, 8, 12, 15, 18, 19, 37, 43; 55, 80; 21; 43; 23.2; 58; 23.4; 42, 43; 24; 3; 25; 3
3325/67	X, Y, Z, V and W v. UK	CD 25, 117; YB 10, 528	6; 35; 7; 15
3347/67	X v. FRG	CD 27, 136	22.4; 50
3374/67	X v. Austria	CD 29, 29; YB 12, 246	22.5; 13; 22.4; 10

TABLE B: EUCM — Judgments, Decisions, and Reports Cited

Application	Applicant and State	Decision	Report	§; n.
3376/67	Rosenbaum v. FRG	CD 29, 31 / YB 12, 250		14.2; 117, 119
3435/67 3436/67 3437/67 3438/67	W, X, Y and Z v. UK	CD 28, 109 / YB 11, 562		18; 69, 70, 92 / 22.4; 50 / 23.2; 49
3444/67	X v. Norway	CD 35, 37 / YB 13, 302		22.4; 61
3448/67	Wemhoff v. FRG	CD 30, 56		14.3; 49 / 23.2; 17
3457/68	De Courcy v. UK	CD 29, 50 / YB 12, 284		14.2; 142
3603/68	X v. FRG	CD 31, 48 / YB 13, 332		23.2; 15, 47
3637/68	X v. FRG	CD 31, 51 / YB 13, 438		14.2; 117, 119, 121
3717/68	X v. Ireland	CD 31, 96 / YB 13, 528		8; 70
3788/68	X v. Sweden	CD 35, 56 / YB 13, 548		23.2; 59 / 23.2; 64
3798/68	Church of X v. UK	CD 29, 74 / YB 12, 306		7; 21 / 20; 5, 12 / 22.4; 34, 50 / 23.3; 8
3819/68	X v. FRG	CD 32, 33		8; 97
3868/68	X v. UK	CD 34, 10 / YB 13, 600		23.2; 14 / 14.2; 117
3898/68	X v. UK	CD 35, 102 / YB 13, 666		23.2; 45

Application	Party	Citation	References
3911/69	X v. FRG	CD 30, 76; YB 12, 324	7; 12 / 14.2; 57, 113 / 22.4; 89, 90
3914/69	X v. Belgium	CD 34, 20	23.4; 25
3959/69	X v. Austria	CD 35, 109	22.4; 50
3962/69	X v. FRG	CD 32, 68	14.4; 19
3973/69	X v. UK	CD 32, 70	14.3; 65
3994/69	X v. FRG	CD 33, 15	14.2; 117
4004/69	W.X and H.X v. UK	CD 33, 18	23.2; 54
4050/69	X v. FRG	CD 34, 33	7; 20
4101/69	X v. FRG	CD 34, 38; YB 13, 720	8; 97
4124/69	X v. FRG	CD 35, 132	22.6; 1, 2, 3
4125/69	X v. Ireland	CD 37, 42	4; 18
4130/69	X v. Netherlands	YB 14, 198; CD 38, 9	24; 28 / 7; 20
4137/69	X v. Ireland	YB 14, 224; CD 35, 137; YB 13, 792	23.4; 17
4144/69	X v. Luxembourg	CD 33, 27	8; 97
4162/69	X v. FRG	CD 32, 87; YB 13, 806	14.3; 48
4185/69	X v. FRG	CD 35, 140	23.2; 47, 54
4203/69	X v. UK	CD 34, 48; YB 13, 836	14.1; 14 / 14.3; 49
4220/69	X v. UK	CD 37, 51; YB 14, 250	14.2; 98
4225/69	X v. UK	CD 33, 34; YB 13, 864	14.2; 132
4256/69	X v. FRG	CD 37, 67	14.4; 19
4274/69	X v. FRG	CD 35, 158; YB 13, 888	22.5; 10

Application	Applicant and State	Decision	Report	§; n.
4280/69	X v. Austria	CD 35, 161		7; 12, 15
4284/69	X v. FRG	CD 37, 74		23.2; 53, 54
4288/69	X v. UK	CD 33, 53 / YB 13, 892		7; 20
4314/69	X v. FRG	CD 32, 96 / YB 13, 900		14.3; 48
4338/69	X v. Austria	CD 36, 79 / YB 13, 904		22.6; 30
4340/69	Simon-Herold v. Austria	CD 38, 18 / YB 14, 352	19 December 1972	14.1; 15
4372/70	X v. Belgium	CD 37, 101 / YB 14, 398		7; 15, 21
4403–19/70 4422–23/70 4434/70 4476–78/70 4486/70 4501/70 4526–30/70	Patel et al. v. UK ('East African Asians Case')	CD 36, 92 / YB 13, 928	3 EHRR 76	14.3; 57, 58 / 14.4; 33
4428/70	X v. Austria	CD 40, 1		22.4; 62
4445/70	X v. FRG	YB 15, 264		22.6; 55
4451/70	Golder v. UK	CD 37, 119 / YB 14, 416	1 June 1973	23.2; 59 / 22.4; 6, 11 12
4464/70	National Union of Belgian Police v. Belgium	YB 14, 308	27 May 1974	23.2; 60 / 7; 18
4505/70	X v. FRG	CD 39, 51 / YB 14, 522		24; 21 / 22.4; 50
4515/70	X v. UK	CD 38, 86 / YB 14, 538		23.4; 19, 67

Application No.	Case	Citation		References
4517/70	*Huber v. Austria*	CD 38, 90; YB 14, 548	DR 2, 11	8; 97 / 22.4; 91 / 23.4; 23 / 22.4; 50
4523/70	*X v. FRG*	CD 38, 115; YB 14, 622		23.4; 50
4561/70	*X v. FRG*	CD 39, 58		7; 12
4622/70	*X v. Austria*	CD 40, 15		22.4; 28
4623/70	*X v. UK*	CD 39, 66; YB 15, 376		
4626/70	*35 East African Asians v. UK*	DR 13, 5		14.2; 7
4649/70	*X v. FRG*	CD 46, 1		22.4; 85
4653/70	*X v. FRG*	CD 46, 22; YB 17, 148		7; 11, 20 / 18; 78, 83 / 21; 20
4681/70	*Murphy v. UK*	CD 43, 1		22.5; 8 / 7; 10
4715/70	*3 East African Asians v. UK*	DR 13, 17		14.2; 7 / 14.3; 59 / 20; 10
4783/71				
4827/71				
4733/71	*X v. Sweden*	CD 39, 75; YB 14, 676		23.4; 66
4750/71	*X v. UK*	CD 40, 29		22.4; 54
4764/71	*X v. Denmark*	CD 39, 87		8; 101
4771/71	*Kamma v. Netherlands*	CD 42, 22	DR 1, 4	14.2; 1 / 14.3; 42
4833/71	*X v. FRG*	CD 38, 130		14.2; 141, 142
4897/71	*Gussenbauer v. Austria*	CD 42, 41		18; 85
4962/71	*X v. Netherlands*	CD 40, 42		14.2; 119
4984/71	*X v. FRG*	DR 43, 28		21; 22 / 25; 6
4991/71	*Mr and Mrs X v. UK*	CD 45, 1; YB 16, 82		22.4; 60

Application	Applicant and State	Decision	Report	§; n.
5025/71	X v. FRG	CD 39, 95		7; 12
		YB 14, 692		14.2; 153
5029/71	Klass v. FRG	DR 1, 20	9 March 1977	6; 35
		YB 17, 178		23.2; 66
5078/71	X v. Italy and FRG	CD 46, 42		22.4; 85, 90
5095/71	Kjeldsen et al. v. Denmark	YB 15, 482	21 March 1975	7; 21
5920/72				20; 8
5926/72				23.2; 41
5100/71	Engel et al. v. Netherlands	YB 15, 508	19 July 1974	8; 43, 44, 45, 101
5101/71				14.2; 1, 42, 136, 141
5102/71				22.4; 25, 30, 50
5354/72				23.4; 6, 62
5370/72				
5124/71	X v. UK	CD 42, 135		22.6; 8
5155/71	X v. UK	DR 6, 13		25; 15
5178/71	De Geillustreerde Pers N.V. v. Netherlands	DR 3, 5	DR 8, 5	7; 8, 17
5207/71	X v. FRG	YB 16, 124		23.4; 69
		CD 39, 99		14.1; 13
5212/71	X v. Austria	YB 14, 698		22.4; 32
5217/71	X and Y v. FRG	CD 43, 69		22.6; 36
5376/72		CD 42, 139		
5229/71	X v. UK	CD 42, 140		23.2; 47
5269/71	X and Y v. UK	CD 39, 104		23.2; 31, 44
		YB 15, 564		
5270/71	X v. UK	CD 46, 54		23.4; 23
5282/71	X v. UK	CD 42, 99		22.6; 27
5301/71	X v. UK	CD 43, 82		23.2; 43, 44

Application	Case	Citation	Date	References
5302/71	X and Y v. UK	CD 44, 29		14.2; 7 / 14.3; 59 / 21; 40 / 22.4; 32 / 23.2; 32 / 25; 8
5310/71	Ireland v. UK	YB 19, 82	25 January 1976	7; 12 / 11; 14, 17 / 14.3; 3, 19, 38, 42, 43, 44, 45
5339/72	X v. FRG	CD 43, 156		23.2; 22
5428/72	X v. FRG	CD 44, 49		22.4; 50
5442/72	X v. UK	DR 1, 41		23.4; 27
5445/72	X and Y v. UK	CD 42, 146		23.2; 44
5446/72	X and Y v. UK	CD 40, 75		23.2; 59
5459/72	Firestone Tyre and Rubber Co. Ltd. and International Synthetic Rubber Co. Ltd. v. UK	CD 43, 99		22.4; 113
5460/72		YB 16, 152		
5481/72	X v. Austria	CD 44, 127		22.4; 103
5492/72	X v. Austria	CD 44, 63		7; 21 / 20; 1
5493/72	Handyside v. UK	CD 45, 23 / YB 17, 228	30 September 1975	8; 3, 21, 22, 24, 28, 52, 74 / 22.6; 6 / 23.4; 2, 28, 29, 30, 36, 37, 63
5523/72	Huber v. Austria	CD 46, 99 / YB 17, 314		22.4; 105
5532/72	X v. UK	CD 43, 119		23.2; 31 / 4; 16 / 7; 18
5589/72	Schmidt and Dahlström v. Sweden	YB 15, 576	17 July 1974	24; 29

TABLE B: EUCM   *Judgments, Decisions, and Reports Cited*

Application	Applicant and State	Decision	Report	§; n.
5591/72	X v. Austria	CD 43, 61		18; 93 23.3; 4
5593/72	X v. Austria	CD 45, 113		7; 20
5608/72	X v. UK	CD 44, 66		8; 50, 67 23.2; 54
5614/72	Svenska Lokmannaforbundet v. Sweden	YB 15, 594	27 May 1974	7; 18
5620/72	X v. FRG	CD 46, 110		22.6; 7
5712/72	X v. UK	CD 46, 112		8; 58 23.2; 47
5763/72	Mrs X v. Netherlands	CD 45, 76 YB 16, 274		9; 6
5767/72 5922/72 5929/72 5953–57/72 5984–88/73 6011/73	16 Austrian Communes and some of their Councillors v. Austria	CD 46, 118 YB 17, 338		23.4; 7
5849/72	Müller v. Austria	DR 1, 46 YB 17, 374	DR 3, 25	6; 44 7; 4. 20 21; 4, 12 22.4; 18
5856/72	Tyrer v. UK	CD 46, 146	14 December 1976	14.3; 52, 68
5874/72	Monika Berberich v. FRG	YB 17, 386		14.2; 117
5877/72	X v. UK	CD 45, 90		14.2; 7 23.2; 21
5913/72	X v. Ireland	CD 45, 95		7; 15, 20
5916/72	X v. UK	CD 46, 165		9; 6
5923/72	X v. Norway	DR 3, 43		22.6; 32, 36

Application	Case	Report citation	Decision	References
5934/72	X v. UK	CD 45, 116		22.4; 50
5935/72	X v. FRG	DR 3, 46		7; 15
5947/72, 6205/73, 7052/75, 7061/75, 7107/75, 7113/75, 7136/75	Silber et al. v. UK	YB 19, 276; DR 5, 8	11 October 1980* 3 EHRR 475	23.2; 9 / 6; 41 / 8; 8, 12, 49, 99 / 23.2; 59, 62
5961/72	Amekrane v. UK	YB 16, 356	19 July 1974	14.5; 5
5962/72	X v. UK	DR 2, 50		20; 6
6040/73	X v. Ireland	YB 16, 388; CD 44, 121		4; 20 / 14.1; 12
6061/73	X v. Netherlands	CD 45, 120		23.2; 53
6066/73	Levy v. FRG	YB 16, 394	9 July 1975	14.2; 117, 120, 121 / 8; 36, 60
6084/73	X v. UK	DR 3, 62		23.2; 59
6087/73	X v. Austria	DR 5, 10		7; 20
6094/73	X v. Sweden	DR 9, 5		7; 18 / 24; 7, 10
6148/73	X v. UK	DR 6, 19		23.2; 56
6163/73	X v. Austria	DR 1, 60		7; 20
6167/73	X v. FRG	DR 1, 64		17; 12
6181/73	Hätti v. FRG	DR 6, 22; YB 17, 430	DR 6, 22	22.4; 84, 90
6185/73	X v. Austria	DR 2, 68		22.6; 22, 66
6189/73	X v. Austria	CD 46, 214		14.4; 36
6202/73	X v. Netherlands	DR 1, 66		7; 15, 20
6210/73, 6877/75, 7132/75	Luedicke, Belkacem and Koç v. FRG	DR 4, 200; YB 19, 290	18 May 1977	22.4; 67 / 22.6; 62

Application	Applicant and State	Decision	Report	§; n.
6224/73	*Kiss v. UK*	DR 7, 55; YB 20, 156		14.3; 51; 22.4; 17, 27, 32
6231/73	*Hess v. UK*	DR 2, 72; YB 18, 146		6; 30
6242/73	*Brückmann v. FRG*	CD 46, 202; DR 6, 57; YB 17, 458	DR 6, 57	14.3; 47; 14.4; 35
6289/73	*Airey v. Ireland*	DR 8, 42; YB 20, 180	9 March 1978	22.4; 14
6301/73	*Winterwerp v. Netherlands*	DR 5, 35; YB 18, 192	15 December 1977	14.2; 145
6315/73	*X v. FRG*	DR 1, 73; YB 17, 480		14.3; 48
6337/73	*X v. Belgium*	DR 3, 83		14.3; 51
6357/73	*X v. FRG*	DR 1, 77		23.2; 45
6482/74	*X v. Belgium and Netherlands*	DR 7, 75		17; 8; 23.2; 31, 51
6501/74	*X v. FRG*	DR 1, 80		22.6; 25
6541/74	*X v. FRG*	DR 3, 86		14.2; 121
6564/74	*X v. UK*	DR 2, 105		14.3; 51; 17; 9
6572/74	*X v. FRG*	DR 8, 70		23.2; 15; 21; 36
6573/74	*X v. Netherlands*	DR 1, 87		7; 22; 23.4; 16
6659/74	*Liebig v. FRG*	DR 17, 5		25; 5; 22.6; 4
6683/74	*X v. UK*	DR 3, 95		22.5; 7
6692/74	*X v. Belgium*	DR 2, 108		14.2; 141
6694/74	*Artico v. Italy*	DR 8, 73	8 March 1979	22.6; 30, 31

No.	Case	Reference	Date	Citations
6699/74	X v. FRG	DR 11, 16		14.3; 60
				23.2; 4
6728/74	X v. UK	DR 14, 26		22.4; 86
6741/74	X v. Italy	DR 5, 83		7; 16, 17, 18
6742/74	X v. FRG	DR 3, 103		25; 17
6745/74 }	W, X, Y and Z v. Belgium	DR 2, 110		7; 22
6746/74		YB 18, 236		25; 4, 9, 14
6753/74	X and Y v. Netherlands	DR 2, 118		6; 35
				8; 65
				23.2; 54
6776/74	X v. Sweden	DR 2, 123		22.4; 50
6780/74 }	Cyprus v. Turkey	DR 2, 125	10 July 1976	6; 26
6950/75 }				11; 20
				14.1; 19
				18; 80
6782/74 }	X, Y and Z v. Belgium	DR 9, 13		7; 17
6783/74 }				8; 53
6784/74 }				23.4; 36
6794/74	X v. FRG	DR 3, 104		23.2; 19
6821/74	Huber v. Austria	DR 6, 65		14.2; 151
6825/74	X v. Iceland	DR 5, 86		23.2; 7, 12
		YB 19, 342		
6833/74	Marckx v. Belgium	DR 3, 112	10 December 1977	7; 15, 20
		YB 18, 248		8; 31
				17; 72, 74
				21; 5, 19
				23.1; 1
				23.2; 30, 33, 34, 35
6839/74	X v. Belgium	DR 3, 139		14.2; 145
6850/74	Association X, Y and Z v. FRG	DR 5, 90		23.3; 11
				25; 11

Application	Applicant and State	Decision	Report	§; n.
6871/75	Caprino v. UK	DR 12, 14 / YB 21, 284	17 July 1980	8; 4 / 14.2; 45, 78, 79, 80, 81, 134, 135
6878/75, 7238/75	Le Compte, Van Leuven and de Meyere v. Belgium	DR 6, 79 / YB 20, 254	14 December 1979	22.4; 40, 72, 102 / 111
6886/75	X v. UK	DR 5, 100		24; 8 / 8; 58, 69
6946/75	X v. FRG	DR 6, 114		23.3; 16
6958/75	X v. Switzerland	DR 3, 155		22.4; 87
6959/75	Brüggemann and Scheuten v. FRG	DR 5, 103	DR 10, 100 / 3 EHRR 244	22.4; 59 / 14.1; 6 / 23.2; 8, 11
6998/75	X v. UK	DR 8, 106 / YB 20, 294	16 July 1980	14.2; 74, 102, 103
7008/75	X v. Austria	DR 6, 120		25; 10
7010/75	X v. Belgium	DR 3, 162		20; 7
7011/75	Becker v. Denmark	DR 4, 215 / YB 19, 416		14.3; 46
7034/75	X v. Austria	DR 10, 146		14.4; 37
7048/75	X v. UK	DR 9, 42		14.2; 54
7050/75	Arrowsmith v. UK	DR 8, 123 / YB 20, 316	DR 19, 5 / 3 EHRR 218	23.2; 42 / 7; 16, 17 / 8; 10, 11, 23, 28, 44 / 14.2; 6 / 23.3; 3
7052/75	Carne v. UK	DR 10, 154		23.4; 36
7096/75	X v. UK	DR 3, 165		23.2; 59
7113/75	McMahon v. UK	DR 10, 205		25; 16
7114/75	Hamer v. UK	DR 10, 174	13 December 1979	23.2; 59 / 17; 4, 9, 14

Application	Case	Reports	Cited at
7116/75	X v. FRG	DR 7, 91 YB 21, 302	22.4; 17, 45
7138/75	X v. Austria	DR 9, 50	7; 13 22.6; 27
7140/75	X v. UK	DR 7, 95	25; 13
7151/75	Sporrong and Lönnroth v. Sweden	DR 15, 15 8 October 1980*	6; 37, 45 7; 5
7152/75		YB 22, 110	8; 74, 87 21; 18, 39 22.4; 49, 50
7154/75	Association X v. UK	DR 14, 31	4; 13 14.1; 17 23.2; 26
7215/75	X v. UK	DR 11, 36 DR 19, 66 YB 21, 354 3 EHRR 63	7; 15, 23 8; 22, 52, 58 23.2; 9
7216/75	X v. FRG	DR 5, 137	23.4; 8 14.3; 46
7229/75	X and Y v. UK	DR 12, 32	17; 7
7289/75	X and Y v. Switzerland	DR 9, 57 YB 20, 372	23.2; 31, 42 14.3; 51 23.2; 32, 43
7349/76			
7306/75	X v. UK	DR 7, 115	22.4; 63
7317/75	Lynas v. Switzerland	DR 6, 141 YB 20, 412	14.3; 46
7334/76	X v. FRG	DR 5, 154 DR 15, 35	14.3; 48 6; 38 7; 12
7341/76	Eggs v. Switzerland	DR 6, 170 YB 20, 448	14.2; 39, 40, 47 50, 51, 53 14.3; 51 22.4; 32

Application	Applicant and State	Decision	Report	§; n.
7360/76	Zand v. Austria	DR 8, 167	DR 15, 70	22.4; 102, 105, 107 24; 22
7361/76	Trade Union X v. Belgium	DR 14, 40		
7367/76	Guzzardi v. Italy	DR 8, 185 YB 20, 462	7 December 1978	14.2; 35, 36 23.2; 50
7370/76	X v. Switzerland	DR 9, 95		22.4; 58, 97
7374/76	X v. Denmark	DR 5, 157		22.4; 50 23.3; 6
7376/76	X and Y v. Sweden	DR 7, 123		14.2; 141
7408/76	X v. FRG	DR 10, 221		14.3; 51
7412/76	Haase v. FRG	DR 7, 127 YB 20, 494	DR 11, 78	14.2; 117 22.4; 84
7427/76	Four Companies v. Austria	DR 7, 148		7; 11, 20 18; 87 21; 40
7434/76	X v. UK	DR 9, 103		23.2; 54
7456/76	Wiggins v. UK	DR 13, 40		6; 33 7; 15, 20 8; 62, 75 21; 3, 15, 13 23.2; 55
7465/76	X v. Denmark	DR 7, 153		14.3; 48
7511/76 7743/76	Campbell and Cosans v. UK	DR 12, 49 YB 21, 396	16 May 1980* 3 EHRR 531	14.3; 65, 69 20; 17
7512/76	X v. Netherlands	DR 6, 184		22.5; 9
7525/76	Dudgeon v. UK	DR 11, 117 YB 22, 156	13 March 1980 3 EHRR 40	7; 15 8; 51, 61 23.2; 9
7527/76	X and Y v. UK	DR 11, 147		20; 12
7566/76	X v. UK	DR 9, 121		7; 22 25; 4, 8

No.	Case	Reference	Date	Citations
7567/76	*X v. Denmark*	DR 9, 117		7; 16
7572/76 7586/76	*Ensslin, Baader and Raspe v. FRG*	DR 14, 64 YB 21, 418		14.3; 51 22.4; 61 22.6; 4, 35, 37 22.4; 9, 47, 52
7598/76	*Kaplan v. UK*	DR 15, 120 YB 22, 190	17 July 1980	4; 17 6; 45
7601/76 7806/77	*James, Young and Webster v. UK*	DR 9, 126 YB 20, 520	14 December 1979 3 EHRR 20	24; 19, 30, 31
7602/76	*X v. Netherlands*	DR 7, 161		14.3; 65 18; 86
7604/76 7719/76 7781/77 7913/77	*Foti et al. v. Italy*	DR 14, 133	9 March 1981*	22.4; 91, 92
7620/76	*X v. Austria*	DR 11, 156		22.4; 42 7; 20
7624/76	*X v. Austria*	DR 19, 100		21; 13
7626/76	*X v. FRG*	DR 14, 175		23.2; 54
7627/76	*X v. UK*	DR 11, 160		20; 9
7628/76	*X v. Belgium*	DR 9, 169		22.6; 24
7629/76	*Krzycki v. FRG*	DR 9, 175 YB 20, 564	DR 13, 57	7; 12 14.2; 55
7630/76	*Reed v. UK*	DR 19, 113	17 December 1981 3 EHRR 136	14.3; 62 22.4; 4
7640/76	*Geerk v. Switzerland*	DR 12, 103 YB 21, 470	DR 16, 56	22.6; 64 23.4; 40
7641/76	*X and Y v. FRG*	DR 10, 224		18; 76, 77, 83 21; 21
7648/76	*Christinet v. Switzerland*	DR 11, 175	DR 17, 35	14.2; 54, 140
7654/76	*Van Oosterwyk v. Belgium*	DR 11, 194 YB 21, 476	1 March 1979 3 EHRR 57	17; 2, 5, 6, 12 13 23.2; 4, 20

Application	Applicant and State	Decision	Report	§; n.
7655/76 ⎫ 7656/76 ⎬ 7657/76 ⎭	X, Y and Z v. FRG	DR 12, 111		21; 11
7680/76	X v. FRG	DR 9, 190		14.2; 69, 117 14.4; 19
7694/76	X v. FRG	DR 12, 131		7; 20
7697/76	X v. Belgium	DR 9, 194		14.3; 65
7705/76	X v. FRG	DR 9, 196		22.5; 10 23.3; 5
7710/76	Schiesser v. Switzerland	DR 10, 238	9 March 1978	14.2; 107
7721/76	X v. Netherlands	YB 20, 574 DR 11, 209		7; 14 22.5; 3, 4, 5
7729/76	Agee v. UK	DR 7, 164		7; 12, 13, 15, 17 14.2; 7 14.3; 48, 65 22.4; 10, 32, 50 23.2; 44, 45 23.4; 22 24; 13
7736/76	X v. Switzerland	DR 9, 206		8; 14 23.2; 59
7742/76	AB and Company AS v. FRG	DR 14, 146 YB 21, 492		7; 20
7743/76	Cosans v. UK	DR 12, 140	16 May 1980*	14.3; 69
7754/77	X v. Switzerland	DR 11, 216		14.2; 41
7755/77	X v. Austria	DR 9, 210		14.2; 63
7758/77	X v. Switzerland	DR 9, 214		23.4; 15
7770/77	X v. FRG	DR 14, 175		23.2; 52, 54

No.	Case	Reference	Citations
7782/77	X v. UK	DR 14, 179	7; 21 — 20; 1
7816/77	X and Y v. FRG	DR 9, 219	23.2; 45
7819/77	Campbell v. UK	DR 14, 186 — YB 22, 256	22.4; 8
7823/77	48 Kalderas' Gypsies v. FRG and Netherlands	DR 11, 221	14.3; 61
7824/77			23.1; 1 — 23.2; 33
7830/77	X v. Austria	DR 14, 200	22.4; 44
7854/77	Bonzi v. Switzerland	DR 12, 185	14.3; 49 — 22.6; 37
7878/77	Fell v. UK	14 March 1981	22.6; 37
7900/77	X v. FRG	DR 13, 70	22.5; 6, 30
7902/77	X v. UK	DR 9, 224	22.4; 50
7906/77	Van Droogenbroek v. Belgium	DR 17, 59 — 9 July 1980*	14.2; 49, 54, 133, 146 — 18; 71, 89
7911/77	X v. Sweden	DR 12, 192	23.2; 54
7945/77	X v. Norway	DR 14, 228	22.4; 54 — 23.2; 20
7973/77	X v. Sweden	DR 17, 74	7; 13
7986/77	Krause v. Switzerland	DR 13, 73 — YB 21, 516	14.3; 49 — 22.4; 61 — 22.6; 4
7987/77	X v. Austria	DR 18, 31	7; 20 — 21; 31
7990/77	Gallogly v. UK	11 May 1981	22.4; 49, 50
7992/77	X v. UK	DR 14, 234	24; 23 — 8; 55 — 23.3; 12
7994/77	Kotalla v. Netherlands	DR 14, 238 — YB 21, 522	14.3; 51, 54
8000/77	X v. Switzerland	DR 13, 81	22.4; 44

Application	Applicant and State	Decision	Report	§; n.
8003/77	X v. Austria	DR 17, 80	3 EHRR 285	7; 20 8; 74, 87 21; 6, 17, 34
8041/77	X v. FRG	DR 12, 197		23.2; 45
8042/77	Hagmann-Hüsler v. Switzerland	DR 12, 202		7; 15
8065/77	X v. UK	DR 14, 246		8; 58 23.2; 16
8130/78	Eckle v. FRG	DR 16, 120	19 February 1981*	22.4; 91
8142/78	X v. Austria'	DR 18, 88		6; 35 14.3; 65 22.4; 32, 50
8149/78	X v. Austria	DR 14, 252		22.4; 50
8160/78	Ahmad v. UK	12 March 1981		23.3; 1, 7 7; 15
8166/78	X and Y v. Switzerland	DR 13, 241		17; 4 23.2; 15
8186/78	Draper v. UK	1 May 1979	10 July 1980	17; 4
8191/78	Rassemblement Jurassien and Unité Jurassienne v. Switzerland	DR 17, 93		8; 29, 95 24; 1
8208/78	X v. UK	DR 16, 162		22.4; 50
8209/78	Sutter v. Switzerland	DR 16, 166		22.4; 106
8224/78	Bonnechaux v. Switzerland	DR 15, 211	3 EHRR 259	14.2; 64
8233/78	X v. UK	DR 17, 122	3 EHRR 271	14.2; 112 22.4; 22, 88
8239/78	X v. Netherlands	DR 16, 184	DR 20, 29	22.6; 12
8244/78	Uppal et al. v. UK	DR 17, 149	3 EHRR 391	6; 41 7; 15 22.4; 50
8257/78	X v. Switzerland	DR 13, 248		8; 58 23.2; 7, 30, 54
8261/78	Kofler v. Italy	8 July 1981		22.4; 91

8269/78	*Adolf v. Austria*	8 October 1980*	DR 17, 171	22.4; 23
				22.6; 5
8278/78	*X v. Austria*		YB 22, 324	8; 64
			DR 18, 154	14.2; 43
				23.2; 27
8282/78	*Church of Scientology v. Sweden*		DR 21, 109	23.3; 8
8289/78	*X v. Austria*		DR 18, 166	22.4; 58
8290/78	*A, B, C and D v. FRG*		DR 18, 176	8; 34, 46
				23.2; 68
8304/78	*Corigliano v. Italy*	16 March 1981*	DR 21, 116	22.4; 80
8307/78	*Deklerck v. Belgium*		DR 20, 44	8; 56
8317/78	*McFeeley et al. v. UK*	3 EHRR 161		7; 6, 15, 16
				8; 48, 99
				14.3; 63, 65
				23.2; 18, 48
				23.3; 18
				24; 12
8329/78	*Schertenleib v. Switzerland*		DR 17, 180	14.2; 64, 66
				22.6; 37
8346/78	*X v. Austria*		DR 19, 230	21; 22
8348/78	*Glimmerveen and Hagenbeeck v.*		DR 18, 187	9; 2, 4
8406/78	*Netherlands*			23.4; 65
				25; 7
8363/78	*X v. FRG*		DR 20, 163	21; 7, 37
8378/78	*Kamel v. UK*		DR 20, 168	23.2; 46
8383/78	*X v. FRG*		DR 17, 227	23.2; 65
				23.4; 18
8386/78	*X v. UK*		DR 21, 126	22.6; 34
8410/78	*X v. FRG*		DR 18, 216	7; 20
				18; 84
				21; 8

527

Application	Applicant and State	Decision	Report	§; n.
8414/78	X v. FRG	DR 17, 231		22.4; 62 22.6; 56
8416/78	X v. UK	DR 19, 244		8; 63, 100 14.1; 7 17; 11 23.2; 36
8440/78	Christians against Racism and Fascism v. UK	DR 21, 138		24; 1
8463/78	Kröcher and Möller v. Switzerland		9 July 1981	14.3; 49
8496/79	X v. UK	DR 21, 168		22.4; 50 7; 11
8500/79	X v. Switzerland	DR 18, 238		8; 47 14.2; 73 18; 90
8518/79	X v. FRG	DR 20, 193		23.2; 24
8544/79	Öztürk v. FRG	15 December 1981		14.3; 65
8604/79	X v. FRG	DR 20, 206		22.6; 64
8660/79	Minelli v. Switzerland	DR 21, 199	6 May 1981*	23.2; 38 22.6; 6
8691/79	Malone v. UK	13 July 1981		8; 18
8692/79	Piersack v. Belgium	DR 20, 209	15 May 1981*	23.2; 25, 66, 67 22.4; 102, 111, 112 7; 22
8701/79	X v. Belgium	DR 18, 250		25; 4, 5
8707/79	X v. Belgium	DR 18, 255		23.2; 13
8724/79	X v. FRG	DR 20, 226		21; 23
8765/79	Liberal Party et al. v. UK	DR 21, 211		25; 13
8919/80	Van der Mussele v. Belgium	17 March 1981		18; 85 21; 20
9019/80	Luberti v. Italy	7 July 1981		14.2; 75, 145
9117/80	Barclay-Maguire v. Italy	17 December 1981		14.2; 75, 145

EUCT

EUCT publishes its *Judgments and Decisions* individually in 'Series A', and the relevant *Pleadings, Oral Arguments and Documents* (which include the Reports of EUCM on the cases referred to the Court), likewise individually, in 'Series B'. All the Court's judgments and decisions are now being republished in the European Human Rights Reports (abbreviated in the present work to 'EHRR'). Where a judgment appears there, that is the only reference given in the appropriate footnote. Any judgment not reprinted in any of the three volumes of EHRR published before this book went to press is referred to in the footnotes only by its date.

In order not to offend the susceptibilities of those who continue to believe that an international court cannot be a forum for the adjudication of a dispute between a private individual and a State, EUCT has followed the convention of giving the names of both parties in the formal titles of its judgments only when they are both States — as in *Ireland* v. *United Kingdom*. In other cases, the title gives only the name of the original applicant to the Commission (though he cannot himself be a formal party to the proceedings before the Court: see §28.6), and not that of the respondent State (which *is* a party) — for example *'The Sunday Times Case'*.

However, for ease of reference and in order to reflect the realities of the situation — even at the risk of offending some purists — all EUCT judgments are referred to throughout the present work by the names of both the original applicant and the respondent State. (Whether by oversight or design, the Court has itself given the title *'Case of X v. United Kingdom'* to the last judgment it delivered in 1981.) Again, although the Court does not continue to attach to its cases the application numbers assigned to them when they were before the Commission, these numbers are nonetheless cited in the present work for ease of cross-reference.

The list which follows is arranged in the alphabetical order of the applicants' names.

Applicant and State	EUCM Application number	Date of Judgment	Series A number	EHRR Reference	§; n.
Airey v. Ireland	6289/73	9 October 1979	32	2, 305	4; 14 22.4; 14, 39, 59 22.6; 30 23.2; 3
Artico v. Italy	6694/74	13 May 1980	37	3, 1	22.4; 54 22.6; 33
'Belgian Linguistic Case' *(6 Groups of Belgian* *Citizens v. Belgium)*	1474/62 1677/62 1691/62 1769/63 1994/63 2126/64	23 July 1968	6	1, 252	7; 3, 5, 6, 7, 9, 15, 21 8; 31 20; 1, 3, 4, 15 22.4; 13 23.2; 2, 40 26; 8
Buchholz v. Federal *Republic of Germany*	7759/77	6 May 1981	42	3, 597	22.4; 79, 96, 98
De Becker v. Belgium	214/56	27 March 1962	4	1, 43	8; 28, 58 23.4; 31, 41
Delcourt v. Belgium	2689/65	17 January 1970	11	1, 355	22.4; 18, 31, 55, 111
Deweer v. Belgium	6903/75	27 February 1980	35	2, 439	22.4; 16, 24, 29
De Wilde, Ooms and Versyp *v. Belgium*	2832/66 2835/66 2899/66	18 June 1971	12	1, 373	6; 38 8; 15, 58 14.2; 76, 142, 147 18; 88 23.2; 59
Dudgeon v. United Kingdom	7525/76	22 October 1981			8; 22, 30, 54 23.2; 10

Case	Application no.	Date			References
Engel et al v. Netherlands	5100-2/71, 5354/72, 5370/72	8 June 1976	22	1, 647	7; 12, 13, 17 / 8; 43, 44, 88 / 14.2; 39, 47, 52, 58, 59 / 22.4; 26, 72, 105 / 22.6; 7 / 23.4; 6, 36, 64 / 24; 14
Golder v. United Kingdom	4451/70	21 February 1975	18	1, 524	8; 24, 71 / 22.4; 4, 7, 12, 13, 93 / 23.2; 61
Guzzardi v. Italy	7367/76	6 November 1980	39	3, 333	14.2; 5, 35, 36, 42, 48, 68, 77
Handyside v. United Kingdom	5493/72	7 December 1976	24	1, 737	7; 17, 20 / 8; 53, 89
Ireland v. United Kingdom	5310/71	18 January 1978	25	2, 25	22.4; 2 / 23.4; 28, 29, 30, 36, 37 / 6; 27 / 7; 12, 13 / 8; 80, 90, 91 / 11; 4, 7, 8, 9, 12, 14, 15 / 14.3; 3, 10, 12, 13, 16, 19, 40, 43, 45, 56, 81
James, Young and Webster v. United Kingdom	7601/76, 7806/77	13 August 1981	44		4; 16 / 6; 28, 45 / 8; 22, 24, 25, 26, 27, 30 / 24; 6, 32

Judgments, Decisions, and Reports Cited

Applicant and State	EUCM Application number	Date of Judgment	Series A number	EHRR Reference	§; n.
Kjeldsen et al. v. Denmark	5095/71 5920/72 5926/72	7 December 1976	23	1, 711	7; 21 20; 11, 13, 14, 15
Klass v. Federal Republic of Germany	5029/71	6 September 1978	28	2, 214	6; 34, 36, 39, 42 8; 5, 16, 18, 22, 34 22.4; 32, 50 23.2; 25, 57, 66 22.4; 36, 40, 94, 95
König v. Federal Republic of Germany	6232/73	28 June 1978	27	2, 170	8; 77 9; 5 11; 2, 5, 6, 8, 10, 13, 19, 21
Lawless v. Ireland	322/57	1 July 1961	3	1, 15	14.2; 60, 61 22.5; 11
Le Compte, Van Leuven and De Meyere v. Belgium	6878/75 7238/75	23 June 1981	43		22.4; 19, 38, 40 51, 73
Luedicke, Belkacem and Koç v. Federal Republic of Germany	6210/73 6877/75 7132/75	28 November 1978	29	2, 433	24; 9 22.6; 63, 64, 65
Marckx v. Belgium	6833/74	13 June 1979	31	2, 330	4; 15 7; 15 17; 72, 74 23.1; 1 23.2; 33, 34, 35, 37

Case	Application	Date			Citations
Matznetter v. Austria	2178/64	10 November 1969	10	1, 198	14.2; 117, 118, 119
National Union of Belgian Police v. Belgium	4464/70	27 October 1975	19	1, 578	4; 16 7; 18 24; 18, 20, 25, 27
Neumeister v. Austria	1936/63	27 June 1968	8	1, 91	14.2; 70, 116, 117, 132, 136, 139 22.4; 55, 82, 89
Neumeister v. Austria (No. 2)	1936/63	7 May 1974	17	1, 136	14.2; 152
Ringeisen v. Austria	2614/65	16 July 1971	13	1, 455	22.4; 35, 41, 82, 89, 102
Schiesser v. Switzerland	7710/76	4 December 1979	34	2, 417	14.2; 107, 108
Schmidt and Dahlström v. Sweden	5589/72	6 February 1976	21	1, 637	7; 18 24; 21, 22, 26
Stögmüller v. Austria	1602/62	10 November 1969	9	1, 155	14.2; 65, 71, 117, 118
Sunday Times v. United Kingdom	6538/74	26 April 1979	30	2, 245	8; 6, 7, 9, 13, 24, 72, 73, 94 23.4: 4, 38
Svenska Lokmannaforbundet v. Sweden	5614/72	6 February 1976	20	1, 617	7; 18 24; 18, 21, 22, 24, 26
Tyrer v. United Kingdom	5856/72	25 April 1978	26	2, 1	6; 31 14.3; 3, 25, 52, 66, 67, 69, 70, 71, 72
Van Oosterwyk v. Belgium	7654/76	6 November 1980	40	3, 557	17; 3 23.2; 5
Wemhoff v. Federal Republic of Germany	2122/64	27 June 1968	7	1, 55	14.2; 56, 111, 116, 119, 130 22.4; 82, 89

533

Applicant and State	EUCM Application number	Date of Judgment	Series A number	EHRR Reference	§; n.
Winterwerp v. Netherlands	6301/73	14 October 1979	33	2, 387	8; 92 14.2; 2, 46, 74, 88, 137, 143 22.4; 48
X v. United Kingdom	6998/75	5 November 1981			8; 93 14.2; 46, 75, 92, 102, 103, 135, 136, 138, 144

EUCE

For every successive 'supervision cycle' under *ESC* Part IV (see § 32), CE's Division of Social Affairs publishes a volume of EUCE's Conclusions, bearing the number of the cycle. Citations from these Conclusions in Part III of the present work are noted by reference to their volume (in roman figures) and page number (in arabic ones); so, for example, 'III, 64' is a reference to page 64 of volume III of EUCE's Conclusions, expressed in the course of the third supervision cycle.

CE has also published a useful volume entitled *Case Law on the European Social Charter*, which abstracts the more important views expressed by EUCE in volumes I to V inclusive of its Conclusions, as well as the subsequent comments on these by the Governmental Committee, the Parliamentary Assembly, and the Committee of Ministers of the CE. Since these latter comments emanate from political, rather than independent, institutions they are not noted in the present work.

EUROPEAN COURT OF JUSTICE

Parties	Report	§; *n.*
Rutili v. *Minister of Interior, France*	[1975] ECR 1219	14.4; 15

IACM

IACM's jurisprudence is to be found in two series of its publications: its Annual Reports to the OAS, and its individual 'country studies' (generally entitled 'Report on the Situation of Human Rights in ...').

Within an Annual Report, jurisprudence may appear in several places, notably in the chapter where the Commission reports its observations on specific communications it has received, and what violations (if any) these disclose of specific Articles of *ADRD*, *AMR*, or both (see § 29). Other jurisprudence is sometimes included in a chapter dealing with the situation of human rights in various countries.

The 'country studies' are internally organized by reference to different groups of human rights, and sometimes include jurisprudence relevant to those rights.

Where any IACM jurisprudence noted in Parts II or III of the present work arises from consideration of a specific communication, the Commission's Case Number and the country concerned are included in the reference given. These are listed below: so are the country studies cited. For all citations, the year of the Annual Report (e.g. AR 1977) or an abbreviated reference to the country study (e.g. 6 Cuba) are given, followed by the relevant page number in the publication concerned.

CASES

Case No.	Country	Annual Report, p.	§; n.
1702 ⎫ 1748 ⎬ 1755 ⎭	Guatemala	1975, 67	4; 21 14.1; 20 14.2; 10
1742	Cuba	1975, 37	14.4; 18
2141	USA	6 March 1981	6; 19 14.1; 4 16; 2 17; 27 22.3; 4
2509	Panama	1979/80, 63	14.2; 9 14.4; 34 22.4; 20
2719	Bolivia	1978, 54	14.4; 32
2723	Bolivia	1978, 62	14.4; 32
2760	Bolivia	1978, 75	14.4; 32
3411–16 ⎫ 3418–19 ⎪ 3428 ⎪ 3434–6 ⎬ 3440–4 ⎪ 3446 ⎪ 3498 ⎪ 3548 ⎭	Chile	1978, 83	14.4; 33

'COUNTRY STUDIES'

Title	Year	IACM Document No.	Cited as	§; n.
[Third] Report on the Development of the Situation of Human Rights in Chile	1977	AR 1977, 77–99	3 Chile	22.1; 1
[Third] Report on the Situation of Human Rights in Paraguay	1978	OEA/Serv.L/V/II.43, doc. 13	3 Paraguay	22.6; 42
Report on the Situation of Human Rights in El Salvador	1978	OEA/Ser.L/V/II. 46, doc. 23	El Salvador	17; 21, 27 22.3; 3
[First] Report on the Situation of Human Rights in Nicaragua	1978	OEA/Ser.L/V/II.45, doc. 16	1 Nicaragua	23.3; 20
[Fourth] Report on the Situation of Human Rights in Haiti	1979	OEA/Ser.L/V/II.46, doc. 66	4 Haiti	25; 23
Sixth Report on the Situation of Political Prisoners in Cuba	1979	OEA/Ser.L/V/II.48, doc. 7	6 Cuba	14.4; 17 18; 79 14.5; 3 22.6; 43
Report on the Situation of Human Rights in Argentina	1980	OEA/Ser.L/V/II.49, doc. 19	Argentina	
[Second] Report on the Situation of Human Rights in Nicaragua	1981	OEA/Ser.L/V/II.53, doc. 25	2 Nicaragua	22.4; 61, 104 22.6; 17, 26, 58, 79 23.4; 32

537

ANNUAL REPORTS

Year	IACM Document No.
1969/70	OEA/Ser.L/V/II.25, doc. 9
1971	OEA/Ser.L/V/II.27, doc. 11
1972	OEA/Ser.L/V/II. 29, doc. 41
1973	OEA/Ser.L/V/II.32, doc. 32
1974	OEA/Ser.L/V/II.34, doc. 31
1975	OEA/Ser.L/V/II.37, doc. 20
1976	OEA/Ser.L/V/II.40, doc. 5
1977	OEA/Ser.L/V/II.43, doc. 21
1978	OEA/Ser.L/V/II.47, doc. 13
1979/80	OEA/Ser.L/V/II.50, doc. 13

IACT

IACT has published its first Annual Report[3] (for 1980) to the General Assembly of the OAS, but has not so far delivered or published any judgments. However, an interlocutory decision (No. G. 101/81) is reported at 2 *Human Rights Law Journal* 108 and noted in § 29.2.6 above.

BRITISH COMMONWEALTH

The cases listed here are divided by countries (in alphabetical order), and arranged within those in the alphabetical order of the appellants' or plantiffs' names. Unless otherwise indicated, the decision is that of the Supreme Court of the country concerned. Decisions of the Judicial Committee of the Privy Council (which are listed first) show the country from which the appeal came. All references are to standard series of law reports, in the usual form of citation; where a case appears in the All England Law Reports as well as the official series, only the All England reference is given in the relevant footnotes.

---

[3] OEA/Ser.L/V/III.3, doc. 13, corr. 1 (OAS).

Parties	Country	Report	§; n.
JUDICIAL COMMITTEE OF THE PRIVY COUNCIL			
Akar v. Attorney-General of Sierra Leone	Sierra Leone	[1970] AC 853 [1969] 3 All ER 384	7; 29
Attorney-General of Antigua and another v. Antigua Times Ltd.	Antigua	[1976] AC 16 [1975] 3 All ER 81	23.4; 5, 46, 55
Collymore v. Attorney-General	Trinidad and Tobago	[1970] AC 538 [1969] 2 All ER 1207 (1969) 15 WIR 229	24; 11
Francis v. Chief of Police	St Christopher, Nevis and Anguilla	[1973] AC 761 [1973] 2 All ER 251	23.4; 58
Harrikisson v. Attorney-General	Trinidad and Tobago	[1979] 3 WLR 62	21; 9
Liyanage et al. v. The Queen	Ceylon	[1967] AC 259 [1966] 1 All ER 650	22.5; 29
McPherson v. McPherson	Alberta	[1936] AC 197 [1935] All ER 105	22.4; 77
Maharaj v. Attorney-General of Trinidad and Tobago (No. 2)	Trinidad and Tobago	[1979] AC 385 [1978] 2 All ER 670	14.2; 97
Minister of Home Affairs v. Fisher	Bermuda	[1979] 2 WLR 889 [1979] 3 All ER 21	17; 28
Olivier et al. v. Buttigieg	Malta	[1967] 1 AC 115 [1966] 2 All ER 459	23.4; 45
Runyowa v. The Queen	Southern Rhodesia	[1967] 1 AC 26 [1966] 1 All ER 633 [1966] RLR 42	14.3; 53

Parties	Court	Report	§; n.
CANADA			
Brownridge v. The Queen		[1972] SCR 926	22.6; 44
Canard v. Attorney-General of Canada	Court of Appeal, Manitoba	[1972] 5 WWR 678	22.3; 20
Curr v. The Queen		[1972] SCR 889	22.6; 76
Dowhopoluk v. Martin	High Court, Ontario	[1972] 1 OR 311	14.3; 22
In re Drummond Wren	High Court, Ontario	4 Ont. Rep. 778	6; 6
Gilberg v. Attorney-General for Alberta	Supreme Court, Alberta	[1974] 2 WWR 474	22.6; 48
Re Laporte and the Queen	Court of Queen's Bench, Quebec	(1972) 8 CCC (2nd) 343	14.3; 22
R v. Balkan	Supreme Court, Alberta	(1973) 6 WWR 617	22.6; 46
R v. Bruce et al.	Supreme Court, British Columbia	(1977) 36 CCC (2nd) 158	14.3; 22
R v. Buchler	Provincial Court of Middlesex, Ontario	(1970) 2 CCC (2nd) 4	14.3; 22, 26, 54
R v. Burnshine	Court of Appeal, Manitoba	[1974] 4 WWR 49	22.3; 23
R v. Drybones		(1970) 3 CCC (2nd) 355	7; 25
R v. Irwin		[1974] 5 WWR 744	22.6; 46
R v. Krenn et al.	Supreme Court, British Columbia	(1976) 27 CCC (2nd) 168	22.3; 21
R v. MacDonald	Supreme Court of Nova Scotia	(1975) 22 CCC (2nd) 350	14.2; 67
R v. McGuirk	Supreme Court, Prince Edward Island	(1976) 24 CCC (2nd) 386	22.6; 46
R v. Makismchuk	Court of Appeal, Manitoba	[1974] 2 WWR 668	22.6; 46
R v. Martel	District Court, Alberta	(1968) 64 WWR 152	22.6; 45
R v. Miller	Court of Appeal, British Columbia	(1975) 24 CCC (2nd) 401	14.3; 34

R v. Odgers	Supreme Court, Alberta	(1978) 37 CCC (2nd) 554	22.3; 22
R v. Paterson	High Court, Ontario	(1978) 39 CCC (2nd) 355	22.6; 46
R v. Penner	Court of Appeal, Manitoba	[1973] 6 WWR 94	22.6; 46
R v. Shand	Court of Appeal, Ontario	(1976) 30 CCC (2nd) 23	14.3; 26
R v. Straightnose	District Court, Saskatchewan	[1974] 2 WWR 662	22.6; 47
Stewart v. Public Service Staff Relations Board	Federal Court of Canada	[1978] 1 FC 133	23.4; 59

CEYLON (SRI LANKA)

In re Agnes Nona		53 NLR 106	22.4; 110
Aseeruvatham v. Permanent Secretary, Ministry of Defence and External Affairs et al.		6 J. International Commission of Jurists 319	14.4; 28
Corea v. The Queen		55 NLR 457	14.2; 94
Gooneratne v. Permanent Secretary, Ministry of Defence and External Affairs et al.		6 J. International Commission of Jurists 320	14.4; 28
Kolugala v. Superintendent of Prisons		66 NLR 412	14.2; 148
Premaratne v. Gunaratne		71 NLR 113	22.6; 51
Premasiri v. Attorney-General		70 NLR 193	14.2; 114
Satharasinghe v. Jurianz		66 NLR 490	22.4; 69
Senadhira v. Bribery Commission		63 NLR 313	22.4; 108
Subramaniam v. Inspector of Police, Kankesanturai		71 NLR 204	22.6; 50
The Queen v. Guanaseeha Thero et al.		73 NLR 154	14.2; 93
The Queen v. Liyanage et al.		64 NLR 313	22.4; 109
The Queen v. Liyanage et al.		65 NLR 337	22.6; 19
In re Ratnagopal		70 NLR 409	14.4; 21

Parties	Court	Report	§; n.
Wickremanayake v. The State	Court of Appeal	*Hansard*, 2 October 1979, 407	14.3; 53
CYPRUS			
Costas Tsirides v. The Police		[1973] 2 CLR 204	14.2; 119
Elia v. The Police		[1980] 2 CLR 118	14.4; 14
Kantara Shipping Ltd. v. Republic of Cyprus		[1971] 3 CLR 176	22.4; 50
Kouphs v. The Republic		(1977) 11 JSC 1860	22.4; 68
Sofroniou et al. v. Municipality of Nicosia		(1976) 6 JSC 874	21; 38
In the matter of an application by Ioannis Ktimatias		(1977) 6 JSC 1043	22.6; 56
Papadopoulou et al. v. Republic of Cyprus		[1971] 3 CLR 317	21; 32
GUYANA			
Hope v. New Guyana Co. Ltd. and Teekah	Court of Appeal	Civil Appeal No. 33 of 1976	23.4; 56
Jagan v. Burnham	Court of Appeal	(1973) 20 WIR 96	23.4; 54
Lilleyman et al. v. Inland Revenue Commissioners et al.		(1964) 13 WIR 224	21; 41
R v. Edwin Ogle		(1966) 11 WIR 439	22.4; 100
The State v. Cleveland Clarke	Court of Appeal	(1976) 22 WIR 249	22.6; 59
The State v. Fitzpatrick Darrell	Court of Appeal	(1976) 24 WIR 211	22.6; 60
INDIA			
AIBE Association v. NI Tribunal		AIR [1962] SC 171	24; 10
A. P. Grain & Steel Merchants Association v. Union of India		[1971] 1 SCR 166	22.3; 9
Abbas v. Union of India		[1970] 2 SCR 780	22.3; 9
Ameerunnissa Begum v. Mahboob Begum		[1953] SCR 404	22.3; 16
B.I.C. v. Collector, Control Excise		[1963] 3 SCR 642	22.3; 9
Balaji v. I.T. Officer		[1962] 2 SCR 983	22.3; 9

Case	Citation	References
Bennett Coleman & Co. v. Union of India	[1962] 3 SCR 842	23.4; 48
Bhawarlal Garashmalji v. State of Tamil Nadu	AIR [1979] SC 541	14.2; 95
Bombay v. Balsara	[1951] SCR 682	22.3; 9, 15
Bombay v. Kathi Kalu Oghad	[1962] 3 SCR 10	22.6; 75
Brij Bhushan v. State of Delhi	[1950] SCR 605	8; 37
		23.4; 39
Budhan Choudry et al. v. Bihar	[1955] 1 SCR 1045	22.3; 10, 15
Chief Inspector of Mines v. Thapar	[1962] 1 SCR 9	22.5; 16
Chiranjitlal Chowdhri v. Union of India	[1950] SCR 869	22.3; 15
Cooper v. Union of India	[1971] 1 SCR 512	14.2; 13
		14.4; 10
Dana v. Punjab	[1959] Supp 1 SCR 274	22.6; 81
Dhirendra Krishna Mandal v. The Superintendent and Remembrancer of Legal Affairs	[1955] SCR 224	22.3; 17
Dwarka Prasad Laxmi Narain v. Uttar Pradesh	[1954] SCR 803	22.3; 17
Ebrahim Vazir Mavat v. State of Bombay and others	[1954] SCR 933	14.4; 16
Gopalan v. State of Madras	[1950] SCR 88	14.2; 13, 89
Hamdad Dawakhana (Wakf) Lal Kuan, Delhi v. Union of India	[1960] 2 SCR 671	23.4; 12
Harakchand Ratanchand Banthia v. Union of India	[1970] 1 SCR 479	22.3; 9
Harman Singh v. R.T.A.	[1954] SCR 371	22.3; 8
Himat Lal K. Shah v. Commissioner of Police	[1973] 1 SCR 227	24; 2
Hussainara Khatoon v. Home Secretary, State of Bihar	AIR [1979] SC 1369	22.4; 81
Joshi D.P. v. M.B. State	[1955] SCR 1215	22.3; 7
Kalawati v. H.P. State	[1953] SCR 546	22.6; 77
Kameshar Prasad v. State of Bihar	AIR [1962] SC 1166	23.4; 13

543

Parties	Report	§; n.
Kathi Raning Rawat v. Sanrashtra	[1952] SCR 435	22.3; 18, 19
Katra Education Society v. Uttar Pradesh	[1966] 3 SCR 328	22.3; 9
Kedar Nath Bajoria v. West Bengal	[1954] SCR 30	22.3; 15 22.5; 31
Kharak Singh v. State of Uttar Pradesh et al.	[1964] 1 SCR 332	14.2; 13, 15, 38 14.4; 7, 8, 9
Lachman Das v. Punjab	[1963] SCR 925	22.3; 9
Lohia v. State of Bihar	[1966] 1 SCR 709	8; 40
Madhya Pradesh v. Mandawar	[1955] SCR 599	22.3; 7
Madhu Limaye v. Subdivisional Magistrate, Monghyr	[1971] 2 SCR 711	8; 41
Madhyn Pradesh v. Bhopal Sugar Industries	[1964] 6 SCR 846	22.3; 9
Mahant Moti Das v. Sahi	[1959] Supp 2 SCR 563	22.3; 8
Makhan Lal Malhotra v. Union of India	[1961] 2 SCR 120	22.3; 9
Maneka Gandhi v. Union of India and Another	[1978] SCR 312	14.2; 13, 16, 17, 34, 91
Matajog Dobey v. Bhari	[1955] SCR 925	14.4; 5, 10, 27
Mohanlal Jain v. Man Singhji	[1962] 1 SCR 702	22.3; 9
Mohd. Sahed Mahboob Medico v. Dy. Custodian-General	[1962] 2 SCR 371	22.3; 9
Muthamma v. Union of India	AIR [1979] SC 1868	7; 24
Nagaland v. Ratan Singh	[1966] 3 SCR 830	22.3; 7
Nandini Satpathy v. Dani	AIR [1978] SC 1025	22.6; 49
Narottam Kishore v. Union of India	[1964] 7 SCR 55	22.3; 9
Nav Rattanmal v. Rajasthan	[1962] 2 SCR 324	22.3; 9
Prabhakar Rao N. Mawle v. Andra Pradesh	[1965] 3 SCR 743	22.3; 8
Pratap Singh v. State of U.P.	[1961] 2 SCR 509	22.3; 9
Punjab v. Ajaib Singh	[1953] SCR 254	22.3; 7
Purushottam Govindji Halai v. Desai	[1955] SCR 887	22.3; 7
Rajasthan v. Rao Manohar Singh Ji	[1954] SCR 996	22.3; 7

Case	Citation	References
Ramesh Presaad Singh v. State of Bihar	AIR [1978] SC 327	7; 6
Ramprasad Narain Sahi v. Bihar	[1953] SCR 1129	22.3; 16
Ram Parshad v. Punjab	[1966] 3 SCR 486	22.3; 9
Rao Shiv Bahadur Singh v. Vindhya Pradesh	[1953] SCR 394	22.5; 16, 21
Rashid and Sons v. I.T. Officer	[1964] 6 SCR 826	22.3; 8
Ratilal Panachand Gandhi v. State of Bombay	AIR [1954] SC 388	23.3; 9
Rehman Shagoo v. State of J.K.	[1960] 1 SCR 680	22.3; 9
Romesh Thappar v. State of Madras	37 AIR (1950) SC 124	23.4; 9
Roshan Lal Mehra v. Ishwar Das	[1962] 2 SCR 947	22.3; 8, 9
Sakal Papers (P) Ltd. v. Union of India	[1962] 3 SCR 842	23.4; 47
Satwant Singh Sawhney v. Ramartham	[1967] 3 SCR 525	14.2; 17
		14.4; 5, 21
Sharma et al. v. Satish Chandra et al.	[1954] SCR 1077	22.6; 72, 74
Shri Krishan Singh v. Rajasthan	[1955] SCR 531	22.3; 7
Shri Ram Krishna Dalmia v. Shri Justice S.R. Tendolkar et al.	[1959] SCR 279	22.3; 11
Sobraj v. Superintendent, Central Jail, Tihar	AIR [1978] SC 1514	14.2; 33
State of J & K v. Khosa	[1974] 1 SCR 19	22.3; 12
Uttar Pradesh v. Kaushliya	[1964] 4 SCR 1002	22.3; 9
West Bengal v. Anwar Ali Sarkar	[1952] SCR 284	22.3; 17
Western India Theatres v. Cantonment Board	[1959] Supp 2 SCR 63	22.3; 9
V.M. Syed Mohammad & Co. v. State of Andhra	[1954] SCR 1117	22.3; 15

JAMAICA

Case	Citation	References
Banton et al. v. Alcoa Minerals of Jamaica et al.	(1971) 17 WIR 275	24; 21
Re Eric Darien	(1974) 22 WIR 323	8; 42

KENYA

Case	Citation	References
Madhura v. City Council of Nairobi	[1968] EA 406	7; 27
Republic v. Khadi, Kisumu, ex p. Nasreen	[1973] EA 153	18; 72

545

Parties	Court	Report	§; n.
Shah Vershi v. Transport Licensing Board		[1971] EA 289	7; 28
MAURITIUS			
Hawoldar v. Government of Mauritius		SCR 19985, No. 54 of 1978	21; 42
NIGERIA			
Awolowo v. Sarki		[1966] 1 All NLR 178	22.6; 52
DPP v. Obi		[1961] All NLR 186	23.4; 53
The Queen v. Eguabor		[1962] 1 All NLR 287	22.6; 69
Yanor v. The State		[1965] 1 All NLR 193	22.6; 61
NEW ZEALAND			
R v. Woolnough		[1977] 2 NZLR 408	14.1; 9
SIERRA LEONE			
Buckle v. Commission of Police		[1964-66] ALR S.L. 265	22.5; 38
Macauley v. Attorney-General		[1968-69] ALR S.L. 58	22.6; 20
TRINIDAD AND TOBAGO			
Re Ramesh L. Maharaj		No. 974 of 1975	14.2; 151
Thornhill v. Attorney-General		(1974) 27 WIR 281	22.6; 46
Re Weekes		(1972) 21 WIR 526	22.4; 76
UGANDA			
Shah v. Attorney-General		[1970] EA 523	21; 10
UNITED KINGDOM			
Christie v. Leachinsky	House of Lords	[1947] AC 573	14.2; 98
		[1945] 2 All ER 395	

Case	Court	Citation	Reference
Re D (a minor)	High Court	[1976] Fam D 185 [1976] 1 All ER 326	14.1; 11
Entick v. Carrington	Court of Common Pleas	(1765) 19 ST 1030	23.4; 1
Hubbard v. Pitt	Court of Appeal	[1976] QB 142 [1975] 1 All ER 1056	24; 5
Leach v. Money	Court of King's Bench	(1765) 19 ST 1002	23.4; 1
Malone v. Metropolitan Police Commissioner (No. 2)	High Court	[1979] Ch 344 [1979] 2 All ER 620	4; 9
Paton v. British Pregnancy Advisory Service Trustees	High Court	[1978] 3 WLR 687 [1978] 2 All ER 987	17; 10
R v. McCormick et al.	Court of Appeal, Northern Ireland	[1977] 4 NIJB 105	14.3; 8
Stockdale v. Hansard	Court of Queen's Bench	(1839) 8 LJQB 294	23.4; 1
Waddington v. Miah	House of Lords	[1974] 1 WLR 683 [1974] 2 All ER 377	4; 9 22.5; 28
Wilkes v. Wood	Court of Common Pleas	(1763) 19 ST 1153	23.4; 1

WEST INDIAN ASSOCIATED STATES

Case	Court	Citation	Reference
Attorney-General v. Reynolds	Court of Appeal	(1977) 24 WIR 552	22.4; 21
Herbert v. Phillips and Sealey	Court of Appeal	(1967) 10 WIR 435	14.2; 95
Camacho & Sons Ltd. et al. v. Collector of Customs	Court of Appeal	(1971) 18 WIR 159	7; 26

ZAMBIA

Case	Court	Citation	Reference
In the matter of Simon Kapepwe	Court of Appeal	[1972] ZR 248	14.2; 95

USA

The cases listed here are arranged in the alphabetical order of the appellants' names. With one exception, all of them are decisions of the US Supreme Court, and the references are to the standard series of 'United States Reports', but without the addition of the year.

Parties	Report	§; n.
Addyston Pipe & Steel Co. v. *United States*	175 US 211	14.2; 24, 25
Adkins v. *Children's Hospital of District of Columbia*	261 US 525	14.2; 24
Advance-Rumely Thresher Co. v. *Jackson*	287 US 283	14.2; 24
Allgeyer v. *Louisiana*	165 US 578	14.2; 13, 24, 25, 30
Aptheker v. *Secretary of State*	378 US 500	14.2; 32 14.4; 3, 4, 24
Bachellar v. *Maryland*	397 US 564	23.4; 3
Badders v. *United States*	240 US 390	14.3; 26
Bayside Fish Flour Co. v. *Gentry*	297 US 422	14.2; 24
Beazell v. *Ohio*	269 US 167	22.5; 21
Board of Regents v. *Roth*	408 US 564	14.2; 13, 14, 19, 24, 25, 27, 29
Bolling v. *Sharpe*	347 US 497	14.2; 27
Booth v. *Illinois*	184 US 425	14.2; 13, 24, 25, 31
Bowie v. *Columbia*	378 US 347	22.5; 19
Boyd v. *United States*	116 US 616	22.6; 73
Bugajewitz v. *Adama*	228 US 585	22.5; 20
Burgess v. *Salmon*	97 US 381	22.5; 20
Joseph Burnsteyn, Inc. v. *Wilson*	343 US 495	14.2; 20
Calder v. *Bull*	3 US 386	22.5; 22, 31
Cantwell v. *Connecticut*	310 US 296	14.2; 19
Chicago B. & Q.R. Co. v. *McGuire*	219 US 549	14.2; 24
Cleveland Board of Education v. *La Fleur*	414 US 632	14.2; 29
Coker v. *Georgia*	433 US 584	14.3; 27, 34
Cook v. *United States*	138 US 157	22.5; 21
Cummings v. *Missouri*	71 US 277	22.5; 25
Dobbert v. *Florida*	432 US 282	22.5; 23, 24, 37
Donald v. *Massachusetts*	180 US 311	22.5; 37
Duncan v. *Missouri*	152 US 377	22.5; 21
Dunn v. *Blumstein*	405 US 330	14.4; 3, 12
Estelle v. *Williams*	425 US 501	14.2; 18
Filartiga v. *Pena-Irala*	630 F (2nd) 876	5; 9 6; 7 14.3; 21

Parties	Report	§; n.
Flemming v. *Nestor*	363 US 603	22.5; 20
Fletcher v. *Peek*	10 US 87	22.5; 27
Furman v. *Georgia*	408 US 238	14.3; 25, 28, 29, 33, 35
Galvan v. *Press*	347 US 522	22.5; 20
Ex parte Garland	71 US 333	22.5; 25
Garner v. *Board of Public Works*	341 US 716	22.5; 25
Gibson v. *Florida Legislative Investigation Committee*	372 US 539	14.2; 19, 21
Gitlow v. *New York*	268 US 652	14.2; 20
Graham v. *West Virginia*	224 US 616	14.3; 26
Greene v. *McElroy*	360 US 474	14.2; 25
Gregg v. *Georgia*	428 US 153	14.3; 34
Griffin v. *Breckenridge*	403 US 88	14.4; 3
Re Griffiths	413 US 717	14.2; 26
Gryger v. *Burke*	334 US 728	22.5; 37
Gulf C. & S.F.R. Co. v. *Ellis*	163 US 150	22.3; 6
Gut v. *State*	76 US 35	22.5; 21
Hall v. *Geiger Jones Co.*	242 US 539	14.2; 24
Hardware Dealers Mut. Fire Ins. Co. v. *Glidden Co.*	284 US 151	14.2; 24
Harisiades v. *Shaughnessy*	342 US 580	22.5; 20
Hawker v. *New York*	170 US 189	22.5; 37
Highland v. *Russell Car & Snow Plow Co.*	279 US 253	14.2; 24
Holden v. *Minnesota*	137 US 483	22.5; 35
Hopt v. *Utah*	110 US 574	22.5; 21
Howard v. *Fleming*	191 US 126	14.3; 26
Hughes v. *Superior Court of California*	339 US 460	14.2; 22
Jacobson v. *Massachusetts*	197 US 11	14.2; 31
Johannessen v. *United States*	225 US 227	22.5; 26
Jurek v. *Texas*	428 US 262	14.3; 34
In re Kemmler	136 US 436	14.3; 23
Kent v. *Dulles*	357 US 116	14.2; 32 14.4; 4, 20, 23
Kring v. *Missouri*	107 US 221	22.5; 23
Lindsey v. *Washington*	301 US 397	22.5; 32, 33
Louisiana v. *Resweber*	329 US 459	14.3; 23
Lovell v. *Griffin*	303 US 444	14.2; 20
Loving v. *Virginia*	388 US 1	14.2; 29
Mahler v. *Eby*	264 US 32	22.5; 20
Mallet v. *North Carolina*	181 US 589	22.5; 21
Malloy v. *South Carolina*	237 US 180	22.5; 22, 37
McDonald v. *Massachusetts*	180 US 311	14.3; 26
McElvaine v. *Brush*	142 US 155	22.5; 35
Re Medley	134 US 160	22.5; 31, 35 36
Meyer v. *Nebraska*	262 US 390	14.2; 13, 19, 24, 25, 27, 29
Middleton v. *Texas Power and Light Co.*	249 US 152	22.3; 13
Mills v. *Alabama*	384 US 214	23.4; 11

Parties	Report	§; n.
Muller v. *Oregon*	208 US 412	14.2; 24
Munn v. *Illinois*	94 US 113	14.1; 23, 24
Murphy v. *Ramsay*	114 US 15	22.5; 37
NAACP v. *Alabama*	357 US 449	14.2; 20
Near v. *Minnesota*	283 US 697	14.2; 20
New York ex rel. Bryant v. *Zimmerman*	278 US 63	14.2; 21
New York Life Ins. Co. v. *Dodge*	246 US 357	14.2; 24
New York Times v. *Sullivan*	376 US 254	23.4; 3
Northwestern Nat. Life Ins. Co. v. *Riggs*	203 US 243	14.2; 24, 25
O'Neil v. *Vermont*	144 US 323	14.3; 26
Oyama v. *California*	332 US 633	6; 5
Paris Adult Theatre I v. *Slaton*	413 US 49	14.2; 23
Patterson v. *Bark Eudora*	190 US 169	14.2; 24
Paul v. *Davies*	424 US 693	14.2; 34
Pierce v. *Society of Sisters*	268 US 510	14.2; 28
Powell v. *Texas*	392 US 514	14.3; 31
Profitt v. *Florida*	428 US 242	14.3; 34
Radice v. *New York*	264 US 294	22.3; 14
Stanislaus Roberts v. *Louisiana*	428 US 325	14.3; 36
Roberts v. *Louisiana*	431 US 633	14.3; 36
Robinson v. *California*	370 US 660	14.3; 24, 30, 31
Roe v. *Wade*	410 US 113	14.2; 23
Rooney v. *North Dakota*	196 US 319	22.5; 35, 37
Ross v. *Oregon*	227 US 150	22.5; 18
Roth v. *United States*	354 US 476	23.4; 3
Rudolph v. *Alabama*	375 US 889	14.3; 32
Re Savage	134 US 176	22.5; 36
School District of Abington Township v. *Schempp*	374 US 203	14.2; 19
Shapiro v. *Thompson*	394 US 618	14.4; 3, 11, 55 19; 13
Smith v. *California*	361 US 147	14.2; 20
Southern Railway Co. v. *Greene*	216 US 400	22.3; 5
Staub v. *Baxley*	355 US 313	14.2; 20
Street v. *New York*	394 US 576	23.4; 3
Stromberg v. *California*	283 US 359	14.2; 20
Talley v. *California*	362 US 60	23.4; 11
Taylor v. *Mississipi*	319 US 583	14.2; 20
Terminiello v. *Chicago*	337 US 1	23.4; 2
Thompson v. *Missouri*	171 US 380	22.5; 21
Traux v. *Raich*	239 US 33	14.2; 26
Trop v. *Dulles*	356 US 86	14.3; 25, 28
United States v. *Guest*	383 US 745	14.4; 3, 12
United States v. *Laub et al.*	385 US 475	14.2; 32 14.4; 20, 26
United States v. *Robel*	389 US 258	14.2; 25
Warden, Lewisburg Penitentiary v. *Marrero*	417 US 653	22.5; 34

Parties	Report	§; n.
Weeks v. *United States*	232 US 383	22.6; 73
Weems v. *United States*	217 US 349	14.3; 25, 26
Wilkerson v. *Utah*	99 US 130	14.3; 23
Williams v. *Fears*	179 US 270	14.2; 13, 24, 25, 30
Wolf v. *Colorado*	383 US 25	14.2; 23
Woodson v. *North Carolina*	428 US 280	14.3; 34, 35
Yick Wo v. *Hopkins*	118 US 356	22.3; 5
Zemel v. *Rusk*	381 US 1	14.2; 32
		14.4; 4, 13, 25

EUROPE

References to decisions of national courts of European countries[4] are listed in the order of their dates (which is how they are generally cited[5]), with an indication of the court or tribunal concerned, and either the journal in which the decision is reported or the case reference.

EUCM has published an unpaginated 'Collection of Decisions of National Courts' in the English language, and four later (and paginated) Supplements to it. Where a national decision is reported in one of these, the reference is given as 'CDNC', followed (where appropriate) by the Supplement and page numbers; that is then the only reference in the relevant footnote, but in this Table the appropriate national reference is also given. References to EUCM's Yearbooks (cited as 'YB') indicate that English and French translations of relevant portions of the decision concerned may be found there.

References to the *Europäische Grundrechtzeitung* are abbreviated as *EuGRZ*.

---

[4] For convenience, the two cases from Israel are included in this part of the Table.
[5] Except for Ireland and Israel, which follow the Anglo-Saxon system of citation.

AUSTRIA

The following abbreviations are used for the courts whose decisions are cited:

Oberster Gerichtshof	(Supreme Court)	OGH
Verfassungsgerichtshof	(Constitutional Court)	VfGH

Decisions cited are reported in the following journals:

Juristische Blätter	*JB*
Österreichische Juristen-Zeitung	*ÖJZ*

Date	Court	Reference	§; *n.*
3 July 1965	VfGH	G 26/64; G 10/65, 11 YB 8, 530	22.4; 102
12 October 1965	VfGH	*ÖJZ* 1966, 400	23.2; 23
14 October 1965	VfGH	*ÖJZ* 1966, 248 YB 9, 734	22.4; 46
11 February 1970	OGH	*ÖJZ* 1970, 411	22.6; 55
8 June 1970	OGH	*ÖJZ* 1971, 158	23.2; 28
19 June 1970	OGH	*JB* 1970, 629	23.4; 36
29 September 1970	VfGH	*ÖJZ* 1971, 413	22.4; 50
14 January 1971	OGH	*ÖJZ* 1971, 469	22.6; 9
8 March 1971	VfGH	*JB* 1972, 311	21; 16
10 May 1971	VfGH	*ÖJZ* 1972, 305	18; 87
17 July 1971	VfGH	*ÖJZ* 1972, 306	23.4; 26
27 July 1972	OGH	*ÖJZ* 1973, 127	22.6; 23
16 October 1972	VfGH	*JB* 1972, 196	23.4; 44
11 October 1974	VfGH	*EuGRZ* 1975, 74	14.1; 8
11 June 1977	VfGH	*JB* 1978, 311	14.1; 18
6 October 1977	VfGH	*JB* 1978, 312	14.3; 64

Date	Court	Reference	§; n.
BELGIUM			
24 March 1961	Conseil d'Etat	No. 8500	23.4; 42
8 November 1966	Tribunal de Première Instance de Bruxelles	CDNC YB 9, 746	23.4; 17
26 January 1967	Tribunal de Première Instance de Bruxelles	Parquet No. 4506/SOC/65	22.6; 53
10 August 1968	Bureau d'assistance judiciaire du Tribunal de Bruxelles	Journal de Droit International No. 4, 1971, 856	22.6; 68
27 January 1970	Cour de Cassation	No. 5280	22.6; 67
30 January 1970	Tribunal de Première Instance de Bruxelles	CDNC 1, 55	23.4; 2
20 April 1970	Cour de Cassation	Pas. belge 1970, 724	22.4; 32
7 January 1971	Cour de Cassation	Pas. belge 1971, 419	22.4; 64
8 June 1971	Cour de Cassation	Cassation, 1st Chamber, No. F 361 N	22.4; 50
27 September 1971	Cour de Cassation	Pas. belge 1972, 87	23.2; 56
29 October 1971	Cour de Cassation	Pas. belge 1972, 213	22.4; 50
14 March 1972	Cour de Cassation	Cassation, 2nd Chamber, No. 1248	22.6; 64
20 March 1972	Cour de Cassation	Cassation, 2nd Chamber, No. 6401	14.2; 122 22.4; 57
8 September 1972	Cour de Cassation	Cassation, 1st Chamber, No. 7.D.7783	22.4; 50
20 November 1972	Court Martial of Liège	Journal des Tribunaux, 3 March 1973, 148	14.3; 14
17 December 1972	Cour de Cassation	Cassation, 2nd Chamber, No. 7.D.8081	22.6; 21
DANZIG			
Zappot Street Crossing Case		Annual Digest 1933–4, No. 104	1; 21

FEDERAL REPUBLIC OF GERMANY

The following abbreviations are used for the courts whose decisions are cited:

Bundesverfassungsgericht	(Federal Constitutional Court)	BVfG
Bundesgerichtshof	(Federal Supreme Court)	BG
Bundesverwaltungsgericht	(Federal Administrative Court)	BVwG
Bundesarbeitsgericht	(Federal Labour Court)	BAG
Bundessozialgericht	(Federal Social Court)	BSG
Oberlandesgericht	(Court of Appeals)	OLG
Kammergericht	(Court of Appeals, Berlin)	KG
Oberverwaltungsgericht	(Administrative Court of Appeals)	OVwG
Landgericht	(High Court)	LG
Verwaltungsgericht	(Administrative Court)	VwG
Amtsgericht	(Local Court)	AG

Decisions cited are reported in the following journals:

Deutsches Verwaltungsblatt	*DVwB*
Entscheidungen des Bundesgerichts in Zivilsachen	*E/BG/Z*
Entscheidungen des Bundesverfassungsgerichts	*E/BVfG*
Entscheidungen des Bundesverwaltungsgerichts	*E/BVwG*
Neue Juristische Wochenschrift	*NJW*
Die öffentliche Verwaltung •	*ÖVw*
Verwaltungsrechtssprechung	*VwRS*

Judgments, Decisions, and Reports Cited

Date	Court	Reference	§; n.
6 November 1953	VwG Stuttgart	ÖVw 1954, 223	14.3; 48
12 August 1955	LG Mannheim	NJW 1956, 384	23.4; 61
13 September 1955	OVwG Münster	ÖVw 1956, 381	14.3; 46
15 December 1955	BVwG	E/BVwG 3, 58	14.3; 48
10 January 1956	VwG Württemberg/Baden	VwRS 8, 859	14.3; 46
10 May 1957	BVwG	E/BVfG 6, 389 YB 2, 594	14.1; 25
27 June 1957	BG	NJW 1957, 1480 YB 2, 596	22.4; 74
20 May 1958	BG	E/BG/Z 27, 284	23.2; 68
8 October 1959	VwG Bremen	NJW 1960, 400	14.1; 22
27 September 1960	OVwG Berlin	YB 3, 638	14.3; 46, 48
25 October 1960	BVwG	NJW 1961, 571	22.6; 13
22 February 1962	BVwG	NJW 1962, 1532	17; 15
18 October 1962	AG Bremerhaven	NJW 1963, 827	22.6; 64
25 January 1963	AG Wiesbaden	NJW 1963, 967	14.3; 73
10 June 1963	OLG Köln	NJW 1963, 1748	14.3; 53, 74
13 June 1963	OLG Hamburg	NJW 1963, 1840	14.3; 49
16 January 1964	BVwG	DVwB 1968, 983 CDNC 2, 4	14.1; 1, 22
14 February 1964	BSG	NJW 1964, 1691	23.4; 51
16 October 1964	OLG Hamburg	NJW 1965, 357	14.3; 50
31 January 1965	BG	NJW 1966, 1021 YB 9, 782	14.2; 150, 151
10 March 1965	AG Köln	5 XIV 691 B YB 8, 558	14.2; 82
9 December 1965	KG	NJW 1966, 1088	14.3; 51
4 October 1967	AG Berlin-Tiergarten	NJW 1968, 61	14.3; 74
2 July 1969	BG	NJW 1969, 2107	22.4; 75

Date	Court	Citation	
10 March 1971	OLG Celle	NJW 1971, 1665	22.6; 14
		CDNC 3, 25	
17 March 1971	BG	NJW 1971, 1097	22.4; 65
4 May 1971	BVfG	NJW 1971, 1509; 2121	17; 12
18 June 1971	OLG Celle	NJW 1971, 2180	22.6; 15
21 June 1971	AG Geilenkirchen	NJW 1971, 2320	22.6; 64
14 July 1971	BG	NJW 1971, 20	14.3; 73
13 October 1971	OLG Koblenz	NJW 1972, 404	22.4; 99
10 November 1971	BG	NJW 1972, 402	22.4; 99
1 December 1971	LG München	NJW 1972, 405	22.6; 21
10 January 1972	OLG Karlsruhe	ISs 220/71;	22.4; 99
		Justiz 1972, 120	
22 October 1975	OLG Bayern	NJW 1976, Heft 11 S, 483	14.2; 97
		YB 19, 1126	
14 December 1976	OLG Bayern	Bay. VB 1977, Heft 1, 24	14.2; 97
		YB 20, 764	
26 August 1977	VwG Berlin	NJW 1978, 68	14.4; 15
		YB 21, 747	
16 October 1977	BVfG	1 BVQ 5/77	14.1; 18
10 June 1980	BAG	1 AZR 168/79	24; 73
10 June 1980	BAG	1 AZR 822/79	24; 73

FRANCE

Date	Court	Citation	
15 January 1975	Conseil Constitutionnel	EuGRZ 1975, 54	14.1; 8
31 October 1980	Conseil d'Etat	6 Human Rights Review 75	8; 63
			17; 11
			23.2; 36

GREECE

Date	Court	Citation	
5 December 1960	Council of State	No. 35/1961	14.2; 62

Judgments, Decisions, and Reports Cited

Date	Court	Reference	§; n.
LUXEMBOURG			
26 June 1972	Cour Supérieure de Justice	Pas. Lux. 1973, 216	23.2; 59
ICELAND			
25 June 1963	Supreme Court	No. 66/1063	21; 24
IRELAND			
The State v. John Frawley	High Court	[1976] IR 365	14.3; 14
ISRAEL			
Rufeisen v. Minister of the Interior	Supreme Court	(1962) 16 PD 2428	26; 1
Shalit v. Minister of the Interior	Supreme Court	(1969) 23 PD 477	26; 1
ITALY			
29 May 1970	Court of Appeal, Milano	No. 1313/70 CDNC 1, 56	23.4; 60
11 October 1972	Corte Suprema di Cassazione	No. 6588 YB 19, 1132	14.2; 105
12 October 1972	Corte Suprema di Cassazione	No. 1475 CDNC 4, 41	25; 12
18 February 1975	Corte Constituzionale	*EuGRZ* 1975, 172	14.1; 8

NETHERLANDS

Decisions cited are reported in the following journals:

Nederlands Jurisprudentie	*NJ*
Netherlands Yearbook of International Law	*NYIL*
Militair Rechtelijk Tijdschrift	*MRT*

Date	Court	Reference	§; *n.*
22 March 1960	Hoge Raad	*NJ* 1960, 707	23.4; 10
19 January 1962	Hoge Raad	*NJ* 1962, 417	8; 39
25 June 1963	Hoge Raad	*NJ* 1964, 595	8; 17
25 May 1964	Gerecht in eerste aanleg	*NJ* 1965, 412	23.4; 68
25 June 1965	Hoge Raad	*NJ* 1966, 115	23.4; 69
24 January 1967	Hoge Raad	*NJ* 1967, 747	23.4; 13
30 May 1967	Hoge Raad	*NJ* 1968, 14	23.4; 13
30 May 1967	Hoge Raad	*NJ* 1968, 18	23.4; 52
7 November 1967	Hoge Raad	*NJ* 1968, 266	23.4; 13
30 January 1968	Hoge Raad	*NJ* 1968 199	8; 53 23.4; 36
6 February 1968	Hof van Justitie, Nederlands Antilles	*NJ* 1969, 128	23.4; 49
4 November 1969	Hoge Raad	*NJ* B/z. 3298, No. 127 CDNC 1, 52	23.3; 10
14 August 1970	Koninklijk Besluit	*NYIL* Vol. III, 1973 CDNC 3, 40	23.2; 56
26 April 1971	Rechtbank Breda	*NYIL*, Vol. III, 1973 CDNC 3, 35	22.6; 21
19 May 1971	Rechtbank Amsterdam	*NYIL*, Vol. III, 1973 CDNC 3, 36	22.6; 21
22 June 1971	Hoge Raad	*NJ* No. 22, 1970 CDNC 3, 41	23.3; 14
3 December 1971	Hoge Raad	*NJ* 1972, 137	22.4; 66
18 January 1972	Hoge Raad	*NJ* 1972, 545	23.4; 36
2 February 1972	Hof Den Bosch	*NJ* No. 263, 1972 CNDC 4, 30	22.6; 21
12 April 1972	Hoog Militair Gerechtshof	*MRT* 1972, 338	23.4; 36
9 July 1974	Hof Arnhem	YB 18, 427	23.4; 20
15 April 1975	Hoge Raad	*NJ* No. 3, 1976 YB 19, 1147	23.4; 14
27 February 1976	Court of Appeal	*NYIL*, Vol. VIII, 1978 YB 20, 772	14.3; 54

SWITZERLAND

All the decisions listed here are by the Bundesgericht (Federal Court), Lausanne.

Date	Reference	§; n.
14 July 1976	PE 2/76 he	14.2; 109
	YB 20, 793	
19 July 1976	750/76	14.1; 18
3 November 1976	YB 20, 801	14.2; 109, 110, 131, 132

SELECTED BIBLIOGRAPHY

This is only a very small selection from the available literature, confined to *books* in the *English* language, published before 1 January 1982, and dealing mainly or entirely with *substantive international* human rights *law*. Where other sources have been used, their references are given in the appropriate footnotes.

Brownlie, I. (ed.), *Basic Documents on Human Rights* (Oxford, 1st ed. 1971, 2nd ed. 1981).

Carey, J., *UN Protection of Civil and Political Rights* (New York, 1970).

Castberg, S., *The European Convention on Human Rights* (Leyden, 1974).

Fawcett, J. E. S., *The Application of the European Convention on Human Rights* (Oxford, 1969).

International Commission of Jurists, *The Rule of Law and Human Rights: Principles and Definitions* (Geneva, 1966).

Jacobs, F. G., *The European Convention on Human Rights* (Oxford, 1975).

Jenks, C., *Human Rights and the International Labour Standards* (New York, 1960).

Joyce, J. A., *Human Rights: International Documents* (3 vols., Alphen aan den Rijn, 1978).

Lauterpacht, H., *International Law and Human Rights* (London, 1950; reprinted 1968).

Lillich, R. and Newman, F. (eds.), *International Human Rights: Problems of Law and Policy* (Boston, 1979).

Luard, E. (ed.), *The International Protection of Human Rights* (New York, 1967).

Ramcharan, B. G. (ed.), *Human Rights: Thirty Years after the Universal Declaration* (The Hague, 1979).

Robertson, A. H., *Human Rights in the World* (Manchester, 1972).

Robertson, A. H., *Human Rights in Europe* (2nd ed., Manchester, 1977).

Robertson, A. H. (ed.), *Human Rights in National and International Law* (Manchester, 1968).

Schreiber, A., *The Inter-American Commission on Human Rights* (Leyden, 1970).

Schwelb, E., *The influence of the Universal Declaration of Human Rights on international and national law* (New York, 1959).

Schwelb, E., *Human Rights and the International Community* (Chicago, 1964).

Sohn, L. and Buergenthal, T. (eds.), *International Protection of Human Rights: Basic Documents* (Indianapolis, 1973).

United Nations, *Human Rights: A Compilation of International Instruments* (New York, 1978).

United Nations, *UN Action in the Field of Human Rights* (New York, 1980).

Vallat, F. (ed.), *An Introduction to the Study of Human Rights* (London, 1972).

Vasak, K. (ed.), *The International Dimensions of Human Rights* (Unesco, 1979).

INDEX OF ARTICLES

This index lists, in their original numerical order, the Articles of the major international instruments reproduced in Parts II, III, and IV of this book, and shows the sections and sub-sections where they appear. For the full texts of these instruments (other than [AFR]), including their Preambles and transitional provisions, the reader is referred to I. Brownlie (ed.), *Basic Documents on Human Rights* (2nd ed. 1981). The full text of [AFR] is reprinted in *The Review* of the International Commission of Jurists, No. 27, December 1981.

UNCH

Article	§	Article	§
55	6.1.1	56	6.1.1

UDHR

Article	§	Article	§
1	23.1.1	19	23.4.1
2	6.5.1; 7.0.1	20(1)	24.1.1; 24.2.1
3	14.1.1; 14.2.1	(2)	24.2.1
4	18.4.1	21	25.0.1
5	14.3.1	22	19.0.1
6	22.2.1	23(1)	18.1.1; 18.2.1
7	7.0.1; 22.3.1	(2)	18.2.1
8	6.6.1	(3)	18.2.1
9	14.2.1; 14.4.1	(4)	24.3.1
10	22.4.1	24	18.3.1
11(1)	22.6.1	25(1)	15.0.1; 16.0.1; 19.0.1
(2)	22.5.1	(2)	17.2.1
12	23.2.1	26	20.0.1
13	14.4.1	27	23.5.1
14	14.5.1	28	26.2.1
15	22.1.1	29(1)	8.0.1; 23.1.1
16	17.1.1	(2)	8.0.1
17	21.0.1	(3)	9.0.1
18	23.3.1	30	9.0.1

ADRD

Article	§	Article	§
I	14.1.1; 14.2.1	VI	17.1.1
II	7.0.1; 22.3.1	VII	17.2.1
III	23.3.1	VIII	14.4.1
IV	23.4.1	IX	23.2.1
V	23.2.1	X	23.2.1

Index of Articles

(Other qualifications set out in the Appendix are reproduced with the specific provisions of *ESC* to which they are expressed to refer.)

[*AFR*]